V&R

Lublin Theological Studies

Volume 4

Marek Jagodziński

The Holy Spirit of Communion

A Study in Pneumatology and Ecclesiology

VANDENHOECK & RUPRECHT

Reviewers of the book:
Prof. Bogdan Ferdek (Pontifical Faculty of Theology in Wrocław)
Prof. Andrzej Perzyński (Cardinal Stefan Wyszyński University in Warsaw)

Bibliographic information published by the Deutsche Nationalbibliothek:
The Deutsche Nationalbibliothek lists this publication in the Deutsche Nationalbibliografie; detailed bibliographic data available online: https://dnb.de.

Typesetting: le-tex publishing services, Leipzig
Cover design: SchwabScantechnik, Göttingen
Printed and bound: Hubert & Co, Göttingen
Printed in the EU

Vandenhoeck & Ruprecht Verlage | www.vandenhoeck-ruprecht-verlage.com

ISBN 978-3-525-50021-7

Table of Contents

Introduction

Understanding God as self-giving love lies at the horizon of understanding His reality not so much as substance (as the Aristotelian account would suggest), but as relation. In contemporary theology we can notice a clear mark of the trinitarian understanding of God, who "in Himself is the mutually directed love of the Father and the Son in the common Spirit of that love, is pure life in this relation, the infinitely complete becoming of that relation, the communion, the communion of the Giver (the Father), the Receiver (the Son) and the Uniter (the Holy Spirit). The essence of God, then, is Communication of love – Communion – sustained in varied ways by the Divine Persons.[1] The Father is the proper source of the Communication-Communion of love, which continually spouts life. The Son is (from the perspective of the salvific economy) the Word made Flesh. The Holy Spirit, as the personified love of the Father and the Son, is also the personified Communication of love. Moreover, the Holy Spirit[2], as the intrinsically trinitarian bond of love, in an economic-salvific inversion is oriented towards man and is the personal medium of the communication-communion of love between man and Christ – to the glory of the Father".[3]

From the very beginning of Christianity, the Holy Spirit has occupied an important place in the Christian faith. In the Hebrew tradition of prophets and kings, the term "Christ" itself meant someone anointed by the Spirit (κεχρισμένος, χριστός), except that Jesus was the Messiah – the ultimate, eschatological prophet or king who was not only to receive upon Himself the fullness of God's Spirit, but also

1 See Marek Jagodziński, *Trynitologia komunijna* (Lublin: Wydawnictwo KUL, 2021), 96–126.

2 The essence of God transcends the question of gender. God is completely above such distinctions. Some try to apply feminine nomenclature to the Holy Spirit, but the author of this study consistently follows the oldest, most widespread, and fine Christian and academic tradition, which uses the vocabulary of the masculine gender when referring to the Holy Spirit.

3 Jagodziński, *Węzłowe zagadnienia chrystologii komunijnej* (Radom: Wydawnictwo Diecezji Radomskiej AVE, 2013), 5–6. This is well illustrated in the schema of the trinitarian "structure of reference" proposed by Medard Kehl, in which the "Father" is the beginningless and incommunicable "Wherefrom" of infinitely self-giving love, the "Son" is the "Whereto" of infinitely received love coming from the Father and imparted through Him, and the Holy Spirit is the "Wherein" of that infinite love that unifies, mediates between the Father and the Son and mediates through Them. Love, in turn, is ultimately the "What" – the content of the references between the Father, the Son and the Holy Spirit – and as such is identical with the "essence" of God. Cf. Medard Kehl, "Kirche als Institution – eine theologische Begründung," in *Kirche als Institution*, *Studienbrief* II/1, ed. Kehl and Norbert Glatzel, and Norbert Mette (Tübingen: "Deutsches Institut für Fernstudien an der Universität Tübingen. Fernstudium Katholische Religionspädagogik," 1984), 121.

to give it to others as a gift of the last days (cf. Joel 3:1-5). Jesus' resurrection was proof that he was indeed this eschatological Messiah and was therefore linked to the pouring of the Holy Spirit first upon the disciples and then upon "all flesh" at Pentecost (Acts 2:17). The delay of the Parousia did not leave Christians "orphaned" but meant that another "Comforter" (παράκλετος) would undertake to guide and strengthen Christians until Christ's return (John 14:18). For this reason, the role of the Holy Spirit was decisive for Christian existence between the resurrection and the second coming of Christ. The fact that the Holy Spirit was already given and doing His work after the Resurrection and Ascension meant that His eschatological gifts were already present in the Christian community. The members of the Church had become "spiritual" (πνεματικοί). On the occasion of a certain dispute among Christians in Corinth concerning the "degrees" of spirituality, St. Paul taught that all members of the Church in one way or another are bearers of the Spirit and His gifts, and that true Christian spirituality does not allow discrimination that would place one gift above the others, just as one member of the body could not despise the others or exist independently of the other members. The highest form of spirituality is love (1 Cor 13:13), because the Spirit is communion. Therefore, Christian spirituality could not be experienced outside of a community that encompassed multiple and diverse spiritual charisms. Individualism is incompatible with Christian spirituality. No one can possess the Spirit as an individual – one can only possess Him as a member of the community. When the wind of the Holy Spirit "blows", the result is never good individual Christians, but members of the community.[4]

Because the Holy Spirit was considered a "communion" and His gifts were by nature collective, the age of the Spirit was, in a profound sense, the age of the Church, the community of those who, as one Body, were incorporated into Christ. Life in the Spirit was identified with belonging to the community of the Messiah, formed through the gifts of the Spirit and by the Spirit. The Church was regarded as the eschatological community that the resurrected Lord would gather around Him at the Parousia and with which He would be fully identified (Matt 25:30-31; Acts 9:5). In this sense, the Church as the Body of the resurrected Christ and the Church as the communion of the Spirit are one and the same. The Holy Spirit built the Body of Christ and did not act independently of the Person and "Body" of Christ, and Christ too was incomprehensible as an individual, but could only be apprehended "in the Spirit" – as a collective Person made up of many at the same time. Similarly, the "many" Persons could not be understood apart from one – Christ. Christian spirituality was ecclesial in nature. The Church was not a means by which one could

---

4 Cf. John D. Zizioulas, *The One and the Many: Studies on God, Man, the Church, and the World Today* (Los Angeles: Sebastian Press, 2010), 151–2.

become spiritual in the sense that it provided the necessary instruction, worship, grace etc., but a set of relations that gave an individual a new identity, different from the identity conferred by natural birth or society. For this reason, being a spiritual person in early Christianity was primarily associated with "a new birth", being born by the Holy Spirit (John 3:3).[5]

The person's ability to listen and open up to others – to communicate – leads to the establishment of a communion (*koinonia* – *communio*) in both the human and divine dimension. In its original usage, *communio* meant "participation" in the sense of having a share and providing it in the community. In the New Testament, however, this communion is not the work of men, but – through the Eucharistic community of Christians – derives form participation in Christ, as participation "in the Blood of Christ" and "in the Body of Christ" (cf. 1 Cor 10:16). St. Paul also refers to communion in the Holy Spirit as sharing in Him, which also means sharing spiritual and material gifts. Thus, *koinonia* means a reality existing through the community of believers who participate in the common reality given to them.[6]

Communio is a dynamic reality – a communication, a process, a life – thus reducing it to something akin to other human communities is restrictive and misleading. What is meant by this concept is an extraordinarily intense form of reference, love, communion, which from the theological perspective is most closely linked to the Eucharistic understanding of "communion" – being close to one another, unity of life, mutual penetration, the closest union. This concept seems to be the most accurate paradigm drawn from the created world to help one understand the inner

5 Cf. Zizioulas, *The One and the Many*, 152.

6 Jagodziński, *Węzłowe zagadnienia chrystologii komunijnej*, 6–7. "In the translations of the New Testament into Latin, the meaning of *koinonia* is rendered by the words *communio* and *communicatio*. The first and most direct equivalent of *communio* is communion, with two significant metaphorical connotations: *communio* points to the root "-mun-" meaning, more or less, an embankment gathering people in a common space of life and uniting them through mutual orientation towards each other – this root can also be found in the word *munus* (task, service, but also gift, offering) denoting a commitment to mutual service on the basis of a gift received that should subsequently be passed on. Both connotations point to the notion of *communio* as a mediated reality, which does not arise as a derivative of the sum of individuals, but from the beginning exists with them" (ibid., 8). Cf. Gisbert Greshake, "Communio – Schlüsselbegriff der Dogmatik," in *Gemeinsam Kirche sein. Theorie und Praxis der Communio. Festschrift der Theologischen Fakultät der Universität Freiburg i. Br. für Erzbischof Dr. Oskar Saier*, ed. Günther Biemer and Bernhard Casper, and Josef Müller, (Freiburg-Basel-Wien: Herder, 1992), 90–121.

life of God;[7] it is the key concept of faith and theology,[8] ingenious in relation to the mystery of the Holy Trinity[9] and analogously appropriate to the mystery of the Church.[10]

This monograph focuses precisely on the Holy Spirit, who – as theologians do not hesitate to say – is the Communion within the reality of the Trinity and forms the communion between God, man and the world, as well as within the reality of this world. The reflection on the Holy Spirit presented here, using the pneumatological potential available in the theological literature, in the context of the deepest and broadest understanding of communion, is intended to lead to the foundation of a fairly comprehensive study of pneumatology of communion.

Chapter One presents the Holy Spirit in the Communion of the Holy Trinity. First, the chapter outlines the communion-guided pneumatological potential extracted from the biblical texts, and then isolates the communional aspects of the historical development of pneumatology, showing first the communional position of the Holy Spirit in the light of the first trinitological concepts, and then the communion-oriented pneumatological aspects in the further development of trinitology (including the communional dimension of the *Filioque* debate), through medieval pneumatology to the pneumatology of the last council and post-conciliar theology. The chapter focuses particularly on the Holy Spirit as a Person in the Communion of the Holy Trinity and will show him first in the context of the Persons of the trinitarian Communion, the communional trinitarian perichoresis and the communional unity and plurality of the Persons in the Holy Trinity. Subsequently, the issues of the origin of the Holy Spirit in the trinitarian Communion, the problems associated with the traditional view of the Persons of the Trinity, and the issues of the specificity of the Holy Spirit in the trinitarian Communion and the

---

7 Zizioulas writes that life in the biblical sense "is rather to be understood as springing from a *relational* situation, from a relationship of *persons*. Life in this sense is the *event of communion of persons*, i. e., a situation in which all the divisions, individualizations, and fragmentations of existence (natural, moral, social, etc.) which threaten existence with decomposition and hence with death, are transcended in a communion of *freely loving* beings. Life as the overcoming of death – and truth which is life – is thus ultimately expressed in God understood not in a deistic but in a *Triadological* sense, i. e., as a relationship of persons, as 'communion' in an ultimate ontological sense" (Zizioulas, *The One and the Many*, 215).

8 Cf. Greshake, *Trójjedyny Bóg. Teologia trynitarna* (Wrocław: Wydawnictwo Wrocławskiej Księgarni Archidiecezjalnej, 2009), 339–45.

9 In his "Trinitarian theology," Greshake emphasises the dimension of communion in the Trinity and regards it as the centre and key to understanding the Christian faith. Cf. Greshake, *Trójjedyny Bóg*, 190.

10 Cf. Robert Skrzypczak, *Osoba i misja. Podstawy eklezjologii misyjnej w świetle personalizmu papieża Jana Pawła II* (Warszawa: Wydawnictwo Sióstr Loretanek, 2005), 331–3; Jagodziński, *Węzłowe zagadnienia chrystologii komunijnej*, 8–9.

communional view of the properties of the Holy Spirit are discussed. The chapter concludes with the presentation of a communicative-communional view of the reality of the Holy Spirit.

Chapter Two discusses of the communional and trinitarian aspects of the Holy Spirit's action in the history of salvation. First, the chapter addresses the question of so-called Christological pneumatology or, put differently, pneumatological Christology. This is followed by a presentation of the Holy Spirit in the revelation of and joint action with the Son, as well as the Holy Spirit's work in Christ's mysteries. The chapter also presents a reflection on the pneumatological dimensions of human life in communion with Christ and of theology, with particular emphasis on the communional aspects of contemporary pneumatological thought.

Chapter Three discusses the pneumatological-sacramental structure of the Church's communion. First, the Holy Spirit is presented as the co-creator of the Church's communion and the pneumatological dimensions of faith and the Word of God are delineated. Further, a vision of the Church as the sacrament of the Holy Spirit, with particular emphasis on the pneumatological-communional dimension of the Church as institution, which serves its identity, unity and freedom, is presented. The chapter also discusses the implications arising from the pneumatological-sacramental vision of the Church. Finally, the pneumatological dimension of the sacraments as sacraments of communion are outlined.

Chapter Four addresses the pneumatological-communicative dimensions of the Church's unity in terms of the communion of the faithful, the communion of particular Churches and the hierarchical communion. The chapter concludes with the presentation of the pneumatological dimensions of the common ecumenical vision of the Church as communion.

1. The Holy Spirit in the Communion of the Holy Trinity

The Church's teaching about God does not produce a new concept of God, but rather provides a continuation for the faith of Israel modified by Jesus Christ. God is transcendent, absolutely free, personal and reveals himself in history through His rulings. Christ is the Lord who sits at the right hand of God (cf. Ps 110:1), receives all honour and glory, but while departing to the Father He said: "I will not leave you orphaned; I am coming to you. [...] But the Advocate, the Holy Spirit, whom the Father will send in my name, will teach you everything, and remind you of all that I have said to you" (John 14:18, 26). As Christ sits at the right hand of God, the Father sends another Helper – the Spirit of Truth. The coming of the Third Person – the Holy Spirit – opened a new relationship of people to God. His Person verifies the presence of God Himself, gives gifts and reveals a power that can only be the power of God Himself. The first disciples were compelled to find a space in their understanding of God for the experience of the Holy Spirit's company through which Christ breaks down the barriers of nature and creates the Church. Before the coming of the Spirit of Christ, the world had not known a community that could surpass all the divisions of creation.[1]

God has revealed Himself in Jesus Christ as the mystery of the Trinity[2], and the experience of the Church as communion has made it possible to show convincingly that God's existence is a perfect communion through personal relationships and interpersonal love.[3] At the same time, the confession of a historico-salvific (economic) Trinity was never regarded by Christians as a limitation or abandonment of strict monotheism,[4] nor as an "extra" feature of the newly created faith. For them, the

1 Cf. Jagodziński, *Trynitologia komunijna*, 153–5.

2 Hans Urs von Balthasar, *Teologika*, vol. II: *Prawda Boga* (Krakow: WAM, 2004), 117: "There is [...] no other approach to the trinitarian mystery than its revelation in Jesus Christ and the Holy Spirit, and no statement about the immanent Trinity can distance itself even a step from the foundation of the New Testament, if it does not want to plunge into the emptiness of abstract theses which have no meaning in the historico-salvific perspective. Only the behaviour of Jesus towards his Father and the Holy Spirit tells us something about the intra-trinitarian relationships of life and love in the one and only God."

3 G. Greshake writes that "the development of the theology of the Trinity 'would not have been possible without the experience of the Church's existence.... The Son of God is a relational being: without the idea of *Communio*, it would not be possible to speak of God's being'" (Greshake, *Trójjedyny Bóg*, 46 – the quotation comes from Zizioulas, *Being as Communion. Studies in Personhood and the Church* (Crestwood-New York: St. Vladimir's Seminary Press, 1985), 16–8).

4 See Jean Daniélou *Teologia judeochrześcijańska. Historia doktryn chrześcijańskich przed Soborem Nicejskim*, (Kraków: WAM, 2002).

one God was always the Trinity, the communion,[5] although there were problems in relating this faith to the clearly formulated Old Testament truth of the one God and to monotheistic religiosity and pagan philosophy.[6] The symbols of faith, the baptismal formulas and the writings of the apologists have always expressed the trinitarian awareness of the Church's faith.[7] Faith in God was thus deepened by the figure of Jesus Christ and the work of the Holy Spirit – with the Holy Spirit Himself (accessible only through Christ) being the crucial experience of understanding Christ.[8] In the introduction to the section on the Holy Spirit, the *Catechism of the Catholic Church* includes the following words: "Now God's Spirit, who reveals God, makes known to us Christ, his Word, his living Utterance, but the Spirit does not speak of himself. The Spirit who 'has spoken through the prophets' makes us hear the Father's Word, but we do not hear the Spirit himself. We know him only in the movement by which he reveals the Word to us and disposes us to welcome him in faith. The Spirit of truth who 'unveils' Christ to us 'will not speak on his own'" (John 16:13) (CCC 687). "The One whom the Father has sent into our hearts, the Spirit of His Son, is truly God. Consubstantial with the Father and the Son, the Spirit is inseparable from them, in both the inner life of the Trinity and his gift of love for the world. In adoring the Holy Trinity, life-giving, consubstantial, and indivisible, the Church's faith also professes the distinction of Persons. When the Father sends his Word, He always sends his Breath. In their joint mission, the Son and the Holy Spirit are distinct but inseparable. To be sure, it is Christ who is seen, the visible image of the invisible God, but it is the Spirit who reveals Him" (CCC 689).

1.1 The Communion-based Pneumatological Potential of Biblical Texts

Biblical pneumatology plays an important role in the process of producing a treatise on the Holy Spirit. It usually takes the form of an account of the pneumatological

5 Cf. Walter Kasper, *Bóg Jezusa Chrystusa* (Wrocław: TUM Wydawnictwo Wrocławskiej Księgarni Archidiecezjalnej, 1996), 302–12.

6 Cf. Greshake, *Trójjedyny Bóg*, 46–7.

7 Cf. Eligiusz Piotrowski, "Traktat o Trójcy Świętej," in *Dogmatyka*, ed. Elżbieta Adamiak and Andrzej Czaja, and Józef Majewski (Warszawa: Więź, 2007), 4: 60–87; Jagodziński, *Węzłowe zagadnienia chrystologii komunijnej*, 15–6.

8 This is why F. Courth wrote about the revelation of the Father in the Son and the revelation of the Son in the Holy Spirit (Franz Courth, *Bóg trójjedynej miłości* (Poznań: Pallottinum, 1997), 299–305). Cf. Cornelius Keppler, "Der Heilige Geist – tatsächlich Gott, Person und Herr? Eine Spurensuche," *Stimmen der Zeit* 3 (2016), 187–8.

content of particular groups of New Testament writings,[9] accompanied by questions concerning the relationship of the Holy Spirit to the other Divine Persons.[10] The beginnings of trinitarian pneumatology, in the context of the Christologically relevant question of the interrelation between the Son and the Holy Spirit,[11] as well as the joint salvific action of both, could be seen in St. John.[12] Similarly to St. Paul, St. John did not present a speculative perspective of the biblical tradition, but a historical and practical perspective. In the farewell speeches, it is not the Persons but their functions that are revealed. The concept of person is unfamiliar to both the New and Old Testament, and in the biblical thought it is the function that defines the identity of a character. A change in the global cultural context was thus needed for trinitarian reflection to emerge.[13]

God reaches us through His Son Jesus Christ in the Holy Spirit, who is also the Spirit of His Son. The Holy Spirit – the Spirit of the Father and the Son – is given to us as the principle of unity and love.[14] The biblical image presents the Father as the fullness of life, who "saved us […] according to his mercy, through the water of rebirth and renewal by the Holy Spirit. This Spirit he poured out on us richly through Jesus Christ our Savior (Titus 3:5-6).[15] According to the Gospel of St. John, the Holy Spirit "comes from the Father" (John 15:26). Jesus said of Him: "the heavenly Father will give the Holy Spirit to those who ask Him" (Luke 11:13) – "the Holy Spirit, whom the Father will send in my name, will teach you everything, and

9 Cf. e.g. Max-Alain Chevalier, "Biblische Pneumatologie," in *Neue Summe Theologie*, vol. 1: *Der lebendige Gott*, ed. Peter Eicher (Freiburg-Basel-Wien: Herder, 1988), 341–78; Manuel Isidro Alves, "Dam wam Ducha nowego," *Communio. Międzynarodowy Przegląd Teologiczny* 8/1 (1988) 14–31. Y. Congar presents the Holy Spirit in a more systematic form as the "Breath of the Word" and the "Spirit of the Son" and also writes about pneumatic Christology. Cf. Yves Congar, "Systematische Pneumatologie," in *Neue Summe Theologie*, vol. 1: *Der lebendige Gott*, ed. Eicher (Freiburg -Basel-Wien: Herder, 1988), 393–9; Zdzisław Józef Kijas, *Traktat o Duchu Świętym i łasce* (Warszawa: Więź, 2007), 348–82.

10 Cf. Jagodziński, *Trynitologia komunijna*, 25–36.

11 Cf. Krzysztof Guzowski, *Duch Dialogujący. To dialegomenon Pneuma. Zarys pneumatologii dialogalnej* (Lublin: Wydawnictwo KUL, 2016), 142–4.

12 See the collection of testimonies deriving from the Scriptures on the union of Word and Spirit in Congar, *Słowo i Tchnienie* (Kraków: WAM, 2018), 34–9.

13 Cf. Chevalier, "Biblische Pneumatologie," 370.

14 After Easter, the being of the faithful introduced into the relationship of Jesus to the Father and participation in the power of God is attributed to the action of the Holy Spirit (Kasper, *Bóg Jezusa Chrystusa*, 303–4). For the names of the Divine Persons, see Józef Warzeszak, *Bóg Jedyny w Trójcy Osób* (Warszawa: Wydawnictwo Archidiecezji Warszawskiej, 2006), 214–9; Janusz Królikowski, *Tajemnica Trójjedynego. Studia z teologii trynitarnej* (Kraków: Wydawnictwo Naukowe UPJP II, 2015), 113–5.

15 Cf. Jan Daniel Szczurek, *Bóg Ojciec w tajemnicy Trójcy Świętej. Elementy patrylogii* (Kraków: Wydawnictwo M, 2003), 124–6.

remind you of all that I have said to you" (John 14:26). This is why the Epistle to the Ephesians reminded the believers: "In him you also [...] were marked with the seal of the promised Holy Spirit; this is the pledge of our inheritance toward redemption as God's own people, to the praise of his glory" (Eph 1:13-14).[16] The Christian tradition has spoken much about how we are related to the Father and the Son through the Holy Spirit, who is the centre of this relationship.

The Scriptures in the Old Testament use the word *ruah* in relation to God, His life and His creation of life, and in relation to human beings – designating in this way the God-given element that is the basis of life. God is breath as Creator (Ps 33:6; 104:29; Job 34:14). He acts as Spirit in the history of Israel (Isa 11:2; 42:1; 61:1) and in the hearts of people (Ezek 36:26-27; Joel 3:1-2). Particularly in the Book of Wisdom, *pneuma* conveys wisdom (Wis 7:2-3).[17] The New Testament sees Jesus as the Spirit-filled Messiah who also imparts the fullness of the Spirit (Rom 1:3; cf. 1 Pet 3:18; 1 Tim 3:16). This is based on the belief, strongly entrenched in the Old Testament, that the Spirit is the essence of the living God. Thus, when Jesus is referred to as the One who has the Spirit in Him and who gives the Spirit, His divinity is affirmed. But a new light is also shed on the essence of *Pneuma*. According to St. Paul, the Christian life is to be defined as abiding in Christ and in the Holy Spirit. The Spirit is a gift of God, another reality. Neither is it simply identical with God, nor is it our spirit.[18] In a particular way, it appears as a gift of love, which in a specific way characterises the essence of the mysterious Third Person between the Father and the Son, and Their action for the salvation of the world.[19]

The Holy Spirit reveals Himself as the source of life by collaborating in the Incarnation (Luke 1:35) – He descends upon Mary and gives human life to her Son without the intermediacy of a man. St. John interprets Christ's words: "Let anyone who is thirsty come to me, and let the one who believes in me drink!" as referring to the Spirit (John 7:37-38). The condition for eternal life is precisely the new birth of water and Spirit (John 3:5). Water is the visible sign of mortal life, hence it has a similar function for the invisible source of eternal life, which is the life-giving Holy Spirit (cf. John 6:63). Having life by the Spirit obliges one to be submissive to Him

16 Cf. Szczurek, *Bóg Ojciec w tajemnicy Trójcy Świętej*, 152–7.

17 Cf. Kasper, *Bóg Jezusa Chrystusa*, 253–4; Kijas, *Traktat o Duchu Świętym i łasce*, 327–348; Guzowski, *Duch Dialogujący*, 121–8.

18 Cf. Warzeszak, *Bóg jedyny w Trójcy Osób*, 160.

19 Cf. Wilhelm Breuning, *Nauka o Bogu* (Kraków: Wydawnictwo M, 1999), 45–8; Warzeszak, *Bóg jedyny w Trójcy Osób*, 156–63; Szczurek, *Bóg Ojciec w tajemnicy Trójcy Świętej*, 91–109; Guzowski, *Duch Dialogujący*, 41–50.

(Gal 5:25). The life-giving Holy Spirit is also the source of the Church's life, which can be seen in the remarkable episode with Ananias and Sapphira (Acts 5:1-11).[20]

The Gospels are keen to present the outpouring of the Holy Spirit as a consequence of Jesus' exaltation: "For as yet there was no Spirit, because Jesus was not yet glorified" (John 7:39). The resurrected Jesus stood among the disciples and bestowed the Holy Spirit on them: "When he had said this, he breathed on them and said to them, 'Receive the Holy Spirit'" (John 20:22; cf. 7:37-39; 4:16.26; 15:26; 16:13).[21] St. Luke explains the trinitarian meaning of the mystery of Pentecost: "This Jesus God raised up, and of that all of us are witnesses. Being therefore exalted at the right hand of God, and having received from the Father the promise of the Holy Spirit, he has poured out this that you both see and hear" (Acts 2:32-33).[22]

According to Luke's theology, the Holy Spirit belongs to the essence of God (the Father) and manifests Himself at the moment of the execution of the salvific work for the world. He appears to be the world-directed dimension of the intra-divine Father-Son relationship: the powerful action of the Father with the Holy Spirit seeks to reveal the essence of Christ calling the world into communion with God (Acts 2:36). In such a context, the famous passage from Joel's prophecy receives its full meaning: "In the last days [...] I will pour out my Spirit upon all flesh" (Acts 2:17). The Spirit of Yahweh, whom the prophet foreshadowed as an eschatological gift (Joel 3:1-5), now turns out to be the Spirit of the Father and the Son, through whom the Crucified One became the Messiah, by whose power the newly created Israel finally abides in union with God.[23]

The testimony of the New Testament in many places links the Holy Spirit to the salvific work of the Father and the Son. The resurrection of Jesus was a mighty act of the Father: "you killed the Author of life, whom God raised from the dead" (Acts 3:15). St. Paul also believes that it was the Father – God – who "raised" the Son (cf. Rom 10:9; 1 Cor 6:14; 1 Cor 15:15; Gal 1:1 etc.). However, the medium of this resurrection and its cause is the Holy Spirit: "If the Spirit of Him who raised Jesus from the dead dwells in you, He who raised Christ from the dead will give life to your mortal bodies also through His Spirit that dwells in you" (Rom 8:11). In

---

20 Cf. Szczurek, *Trójjedyny. Traktat o Bogu w Trójcy Świętej jedynym* (Kraków: Wydawnictwo Naukowe PAT, 2003), 148.

21 K. Guzowski combines the evangelists Mark and John (Guzowski, *Duch Dialogujący*, 130–5), as well as Matthew and Luke (ibid., 135–137) while discussing the pneumatological message of the New Testament. Simultaneously, he separately presents the message of Acts (ibid., 137–140) and St. Paul (ibid., 141–8) – distinguishing the themes concerning the relationship between Christ and the Holy Spirit, the Church and the Holy Spirit, and the Holy Spirit and charisms.

22 Cf. Bertram Stubenrauch, *Pneumatologia – traktat o Duchu Świętym* (Kraków: Wydawnictwo M, 1999), 47–9.

23 Cf. Stubenrauch, *Pneumatologia*, 49; Congar, *Wierzę w Ducha Świętego. Duch Święty w „ekonomii" Objawienia i doświadczenie Ducha*, vol. I (Warszawa: Wydawnictwo Księży Marianów, 1995), 85–90.

this context, the Holy Spirit is also assigned a role in the relationship between the Father and the Son, and between the Father and the people of God chosen in the Son. The resurrection marks the beginning of the work of the Holy Spirit, which is aimed at incorporating believers, formed in the Son's likeness, into the life of God.[24]

The resurrection of Jesus in the Spirit is also mentioned in 1 Peter 3:18: "For Christ also suffered for sins once for all, the righteous for the unrighteous, in order to bring you to God. He was put to death in the flesh, but made alive in the Spirit". The sharp body-spirit antithesis arose from the desire to characterise the life of the Resurrected One as a new mode of existence in the divine realm, incomparable to earthly life, one in which the Holy Spirit is the animating element. In this sense, Paul could say of Christ that He is the "animating spirit" as the exalted *Kyrios*, endowed with the life-giving elixir of divine love, by virtue of which the old, mortal Adam became the new, immortal Adam (1 Cor 15:45-50). The Holy Spirit, as an autonomous power, comes from within God and, as the Bearer of God's imperishable life, brings about the exaltation of the Crucified One. Being at the same time the Gift of the Exalted One – the Spirit leaves with Him the divine realm in order to bestow life on those who confess the Exalted One as their Lord.[25]

The New Testament writings direct their attention to the earthly life of Jesus in the Easter context: He is the Spirit-filled true Messiah, the Son; the fact of possessing the Holy Spirit distinguishes the conduct and essence of the Nazarene, so that even His origin can only be understood through the Holy Spirit.[26] The mystery of the Holy Spirit cannot be separated from either the Son or the Father – it can only be grasped indirectly, through the trinitarian aspect. Although They are inseparably united in action and existence, the Father, the Son and the Holy Spirit are distinct; someone else is the Father, someone else is the Son, someone else is the Holy Spirit.[27] Convinced of the momentousness of this Spirit, the Gospels interpret the historical biography of Jesus in two strands of narrative – in the accounts of Jesus' baptism (given by the Synoptics and in the Gospel of John) and in the Gospels of Matthew and Luke (in the so-called childhood accounts which describe, inter alia, the conception and birth of Jesus.[28]

---

24 Cf. Stubenrauch, *Pneumatologia*, 50–1; Congar, *Wierzę w Ducha Świętego. Duch Święty w „ekonomii" Objawienia*, 67–84; Kasper, *Bóg Jezusa Chrystusa*, 255.

25 Cf. Stubenrauch, *Pneumatologia*, 51–2.

26 Cf. Bernd Jochen Hilberath, "Pneumatologie," in *Handbuch der Dogmatik*, ed. Theodor Schneider (Düsseldorf: Patmos, 1992), 1: 464, 466–7, 473–9, 482–8.

27 Cf. Hilberath, "Pneumatologie," 488–9.

28 Cf. Stubenrauch, *Pneumatologia*, 53–5; Congar, *Wierzę w Ducha Świętego. Duch Święty w „ekonomii" Objawienia*, 52–63.

"In those days Jesus came from Nazareth of Galilee and was baptized by John in the Jordan. And just as he was coming up out of the water, he saw the heavens torn apart and the Spirit descending like a dove on him. And a voice came from heaven, 'You are my Son, the Beloved; with you I am well pleased'" (Mark 1:9-11). Henceforth begins the fulfilment of John's prediction that Jesus would baptise with the Holy Spirit – based on His anointing with the Holy Spirit, the Messiah is sufficiently entitled to this mission.[29]

The pneumatological components of the baptism scene are best visible in Luke's Gospel. First, it clearly emphasises the intimacy between the Father and the Son by mentioning that Jesus received the Holy Spirit when 'praying' (cf. Luke 3:21). In this way, the Spirit is intimately linked to the divine sonship of Jesus, expressed most pristinely in prayer, and especially in Jesus' form of address to the Father: *Abba*; the Spirit has its place in the Father-Son relationship. But Luke is equally emphatic about the reality of Jesus' anointing with the Holy Spirit and the peculiar reality of the Holy Spirit Himself. This is done through a supremely realistic understanding of the symbol of the dove: The Holy Spirit descends upon Jesus "visibly", literally, "in bodily form" (Luke 3:22).[30]

Only Matthew and Luke convey recollections of Jesus' childhood and provide statements about His earthly beginning. In the descriptions of the Annunciation, the Holy Spirit is gradually assigned the task of helping Jesus to realise his role as being the Son in an earthly existence. Therefore, it can be said that we come to know Jesus' "filial relationship" to God through the mediation of the Holy Spirit, i. e. through the manifesting presence of God. This is mainly described in Mattew 1:18-24 and Luke 1:26-38. Matthew, who unlike Luke says nothing about the annunciation, states emphatically that Jesus was conceived "from the Holy Spirit" (Matt 1:18-20). In Luke's version (1:26-38), the origin of Jesus from the Holy Spirit is more clearly linked to His virgin conception and His dignity as the Son of God: "The Holy Spirit will come upon you, and the power of the Most High will overshadow you; therefore the child to be born will be holy; he will be called Son of God" (Luke 1:35; cf. also Luke 1:32 – "He will be great, and will be called the Son of the Most High").[31]

With reference to the description of the baptism, all the synoptics include the remark that Jesus, "full of the Holy Spirit" (Luke 4:1), was led into the wilderness (cf. also Mark 1:12 – "the Spirit immediately drove him out"; Matt 4:1 – "Jesus was led up by the Spirit"). They thus place the earthly life of Jesus under the sign of the Holy Spirit. Meanwhile, advanced pneumatology, especially that of the Gospel of Luke, avoids describing Christ as a pneumatic. Jesus had the sovereign power to dispose of

29 Cf. Stubenrauch, *Pneumatologia*, 55–8.

30 Cf. Kasper, *Bóg Jezusa Chrystusa*, 254–5; Stubenrauch, *Pneumatologia*, 58.

31 Cf. Stubenrauch, *Pneumatologia*, 59–61.

the Holy Spirit, He is the Lord of *Pneuma*, and consequently He is not endowed with the Holy Spirit in the same way as the great Old Testament figures or Christians, but in a totally extraordinary way – Jesus is so closely united to the Father in the Spirit that He alone can establish His reign in the world. This is evident in Luke's very carefully crafted summary in the Acts: Peter alludes to the resurrection of Jesus, but the Holy Spirit is mentioned not in connection with the resurrection, but in relation to the earthly life of the Exalted One – "That message spread throughout Judea, beginning in Galilee after the baptism that John announced: how God anointed Jesus of Nazareth with the Holy Spirit and with power; how he went about doing good and healing all who were oppressed by the devil, for God was with him" (Acts 10:37-38). Luke only occasionally introduced the subject of the Holy Spirit into the proper story of Jesus, but he did this in such a way that the result was a compact and comprehensive picture. Christ and the Holy Spirit relate to each other synergistically, in a mutually compatible way – the appearance of Jesus was prepared, enabled and attested by the Holy Spirit. On the other hand, however, the independence of Jesus' teaching and some direct statements make it possible to recognise the work of the Holy Spirit.[32]

Other textual passages shed light on the opposite situation – Jesus' actions and speeches reveal the Holy Spirit. The passage from Luke 10:21 is significant here: "At that same hour Jesus rejoiced in the Holy Spirit and said, 'I thank you, Father, Lord of heaven and earth, because you have hidden these things from the wise and the intelligent and have revealed them to infants". Unlike Matthew, who conveyed these words without mentioning the Holy Spirit (Matt 11:25), Luke regards the Holy Spirit as the author of these words – and, in turn, Jesus as one filled with the Holy Spirit in a prominent sense. Thus, the Holy Spirit once again, as in the baptism scene, is shown to be the power in which the Father and the Son form an inner communion. In the Spirit the Son knows the Father, and in the Spirit the Son receives the mandate to reveal the Father in the world. The joyful confession is followed by a very surprising revelation for the synoptics: "All things have been handed over to me by my Father; and no one knows who the Son is except the Father, or who the Father is except the Son and anyone to whom the Son chooses to reveal him" (Luke 10:22). At the same time, from the revealing mission of the Son stems His knowledge of the significance of the Holy Spirit. This is what the disciples should ask for, since He is the Father's greatest gift (Luke 11:13) and the Comforter who, in moments of crisis and trial, "teaches" Christians what to say in order to bear witness to the faith (Luke 12:12; cf. Mark 13:11).

32 Cf. Stubenrauch, *Pneumatologia*, 63–5.

According to the first chapter of the Acts, the Resurrected One announces the sending of the Holy Spirit. This should take place on the day of Pentecost (cf. Acts 1:4-8; 2:33).

The other synoptics make rather modest statements on this subject. Exceptions include the logion concerning sin against the Holy Spirit, the evaluation (omitted by Luke) of Jesus' casting out of demons by the power of the Holy Spirit, and the so-called final command concerning the administration of baptism (Matt 28:19).[33]

The divinity of the Holy Spirit is also revealed in the teaching of St. Paul[34]. He reminds Christians: "Do you not know that you are God's temple and that God's Spirit dwells in you? If anyone destroys God's temple, God will destroy that person" (1 Cor 3:16-17). In another place he writes that human body is the temple of the Holy Spirit (1 Cor 6:19-20). So if we are the temple of the Holy Spirit, it means that He is true God.[35]

In the First Epistle to the Corinthians, Paul begins the list of charisms with a three-part formula that juxtaposes the action of "God" with three specific images of "Father", "Son" and "Holy Spirit". Thus, the charisms appear as the result of the action of the triune God: "Now there are varieties of gifts (*charismata*), but the same Spirit (*pneuma*); and there are varieties of services (*diakoniai*), but the same Lord (*Kyrios*); and there are varieties of activities (*energemata*), but it is the same God (*Theos*) who activates all of them in everyone" (1 Cor 12:4-6). The question of the Spirit (*Pneuma*) cannot be resolved simply by regarding Him as the result of the action of one power of the Father and the glorified Son. Therefore, in his various letters, the apostle speaks of "the Spirit of God" (1 Cor 3:16; 7:40; Rom 8:14; 2 Cor 3:3) and, at the same time, of "the Spirit of Jesus Christ" (Phil 1:19), of "the Spirit of the Lord" (2 Cor 3:17) or of "the Spirit of the Son" (Gal 4:6). Paul further refers to the personal dimension of the Holy Spirit. He unquestionably assumes His self-subjectivity: the Holy Spirit acts by His own will (1 Cor 12:11); He forms the baptised into a community by "dwelling" in them (cf. 1 Cor 3:16); He prays with the believers in such a way that He calls to God "Abba" together with them and calls Him the "good Father" of the community (cf. Gal 4:6; Rom 26-27). Logical conclusions about the direct affinity of the Holy Spirit to God's essence and activity, taking into account the Holy Spirit's own "person", were obviously the task of John's theology and, above all, of the early Church. Paul himself was not (yet) interested in systematically defining the relationships in God.[36]

The Gospel of St. John conveys a particularly insightful meditation on the relationship of the exalted Lord to the Holy Spirit that was promised and sent by

33 Cf. Stubenrauch, *Pneumatologia*, 65–8.

34 Cf. Warzeszak, *Bóg jedyny w Trójcy Osób*, 159–160.

35 Cf. Szczurek, *Trójjedyny*, 149.

36 Cf. Stubenrauch, *Pneumatologia*, 89–90.

Him.[37] Furthermore, more than the other New Testament testimonies, it addresses the "personal essence" of the Holy Spirit and His revealing work within the faithful community of the Church.[38] The Spirit is promoted later in John's Gospel to the status of the "Spirit of Truth" (cf. John 14:17; 15:26; 16:13). Christ is uniquely filled with the Spirit (cf. John 3:34) and is also the giver of the Holy Spirit. Jesus' death on the cross and His last breath of life provides John with the premise that the Holy Spirit comes and unfolds Jesus' action. Only through Him would the essence of the Son be fully revealed. The Holy Spirit is sent by the resurrected and exalted Lord when Jesus has completed His work and has been "glorified".[39]

The Gospel of St. John presents the Holy Spirit as a self-acting agent who guides all things to good. In this sense also, the concept of ,"paraclete" was applied to Jesus by John's communities: "But if anyone does sin, we have an advocate [paraclete] with the Father, Jesus Christ the righteous" (1 John 2:1). The texts give clear information about the origin of the Paraclete – he comes from the Father and is His "Gift", is "sent" by Him and proceeds from Him. God gives Himself and reveals Himself in Him as "Giver" and "Gift". However, this Advocate and Giver of courage comes at the initiative of Jesus. Moreover, the Paraclete is sent by the glorified Christ. This takes place, admittedly, "from the Father", but through the Son, who previously has to "depart" into the inaccessible light of God and from there sends the Advocate.[40]

The Holy Spirit derives from the unity of the Father and the Son and comes from the Father as well as from the exalted Son, since He "takes from that" which "belongs to the Son". The Son, however, has everything from the Father and in common with Him (cf. John 16:14-15). By making parallels between the sending of the Spirit and the sending of the Son, John acknowledges the origin of the Spirit from within the Father. In this way, the Holy Spirit – no less than the Son – is defined as God's Gift. The greatest and all-embracing Gift of the Father to the mankind in need of redemption is His Son. This giving of God is accomplished through the giving of the Spirit through the Son (John 16:16). The Spirit thus continues the Son's salvific work. He is in a direct and intimate relationship with both the Father and the Son, which makes Him a co-knower and co-bearer of God's single salvific initiative. In this sense, the Holy Spirit is placed on the divine plane, even though the Evangelist – unlike in relation to the Son – does not at any point call Him "God" (cf. John 1:1,18). It is only through His knowledge of the mysteries of God that the Holy Spirit is able to "teach" (14:26) the disciples what He Himself has "heard"

---

37 Cf. Kasper, *Bóg Jezusa Chrystusa*, 258–9.

38 Cf. Congar, *Wierzę w Ducha Świętego. Duch Święty w ekonomii Objawienia*, 91–102.

39 Cf. Stubenrauch, *Pneumatologia*, 95–102.

40 Cf. Stubenrauch, *Pneumatologia*, 104–5.

(16:13) from God and, after "surrounding the Son with glory" (16:14) "guide [the community of disciples] into all truth" (16:13).[41]

The person of the Holy Spirit is revealed in texts that attribute personal properties and activities to Him: defence, teaching the truth and others. The personal existence of the Holy Spirit derives from the revealed truth that He is the source of freedom. "Holy Spirit" is a proper name, not the name of a divine power. The personality of the Holy Spirit is also evidenced by the attribution to Him of the title *parakletos*, which roughly corresponds to the terms "comforter", "defender", "advocate" (John 14:16,26; 15:26; 16:7), and furthermore, by describing His actions using personal categories: teaching the truth (John 14:26; 16:3), bearing witness to Christ (John 15:26), revealing God's mysteries (1 Cor 2:10), explaining future events (John 16:13; Acts 21:11), ordaining bishops (Acts 20:28), speaking (Acts 4:25; 28:25), dwelling in us (1 Cor 3:16) like God and Christ (Rom 8:26). The personality of the Holy Spirit is also evidenced by the use of the word "name" in the so-called baptismal formula in Matthew 28:19. According to it, Christ commands to baptize nations in the name of the Father, and of the Son, and of the Holy Spirit – if the Holy Spirit were only a supernatural power, He would not have a proper name, but a designation. In the light of the New Testament revelation, the Holy Spirit is also the giver and guarantor of freedom: "where the Spirit of the Lord is, there is freedom" (2 Cor 3:17), and those having the Spirit of the Lord are truly free children of God and have access to God (cf. Rom 8:15,26; Gal 4:6). Another important personal title is "Lord". By contrast, the phrase "Now the Lord is the Spirit" in 2 Cor 3:17 is not entirely clear, since it is ambiguous to whom this title refers: to Christ or to the Spirit. The personal distinctiveness of the Holy Spirit is thus evident from the passages that speak of His origin from the Father, His being sent by the Father and the Son, and that He is the Spirit of both.[42]

In his farewell speech, Jesus promises the Spirit whom he will send, and "who comes from the Father" (John 15:26). It follows that the Holy Spirit is a person distinct from Christ – He is sent by Christ and, after all, no one sends oneself. He is also different from the Father because He comes from Him. On the basis of the revelation of the origin and sending of the Holy Spirit, we must recognise that He is someone distinct from the Father and the Son. The origin of the Holy Spirit from the Father is clearly revealed in the words: "[the Holy Spirit] who comes from the Father" (John 15:26). His origin from the Son, on the other hand, is not so clearly revealed. It can be inferred from the words in which Jesus announces that the Holy Spirit would reveal future things to the Church: "The Spirit of truth [...] will take what is mine and declare it to you" (John 16:13-14). The origin of the Holy Spirit

41 Cf. Stubenrauch, *Pneumatologia*, 105–6.

42 Cf. Szczurek, *Trójjedyny*, 149–150; Kijas, *Traktat o Duchu Świętym i łasce*, 382–5.

from the Son is also evident from the words in which Jesus justifies that all that the Father has is His (John 16:15). As a result of being begotten by the Father, the Son possesses all that the Father has. Therefore, the Son also has the power to give the Holy Spirit – just as the Father, also the Son has the power to breathe the Holy Spirit.[43]

The relationship of the Holy Spirit to the Father and to the Son is also evidenced by Jesus' words: "All things have been handed over to me by my Father" (Matt 11:27) – including the fact that the Holy Spirit comes from Him. Sending Him into the world by both of Them also testifies to this: "But the Advocate, the Holy Spirit, whom the Father will send in my name, will teach you everything, and remind you of all that I have said to you" (John 14:26; cf. v. 16); "When the Advocate comes, whom I will send to you from the Father, the Spirit of truth who comes from the Father, he will testify on my behalf" (John 15:26; cf. John 16:7; Luke 24:49; John 20:22). Two elements are crucial here – the sending and the origin. The sending of the Holy Spirit into the world is intended to continue and complete the work done by Christ. It is a temporal revelation of the intrinsic and extra-temporal origin of the Holy Spirit from the Father and the Son. It also results from the fact that the Holy Spirit is first the Spirit of the Father: "do not worry [...] for it is not you who speak, but the Spirit of your Father speaking through you" (Matt 10:19-20). The Holy Spirit, however, is not only the Spirit of the Father, but at the same time the Spirit of the Son: "And because you are children, God has sent the Spirit of his Son into our hearts, crying, 'Abba! Father!'" (Gal 4:6). Other New Testament texts call him the Spirit of Jesus (Acts 16:7), the Spirit of Christ (Rom 8:9), or the Spirit of Jesus Christ (Phil l:19).[44]

1.2 The Communional Aspects of the Historical Development of Pneumatology

The meditation on the triune nature of God took place in the early days of theology in the context of contemporary experience and thought, the specific worldview, language and concepts that were influenced by the philosophies of Middle Platonism and Neoplatonism. These emphasised the absolute transcendence of the only, supreme, incomprehensible and unchanging deity vis-à-vis the manifold and changeable world of matter. However, they also embraced the concept of the de-

43 Cf. Szczurek, *Trójjedyny*, 151.

44 Cf. Szczurek, *Trójjedyny*, 151–2; Warzeszak, *Bóg jedyny w Trójcy Osób*, 160–163; Piotrowski, *Traktat o Trójcy Świętej*, 51–2.

scending, receding mediations of the divine towards the world and, at the same time, the ascending of the world towards the divine.

1.2.1 The Communional Position of the Holy Spirit in the Light of the First Trinitological Concepts

In the first two centuries' attempts at systematisation, one can see the conceptual and theological struggles concerning the definition of the relationship between the Holy Spirit and Christ, especially in view of Christ's pre-existence in the bosom of the Father. However, Christian writings of this period referred the term *pneuma* to the pre-existent Christ, which gave rise to specific binitarianism, as the term "spirit" usually referred to the pre-existence of Christ. The distinction of the "Three" began after the incarnation. The Holy Spirit was also perceived as the creator of the Church and its unity in the relationship between the particular persons and the two components – charismatic and institutional. According to the *Didache*, the charismatic function of prophets and teachers was shared by apostles, missionaries, prophets, as well as bishops and deacons. Those who proclaim the Good News and the coming of the Kingdom of God are filled by the Holy Spirit and given His power. From the Holy Spirit comes the inspiration of the Scriptures, the preaching of the prophets and the valour of the apostles. The Church Fathers saw in the Holy Spirit the principle of sanctification and the indestructibility of the body of Christ. The Holy Spirit accomplishes the purification of the Church in history. Confession of faith in the Holy Spirit was usually linked to the idea of new life as the fruit of baptism. Life in the Spirit opens to the ultimate goal – the resurrection of bodies. This "new life" was understood primarily in a personal sense, as a new way of existence, which commences sacramentally through baptism and leads to the fullness of filial life in close intimacy with the Father and the Son by the power of the Holy Spirit.[45]

In his first attempts at trinitological systematisation, St. Irenaeus overcame the "binitarianism" of the early apologists and emphasised the presence of the divinising Holy Spirit in the Church. The Church preserves the Gospel containing the Holy Spirit; in the Church one receives the Holy Spirit and a new life through baptism; in the Church the work of sanctification, purification of man and elevation to divine life is fulfilled through the Holy Spirit; the Holy Spirit ensures the eternal youthfulness of faith in the Church; in the Church the Word and the Spirit work together to fulfil the work of the Trinity, i. e. to form the new man, redeemed by Christ, filled with life by the Spirit and made an adoptive son of the Father. The Holy Spirit gives man a new shape of personal life and new dignity. "Spiritual man"

---

45 Cf. Guzowski, *Duch Dialogujący*, 151–2.

is the "new man" living in the Spirit as His masterpiece. The created man is an imperfect image made perfect by the likeness obtained through the Holy Spirit. The filling with the Holy Spirit of the sanctified man is called by Irenaeus "implantation in the Holy Spirit".[46]

St. Hippolytus compared the Holy Spirit to the fragrant breath given by the Father to the Son to be poured out upon the new creation. Hanging on the cross, Christ gave off a fragrance similar to an apple tree, and after the resurrection, the community took on the new garment of the Holy Spirit, which knows no corruption; with the attainment of new life in the Spirit, the Church appears like a lily to which, lured by the fragrance, the sojourners from far away in the desert approach and receive by grace the citizenship with the saints. This vision of the Church is pneumatic, it is a community organised on the basis of the apostolic order and tradition. Church services are preceded by charisms, while the Church's worship and liturgical life are the fruit of the Holy Spirit. Tertullian introduced the term *Trinitas* (Trinity) to describe the three "persons". He saw a numerical distinction in the Trinity but did not recognise a separation due to the unity of substance. He taught that the Holy Spirit comes from the Father through the Son.[47]

Origen gives the Holy Spirit a third place and calls Him the third "hypostasis". He also calls Him the "Gift" and recognises that all gifts come from Him. One of Origen's significant works in pneumatology is his concept of the spiritual exegesis of the Gospels. Because it was written under the inspiration of the Spirit of God, the Holy Spirit imparts Himself in it, while its truth can only be known by those who have the Spirit of Christ and are able to transform the sensual Gospel into the spiritual Gospel. The Holy Spirit sanctifies and enlightens man. The Son and the Spirit reveal God: the Son is the objective revelation – the image of the Father, and the Spirit is the light by which the soul can see the image of the Son and in it contemplate the face of the Father.[48]

Within such a framework, there was an attempt to interpret first the "Son", and then the "Spirit", as a subordinate mediating quantity between the Father-God and the world, which was the essence of the view known as subordinationism. The second problem was monarchianism. Since the Father, the Son and the Holy Spirit do not stand in a hierarchical relationship to each other – perhaps they are one (*monos*) with no real distinction? The Gospels vividly show the difference (and indeed the contrast between the Father and the Son), although equally apparent is their unity, which does not erase the difference. However, this led to further reflection: Is the difference only conditioned "economically" – referring only to the

46 Cf. Guzowski, *Duch Dialogujący*, 152–4.
47 Cf. Guzowski, *Duch Dialogujący*, 154–6.
48 Cf. Guzowski, *Duch Dialogujący*, 156–8.

history of salvation, or does it exist in God Himself – "theologically" (immanent) in the Holy Trinity? The Christian answer was that God not only manifests Himself as the Father, the Son and the Holy Spirit, but that He Himself is triune.[49] Alongside the subordinationist tendency, there was also the theory that the Son and the Spirit are not subordinate to the Father, but are merely external modes of manifestation as historical figures of revelation (*modi*) of the One, hidden and incomprehensible God, who hides completely "behind" His epiphanies – i. e. modalism.[50]

In the face of these imperfect attempts, the great breakthrough came with the work of the Council of Nicea (325) and the Council of Constantinople (381). The starting point was not the stagnant forms of philosophical monotheism, but the experience of faith evoked by the Revelation. God is not an abiding or a circulating monad, but multiplicity, life, communication, communion. The Father sends his consubstantial Son (*homooúsios tô patrí*) – and, as a result, the Holy Spirit – so that man can encounter God in Them and gain a share in the divine life.[51] The Greek notion of God as untouched, undefiled by the world, completely identical with Himself and unmoved by the *arché* has been corrected. There is communication in true God, because only then can He be conceived of as giving Himself to the world through His Son and the Spirit.[52]

The abandonment of the rigid monarchical image of God resulted in the rejection of tritheism, subordinationism and modalism. After heated debates, the Church accepted the claim that God is one in his substance and triune in persons

---

49 Cf. Breuning, *Nauka o Bogu*, 145–8. "The whole dispute provoked by the debate over monarchianism has become complicated by two circumstances. The first is a rather linguistic problem – the issue of translation. From a purely philosophical point of view, the Greek terms *prosopon, hypostasis, ousia* and the Latin *persona, substantia* are related words. The second circumstance is rather of substantive nature, but is also somewhat due to the differences in mentality between the Christian East and the Christian West, and the different course of dogmatic disputes also had an additional influence on it. In the West, the struggle against modalism left a strong mark; it was necessary to present the internal differences in the Trinity between the Father, the Son and the Holy Spirit in such a way that Their unity (*Trinitas*) remained intelligible. This was achieved by emphasising the equality of the Persons and substantiality as its basis. Then, however, the personality remains almost necessarily in the shadows. In the East, on the other hand, speculation focused on overcoming the destructive effects of subordinationism. It can be overcome when the focus is put the unity of the Persons in essence. The theologians of the East, however, saw then that the differentiation of the Persons becomes vague, thus they sought to emphasise the conduct of the Persons. Then, however, the Father must be seen as the Beginning, as the One from whom the Son (and the Holy Spirit) come, and there lies a danger that the unity becomes blurred" (Jagodziński, *Węzłowe zagadnienia chrystologii komunijnej*, 19).

50 Cf. Greshake, *Trójjedyny Bóg*, 49.

51 Cf. Courth, *Bóg trójjedynej miłości*, 179–82; Breuning, *Nauka o Bogu*, 152–6.

52 Cf. Peter Hünermann, *Jesus Christus. Gottes Wort in der Zeit* (Münster: Aschendorff, 1994), 145; Jagodziński, *Trynitologia komunijna*, 46–8.

(hypostases).[53] This, however, is connected with the central problem of the relation between unity and trinitarian multiplicity in God.[54]

Western thought about the triune God has always been characterised by specific "unitarianism". Although theology explained that intra-trinitarian references could not be understood subordinationistically, as if the Son (and the Spirit) did not possess full divinity, the Platonic and Neoplatonic way of thinking and representation was nevertheless preserved. According to it, the Son and the Holy Spirit – equal in nature – had for centuries been "derived" from the unity of the Father, and accordingly the Neoplatonic image of the *fontalis plenitudo* as the ultimate and supreme unity from which everything else "flows" was also transferred to the Father. This, however, resulted in the incomprehensibility of the intra-divine "genesis" (even understood as eternal) of the trinity from the unity in which the Father has given birth to the Word and breathed the Spirit of love for ages. This hindered the communal understanding of the Trinity, according to which unity and plurality in the Trinity mutually constitute each other, and the plurality can be understood as the inter-personal unity of God that constitutes the exchange of Divine Persons[55].

If a "philosophical" approach to God prevailed among theologians, which looked at Him not in terms of His historico-salvific action but in terms of the metaphysics of being, He appeared as the "supreme substance", the only and highest principle of the world. In the history of the revelation of this God, the personal agencies (Son, Holy Spirit) were somehow incorporated into this assumed form of substantial unity – with the form itself experiencing no change or modification – and the triplicity was attempted to be conceived as added to the pre-existing substantial unity. Here, however, a central problem arose: What is the difference of the Persons in the assumed unity of God? Especially given the fact that the theology of the Trinity realised that the differences in God are realised (through the begetting of the Son and the breathing of the Holy Spirit) most often without relating Them to how the differences, as it were, "return" to unity (through the reciprocity of knowledge and love).

Under the influence of St. Augustine, a view of the triune God as *una trinitas, una divina substantia* (even in widespread prayer) spread astonishingly quickly in the West, while the historico-salvific view of the three Persons receded into the background (although it did not disappear completely). St. Thomas Aquinas was not even afraid to consider as correct the formula claiming that God is *una*

53 Cf. Kasper, *Bóg Jezusa Chrystusa*, 319–24; Czesław Stanisław Bartnik, *Dogmatyka katolicka* (Lublin: Wydawnictwo KUL, 2000), 1: 201–2; Piotrowski, *Traktat o Trójcy Świętej*, 97–133.

54 Jagodziński, *Węzłowe zagadnienia chrystologii komunijnej*, 20–1.

55 Cf. Greshake, *Trójjedyny Bóg*, 55–7; Jagodziński, *Węzłowe zagadnienia chrystologii komunijnej*, 21–2.

persona[56] – although the ancient Church considered it heretical.[57] This related to the danger of showing the essence of God as something "fourth", "above", "beside" or "behind" the three Persons.[58] This unitarianism led scholastic theology to produce the treatise *De Deo uno*, where the general doctrine of God was considered without the trinitarian "differentiation"; the previously appended *De Deo trino* was produced separately. As a result, the trinitarian image of God gave way ontologically and cognitively, as well as existentially, to a monarchianistic concept of God. This tendency could be expressed in the highly simplified formula *Unum in Trinitate*, i. e. God was presented first as pre-personal substance that additionally appears in the trinitarian Persons – with the unintentional danger of modalism.[59]

There is still an alternative form of Eastern theology, inclined to see God as *Unus in Trinitate* – to see Him as a unity realised personally in the Father – the Father communicates to the Son and the Holy Spirit the essence He possesses intrinsically, so that the one God lives and acts in a trinitarian-relational structure. Indeed, in the New Testament, the name "God" almost always signified the Father as the beginning of creation and salvation history, and assuming that God appears in the history of salvation as He is, the person of the Father is also the intrinsically trinitarian beginning and source of the Son and the Holy Spirit. This concept cannot be questioned, but it carries with it the dangerous tendency to consider the person of the Father and the unity embodied in Him independently of the other Persons, and to see the Son and the Holy Spirit as subordinate, "consequent complements" of the God-Father already constituted in Himself. This in turn opens the way to the specifically Eastern danger – subordinationism.[60]

Therefore, at the core of trinitology lay a narrowing of the field of vision, which resulted in "inferring" the intrinsic essence of God on the basis of certain connections in the history of salvation, while ignoring the other connections.[61]

---

56 Cf. STh III, 3, 3, ad 1, 2: *ita exclusis per intellectum proprietatibus personalibus, remanebit in consideratione nostra natura divina, ut subsistens, et ut persona* [...] *remanebit in intellectu una personalitas Dei....*

57 Cf. Josef Ratzinger, *Dogma und Verkündigung* (München-Freiburg: Wewel, 1973) 223.

58 Cf. Greshake, *Trójjedyny Bóg*, 58–9.

59 In modern times, the notion of person as subject has additionally developed, whose essential features are being in and for oneself, self-consciousness, self-determination and freedom – this makes it difficult to transfer the notion of person to the triplicity of the Divine Persons, leaving barely the possibility of relating the notion of person to the one God as the "absolute subject." The trinitarian distinction in God is in this situation either completely stripped of its reference to the person or robbed of its vital sense, and the advantage is given – by force of circumstance – to the unitarian aspect of the image of God. Cf. Greshake, *Trójjedyny Bóg*, 59–60.

60 Cf. Greshake, *Trójjedyny Bóg*, 61.

61 Cf. Jagodziński, *Węzłowe zagadnienia chrystologii komunijnej*, 22–4.

1.2.2 The Communion-based Pneumatological Aspects in the Further Development of Trinitology

The trinitarian faith, as the first experience of faith and of the Church, has always been firmly rooted in the consciousness of the community, even before any scientific findings of theological reflection, and present in liturgy and meditation.[62] It carried within it the awareness that the one God has always been a Holy Trinity, a relational entity, a Communion.[63] What was needed, however, was a deepening that took into account the explicitly internal references between the Father, the Son and the Holy Spirit. Once the erroneous concepts of origins had been dealt with, a breakthrough was made. This consisted in no longer starting from the stagnant forms of philosophical monotheism but focusing on the Revelation. The One God is thus not a monad, but a multitude – life, love, communion. [64] The Father sent the consubstantial Son and the consubstantial Spirit into history so that we might encounter God Himself and gain a share in His life.[65] Once the problem of the

---

62 Cf. Jürgen Werbick, "Trinitätslehre," in *Handbuch der Dogmatik*, ed. Schneider (Düsseldorf: Patmos, 2000), 2: 491–2; Królikowski, *Tajemnica Trójjedynego*, 143–55.

63 Cf. Courth, *Bóg trójjedynej miłości*, 71–5, 139–46; Greshake, *Trójjedyny Bóg*, 46–7; Szczurek, *Trójjedyny*, 165–9; Warzeszak, *Bóg jedyny w Trójcy Osób*, 201–2. See Michael Fiedorowicz, *Teologia ojców Kościoła. Podstawy wczesnochrześcijańskiej refleksji nad wiarą* (Kraków: Wydawnictwo UJ, 2009).

64 Cf. Kasper, *Bóg Jezusa Chrystusa*, 367–71. J.D. Zizioulas emphasises that the primary reality of God is not substance but person: "In God [...] it is not divine nature that is the origin of the divine persons. It is the person of the Father that 'causes' God to exist as Trinity. However, 'Father' has no meaning outside a relationship with the Son and the Spirit, for he is the Father *of* someone. This plurality and interdependence of the persons is the basis of a new ontology. The one essence is not the origin or cause of the being of God, it is the person of the Father that is the ultimate agent, but since 'Father' implies communion he cannot be understood as a being in isolation. Personal communion lies at the very heart of divine being. [...] The Church [...] insisted [...] that the phrase 'God is love' means that God is constituted by these personal relationships, God is communion: love is fundamental to his being, not an addition to it. [...] That 'God is love' means that God is the communion of this Holy Trinity. God the Father would lose his identity and being if he did not have the Son, and the same applies to the Son and to the Spirit. If we took away the communion of the Trinity to make God a unit, God would not be communion and therefore would not be love. [. . .] God is love in his very being. It is not however himself that he loves, so this is not self-love. The Father loves the Son and the Spirit, the Son loves the Father and the Spirit, the Spirit loves the Father and the Son: it is another person that each loves. It is the person, not the nature or essence, who loves, and the one he loves is also a person. Because divine love is a matter of personal communion this love is free: each person loved is free to respond to this love with love" (Zizioulas, *Lectures in Christian Dogmatics*, (London-New York: T&T Clark, 2009) 53–4).

65 St. Athanasius and the Cappadocian Fathers created the foundations of a metaphysics built on evangelical meditation, but their efforts did not deprive the theology they created of its basic phenomenological approach. According to J.-L. Marion, Saints Basil the Great and Augustine proposed an elaborate phenomenological model for trinitarian theology. Basil wanted to trace the

Son's relationship to the Father had been clarified, the pneumatological question became pressing.[66]

St. Athanasius rejected the thesis that the Holy Spirit is different in essence from the Father and the Son, because it would destroy the historico-salvific dynamics of the process of deification. After all, according to St. Paul and St. John, the Holy Spirit makes us similar to Christ. He is the image of Christ in us, just as the Son is the image of the Father. Thus, the Holy Spirit is God just as the Father and the Son are God. St. Basil argued similarly, beginning with the liturgy of baptism administered in the name of the Father, and of the Son, and of the Holy Spirit. Since we receive divine life through the Holy Spirit, He cannot be a creation. This followed even more clearly from the doxology.[67]

After the Council of Nicaea, the relevant problem was the precise clarification of the terms *ousia* and *hypostasis*. God is only one. One being not only "acts as" Father, Son and Holy Spirit – there are real differences in the very life of God, the "names" of the divine Persons are therefore distinguishable vehicles for this being.[68] The titles of the Holy Spirit from the pneumatological addendum of the First Council of Constantinople (381) to its *Creed* are "Lord" and "Live-Giver"

---

question of the manner in which Christ is the image of the invisible Father. The work of Father's revelation in the incarnate Son was made possible by the special activity of the Holy Spirit, who made the body of Jesus an icon of the mystery of the Father. The revelation of the Holy Trinity became a drama in which all the Persons participate. The Son reveals the Father, the Father becomes visible in the Son and in the whole of the Son's life, and all this is made possible by the light of the Holy Spirit who constitutes the revealed corporeity of the Son and transforms the eyes of the one who looks at the Son. This is a basic and crucial schema in Basil's trinitarian theology that has not been noticed until now. Cf. Robert J. Woźniak, *Praca nad dogmatem. Wybrane aspekty odnowy teologii dogmatycznej* (Kraków: WAM, 2022), 229–30.

66 Cf. Kasper, *Bóg Jezusa Chrystusa*, 321, see Kijas, *Traktat o Duchu Świętym i łasce*, 386–419.

67 Cf. Breuning, *Nauka o Bogu*, 156–8; Szczurek, *Trójjedyny*, 185–6; Guzowski, *Duch Dialogujący*, 160–2.

68 Cf. Courth, *Bóg trójjedynej miłości*, 154–64. "As conceptual material, the words *ousia* and *hypostasis* (to some extent also *prosopon*) were available. All, however, were inadequate and all were sometimes rejected: *homoousios, treis hypostaseis, prosopon.* Each of the concepts from which the grammar of faith was ultimately constructed was sometimes first rejected, which, from the historical point of view, showed its only analogous utility. The formula in which the great Cappadocian Fathers ultimately framed the Church's faith is, in the thought of Late Antiquity, at first a veritable paradox: one *ousia,* three *hypostasis* – back then, there was no unambiguous distinction between *ousia* and *hypostasis*, thus it became directly apparent that belief in the triune God must postulate a new order that demands a distinction that had not existed before. [...] the separation of the two planes, *ousia* and *hypostasis*, thus effected, with a simultaneous complete unity, or the creation of *persona* as a concept opposed to *essentia*, was an event of fundamental importance in the history of the spirit. Thus unveiled was a new dimension of thinking which had hitherto been touched at best in the dark, namely, the dimension of the personal, which for the first time was clearly distinguished from the 'physical', the material, from the general essence" (Ratzinger, "O kwestii historyczności dogmatów,"

(*to kyrion* – ruling, *to zoopoion* – life-giving[69]). The distinction between the Holy Spirit and Christ (*Kyrios*) was made explicit and the divine plane of dominion was retained (cf. 2 Cor 3:17; John 6:63; Rom 8:2; 2 Cor 3:6). The concept of origin from the Father is based on John 15:26 (cf. 1 Cor 2:12) and speaks of the internal relations of the Holy Trinity.[70] The Father is the origin in relation to the Son and the Holy Spirit. But the Holy Spirit is not begotten by the Father but comes from Him,[71] hence he is not identical with the Son and is also not a creation.[72] He receives jointly with the Father and the Son the same honour and glory and is therefore not on a lower plane of existence than the Father and the Son. He also shares in revelation (cf. 2 Peter 1:21). However, in this *Creed* there is no mention of the identity of the Holy Spirit as to His essence.[73]

The differentiation of Persons has been expressed by the term "hypostasis" or "person". One being does not abolish or exclude the possibility of hypostatic differentiation. Hypostasis is the way in which being God is realised in the Father, the Son and the Holy Spirit.[74] The difference in the Holy Trinity is thus the difference in the relations of the Three Persons to each other, and the autonomy of the divine Hypostases goes together with the inseparability of being God. In Eastern theology the doctrine of "perichoresis" is based on this assumption.[75] The terms "being unbegotten" or "being without beginning" in relation to the Father do not, therefore, speak of a lack of relationship. In Cappadocian trinitarian theology, not having a beginning defines the property of the first Person in relation to the other two. The first Hypostasis has no beginning as the Father – and it is here that the unambiguity about the nature of the two other Hypostases has its roots. Besides, the Cappadocian Fathers were aware that in God's outward action the Hypostases are inseparably united. They explained that the Hypostasis of the Holy Spirit has

---

in Ratzinger, *Opera omnia*, ed. Krzysztof Góźdź and Marzena Górecka (Lublin: Wydawnictwo KUL, 2018), IX/1: 536–7.

69 Cf. Courth, *Bóg trójjedynej miłości*, 182–5; Ysabel de Andia, ""Święty, Pan i Dawca życia,"" *Communio. Międzynarodowy Przegląd Teologiczny* 8/1 (1988) 32–48.

70 Cf. Warzeszak, *Bóg jedyny w Trójcy Osób*, 203–4; Piotr Liszka, *Duch Święty, który od Ojca (i Syna) pochodzi* (Wrocław: Papieski Wydział Teologiczny, 2000), 25–38.

71 Cf. Szczurek, *Bóg Ojciec w tajemnicy Trójcy Świętej*, 178–83; Liszka, *Duch Święty, który od Ojca (i Syna) pochodzi*, 64–70.

72 See Szczurek, *Bóg Ojciec w tajemnicy Trójcy Świętej*, 184–194.

73 Cf. Kasper, *Bóg Jezusa Chrystusa*, 265–27; Breuning, *Nauka o Bogu*, 158–62; Warzeszak, *Bóg jedyny w Trójcy Osób*, 178–80; Piotrowski, *Traktat o Trójcy Świętej*, 128–33; Królikowski, *Tajemnica Trójjedynego*, 157–83; Guzowski, *Duch Dialogujący*, 167–8.

74 Cf. Breuning, *Nauka o Bogu*, 163–4; Warzeszak, *Bóg jedyny w Trójcy Osób*, 194–200; Kijas, *Traktat o Duchu Świętym i łasce*, 394–402.

75 Cf. Szczurek, *Trójjedyny*, 221–3; Jagodziński, *Węzłowe zagadnienia chrystologii komunijnej*, 35–7; Bruno Forte, *Istota chrześcijaństwa* (Lublin: Wydawnictwo KUL, 2007), 102–13.

its origin in the Father. In contrast to the beginning of the Son, they spoke not of begetting, but of origin. The Holy Spirit is thus not a second Son.[76]

The Western bishops at Rome (328) confirmed the teaching of the Council of Constantinople: The Holy Spirit is of one power and essence with the Father and the Son – thus they applied the term *homoousios – unius substantiae* to the Holy Spirit, stating that He possesses the same essence as God the Father and the Son of God; the Holy Spirit comes from the Father truly and in His own way, as the Son, of Divine essence, is truly God – the Council called the Holy Spirit directly God and not merely Lord. The Father, the Son and the Holy Spirit possess one deity, one power, one majesty, one authority, one glory, one dominion, one kingdom, one will and one truth – each Divine Person thus possesses all the absolute attributes in a perfect manner; the Father, the Son and the Holy Spirit – each is eternal; the Son is begotten of the Father, viz. from His Divine essence; the Father, the Son and the Holy Spirit – each can do all things, knows all things and is equal to each Person, present everywhere; God the Father created all things, visible and invisible things through the Son and the Holy Spirit. The Council affirms here the unity of action of the Holy Trinity, which results from having one and the same nature; the Father, the Son and the Holy Spirit are equal, they are living, they judge all things, they bring all things to life, they create all things, they save all things; we are baptised in the Father, the Son and the Holy Spirit and not in angels; we believe in the Holy Trinity, i. e. in the Father, the Son and the Holy Spirit, and in Their Name we are baptised; the Holy Spirit is to be worshipped as much as the Father and the Son; all the Divine Persons have one true deity, power and substance.[77]

The most significant impetus for the conceptual apprehension of unity and difference in the Holy Trinity came when St. Augustine adopted and then developed the concept of relation (*relatio*).[78] Following Aristotle, he stated that God is His very own essence, absolute substance, and there is nothing accidental in Him. However, we know from the Bible that one God is the Father, the Son and the Holy Spirit. These cannot be properties added to the divine substance. They are something real and bring distinction to God. The Father is not the Son, the Son is neither the Father nor the Holy Spirit. The only philosophical possibility to explain such a situation was to reach for the category of relation, which is theologically appropriate because it is not accidental and is immutable. Divine substance is thus an arrangement of relations.[79]

---

76 Cf. Breuning, *Nauka o Bogu*, 162–6; Warzeszak, *Bóg jedyny w Trójcy Osób*, 175–7; Szczurek, *Trójjedyny*, 186–190; Guzowski, *Duch Dialogujący*, 162–7.

77 Cf. Warzeszak, *Bóg jedyny w Trójcy Osób*, 181–2.

78 Cf. Guzowski, *Duch Dialogujący*, 171–4.

79 See Courth, *Bóg trójjedynej miłości*, 245–6. St. Augustine considered this interpretation to be clearer than the reflection using the concept of person since theology of the time had not yet developed

When we speak of God – we become aware of His unity. We perceive difference when we speak of God the Father, God the Son and God the Holy Spirit. Each is not "something different" (*aliud*), but each is "different/other" (*alius*). And because they are always such, Their being the Father, the Son, and the Holy Spirit is not accidental. The fact of being other can be described as a relation. The first two designations are clearly concepts that define mutual relations. The peculiarity of the Holy Spirit is that He is the gift of the Father to the Son and of the Son to the Father, the love that unites them, and love unambiguously constitutes a relation and is not the perfection of relations in general.[80]

The *Quicumque Creed* (5th century) provides a fairly comprehensive explanation of the faith in the categories developed by St. Augustine. There is one God in the Trinity and the Trinity in unity. Starting from the affirmation of the existence of one God, the text proceeds to distinguish the three divine Persons and re-emphasises the unity of God's essence: one deity, equal glory, co-eternal majesty of the three Persons. It then emphasises the divine attributes of the three Divine Persons: the uncreated, boundless, eternal, omnipotent Father, Son and Holy Spirit – but this does not mean that the Three are uncreated – there is one eternal, one uncreated, one boundless, simply one God. In turn, the creed emphasises what is different about the individual Divine Persons: i. e. the Father proceeds from no one, the Son proceeds from the Father by begetting, the Holy Spirit proceeds from the Father and the Son.[81]

1.2.3 The Communional Dimension of the Filioque

The *Filioque* was first and foremost supposed to emphasise the Deity of the Son, but it also expressed a demand for a more precise definition of the origin of the third Divine Hypostasis.[82] The Son comes from the beginningless Father, and certainly this also applies to the Holy Spirit. But in what relation does the Holy Spirit stand

---

a precise distinction between person, substance and hypostasis. It was only because of linguistic difficulties that Augustine acquiesced to the use of the term "person" in trinitology. Cf. Breuning, *Nauka o Bogu*, 170–1; Szczurek, *Trójjedyny*, 208–15.

80 Cf. Breuning, *Nauka o Bogu*, 171–3; Greshake, *Trójjedyny Bóg*, 89; Jagodziński, *Trynitologia komunijnu*, 49–52.

81 Cf. Courth, *Bóg trójjedynej miłości*, 212–14; Warzeszak, *Bóg jedyny w Trójcy Osób*, 182.

82 Cf. Courth, *Bóg trójjedynej miłości*, 187–91; Leo Scheffczyk, "Sens Filioque," *Communio. Międzynarodowy Przegląd Teologiczny* 8/1 (1988) 49–60; Hilberath, "Pneumatologie," 506–11; Harald Wagner, *Dogmatyka*, (Kraków: WAM, 2007), 119–20; Królikowski, *Tajemnica Trójjedynego*, 219–41. Gerhard Ludwig Müller, *Dogmatyka katolicka* (Kraków: WAM, 2015), 476–8. For the discussion of the origin of the Holy Spirit in the Western tradition, see Liszka, *Duch Święty, który od Ojca (i Syna) pochodzi*, 71–86; in the Eastern Tradition, see Hilberath, "Pneumatologie," 511–4; Guzowski, *Duch Dialogujący*, 377–81. J.D. Zizioulas wrote that the history of the *Filioque* is so saturated with polemic that it is

to the Son? In the order of economy, no difficulties have arisen – the relation to the Father and the Son is the gift of the Holy Spirit, He Himself being their salvific Gift. According to the Scriptures, the Son sent by the Father gives us the Holy Spirit, hence the Holy Spirit comes from the Father through (*para, dia*) the Son. St Augustine's speculation on love as the intra-trinitarian communal bond[83] showed the origin of the Holy Spirit from the two first Hypostases as self-evident. The proper origin is the Father – from Him come "primordially" the Son and the Holy Spirit ("primordially" in this case, since the Holy Spirit also comes from the Son).[84]

The *Quicumque* symbol also contains the teaching of the *Filioque* in a moderate formulation, which came along with the question of the origin of the Holy Spirit and His relation to the Son. The Greeks and Latinists first unanimously spoke of the origin of the Holy Spirit from the Father through the Son. They wanted to show that the only source of the Divinity is the Father alone, while the Spirit – according to information contained in the Scriptures – is mediated by the Son, i. e. He proceeds from the Father and is transmitted to the world through the Son. In addition to this, Eastern and Western theologians also taught about the origin of the Holy Spirit from the Father and the Son. St. Cyril of Alexandria believed that the Spirit was the "property" of the Son and came "from both", but he did not have in mind the close relationship of the Son and the Holy Spirit, but the dignity of Divine existence of the Holy Spirit and wanted to defend His equality with the Son's nature against the Arians. The *Filioque* (in the material, not necessarily literal, sense) thus fulfilled a variety of theological functions for a long time and was sometimes perceived as absolutely false or constraining.[85]

The problem was initiated by St. Augustine's trinitarian theology. Since he understood the Holy Spirit as that which is common between the Father and the Son – as their reciprocal Gift – the source of His origin had to be sought in both of Them. Augustine was bolder than the Eastern theologians in drawing conclusions about the intrinsically trinitarian existence of God. His trinitarian model of thought, however, makes it possible to assume a circular rather than linear dynamic, which does not proceed, as Eastern thought did, from the Father to the Son and then to the Holy Spirit, but proceeds from the Father in the Spirit to the Son and vice versa. Originally, the great confession of faith spoke of the origin of the Holy Spirit "from the Father". In the Latin translation of the symbol in the Frankish area, the expression

---

impossible to evaluate it without making an effort to "demythologise" it (Zizioulas, *The One and the Many*, 13).

83 Cf. Wagner, *Dogmatyka*, 121.

84 Cf. Breuning, *Nauka o Bogu*, 173–6; Szczurek, *Trójjedyny*, 198–203.

85 Cf. Stubenrauch, *Pneumatologia*, 152–5; Congar, *Wierzę w Ducha Świętego. Rzeka życia płynie na Wschodzie i na Zachodzie (Ap 22,1)*, vol. III (Warszawa: Wydawnictwo Księży Marianów, 1996), 70–8.

"Filioque" was present as early as from the Eighth Council of Toledo (653).[86] Saints Maximus the Confessor and John of Damascus recognised the Western concern for the unity and equality of God's essence, which was expressed in the *Filioque*, and which they themselves shared, but they also insisted on the preservation of the existing doctrine. They emphasised the absolute primordiality of the Father and the sole *arche* and the self-existent status of the three Hypostases, but they did not deny the Son's participation in the mediation of the Holy Spirit – John Damascene in particular believed that He should even be called the Spirit of the Son. The rupture of ecclesiastical communion between East and West led to many disagreements concerning the *Filioque*.[87]

Latinists sought to refute the allegation that the *Filioque* postulated two primary principles for the origin of the Holy Spirit instead of one. The Council of Lyons II taught that the Holy Spirit eternally proceeds from the Father and the Son not as from two principles, but as from one principle. However, unification did not take place. The success achieved at the Council of Florence did not last long either, although its teachings did try to meet the Greek thought by revealing the precise sense of the theological content of the phrases "from the Father through the Son" and "from the Father and the Son" and paved the way for reconciliation.[88] As a theological issue, the question of *Filioque* reappeared in the 20th century, when Russian emigrants brought Slavophile theology to the West. The main representative of this theology, Vladimir Lossky, put it at the centre of the debate and this brought the controversy back.[89]

As it has already been mentioned, from a theological point of view, the *Filioque* was based on St. Augustine's position that within the Holy Trinity the Son – as Logos – represents the knowledge of God, while the Holy Spirit is the love of God. Thus, just as knowledge precedes love, so the Son preceded the Spirit. On this basis, Augustine attributed priority to the Son over the Spirit and made the Son – alongside the Father – the source of the origin of the Holy Spirit. The second basis of the *Filioque* was the conviction that – according to Augustine's view – in God the "substance" is primary to the person. One God means a substance in which three relations subsist: Father (memory), Son (knowledge) and Spirit (love). According to scholastic theologians, the complete relations must also be reciprocal

86 Cf. Congar, *Wierzę w Ducha Świętego. Duch Święty w ekonomii Objawienia*, 157–60.

87 For the origin of the Holy Spirit according to the Eastern Tradition, see Liszka, *Duch Święty, który od Ojca (i Syna) pochodzi*, 91–137.

88 Cf. Kasper, *Bóg Jezusa Chrystusa*, 267–76; Stubenrauch, *Pneumatologia*, 155–9; René Laurentin, *Nieznany Duch Święty. Odkrywanie Jego doświadczenia i Jego Osoby* (Kraków: Znak, 1998), 357–8, 362–4. For a discussion of contemporary Eastern pneumatology, see Congar, *Wierzę w Ducha Świętego. Rzeka życia płynie*, 95-102, 207–51.

89 Cf. Zizioulas, *Lectures*, 77.

and thus must occur in pairs. The Spirit, therefore, cannot come from one Person, but from the relationship of two Persons. If the Son is the only second Person, the *Filioque* appears to be a necessity.[90]

The Reformation brought a different approach to the problem of the origin of the Holy Spirit. Protestants denounced any theology that spoke of God's "being", treating it on par with metaphysics, and maintained that we only know God through His work in history – through His economic action. Therefore, since the Trinity shows itself economically in history because the Father sends the Son and the Son sends the Spirit, the Spirit is given to us by the Son. Assuming, then, that all our knowledge of God depends on the economy of salvation, we must agree that the Spirit also depends on the Son and not only on the Father. The result of such reasoning clearly contributed to the support for the doctrine of the *Filioque*.[91]

According to J.D. Zizioulas, Protestants succumbed to confusion similarly to 14th-century theologians who were unable to distinguish between the two types of trinitarian processes: "origin" and "being sent". "Origin" refers to the eternal relationship between the Father, the Son and the Spirit. The Spirit originates in eternity directly from the Father. In the economy of salvation, by contrast, the Son sends us the Spirit – gives us the Spirit. Clearly the Son has something to do with the economic manifestation of the Spirit. Zizioulas recalls at this point that the Greek-speaking East used the term "come from" (εκπορεύεται) only to refer to the eternal immanent Trinity. In Latin it was not easy to distinguish precisely between these aspects. From the 4th century onwards, the Greek *ekporeuetai* (come from) and *pemptai* (be sent) were translated as *procedere* in Latin texts. From the beginning, therefore, the West used the *Filioque* in both the theological (immanent) and the economic sense – and that is why this triggered mutual misunderstandings, which fuelled the aforementioned controversy.[92] The second area of difficulty concerned the Augustinian trinitarian analogies mentioned above.[93]

The East did not place the nature of God before the person. It was believed that if the Father is God, then making the Son the source of the origin of the Spirit on an equal footing with the Father would be tantamount to recognising the existence in the Trinity of two ontological origins and hence two Gods. The unity of God

---

90 Cf. Zizioulas, *Lectures*, 77.

91 Cf. Zizioulas, *Lectures*, 77–8.

92 Cf. Zizioulas, *Lectures*, 78.

93 "In the view of the Greek Fathers such arguments give no support to the *Filioque*. The only thing we can say about the Father, the Son and the Spirit is that the Father is Unbegotten and that he is the Father of the Son; the Son is begotten and is the Son of the Father; and the Spirit 'proceeds from' the Father and that he is the Spirit, not the Son. These characteristics, which derive from the very being of these persons, tell us *how* they are and thus *who* they are. We cannot say anything about the other characteristics that belong to each of the persons" (Zizioulas, *Lectures*, 78).

is thus secured by the Father, who is the sole source and cause, from whom all the life and being of God is derived. God's absolute sovereignty is guarded by the Father's sole principle (*monarchia*), and the *Filioque* would introduce a second source (*arché*) alongside the Father.[94] Zizioulas also considers the Augustinian argument – that knowledge precedes love and therefore the Spirit can only follow the Son – unjustified. He stresses that knowledge is intrinsically linked to love and communion, and thus we can only know a person to the extent that we love them, that is, we are in communion with them.[95]

Zizioulas finally concludes that the *Filioque* can be accepted if it is understood correctly. The first issue concerns the clear distinction between "origin" and "being sent" in relation to the eternal and economic Trinity. In the economy of salvation, the Holy Spirit does indeed depend on the Son, but it is quite different in the case of the immanent Trinity, where no *Filioque* can be spoken of, since there the Father alone is the sole cause of the Spirit. However, he adds, the Greek Fathers made a distinction which leaves a certain role for the Son in the eternal origin of the Holy Spirit. St. Gregory of Nyssa wrote that the difference between the Father, the Son and the Holy Spirit is that the Father is the cause, while the Son and the Spirit are the fruits of that cause. The cause is the person, the agent who takes free initiative. This distinction between the cause and that which is its effect is most important. St. Gregory writes that the Son proceeds directly from the Cause, while the Spirit proceeds through the One who proceeds directly from the Cause, i. e. through the mediation of the Son.[96] This mediation of the Son in the origin of the Spirit is sanctioned by the fact that the Son is the only begotten One, i. e. He is the only Son, and the Spirit is no other son besides Him. The mediation of the Son does not alter the fact that the Spirit has a direct relationship to the Father, and St. Gregory emphasises that the mediating role of the Son in the origin of the Spirit sanctions this direct relationship. Thus, as long as we are aware that the Son is not the cause, His role in the origin of the Spirit is permissible. However, in the immanent life of God, the Spirit does not come from the Son. Since in the immanent Trinity the relations are entirely ontological, the cause (the agent) must be the Father. From the economic perspective, it can be said that the Spirit depends on the Son, is sent by the Son and given by the Son to the Church.[97] From this it follows that, with

94 Cf. Zizioulas, *Lectures*, 78–9.

95 Cf. Zizioulas, *Lectures*, 79.

96 Cf. St Gregory of Nyssa, *Ad Ablabium*, PG 45, vol. II, 133.

97 Cf. Wacław Hryniewicz, "Duch Święty – Mistagog Bożego Królestwa," in *Duch Święty w tradycji prawosławnej*, ed. Paul Evdokimov (Poznań: W drodze, 2012), 20–3.

the distinction between the eternal plane and the economic plane, the origin of the Spirit from the Father "and the Son" is also acceptable in the Eastern Tradition.[98]

Zizioulas adds that the Council of Florence (1438-1439) wanted to prevent a division of the Church on this issue and proposed that if both sides wanted to accept the expression "through the Son" instead of "from the Son", there could be a basis for agreement. However, neither side was willing to take the decisive step. The West consolidated its position by adopting the expression "from the Father and the Son" and did not want to withdraw it or replace it with the phrase "through the Son". However, Zizioulas believes that the *Filioque* issue can be resolved by the Churches of East and West and that the dialogues undertaken can lead to success on this issue. [99] He only stresses that we must avoid anything that would contradict the principle that in the Trinity only the Father is the acting cause. He believes that we all can contribute to the understanding of the place of the *Filioque* in the doctrine of God as the Church did in the era of St. Maximus the Confessor.[100]

The Symbol of Faith of the Council of Toledo (675) clarifies the question of the intra-divine origin of the Divine Persons. The Son comes by being begotten from the essence of the Father. The Holy Spirit proceeds from the Father and the Son in the manner of the will, since it is love or holiness of both Divine Persons. The Symbol introduces the conceptual designation for the Persons: to the Father it attributes (following earlier Church documents) the name *Ingenitus* - Unbegotten as His personal characteristic; the Son is *Genitus* - Begotten; the Holy Spirit proceeds from both, He is the Spirit of both, i. e. He is the Spirit of the Father and of the Son. The consequence of His origin from the two Divine Persons is that He is sent out by Them.[101]

---

98 Cf. Zizioulas, *Lectures*, 79–80. See Chapter I in the second part of Evdokimov's work, *Duch Święty w tradycji prawosławnej*, entitled "The Pneumatology of the Fathers in the Economy of Salvation," 115–34.

99 See Evdokimov, *Duch Święty w tradycji prawosławnej*, 102–14, 149–54.

100 Cf. Zizioulas, *Lectures*, 82. "In the seventh century, as word was getting around that the *Filoque* being used in the West, Saint Maximus was asked for his opinion on this matter. He replied that he had looked into it, and found that the Latin-speaking Romans did not have respective words for expressing the two notions of *proceeding from* and *sent out by* (*ekporeuetai* and *pempetai*), so they used only one word, *proceeds* and this gave rise to confusion. In the same letter to Marinus, Saint Maximus noticed that Roman Christians referred to Saint Cyril of Alexandria, whose writings seemed to give the *Filioque* some support in the eternal Trinity. [...] he discussed the issue with Christians in Rome and concluded that they did not mean that the Son is the cause, so Maximus said that there was no heresy involved. That was how the situation was left in the seventh century" (Zizioulas, *Lectures*, 80–2).

101 The Council clarifies the concept of the Divine Person in the Holy Trinity. It uses it not in the generic or individual sense, because the Divine Persons are not different in terms of Their being but are the same Divine being. The trinity of the Divine Persons does not preclude the fact that there is one God. Cf. Courth, *Bóg trójjedynej miłości*, 214–18; Warzeszak, *Bóg jedyny w Trójcy Osób*, 183–4.

There are two ways of approaching the study of the mystery of the Trinity.[102] When the aim is to show unity, the consideration starts from the life process constituting the Persons as unity – this path is followed especially in the theology of the Eastern Churches: the "monarchy" of the Father is at the top, even when describing intra-trinitarian relations; the Father is the only source of divine life, and the Holy Spirit owes His being God only to Him – the Son has at most a mediating ("through") function. However, when one wants to show the equality in essence of the (distinct) Persons and from this point of view see the unity as grounded in God – this perspective has become dominant in Latin theology – the Father and the Son are united in that in relation to the Holy Spirit They function as the beginning, for how else could one precisely call the relationship of the Son to the Holy Spirit? The function of the beginning is not fully identical in the case of the Father and the Son, which had already been noticed by St. Augustine: the Father is *principium non de principio* – He is the beginning without a beginning, the Son is *principium de principio* – He is the beginning with an origin. Recent Western theology tends to assess the different explanations of the origin of the Spirit as complementary ways of seeing, deeply conceived but not alternatives to each other.[103] The complementary view of the two theological narratives should be interpreted in mutual dependence according to the hermeneutics of aesthetic polyphony.[104] The Eastern assessment of this issue is obviously more sceptical.[105]

---

102 For more on Greek and Latin contributions to dogmatic theology, see Congar, *Wierzę w Ducha Świętego. Rzeka życia płynie*, 9–16; Piotrowski, *Traktat o Trójcy Świętej*, 149–63. For a critical juxtaposition of the principles of Eastern Trinitarianism with Western Trinitarianism, see Evdokimov, *Duch Święty w koncepcji prawosławnej*, 96–102.

103 See Pontifical Council for Promoting Christian Unity, *Greek and Latin Traditions Regarding the Procession of the Holy Spirit* (1995). Cf. Jerzy Szymik, "Filioque i dia tou Hyiou u progu trzeciego tysiąclecia," in *Duch Odnowiciel*, ed. Lucjan Balter et al. (Poznań: Pallottinum, 1998), 83–90; Daniel Munteanu, "Das Filioque – ewige Streifrage oder Herausforderung der ökumenischen Trinitätslehre?," in *Der lebendige Gott. Auf den Spuren neueren trinitarischen Denkens*, ed. Rudolf Weth (Neukirchen-Vluyn: Neukirchener Verlag, 2005), 233–249; Bernhard Nitsche, "Pneumatologie", in *Dogmatik heute. Bestandsaufnahme und Perspektiven*, ed. Thomas Marschler and Thomas Schärtl (Regensburg: Pustet, 2014), 340–347.

104 Cf. Jan Strumiłowski, *Między Bogiem a człowiekiem. Teologia relacji w kontekście późnej nowoczesności* (Kraków: WAM, 2018), 46.

105 Cf. Breuning, *Nauka o Bogu*, 176–8; Warzeszak, *Bóg jedyny w Trójcy Osób*, 207–14; Kijas, *Traktat o Duchu Świętym i łasce*, 455–62; Evdokimov, *Duch Święty w koncepcji prawosławnej*, 102–14. See Zizioulas, *The One and the Many*, 41–5.

1.2.4 The Communional Aspects of Medieval Pneumatology

St Augustine's reflections on the language of theology, pneumatology and the doctrine on relations were adopted and consistently elaborated on in the Middle Ages[106] by St. Thomas Aquinas,[107] who emphasised that the Father is also the origin of the Holy Spirit coming from the Son. The monarchy of the Father is thus preserved: The Father speaks the Word which breathes Love.[108] Thomas did not so much seek to describe how the triune God is one, but how one God is triune. This made the Divine nature in his writings appear as if It were one person, and the intra-trinitarian communion becomes a side topic. Thomas devotes the most beautiful pages to the characterisation of the Holy Spirit as Love and as Gift – both qualities mutually condition each other. In describing the Holy Spirit as Love he nevertheless differs from St. Augustine. He makes a distinction between essential love – referring to the three Persons of God – and personal love – which in the proper sense is the Person of the Holy Spirit. If the Holy Spirit is personal and subsistent (hypostatic) Love, then everything that God gives outside of Himself in the order of creation and grace is to be attributed to the Spirit (based on the principle of appropriation). The Holy Spirit, as Gift, is the fruit of the eternal endowment of the Father and the Son and is at the source of all gifts given to people. Thus, in the third Person, the circle of Divine life is closed – the Father and the Son love each one in the Spirit, and in Him also the Father and the Son give us love.[109]

Richard of Saint Victor († 1173) developed the original version of Augustine's trinitarian theology.[110] He included the observation that from the definition of God as Love, the *ternion* can be derived: Loving, Beloved, Love. In God, the Father is Loving, the Son is Beloved. However, he does not call the third Person Love, but the "Co-Beloved" (*condilectus*). Between two Persons, love is not yet complete, for it becomes perfect only in its opening to the third Person. Thus, each of the Divine Persons possesses all love in an unconvertible way. The Father is the giver, the Son as the receiver exists through the Father and is simultaneously the giver, and finally the Holy Spirit is only the receiver. The three Persons are at the same time involved in the same event and only in it and owing to it are thus Love that is God.[111] In this

106 On the output of trinitology in the period from the Middle Ages to modernity as a background for the contemporary development of communion-based reflection, see Jagodziński, *Trynitologia komunijna*, 52–60.

107 Cf. Courth, *Bóg trójjedynej miłości*, 220–232; Guzowski, *Duch Dialogujący*, 177–9.

108 Cf. Warzeszak, *Bóg jedyny w Trójcy Osób*, 192–4.

109 Cf. Guzowski, *Duch Dialogujący*, 177–9.

110 See Werbick, "Trinitätslehre," 508–11; Müller, *Dogmatyka katolicka*, 466–7.

111 Cf. Guzowski, *Duch Dialogujący*, 180–1.

way Richard avoided tritheism and situated himself close to the Greek model of the monarchy of the Father.[112]

For Richard, the Boeotian definition of person was inadequate for the Persons comprising the Holy Trinity, since the substance of God is spiritual and individual, but He is not a person. The trinitarian being of the Person must go beyond the individuality of *substantia rationalis naturae*: "The Divine person is the incommunicable existence of the Divine nature".[113] A linguistic analysis of the word *existentia* shows that "sistere" denotes a mode of being and "ex" a primary relation of "wherefrom". *Ex-sistentia* thus means being oneself for the sake of another. In this case, the Divine Persons are co-constituted in Their being by the relation "wherefrom", and this means that "the relation of a person to those persons who are its primary cause is co-extensive with the determination of the essence of a person",[114] that this definition assumes an intrinsic and person-specific relationality.[115] Richard showed the realisation of this relationality primarily through the structure of God-realised supreme love, which must be reciprocal and – if it is to correspond to God's perfection and be ordered – must be a Divine Person. However, love only between two persons cannot yet be the highest realisation of reciprocal love, and must therefore open itself to the Third – it is only in Him, the Co-Beloved (*condilectus*), that the proper selflessness and greatness of love is manifested, which desires to communicate common happiness to the Third and attains its fullness.[116] In such a phenomenology of perfect love, the Persons in God appear as triple-relational realities: *diligens, dilectus, condilectus*. The Father is bestowing love, the Son is receiving and simultaneously bestowing love, the Holy Spirit is pure receiving love[117] – but

112 Cf. Breuning, *Nauka o Bogu*, 183–4.

113 *De Trinitate* (Richard de Saint-Victor, *De Trinitate. Texte critique avec introduction, notes et tables* (Paris: Librairie Philosophique *J. Vrin*, 1958) IV, 20 (quoted in Greshake, *Trójjedyny Bóg. Teologia trynitarna*, 92).

114 Heribert Mühlen, *Der Heilige Geist als Person. Beitrag zur Frage nach der dem Heiligen Geiste eigentümlichen Funktion in der Trinität, bei der Inkarnation und im Gnadenbund* (Münster: Aschendorff, 1989) 40, footnote 65 (quoted in Greshake, *Trójjedyny Bóg*, 92).

115 Cf. Greshake, *Trójjedyny Bóg*, 92. According to Richard of Saint Victor, "the person is 'naturae intellectualis incommunicabilis existentia'. The person is in an unalterable and unique way a specific *incommunicabilis*; but it is not when it closes in on itself, only when it is an existence, i. e. an existence *from* something else *towards* something else. While Thomas Aquinas essentially referred to Boethius, Duns Scotus developed and deepened the relational concept of person proposed by Richard of Saint Victor" (Kasper, *Jezus Chrystus* (Warszawa: Pax, 1983), 249).

116 Cf. Greshake, *Wierzę w Boga trójjedynego. Klucz do zrozumienia Trójcy Świętej* (Kraków: Znak, 2001), 33–4.

117 Cf. Richard of St. Victor, *De Trinitate* III, 11, 14–5. On the development of these ideas in trinitarian anthropology, see Jörg Splett, "Dialektik des Tuns – Dialog – Person-Sein in trinitarischer Analogie: L'Action (Blondel) als con-dilectio (Richard v. St. Victor)?," *Theologie und Philosophie* 61 (1986), 171–3.

all Three are one and the same love in three rhythms[118] (the first rhythm is the Father as the unbegotten Person).[119]

According to St. Thomas Aquinas, the Father sends the Son in incarnation and gives the Holy Spirit as gift. The intra-divine event is the origin.[120] The Son (Logos) originates in the way of reason and the Holy Spirit in the way of will – love. Thus, the origins were distinguished to avoid speaking of two Sons. The Persons differ in origin, and the origin of each characteristically defines their mutual relations.[121] The Father, the Son and the Holy Spirit are differentiated by their mutual relations, which do not violate the common essence of God.[122] If we think of a reality that encompasses two others standing in a reciprocal relation, rather than merely defining their identity, it will be a subsistent relation – existing in itself, being purely referential, i. e. directed towards and from something. The statements contained in the Scriptures about God mandate an explanation of the differences between the Persons as arising from relations. The two modes of origin give rise to four relations, but only three of them form real existing references, differing from one another as respectively opposite. They correspond to the three Persons, for since faith knows three Persons and they are relations, the Person and the existing relation must be the same thing. The following relations result from this: active begetting – the Father begets the Son (fatherhood), passive begetting – the Son is begotten by the Father (sonship/filiation), active spiration – the Father and the Son breathe the Holy Spirit, passive spiration- the Holy Spirit is breathed by the Father and the Son (being

118 Cf. Szczurek, *Bóg Ojciec w tajemnicy Trójcy Świętej*, 263–70; Greshake, *Trójjedyny Bóg*, 165–6: "Today these trinitarian relations [...] are not considered from a conventional constitutional-hermeneutic point of view (Where do the Son and the Spirit 'come from'?), but on the ground of relational correlation, where it is a mutual mediating event, which excludes any *reductio in unum*. Therefore, it is better to begin the consideration of the trinitarian event from the Father's side, which allows us to define it as the eternal 'rhythm of love', and the individual persons fulfilling this rhythm as rhythms = specific shapes of fulfilment, in a sense as 'nodal points' of this event of love. Each person is in its own way entirely of and for other persons: giving/receiving – receiving/giving – uniting/receiving/giving back, so that each person is themselves only in others and in the fulfilment of their own being a person includes and embraces others (perichoresis). Thus – as Balthasar aptly formulates – 'all three .... are one and the same love in the three modes of being that are necessary for there to be love at all in God, namely… supreme, most selfless love.'" Cf. Greshake, *Trójjedyny Bóg*, 91–7; Jagodziński, "Trialogiczno-komunijna koncepcja trynitologii," *Studia Diecezji Radomskiej* 10 (2010/2011), 60–4. The background for such a trinitarian view is the dialogical and trialogical understanding of the person developed in modern philosophy – cf. Greshake, *Trójjedyny Bóg*, 134–44.

119 Cf. Greshake, *Wierzę w Boga trójjedynego*, 35; Jagodziński, "Trialogiczno-komunijna koncepcja trynitologii," 69; Jagodziński, *Węzłowe zagadnienia chrystologii komunijnej*, 38–9.

120 Cf. Kasper, *Bóg Jezusa Chrystusa*, 344–5.

121 Cf. Courth, *Bóg trójjedynej miłości*, 244–5; Szczurek, *Trójjedyny*, 195–7.

122 Cf. Szczurek, *Trójjedyny*, 203–8.

breathed). It is thus apparent that the distinction in God is only possible because of the different relations of origin. Fatherhood characterises the Father, filiation – the Son, being breathed – the Holy Spirit. With this, the individual Persons are realistically different from one another. Everything else is common to them, they are God in the same way. The essence of God has nothing that exists "beyond" that which subsists as relations. God is His own being, subsisting realistically threefold in relations – beyond this there is no other mode of subsistence in God.[123]

"Person" is a term for the differing (by realtion) bearers of the name of God (the Father, the Son, the Holy Spirit). It expresses what differentiates Them, but in the case of God one must always immediately think of what they simultaneously have in common. In theology, this concept has its own meaning that makes it distinct from the general philosophical connotations. In Western philosophy, the definition proposed by Boethius stated that "a person is an *indivisible* individual substance of rational nature" (*persona est naturae rationalis individua substantia*), characterised by self-existence, self-consciousness and irreplaceable and indivisible uniqueness.[124] However, it was necessary to find terms that could also be valid in relation to God in three Persons. The concept of person was in principle adequate, but God is spirit. The only problem was that trinitarian theology did not make the distinction between genus and individual: the essence of God is not something – as we read in the decisions of the Second Lateran Council – that is distinct from the Divine Persons.[125]

The Persons of the Holy Trinity are the concrete realisation of being God. Richard of Saint Victor first removed the notion of substance from Boethius' definition, because substance is something general, whereas person is something individual and unique. What is the property of this and where does it come from? Richard thought he had found the answer by introducing the concept of *existentia* – existence. He offered the following statement as a definition: "A person is one who exists for himself according to a unique mode of rational existence". Relations within the Holy Trinity differ from relations between created persons not because of the quality of persons, but solely because of origin. God encompasses that which is common to many (essence) and that which is absolutely incommunicable (relation of origin). With reference to God, according to Richard's definition, a person is a divine existence (essence) which it possesses as an incommunicable property.[126]

St. Thomas adopted Boethius' definition but interpreted his notion of substance not as an abstract "essence" but as self-existence – *subsistentia* (in the sense of *hypostasis* distinguished from the static *ousia*). Therefore, for Thomas, a person is a

123 Cf. Breuning, *Nauka o Bogu*, 186–92; Szczurek, *Bóg Ojciec w tajemnicy Trójcy Świętej*, 270–7.

124 Cf. Greshake, *Trójjedyny Bóg*, 89–91.

125 Cf. Breuning, *Nauka o Bogu*, 192–3.

126 Cf. Breuning, *Nauka o Bogu*, 193–4. See Greshake, *Trójjedyny Bóg*, 91–7.

specific nature existing of itself, and thus superior to all others in dignity. Therefore, a person can learn and want, dispose of truth and freedom. Persons are not merely objects of action like other things but act themselves – they are subjects.[127]

According to St. Thomas, the relations in the Holy Trinity are personal, and the relative opposites in God consist in the manner in which the divine essence is given and received, and justify the personhood of the Persons, i.e. their relative separateness. Accordingly, five different personal properties (*proprietas*) can be distinguished: The Father (1) has no beginning; He is the One who (2) begets and (3) breathes; the Son is (4) begotten and (3) breathes; the Holy Spirit is (5) breathed. Substantively identical to the five properties are the *notiones* – the "names" of the vital processes in God, which render the properties as relations: being without beginning, active and passive begetting, active and passive breathing. "Notional acts" are then actions corresponding to origin – in the language of St. Augustine these are knowledge and love.[128]

The transition to the early Middle Ages is characterised by the adoption of the achievements of past epochs and does not present any original pneumatological thought. It was then that the process of a certain oblivion of the Holy Spirit began. The Scholastic doctrine of God had in mind not so much the Persons and their ontic equality, but rather the existence of a single Deity (*una deitas*). However, whether the origin of the Holy Spirit was derived psychologically from the unity of reason, cognition and willing, or from the conviction that in the Holy Spirit the reciprocal love of the Father and the Son meet – the Holy Spirit remained the measure of the intra-divine exchange of love.[129]

This can already be seen in the teaching of St. Anselm of Canterbury – in the Holy Spirit the Father loves the Son and vice versa. This love, however, is identical to the one essence of God. Therefore, the Holy Spirit proceeds from the Father and from the Son, who are One and therefore constitute for the Holy Spirit the self-same principle of the one Deity.[130] St. Thomas Aquinas also taught that – since

127 Cf. Greshake, *Trójjedyny Bóg*, 100–11.

128 Cf. Szczurek, *Trójjedyny*, 215–6.

129 Cf. Stubenrauch, *Pneumatologia*, 159–62. L. Bouyer noted that Bulgakov, "while, in a sense, acknowledging the Augustinian identification of the Holy Spirit with Divine love, at the same time opposes Western trinitology taking its origin from St. Augustine with its 'origin' of the Son by reason and the origin of the Spirit by will. He argues that love, or at least the love in question here, is something quite different from a matter of the will. A more accurate observation could hardly be made. Let us add that, despite the simultaneous reference to the second Divine Person as 'Son' and 'Logos', God's 'reason', his 'self-consciousness', cannot be placed on a par with begetting, which makes God first and foremost the Father" (Louis Bouyer, *Duch Święty Pocieszyciel. Duch Święty i życie w łasce* (Kraków: Wydawnictwo M, 2000), 529). Cf. Congar, *Wierzę w Ducha Świętego. Rzeka życia płynie*, 134–42.

130 Cf. Congar, *Wierzę w Ducha Świętego. Rzeka życia płynie*, 121–7.

the separateness of the Divine Persons derives solely from other relations – it would not be possible to tell the difference between the Holy Spirit and the Son if the Holy Spirit did not also proceed from the Son.[131] Richard of Saint Victor associated the tri-personal existence of God with the reality of "love" in a new way. Since perfect love operates in God by means of dialogue, it flows from one "Person" to another, from the Lover to the Beloved. However, this cannot be constrained to the duality, because then one would be enclosed in the other, and this would result in a relationship of "egotism in two". It is also for this reason that the Father and the Son turn towards the Third – Richard called Him *condilectus*, "Co-Beloved", because the measure of perfect love is the willingness to pass it on. From this identification of the Holy Spirit as the Co-Beloved, who entirely originates from the mutual love of the Father and the Son, and in a way gives rise to it Himself and directs it to both, derives the self-existence of the Holy Spirit: He is the Gift and the Flame. In him, the Father and the Son give themselves to one another; in Him, trinitarian love also opens up to creation and is passed on it. While the creation is not a suitable partner for intra-divine love, it is certainly the recipient of Creator's gracious love.[132] The path of Richard's reasoning was continued by William of Auxerre and St. Bonaventure.[133] From the Pseudo-Areopagite, scholasticism took over the notion that goodness necessarily spills outwards (*bonum diffusivum sui*). In medieval theology, this image receives an intra-trinitarian interpretation, with the Holy Spirit being treated as the fruit of the ecstatic, self-transcending goodness of the Father and the Son.[134]

Within Protestantism, Calvin showed the dynamism of the economy of the Holy Spirit in the life of the Church and the faithful. He adopted the principles of Western pneumatology and emphasised the joint action of the Holy Spirit and Christ. Christ as the Eternal Word created the world by the Spirit and preserves the world in existence, He also brings salvation to men. The same Spirit who gave the Scriptures also makes it possible to understand and accept it. This inner work of the Spirit, which enlightens us to accept the true message of the Divine Word and to convince ourselves of its truthfulness and our salvation, is called by Calvin "the inner testimony of the Holy Spirit". Among the strongest points of Calvin's ecclesiology is the emphasis on the relationship between the Church and the Holy Spirit. God transform us inwardly by his Spirit and outwardly by His word and sacraments. The Church depends on the Holy Spirit in every sacrament, in the Eucharist Christ gives Himself to us in His mysterious power. This "spiritualisation"

131 Cf. Stubenrauch, *Pneumatologia*, 162–3; Congar, *Wierzę w Ducha Świętego. Rzeka życia płynie*, 143–55.

132 Cf. Congar, *Wierzę w Ducha Świętego. Rzeka życia płynie*, 128–33.

133 Cf. Congar, *Wierzę w Ducha Świętego. Rzeka życia płynie*, 134–42.

134 Cf. Stubenrauch, *Pneumatologia*, 163–5; Guzowski, *Duch Dialogujący*, 181–2.

of the sacrament of the Last Supper seems insufficient in terms of interpreting the merely spiritual presence of Christ in the Eucharist. Calvin's point was to emphasise that the Church has no sacramental power, but the Holy Spirit, who dwells in our hearts, enables us to know the power of Jesus Christ, enlightens us in order to learn His graces, imprints them in us and makes them effective. Through the Holy Spirit we receive all the gifts from Christ – especially the new birth.[135]

In the Church life and the doctrine dominated at that time by the influence of the Council of Trent, especially in ecclesiology, there was a lack of an in-depth reflection on the Holy Spirit. He was only portrayed as acting and animating ecclesial structures. The Scriptures do not exist without the Church reading and interpreting them in the light of the Holy Spirit, in accordance with the living tradition of faith. In the polemic against the Reformation, theology placed too much emphasis on the institutional dimension of the Church and the role of the Teaching Office, which in turn was credited with an almost unconditional guarantee of being guided by the Holy Spirit. Apart from a few texts linking the nature of the Church to the Holy Spirit, we had to wait until the Second Vatican Council and the new framing of the Church.[136] However, it is worth mentioning two theologians that were prominent in the field of pneumatological ecclesiology – Johann Möhler and Henry Edward Manning – as well as Leo XIII's encyclical *Divinum illud munus* (1897).[137]

1.2.5 The Communional Aspects of Pneumatology of the Last Council and Post-Conciliar Theology

Instead of speaking of God in a general way, the Second Vatican Council preferred to speak of the Trinity – the Father, the Son and the Holy Spirit. In this way, theology recovered important perspectives from the patristic tradition, mainly rich Eastern pneumatology.[138] The expression "to the Father through the Son in the Holy Spirit" returns several times, the Church was defined in a trinitarian way, the Holy Trinity is pointed out as the model of the Church, the Holy Spirit as the Lord and creator of history through the Church. According to more recent theology, there is a strong dependence of the mystery of the Church as communion on the Holy Spirit being

135 Cf. Guzowski, *Duch Dialogujący*, 185–9.

136 On preconciliar pneumatology, see Miguel de Salis, *Kościół wcielony w historii. Elementy do ponownego odczytania Konstytucji dogmatycznej o Kościele Lumen gentium* (Kraków: WAM, 2021), 142–66.

137 Cf. Guzowski, *Duch Dialogujący*, 190–4.

138 Cf. de Salis, *Kościół wcielony w historii*, 166–8. According to G. Florowski, the Holy Spirit coordinates all acts of love in the Church and makes it something more than just a community – it is a sacrament of communion with God.

"Communion". In the communion of the Church, He implants people into the Communion of the Persons of the Holy Trinity and unites Them among Themselves. The ultimate goal is to make people partakers of the Communion that exists between the Father and the Son in the Spirit of love. Although the pneumatology of the Second Vatican Council is found mainly in the ecclesiological texts, it is also important to note the pneumatological revolution in trinitarian theology, Christology and liturgical theology. The Holy Spirit is also portrayed as the Spirit of Christ, the Spirit of the Body of Christ. The Council shows Christocentrism in the pneumatological perspective, for Christ in the Holy Spirit and together with Him is the dynamic centre of history and the universe.[139]

The renewal of pneumatology took place on several levels: the experience of the work of the Holy Spirit through the revival of charisms, the emergence of new spiritual groups, in academic theology and in the documents of the Church.[140] The Council was called the "new Pentecost" and marked the beginning of a new experience of new ways of the Holy Spirit's presence in the Church and the world. The most seminal document was John Paul II's encyclical *Dominum et Vivificantem* (1986). According to the historico-salvific pneumatology of this document, "Jesus himself, is the first Counselor, being the first bearer and giver of the Good News. The Holy Spirit comes after him and because of him, in order to continue in the world, through the Church, the work of the *Good News of salvation*".[141] Numerous pneumatological studies show that Catholic theology is still searching for a comprehensive conceptual internalisation of the theology of the Holy Spirit.[142]

The influence of Orthodox pneumatology is also significant in this period. The main salvific work of the Holy Spirit is to divinise, perfect, adopt and sanctify people. The Church#s# is the Body of Christ and the fullness of the Holy Spirit. The Christ's work is embedded in the economy of the Spirit. As a result, the Church is one and diverse at the same time. The Christological aspect guarantees constancy while the pneumatological aspect ensures the dynamism of the Church.[143]

139 Cf. Guzowski, *Duch Dialogujący*, 195–6.

140 Cf. de Salis, *Kościół wcielony w historii*, 168–77.

141 John Paul II, Encyclical *Dominum et Vivificantem* (1986), 9. Cf. Guzowski, *Duch Dialogujacy*, 197–9.

142 Cf. Nitsche, "Pneumatologie," 321–31.

143 Cf. Guzowski, *Duch Dialogujący*, 199–203. M. de Salis considers that there is still no consensus today on whether the Second Vatican Council overcame the imbalance between the Christological and pneumatological dimensions in ecclesiology (cf. de Salis, *Kościół wcielony w historii*, 177–9).

1.3 The Holy Spirit as a Person in the Trinitarian Communion

Emphasising the transcendence of Divine love, L. Bouyer wrote that the essence of the Father is personal *agape* and added the important comment that it is a Person in the full sense of the word, most important and unique in and through itself, since it is the offering of itself in the Son. For this reason, in its entirety love resides in the Father and overflows into the Son as the only one and absolutely beloved and loving in return, together with the Holy Spirit as love simultaneously received and given back. This love is in the Father, the first and primary Source of love.

> "Therefore, it cannot be said [...] that the Spirit is personal love in God, because love which is the life of God, which is the Father in his very paternity, which is the Son as the beloved and mutually loving, is completed in the Spirit of the Father which is the very Spirit of adoption, resting on the Son as the Spirit of voluntary reciprocity, through whom the same is at the same time loving and beloved in the highest degree. In this sense, the Spirit, as its name indicates, is the breath of divine life, or in other words, he appears to be the heart of the Deity, the heart of the Father, which is at the same time the heart of the Son, the life-giving gift, making it possible to love with the love with which one is loved. The life of God is thus perfect in itself as a life of love, [...] which, [...] must exist between the two Persons, and which, between the two who are one – the Father and the Son, we do not say that it enters as a third Person, which would be the greatest nonsense, but – that it is the seal of Their closeness and the inexhaustible source of Their infinity. Therefore, this Spirit, in which the love of God, the love that is God, manifests itself in its perfection, in its holiness beyond all definitions, because beyond all limitations – is also the One in that the absolute freedom of God is manifested, not against the sole necessity of this only necessary being, but as the very necessity of its existence, being the existence of the One beyond unity and beyond plurality"[144]

---

144 Bouyer, *Duch Święty Pocieszyciel*, 535–6. The author completes this statement with the reflection on the kenosis of the Holy Spirit, in which He also reveals Himself to the creation: "The Spirit is that personality of God which manifests itself as love at its end, making the beloved and the lover one, where the beloved is one such precisely by virtue of reciprocity, just as the person of God the Father, visible only in the Son, in whom He manifests Himself through the Spirit, is love in its one and only eternal source, essential or "superessential," as Pseudo-Dionysius would say. All the more so, then, the Holy Spirit should be the One in whom the Wisdom of creation, in its voluntary distinction from the creative Word, is called to be one with the Word, in a spousal love that brings it to the plane of filial love, allowing it to rest together with the Son, through the Spirit, in the bosom of the Father. To this end, it began, in the same Spirit, to be maternal Wisdom towards each individual creature and, even more, towards all creation, gathered into one by and in the Creator. As a result, between them, at the place where they meet, the cross on which the Creator in His love, in that love which is Himself, makes Himself one with the creation, in its twofold infinite remoteness from God, if we may say so, bearing in mind the creation of the world in the limited order and its

The concept of person thus occupies a key role in trinitology. According to Joseph Ratzinger

> a person is not just an individual, not a duplicated copy, formed by the division of ideas in matter, but precisely a 'person'. The Greek thought has always regarded individual beings, including individual people, only as individuals. They arise as a result of ideas breaking through matter [...] A Christian sees in man not an individual but a person [...] this leap from an individual to a person contains the whole span of the transition from Antiquity to Christianity, from Platonism to faith.[145]

In reflection on the Christian God, the concepts of *ousia* (essence/substance, *substantia*) and *hypostasis/prosopon* (person, *persona*) pertaining to the Holy Trinity were clearly distinguished and placed fundamentally on the same level.[146] Prior

---

fall – that cross is the most eloquent sign of the Spirit for faith. Similarly, the resurrection of the Crucified One, continued by the universal resurrection on the day of the Parousia, will become the glory prepared by this kenosis of the Holy Spirit, the glory in which faith fades away because it becomes a vision" (Bouyer, *Duch Święty Pocieszyciel*, 545–6). Cf. Laurentin, *Nieznany Duch Święty*, 369–373; Nitsche, "Pneumatologie," 331–9.

145 Ratzinger, *Wprowadzenie w chrześcijaństwo* (Kraków: Znak, 1994), 148–9.

146 Bartnik, *Personalizm* (Lublin: Wydawnictwo KUL, 2008), 174: "a substance is the structure of being independent in its *essence*, while subsistence means independence in *existence*." Analysing the notion of person, Fr. Bogumił Gacka distinguished two approaches to this reality in J. Ratzinger's theological thought: as subsistence (translation of the Greek term *hypostasis* – St. Rufinus) and as relation. The trinitological and Christological battle showed how great an effort was required to elaborate this concept not in substance-related terms, but from an existential point of view, in terms of subsistence, self-existence, life. Boethius' definition remained entirely at the level of substance and was unable to express the truth of God: "*substance* in the Western tradition meant rather being in the aspect of its form, essence, nature, almost as a *piece of nature*. *Subsistence*, on the other hand, means rather a being in its existential, dynamic aspect, which has to be translated into Polish as *samoistność* [*self-existence*]. This is why Pope John II, following the Roman centre, in 534 translated the Greek *hypostasis*, which meant person, as *subsistentia* and not as *substantia* (DH 401), although the construction of the term *hypostasis* corresponds more closely to the word *substantia*. For the word *substantia* comes from *sub – stare*, meaning to *stand in oneself*, which rather expresses the static and reistic aspect. By contrast, *subsistence* comes from *sub – sisto*, *sub – existo* and conveys rather the meaning of *existence in oneself*, i. e. self-existence, the real subjectification of substantial existence" (Bartnik, "Osoba a dusza", *Personalizm* 12 (2007), 25. Cf. Bogumił Gacka, *Znaczenie osoby w teologii Josepha Ratzingera – Benedykta XVI* (Warszawa: Wydawnictwo UKSW, 2010), 25–30, 124–5. The understanding of person as subsistence opened new perspectives for understanding person as relation. "A Person in God implies Relation. A *relation*, being a reference, is not something secondary, secondary to the person, but is the person. A person exists here because of its subsistence only as a relation. A person is a pure relation of referring to someone. This can be expressed in the sense that the Person of the Father begets the Son, not in the sense that the act of begetting is something additional to the entire, complete person, but in the sense that this begetting *is* a total surrender, an offering, a self-giving that is conscious and loving. The paternal

to the Council of Nicea, it was difficult to distinguish between the sending of the Logos outwardly and His intrinsically divine mode of being, but since that Council it has been argued in principle – as a result of the dispute with Arianism – that the personal distinction in God not only lies on the plane of intra-divine being, but is identical with divine being itself, or more precisely that God's very being and essence are determined by personal relations.[147]

God Himself is His essence, the absolute substance, and there is nothing accidental in Him. However, we know from the Bible that the one God is the Father, the Son and the Holy Spirit. They cannot be properties added to the divine substance. They are something real, bringing distinction to God. The only philosophical way of explaining this, as already mentioned, was to reach for the category of relation, which is theologically appropriate because it is not accidental and is immutable. Divine substance is thus an arrangement of relations[148].

What does the concept of *relatio* bring to the explanation of the doctrine on the holy Trinity? When we speak of God, we can take two points of view. Starting from the first, we become aware of His unity (when we think of His goodness, wisdom, infinity). The second point of view allows us to see the diversity when we speak of God the Father, God the Son and God the Holy Spirit. Each of them is not something different (*aliud*), but rather each is other (*alius*). And because they are always such, the being of the Father, the Son and the Holy Spirit is not accidental. This fact of being different can be described as "relation" (the first two names – the Father and the Son – are clearly terms that designate mutual relations).[149] Based on these reflections, St. Augustine formulated a principle that would later be adopted by the Council of Florence as a theological certainty, which states that in the Holy Trinity "all things are one except where there is opposition of relation".[150]

---

giving of self is a pure act of giving and is not something added. Thus, the Person of the Father does not beget the Son in the sense that there is an added act of giving birth to an already full person, but *is* the eternal act of begetting as a complete giving of self" (ibid., 31).

147 Cf. Bartnik, *Dogmatyka katolicka*, 1: 220–5; Greshake, *Trójjedyny Bóg. Teologia trynitarna*, 78; Balthasar, *Teologika*, vol. II: *Prawda Boga*, 120–5.

148 Cf. Courth, *Bóg trójjedynej miłości*, 203–5; Ignacy Bokwa, *Trynitarno-chrystologiczna interpretacja eschatologii w ujęciu Hansa Ursa von Balthasara* (Radom: Radomskie Wydawnictwo Diecezjalne AVE, 1998), 87–8; Woźniak, *Praca nad dogmatem*, 185–90. St. Augustine considered this interpretation less ambiguous than using the concept of person (theology at that time had not yet developed a precise distinction between person, substance and hypostasis). Because of linguistic difficulties, Augustine acquiesced to the use of the term "person," explaining that each (Divine) person is defined with respect to another as standing in some kind of relation to it.

149 Cf. Johann Auer, *Gott – Der Eine und Dreieine* (Regensburg: Pustet, 1978), 311–8.

150 Cf. Auer, *Jesus Christus – Gottes und Mariä "Sohn"* (Regensburg: Pustet, 1986), 282–99; Breuning, *Nauka o Bogu*, 170–1; Warzeszak, *Bóg Jedyny w Trójcy Osób*, 194–200; Hryniewicz, *Pascha Chrystusa w dziejach człowieka i wszechświata. Zarys chrześcijańskiej teologii paschalnej – tom 3* (Lublin: TN KUL, 1991), 66–70. Hryniewicz writes about a very important clue contained in the very etymology

of the word *prósopon*, which guides the theological interpretation of the truth about person as a relational reality. "The original function of the word *prósopon* was to denote a direct relationship. It is composed of the preposition *pros* (towards, in relation to, relative to) and the noun *he ōps* (accus. *ōpa*, plur. *ta ōpa*), denoting face, countenance, appearance, eye, gaze. The compounding of the two segments into one word gives it a relational character. It conveys the meaning of turning one's face or gaze towards someone or something, of finding oneself facing someone or something. *Prósopon* means being in relation to someone or something. The original content of the word precludes the understanding of a person as an entity in itself, without any reference to another reality. The concept of person is inextricably linked to relation and reference. Relation defines a person, its generic difference. It should be emphasised, however, that it is a matter of understanding relation in the sense of an event that brings a person into a state of reference to someone or something. The concept of person is a relational ontological concept. The reality of a person presupposes a relation to another subject or object. This dimension belongs to the ontology of a person. Therefore, by its very definition, a person must be understood as an existential relation, as a specific mode of existence of nature, manifested in relation and the ability to enter into contact and community. A person is a reality irreducible to anything, incomparable and unlike any other. It can only be known through relation. It is not a self-contained monad or an end in itself. This is what distinguishes it from an individual. [...] The Greek Fathers made a bold attempt to revise Greek ontology in order to apply it to the considerations on the Holy Trinity. [...] *Hypóstasis* was identified with the concept of person (*prósopon*), which, since its application to trinitarian theology, was eminently relational. [...] According to the Cappadocian Fathers, 'to be' always means 'to be in relation'. For one to truly be, one must fulfil two essential conditions: a) to be oneself, to sustain one's own essence (*hypó-stasis*), b) to be in relation, to be oneself (*prósopon*), i. e. to have the capacity to come out of oneself (*ek-stasis*). Only in relation does identity reveal its ontological meaning. On the other hand, a relation would not be a true relation if it did not contain an ontologically significant identity. Thus, we already deal with Christian ontology, based on the concept of God's very being. It is therefore understandable that in the Eastern tradition, greater priority will henceforth be given to the category of person (and not essence, as in the trinitarian doctrine in the West). The causal principle (*archè*) and ultimate raison d'être of God's being is, in this perspective, the person of the Father. Not essence (*ousia*), but person (*hypóstasis – prósopon*) thus becomes the expression of the ultimate rationale of God's being. Thus, the most fundamental ontological claim about God concerns not the one nature of God, but the person of the Father. God is the fullness of personal existence in community. Each person bears witness to the others in constant and mutual *perichóresis*. God's ultimate being is first identified with the person. God's existence is an ecstatic existence, which is shared in a personal relation. [...] The traditional doctrine on the Holy Trinity, prevalent in the West since the time of St. Thomas Aquinas, used the concept of *relatio subsistens* in explaining the differentiation of the divine persons. However much criticism can be levelled at relational theology, one thing seems to still hold true. Defining the Divine persons as 'self existent relations' emphasised the conviction that the person in the sphere of divine existence is the negation of existential self-sufficiency and of any 'bending' towards itself (Augustine's 'incurvatio in seipsum'). The whole reality of a person is expressed by its orientation towards other persons. Each is self-contained and independent, existing together entirely in relation to the other persons. This expresses a very important element of the very ontology of person. [...] The divine persons exist in mutual relation to one another. [...] By introducing the concept of person into ontology, the Cappadocian Fathers emphasised that it is a proper feature of existence (*idiádzon*), something indescribable, a total otherness. The ontological content of a person is its absolute otherness, distinct from the common features of

In his teaching on the persons of the Holy Trinity as relations of origin, St. Thomas Aquinas elaborated on the tradition of St. Augustine and, differentiating the Aristotelian notion of relation, he supplemented mental relations with "self-existent relations". The existence of such relations is reflected precisely in the trinitarian origins.[151] Four relations correspond to the two origins in God, but only three of them are distinct from each other and thus self-existent. And since distinction in God is only possible based on the relations of origin, they constitute and characterise the trinitarian Persons: the fatherhood of the Father, the sonship of the Son and the being breathed of the Holy Spirit (passive spiration).[152]

1.3.1 The Holy Spirit in the Personal Relations of the Trinitarian Communion

Early Christian endeavours to properly understand the Holy Trinity led not only to the discovery that person is a unique, incommunicable reality, but also to the

---

nature or essence, existing in persons (*en prosópois*). The person has priority over the essence, as it represents the absolute otherness of existence compared to the common features of essence or nature. A person's mode of existence is characterised by uniqueness, singularity and dissimilarity. It is impossible to define this *proprium* (*idiádzon*) of a person. One can only experience its otherness as an event and a unique relation. The otherness of a person is relational. It can only be grasped in relation. A person is a mode of existence that realises and manifests itself as a dynamic relation to other persons. A person has the capacity to define its nature and to conform it to the Divine Principle. This brings us to a very important statement. The realisation of a person's otherness is accomplished by their stepping out of their own objectivity and entering the realm of existential relation. It involves a certain ontological *exodus* on the personal plane. It can be described as an event of ecstasy (*ek-stasis*), i. e. an exit from the self. A person is not an intelligible reality in itself. It is not merely the capacity to think consciously about itself or others. Self-consciousness and the ability to think do not exhaust the most essential properties of a person." The concept of person, however, has not been defined once and for all. Since the Enlightenment (and especially since Kant), consciousness thinking of itself has been indispensably linked to the concept of person – person is equated with being a subject. In this modern terminology, the statement of the ancient Church about the Holy Trinity would be heresy. That "there are three Persons in God" would now mean that "there are three different centres of action and consciousness in God" – which would end in tritheism. In today's language, one would rather say "God is one Person (one subject, one will, one love, one freedom) in three distinguishable subjects." But this way of speaking is also wrong (cf. Breuning *Nauka o Bogu*, 196). For a detailled discussion of proposals formulated by K. Barth and K. Rahner, see Hryniewicz, *Pascha Chrystusa w dziejach człowieka i wszechświata*, 219–20. The context of the modern discussion on this topic is outlined in: Courth, *Bóg trójjedynej miłości*, 307–8; Kasper, *Bóg Jezusa Chrystusa* 353–60.

151 Cf. Auer, *Gott – Der Eine und Dreieine*, 286–99.

152 Cf. Courth, *Bóg trójjedynej miłości*, 227–8; Breuning, *Nauka o Bogu*, 170–1; 189–92; Kasper, *Bóg Jezusa Chrystusa*, 345–7; Jagodziński, *Węzłowe zagadnienia chrystologii komunijnej*, 25–9.

discovery of its relationality and interpersonal-communal structure.[153] Thus, in the Trinity there is no true existence of the individual in himself without communion.[154] Already Tertullian steered towards a communal view of person: God is not a monad, but an originally distinguishable plurality of three Persons: *Tres unum sunt, non unus*.[155] Not only are there three individual and peculiar realities in God, but this also presents the interpersonal conception of person.[156] The three Persons have their independence – but only within the relational structure.[157] Thus, Person is "an irreplaceable bearer of an irreversible role in an interpersonal and interactional play of roles, [...] an independence in relation".[158] According to the Council of Nicaea, the Son is consubstantial with the Father[159] – and thus movement was somehow added to the concept of God. Therefore, there was an attempt to replace the Greek concept of God with biblical thinking and to conceive of being not as a thinking being, but as a personal relation. The Cappadocian Fathers (in particular St. Gregory of Nazianzus) emphasised the *schésis* – the reciprocal relationality of the Hypostases in God. On that basis, they said that the divine Persons show conformity of will, communion in action, unified orientation, real interaction and communion of Hypostases. Divine Communion (*koinonia tes ousias*) is not a collective unity of individual Persons, but neither can it be separated into individual Persons – it is a unity of essence (*ousia*). This essence is originally realised in the Father and transmitted to the Son and the Holy Spirit, through each of the Hypostases it becomes perfect and is preserved, and therefore the life of God is a kind of "pulsation" in which "unity becomes triplicity and triplicity reverts back to unity".[160]

---

153 Cf. Kasper, *Bóg Jezusa Chrystusa*, 247–9; Ratzinger, *Wprowadzenie w chrześcijaństwo*, 170–4; Teofil Wilski, ""Tajemnica osoby" – klucz do rozumienia siebie i Boga," *Communio. Międzynarodowy Przegląd Teologiczny* 2/2 (1982), 24–44; Guzowski, *Duch Dialogujący*, 362–5.

154 I draw here on my own study, Jagodziński, *Węzłowe zagadnienia chrystologii komunijnej*, 9–30.

155 Tertulian, *Adversum Praxean* 3 (CCL 1, 282). Cf. Guzowski, *Duch Dialogujący*, 367.

156 Cf. Kasper, *Bóg Jezusa Chrystusa*, 347–9.

157 Cf. Bartnik, *Dogmatyka katolicka*, 1: 212–4.

158 Hilberath, *Der Personbegriff der Trinitätstheologie in Rückfrage von Karl Rahner zu Tertullians "Adversus Praxean"* (Innsbruck-Wien: Tyrolia, 1986), 230 (quoted in Greshake, *Trójjedyny Bóg. Teologia trynitarna*, 80).

159 Cf. Ratzinger, *Bóg Jezusa Chrystusa. Medytacje o Bogu Trójjedynym* (Kraków: Znak, 2006), 85–92.

160 Ἐκ μονάδος Τριάς ἐστί καί ἐκ Τριάδος μονάς αὖθις ... (St. Gregory of Nazianzus, *Carmina dogmatica* I, 1, 3: PG 37, 413). Cf. Guzowski, *Duch Dialogujący*, 366–7. Greshake notes that "Augustine's understanding of person, despite its allowance for the relational moment, is rather evocative of that direction which emphasises the unity of God as well as the singularity and specific independence of persons. At the same time, his 'primordial vision', according to which the unity of God lies in the Divine substance, but diversity in God is understood – on the basis of *processiones* – as relation, influenced an entire epoch and indeed led later to a relational understanding of person, on the basis of which God himself – formally speaking – is a 'relational structure' or, less abstractly, is perfect

When attempting to describe the relationship between the three divine Persons, a critical assessment of the Boeotian substantialisation of person often arises because, according to J. Tischner, it makes these Persons

> signs without expression, it objectifies them, prevents access to an understanding of the reciprocal relation between them, excludes the framing of their action in historical and event-typical terms, and finally, it does not eliminate the possibility of thinking of the Trinity in terms of the coexistence of three gods.[161]

This is why Tischner proposed the category of "dialogue"[162] as a tool that facilitates gaining insight into the interior of the Holy Trinity.

1.3.2 The Holy Spirit in the Communional Trinitarian Perichoresis

The relational-communional understanding of the Persons in the Holy Trinity is closely linked to the concept of *perichoresis*[163] (the Latin *circumincessio* emphasises the mutual dynamic interpenetration of the Persons, *circuminsessio* emphasises the permanent presence of one Person in the other, inherence, static continuance; *circumincessio* also points to the ecstatic movement of the Persons towards each

---

being and life through the relations between the persons: *Communio*" (Greshake, *Trójjedyny Bóg*, 88). Cf. ibid., 84–8.

161 Jarosław Jagiełło, "Metodologiczna odnowa dogmatyki: egzystencjalno-antropologiczny punkt widzenia," in *Dogmat i metoda. Wprowadzenie do badań interdyscyplinarnych w teologii dogmatycznej*, ed. Woźniak (Kraków: WAM, 2020), 225.

162 Jagiełło, "Metodologiczna odnowa dogmatyki: egzystencjalno-antropologiczny punkt widzenia," 226: "all that is in God is God, God is a 'conversation', or the eternal 'choosing of choice'. [...]. The concept of dialogue as 'choosing a choice', in the case of the persons of the Holy Trinity, exposes their variety, their radical otherness in relation to one another. But in this otherness, at the same time, their radical essential similarity is revealed. This is why Tischner, undoubtedly following St. Bonaventure and Hans Urs von Balthasar, emphasises that 'in God, infinite otherness is joined by the infinite similarity of the Persons. [...] This sounds like a contradiction. But there are contradictions that open up new horizons. When the Father 'gazes' at the Son whom he begot, he sees infinite otherness and simultaneously infinite likeness, leading all the way to identity. Similarly, when the Son gazes at the Father. It is no different with the Holy Spirit. For what we experience on earth, when we encounter otherness, is only a distant reflection of that Otherness...' According to Tischner, the dialogical relation between the Divine Persons is thus a dialectical relation, the existence of which is based on a paradox: the greater the similarity, the greater the otherness, and the greater the identity, the greater the difference."

163 See Jürgen Moltmann, "Der dreieinige Gott", in *Der lebendige Gott. Auf den Spuren neueren trinitarischen Denkens*, ed. Weth (Neukirchen-Vluyn: Neukirchener Verlag, 2005), 181–6.

other – not only *ad aliam*, but also *in aliam* and thus also *in alias*[164]).[165] Originally, perichoresis meant the mutual whirling of the dancers around each other; in Stoic and Neoplatonic thought, it referred to the union and mutual interpenetration of soul and body in man. In trinitarian theology, it means that the Father, the Son and the Holy Spirit are so closely united that they perfectly comprehend and interpenetrate one another, keep nothing to Themselves, but mutually order all that They are and mutually grant it to one another. Metaphorically, this can be shown precisely as a common dance of the Persons.[166] The Council of Florence drew a consistent conclusion from the truth of *circumicessio*: "The Father is whole in the Son, whole in the Holy Spirit, the Son is whole in the Father, whole in the Holy Spirit, the Holy Spirit is whole in the Father, whole in the Son".[167]

The Cappadocian theologians said that the life of God is like a "pulsation" in which "unity gives rise to the Trinity and the Trinity gives rises to unity".[168] Perichoresis metaphorically conceptualises the Persons of God as "dancers whirling in the common dance": The Son is whole in the Father, the Father is whole in the Son and with the Son, and the basis of their unity is the bond in the one Holy Spirit. This is consistent with the *Prologue* of St. John's Gospel, which says of the Son that He is "the only-begotten God who is in the bosom of the Father" (John 1:18). Therefore, Jesus could say that "the Son can do nothing on his own, but only what he sees the Father doing; for whatever the Father does, the Son does likewise" (John 5:19). He could say to the Father "All mine are yours, and yours are mine" (John 17:10); the disciples should know "the Father is in me and I am in the Father" (John 10:38). The Son and the Father are then a perichoretic unity in the Holy Spirit.[169]

The concept of "person" is not "flat" in relation to the dynamics of perichoresis, since each Person in the historico-salvific Trinity has revealed Their own Person and the divinity common to the three Persons, and therefore the concept of person captures the richness of intra-trinitarian life as the Communion of the three Persons.[170] Within the communional (perichoretic) model of the trinitarian unity, G. Greshake emphasises that unity in the Trinity cannot be considered as something existing prior to the Persons (an essentialist view) or as something following the

164 Cf. Greshake, *Trójjedyny Bóg*, 82, footnote 244.

165 Cf. Auer, *Gott - Der Eine und Dreieine*, 318–22; Bartnik, *Dogmatyka latolicka*, 1: 215–6; Warzeszak, *Bóg Jedyny w Trójcy Osób*, 219.

166 I draw here on my book: Jagodziński, *Węzłowe zagadnienia chrystologii komunijnej*, 35–7.

167 Sobór w Bazylei – Ferrarze – Florencji – Rzymie. *Bulla unii z Koptami* (*"Cantate Domino"* also called *Decretum pro Jacobitis*) (1442), in *Dokumenty Soborów Powszechnych. Tekst łaciński, grecki, arabski, ormiański, polski*, vol. III (1414–1445), ed. Arkadiusz Baron and Henryk Pietras (Kraków: WAM, 2003), 580–1. Cf. Greshake, *Trójjedyny Bóg*, 82–3; Kasper, *Bóg Jezusa Chrystusa*, 351–2.

168 St. Gregory of Nazianzus, *Carmina dogmatica* I, 1, 3, PG 37, 413.

169 Cf. Greshake, *Wierzę w Boga trójjedynego*, 29–30.

170 Guzowski, *Duch Dialogujący*, 376, 381–2.

Persons (an interpersonal view), since it takes place precisely "in" and "through" the perichoresis of the Persons. The concept of perichoresis serves "to understand *communio* as *communicatio*". He further considers that, according to the original meaning of the traditional concept of perichoresis, references to the other Persons are present in each Person. The very association of the concept of unity with nature (essence) had a philosophical basis at the time, for "one nature" of God meant a communion of love between the Persons. According to this, the biblical formula "God is Love" (1 John 4:8,16) expresses the highest form of unity and not merely subjective goodness. In this way, theological and personalistic mention of unity (not purely philosophical) is a way of expressing both the deity and the unity of God. In this view on the dynamics of Divine Communion, it is also easier to understand why God ecstatically leans towards the creation, as well as invites and includes human persons in the dialogue.[171]

K. Hemmerle emphasised that – in contrast to human interpersonal reality, in which it is impossible to overcome the diversity of persons because it is constitutive of what is common to persons while difference is perceived as enrichment – the essential communion of the Divine persons is not a communion (*koinonia*) of complementarity, but a communion of perichoresis.[172] W. Kasper believes that only the trinitarian doctrine specifies the abstract idea of singularity and unity in God. Unity is defined as the communion between the Father, the Son and the Holy Spirit – unity in love. In relation to God, one should say that He "is" love, not that He "has" love.[173]

J. Moltmann also adopted the perichoretic model of the unity of the Trinity as the most adequate and synthetic account, since speaking of the unity of God in a static and essential sense carries the danger of modalism, whereas the perichoretic picture captures the personal dynamics of the Holy Trinity. The trinitarian Persons establish through Themselves Their own unity within the circle of Divine life. Each exists outside of itself in the other two. The power of perfect love makes each of them go out of Themselves and is completely present in the others. This means, in a reverse setting, that each Person of the Holy Trinity is not only a person but is also the living space for the other two. The basis of the immanent unity of the Trinity is neither nature – as in the Latin tradition – nor person – as in the Eastern tradition (the monarchy of the Father). Furthermore, the Persons of God should not be reduced to the three modes (*modus*) of being of one Divine subject (contrary to the concepts postulated by K. Barth and K. Rahner), especially since the same Persons form proper differences and proper unity. On a perichorectic approach, God's life

171 Cf. Guzowski, *Duch Dialogujący*, 382–3.

172 Cf. Klaus Hemmerle, *Thesen zu einer trinitarischen Ontologie* (Einsiedeln: Johannes Verlag, 1976), 44.

173 Cf. Guzowski, *Duch Dialogujący*, 383–4.

is not actualised monadically by a single Person, but precisely in a Communion of three Persons facing each other and existing in each other. Therefore, Moltmann did not see unity in the domination of one Person, but in the union of the Tri-unity. Since the discussion around the *Filioque* raised the issue of the distinction (by St. Augustine) between the relations of origin that are constitutive of the Persons in the Trinity and the intra-trinitarian relations, Moltmann drew a distinction between the constitutive "origin" of the Trinity, which is the Father (the monarchy of the Father), and the life of the Trinity, in which the three Persons are equal in Their mutual relations. In the light of this, the Holy Spirit is not the "third" Person in the dynamics of this life. Moltmann emphasised that on the perichoretic plane there is no precedence of any Person over the others. The Holy Trinity is not a hierarchical community and it is not the Holy Spirit in the unity of the Father and the Son that constitutes the node of the unity of the Trinity. "In the Trinity, it is not the subject that represents unity, but every triadic inter-subjectivity, which we call *perichóresis*".[174]

When we look at the mystery of the Holy Trinity in terms of trinitarian life rather than static mental constructs, unity will not be something abstract, but precisely life in unity, a perichoresis of the Persons. Unity in God can be understood neither as a nature preceding the self-existent Divine Hypostases (*una substantia – tres personae*), nor as a subject whose modes of being constitute a triplicity rather than a Trinity. This unity is the Communion of Persons which is the communion of life[183]. It should therefore be understood as a unity that is welcoming, open and capable of exchange. The one God is the unifying God. Unity is an expression of the capacity for unifying and self-giving to others and it lies in persons. Only persons can be one, not ways of being (this is a reference to K. Rahner's criticised proposal).

1.3.3 The Holy Spirit in the Communional Unity and Plurality of the Persons of the Holy Trinity

In the Middle Ages, under the influence of St. Augustine, the official teaching of the Church emphasised the relationality of the three Persons comprising the Holy Trinity,[175] but theological reflections tended to emphasise their specific, individual singularity. Therefore, recourse was made to the concept of person developed by Boethius, according to whom a person is an individuality of spiritual nature.[176]

---

174 Moltmann, *Bóg nadziei* (Lublin: Wydawnictwo KUL, 2006), 130. Cf. Guzowski, *Duch Dialogujący*, 384–6.

175 Cf. Guzowski, *Duch Dialogujący*, 367.

176 Cf. Kasper, *Bóg Jezusa Chrystusa*, 248–9: "A step further was taken by Leontius of Byzantium: to be a person – according to him – means 'to be for oneself' [...] 'to exist for oneself' [...]. Similarly, Deacon Rusticus defines person as 'remaining in oneself' [...]. In this way, it was clarified that

It must be remembered, however, that in this definition two aspects of a person's identity meet – the individual and the general. The individual being of a person is constantly linked to being with others who share the same nature. Therefore, the nature of person encompasses the openness to and reference to the whole, thus Boethius' definition includes – still inexplicitly and indirectly – a relational element that was not yet able to express the specific personal relationality at that time.[177] Besides, Boethius developed his notion of person in the current of philosophical and Christological rather than trinitarian considerations. Within trinitology, the person pointed to that which is distinctive, whereas in Christology it was defined precisely as the principle of the unity of the two natures. Nevertheless, both were concerned with the proper distinction between nature and person, albeit the context of the problem was different or even opposite.[178]

According to Richard of Saint Victor, the Boeotian definition of person was inadequate for the Persons of the Holy Trinity since the substance of God is spiritual and individual, and is not a person. The trinitarian being of Person must therefore go beyond the individuality of *substantia rationalis naturae*. Therefore, "the divine person is the incommunicable existence of divine nature".[179] What is special here is the notion of existence – it is substance, but not a general essence; a concrete property that makes a being itself. Besides, as already pointed out, "sister" denotes a mode of being, and "ex" – the primary relation of "wherefrom". *Ex-sistentia* thus means being oneself for the sake of another. In this case, the Divine Persons in their being are co-constituted by the relation "wherefrom", and this means that "the relation of a person to those persons who are their primary cause is co-constitutive in the determination of the essence of that person".[180] Thus, this definition involves, in a significant way, the person's own and peculiar relationality.[181]

---

this individuality is not accidentally received by person from outside, but person has it within themselves. It is precisely this that allows the Divine Person to unite itself, as closely as possible, with human nature, while still retaining its own free existence. This doctrine of hipostatization, developed by Leontius, i. e. of the immanent existence of human nature in the Divine Hypostasis, must therefore be considered in view of its dialectical character, according to which unity and difference grow in equal and not inverse relation. At the end of the Age of the Fathers, Maximus the Confessor formulated this dialectical principle: 'There clearly occurs a unification of things to the extent that their physical difference is preserved.'"

177 Cf. Guzowski, *Duch Dialogujący*, 368.

178 Cf. Greshake, *Trójjedyny Bóg*, 89–91. The quoted content is taken from my monograph: Jagodziński, *Węzłowe zagadnienia chrystologii komunijnej*, 37–8.

179 *De Trinitate* IV, 20 (quoted in Greshake, *Trójjedyny Bóg*, 92).

180 Mühlen, *Der Heilige Geist als Person*, 40, footnote 65 (quoted in Greshake, *Trójjedyny Bóg*, 92).

181 Cf. Greshake, *Trójjedyny Bóg*, 92. According to Richard of Saint Victor, "person is 'naturae intellectualis incommunicabilis existentia'. Person is – in an unalterable and unique way – a peculiar *incommunicabilis*; but it is not person when it closes in on itself, but when it is an existence, that is, an existence *from* something else *towards* something else. While Thomas Aquinas essentially

Richard showed the realisation of such relationality mainly in the structure of God-realised supreme love, which must be reciprocal and – if it is to correspond to God's perfection and be ordered – must be a Divine Person. And since love between two cannot yet be the highest realisation of reciprocal love, it must hence open itself to the third – it is only in Him, the Co-Beloved (*condilectus*) – that the proper selflessness and greatness of trinitarian love, which desires to communicate its common happiness to the third, is manifested and only then does it reach its fullness.[182] In such a phenomenology of the perfect love of the Persons in God, the triple-relational realities of *diligens*, *dilectus* and *condilectus* are revealed: the Father is the bestowing love, the Son is both the receiving and bestowing love, the Holy Spirit is the pure receiving love[183] – but all Three are one and the very same love in three rhythms.[184] The first rhythm is, of course, the Father as the unbegotten Person.[185]

---

referred to Boethius, Duns Scotus developed and deepened the relational notion of person proposed by Richard of Saint Victor" (Kasper, *Bóg Jezusa Chrystusa*, 249). Cf. Guzowski, *Duch Dialogujący*, 368.

182 Cf. Greshake, *Wierzę w Boga trójjedynego*, 33–4.

183 Cf. Richard of Saint Victor, *De Trinitate* III, 11, 14–5. On the development of these ideas in trinitarian anthropology, see Splett, "Dialektik des Tuns – Dialog – Person-Sein in trinitarischer Analogie," 171–3.

184 Cf. Greshake, *Trójjedyny Bóg*, 165–6: "Now, these trinitarian relations – explicated entirely within the framework of the traditional doctrine on relations – are not considered from a conventional constitutional-hermeneutic point of view (Where do the Son and the Spirit 'come from'?), but on the ground of the correlation of relations, with the focus on a mutual mediating event that excludes any *reductio in unum*. Hence, it is better to begin the consideration of the trinitarian event from the Father's side, which allows us to define it as the eternal 'rhythm of love', and the individual persons fulfilling this rhythm as rhythms = specific shapes of fulfilment, in a sense as 'nodal points' of this event of love. Each person is in its own way entirely of and for the others: giving/receiving – receiving/giving – uniting/receiving/giving back, so that each is itself only in others and in the fulfilment of its own being a person includes and embraces others (perichoresis). Thus, as Balthasar aptly formulates, they are 'all three .... one and the same love in the three modes of being that are necessary for there to be love at all in God, i. e. the supreme, most selfless love.'" Cf. Greshake, *Trójjedyny Bóg*, 91–7; Jagodziński, "Trialogiczno-komunijna koncepcja trynitologii," 60–4. The background for such a trinitarian account is the dialogical and trialogical understanding of person developed in modern philosophy. Cf. Greshake, *Trójjedyny Bóg*, 134–44.

185 Cf. Greshake, *Wierzę w Boga trójjedynego*, 35. "The Father is, in the rhythm of love, the Original Gift. This expresses the truth that he never existed without the Son (and the Holy Spirit), to whom He gives Himself, and thus cannot even be mentally 'isolated' from the two other Persons as their unthinkable original foundation. He has His own 'identity' precisely in the giving of Himself, that He is always directed towards the others and at the same time 'obtains' His identity from Them in this way. In this possession of the self in being directed towards the others, from the beginning – together with identity – a difference is also established, the 'God's distance from God', the initial 'no' (not in oneself but in the others), which signifies both the infinite confirmation of the self and the others – a 'no' in 'confirmation'. 'No' as difference and otherness thus occurs

In terms of the reciprocal mediation of the unity and plurality of the Persons of the Holy Trinity, it is important to conceive of the Trinity as Communion. God, who is Communion, realises His being in the dialogue of the three Persons. The trinitarian logic of faith makes it possible to infer from the interpersonality of the historico-salvific Trinity about Their immanent life. At the same time, the Communion paradigm overcomes the ancient dangers of associations with subordinationism, modalism or tritheism.[186]

God is Communion. There is no essence of God that can only be conceived independently of the structure of the Persons, and there is no Person that could exist independently of the binding relationship with the other Persons. The eternal, constitutive mutual being with each other of the three Persons, in their mutual being "from each other" and "for each other", exists in the inseparable being together in self-union – through self-differentiation from the others – and union – through merging with them. The being of the triune God thus turns out to be the realisation of self-giving.[187] Here, G. Greshake writes specifically:

> The Divine essence neither has its selfhood 'in itself' nor above or beside the three persons, but is what happens 'in' and 'between' the three persons [...] whatever takes place in various ways in and through the Three jointly is [...] the content of their being a person and of their interpersonal perichoresis. On such an assumption, [...] the action of the three Divine persons, insofar as they perichoretically interpenetrate each other, can be attributed to one divine essence, or one divine nature, and properties can also be stated through them, as long as it is guaranteed that it is not something fourth, which – even if only "logically" – precedes the persons or follows them, but is precisely the fulfilment of their perichoretic communion: *Communio*. Thus *essentia divina*, the one Divine essence, is the *Communio* that exists only in the exchange of the Father, the Son and the Spirit. Each of the Divine persons is turned towards the other, i. e. is correlative when it simultaneously gives and receives: The Father fulfils His own Son when he completely gives Himself to the other as Son (thus He possesses his Divinity 'only as given', but at the same time receives from Him being the Father); the Son when He receives Himself completely from the

---

not only in the appearance of finiteness (manifested through a lack in being and negativity), but is given prior in the life of God in the form of purest positivity. Existing as the bottomless and incomprehensible mystery of being a gift, the Father gives the foundation and sustains the entire *Communio*, He carries it and maintains it in its entirety in such a way that the other Persons light up in His centre. However, this does not mean that He is the ontological basis of the genetic process, or that it is possible to think of Him in this way" (Jagodziński, "Trialogiczno-komunijna koncepcja trynitologii," 69). Cf. Jagodziński, *Węzłowe zagadnienia chrystologii komunijnej*, 38–9.

186 G. Greshake emphasises that, given the capacity of human experience, the simplest form of communion involves three persons (cf. Greshake, *Trójjedyny Bóg*, 161).

187 Cf. Greshake, *Trójjedyny Bóg*, 161–2; Jagodziński, *Węzłowe zagadnienia chrystologii komunijnej*, 41–2.

> Father and gives Him 'glory'; the Spirit when He receives Himself from the relationship of the Father and the Son as the 'Third' and at the same time glorifies both. In this way, the three persons in God do not hold their self-existence against one another, but only for the sake of one another, with one another and for one another. Each of the three persons thus reflects the totality of the trinitarian event in Their own way. [...] on the ground of the radical mediation of each person by the other and thus the radical mutual 'entanglement', where the one divine person is involved the other two are also given there together. Since the fullness of love blossoms in the Spirit, and insofar as the unity of oneness and plurality of the Father and the Son remains open to a certain extent, also from His side, i. e. from the perspective of the Spirit, it is possible to capture the totality of the trinitarian life as perfect love.[188]

1.3.4 The Origin of the Holy Spirit in the Trinitarian Communion

Concerning the difference of the Persons comprising the Holy Trinity, traditional teaching pointed to the personal qualities rooted in the "origins":[189] the (original) paternity, the (begotten) sonship and the (breathed) origin of the Holy Spirit.[190] The creeds and theological explanations emphasised that the Father is God who originates from no one and is, as His very name indicates, the Source of the origin of the Son (and the Holy Spirit).[191]

The problem of the origin of the Son was relatively easy to solve. It was more difficult to explain the origin of the Holy Spirit. The fact that the Holy Spirit comes from the Father was made clear by Jesus Himself when bidding farewell to his disciples: "When the Advocate comes, whom I will send to you from the Father, the Spirit of truth who comes from the Father, he will testify on my behalf" (John 15:26). The Constantinian Creed takes up this very statement of Jesus. The question immediately arises as to what distinguishes the Holy Spirit from the Son, since they both come (equally) from the Father and constitute, as St. Irenaeus proclaimed, "the two hands of the Father". The answer, developed by the Christian East and West and later sustained in the West, is that the only basis for the Holy Spirit's distinctiveness

---

188 Greshake, *Trójjedyny Bóg*, 164–166. For a more detailed analysis of the Holy Trinity as Communion, see ibid., 150–76.

189 See Jagodziński, *Trynitologia komunijna*, 81–6.

190 Cf. Auer, *Gott – Der Eine und Dreieine*, 305–11; Breuning, *Nauka o Bogu*, 188–97; Kasper, *Bóg Jezusa Chrystusa*, 344–5; Bartnik, *Dogmatyka katolicka*, 1: 210–11; Scheffczyk, *Der Gott der Offenbarung. Gotteslehre* (Aachen: MM Verlag, 1996), 350–7.

191 Cf. Jagodziński, *Węzłowe zagadnienia chrystologii komunijnej*, 42. Origins are justified by specific (substantive) relations and thus the distinguished Persons. This doctrine, however, is not unproblematic, with two problematic circles: the traditional view of Persons and the specificity of the Son in the Communion of the Holy Trinity (ibid., 46).

from the Son can be found in His origin. This is supported by other statements made by Jesus in the same farewell speech, e. g. "He will glorify me, because he will take what is mine and declare it to you" (John 16:14). Western theologians started to emphasise more and more strongly that the Holy Spirit cannot "take" anything from the Son except origin, since they have everything in common except different origin. The validity of the above conclusion is also supported by several other statements made by Jesus: "But the Advocate, the Holy Spirit, whom the Father will send in my name, will teach you everything, and remind you of all that I have said to you" (John 14:26); "Nevertheless I tell you the truth: it is to your advantage that I go away, for if I do not go away, the Advocate will not come to you; but if I go, I will send him to you" (John 16:7). Jesus says that the Father will "send" the Spirit in His name and that He Himself will "send" from the Father the One "who comes from the Father" (John 15:26). The possibility of "sending", expressed so unambiguously, can only be derived from the fact of "origin". Thus the statement, which was finally clarified at the medieval councils, is: "The Holy Spirit proceeds from the Father and the Son as from one principle and by a single spiration". Western theologians added that it is an origin "by an action of the will – in the way of love".[192]

Theologians could deal with "God Himself" only because He had revealed Himself to man. Initially, no distinction was made between these two planes and thus the theology practised by the most ancient Church Fathers was simply the "economy of salvation". It was only in the course of time that some real distinction was realised between "God for us" and "God in Himself". Focusing on the action of God "outwardly", the Greek Church Fathers spoke of "energies" as the joint action of the Holy Trinity manifested in creation,[193] while the West developed the Scripture-based

192 Cf. Courth, *Bóg trójjedynej miłości*, 244–5; Balthasar, *Teologika*, vol. II: *Prawda Boga*, 144–51. In the view of F. Courth, according to H.U. von Balthasar, "the whole Augustinian-Thomistic system suffers from the difficulty of being unable to explain the relations inside the divine substance as relations between persons. On the other hand, the adoption of Platonic *bonum diffusivum sui*, the divine self-giving, must in turn limit *opera Trinitatis ad extra* (the works of the Holy Trinity outwardly), since the Son comes 'in the way of knowledge' and the Holy Spirit 'in the way of love'. Balthasar believes that, on this view, one can only with difficulty explain, as a manifestation of the immanent trinitarian relation, that phrase from the farewell speech when Jesus says: 'All mine are yours, and yours are mine' (John 17:10). A more relational understanding of the trinitarian Persons than in the Augustinian tradition, according to the Swiss theologian, is conveyed to contemporary personalist thought by Richard of Saint Victor. He treats the relation of 'I' to 'you' as essentially belonging to a person. Man as a person is not defined by 'I' to which 'you' is added; but rather, 'you' belongs to 'I'; it is the fruit of the loving call and surrender of 'you'. In this perspective, the relation between persons in Balthasar's work enters "into the first rank of images and likenesses of God's essence – after all, relation is the most noteworthy within creation – and can be used as an aid to understanding, like a psychological schema, if only it were prepared to allow itself (as the last!) to be critically evaluated in its momentousness"' (Courth, *Bóg trójjedynej miłości*, 287–9).

193 See Courth, *Bóg trójjedynej miłości*, 250–2.

doctrine of the messages of Divine persons.[194] Indeed, Jesus repeatedly said of himself that he was sent by the Father: "he sent me" (John 8:42); "the one who sent me is true" (John 8:26); "the one who sent me is with me" (John 8:29); "the Father who sent me has himself given me a commandment about what to say and what to speak" (John 12:49); "whoever sees me sees him who sent me" (John 12:45); "But now I am going to him who sent me" (John 16:5) etc. Jesus made similar statements about the Holy Spirit. Based on these and similar texts, Western theology developed the idea of the message of the Divine Persons.[195]

In doing so, a distinction was made between intra-trinitarian (internal) and so-called external messages. The former were treated as identical to origins. Being the basis of the external messages, they would point to the mystery of "God in Himself". We learn of their actual existence in God only from external messages. For this reason, over the centuries Western theology have examined the claims concerning the messages of the Divine Persons in parallel with the claims about their origins: "God the Father sends but is not sent; the Son of God sends and is sent; the Holy Spirit is sent but does not send". "External" messages, in turn, were divided into visible and invisible ones. When it comes to the Holy Spirit, theologians have sometimes listed as many as four of His visible messages – two of which refer to Christ and two to the Apostles. The Spirit's first message referring to Christ is connected with Jesus' baptism in the Jordan: "Now when all the people were baptized, and when Jesus also had been baptized and was praying, the heaven was opened, and the Holy Spirit descended upon him in bodily form like a dove. And a voice came from heaven, 'You are my Son, the Beloved; with you I am well pleased'" (Luke 3:21-22). The second, more symbolic sending of the Holy Spirit takes place at the moment of transfiguration: "While he was still speaking, suddenly a bright cloud overshadowed them, and from the cloud a voice said, 'This is my Son, the Beloved; with him I am well pleased; listen to him!'" (Matt 17:5). To the Apostles refers the message of the Holy Spirit from the first meeting of the resurrected Lord with the disciples in the Cenacle, when Jesus "said to them again: 'Peace be with you. As the Father has sent me, so I send you'. When he had said this, he breathed on them and said to them, 'Receive the Holy Spirit'" (John 20:22-23), and from the scene of sending of the Holy Spirit at Pentecost: "And suddenly from heaven there came a sound like the rush of a violent wind, and it filled the entire house where they were sitting. Divided tongues, as of fire, appeared among them, and a

194 Cf. Auer, *Gott – Der Eine und Dreieine*, 300–4; Scheffczyk, *Der Gott der Offenbarung*, 358–65; Warzeszak, *Bóg Jedyny w Trójcy Osób*, 223–4.

195 Cf. Kasper, *Bóg Jezusa Chrystusa*, 343–4.

tongue rested on each of them. All of them were filled with the Holy Spirit [...]" (Acts 2:2-4).[196]

1.3.5 Problems in the Traditional View of the Persons of the Holy Trinity

The terms Father, Son and Holy Spirit come from the history of salvation – they are thus the names of the economic Trinity. They can be transferred to the inner life of God, but historically contingent elements – e. g. temporal forms, shapes, categories, images – can also be transferred with them, and the "ontological difference" (i. e. their analogical character and especially their contradictory dimension) contained in them must be considered. But if God reveals Himself as He is in Himself, then the historico-salvific being of the Father, the Son and the Holy Spirit must have a real and not merely metaphorical counterpart in the inner life of God[197]. The ancient creed attempted to articulate positive counterparts and, at the same time, negations, similarities and dissimilarities. The danger has always been that the negations, paradoxes and biblical ways of speaking contained in these statements turn into affirmations.

The accounts of the beginning of the immanent Trinity reconstructed from the history of salvation are understood very unilaterally in the theological tradition. St. Augustine spoke rightly of the Son being send by the Father (begetting) and of the Holy Spirit being given by the Father and the Son (breathing). However, other still historico-salvific facts were not taken into account or appreciated. After all, according to the New Testament, the Holy Spirit is not only "sent" by the Son, but the Son is also to some extent sent by the Spirit, who realised the coming of the Son in flesh ("by the power of the Holy Spirit He became incarnate of the Virgin Mary and was made man" – "who was conceived by the Holy Spirit") and led ("Jesus was led up by the Spirit into the wilderness" – Matt 4:1; "Jesus, filled with the power of the Spirit, returned to Galilee" – Luke 4:14), enabled Him to offer His life ("who through the eternal Spirit offered himself without blemish to God" – Heb 9:14), raised from the dead ("He was revealed in flesh, vindicated in spirit, seen by angels, proclaimed among Gentiles, believed in throughout the world, taken up in glory" – 1 Tim 3:16; "He was put to death in the flesh, but made alive in the spirit" – 1 Pet 3:18; also Rom 6:4 – "Christ was raised from the dead by the glory of the Father") and surrounds Himself with glory ("the Spirit of truth [...] He will glorify me" – John 16:13-14). Paul Evdokimov even spoke of the Son's origin "ex Patre Spirituque". The historico-salvific accounts thus point

196 Cf. Courth, *Bóg trójjedynej miłości*, 247–9; Jagodziński, *Węzłowe zagadnienia chrystologii komunijnej*, 43–6.

197 Cf. Greshake, *Trójjedyny Bóg*, 177.

to a "reciprocal reference" between the Son and the Holy Spirit[198], and since the traditional formulation "Credo [...] in Spiritum Sanctum [...] qui ex Patre Filioque procedit" does not explain this sufficiently,[199] it should be supplemented by the clarifications cited above.[200] A debatable point of H.U. von Balthasar's trinitarian theology is the introduction of the notion of "intra-trinitarian kenosis"[201] and the

---

198 The Son receives from the Father and returns gratitude to the Father. "This reciprocal action of the Son signifies a 'return of gratitude, being at Father's disposal, commitment'. Through this, the gift 'becomes' the gift and the Father becomes the Father – in a strictly correlative movement. This is only possible because the Father and the Son are, in their being 'the other', united in oneness by their relation to the Holy Spirit, whereby the Son can be grasped in the proper sense as 'fruit' – 'begotten of the Father' and united with Him by the action of the ecstatic Spirit and His unifying action. But the Son is not only 'being in receiving', 'being in giving', he is also in 'giving forth' (to the Holy Spirit) and thus the principle of communication (Logos) – and thus even more 'the image of the Father'" (Jagodziński, *Węzłowe zagadnienia chrystologii komunijnej*, 51).

199 G. Greshake cites Wolfhart Pannenberg's claim (*Systematische Theologie*, (Göttingen: Vandenhoeck & Ruprecht, 1993), 3: 21) that the origin of the Holy Spirit from the Son is only a momentous point in the history of salvation since in the New Testament view, the reverse movement is much more emphatically underlined. Therefore, "in the trinitarian life of God, the Son in eternity is the recipient of the Spirit coming from the Father" (cf. Greshake, *Trójjedyny Bóg*, 180, footnote 649).

200 Cf. Greshake, *Trójjedyny Bóg*, 179–80.

201 Cf. Piotrowski, *Traktat o Trójcy Świętej*, 212–3: "The Father divests himself of His Deity and hands it over to the Son: He does not share with the Son, but gives His all to the Son (cf. John 17:10). God (as the Father) gives His Deity, and God (as the Son) has it in a 'consubstantial' way. This reveals the ineffable 'separation' of God from Himself. In giving Himself to the Son, the Father does not lose Himself; nor does He keep anything for Himself. He thus reveals Himself in this self-giving, which is the whole essence of God. Here God's infinite omnipotence and at the same time His impotence are revealed, for He is God only in such intra-trinitarian kenosis. The measure of this omnipotence is that He can beget a consubstantial, and thus uncreated God, in total self-surrender. The Son thus possesses Deity in the manner of assuming this unity between the omnipotence and impotence of the Father. The drama (in the sense of an event happening with unprecedented intensity) in God continues eternally because the Father was never without the Son, the Father and the Son never existed without the Spirit. The Father is also the eternal source of the opportunity given to the Son to be, together with Him, the (co-)source of origin of the Spirit. This event gives the Son's willingness to let Himself be guided by the Spirit, whom He possesses in all fullness (cf. John 3:34). Nevertheless, on the other hand, for methodological and substantive reasons, it must be borne in mind that the historico-salvific Trinity cannot be simply identified with the immanent Trinity, since the immutability of God must be reconciled with His evident historico-salvific mutability, without falling into heresy at the same time. Speaking of the Father's kenosis is made possible by Jesus' revelation of Him. The Father, who sends the Son, is thus present in the Son's message, although He is not identical with Him. The first kenosis of the Father becomes the kenosis of the whole Trinity, because the Son is consubstantial with the Father in the total renunciation of Himself. Also the Spirit, as the "We" of the Father and the Son, being the seal of their self-resignation, is not in the least degree for Himself, but only wants to be the very revelation and bestowal of love between the Father and the Son. This kenotic attitude of the Spirit (in the Trinity) is evidenced by His revelation in the world (cf. John 13:31-16:33). The kenosis is God's self-constraint: the first is the bestowal

cross to the immanent Trinity,[202] while J. Moltmann's concept describes the virtual breach of intra-trinitarian Communion on the cross.[203]

The concept of "trinitarian ontology" is noteworthy here. The persons of the Trinity are distinguished only by their mutual and distinctive relations. The Father is characterised by unbegottenness, paternity and (together with the Son) spiration, the Son – by filiation and (together with the Father) spiration, while the Spirit is characterised by origin alone (from the Father and the Son, insofar as one accepts the *Filioque*). These differences do not compromise the full identity of nature. This means that at the very heart of the doctrine on the Holy Trinity lies the category of relation. The use of the category of relation in Christian theology to describe God was something absolutely unexpected on the grounds of classical metaphysics. The Greeks quite commonly regarded relations as the weakest kind of being. The reason for the disregard of relations was the conviction that they were ontologically secondary not only to substance, but also to other kinds of accidents. Trinitarian theology gave the category of relation a completely different status. In the Holy Trinity, relations are understood as essential to its members – the Persons of the Trinity do not so much enter into relations as are constituted by them (or are identified with them). As J. Ratzinger wrote, the supremacy of substance was broken. Relation was discovered as an equal, primary existential mode of reality and a new plane of being was revealed. It was the notion of relation that became the foundation of a new trinitarian ontology, the development of which was started by K. Hemmerle with reference to H.U. von Balthasar, and continued by P. Coda, G. Maspero and J. Milbank – although the links between metaphysics and dogmatics are always rather ambivalent.[204]

---

of freedom on the creation, the second is the establishment of the covenant with Israel, which is irresolvable on God's part, while the third, clearly trinitarian self-constraint, is the incarnation of the Son."

202 See the critical comments in Courth, *Bóg trójjedynej miłości*, 289–90.

203 Cf. Moltmann, *Trinität und Reich Gottes* (München: Kaiser, 1980), 96: On J. Moltmann's system and the related E. Jüngel's system, see Courth, *Bóg trójjedynej miłości*, 294–8. The comments on the problems cited here are taken from Jagodziński, *Węzłowe zagadnienia chrystologii komunijnej*, 46–50. K. Guzowski pointed out that within trinitarian theology Moltmann discovered the dialogical dimension of person – mainly under the influence of Martin Buber's dialectical personalism (Guzowski, *Duch Dialogujący*, 371).

204 Cf. Paweł Rojek, "Dogmatyka a metafizyka. Założenia i implikacje teologii trynitarnej," in *Dogmat i metoda*, 252–70.

1.3.6 The Specificity of the Holy Spirit in the Trinitarian Communion

The trinitarian understanding of God[205], who in Himself is the mutually directed love of the Father and the Son in the common Spirit of that love, is the pure life in relation, the infinitely complete becoming out of relation, the community, the communion of the Giver (the Father), the Receiver (the Son) and the Uniter (the Holy Spirit),[206] has been firmly established in contemporary theology. The essence of God is thus a Communication of love[207] – a Communion – sustained in various ways by the Divine Persons. The Father is the proper source of the Communication-Communion of love, which spouts continually with life. The Son is (from salvific economy) the Word made Flesh for the salvation of the world. The Holy Spirit, as the personified love of the Father and the Son, is also the personified Communication of love. Moreover, the Holy Spirit, as an intra-trinitarian bond of love, is oriented in an economic-salvific inversion towards people and is the personal medium of communication-communion of love between people and Christ – to the glory of the Father.[208] As J. Szymik wrote, "communion flows into our world – into man, into people, into all reality – from the source, from God. The Holy Spirit is the communion in God. He is the *communio* of the Father and the Son; this constitutes His essence: to be the unifying communion of the Father and the Son".[209] J.D. Zizioulas writes that communion with others requires the kenosis of the Incarnation and the experience of Christ's cross, while the breath of the Holy Spirit creates a communion that transforms everything He touches into relational existence.[210] "In this light, the Holy Spirit appears as a superabundance of Divine

205 Cf. Raimund Lachner, "Communio – eine Grundidee des christlichen Glaubens. Ein Beitrag zur Elementarisierung im Fach Dogmatik," in *Qualitätsmanagement in der Theologie. Chancen und Grenzen einer Elementarisierung im Lehramtsstudium*, ed. Lachner and Egon Spiegel (Kevelaer: Butzon & Bercker, 2003), 235–8; Guzowski, *Bruno Symbolika trynitarna Brunona Fortego* (Lublin: Wydawnictwo KUL, 2004), 23–4; Skrzypczak, *Osoba i misja*, 93–5.

206 Cf. Paul Josef Cordes, *Communio – Utopie oder Programm?* (Freiburg-Basel-Wien: Herder, 1993), 147–156. On so-called analytic metaphysics of the Trinity and its main contemporary representatives (Richard Swinburne, Brian Leftow, Jeffrey Brower and Michael Rea), see Rojek, "Dogmatyka a metafizyka. Założenia i implikacje teologii trynitarnej," 242–51.

207 Cf. Matthias Scharer and Hilberath, *Kommunikative Theologie. Eine Grundlegung* (Mainz: Grünewald, 2002), 76–85.

208 Cf. Kasper, *Bóg Jezusa Chrystusa*, 382–3. This is clearly shown by the schema of the trinitarian "structure of references" based on the model of communicative action. Cf. Kehl, "Kirche als Institution – eine theologische Begründung", 121.

209 Szymik, "Pneumatologiczna communio. Po stronie Logosu (pistis), przeciwko anarchii (gnosis)," in *Duch Kościoła. Kościół Ducha*, ed. Andrzej Proniewski (Białystok: Wydawnictwo Uniwersytetu w Białymstoku, 2014), 21.

210 Cf. Zizioulas, *Communion and Otherness. Further Studies in Personhood and the Church* (London-New York: T&T Clark, 2006), 5–6.

love, an overflowing fullness, a generous and selfless excess of radiant communion: Holy Spirit the Creator, the gift of the Most High, the fountain and overflowing fire of life (cf. the Western hymn *Veni Creator*)".[211]

In the trinitarian rhythm of love, the Holy Spirit is, on the one hand, pure receiving, because it is the gift of the Father and the Son (in a different way) and a loving response in praise and worship. On the other hand, it is the knot of love between the Father and the Son that unifies Them in oneness of being. He is the 'Third' (according to Richard of Saint Victor) who in the fire of selfless love unites the incomprehensible being the other of the Father and the Son as Their "unity in opposition", the "objectification of Their subjectivity", by which He acts against the possibility of Their blending or separation and directs Them towards each other. Thus the Holy Spirit, by being the gift of the Father to the Son and of the Son to the Father, and hence confirming the identity of the givers – confirms the identity in the difference of the Father and the Son, and hence the identity in the difference of the Divine Communion of love. Despite the dual character of the knot of love between the Father and the Son and the fruit of that love – as the Third guarantor of that love – the Holy Spirit is no duality. This dual character is two aspects of the same content in which He expresses the Divine 'We' of love. The Holy Spirit is the Person in whom the Communion of Divine love finds its full shape, and even more – in it, in going "beyond oneself", the "split" of the Father and the Son takes place. In the Spirit, the personal totality of the Divine life becomes comprehensible.[212] In his conception of trinitarian communion, G. Greshake paid more attention precisely to the Holy Spirit,

> who is both the bond and the fruit of the love of the Father and the Son. The common Divine 'We' of love is only fully expressed in the Spirit, that Third in love. He is that Person in the *communio* of Divine love in whom the Father and the Son are 'set apart' towards 'more'. The Spirit, therefore, as a Person becomes communion.[213]

---

211 Forte, *Istota chrześcijaństwa*, 93. "In Him, the Three Divine Persons open Themselves to that which is not Divine. In Him, God dwells where, in a certain sense, He is 'outside Himself'. That is why He has been called 'love'. He is God's 'ecstasy' towards man 'other' than Him. The third figure of the trinitarian symbolism excludes the possibility of a 'narcissistic' interpretation of the relation between the first two figures: God is the Opening, the connection, He is the source of life and sharing'" (Forte, *Istota chrześcijaństwa*, 93).

212 Cf. Greshake, *Der dreieine Gott*, 210–1; Stubenrauch, *Pneumatologia*, 221–36.

213 Guzowski, *Duch Dialogujący*, 88. "Greshake's proposal is interesting insofar as he wishes to break the Neoplatonic schema about the origin of the Persons. By defining each of the Persons in the Divine *communio* as the Gift giving itself and receiving into itself, he pushes away the genetic schema and replaces it with a schema of reciprocity in the perichoresis of the gifts. Although the Father is called the Original Gift, he cannot be conceived of in isolation from the other Persons, since the mystery of love is the mystery of the Persons who are a gift to each other. In the intra-divine

H. Mühlen was not so much interested in the structure of the intra-trinitarian unity, but rather in the dynamics of unity. Since in his approach the salvific mediation and the active principle of the Holy Spirit's presence become clearer, his schema is useful in the reinterpretation of trinitarian economy from a trinitarian-personal perspective. The image of the Holy Spirit as the most active Person in our history as subjects is revealed through the symbolism of the inter-personal dialogue in the Trinity. In the Trinity, the Holy Spirit is one Person in two persons, and in the Church, the Holy Spirit is one Person in many persons. The relationship between the Father and the Son is the "I-You" or "Me-You" relation, as e. g. in John 17:21-26. It is impossible to characterise the relationship of the Father and the Son with the Holy Spirit as "We-You" relation and, correspondingly, the relationship of the Spirit in reference to the Father and the Son as "I-You (plural)" relation. The Holy Spirit appears as the personal "We" between the "I" of the Father and the "You" of the Son, as the one who unites them in "We". On the basis of biblical analysis, the Father and the Son appear as two "I" who maintain an "I-You" relationship between them. In the trinitarian context, the Father is the fundamental "intra-trinitarian I", while the Son is the fundamental "intra-trinitarian You". When Jesus utters "We", he does so in a double sense: he includes the Father, but never the people, and He includes the Father and the Holy Spirit (cf. John 14:23). "We" involving the Holy Spirit points to Him as a dialogical Person, in the light of which He would be the "intra-trinitarian We". This claim is based on the Western doctrine on the origin of the Holy Spirit, which emphasises that in the Trinity we have *duo spirantes sed unus spirator* – this refers to active spiration. The action of the Father and the Son is in any case a subsistent act of "We", since it is performed by two Persons. The expression of this act from the side of the passive spiration is the Holy Spirit, who as the personal "Act-We" subsists between the Father and the Son. On the other hand, the consequence of the Spirit's relationship with the Father and the Son is the "I-You (plural)" relation. The Holy Spirit is the *nexus* of the Father and the Son. This paints a picture of two forms of intra-trinitarian perichoresis – one occurring between the Father and the Son, and the other occurring between the Father along

---

bestowal there is neither loss nor growth. In spite of its many virtues, however, this proposal in some points imitates the scheme of origin, when Greshake describes the Father as the 'Pre-basis' of the other Persons, the Son as the 'reception', the Spirit as the 'pure reception'. Nonetheless, in this *communio* schema, the Father is seen as the Centre rather than the beginning of the origin. Moreover, from trinitology Greshake draws the inspiration for his trialogical concept of the human person, for the human person is a reflection of the trinitarian Communion and thus serves as *locus theologicus*" (Guzowski, *Duch Dialogujący*, 388–9).

with the Son and the Holy Spirit. Therefore, according to this view, the Holy Spirit is a Person in two Persons.[214]

In order to properly capture the truth about the Holy Spirit as a person of the Trinity, C.S. Bartnik adopted a modified personalistic model of the Holy Trinity:

> In the Father as *Principium sine principio* it is the primordial realisation of essence in person. The Person of the Son is the essence that is begotten and 'reciprocal' with respect to the Person of the Father. The Person of the Spirit is the same essence, breathed between the Person of the Father and the Person of the Son. At the same time, the Begotten Person allows the One that Begets to become a Person, and the Breathed Person reciprocally completes the Communion of Person and Being. Consequently, in the Trinity, no Person would be itself without the other two and without the identity of Nature.[215]

---

214 Cf. Guzowski, *Duch Dialogujący*, 389–91. Mühlen extends his assumptions to encompass the reality of the Church. Just as in the Trinity the Holy Spirit is the bond between the persons and is "We," so in the Church He is identical in Christ and in a Christian: "he is one Person in many persons." Mühlen develops and interprets the formula found in the encyclical *Mystici corporis*, which speaks of the Spirit as *una Persona Mystica*. This concept enriches traditional pneumatology – it draws attention to the dialogical dimension of the trinitarian person and the human person; it reveals the mystery of the Holy Spirit as acting in a personal and direct way in the lives of people; it also revitalises the vision of the Trinity acting in the Church and in the world. The shortcomings are that, in his anthropological-grammatical analysis of personal pronouns, Mühlen focused too much on "We" and "You" without reaching sufficiently for the pronoun "He," and though in the Bible the Holy Spirit is spoken of primarily in the third person – especially when mentioned by Jesus. There has also been a lack of consistency in the personalistic approach, since the Holy Spirit is not only a bond of love between the Father and the Son, but also the Spirit of Dialogue. The revelation speaks of God-Love, in which love is a reciprocity of gift, and here the Holy Spirit is merely someone receiving and participating. Any trinitarian-personalist analysis should, after all, take into account the characteristics of intra-trinitarian life as love that is constitutive for persons. Nevertheless, this concept appears as a perfect illustration of the continuity between the role of the Holy Spirit in the inner life of the Trinity and the mission He fulfils in the world. As a Person of the Trinity, He at the same time unifies the Persons and personalizes the ecclesial community He creates. Cf. Guzowski, *Duch Dialogujący*, 391–2.

215 Bartnik, *Personalizm*, 304–5. "Contemporary personalism precisely portrays person as a social entity, for it is not a general entity. In the Trinity, each person is communion, relation and communication. What used to refer to nature, today refers to person. In the world of non-personal entities, we can observe a kind of perichoresis, i. e. qualities common to many individual entities which interpenetrate each other and blend together. However, it is only in the world of persons that the interpenetration of individual qualities constitutes a constant dynamic of perichoresis of the individual and the common. A person as a spiritual subject realises and expresses itself in community with others, in establishing communication and its constant maintenance. This is a feature of its nature. However, for many centuries it had been imagined that the essential feature of a person was their separateness, individuality and 'solitary' existence. For this reason, Mounier and Maritain juxtaposed two concepts: *individual* and *person*, until finally, in our intellectual culture, the concept of person has started to mean communication, unity and community, which

Person is thus intrinsically social, presupposes a communal existence, completes and names it. This communionality determines the unity of the nature of God, and besides this, the idea of person resolves the antinomy of unity and plurality. Its basic structure is being "for" – for oneself as a person and for the other person. Person also contains in its structure the dialectic of personhood and communion: one is a person by virtue of communion and one is in communion by virtue of personhood. In the Holy Trinity, each Person divests Himself so that the other may dwell in Him: The Father is whole to the Son and the Son is whole to the Father. Together they are whole for the Holy Spirit, and the Holy Spirit is communion towards the Father and the Son. Each of these Persons constitutes "I" in God and together they constitute Divine "We", and the principle of this transition is one and the same Nature. Existence in the Trinity is thus relational, and the three Persons are not only categories, similar to the modes of our perception, but above all personal realities.[216]

While discussing the significance of the Holy Spirit's being a person, Cornelius Keppler notes that it is necessary to start from such a conception of person that is less characterised by its shape and more by its action, and distinguishes different perspectives or dimensions of this. The first dimension is the personalising reception of the self – being a person in relation to the Holy Spirit means a pure reception of the self – a relational ex-sistence (subsistence) from the Father through the Son (passive spiration), manifested in being sent by the Father and the Son.[217] This passive spiration, however, is not passivity at all, but passive self-realisation, since the Holy Spirit is constituted by actively accepting His passive reception of Himself as person.[218] The second dimension focuses on understanding the Holy Spirit as a reference; from the intra-trinitarian perspective – as a reference between the Father and the Son, and inner-worldly as a reference between God and people. Keppler cites Greshake, who writes that the specific work of the Holy Spirit is that he "personalises" the unity and differentiation of the Father and the Son, guaranteeing their personhood in their own state and relationality from the beginning, for the one who personalises cannot be less than what the work he performed – i. e. the

---

we owe to the natural characteristics of a person. In Bartnik's view, the identification of personalism with individualism and subjectivism, has had a profound influence – until our time – not only on trinitology but also on the belief in the Trinity of Persons" (Guzowski, *Duch Dialogujący*, 374).

216 Cf. Guzowski, *Duch Dialogujący*, 374–5.

217 Cf. Michael Schulz, *Sein und Trinität: Systematische Erörterungen zur Religionsphilosophie G.W.F. Hegels im ontologiegeschichtlichen Rückblick auf J. Duns Scotus und I. Kant und die Hegel-Rezeption in der Seinsauslegung und Trinitätstheologie bei W. Pannenberg, E. Jüngel, K. Rahner und H.U. v. Balthasar* (St. Ottilien: EOS Verlag, 1997), 947.

218 Cf. Keppler, "Der Heilige Geist – tatsächlich Gott, Person und Herr?," 185–6.

person.[219] Keppler also notes that J. Werbick noticed in God a boundless capacity and will of referentiality that is person in the Holy Spirit.[220] This means that the Holy Spirit – as a personalising reference – builds a bridge between the loving God and the beloved man.[221] The third dimension sees the Holy Spirit as a personalising person. Keppler evokes here the thought of F.-X. Durwell, who wrote that the Father begets in the Spirit and thus constitutes Himself as person, the Son is begotten in the Spirit and thus also constitutes Himself as person; in the same way the world is personalised through the action of the Holy Spirit.[222]

1.3.7 A Communional View of the Properties of the Persons of the Holy Spirit

There is nothing in the triune God that is not inherent in the communal act of love. Therefore, the so-called attributes of God's essence do not refer to the abstract nature of God, but they have their meaning because of their trinitarian reality and are only real in their relational, i. e. personal specificity. Each attribute is revealed in a different way in the Father, the Son and the Holy Spirit – not statically or essentially, but as pulsating life in the very specific personal exchange of God's Communion, in the perichoretic-communal being with each other. This is why the teaching on appropriation, based on the conviction that in the world God acts as a single entity and that individual actions point only to one of the Persons and on that basis are attributed to (appropriated by) that Person, must be treated differently.[223] However, the procedure of appropriation has often been characterised by arbitrary associations. Meanwhile, it is not important to attribute the properties

---

219 Cf. Greshake, *Der dreieine Gott. Eine trinitarische Theologie*, 211.

220 Cf. Werbick, "Trinitätslehre," 481–576.

221 Cf. Keppler, "Der Heilige Geist – tatsächlich Gott, Person und Herr?," 186.

222 Cf. François-Xavier Durwell, *L'Esprit Saint de Dieu* (Paris, *Cerf*, 1983), 54; Keppler, "Der Heilige Geist – tatsächlich Gott, Person und Herr?," 186.

223 "The study of appropriations has been developed in the West since the time of St. Thomas Aquinas and St. Bonaventure. Its theological basis is the statement of the Council of Florence that in God all things are one, except for the opposing relations. Thus, instead of speaking, as the East did, of energies that manifest attributes or of the personal specificity of individual hypostases, certain properties of action were attributed to the individual Divine Persons as more 'befitting' them. Recently, under the influence of the ecumenical dialogue with the East, Western theologians have been trying to move away from the system of appropriation and to speak (perhaps not always accurately) of *proprium*, i. e. of something 'specific' (of personal specificity, also expressed in external action) of the individual Divine Persons. A specific kind of appropriation was the attribution – treated as common to the whole Trinity – of specific historico-salvific works to the individual Divine Persons. To the Son of God was thus attributed the work of redemption (salvation of man), and to the Holy Spirit – the work of sanctification (of the world and of man)" (Jagodziński, *Węzłowe zagadnienia chrystologii komunijnej*, 52–3).

of God's essence to a particular Person, but rather the opposite should apply: the specificity of a particular Person must be seen in the context of perichoretic unity or the properties of God must be considered each time as specifically realised in particular Persons. In the perichoretic exchange of life and love, each Person brings (as a specific pre-rhythm) a specific property (*proprium*). Each essential *proprium* in God is mediated by the *propria* of the other Persons – as a property of Divine Communion. Each Person brings its *proprium* to the whole, which is also present and efficacious in the individual Persons in different ways – thus they all have dimensions and properties of action in a specific way, each time differently. This understanding of the Holy Trinity as a Communion of Persons is also the key to a deeper understanding of faith and experience of reality.[224]

1.4 A Communicative-Communional Account of the Holy Spirit

As part of the contemporary rediscovery of trinitarian discourse on God, a new ontology was developed – metaphysics of substance was replaced by ontology of relations. The shift in perspective, which placed the plurality of the Persons and their relations at the centre, revealed the social dimensions of trinitology and made it possible to speak of social trinitology.[225] The point of departure of the new trinitarian thinking is the inter-personal and communicative action of the Divine Persons that is mentioned in the Scriptures.[226] To arrive at a clear view on this matter, it is necessary to examine to what extent the communicative relations discovered in the reality of the world agree with the Christian understanding of God.[227]

Since God is perfect love, the Holy Spirit is the environment (medium) of the love of the Father and the Son, uniting them by a knot, referred to, following St. Augustine, as "Communion in God", mediating the unity and diversity of the Persons. Why is the Holy Spirit a Person in God, why cannot He be conceived as an impersonal medium of communication between the Father and the Son? M. Knapp points here to the proposal put forward by Richard of Saint Victor, which

224 Cf. Greshake, *Trójjedyny Bóg*, 188–90. On the concept and reality of communion, see Jagodziński, *Trynitologia komunijna*, 60–7.

225 Cf. Ulrike Link-Wieczorek, "Warum trinitarisch von Gott reden? Zur Neuentdeckung der Trinitätslehre in der heutigen Theologie," in *Der lebendige Gott*, ed. Weth, 22.

226 Cf. Moltmann, "Der dreieinige Gott," 178.

227 Cf. Markus Knapp, "Trinitätslehre und Handlungstheorie," in *Gottesrede – Glaubenspraxis. Perspektiven theologischer Handlungstheorie*, ed. Edmund Arens (Darmstadt: Wissenschaftliche Buchgesellschaft, 1994), 55–6; Arens, "Was kann Kommunikation?," *Stimmen der Zeit* 6 (2002), 414–7; Jagodziński, "Teologia a komunikacja," *Studia Theologica Varsaviensia* 41/2 (2003), 76–80.

showed the Third Person as a necessary consequence of conceiving of the Holy Trinity as an event of God's intrinsic love. For love is not only the pure self-giving (the Father) and the corresponding reciprocal self-giving (the Son), but it is also necessarily realised in the pure receiving – in the opening oneself to be bestowed upon. Hence, the realisation of perfect love requires the Third – the Co-Loving and Co-Beloved One (*Condilectus*). In the person of the Holy Spirit, God is perfect love as the receiver – but without any dependence – and at the same time this love opens beyond itself. The essence of God, then, is love, which brings about the unity of the Persons in Their reciprocal communicative reference.[228]

Knapp emphasises that the notion of "person", which is disputed in contemporary theology, only becomes legitimate if the person is understood as a purely relational being.[229] For the Father, the Son and the Holy Spirit are an eternal act of responding to one another, and the tritnitarian process of life as perfect love is realised as an event in which each Person "is in the others Themselves". It is to such mutual interpenetration (*circumincessio* and indwelling (*circuminsessio*) that the traditional concept of perichoresis is directed.[230] The experience of perichoretic unity ultimately leads to a new understanding of the trinitarian concept of person.[231]

The trinitarian reality of the Holy Spirit can be understood in relational terms as a unity, as the personified *Unio* and *Communio* of the simultaneously given and received love in God. The Holy Spirit constitutes the intra-trinitarian, eternal and mediating "medium", the "space" of mutual love between the Father and the Son. God is "Spirit" – the Spirit of love of the Father and the Son and only in this common Spirit which is both the "space" and the "maternal bosom" (Y. Congar) of God's love. At the same time, the Holy Spirit grows out of this mutual devotion as its "result" ("who proceeds from the Father and the Son"). In Him, the reciprocal reference (devotion) of love between the Father and the Son finds a "form" of unity that is different from them – embracing, uniting and transcending them; it takes the shape of "We" which, with all its dependence on the Father and the Son, retains a relative self-existence transcending them both ("who with the Father and the Son is adored and glorified"). This is why the Tradition of the Church defines the

---

228 Cf. Knapp, "Die Theorie des kommunikativen Handelns als Denkmodell für den trinitarischen Gottesbegriff?," in *Communio Sanctorum. Einheit der Christen – Einheit der Kirche*, ed. Josef Schreiner and Klaus Wittstadt (Würzburg: Echter, 1988), 336; Knapp, "Trinitätslehre und Handlungstheorie," 57–8.

229 Cf. Knapp, "Trinitätslehre und Handlungstheorie," 58. On the relational concept of person, see Jagodziński, *Trynitologia komunijna*, 70–81.

230 Cf. Knapp, "Trinitätslehre und Handlungstheorie," 58–9; Moltmann, " Der dreieinige Gott," 182–6.

231 Cf. Moltmann, "Der dreieinige Gott," 185; Miroslav Volf, *Trinität und Gemeinschaft. Eine ökumenische Ekklesiologie* (Mainz – Neukirchen-Vluyn: Neukirchener Verlag, 1996), 199–203.

specifically personal character of the Holy Spirit with the word "Gift" – the mutual devotion of the Father and the Son culminate in Him, "concretise" and take the form of mutually given communion and joy. The Triune God offers Himself to the creation by coming to it as this "Gift", as the power of the Holy Spirit to initiate communion with God and with all human beings. This event of the accepted "Gift of God" is called the "Church".

The trinitarian context is characterised by yet another aspect of the Holy Spirit as the unifying love of God: The Father and the Son – as the poles of mutual reference – do not overlap in Him, but, on the contrary, show Their nonconvertible personal difference. This fact formed the basis of the Western understanding of person, freedom, love and unity – the deeper the unity between loving persons, the greater the guarantee of freedom to be different. The original trinitarian model of this apparent paradox makes it possible to preserve the highest personal differentiation in the closest mutual communication – this regularity is, at the same time, the basis for the pivotal importance of pneumatology in ecclesiology.[232]

From the cognitive perspective, the Holy Spirit is only accessible through the historical and exalted Jesus. On the other hand, He is at the same time the "transcendental" condition that makes faith in Jesus Christ possible – hence Christology implies pneumatology as a condition for its existence (the Holy Spirit is the "space" of faith).[233]

To explain the unity and differentiation in the trinitarian "structure of references", Medard Kehl used a schema drawn from the model of communicative action: "the Father" is the subject and source ("Wherefrom") of infinitely offering love, "the Son" is the Father-derived goal and partner ("Whereto") of infinitely received love. "The Holy Spirit" is the unifying and mediating environment ("Wherein") of this infinite love. And finally, love itself is the content ("What") of that which exists between the Father, the Son and the Holy Spirit and is identical with the Divine "essence".[234]

232 Cf. Kehl, *Die Kirche. Eine katholische Ekklesiologie* (Würzburg: Echter, 1994), 68–73; Jagodziński, "Trynitarne podstawy Kościoła jako komunii," *Studia Theologica Varsaviensia* 42/1 (2004), 59–60; Jagodziński, "Teoria komunikacyjnego działania w nauce o Trójcy Świętej," *Studia Koszalińsko-Kołobrzeskie* 15 (2010), 60–1; Wagner, *Dogmatyka*, 81.

233 Cf. Kehl, *Die Kirche*, 68–70; Jagodziński, "Teoria komunikacyjnego działania w nauce o Trójcy Świętej," 61–2.

234 Cf. Kehl, "Kirche als Institution – eine theologische Begründung," 121; Jagodziński, *Communio dzięki komunikacji. Teologiczny wymiar teorii komunikatywnego działania w eklezjologii Medarda Kehla SJ* (Radom: Wydawnictwo Diecezjalne w Sandomierzu, 2002), 343; Jagodziński, *Komunijna wizja Kościoła według Medarda Kehla SJ* (Kraków: Unum, 2009), 17; Jagodziński, "Teoria komunikacyjnego działania w nauce o Trójcy Świętej," 63.

Tradition has often referred to the Holy Spirit as "Unity" (*unio*) or "Communion" (*communio*) in God.[235] Since the communion between the Father and the Son is a relatively independent existence (as Person) of Divine Love – the Holy Spirit constitutes the "We" in God (H. Mühlen).[236] The Divine Communion between the Father and the Son (equal to the Holy Spirit) has primordial and exemplary property of the mediating "Wherein", because God in Himself, in the Holy Spirit, is a mediating event. On the one hand, the unity between the Father and the Son is always the pre-existing common "Space" (Spirit) of Their reference, but on the other hand, the common Spirit is established only through the mutual reference of the Father and the Son, and without this reference there would be no communional "We". The Holy Spirit, however, does not enter into these two "poles" and Their mutual reference, but creates its own distinct mode of Divine love. If man allows himself to be embraced by this reciprocal reference of the Father and the Son – he is welcomed "into" the Holy Spirit, into this Communion; this is why the Bible speaks of the gift of the Holy Spirit as "receiving the Holy Spirit" and "being filled by the Holy Spirit".[237]

Since the Holy Spirit is a mediating "communion" between the Father and the Son, admission to it is communion-based and generates communion. The Holy Spirit as Communion in God is the proper theological foundation of ecclesial communion, and it is precisely because of this that this communion is fundamentally different from other communions. The prior gift of the common "space of life" of faith is thus not based on the human will which longs for communion, but on the gift of the Holy Spirit, the gift of participation in the communion in God, and the Church becomes the historical sign of intra-divine Communion – the "sacrament of the Holy Spirit".[238]

The Holy Spirit is the mediating "Wherein" in the history of salvation, the mediating power in and through which Jesus Christ comes inwardly to man. He mediates as the "environment of meaning"[239] given beforehand and permanently, yet simultaneously given each time, uniting the subject and the object. He is the "environment of meaning" of the mutual love of the Father and the Son, as well Their "social

---

235 Cf. Kehl, *Die Kirche*, 70–3.

236 Cf. Kehl, "Kirche als Institution – eine theologische Begründung," 136.

237 Cf. Kehl, "Kirche als Institution – eine theologische Begründung," 122; Kehl, "Kirche – Sakrament des Geistes," in *Gegenwart des Geistes. Aspekte der Pneumatologie*, ed. Kasper (Freiburg-Basel-Wien: Herder, 1979), 158–9; Jagodziński, "Trynitarne podstawy Kościoła jako komunii," 61.

238 Cf. Kehl, "Kirche – Sakrament des Geistes," 155–61; Kehl, "Kirche als Institution," in *Handbuch der Fundamentaltheologie*, vol. III: *Traktat Kirche*, ed. Walter Kern and Hermann Josef Pottmeyer, and Max Seckler (Freiburg-Basel-Wien: Herder, 1986), 140–1; Jagodziński, "Trynitarne podstawy Kościoła jako komunii," 61–2.

239 Cf. Kehl, "Kirche – Sakrament des Geistes," 157.

form" which is revealed in Him and unites Them.[240] Through Him, the history of humanity is incorporated into the event of this love in order to become the perfect historical form of the communion that is identical with Him – the "social form" of God's love. This mediating power of the Holy Spirit aims at extending the love of the Father and the Son into a universal communion of people with God and among people.[241]

240 Cf. Kehl, "Kirche – Sakrament des Geistes," 159.

241 Cf. Kehl, "Kirche – Sakrament des Geistes," 159–60; Kehl, "Kirche als Institution," 190; Jagodziński, "Trynitarne podstawy Kościoła jako komunii," 62; Jagodziński, "Teoria komunikacyjnego działania w nauce o Trójcy Świętej," 62–4.

2. The Communional-Trinitarian Aspects of the Holy Spirit's Work in the History of Salvation

From the very beginning of God's history with people, we can affirm the presence of the Holy Spirit in it (cf. CCC 702-16). The Spirit of God worked after Christ and before Him, so that Jesus Himself, formed by the Spirit of the Father, began His activity in Nazareth in the Holy Spirit, received the same Spirit in the Jordan (cf. CCC 727-30), and having been exalted at the right hand of the Father, having Him fully, sent Him upon believers (Acts 2:33) (cf. CCC 731-6). The Spirit walked the ways of Christ from conception to glorification, and thus, in a wonderful way, He walks with all who receive Him – even preceding baptism and being with those who are preparing for it. He accompanies us throughout our lives and at the moment of death that leads us to the Father's house.[1]

From the Incarnation onwards, the Son of God completely "transposes" His life onto human history, He lives His intra-trinitarian "otherness" in human ways. Just as in eternity He receives his Divine life in Communion with the Father and the Holy Spirit, so now – as a human – He receives his life from the Father and the Holy Spirit and gives Himself to them in obedience to creation.[2] G. Greshake interprets the Incarnation pneumatologically, emphasising that in order for the Son of God to unite Himself with humanity, He needed a human nature open to Him, and it is the Holy Spirit, residing constantly in creation, who develops the dynamic of a human nature directed beyond itself. The Holy Spirit is the author of this "convergent" movement "from above" – the Son of God was sent by the Father "into" humanity. As a result, the Son and creation were united by the Holy Spirit – but not blended, since it is the Spirit who unifies diversity. Therefore, the Christological axiom proclaiming that Christ's human nature was created by the

1 Cf. Piet Schoonenberg, "Duch Boży w historii zbawienia," *Communio. Międzynarodowy Przegląd Teologiczny* 8/1 (1988), 86.

2 Cf. Greshake, *Trójjedyny Bóg*, 63. "Through the Incarnation of the Son, the life of the Creator and His creation are joined together in a special and inseparable way. The Son of God remains forever truly human, the Spirit plunges into the innermost abysses of creation, and through both of them the Father has united Himself with us in a new way, that is to say, by God's free decision, the 'previous' intra-trinitarian life (in the proper language of theology: the immanent Trinity) has completely and for all time opened up to us, the creation (the immanent Trinity has become the historico-salvific Trinity). From that moment on, God lives his own inner life among us and with us, for the reason that in and through the incarnate Son, through and in the world-filling Spirit, he has completely and utterly 'entangled Himself' in the affairs of this world" (Greshake, *Trójjedyny Bóg*, 64). Cf. Jagodziński, *Węzłowe zagadnienia chrystologii komunijnej*, 76.

Son's assumption of it must be supplemented by the statement that human nature was infused by the Holy Spirit with such openness and movement directed towards its transcendence that it could become the form and expression of the eternal Logos.[3]

At the same time, the Holy Spirit guided in depth the human destiny of the only Son of God. He gave the grace and gifts to His humanity that were necessary to live according to Divine love and thus made Christ the prototype of the new man, divinized in human weakness; by Spirit's grace His humanity was adapted to Divine life. The Spirit granted Christ the supreme charismatic grace that made Him the Head of humanity and of the Mystical Body. The Spirit guided and inspired Christ throughout His mission. During the Passion, the Spirit remained in communion and deep compassion with the Son (and the Father) and gave the inspiration to accomplish and fulfil everything (Luke 22:37; 24:44; John 17:12; 18:9,32; 19:24,28,30,36).[4]

On the day of Pentecost, the Holy Spirit caused the birth of the Church and brought it together in unity and holiness and gave it its universal and apostolic dimension. "Wherever the Holy Spirit blows, the immediate result is that the eschaton enters into history and people are brought into communion among themselves with God in the form of a community".[5] Not only does the Spirit continually give the Church Divine life, but also the sacraments, which resulted in charisms and triggered the first evangelisation. Through the epiclesis, which invokes the Holy Spirit at the breaking of bread (Acts 2:42), the Body of Christ appears and the Mystical Body grows. It is He who ensures Christ's presence with us until the end of the world.[6]

The Holy Spirit induces a new creation that will last until Christ's return in glory. The Lord will then visibly announce and fulfil the invisible judgement of the Spirit which is already taking place in the world (John 16:8,11), He will place all fulfilment in the hands of His Father, wipe away every tear (Rev 7:17; 21:4) and become all in all. Currently, however, the Spirit spreads the energy needed for spiritual warfare and records the God-bound destiny of all people and the whole world.[7] The basis

---

3 Cf. Greshake, *Trójjedyny Bóg*, 319; Jagodziński, *Węzłowe zagadnienia chrystologii komunijnej*, 79–80.

4 Cf. Laurentin, *Nieznany Duch Święty*, 395.

5 Zizioulas, *The One and the Many*, 182. "We see this happen par excellence on the day of Pentecost as described in Acts 2, where the descent of the Spirit upon the Disciples and those who are with them in the Upper Room is seen as a purely eschatological event bringing 'the last days' into history (Acts 2:17) and, at the same time, as the creation of the community of the Church (Acts 2:241.)." (Zizioulas, *The One and the Many*, 182).

6 Cf. Laurentin, *Nieznany Duch Święty*, 396. On the relationship of the Holy Spirit to the Church, see ibid., 402–7.

7 Cf. Laurentin, *Nieznany Duch Święty*, 396.

of any pneumatology is not only the testimony contained in the Scriptures, but also the experience of the work of the Holy Spirit in the Church. Since the Holy Spirit is only available in His actions (charisms, gifts and fruits),[8] pneumatology must methodologically assume a bottom-up approach in order to recognise in the experienced action – by way of so-called spirit recognition – His identity as the action of God Himself.[9]

2.1 Christological Pneumatology – Pneumatological Christology

At the beginning of the development of theology, the whole space of theological interest was occupied primarily by the subject of the Incarnate Word, but in time a proper synthesis was achieved which showed that Christology and pneumatology must exist simultaneously, and not as separate or successive phases of God's relation to the world.[10] From the beginning of his public activity, Christ appeared as filled with the Holy Spirit. He reveals Christ, and Christ sends Him from the Father. Only in a pneumatological context can the event of Jesus Christ be well understood.[11] Y. Congar once wrote that if he had to summarise the results of his studies on the Holy Spirit in a single conclusion, he would encompass it in the following sentence:

8 CCC 688 points to the Church as the place of knowledge of the Holy Spirit: "- in the Scriptures he inspired; – in the Tradition, to which the Church Fathers are always timely witnesses; – in the Church's Magisterium, which he assists; – in the sacramental liturgy, through its words and symbols, in which the Holy Spirit puts us into communion with Christ; – in prayer, wherein he intercedes for us; – in the charisms and ministries by which the Church is built up; – in the signs of apostolic and missionary life; – in the witness of saints through whom he manifests his holiness and continues the work of salvation."

9 Cf. Josef Freitag, *Geist-Vergessen – Geist-Erinnern. Vladimir Losskys Pneumatologie als Herausforderung westlicher Theologie* (Würzburg: Echter, 1995), 123, footnote 25. Cf. Nitsche, "Pneumatologie," 323: "Prinzipiell steht die Theologie des Heiligen Geistes nicht für sich alleine. Sie kann nicht losgelöst von der Selbstoffenbarung Gottes, also nicht ohne alttestamentliche Glaubensgeschichte, ohne Christologie oder Ekklesiologie usw. ausbuchstabiert werden. Grund dafür ist die spezifische Erschließungs- und Vermittlungsfunktion des Heiligen Geistes. Während Theologische Anthropologie, Spiritualität, Gnadenlehre, Sakramentenlehre und Ekklesiologie vor allen Dingen die subjekthaft vermittelte Ankunft Gottes in der geistlichen Subjektivität und kirchlichen Sozialität der Menschen reflektieren, benennt und bedenkt die Theologie des Heiligen Geistes die objektive Wirklichkeit freier und unverfügbarer göttlicher Selbst-Zuwendung."

10 Cf. Zizioulas, *The One and the Many*, 75–6. Zizioulas, however, considers that the subsequent history of theology until our time has not creatively assimilated this synthesis, especially with regard to ecclesiology (cf. Zizioulas, *The One and the Many*, 77). M. de Salis appreciates the pneumatological contribution of Heribert Mühlen's thought and is critical of Hans Küng's proposal (cf. de Salis, *Kościół wcielony w historii*, 179–85).

11 Cf. Edward Sienkiewicz, *Wspólnota Kościoła* (Szczecin: Feniks, 2013), 292–300. See Jagodziński, *Trynitologia komunijna*, 164–71.

"There is no Christology without pneumatology, and there is no pneumatology without Christology".[12] Many contemporary theologians think similarly;[13] K. Barth even wanted to screen all the truths of the Creed through the prism of pneumatology in order to "baptise" all dogmatics "with the Holy Spirit".[14]

The relationship between Christology and pneumatology, with its implications for spirituality, also occupies an important place in J. Ratzinger's theology.[15] However, if Congar perceived a deficit of pneumatology in Christology, Ratzinger (and following him, J. Szymik) justifies "the pneumatological restraint in theology". Ratzinger directs his reflection to the intra-trinitarian "location" of the Holy Spirit and, in line with the Augustinian tradition, states that "the property of the Holy Spirit is [...] to be that which is common to the Father and the Son. His property is to be unity".[16] Therefore, Christian spirituality is embedded in the Holy Spirit

---

12 Congar, *Słowo i Tchnienie*, 19. "Pneumatological Christology is not the domain of the present time, since the awareness of the constant presence of the Spirit in the life of Christ and of His action in the power of the Spirit has been present for centuries in the writings of the Church Fathers. An example is St. Basil the Great, who has no doubt that the Spirit is present in the whole life of Christ: When one intends to contemplate past things, (...) or that which concerns the coming of the Lord in flesh, everything happens through the Spirit. He was first with the body of the Lord, being the very anointing, and is inseparably with Him, as it is written: 'The One over whom you shall see the Spirit descending and resting upon Him, this is my beloved Son', And also: 'Jesus of Nazareth, whom God has anointed with the Holy Spirit'. Then all the activity unfolds with the Spirit's co-presence. He was also present when [Christ] was tempted by the devil: 'Then the Spirit led Jesus out into the wilderness to be tempted'. And He was inseparably with Him when He performed miracles. 'I, he says, by the power of the Spirit of God cast out evil spirits'. And after Jesus' resurrection, He did not leave Him. And what does the Lord say, breathing on the faces of the disciples, in order to renew man and give him again the grace from the breath of God which he had lost? 'Receive the Holy Spirit! If you forgive the sins of any, they are forgiven them; if you retain the sins of any, they are retained'" (Guzowski, *Duch Dialogujący*, 421–2).

13 "The next challenge facing liberation theology today concerns taking into account – in reflection on the kingdom of God – not only its Christological dimension and character (which was the case in classical liberation theology, which took the person of Christ as the starting point for understanding the kingdom of God), but also the pneumatological dimension and character of the kingdom of God related to the Holy Spirit, His presence and action in history. Therefore, one important task within liberation theology is to enrich Christology and ecclesiology with pneumatology" (Dariusz Gardocki, *Teologia wyzwolenia jako odpowiedź na epokowe wyzwań czasu* (Kraków: WAM, 2020), 74.

14 Cf. Guzowski, *Duch Dialogujący*, 413. On the reasons for the shortcomings in this area, see ibid., 414.

15 Cf. Ratzinger, *Nowe porywy Ducha. Ruchy odnowy w Kościele* (Kielce: Jedność, 2006); Szymik, "'Na bliskość tchnienia': kluczowe tezy pneumatologii Josepha Ratzingera," *Śląskie Studia Historyczno-Teologiczne* 44/2 (2013), 337–51.

16 Ratzinger/Benedict XVI, *Kościół. Pielgrzymująca wspólnota wiary* (Kraków: Wydawnictwo M, 2005), 36.

and is of communional nature. Ratzinger also formulated an important hermeneutical principle proclaiming that "the distinction between Christ and the Spirit is correct only if we can better comprehend their unity".[17] On the oft-raised charge concerning the infrequency of speaking about the Holy Spirit, Ratzinger stated that if pneumatology is to be a correction of one-sided Christology, this correction consists in the fact that the Holy Spirit teaches us to see Christ in the trinitarian mystery – therefore, "the pneumatological restraint of Catholicism" is correct (J. Szymik).[18]

Exegetical discoveries in the 20th century brought the realisation that in various New Testament Christologies, the question of showing Christ in relation to the Holy Spirit occupies a significant place.[19] There is no aspect of Jesus' life in the New Testament that is not related to the Spirit. The depiction of Christ as anointed with the Holy Spirit becomes a central feature of early Christian teaching: "You know the message […] how God anointed Jesus of Nazareth with the Holy Spirit and with power; how he went about doing good and healing all who were oppressed by the devil, for God was with him" (Acts 10:38). The New Testament interpreted Jesus' identity and mission in terms of the working of the Spirit's power in and through Him. Jesus was aware of the work of the Spirit, especially when He fulfilled His prophetic mission and interpreted His death in terms of it. In Jesus' exorcist activity and in the miracles of healing, the reign of God could be felt, the culmination of which is the coming of the Incarnate Son by the power of the Holy Spirit.[20]

An extremely important element needed to reconstruct New Testament Christology in a pneumatological perspective is Isaiah 61, which Christ used at the beginning of his public ministry to affirm his messianic mission in the power of the Spirit. "The Spirit of the Lord is upon me, because he has anointed me to bring

---

17 Ratzinger, *Nowe porywy Ducha*, 22.

18 Cf. Julian Nastałek, "Słowo i Tchnienie. Konieczność duchowości inkarnacyjnej," in *Współczesne oblicza duchowości. Nova et vetera*, ed. Bogdan Ferdek and Paweł Beyga (Wrocław: Papieski Wydział Teologiczny, 2020), 117–8.

19 According to H.U. von Balthasar, Jesus' relationship to God is most fully reflected in the way Jesus addresses God as His Father (*Abba*). It is the result of the Father's accompanying Jesus through the action of the Holy Spirit in Jesus' consciousness. Through him, too, the Father reveals and gives Jesus a mission and specifies His will. On this path, Jesus identifies Himself with the mission which fills His human consciousness. On the other hand, Jesus, through the Holy Spirit, agrees with the Father's will. The Holy Spirit shapes and permeates the consciousness of Jesus. Reaching and explaining the mystery of Jesus' self-consciousness requires taking into account and focusing on the role of the Holy Spirit in Jesus' life. The Father accompanies Him through His Spirit. Jesus, thanks to the inspiration coming from the Holy Spirit, knows that, as Son, he has already consented to the Father's will and carries it out in His assumed humanity. Cf. Gardocki, "Boska świadomość Jezusa w ujęciu współczesnej chrystologii", in *Sens ludzkiej przygody*, ed. Zbigniew Kubacki and Waldemar Cisło (Warszawa: Rhetos, 2008), 172–5.

20 Cf. Guzowski, *Duch Dialogujący*, 414–7.

good news to the poor. He has sent me to proclaim release to the captives and recovery of sight to the blind, to let the oppressed go free, to proclaim the year of the Lord's favour" (Luke 4:18-19). After reading these words, Jesus said: "Today this scripture has been fulfilled in your hearing" (Luke 4:21). The universality of the salvation accomplished by Christ can also be seen in the perspective of the mission of the Holy Spirit. According to the New Testament, the efficacy of the Holy Spirit is directed towards Jesus. He is not only anointed by the Spirit and remains in the Spirit's power, but He is also born of the Spirit (cf. Matt 1:18,20; Luke 1:35). At His baptism in the Jordan He was anointed with the Holy Spirit (cf. Mark 1:10) and His whole activity was marked by the Spirit (e. g. Luke 4:14,18; 5:17; 6:19; 10:2). Another text carrying a similar message is Matthew 11:2-6, in which John the Baptist sends a delegation to Jesus to find out whether He is indeed the expected Messiah. Jesus responds to the disciples John sent with the words from Isaiah 61: "Go and tell John what you hear and see: the blind receive their sight, the lame walk, the lepers are cleansed, the deaf hear, the dead are raised, and the poor have good news brought to them" (Matt 11:4-5). Jesus here portrayed Himself as fulfilling the role of Yahweh's servant, endowed with the Spirit of God, and thus was aware of His unique relationship with the Father and with the Holy Spirit.[21]

Contemporary personalistic Christology links the historicity and uniqueness of Jesus with His intra-trinitarian identity. The Holy Spirit, who mediates between God's inner life and His action in the world, prepares creation for the Incarnation, guides Jesus through earthly life to glory and enables all human beings to participate in the life of the Triune God. The texts of the New Testament reveal the mystery of the person of Jesus Christ acting by the power of the Spirit from His conception from the Virgin until His resurrection by the power of the same Spirit. "You know the message [...] how God anointed Jesus of Nazareth with the Holy Spirit and with power; how he went about doing good and healing all who were oppressed by the devil, for God was with him" (Acts 10:38). Pneumatological Christology reveals the universal and timeless meanings of Jesus for all people. Associated with His mission is the mission of the Spirit and the Kingdom of love, justice and peace emerging through His power. Alongside this universal dimension, the eschatological and salvific dimension of Christ's mission also becomes clear, as the fruits of redemption are born in the lives of people of every era through the Holy Spirit who continues salvation today. In the power of the Holy Spirit, Christ lives in the lives of concrete individuals and peoples.[22]

H.U. von Balthasar wrote about the "trinitarian inversion", i. e. the interchange of roles in the economic Trinity between the Holy Spirit and Christ. Whereas in the

21 Cf. Guzowski, *Duch Dialogujący*, 417–8.
22 Cf. Guzowski, *Duch Dialogujący*, 418–9.

immanent Trinity the Spirit is passive as the breath of the Father and the Son, in the earthly mission of Jesus, the Spirit becomes active and the Son passive. With the resurrection, the Son regains His active role and pours out the Spirit upon the Church. The Holy Spirit is always associated with Christ and vice versa.[23] H. Mühlen emphasised the role of the Holy Spirit as a knot of love and dialogue of unity. Ontologically, the Holy Spirit is "one Person in many persons" and, as during Jesus' earthly life, the Spirit continues to unite the Son with the Father. The culmination of this mission took place at the cross, where the Spirit sustained the unity of Christ and the Father at the moment of Their greatest separation.[24] In pneumatological Christology, J. Moltmann's trinitarian schema of salvation history, which takes a top-down – trinitarian – approach to the whole history of salvation, can be seen as complementary. The Persons of the Trinity always act in unity. Moltmann adopts three periods and patterns of action: 1. In the Old Testament period, the Father gave Israel his Spirit, who spoke through the prophets and prepared the people for the coming of the Son, and the relationship of the Trinity to the world can be illustrated according to the schema: Father → Holy Spirit → Son. 2 Starting from the Incarnation and onwards, the relationship changes, as the Father sent His only begotten Son, who in turn sent the Spirit at Pentecost. This stage can be presented according to the schema: Father → Son → Holy Spirit. 3. In the Church period, the Holy Spirit continues the work of Christ so that through the Son the creation returns to the Father. Here, the pattern of relationships is as follows: Holy Spirit → Son → Father. Therefore, God's plan to bestow trinitarian love upon people and to include them in the life of God can be seen as a great way of exiting and returning from the Father[25] (as in the old schema: *exitus – reditus*).

The baptismal formula of St Matthew's Gospel instructed to baptise "in the name of the Father and of the Son and of the Holy Spirit" (Matt 28:19). A similar formula appeared earlier in St. Paul: "The grace of the Lord Jesus Christ, the love of God, and the communion of the Holy Spirit be with all of you" (2 Cor 13:13). The Holy Spirit also appears there in the third place, while the order of the first two Persons and their names designations changed: "the Lord Jesus Christ" – instead of "the Son", and "God" – instead of "the Father", whereas "grace", "love" and "communion" are associated with the named Persons respectively, with "communion" being associated with the Holy Spirit . A similar version is contained in St. Paul's earlier teaching: "Now there are varieties of gifts, but the same Spirit; and there are varieties of services, but the same Lord; and there are varieties of activities, but it is the same

23 Cf. Balthasar, *Pneuma und Institution. Theologische Skizzen IV* (Einsiedeln: Johannes Verlag, 1974), 224.

24 Cf. Mühlen, *Der Heilige Geist als Person,* 259.

25 Cf. Moltmann, *Trinity and the Kingdom of God: The Doctrine of God* (London 1981), 94; Guzowski, *Duch Dialogujący,* 420–1.

God who activates all of them in everyone" (1 Cor 12:4-6). Jesus as "the Son" (or "the Lord") stands in these texts alongside "the Father" (or "God" – *ho theos*) and "the Holy Spirit" (or "the Spirit").[26] The synoptic Gospels present Jesus as being guided, inspired and empowered by the Spirit of God. For St. Luke in particular, Jesus was the vehicle of the Holy Spirit (e.g. Luke 4:1,14,18-21; 6:19). Probably Jesus Himself spoke of it in such terms (Mark 1:12; 3:22-29), but He never explicitly pointed to His actions as signs of the power of the Holy Spirit or to His awareness of the Holy Spirit, which would be as intense as His awareness of God – "Abba". It was not until the resurrection and exaltation of Jesus that a new, typically Christian way of thinking about the Holy Spirit and the relationship between Jesus and the Holy Spirit was initiated.[27]

The resurrection of Jesus transformed this relationship – it is Jesus who sends or gives the Holy Spirit. St. Paul wrote of the resurrected Christ that he had become "a life-giving spirit" (1 Cor 15:45) and never literally indicates that He sent or will send the Holy Spirit. By contrast, according to St. Luke, Christ "being exalted at the right hand of God, and having received from the Father the promise of the Holy Spirit" sent Him (Acts 2:33; see Luke 24:49); according to St. John, the Holy Spirit comes from Jesus, is sent or given by Jesus (John 7:39; 15:26; 20:22). At the same time, the sending or giving of the Holy Spirit does not imply He is only Jesus' gift – Jesus receives "from the Father" the promised Holy Spirit before pouring Him out on others (Acts 2:33). St. John also wrote of the Father giving the Spirit

---

26 Cf. Gerald O'Collins, *Chrystologia. Jezus Chrystus w ujęciu biblijnym, historycznym i systematycznym* (Kraków: Wydawnictwo Uniwersytetu Jagiellońskiego, 2008), 140–1. Cf. Jagodziński, *Węzłowe zagadnienia chrystologii komunijnej*, 84–90.

27 Cf. Roman Małecki, *Kościół jest wspólnotą. Dogmatyczno-ekumeniczne studium eklezjologii Johna Zizioulasa* (Lublin: Wydawnictwo KUL, 2000), 84–5: "The biblical exegesis, especially of the Gospel of St. Luke, shows Christ as a person 'conceived of the Holy Spirit' (cf. Luke 1:35) in the Mary's womb. Christ's baptism (Luke 3:21-22), the temptation in the desert (Luke 4:1-12), the beginning of his public activity in Nazareth (Luke 4:16-30) and His entire earthly mission can only be understood in this pneumatological context. The Holy Spirit is the one who, in the event of the incarnation, brings Christ into history, while Himself remaining 'outside history'. It is He who anoints Jesus by making Him the Christ (cf. Matt 3:16; Mark l:10; Luke 21-22). Finally, it is by the power of the Holy Spirit that Jesus is raised from the grave (Rom 8:11; 1 Pet 3:18). Although only Christ-Son of God 'becomes history', it is an undeniable fact that the whole Holy Trinity, through its salvific action, is 'brought' into history. The role of the Holy Spirit in the event of the Resurrection is the reverse of His function at the Incarnation: the Holy Spirit is now the one who brings Christ out of the framework of history, making Him the eschatological being *par excellence*. Although the Holy Spirit acts within the framework of visible history, He is always the 'hidden' Spirit. He never reveals His own face in the economy of salvation. While revealing the Father's intention, realised through the Son, the Holy Spirit always remains, as it were, 'in the shadows', bringing God's plan of salvation to completion. It is not in vain that Orthodox theologians speak of a specific 'kenosis of the Holy Spirit' or the 'self-covering' of his own face." Cf. O'Collins, *Chrystologia*, 142.

(John 14:16-17) or sending the Holy Spirit (John 14:26) in response to Jesus' prayer and in Jesus' name. Even when St. Paul depicted Jesus promising to send the Holy Spirit, he clearly wrote: "When the Advocate comes, whom I will send to you from the Father, the Spirit of truth who comes from the Father, he will testify on my behalf" (John 15:26).[28] Paul wrote that "And because you are children, God has sent the Spirit of his Son into our hearts" (Gal 4:6; see 3:5; 1 Cor 2:10). He also used the passive voice: "God's love has been poured into our hearts through the Holy Spirit that has been given to us" (Rom 5:5). Elsewhere, he wrote that Christians "receive" the Spirit (Rom 8:15; 1 Cor 2:12.14; Gal 3:2). He also wrote of "the Spirit of Christ / Christ's Spirit" or "the Spirit of the Son of God" (Rom 8:9; Gal 4:6) – this is an ambiguous form that can be understood in two ways: "the Spirit who comes from God – Christ" or "the Spirit who is God – Christ".[29]

Although the evangelists write that the Holy Spirit was sent by the resurrected and exalted Jesus, none of them made a clear distinction between the Sender and the Sent. St. Luke moved from the statements pointing to the leadership of the exalted Lord (Acts 9:10-16; 18:9-10; 22:17-21) to the statements suggesting the leadership of the Holy Spirit (Acts 8:29; 10:19; 16:6) without making a clear distinction between the two. In St. John, the coming of the Holy Spirit (John 14:16f.,26) seems to be linked to the second coming of Christ (John 14:3,18,23,28). In St. Paul's letters, the Holy Spirit is not only characterised by his relation to Christ, but is virtually identified with Christ in the believers' experience (i. e. the Spirit is Christ or the presence of Christ). The Spirit bears witness to Jesus as the Lord (1 Cor 12:3) and the term saying that the Spirit is "in us" (Rom 5:5; 8:9,11,16; Gal 4:6) is virtually equivalent to saying that we are "in Christ" (Rom 6:3,11,23; 1 Cor 1:30; 4:15; Phil 3:1; 4:1-2).[30]

The biblical authors do not equate Christ with the Holy Spirit. Jesus was begotten by His power (Matt 1:20; Luke 1:35) and this sentence cannot be reversed. The New Testament story of Christ's mission, conception, death, resurrection and their aftermath distinguishes Him from the Holy Spirit.[31] In the Incarnation, the Holy Spirit also acted as a kind of movement prompting God to come out of Himself, as a dynamic that set in motion the process of the trinitarian event of the Incarnation. In the scene of the Annunciation, the angel addresses Mary with the words: "The Holy Spirit will come upon you, and the power of the Most High will overshadow you; therefore the child to be born will be holy; he will be called Son of God" (Luke 1:35)

28 Cf. O'Collins, *Chrystologia*, 142.

29 Cf. O'Collins, *Chrystologia*, 142–3.

30 Cf. Bouyer, *Syn Przedwieczny* (Kraków: Wydawnictwo M, 2000), 400–12; O'Collins, *Chrystologia*, 143.

31 Cf. O'Collins, *Chrystologia*, 144.

and to Joseph: "the child conceived in her is from the Holy Spirit"" (Matt 1:20).[32] The synoptic "bottom-up Christology" (according to Matthew and Luke) explained the origin of Jesus and his personal mystery as God and man by the power of the Holy Spirit, which caused the man Jesus to come into being.[33]

Following the example of the Gospel of St. Mark, Matthew and Luke took the bottom-up route: Jesus appears as the Messiah anointed by the Spirit of God. The (temporal and ontological) beginning, history and completion of Jesus' life have their origin in the action of God's power and the Spirit (Luke 1:35). Therefore, he was the Son of the Eternal Father and appeared as this Son of the Eternal Father (cf. Matt 11:25-27; Luke 10:21-22).[34]

In the Old Testament, there was a reference to the creative action of the Spirit of God in connection with the conception of Isaac in Sarah's womb or St. John the Baptist in Elizabeth's womb – within the possibility of natural motherhood. There, God transcended the limits of the creation and made natural conception possible with the participation of husbands, because nothing is impossible for His word which creates and makes choices (cf. Gen 18:14; Job 42:2; Jer 32:27; Luke 1:38; 18:27; Mark 10:27; Matt 19:26). That the evangelists where not ignorant of the natural conditions of human fertility is evidenced, for example, by Mary's question: "How can this be, since I am a virgin?" (Luke 1:34). The angel's answer also lacked biological explanations. The divine *pneuma* and *dynamis* that "overshadowed" her are not created causes that are subject to empirical verification but describe the life-giving and salvific presence of God. "The shadow of Yahweh" here denotes a kind of theophany: "the cloud" (as an image) obscures the brightness of His glory, while simultaneously revealing it (through the shadow cast). With the sovereign power of the Creator, the Holy Spirit brings into existence the human nature of Jesus within Mary's faith-filled consent.[35]

Matthew's and Luke's testimony to the rise of the Messiah's humanity is not isolated in the development of New Testament Christology. The pre-Paul's "two-tiered messianology" ("[This is] the gospel concerning his Son, who was descended from David according to the flesh and was declared to be Son of God with power according to the spirit of holiness by resurrection from the dead, Jesus Christ our Lord" – Rom 1:3-4; cf. 8:11) speaks of the Messiah's fulfilment in the work of His resurrection, accomplished by the Father through the "Spirit of holiness". If the Holy Spirit, through the resurrection, completes the Messiah in humanity, then this

32 Cf. Bartnik, *Dogmatyka katolicka*, 1: 181–2, 557–8.

33 Cf. Tadeusz Dionizy Łukaszuk, *Ty jesteś Chrystus, Syn Boga żywego. Dogmat chrystologiczny w ujęciu integralnym* (Kraków: Papieska Akademia Teologiczna, 2000), 367–9.

34 Cf. Bartnik, *Dogmatyka katolicka*, 1: 497–8, 506–33.

35 Cf. Auer, *Jesus Christus – Gottes und Mariä "Sohn,"* 299–309; Müller, *Chrystologia – nauka o Jezusie Chrystusie* (Kraków: Wydawnictwo M, 1995), 282–7.

is very close to the idea of the emergence of Jesus' humanity by the power of the Holy Spirit. Both evangelists have thus alluded to the earliest forms of pneumatic messianology. They do not ask how the Son of the Eternal Father became human, but want to answer the question of how, through the power of the Divine Spirit, Jesus could from the very beginning of His humanity be the Messiah. The synoptic accounts of the baptism in the Jordan also show that the basis of Jesus' messiahship is the fullness of the Holy Spirit He received and the His proclamation as "the beloved Son of the Father".

The Evangelists understand Jesus' baptism in a theological way.[36] The apocalyptic motifs – the opening of the heavens, God's voice, the appearance of the promised Holy Spirit – are a sign of the eschatological time of salvation. This is why, in Nazareth, Jesus proclaims the fulfilment of the announcement of Isaiah 61:1: "The Spirit of the Lord is upon me, because he has anointed me to bring good news to the poor. He has sent me to proclaim release to the captives and recovery of sight to the blind, to let the oppressed go free, to proclaim the year of the Lord's favor" (Luke 4:18-19). According to the evangelists, Jesus was God's Anointed One in the pre-Easter period, and his statements about the activity of the Holy Spirit play no part in His preaching (see especially Matt 12:31; Luke 12:10) – "For as yet there was no Spirit, because Jesus was not yet glorified" (John 7:39). However, although according to Luke 11:20, Jesus cast out evil spirits "by the finger of God", Matt 12:28 says otherwise: "if it is by the Spirit of God that I cast out demons […]". Later, St. Luke consistently interpreted Jesus' activity pneumatologically (4:14; 10:21). Both stories of Jesus' childhood (in Matthew and Luke) see Jesus from the moment of His conception not only as God's Anointed One, but also as a creation of the Spirit (Luke 1:35; Matt 1:18,20).

The older New Testament tradition links the work of the Holy Spirit to the raising from the dead and resurrection of Christ. A passage from the old tradition in Rom 1:3-4 is very characteristic: "[This is] the gospel concerning his Son, who was descended from David according to the flesh and was declared to be Son of God with power according to the spirit of holiness by resurrection from the dead […]". Finally, in Hebrews 9:14 it is stated of Jesus that "through the eternal Spirit [Christ] offered himself without blemish to God […]". In doing so, the New Testament did not attempt to harmonise these strands of tradition, but instead very clearly showed their common denominator: In the entirety of His action, life, death and resurrection, in the person and work of Jesus Christ – the Holy Spirit brings everything to eschatological fullness.[37]

---

36 Cf. Bartnik, *Dogmatyka katolicka*, 1: 185.

37 Cf. Kasper, *Bóg Jezusa Chrystusa*, 254–5.

The messianic-functional perspective of Matthew and Luke in ecclesiastical creeds was linked to the relational-personal theology of Paul and John: According to the human nature, the only-begotten Son of the Father "was conceived of the Holy Spirit and born of the Virgin Mary".[38] The humanity of Jesus became the property of the Eternal Son of the Father, was sanctified by the "grace of union", and the Holy Spirit "anointed" it making Him the Messiah, the Christ, the Lord's Anointed.[39] The Church has systematically rejected spiritualist, symbolic-metaphorical interpretations of Jesus' conception from the Holy Spirit and birth from the Virgin Mary. In Jesus, therefore, a mutual revelation of the Father and the Son takes place. The Father is the Revealer of the Son's glory, and the Son reveals the glory of God – the only Son's Father – in the Holy Spirit (cf. John 15:26; 16:13; 20:22; 1 John 3:2-24; 4:7-18).[40]

Reflecting on the Holy Spirit's relation to "theologics" and the knowledge of Christian truth, H.U. von Balthasar quotes John 16:13-15 – "When the Spirit of truth comes, he will guide you into all the truth; for he will not speak on his own, but will speak whatever he hears, and he will declare to you the things that are to come. He will glorify me, because he will take what is mine and declare it to you. All that the Father has is mine. For this reason I said that he will take what is mine and declare it to you" – and emphasises that the most general way to describe the Holy Spirit is as the Teacher leading to the truth. Of course, the Son was an adequate revelation of the Father, but this revelation remained a space closed to men, since "for as yet there was no spirit [...]" (John 7:39).[41] Therefore, the Spirit does not merely give the doctrine (or even the "letter of the Scriptures"), but He introduces us into the communional depths of the living event taking place between the Father and the Son in the innermost part of the hypostatic space. Jesus Christ – the humanised Son of the Father – became human through the Incarnation and was accompanied by the Holy Spirit throughout His entire life. The incarnate Son is the truth of God in earthly form. However, this would not be apparent to us if "the Spirit of truth" (John 14:17; 15:26; 16:13; 1 John 4:6) had not been given to us, so that with Him we might know "the depths of God", which the Spirit alone penetrates: "we have received not the spirit of the world, but the Spirit that is from God, so that we may understand the gifts bestowed on us by God" (1 Cor 2:10,12), "the spirit of truth and the spirit of error" (1 John 4:6), and the abiding of Jesus in us – "And by this we know that he abides in us, by the Spirit that he has given us" (1 John 3:24)".[42]

---

38 Cf. Müller, *Chrystologia – nauka o Jezusie Chrystusie*, 288–9; Bouyer, *Syn Przedwieczny*, 364–74.

39 Cf. Müller, *Chrystologia – nauka o Jezusie Chrystusie*, 289–90.

40 Cf. Jagodziński, *Węzłowe zagadnienia chrystologii komunijnej*, 90–3.

41 Cf. Balthasar, *Teologika*, vol. III: *Duch Prawdy* (Kraków: WAM, 2005), 59–72.

42 Cf. Balthasar, *Teologika*, vol. III: *Duch Prawdy*, 13–20. Thus, Balthasar comments on the essence of Christian theology in a trinitarian way: "The initially 'unknown' God, the Spirit, sheds his light

Balthasar posed the question of the existence of "Christology of the Spirit"[43] and explained that the point of this paradoxical formulation was to integrate Christology into the broader framework of pneumatology. The author mentions three themes that need to come under scrutiny. The first theme concerns the trinitarian relationship of God to the world, and thus also the necessity of the constant presence of the Holy Spirit in the history of salvation.[44] The second theme concerns "trinitarian inversion" – the Christological centre of the economy of salvation must be viewed in the pneumatological context. The third theme, on the other hand, concerns the relationship between the Logos and the Holy Spirit in the formation of the hypostatic union, since from the Middle Ages the personal union of human nature with the Divine "Person" of the Logos seemed at first sight to refer to the Son alone (even if the cooperation of the Father and the Son was recognised) so that the direct co-participation of the Holy Spirit seemed excluded.[45]

Balthasar noticed something akin to Christology of the Holy Spirit already in early Christianity, where the Apostolic Fathers, on the one hand, interpreted freely the biblical concept of the Spirit, including Him in the Divine totality (*ruah Yahweh*, Wisdom), and, on the other hand, knew that God is Spirit (John 4:24), the resurrected "Lord is Spirit" (2 Cor 3:17), the "live-giving Spirit" (1 Cor 15:45), the "Holy Spirit" descended on Mary at the incarnation (Luke 1:35) and the created human being was described by John as "flesh" (*sarx*), while the divine realm was

---

on the 'known', incarnate God, in order to illuminate his meaning as teaching about the invisible (and in this sense 'unknown') Father. It is only because the Son is made known as teaching about the Father as 'another one' (John 5:32), with whom, however, He is 'one' (John 10:30), that He is understood as 'the truth' (John 14:6) and thus His truth (or He in truth) is understood. Therefore, what the Spirit sheds its light on is both the difference and the identity between the Father and the Son: the unity of difference and identity is seen but not recognised to its depths, so that by the explication of the Spirit in the Incarnate, something is made known that is explicable and, at the same time, inexplicable. What is explicable must, up to a certain point, also be cognisable through natural human cognitive abilities; it thus appears it can be isolated and incorporated – though as something extraordinary – into the human sphere: Jesus as a religiously remarkable man and founder of religion, as someone 'endowed with grace', who could regard God as Father [...] This seems to be part of the truth, but it is not part of what Jesus calls the truth and to which the explaining Spirit points. 'It is the spirit that gives life; the flesh is useless. The words that I have spoken to you are spirit and life' (John 6:63). [...] In Christ himself, the *'letter'* is the *'flesh'* (which, as such, is 'of no use'), which, however, must not be transgressed in order to reach what is explicated ('Those who do not eat my flesh have no life in themselves') – which, rather, as the flesh illuminated by the Spirit and containing the Spirit in Christ Himself, belongs inalienably to the 'truth'" (Balthasar, *Teologika*, vol. III: *Duch Prawdy*, 24–5). The reflections quoted in this paragraph are taken from Jagodziński, *Węzłowe zagadnienia chrystologii komunijnej*, 93–102.

43 Cf. Balthasar, *Teologika*, vol. III: *Duch Prawdy*, 28.

44 Cf. Balthasar, *Teologika*, vol. III: *Duch Prawdy*, 30.

45 Cf. Balthasar, *Teologika*, vol. III: *Duch Prawdy*, 28–31.

referred to by the word *pneuma*. What was still lacking at the time was a reflection on the difference between Spirit and Logos in God.[46]

Balthasar took as his starting point the "a priori obedience" of Jesus, who did not "take" humanity for Himself, but "gave" Himself to the Holy Spirit who made Him human. Without threatening the immanent Trinity, the Holy Spirit assumed the role of an active mediator.[47] Balthasar admits that against the claim that the Logos does not take human nature for Himself, one can cite Phil 2:7, where it says that he took "the form of a slave", but the context for this is provided by other statements which say that He allowed the Holy Spirit to be brought into the womb of the Virgin. A more important argument against the activity of the Holy Spirit comes from exegesis, which notes that in the words "the Holy Spirit will come upon you" (Luke 1:35) – *pneuma hagion* comes without an article, which could suggest the phrase was understood in the Old Testament in a colloquial sense – as "the Spirit of Yahweh", a non-personal power (which also seems to be indicated by the phrase "the power of the Most High will overshadow you" – Luke 1:35); it was only at Jesus' baptism that the "Holy Spirit" descended upon him, with an article giving him a personal character (*to pneuma to hagion*). However, Balthasar points out that the article is missing also in many other places that certainly speak of the person of the Holy Spirit.[48] This is sufficient to justify that the Spirit "overshadowing" Mary

---

46 Cf. Balthasar, *Teologika*, vol. III: *Duch Prawdy*, 31–3. Balthasar cites the opinion of W. Pannenberg that any Christology that from the outset notices the presence of the Spirit in Christ falls inevitably into adoptionism (although this does not apply to the aforementioned 'naïve' Christology of the Apostolic Fathers). As a result, ecclesiastical Christology moved rapidly from the *Pneuma-sarx* schema to the *Logos-sarx* schema (ibid., 33). Balthasar believed that the broadest concept of the Christology of the Spirit was presented by Hegel (cf. Balthasar, *Teologika*, vol. III: *Duch Prawdy*, 34–9). Hegel, however, according to another view, although he was a philosopher of the Spirit, forgot the Holy Spirit, he specifically omitted His proper personal mode of existence and twisted the ecclesiastical teaching about Him – cf. Ludger Oeing-Hanhoff, "Hegels Trinitätslehre. Zur Aufgabe ihrer Kritik und Rezeption", *Theologie und Philosophie* 52 (1977), 371 (footnote 30). The dialectical method, however, brought him back to modalism (cf. Balthasar, *Teologika*, vol. III: *Duch Prawdy*, 40). He believed that the protagonists of today's Evangelical and Catholic theology – K. Rahner among them – would be unthinkable without Hegel (Balthasar, *Teologika*, vol. III: *Duch Prawdy*, 34).

47 Cf. Balthasar, *Teologika*, vol. III: *Duch Prawdy*, 41.

48 For example, where "the Resurrected One addresses the disciples with the words: 'Receive the Holy Spirit!' (John 20.22) – the same one whom, when dying, He 'gave up' on the cross along with His mission accomplished in the Spirit: 'then he bowed his head and gave up his Spirit [*to pneuma*]' (John 19:30). And when Jesus, at His first teaching after baptism (Luke 4:18), He refers to the anointing by 'the Spirit of the Lord [without an article]' (Isa 61:1-2) to Himself, he is undoubtedly referring to the Spirit received in baptism. Further, the descent of the Spirit on the day of Pentecost, which Jesus promises to the disciples ('you will receive the *dynamis* of the Holy Spirit [*tou hagiou pneumatos*]', Acts 1:8) is in clear parallel to His descent on Mary. And when in John 7:39 at the promise of 'living water' we read: 'for as yet there was no Spirit *(pneuma)*', this term used without an article denotes without any doubt the personal Holy Spirit, whom Jesus, after His departure to glory,

is the Holy Spirit – the Divine Person, and the concept of the "power (*dynamis*) of the Most High" (Luke 1:35) emphasises His activity at the Incarnation. Although the New Testament does not address the personal (intra-trinitarian) nature of the Holy Spirit, it does distinguish Him as a divine being other than the Father and the Son, who "send" Him (John 14:26; 15:26) – an impersonal power could not be "sent". Thus, the process of incarnation is trinitarian in nature: "the Spirit brings the 'God's seed' (1 John 3:9) – the Son – into the Virgin's womb; the Son, in 'a priori' obedience, agrees to this and thus begins His mission"[49] – the Son was not simply "thrown" into an earthly existence, but it is a result of His obedience. This biblical starting point allows for very far-reaching conclusions relating to Christology. If the Holy Spirit was already personally active at the Incarnation, the Son's entire earthly existence was also marked by this action. This is primarily evident in the description of the baptism in the Jordan, since the visible descent of the Holy Spirit upon Jesus is presented as entering into him (*eis auton*: Mark 1:10) and as hovering over him (*ep 'auton*: Matt 3:16; Luke 3:22; most clearly in John 1:32 "and remained on him"). These expressions are an impenetrable conundrum, which nevertheless calls for deeper reflection within Christology of the Spirit, made possible by economic trinitology. At the same time, Balthasar emphasises the impossibility of objectifying the Holy Spirit, who is not only the fruit but also the gushing source of love between the Father and the Son, and who obtains His supreme revelation (personification) where He most profoundly expresses this ineffable unity.[50]

When introducing the theme of "Christology of the Spirit", Balthasar points to new conceptual stimuli in this area. The first from L. Bouyer's theology:[51] In the history of salvation, it is possible to observe both joint and separate action of the Logos and the Spirit, who come together in Mary who is the supreme efflorescence of the Spirit-Wisdom, ready to receive into herself the incoming Word:

> the ascending Spirit-Wisdom and the descending Word meet in her; 'created wisdom' (Augustine) becomes the eschatological spouse of the Word that becomes flesh from her, while Mary becomes the Church, Bride and Body at the same time. This union of the

---

will give to the Church. The fact that He Himself, while living on earth, possessed the Holy Spirit as a personal 'power' (Jesus 'rejoices in the Holy Spirit [*en to pneumati to hagio*]', Luke 10:21, He begins His teaching 'in the *dynamis* of the Holy Spirit [*tou pneumatos*]', Luke 4:14 etc.) does not prevent Peter from telling Cornelius that God anointed Jesus of Nazareth with the (articleless) 'Holy Spirit and power' (Acts 10:38). Similarly, in Luke 24:49, the 'power from on high' promised to the disciples by Jesus is the same Holy Spirit, whom the same author in Acts 1:8 calls 'the power of the Holy Spirit [*tou hagiou pneumatos*]'" (Balthasar, *Teologika*, vol. III: *Duch Prawdy*, 43).

49 Balthasar, *Teologika*, vol. III: *Duch Prawdy*, 44.

50 Cf. Balthasar, *Teologika*, vol. III: *Duch Prawdy*, 42–4.

51 Bouyer, *Le Consolateur. Esprit Saint et Vie de grace* (Paris: *Cerf*, 1980).

Spirit and the Word results in a return to the Father. Thus, the incarnate Son is the result of the Spirit's action and His fulfilled work, the Church, which at the same time proceeds from the Son.[52]

Bouyer's second theme is intra-trinitarian in nature: Marius Victorinus saw the essence of the biblical God as movement (*esse et moveri*): in the tridynamic God (*tridynamos*), being corresponds to the concept of *status*, life to the concept of *progressio*, cognition to the concept of *regressio*. The Holy Spirit is not only a *copula* between the Father and the Son, but also a fulfilled return to Himself. Balthasar here signals the emergence of the difficult problem of the relationship between the sacredness of the Divine essence and the Holy Spirit.

> Is this Spirit the essence of God or a third Person? Or is there some closer connection between the sentences 'God is love' and 'the Spirit is the bond of love between the Father and the Son'?" If "essence" is not to be understood as something fourth, as neutral outside the Persons, could the Spirit then be not the expression of that which is deepest in God: the 'movement' (Victorinus) that makes the Father come out of himself and beget the Son, by which act he finally becomes the Father – the movement that makes the Son owe everything and return everything to the Father, by which act he finally becomes the Son? Is the earlier distinction between essential love and personal love 'unavoidable'? Should it be said, then, that 'love (which is the very life of God, the Father in His fatherhood, the Son as the beloved and reciprocator of that love) is fulfilled in that Spirit of the Father who can only be the Spirit of childhood, rests on the Son as the free Spirit of reciprocity, so that He Himself is in the highest degree both loving and loved'? Then, 'the Spirit, as His name says, would be the breath of divine life or, which is the same, the heart of divinity, the heart of the Father and in equal measure the heart of the Son, the gift which, by offering Himself, gives life.[53]

Balthasar notes that F.-X. Durwell goes even further at this point.[54] While describing his thought, Balthasar profusely quotes his eloquent formulations:

> 'God is love and the Spirit is love. All the marks of God are embodied in His depths'. [...] 'The Spirit is, in tri-unity, the personifying Person. The Father begets in the Spirit and thereby constitutes Himself as Person, the Son is born in the Spirit and is thus constituted as Person. In the world too, the action of the Spirit takes on the form of a person.... In the Spirit, Jesus the man takes on a divine form, is received into the person of the Logos'. After

52 Balthasar, *Teologika*, vol. III: *Duch Prawdy*, 46.

53 Balthasar, *Teologika*, vol. III: *Duch Prawdy*, 47.

54 Durwell, *L'Esprit Saint de Dieu*.

> all, the Spirit is 'the originator of the Incarnation' and hence the initiator of Christology of the Spirit. In God, the Spirit would thus be [...] 'both at the end and at the beginning': 'The eternal begetting by the Father is an act of His love, and this love in action is the Spirit... The Spirit is at the beginning, in the Father who begets, and is also at the end, in the one who is begotten. Although it comes from both, it comes neither after the Father nor after the Son, because in Him they are Father and Son.' '[...] The begetting of the Son and the origin of the Spirit, though not identical, are mutually contained in each other: the Spirit appears in the act of begetting the Son, He is the Spirit of the Father in His fatherhood. The Father's whole action is the begetting of the Son, and although the Father does not beget the Spirit, the source of the Spirit is contained in His fatherhood... Since the Spirit proceeds from the Father, whose whole action is begetting, and since He is not the Son, He can only be that begetting'. He is 'the fullness in which all things originate and are immersed and fulfilled'. 'In God there is no nature that develops fruitfully in Persons, the nature of God is that He is a Trinity. One of these Persons is the Holy Spirit. He is the bond of unity of the Father and the Son; in Him the attributes of God are personified.[55]

Durwell emphasises that the Son is Son only in the Spirit, as incarnate in the Spirit He gives Himself to the Father, and the supreme act of this giving "through the eternal Spirit" (Heb 9:14) is His death on the cross – and this self-giving is at the same time the Son's Eucharist in relation to the Father and the world. And since this death is the culmination of the incarnation and the revelation of His love for the Father, it is also His fullest act of life, which, in the immortalisation of His humanity by the Holy Spirit, cannot become a thing of the past. This is why, as Balthasar emphasises, there are statements that initially arouse surprise:

> 'The Spirit resurrects Jesus without plucking Him out of death.... He does not lift Him beyond the highest devotion in love, namely beyond death. Death is the mystery of the Incarnation in its ultimate depth, death and glory are aspects of one and the same mystery: the Lamb stands here as slain, in glory that does not follow death, but incorporates it into itself'. 'Jesus does not return after His death, but in the death in which the Spirit elevates Him to glory'. 'Jesus is resurrected without leaving the mystery of His death'. The consequences for the Christian, his 'dying', his (Paul's) living in and out of death, are shown. In essence, this only fully expresses John's 'ascend to glory' as the unity of death and resurrection. And since both the act of death (Heb 9:14; Matt 27:50; John 19:30) and resurrection (Rom 1:4; 8:11) is an act of the Spirit, Christology appears here again as pneumatological Christology.[56]

---

55 Balthasar, *Teologika*, vol. III: *Duch Prawdy*, 48–9.

56 Balthasar, *Teologika*, vol. III: *Duch Prawdy*, 50; cf. ibid., 49–50.

Balthasar also registered doubts about Durwell's trinitology, which does not seem to take sufficient account of the trinitarian "arrangement" (*taxis*). However, he recalled Adrienne von Speyr's reminder that all this cannot be understood in temporal terms, since the origin of the Son and the Holy Spirit is as eternal as their existence.[57]

The most vigorous advocacy of Christology of the Holy Spirit, according to Balthasar, can be seen in W. Kasper,[58] who writes that God who revealed himself in Jesus Christ is love. And since this revelation was ultimately accomplished in Jesus Christ, Jesus and the loving self-giving of God in Him belong to the eternal essence of God. This mediation between God and man in Jesus Christ can only be understood in the sense of trinitarian theology. Jesus Christ – true God and true Man in one person – constitutes the historical exegesis of the Trinity. Besides, the mediation of God and Man in Jesus Christ can only be understood as an event "in the Holy Spirit".[59] Kasper goes on to write that pneumatologically oriented Christology can best express the uniqueness of Jesus Christ and the universal significance of His mediation: The Father in love imparts Himself to the Son, and in the Holy Spirit this love becomes Their inner freedom and through the Spirit it can impart itself externally. However, in the Holy Spirit, there is at the same time a reversed movement – the creation filled with the Divine Spirit gives itself to the Father. This surrender until death "liberates" the Spirit from its particular historical form, so that the death and resurrection of Jesus becomes at the same time a foreshadowing of the ensuing mediation of the Holy Spirit. Jesus Christ in the Spirit mediates between God and man and through the Spirit becomes the universal mediator of salvation.[60]

One of the key theses of J.D. Zizioulas is that Christology must be conditioned by pneumatology. Christology and pneumatology condition each other. There is

57 Cf. Balthasar, *Teologika*, vol. III: *Duch Prawdy*, 50–1.

58 Kasper, *Jezus Chrystus* (Warszawa: Pax, 1983).

59 Cf. Kasper, *Jezus Chrystus*, 258. "Because of its one-sided metaphysical assumptions, where the very essence of God is taken as the basis, scholastic theology was unable to make sense of the pneumatological aspect of the incarnation. It could only attribute the incarnation as a work of God's love to the Holy Spirit (*appropriation*). Since the Spirit is an expression of the grace of God's incarnation, scholastic theology spoke quite matter-of-factly of Him, using the term *gratia unionis* or, in the more figurative language of the Church Fathers' theology, 'anointing'. Usually, however, it usually attributed both to the Logos who, through His hypostatic union with human nature, endows that nature in a substantive way with grace and, as it were, anoints it with fragrant oil (*perichoresis*). Through this anointing, according to the opinion of many Church Fathers, the humanity of Jesus is even divinised. This profound union of the Logos with the humanity of Jesus has, according to scholastic theology, the effect that the Holy Spirit rests fully on Jesus' humanity, and even further – that 'God anointed him with the Holy Spirit and with power' (Acts 10:38; cf. Isa 61:1f.; Luke 4:21)." (Kasper, *Jezus Chrystus*, 259; cf. ibid., 260–1).

60 Cf. Kasper, *Jezus Chrystus*, 261.

no Christ without the Holy Spirit and no Holy Spirit without Christ – He is the "pneumatic Christ". Even the Body of Christ in the Christological (incarnational) and ecclesiological sense is a historical reality "only in the Holy Spirit". Any separation between Christology and pneumatology disappears in the Holy Spirit.[61] Zizioulas writes that for some people (even for whole traditions), the Spirit plays the role of Christ's mediator. He is the doorkeeper who opens the door and lets people into Christ, He prepares our hearts to hear the word of God and assent to it in faith, He is the animator or soul of the Body of Christ. But in all this we forget that the Spirit is above all the one who makes Christ who He is – the Messiah, the Saviour. He gives Christ His personal identity because Christ was born of the Spirit and by the Spirit rose from the dead. It must always be remembered that death was not defeated in Christ's resurrection by virtue of *communicatio idiomatum* of Christ's two natures; it was not a miracle of Christ's divine nature, but the result of the Holy Spirit's intervention. Both the historical and the eschatological Christ owes His identity (not His *bene esse*, but His *esse*) to the Holy Spirit.[62]

Y. Congar has shown, on the example of the biblical testimonies, that every action of God in the world takes place by means of two economies – that of the Spirit and that of the Word. The Holy Spirit acts in Jesus, and Jesus by the power of the Spirit proclaims the word of salvation. After the Ascension, the Church was aware

---

61 "*Koinonia* is decisive also in our understanding of the Person of Christ. Here the right synthesis between Christology and Pneumatology becomes extremely important. What does it mean that Christ is a 'Pneumatic' being, a Person 'born by the Spirit', anointed with the Spirit, etc., if not that He is in His very being a relational being? The Spirit is a Spirit of koinonia. If we cannot have Christology without Pneumatology, this means that we must stop thinking of Christ in individualistic terms and understand Him as a 'corporate person', an inclusive being. The 'head' without the 'body' is inconceivable. The Church is the Body of Christ because Christ is a Pneumatological being, born and existing in the *koinonia* of the Spirit" (Zizioulas, *The One and the Many*, 51). Cf. Jeffrey Wong Yee Kheong, *John Zizioulas' Ecclesiology of 'the one and the many'*, Otago (2019), https://ourarchive.otago.ac.nz/bitstream/handle/10523/9239/WongJeffrey2019PhD.pdf?sequence=1&isAllowed=y [8.11.2020], 101–102. Cf. ibid., 106: "According to Zizioulas, when the Holy Spirit blows, He 'creates not good individual Christians, individual 'saints,' but an event of communion, which transforms everything the Spirit touches into a relational being... The Spirit de-individualizes and personalizes beings wherever He operates'. This includes Christ who is not an individual because he has been deindividualised by the Spirit so that he is the pneumatological man in communion with God the Father through the Holy Spirit. Zizioulas even goes on to say that the Holy Spirit makes Christ a person – the 'last Adam', an eschatological being. The Holy Spirit also makes Jesus Christ a catholic being and a pneumatological man. It is the Spirit of God who makes the man Jesus of Nazareth, the Christ – the Anointed One. The Holy Spirit anoints the Christ. There is no Christ without the Holy Spirit. In this sense, Christology is said to be conditioned by Pneumatology. Because the Church is also the Body of Christ, it would naturally follow that if Christology is conditioned by Pneumatology, then ecclesiology will also be conditioned by Pneumatology."

62 Cf. Zizioulas, *The One and the Many*, 138.

that the Holy Spirit was the one acting. One of the most typical characteristics of the Holy Spirit since Antiquity has been the statement that He "spoke through the prophets". The fruit of the Spirit's action is the word of power, which only in Him has its salvific efficacy. After the arrest of Peter and John, Peter "filled with the Holy Spirit" spoke to the elders of the people (Acts 4:8). After Peter's release, the Church prayed mentioning the Holy Spirit (Acts 4:25), and after the prayer "the place in which they were gathered together was shaken; and they were all filled with the Holy Spirit and spoke the word of God with boldness" (Acts 4:31). The Apostles had not only the experience, but also the awareness of the connection between the powerful proclamation of Jesus and the manifestation of the Holy Spirit: "And we are witnesses to these things, and so is the Holy Spirit whom God has given to those who obey him" (Acts 5:32). St. Paul confessed: "because our message of the gospel came to you not in word only, but also in power and in the Holy Spirit and with full conviction" (1 Thess 1:5). Prayer, especially in Acts and Revelation, meant invoking the Holy Spirit, or epiclesis, so that the Spirit would anoint the preacher and the listeners. Through prayer, believers entered into a dialogue with the Holy Spirit, who proclaimed the word of power and life through them. This "active" presence of the Holy Spirit in the proclaimed Word was widely recognised in the theological tradition of the Church Fathers. The quality of the word is not determined by expediency, but by its origin from the Father through the Logos in the Spirit. The Word of God comes from within God and reaches us in the Spirit, thus its understanding is possible through inspiration and enlightenment. St. Augustine wrote about the work of the Holy Spirit as an internal teacher. This idea was also adopted by Luther and Calvin.[63]

---

63 Cf. Guzowski, *Duch Dialogujący*, 423–4. "St. Irenaeus gives an important testimony to the faith of the ancient Church, which found its pillars and its support in the Gospels and the Holy Spirit. Moreover, he writes of the new pagan peoples achieving salvation written for them not on paper and not with ink, but in their hearts by the Spirit. Most important of all is the conviction and constant principle repeated by the Church Fathers and theologians that the Scriptures must be read with the help of that Spirit in whose power it was written. For this reason, the ancient writers practised a spiritual reading of the Scriptures. They not only went beyond the literal sense of the texts, but also beyond the typological sense relating to Christ. However, in their simple faith, they understood that the witness of the Holy Spirit always directed them to the historical witness in the Person of the Word. The two economies of the Spirit and the Word are always present together in the revelation of the Person of the Incarnate Word and in the proclamation of the word of life, between which there is no temporal separation. The inspired Word is the eternal 'now' owing to the fact that the Scriptures, as the word revealed and inspired by the Spirit, is also today the means of God's salvific dialogue with man. The Holy Spirit is in us the closeness and immediacy of the salvation merited by Christ" (Guzowski, *Duch Dialogujący*, 424).

2.2 The Holy Spirit in Revealing and Working Together with the Son

Although the Holy Spirit was seen in the New Testament as descending on Jesus and anointing Him as the Messiah, it was also necessary to go back to the time of the Virgin Birth and the act of the Incarnation itself. All of Jesus' activity took place with the co-presence of the Holy Spirit, who did not abandon the Resurrected One.[64] The active presence of the Holy Spirit on the cross also remains a mystery, in view of which we must content ourselves with the words of Heb 9:13-14: "For if the blood of goats and bulls, with the sprinkling of the ashes of a heifer, sanctifies those who have been defiled so that their flesh is purified, how much more will the blood of Christ, who through the eternal Spirit offered himself without blemish to God, purify our conscience from dead works to worship the living God". H.U. von Balthasar emphasised on this point:

> The complete surrender of the Son to God occurs simultaneously through His blood and through the eternal Spirit, who can be none other than the Holy Spirit that always accompanied Him, by the same *dynamis* which in Heb 7:16 was called 'the power of an indestructible life', so that the bloody death by the power of the presence of the eternal Holy Spirit was itself a positive, eternally living act.[65]

The giving of the Holy Spirit to the Father through the Son marked the completion of the Son's mission. Balthasar also reflected on the role of the Holy Spirit in communicating the offering of the Son's Divinity to the Father and in preserving Their unity. When the mission of the Son was fulfilled, the Holy Spirit should return to the Father. When, after the Resurrection, the Son sent Him to the Church and breathed Him into the disciples,

---

64 The speculative aspects of the role of the Holy Spirit in the incarnation of the Son were presented by von Balthasar in *Teologika*, vol. III: *Duch Prawdy*, 155–62.

65 Balthasar in *Teologika*, vol. III: *Duch Prawdy*, 152. "We have no insight into Jesus' awareness of this inseparable bond with the Spirit. That the resting of the Spirit *over* Him, his knowledge of the Spirit's indwelling *in* Him, is not put in question, is evident from the self-determined character of His actions and words: Jesus acts 'in the Spirit' (Matt 12:27), although this Spirit of His is attuned to the mission of obedience that the Incarnate One is to carry out, at the same time the Spirit of the Father remains 'over' Him, bringing Him commands from the Father. And when Jesus 'is troubled in the spirit' (John 13:21), the unity of this 'in/over' becomes apparent: The Spirit brings from the Father the news of the coming Passion, which is also already felt by the Spirit within, in Jesus' consciousness [...] It is worth noting that in all economic situations there comes to no 'I-You' relation between the Son and the Spirit. Only the Father is 'You' for the Son; and He in the Spirit is this 'You'. (This is why it is difficult to accept the formula proposed by Mühlen, in which the Spirit is immanent to God: 'We-You')" (Balthasar in *Teologika*, vol. III: *Duch Prawdy*, 152–3). See Jagodziński, *Węzłowe zagadnienia chrystologii komunijnej*, 102–7.

> this was akin to 'a reversal of competence': prior to that it was the Spirit who brought the Son into the world, now the Son sends the Spirit into the world, both are 'in seemingly infinite movement, which causes a constant interchange of roles, while the Father contains all this movement within Himself'. However, 'the way of the Spirit to men leads henceforth only through the Son'. He goes, 'sent by the Son, following the Father's will, to men, bearing witness to the Son, strengthening with this testimony the faith of men and thus turning this faith back to the Father'. The Spirit makes the Son's message 'universal, proclaiming all the fullness, the out-of-this-world riches of the Son and His revelation'. But this sending is 'the fruit of the cross' and the sending of the Son back to the Father, in view of which 'the way of the Spirit to men now always leads through the Son', moreover: it takes place inseparably together with the Son, whose corporeality has become something universal: 'the Son in the Eucharist, the Spirit in the outpouring on the whole world'. And at the same time, the one and the other are not side by side: 'the role of the Spirit is made visible' in the transubstantiation, in the linking of the Spirit with 'water and blood' [...] his 'Christhood-shape' comes to the foreground.[66]

In the inseparability of the Son and the Holy Spirit after the Resurrection and His sending to the Church, it is also evident that the mission of the Holy Spirit did not replace that of the Son, but both entered a new stage in which the infinite richness of their relationship is also revealed differently.[67]

Discussing the joint action of the 'dyad' consisting of the Son and the Holy Spirit[68], Balthasar writes that these "'two hands of the Father' do not act in parallel or successively, but they interact with and in each other in very different ways. The Son reveals the Father, the Holy Spirit reveals the Son – but this needs to be more precisely defined". The Father reveals Himself in the Son, who points to the Father, and this mutual pointing (revealing God as love) is indicated by the Holy Spirit.[69] In showing and explaining the movement of the Father to the Son (who becomes man) and of the (resurrected) Son to the Father, the Holy Spirit explains at the same time the significance of the incarnation of the Word for the revelation of the Father and the glory, divinity and intrinsic infinity of the Son (which are revealed in the return to the Father), including the love between the Father and the Son. This is what constitutes the content of "theosis" (esp. in the Eastern tradition) or "incorporation into Christ" (esp. in the Western tradition). On a closer look at the two approaches, the differences between them are almost blurred. "Theosis" is

66 Balthasar, *Teologika*, vol. III: *Duch Prawdy*, 154–5.

67 Cf. Balthasar in *Teologika*, vol. III: *Duch Prawdy*, 155, 227–8.

68 Cf. Balthasar in *Teologika*, vol. III: *Duch Prawdy*, 195–6.

69 Cf. Balthasar in *Teologika*, vol. III: *Duch Prawdy*, 163. One must beware of an overly simple Christology of the Holy Spirit, according to which Jesus' action as man is divine through the Holy Spirit, since a radical formulation of this leads to Nestorianism (cf. ibid., 164).

based on the Incarnation and continues in the Eucharist – to the Father through the Son in the Holy Spirit; "incorporation into Christ" is the only way to participate in the inner life of the triune God – although St. Augustine did not abandon the notion of "theosis" either and emphasised that without the action of the Holy Spirit, the communion of the Body of Christ, which is the Church, would not have taken place at all.[70]

The mutual action of the Son in the Holy Spirit and the Holy Spirit in the Son leads to their inseparability in the sphere of the revelation of theory and practice. The Holy Spirit directs the gaze of the faithful towards the Son so that they may perceive the truth of Christ and, in imitation of the Son's love to the Father, they could love not "in word and speech" but "in truth and action" (1 John 3:18).[71] However, the Holy Spirit

> does not explicate from outside, He does not introduce from outside. He does not refer from Himself to the Son. For He Himself in the Son is already the originator of His incarnation and of all His subsequent teaching about the Father, because *in* the Son (as the Spirit of the Son) and *over* the Son (as the Spirit of the Father and sent by the Father) He co-creates the obedience of the Son, which leads up to the fulfilment of the filial mission, to the witness of the Spirit, water and blood from the open side. [...] the One who accompanies from the beginning is the Spirit Himself 'in Jesus/over Jesus', who precisely by this, from the perspective of the end of the mission, can also become the most experienced Teacher of the work fulfilled between the Father and the Son for the Church and introducing into it...[72]

Jesus' mission was universal and definitive because of the Father's desire and the Holy Spirit's resting on Jesus. Why did Jesus leave the full execution of the mission

70 Cf. Balthasar in *Teologika*, vol. III: *Duch Prawdy*, 164–8.

71 Cf. Balthasar in *Teologika*, vol. III: *Duch Prawdy*, 168–73.

72 Balthasar in *Teologika*, vol. III: *Duch Prawdy*, 170. In an interesting way, Balthasar writes about the Christian "experience" as the result of the Holy Spirit's "guiding" man: "The Spirit [...] introduces into the space between the Father and the Son, [...] this divine space naturally opens up: always from the perspective of the incarnate Son, His word, His deeds, His passion and resurrection, but as a space with the dimension of depth that takes one far and ever further beyond what is purely human. [...] The Spirit, who already rests in the word itself ('The words that I have spoken to you are spirit and life', John 6:63), leads into its space of depths, in which there is truth, and the agreement to show oneself these depths and the personal pursuit of them constitute, in a proper sense, Christian theory, contemplation, meditation. Or, since the speaking word of God is concerned here, listening. [...] It is of course possible, following Thomas Aquinas (*S.th.* I-II 68), to attribute such inclusion into the 'depths of God' [...] to the gifts of the Holy Spirit; but this does not give a separate experience of the Spirit, but lets one penetrate into the triune 'spaces' of God, in which the interpermeating divine hypostases have equal share" (Balthasar in *Teologika*, vol. III: *Duch Prawdy*, 172–3).

to the Holy Spirit? Balthasar answers that the essential task of the Incarnation was to fulfil the trinitarian salvific work within the temporal boundaries of human life (including death), and besides, the universalisation of Christ's achievements assumed by the Holy Spirit could not be realised without the active presence and action of the resurrected Son.[73] This trinitarian event begins the time of the Spirit announced by Jesus to bring about all truth. He, however, is always the Spirit given by Jesus and breathed into the disciples. Although Jesus' earthly mission has been fulfilled, He does not passively observe the process of its universalisation, but He "must reign until he has put all his enemies under his feet" (1 Cor 15:25). This "reigning", however, is in essence a consent to what the Spirit is to do – to unfold for the world the "hidden (in Christ) treasures" of God.[74] The working of the "two hands of the Father" is most evident in the Eucharist, in which – whatever great importance one may attach to the epiclesis – the Spirit works the miracle of making Christ present in an unspeakably profound union with the Son.[75] This becomes even clearer in Christ's identification with the truth – when he included "the truthful God" and the Holy Spirit in His utterance. Here, the Spirit does not play a consecutive or subordinate role – as the Spirit of the Father, He has always communicated Father's will to the Son; as the Spirit of the Son, He has "exercised" Him in obedience – His universality as Paraclete thus demonstrates that it is His own (more specifically trinitarian) universality.[76]

The co-operation of the Holy Spirit also reveals His participation in revealing the truth of Christ.[77] When the eternal Son became man, his (unchangeable!) relationship to the Holy Spirit also had to "change". The Holy Spirit, as it were, now co-experiences being part of creation in relation to God – He is not merely an "external" witness to Jesus' destiny but, as "the Spirit of Christ" (Rom 8:9), He acquires a kind of internal experience. He not only "penetrates the depths of God" but also, as the Spirit of the Son, He travels with the Son through the "abysses of the world".[78]

H. Mühlen defined the Holy Spirit intrinsically as the Divine "We", the intimate union of the Father and the Son , "in Person", "We in Person". In parallel to this intra-trinitarian definition of the Holy Spirit, he explained His historico-salvific

73 Cf. Balthasar in *Teologika*, vol. III: *Duch Prawdy*, 174–6, 261–6.

74 Cf. Balthasar in *Teologika*, vol. III: *Duch Prawdy*, 176.

75 Cf. Balthasar in *Teologika*, vol. III: *Duch Prawdy*, 176–7.

76 Cf. Balthasar in *Teologika*, vol. III: *Duch Prawdy*, 177–9.

77 Cf. Balthasar in *Teologika*, vol. III: *Duch Prawdy*, 179–80.

78 Cf. Balthasar in *Teologika*, vol. III: *Duch Prawdy*, 181.

function: He is the Divine "being-beyond-self", in a way God Himself apparently "coming out of Himself – the Holy Spirit understood as Divine self-giving".[79]

As a gift, the Holy Spirit comes from the Father, while the Father communicates to the Son all that He "possesses" – Himself in love. The Holy Spirit is precisely God's wealth. He proceeds from the perfect self-giving of the substantially personal Father who keeps nothing for Himself but, as "Father", offers everything to the Son and remains "Father". This means that the Son, to whom everything has been given from the Father, also completely offers Himself to the Father. However, as the subject the Son is offered to the Father as "Son". In this way, the mystery of the Holy Spirit is explained: He is the Gift, not like the Father and the Son, who are both Giver and Gift to each other, but the Spirit is pure Gift. The Holy Spirit is the Gift dwelling wholly in the Father and wholly in the Son, making the relationship between Them possible and distinguishing Them from one another. He is also the Gift making God's being Divine in a unique and irreplaceable way, and thus

79 Cf. Stubenrauch, *Pneumatologia*, 215–6; Laurentin, *Nieznany Duch Święty*, 360–62; Congar, *Wierzę w Ducha Świętego. Duch Święty w ekonomii Objawienia*, 64–7; Czaja, *Credo in Spiritum Vivificantem. Pneumatologiczna interpretacja Kościoła jako komunii w posoborowej teologii niemieckiej* (Lublin: Wydawnictwo KUL, 2003), 75–9; Guzowski, *Duch Dialogujący*, 389–92. K. Guzowski presents the theses by H. Mühlen as follows (Guzowski, *Duch Dialogujący*, 390–1): "in the Trinity, the Holy Spirit is one person in two persons [...]." Mühlen "addresses the problem from the perspective of analysing the grammatical and anthropological function of personal pronouns in our verbal paradigms: I-you-he and We-you. The relation between the Father and the Son is an I-you or me-you relation, for example, this is the case in John 17:21-26. It is not possible to characterise the relation of the Father and the Son with the Holy Spirit as a we-you relation and, similarly, the relation of the Spirit to the Father and the Son as a I-you relation. The Holy Spirit appears as the personal We between the I of the Father and the You of the Son, as the one who unites them in We. From the biblical analysis, Mühlen draws the conclusion: The Father and the Son appear as two I's who maintain an I-You relationship between Them. Aware of the trinitarian context of his argument, Mühlen emphasises that the Father is the fundamental intra-trinitarian I, while the Son is the fundamental intra-trinitarian You. When Jesus utters We, it has a double meaning: it includes the Father, but never the people; it includes the Father and the Holy Spirit (cf. John 14:23). This linguistic analysis has a profound cognitive and theological value, since the We involving the Holy Spirit points to Him as a dialogical Person. In our speech, too, We is the most basic way of pointing to a person. In light of this, the Holy Spirit would be the intra-trinitarian We. This claim is based on the Western doctrine of the origin of the Holy Spirit, emphasising that in the Trinity we have *'duo spirantes sed unus spirator'*; this refers to active spiration. The action of the Father and the Son is in any case a subsistent act of We, since it is performed by two persons. The expression of this act from the perspective of passive spiration is the Holy Spirit, who, as a personal Act-We subsists between the Father and the Son. The consequence of the Spirit's relation with the Father and the Son is the I-We relationship. The Holy Spirit is the *nexus* of the Father and the Son. This gives a picture of *two* forms of perichoresis within the Trinity: one occurring between the Father and the Son in the form of I-You, and the other occurring between the Father and the Son, and the Holy Spirit. Therefore, He is one Person in two Persons."

making God's sharing in Himself and externally possible. Since the Father offers Himself completely to the Son and the Son does the same with regard to the Father, and since both in this relationship do not lose Themselves to each other, since as subjects they remain Givers to each other, the pure Gift cannot be thus Their mere reproduction, but is rather something else to them, something "Third". He is the God-Holy Spirit who, as a Person, unites in Himself the Father and the Son, but as a subject He is at the same time the Gift and is also distinct from the Father and the Son.[80]

H.U. von Balthasar believes that the mutual exchange of essence between the Father and the Son leads to their dynamic union in the Holy Spirit. At the root of this union lies the kenotic self-giving. Balthasar emphasises the event-like character of this process. The essence of the love of the Father and the Son is their mutual "collision with one another" in the Holy Spirit, in whom the specification of God's essence is perpetuated. It is He who causes the persistent "exchange" of the Father and Son's mutual being in each other. The dynamism of God's love is expressed precisely in the fact that God's essence has, in relation to each Person, the property of "more and more". The Person of the Holy Spirit contributes to the boundless interpenetration of the Persons in God. He is the source of the energy of the mutual bestowal of the Father and the Son, the embodiment of Their mutual self-giving. The drama of the distance between the Father and the Son finds its solution in the Holy Spirit. Using the paradoxical thought by Adrienne von Speyr, Balthasar argues that in the Third Person of God, the absolute distinction between the Father and the Son becomes ever greater love. The breath of the Spirit is a fertile encounter of giving and receiving love, which seemingly abandons itself to produce the Spirit of love in a common breath of love. In the salvific economy, on the other hand, the Holy Spirit expresses a dynamically "growing" unity as pure distance.[81]

Balthasar emphasises that in the manifestation of the essential union of the Father and the Son, they perceive their unity "as the hypostatic essence of love". The

---

80 Cf. Stubenrauch, *Pneumatologia*, 227–8. Is the monarchy of the Father, and thus the biblical witness, preserved? The Father never becomes the Son, and the Son never becomes the Father. Nor does the Holy Spirit enter, in the manner of the Son, into a Giver-Gift relation towards the Father. Based on this principle, the Father, through his self-giving, begets the Son and not another Father. Nor does the Son reflect Himself in the Father, but treats the Father as a constant dialogue partner. Finally, the Spirit does not "consist" of the Father and the Son – in which case he would not be a Spirit, but a kind of "Father-Son" – instead, He comes as a Gift. This means that He realises God in the form of a pure gift. However, the Father remains *principium non de principio* – a beginning without a beginning. Otherwise, His subjectivity as Father would be reduced to an abstract principle, which could be juxtaposed at will with the names of the Son or the Holy Spirit or some other metaphor, and consequently the essence of the dogma of the Trinity would be violated. Cf. Stubenrauch, *Pneumatologia*, 378–85.

81 Cf. Bokwa, *Trynitarno-chrystologiczna interpretacja eschatologii*, 105–6.

Holy Spirit constitutes the concrete referential reality of the Father and Son's love, becoming "the subjective embodiment of the reciprocal love of the Father and the Son", more than a "mutual inclination" of the Father and the Son, the fruit of Their love – He is the Gift. He enacts Father's love – which gives rise to all reality – giving His whole being to the Son, He is in no way diminished and remains the first, necessary act of the Divine going "outward". The love of the Father and the Son is enclosed in the Person of the Holy Spirit into a whole that "does not threaten Their personal qualities", especially since the Spirit does not wish to be "someone" for Himself, but only a pure declaration of love between the Father and the Son.[82]

Balthasar conceives of the Holy Spirit as a trinitarian duality – the supreme unity of the Father and the Son and the separate, objective, personal "fruit" of Their love, Their eternal begetting, the "result" of that love and its witness. The Third Divine Person exists eternally as the self-contained fecundity of Divine love, the unity of the ineffable love of the Father and the Son. The essence of God's love "imposes" the trinity in God – breathing the Holy Spirit constitutes a "process" that is "necessary" but absolutely free – the Holy Spirit coming from this process is the expression of God's unique freedom. The Spirit of God is identical with Himself and with the essence of God – he is God and, as a Person, he is the "combined breath of the Father and the Son". The relationship between the Father and the Son is described by Balthasar as richness, a gift, a unity, a communion of love. The Spirit of God contains the whole essence of God as love, it is "love as such and absolute", the poured-out totality of being as love. For Balthasar, the Spirit of love is "the essence of God", who is one through the unifying power of the Spirit of love, "the unity of unsurpassable love". The Holy Spirit is the personification, the "prosopon" of the Divine, which in its essence is the pure revealing of itself. He is the "crowning achievement" of God's growing love – Balthasar speaks of the "fecundity of love". It is in the power of the Holy Spirit that God continually "attains" his ultimate eschatological fullness.[83]

The presentation of God as the one and only love, giving itself without reservation, conceals a specific purpose, which is the analogy between the structure of God's absolute love and the personal human encounter. This analogy is reciprocal. In the theological "top-down" path, this means understanding the trinitarian reality of God as the condition that makes love between people possible. However, this analogy is subsidiary and Balthasar's main goal remains the conceptual-imaginative approximation of God's trinitarian essence.[84] Being the love of the Father and the

---

82 Cf. Bokwa, *Trynitarno-chrystologiczna interpretacja eschatologii*, 106.

83 Cf. Bokwa, *Trynitarno-chrystologiczna interpretacja eschatologii*, 106–7.

84 Cf. Bokwa, *Trynitarno-chrystologiczna interpretacja eschatologii*, 107.

Son and the bond of their unity, the Holy Spirit is their eternal communication and, therefore, their communion.[85]

> The Spirit is the communion of the Lover and the Beloved, ensuring also the communion of the Lover with His creation and with the history of their suffering, without excluding the Beloved, but precisely in Him and thanks to Him. [...] The differentiation of the Father and the Son is recognised in the most sublime unity of love, originating in the Father; and this love, bestowed on the Son and reflected in Him, constantly returns to its beginning without beginning: The Spirit is the bond of eternal love. Therefore, the Father remains the beginning, the Son – the manifestation, and the Spirit – Their personal bond in the movement of Divine eternity.[86]

2.3 The Work of the Holy Spirit in Christ's Mysteries

Christ had a special experience of the Holy Spirit, first expressed in the mission undertaken after the anointing with the Spirit in the Jordan. The Holy Spirit then descended upon Him in the form of a dove (cf. Mark 1:10) and the voice of God saying that He is the beloved Son, along with the open heavens, point to Jesus as the Messiah marked by the special presence of the Spirit (cf. Isa 61:1). Christ thus experienced his Sonship to the God of Israel in the Spirit. In the Spirit he also prayed to God, knew the love of the Father and experienced joy. The fact that the Holy Spirit "descended" and "rested" on Him presented the Spirit as the "*shekinah* of God" in Jesus, and thus that the eternal Spirit dwelt and descended, became close to His people in Him, in His history and passion. The Holy Spirit made the person of Christ the "kingdom of God" since it was by the power of the Spirit that Jesus cast out evil spirits, healed the sick and welcomed sinners. Jesus also experienced the presence of the Holy Spirit in temptation and suffering. The Spirit led Him into the desert, where He was tempted, but also in the Spirit Jesus overcame the temptation and, full of His power, returned to Galilee (cf. Luke 4:14). The miracles of healing and deliverance from the power of the devil, which He performed by the power of the Spirit, show that He experienced His special presence.[87]

---

85 Cf. Laurentin, *Nieznany Duch Święty*, 319–20. In the concluding to his work, K. Guzowski wrote that it collects "the best intuitions of the theological tradition and of personalist reflection, which allow us to see the person of the Holy Spirit in the entirety of personal and perichoretic dynamics, in communional unity and relation, and in relational and creative subjectivity" (Guzowski, *Duch Dialogujący*, 425).

86 Forte, *Istota chrześcijaństwa*, 99.

87 Cf. Guzowski, *Duch Dialogujący*, 410.

It was actually only after the last Council that Western theology began to speak of the active role of the Holy Spirit in the incarnation of the Son of God. Prior to this, the act had only been attributed to the Holy Spirit and referred to only objectively as *gratia unionis* or "anointing". H. Mühlen first developed the thought of the encyclical *Mystici Corporis Christi* about the adornment of human nature with the fullness of the Holy Spirit by the incarnate Son. Under the influence of H.U. von Balthasar, however, he began to proclaim that in realising the mystery of Jesus Christ, the Spirit is both the anointment and the Anointing One. The Incarnation, on the other hand, is the work of the Spirit as a form of obedience of the Son to the Father. Both stories of Jesus' childhood already see Him as the "creation of the Spirit" (Luke 1:35; Matt 1:18,20).[88] The Holy Spirit, as mediator between the Father and the Son, is also God's mediator in history. The Son, acting in the Spirit and endowed by Him with openness, obediently responds to the Father.[89] Jesus differs from the prophets in that he experiences the permanent presence of the Spirit. When the Word "became" man, the Holy Spirit became the chrism of anointing, entering the history of salvation as "the Spirit of Christ", becoming in him the fullness of grace.[90]

The New Testament sees in Jesus the bearer of the Spirit and the fulfilled presence and mission of the Spirit.[91] In the Spirit Jesus fulfils His messianic mission; at baptism He is introduced by the Spirit into the messianic office (Mark 1,10),[92] He stays in the desert in the Holy Spirit,[93] in Spirit's power He performs miracles (Luke 4:14,18; 5:17; 6:19; 10:21 and others).[94] On the cross, in the power of God's Spirit, He gives Himself to God in sacrifice (Heb 9:14).[95] By the power of the Spirit He is raised from the dead (Rom 1:4; 8:11; 1 Tim 3:16)[96] and thus becomes a life-giving spirit (1 Cor 15:45). Jesus is associated with the Spirit at every stage of

---

88 Cf. Czaja, *Credo in Spiritum Vivificantem*, 106; see Laurentin, *Nieznany Duch Święty*, 128–43.

89 "The whole existence of the Son of God in humility and submission is marked [...] by the presence and action of the Holy Spirit (Luke 4:1,14; 10:21; Matt 12:28). With unheard-of intuition, the author of the *Epistle to the Hebrews* penetrated this mystery when he wrote that Christ 'through the eternal Spirit offered himself without blemish to God' (Heb 9:14). The inspiration from the Father is thus at the same time the mission of the Holy Spirit, to whom the humbled Son of God showed His obedience in all things" (Hryniewicz, *Chrystus nasza Pascha. Zarys chrześcijańskiej teologii paschalnej – tom 1* (Lublin: TN KUL, 1981), 280).

90 Cf. Czaja, *Credo in Spiritum Vivificantem*, 101–4.

91 Cf. Cirilo Folch Gomes, "Jezus a dar Ducha Świętego," *Communio. Międzynarodowy Przegląd Teologiczny* 7/1 (1988), 7–13.

92 Cf. Laurentin, *Nieznany Duch Święty*, 144–6.

93 Cf. Laurentin, *Nieznany Duch Święty*,146–7.

94 Cf. Laurentin, *Nieznany Duch Święty*, 148–9.

95 Cf. Laurentin, *Nieznany Duch Święty*, 150–2.

96 Cf. Laurentin, *Nieznany Duch Święty*, 152.

life, He speaks in the power of the Spirit. The Spirit is the innermost principle of Jesus' fulfilled life in Him.[97] They work synergistically – the Spirit prepared, enabled and attested Jesus' activity, and the sovereignty of His teaching and some direct statements allow us to recognise the action of the Spirit.[98] From the juxtaposition of the biblical testimonies, it is clear that Matthew and Luke develop a different thought than Paul and John. They do not ask how the Son of the eternal Father becomes man (they do not assume the pre-existence of the Logos), but try to answer the question of how and by what means Jesus the man can be the Messiah. This is also how the pre-Pauline two-stage messianology mentioned earlier develops (Rom 1:3; 8:11). It is concerned with the Father's completion of the Messiah in the work of His resurrection by the power of the "Spirit of holiness", which is the source of Jesus' messianic existence. Matthew and Luke hint at the same thing – the uniqueness of Jesus' coming is not determined by His Virgin birth, but by Yahweh's initiative. His creative power and His Spirit bring Jesus the man into being. The linking of God's eternal salvific will and its realisation in Jesus the Man-Messiah is accomplished by the eternal Spirit of God. The beginning, history and consummation of the life of Jesus have their source in the action of "God's power and the Spirit" (Luke 1:35).[99] The Holy Spirit is the cause of Jesus' holiness; by realising his relationship to the Father, He personifies God's holiness in creation.[100] As an intra-trinitarian "communion in Person" it also enables Jesus to be boundlessly open to people and makes their communion with Him possible.[101]

The question of the relationship between Jesus and the Holy Spirit must be specifically related to the life of Christ and not to abstract nature or human person. Since the way of Jesus was also the way of the Passion, it was also the way of the Holy Spirit who accompanied Jesus. The Holy Spirit was associated with Jesus' destiny. "The Spirit of God" appears clearly as "the Spirit of Christ" and will be invoked together with the name of Christ, although their distinctiveness cannot be overlooked. The Spirit of Christ is therefore the Spirit of the Crucified One and thus Christ did not experience His sacrifice and death in an external way, but it was an experience of internal assent in the power of the Spirit. The Epistle to the Hebrews

97 Cf. Czaja, *Credo in Spiritum Vivificantem*, 104–5.

98 Cf. Stubenrauch, *Pneumatologia*, 64–5.

99 Cf. Czaja, *Credo in Spiritum Vivificantem*, 107; D. Gardocki writes: "the birth of the Son of God from Mary took place through the Holy Spirit before, as the Gospel tells us, she cohabited with Joseph (cf. Matt 1:18). In this way, the chain of human genealogy is broken, making room for the action of the Holy Spirit as the one who permeates history and makes life appear where it was not possible before. Mary, on the other hand, appears as a temple of the Holy Spirit and as a symbol and figure of the New Israel, the new people of God, which, like Jesus, is formed and shaped in her womb by the action of that Spirit" (Gardocki, *Teologia wyzwolenia*, 277).

100 Cf. Czaja, *Credo in Spiritum Vivificantem*, 108.

101 Cf. Czaja, *Credo in Spiritum Vivificantem*, 109.

emphasises the work of the Holy Spirit in Christ's passion and death: "Christ, who through the eternal Spirit offered himself without blemish to God" (Heb 9:14).[102]

The Crucified One releases the Spirit to the Father, which He has given Him, and which will be fully given to Him on the day of the resurrection. Good Friday is the hour of death in God, the abandonment of the Son by the Father in the greatest communion of love. It is the event that completes the surrender of the Spirit to the Father and makes the Son's climactic exit into the otherness of the world possible. If the Spirit had not allowed himself to be "released", the hour of darkness could have been misunderstood as the hour of God's death. In the hour of the cross, the Spirit also makes history – history in God.[103] The cross as the story of the Son, the Father and the Spirit is the trinitarian story of God.[104] The history of the Son, the

102 Cf. Guzowski, *Duch Dialogujący*, 411. "The experience of the Holy Spirit in the life of Jesus is described by all the evangelists. However, Mark's perspective is structured in such a way as to see how the Holy Spirit experiences the story of Jesus with Him. The Holy Spirit permeates the actions and Jesus Himself, accompanying Him in His moments of longing for God, from the desert to the cross. Also, the messiahship of Jesus is shown in Mark from the perspective of His death, and the so-called messianic secret is explained in His passion and death. Jesus experiences the Father through the Spirit. The invocation '*Abba-Father*', the only phrase addressed directly to the Father, is borne by Jesus in the Spirit. In the Garden of Gethsemane, in the face of trial and temptation, He calls out *Abba-Father* in the Holy Spirit. Mark interprets the Passion of Jesus, which begins in Gethsemane with the experience of God's hiding and ends on the cross with the experience of the abandonment by God, in a pneumatological key. 'What began with the baptism in the power of the Spirit ends with the passion in the power of the same Spirit'. In Mark's account, certain parallels are noticeable and worth bringing out: 1. the Holy Spirit is the strength and consolation for Jesus in the moments of temptation: at the beginning of the mission and in Gethsemane, where He urges the apostles to be vigilant so that they 'do not succumb to temptation' (Mark 14:38). While Jesus is strong in Spirit, the Apostles are weak 'in flesh'. 2 At Jesus' baptism, God addresses Jesus as 'my beloved Son'; in Gethsemane, Christ calls out '*Abba*-beloved Father', which can be interpreted as a response. The *Gospel* of Mark thus shows that Jesus is aware of His sonship and His messianic mission, all of which is marked by the guidance of the Spirit. When we realise again that the story of Jesus as Messiah is also the story of the Holy Spirit, it is worth noticing that the Holy Spirit is present in Jesus' suffering and, in a sense, suffers with Him. Such conclusions are justified if we judge everything in terms of the personal presence of the Holy Spirit as a mutual – interpenetrating – experience of the Spirit and Jesus and a mutual relationship" (Guzowski, *Duch Dialogujący*, 412).

103 Discussing J. Moltmann's concept, D. Gardocki writes that "the death of Jesus, when interpreted in a trinitarian key, appears [...] as 'the beginning of a divine event in which from the death of the Son and the pain of the Father emerges the Spirit of love. The Spirit who gives life'" (Gardocki, "Cierpienie Boga w ujęciu Jürgena Moltmanna," *Studia Bobolanum* 1 (2010), 58).

104 Cf. Forte, *Istota chrześcijaństwa*, 67–71. "The cross of the Son reveals the love of the Father (Rom 8:32; John 3:16), which works henceforth in the hearts of men by the power of the Holy Spirit (Rom 5:5). The mystery of the cross thus reveals the whole mystery of the Holy Trinity. The Father is the initiator of the work of salvation: '[...] in Christ God [- the Father] was reconciling the world to himself' (2 Cor 5:19). The witness to the fact that this work has been brought to completion is 'the Spirit of him who raised Jesus from the dead' (Rom 8:11), celebrated in the Eastern tradition

Father and the cross is also the history of the Spirit.[105] The climactic act of release is the sacrificial offering of the Spirit – Jesus "bowed his head and gave up his spirit" (John 19:30). This is the hour of the death in God, the abandonment of the Son by the Father in Their – after all, always greatest – communion of love. The Trinity arrives to a world subjected to sin so that it may return – through the Passover – to the homeland of trinitarian communion.[106]

According to Balthasar, the suffering of God is trinitarian in character. The trinitarian perichoresis provides the basis for speaking of the suffering of the Father and the Holy Spirit in the person of the Son – obviously, following the rules of *communicatio idiomatum*. At the same time, the suffering of the Father has nothing to do with patripassianism, and the Holy Spirit – mediating the suffering of separation – is the principle of the suffering of the triune God.[107] On the day of the Son's surrender of Himself – and the Father's surrender of the Son to death – the Spirit is surrendered by the Son to the Father. Without the surrender of the Spirit, the cross would not have been revealed in all its depth of the trinitarian and salvific event. If the Spirit had not allowed Himself to be "released" in the silence of death, the hour of darkness might have been misunderstood – not as an act in God, as an event of the history of the immortal God's love. In the hour of the cross, the Holy Spirit also makes history in God, because released to the Father, He guarantees the Son's distinctiveness from Him in solidarity with sinners, although remaining in an infinite communion expressed in the sacrificial obedience of the Crucified One.

---

not without reason as 'the Witness of Christ's Passion'. It is not without reason that the juxtaposition of the words 'it is finished' and 'he gave up his spirit' the Gospel of John (19:30) can be seen to have a deeper meaning. The symbolic nature of this Gospel leads one to see in this 'giving up of the spirit' (*parédoken tó pneúma*) something more than just dying (cf. Matt 27:50; Mark 15:37; Luke 23:46). In the indivisible event of Christ's humiliation and exaltation on the cross, the mysterious 'giving up' of the Holy Spirit is already taking place, as if an anticipation of Pentecost. With Christ's final sigh, the Holy Spirit begins His mission (cf. John 7:39), the sign of which is the 'Pentecost of John': The Resurrected One grants the Holy Spirit to his disciples already on the day of his glorification (John 20:22)" (Hryniewicz, *Chrystus nasza Pascha*, 307–8).

105 Cf. Gardocki, "Oblicze współcierpiącego Ojca w ujęciu Jeana Galota," *Studia Bobolanum* 2 (2010), 29. "Galot finally draws attention to the participation of the Holy Spirit in the event of the passion. He views this participation as the co-participation of the Spirit in the sacrifice offered by Jesus. The essence of this co-participation is that Jesus offers Himself through the Holy Spirit who is present during His earthly life – guiding and permeating His activity – as well as during His passion on the cross. Furthermore, if it is accepted that the incarnation was the work of the Trinity, then it is also necessary to accept that the Trinity 'was present in the event of the passion. The Father and the Holy Spirit experienced the salvific drama in deep communion with the suffering Son."

106 Cf. Forte, *Istota chrześcijaństwa*, 70–1.

107 Cf. Bokwa, *Trynitarno-chrystologiczna interpretacja eschatologii*, 200–1.

"The cross, as the history of the Son, the Father and the Spirit, is the trinitarian history of God".[108]

The eternal trinitarian event, in which the Father and the Son give each other the Holy Spirit and are united in Him, is "modalized" on the cross in such a way that, in Jesus' cry, the Holy Spirit (as the bearer of life) is given into God's hands, but this trusting obedience is matched by the Holy Spirit of resurrection (as the "reverse gift" of the Father). For this reason, the relationship between the Father, the Son and the Holy Spirit – since the spatio-temporal life of Jesus ended – has acquired a new "modality": The Son is no longer the Son in the spatial dimension of the world, but "in the glory of the Father".[109]

The impact of past redemptive events on the salvation of people and the world, the living bridge between them and the present experience of redemption, can only be understood by recognising the causality of the triune God and particularly the combined roles of the incarnate and resurrected Christ and the Holy Spirit in their communication with people.[110] The conditions for this effective communication are similar for Christ and the Holy Spirit, but not identical. St. Paul uses the same verb – *exapostellô* (Gal 4:4-6) to describe the sending of the Son and the Holy Spirit, but their missions are different. The Son's mission was related to the Incarnation and acting through Divine authority and nature and through created human authorities. The Holy Spirit does not incarnate or assume a human nature, but acts solely by Divine authority. St. Irenaeus called both "the two hands of God", but the authorities of these hands are radically different.[111]

---

108 Forte, *Istota chrześcijaństwa*, 70–1.

109 Cf. Greshake, *Trójjedyny Bóg. Teologia trynitarna*, 331–3, 351–2.

110 Cf. Bouyer, *Ojciec niewidzialny. Drogi do tajemnicy Boga* (Kraków: Wydawnictwo M, 1998), 254–7. Czaja, (*Jedna Osoba w wielu osobach. Pneumatologiczna eklezjologia Heriberta Mühlena* (Opole: Wydawnictwo Świętego Krzyża, 1997), 381–2) presents H. Mühlen's proposal on this issue: "a concrete example of a brief expression of the revealed truth about the Church is the formulation contained in the encyclical *Mystici Corporis Christi*: 'one mystical person' (*una mystica persona*). He sees its prototype in St. Augustine's utterance of Christ and the Church as 'one and the same person' (*una eademque persona*). From the analysis of his thought, he concludes that the unity of the Head and the members is not the same as the unity of the Son of God and His human nature. In this case, the unity grows out of the mediation of the Holy Spirit. He, one and the same in Christ and Christians, unites all and gives to each the life of Christ that is common to all. Therefore, for the expression of the mystery of the Church, the most adequate formula is: 'One Person (of the Holy Spirit) in many persons (in Christ and Christians)'. Despite its similarity to the conciliar statement of the Holy Spirit as 'one and the same in Head and members' (LG 7), Mühlen's formula has met with great criticism. [...] It has been alleged [...] that it diminishes the role of Christ in the Church and fails to express the distinctiveness of being of the Spirit, of Christ and of Christians."

111 Cf. O'Collins, *Jezus nasz Odkupiciel. Chrześcijańskie ujęcie zbawienia* (Kraków: Wydawnictwo Uniwersytetu Jagiellońskiego, 2009), 178–9; Balthasar, *Teologika*, vol. III: *Duch Prawdy*, 147–9.

The amplification of the human powers of the resurrected Christ, whose power began to exert its full intensity in the new community of believers, does not refer directly to the Holy Spirit. All the Gospels mention the descent of the Holy Spirit upon Jesus at His baptism in the Jordan, but only St. John shows this Spirit "descending and remaining" (John 1:33) on Jesus. Therefore, it is Jesus who "speaks the words of God" and God "gives the Spirit without measure" (John 3:34). God gives the immeasurable gift of the Spirit first to Jesus and through Him to others – thus gifted Jesus will Himself be the source of the Holy Spirit – "Jesus [...] cried out, 'Let anyone who is thirsty come to me, and let the one who believes in me drink. As the scripture has said, Out of the believer's heart shall flow rivers of living water.' Now he said this about the Spirit, which believers in him were to receive; for as yet there was no Spirit, because Jesus was not yet glorified" (John 7:37-39). Jesus was the advocate and representative of the Father, but at the death and resurrection of Jesus, the Holy Spirit will prove to be not only the advocate, spokesperson and representative of Jesus, but also the One who bestows power on Jesus' beloved "community".[112] According to St. Paul, the Spirit is the divine principle or "law" of the new order created by God in Christ or the force enabling to live "according to the Spirit" (cf. Rom 8:1-27). The outpouring of the Spirit (cf. Joel 2:28-29; Luke 2:16-21), which is the essential fruit of Christ's resurrection, is not limited to a single event, but is the power that initiates and continues a certain process.[113]

By raising Jesus from the dead, God apparently gives him back His "spirit", which is now identified with the Divine Spirit, the Spirit of power and glory. Henceforth, the action of the Holy Spirit in the Church would confirm the resurrection of Jesus from the dead and His entry – in human nature – into the sphere of Divine persons, the sphere of the Spirit, God's power and glory. Jesus had to depart so that the Holy Spirit could descend (John 16:7). The resurrection (and ascension) of Christ is not just a Christological event but simultaneously some great epiclesis – the summoning of the Holy Spirit. The resurrected Christ "will ask the Father" to give people "another Advocate", the "Spirit of Truth", who would remain with them forever (John 14:16). In response to this "request" of the first Advocate (cf. 1 John 2:1), the Father grants the Holy Spirit and brings the Church into the sphere of action of eternal Pentecost. The glorified *Kyrios*, to whom all power in heaven and on earth has been given (cf. Matt 28:18), can now Himself send this Spirit from the Father (cf. John 15:26; 16:7). More often, however, Christ's assurance is repeated that the Father would send the Spirit "in his name" to "teach you everything, and remind you of all" (John 14:26) which was the content of His life and preaching.[114]

112 Cf. O'Collins, *Jezus nasz Odkupiciel*, 179–80.

113 Cf. O'Collins, *Jezus nasz Odkupiciel*, 183–4.

114 Cf. Hryniewicz, *Chrystus nasza Pascha*, 370–1.

The resurrection of Jesus was accomplished by the Holy Spirit who is the Giver of life. The life-giving Spirit offers penitent sinners liberation from a state of death (Rom 7:24) and a passage to life and peace; He enables Jesus to be proclaimed Lord (1 Cor 3:2-3), inscribes the image of Christ in human hearts (2 Cor 3:2f.) and takes sanctifying action. He distributes a whole range of gifts to strengthen Christ's Body (1 Cor 12:4-13), joins with Jesus in prayer to the Father, and brings the whole creation to ultimate liberation and transformation (Rom 8:14-30).[115] He is the one who "has been given to us" (Rom 5:5), sent to our hearts (cf. Gal 4:6), "bears witness with our spirit that we are children of God" (Rom 8:16) and imparts profound wisdom (cf. 1 Cor 6-16). The Holy Spirit brings believers to "all the truth": "I still have many things to say to you, but you cannot bear them now. When the Spirit of truth comes, he will guide you into all the truth; for he will not speak on his own, but will speak whatever he hears, and he will declare to you the things that are to come. He will glorify me, because he will take what is mine and declare it to you" (John 16:12-14).[116] The indwelling of the Holy Spirit in man (cf. Rom 8:9-11) and the incorporation of the Holy Spirit into Christ are connected – He has been sent to unite believers with Christ and enable them to live in Him. The Holy Spirit communicates and reveals the presence of the resurrected Christ, awakens faith in Him and prepares hearts to receive Him and give Him a proper response. Chapter 8

115 Cf. O'Collins, *Jezus nasz Odkupiciel*, 184–5. "In the incarnation a unique union of the human nature with the divine nature was accomplished, by which humanity was, in a unique way, deified. The resurrection is the intended consequence, the full realisation and at the same time the most explicit manifestation of this deification. Everything that preceded this transformation was merely a preparation for the birth of the 'new creation' in the resurrected Christ. The humanity of Christ had first to undergo this total transformation itself in order to become – by the power of the Holy Spirit – the source of the total 'novelty' of God's work" (Hryniewicz, *Chrystus nasza Pascha*, 286). "It is about [...]the Church's ontological holiness, that is, its participation in the grace of the Holy Spirit, whose anointing is the indispensable foundation of the Church's existence and communion" (Guzowski, *Duch Dialogujący*, 211).

116 Cf. Balthasar, *Teologika*, vol. III: *Duch Prawdy*, 63: "this does not mean that His earthly instruction must, for external reasons – weaknesses of listening disciples – remain incomplete. This is already contradicted by the fact that the Teacher, the Spirit, fulfils His role essentially as 'remind you of all that I [Jesus] have said to you' (14:26). And when we hear of the Teacher that He 'will speak whatever he hears, and he will declare to you the things that are to come' (16:13), it seems entirely reasonable that by these 'things to come' we should mean first and foremost the future destiny of Jesus, His glorification through the Cross and Resurrection, by which only the Word can be interpreted in its entirety. 'Things to come' in no way imply prophecy in temporal terms, but rather (as in Isa 41:23; 42:23; 44:7) reveal an eschatological dimension, which in the Gospels signifies the ability to read the signs of the times, to recognise the imminence of the end (Matt 24:32f.). 'The whole truth' is therefore not a synthesis of any number of individual truths, but a single truth of teaching about God through the Son in the inexhaustible fullness of His concrete universality." Cf. Balthasar, *Teologika*, vol. III: *Duch Prawdy*, 59–72.

of the Epistle to the Romans shows that by drawing people into the union with the Son, the Holy Spirit gives them the power to love the Father and to return to Him.[117] The inseparability of the Son and the Holy Spirit means that the mission of the Holy Spirit does not replace the mission of the Son, but that both missions have entered a new stage of implementation in which the infinite richness of the relationship of the Son and the Spirit is revealed differently than before.[118]

The inseparable roles of Christ and the Holy Spirit in the act of redemption are most clearly shown in the resurrection and the Eucharist instituted on the eve of the crucial accomplishment of the redemptive work.[119] Christ surrendered Himself completely to His mission in love, and the Father responded by giving the Life-giving Spirit and the immortal life of the resurrection (cf. Rom 8:11-12). Any reflection on the death and resurrection of Jesus without reference to the Father and the Holy Spirit would be theologically impoverished and deaf to the statements of the New Testament, it would also obscure the profound meaning of the mysterious statement in the Epistle to the Hebrews: "the blood of Christ, who through the eternal Spirit offered himself without blemish to God, [will] purify our conscience from dead works to worship the living God" (Heb 9:14). In the resurrection of the crucified Jesus, the manifestation of the triune God reached its peak: "This Jesus God raised up, and of that all of us are witnesses. Being therefore exalted at the right hand of God, and having received from the Father the promise of the Holy Spirit, he has poured out this that you both see and hear" (Acts 2:32-33). Just as the Father and the Holy Spirit were present in the Paschal events, so They are present with the resurrected Christ in the Eucharist which communicates the Paschal mystery to the faithful.[120]

The resurrection of Christ is at the same time the revelation of the Holy Spirit. The fulfilment of the "economy" of the Son of God became the beginning of the "economy" of the Spirit. It is not without reason that the early Church recognised and experienced the Spirit's manifold links with Christ's Pascha. Joy flows from the presence of God's Spirit as "Lord and Life-Giver". The giver of this Spirit is the glorified and exalted Christ who ascended to the Father. The incarnation, cross and resurrection were aimed at the mystery of the personal descent of the Holy Spirit into the human world redeemed by Christ. There is an inseparable link between the mystery of Christ's Pascha and the gift of Pentecost. The resurrection, ascension

117 Cf. O'Collins, *Jezus nasz Odkupiciel*, 185–6.

118 Cf. Balthasar, *Teologika*, vol. III: *Duch Prawdy*, 155.

119 Cf. Balthasar, *Teologika*, vol. III: *Duch Prawdy*, 176–7.

120 Cf. Hryniewicz, *Chrystus nasza Pascha*, 357–61; Kazimierz Matwiejuk, *Liturgiczna celebracja zbawczych ingerencji Boga* (Ząbki: Apostolicum, 2014).

and Pentecost are one mystery of the exaltation of Christ who became the Giver of "the eternal Spirit" (Heb 9:14).[121]

Another way of expressing the dynamic presence of the Holy Spirit in the transmission of new life in Christ presents the image of Christ's ascension. From the theological point of view, the mystery of the Resurrection is identified with the mystery of the Ascension. Of course, this concerns the invisible exaltation and glorification in heaven by the Father, which already took place at the moment of the resurrection. It is the direct consequence and necessary culmination of the resurrection. It is the glorification of Christ, by which He is fully established as the Messiah (Acts 2:36) and "the Son of God with power" (Rom 1:4), able to send the Holy Spirit "from the Father" (John 15:26)[122]. It reveals the predestination of all people to eternal life through participation in the life of the Holy Trinity, which is made possible by the death and resurrection of Christ and the sending of the Holy Spirit. This destiny will be fulfilled to the end when all members of the Body of Christ achieve participation in the life of the Holy Trinity. Through the power of the Holy Spirit, all the people who make up the Body of Christ will ultimately be freed from sin and will joyfully return to the Father.[123]

---

121 Cf. Hryniewicz, *Chrystus nasza Pascha*, 362–3. The author points out that "St. Paul does not show the slightest interest in the question of chronology. According to him, the resurrection of Christ is linked to the Holy Spirit's presence and work. The Father raised the Son from the dead by His Spirit (Rom 8:11). The resurrection is by its very nature a reality inseparable from the Spirit's work, to the extent that the resurrected Christ becomes a 'life-giving spirit' (*pneuma zoopoioún*: 1 Cor 15:45). He is resurrected in a 'spiritual body' (*sóma pneumatikón*: 1 Cor 15:44). The whole new reality of the resurrection is identified, in a way, with the reality of the Spirit: 'Now the Lord is the Spirit' (2 Cor 3:17). The Spirit is not only the instrumental cause of Christ's resurrection from the dead. He is also that new reality into which Christ is introduced by His resurrection from the dead: '[he] was declared to be Son of God with power according to the spirit of holiness by resurrection from the dead' (Rom 1:4). Moreover, 'he was vindicated in spirit' (1 Tim 3:16) throughout his existence, and thus also after his resurrection. The enigmatic text of St. Peter states that 'put to death in the flesh', but 'made alive in the spirit' (*zoopoietheis de pneú nati*: 1 *Pet* 3:18). Henceforth, whoever wishes to live 'in Christ' (*en Christo*) must live at the same time 'in the Spirit' (*en Pneumati*) and according to the demands of the Spirit (cf. Gal 5:16,22,25; 6:1; Rom 8:2,4-5,9,11,14)." (Hryniewicz, *Chrystus nasza Pascha*, 369).

122 Hryniewicz, *Chrystus nasza Pascha*, 363.

123 Cf. O'Collins, *Jezus nasz Odkupiciel*, 187–8. "The relationship of the Holy Spirit to the Paschal mystery is a very fundamental element of Paschal theology. The overcoming of death in the human body of Jesus reveals some immeasurable dynamism and incomprehensible energy of God. They work where the power of the human spirit no longer reaches and where all the achievements of humanity prove powerless. The resurrection of Jesus reveals the power and might of God's Spirit, 'Lord and Life-giver'. It becomes a special 'theological place' (*locus theologicus*) of the divine power of the Spirit, overcoming the reign of death in the world. 'There is only one power of life, the victorious power of resurrection: The Holy Spirit'. The resurrection as the Father's new creative act, manifested in victory over death, was accomplished by the animating power of the Holy Spirit. This

In the Christian experience there is a profound interaction between the Holy Spirit and the resurrected Christ. For St. Paul, the presence of the Holy Spirit "in us" (e. g. Rom 5:5; 8:16) was almost synonymous with being "in Christ" (e. g. Rom 6:3,11,23; 1 Cor 1:30; 3:1). The coming of Christ is associated with the Holy Spirit (cf. Gal 3:1-5), who gives efficacy to the word and strengthens repentance (cf. 1 Thes 1:4-6). Therefore, the Christian experience of the Holy Spirit blends with the experience of the resurrected Christ (cf. 1 Cor 6:11). God's Spirit "in us" seems practically equivalent to "having the Spirit of Christ" or Christ being "in us" (cf. Rom 8:9-11) to such an extent that it is practically difficult to distinguish between Them. However, this does not imply They are identical. It was Jesus who was conceived by the power of the Holy Spirit (cf. Matt 1:20; Luke 1:35), it was the Son who was sent "in the likeness of sinful flesh, and to deal with sin, he condemned sin in the flesh" (Rom 8:3), it was He "who was handed over to death for our trespasses and was raised for our justification" (Rom 4:25), it was His Father who raised Him from the dead (e. g. Gal 1:1), it was He who became "the firstborn within a large family" (Rom 8:29) and "has been raised from the dead, the first fruits of those who have died" (1 Cor 15:20). It is Christ who "holds his priesthood permanently, because he continues forever. Consequently he is able for all time to save those who approach God through him, since he always lives to make intercession for them" (Heb 7:24-25). This intercession "from heaven" differs from that of the Holy Spirit, who "helps us in our weakness; for we do not know how to pray as we ought, but that very Spirit intercedes with sighs too deep for words [...] according to the will of God" (Rom 8:26-27). Therefore, although whole sequences of events and actions are attributed to Jesus or the Holy Spirit, not everything refers to Them interchangeably. Both are revealed, actively communicated in person, but with the specificity of each of Them being preserved.[124]

The Holy Spirit is the Spirit of Christ's resurrection. Through the resurrection He reveals His presence and action in the world, and in this way He reveals his true identity. The descent of the Spirit aims at ultimate fulfilment, just as the ascension is a promise and foreshadowing of Christ's second coming. The power and action of the Spirit are the beginning of this very eschatological fulfilment of history, which is heading towards the final Pentecost. Despite the definitive victory over death, the Church's time is still marked by the earthly kenosis of the Spirit because, as the Spirit of the resurrection, He has been given to the world and is present mysteriously in its history.[125]

power will henceforth operate in a world marked by the presence of sin and death as the principle of new life' (Hryniewicz, *Chrystus nasza Pascha*, 367).

124 Cf. O'Collins, *Jezus nasz Odkupiciel*, 190–2.

125 Cf. Hryniewicz, *Chrystus nasza Pascha*, 367–8.

However, the actions of the resurrected Christ and the Holy Spirit are parallel, complementary and conditional upon each other – especially in the manner of the definitive universalisation of redemption: "All authority in heaven and on earth has been given to me. Go therefore and make disciples of all nations, baptizing them in the name of the Father and of the Son and of the Holy Spirit, and teaching them to obey everything that I have commanded you. And remember, I am with you always, to the end of the age" (Matt 28:18-20). The New Testament also reveals the way in which the Holy Spirit universalises this salvific event of Christ. As the Spirit of love, He communicates life and enlightens the people, who are to form the one Body of Christ, in their pilgrimage to God.[126] This is why in the Pentecost scene, St. Luke portrays the pilgrimage of all nations who are to experience the outpouring of the Holy Spirit, calling all into the communion of Christ (cf. Acts 2:5-11). This Spirit grants life and hope to the entire created world (cf. Rom 8:1-30). Through this action Christ remains lovingly and powerfully present in the Church, humanity and the entire world.[127]

The co-operation of Christ and the Holy Spirit in the salvific work consisted in the fact that, in the passion, the Son offered the blood sacrifice "through the eternal Spirit" (Heb 9:14). This was followed by the transmission of the Holy Spirit from the Father through the Son to the Church, and the Spirit would not speak from Himself, but would continually point to the Son (and the Father). The moment of proximity between the glorified Son and the Holy Spirit becomes most credible in the Eucharist presented as the source of the "one body in Christ" (cf. Rom 12:5). The Holy Spirit also appears as the creator of the Body-Church: "For in the one Spirit we were all baptized into one body […] and we were all made to drink of one Spirit" (1 Cor 12:13). At the moment of His death, the Son gave the Spirit to the Father and to the world – as a trinitarian gift which is the unifying power of the Church, and although Christ is already Lord and Head of the Church, he allows the Holy Spirit to guide Him in His work as He did during His earthly existence.[128]

---

126 Cf. Balthasar, *Teologika*, vol. III: *Duch Prawdy*, 58.

127 Cf. O'Collins, *Jezus nasz Odkupiciel*, 192–3. "The descent of the Spirit and His work in believers has made Christ's presence an internal presence for them henceforth. The descent of the Spirit is thus the mysterious return of the glorified Christ. However, He returns in the Spirit. He is henceforth, by the power of the Spirit, no longer 'before' us, but in us: 'On that day you will know that I am in my Father, and you in me, and I in you' (John 14:20). It is not without reason to suppose that 'that day' is, for Christ's disciples, the day of the descent of the Holy Spirit. For St. John, it is at the same time the day of Christ's resurrection and return to the Father (cf. John 20:22), on which the Paschal gift of the Spirit was given to the disciples. It is only through the Spirit that the presence of the resurrected Christ can be recognised (cf. 1 Cor 12:3). The mystery of Pentecost reveals the lasting meaning of Pascha. It shows what it means for us that Jesus is alive, that the new life has already become a reality for people on earth" (Hryniewicz, *Chrystus nasza Pascha*, 372).

128 Cf. Balthasar, *Teologika*, vol. III: *Duch Prawdy*, 262–6.

The act of sending of the Holy Spirit reveals the theological depth of the events of the cross and resurrection.[129] The Spirit of the Father and of the Son interiorises in believers the salvific event – as the Spirit of Truth, He attests that Jesus is the Son of God who in His historical existence (by "water and blood") came as Saviour (cf. 1 John 5:6). The Holy Spirit also performs the eschatological universalisation of the salvific Paschal event, since God "desires everyone to be saved and to come to the knowledge of the truth" (1 Tim 2:4).[130]

The sending of the Holy Spirit makes the death and resurrection last eternally as an act of God which elevates the whole Paschal mystery to the plane of the eternally lasting "now". Henceforth, the Holy Spirit would actualise and realise in human persons what Christ accomplished for our salvation in the Paschal mystery (cf. John 16:14). Therefore, it can be said that the descent of the Holy Spirit is, in a sense, the culmination and perpetuation of the resurrection (and ascension). The resurrection demands the sending of the Holy Spirit, which is linked to the history of salvation not in some new moment, inherent only in the Spirit, but constitutes an intrinsic dimension of the event of death and resurrection. The paschal mystery is at the same time the beginning of the economy of the Holy Spirit, which in turn becomes the cause of the eternal contemporaneity of Christ's death and resurrection.[131]

The descent of the Holy Spirit gives rise to the New Covenant and a new people, in which the Spirit will represent the mystery of the resurrected Christ. The Holy Spirit restores lost unity, puts an end to the process of division and dispersion, the confusion of languages and the bondage of evil. The gift of tongues no longer divides people but facilitates understanding and reconciliation, which are the beginning of unity (Acts 2:4-12). At the same time, it signifies the sending out to the whole world of the good news that in Christ and the Holy Spirit the Father has reconciled all to Himself (cf. 2 Cor 5:19) and wishes to create a universal unity of people confessing the Lord in the new community of God's people, which is the Church. The vision of the Tower of Babel gives way to the vision of a new unity created by the Spirit but brought about through the voluntary cooperation of human persons, through a personal encounter with the Resurrected One and openness to the Paschal mystery. Experiencing the mystery of Pentecost, the Christian not only recalls the event of

---

129 It was only the gradually developing process of historicising the Paschal mystery that led to its dissection into individual moments and liturgical feasts. However, of far greater significance here is the development of the dogmatic content, in which the Christological and soteriological meaning went hand in hand with the pneumatological meaning. Cf. Hryniewicz, *Nasza Pascha z Chrystusem. Zarys chrześcijańskiej teologii paschalnej – tom 2* (Lublin: TN KUL, 1987), 38–42.

130 Cf. Jagodziński, *Węzłowe zagadnienia chrystologii komunijnej*, 141.

131 Cf. Hryniewicz, *Chrystus nasza Pascha*, 374.

the past, but also experiences its current presence as a privileged moment in which the Church renews its communion with the Holy Spirit.[132]

In connection with the parousia of Jesus Christ, the question of the parousia of the Holy Spirit, which derives from the trinitarian logic of revelation, should also be mentioned. "Being the Father's revelation, the Son and the Holy Spirit are inseparable from each other. According to the Father's will, the Son raises the dead by the power of the Spirit. The parousia of Christ is at the same time the parousia of the Holy Spirit. 'Parousia signifies not only the power of the Incarnation, but also that of Pentecost. It signifies Christ in Glory and Glory in Christ – the manifestation of the Holy Spirit in Him, with Him and through Him'. As the coming of Christ in glory, the parousia is thus also the new and final revelation of the Holy Spirit – a personal and cosmic Pentecost. The Holy Spirit is the glory of the resurrected Christ. This pneumatological thread of Christian eschatology undoubtedly deserves to be brought out of deep oblivion".[133]

2.4 The Pneumatological Dimension of Life in Communion With Christ

In its integral vision of spirituality, contemporary Christian theology tends to give priority to the Holy Spirit who deifies the whole man.[134] Our "communion with the Son" (cf. 1 Cor 1:9) means a participation in Christ given by the Holy Spirit.[135] "Spiritual life means living in the Spirit and according to the Spirit".[136] This thought is based on St. Paul's teaching on the Spirit-induced unity of the Body with Christ. The relationship of the incarnate Son of God to the Father is shared by all who, through faith, are united with Christ by being partakers of His eternal Spirit. Two important theological theses are crucial here – the mediation of the Spirit in the "objective" work of salvation and in the "subjective" reception of it. The Spirit carries out the economy of salvation by overcoming man's opposition, He opens man to receive the gift, makes faith possible and mediates our participation in Jesus' surrender to the Father. It is the Spirit who makes Christ present and brings people to Him and, as the pneumatological mode of existence of the exalted Lord,

132 Cf. Hryniewicz, *Chrystus nasza Pascha*, 376–7.

133 Hryniewicz, *Pascha Chrystusa w dziejach człowieka i wszechświata*, 363.

134 Cf. Guzowski, *Duch Dialogujący*, 285–6.

135 Cf. Werbick, *Den Glauben verantworten. Eine Fundamentaltheologie* (Freiburg-Basel-Wien: Herder, 2000), 778.

136 Congar, *Wierzę w Ducha Świętego. "Panem jest Duch i daje życie" (2 Kor 3,17)*, vol. II, (Warszawa: Wydawnictwo Księży Marianów, 1995), 124.

the Spirit makes the personal encounter with Christ possible, communicates and extends what He Himself has caused in Christ.[137]

> Whoever encounters God in the Holy Spirit, [...] participates in a trinitarian unity that does not nullify the richness of persons and does not destroy separateness; moreover, He is immersed in the movement of love, which is the ecstasy of God from Himself, so that man too can live 'ecstatically' directed towards His God. By the power of the Holy Spirit, the revelation, which culminated in the fullness of the Word, is made present at all times, always ancient and always new, so that the transcendence and openness inherent in the Divine encounter leads to a growing understanding of what is already given, to an exploration of what is hidden in what is revealed. In this way, the revelation releases inexhaustible energies of light and life....[138]

In the East, deification,[139] and in the West, sanctification are essentially synonymous terms; however, deification makes it clear that God's presence in relation to the human person is internal – the salvific and transforming dialogue takes place within the human person and within the Church. Already in the baptismal waters we become deified, and our whole life is based on a covenant guaranteed by the person of the Holy Spirit who always anticipates and prepares us for a salvific dialogue and lasting union. Western theology of grace conveys the same profound mystery of human transformation as the one proclaimed in the theology of deification. Mystics and religious writers have used symbols from everyday life to illustrate the penetrating grace of the Holy Spirit and His transforming power. The human person penetrated by the fire of the Spirit[140] was compared to a glowing iron that

137 Cf. Czaja, *Credo in Spiritum Vivificantem*, 109–12. "In liberation theology, following Jesus is seen as the essence of Christian spirituality. [...] The essence of this pilgrimage consists in 'encountering Christ, living in the Spirit and walking towards the Father'. [...] In turn, the Spirit makes it possible to follow Jesus, opens man to the future and to the new history, in which God is present and constantly reveals Himself in the signs of the times. Moreover, it helps to create history according to the spirit of Jesus. Therefore, the spirituality of liberation is understood as a participation in the history of God Himself received by Him in Jesus Christ and in the Holy Spirit" (Gardocki, *Teologia wyzwolenia*, 289).

138 Forte, *Istota chrześcijaństwa*, 95.

139 See Krzysztof Leśniewski, "Przebóstwienie człowieka w teologii prawosławnej," in *Kościół i człowiek*, ed. Andrzej A. Napiórkowski (Kraków: Salwator, 2021), 191–208.

140 This symbolism is referred to in a contemporary song about the Holy Spirit – "Duchu Ogniu, Duchu Żarze," the text of which is an excellent illustration of His action. English translation of the Polish text: "Ref. Spirit of Fire, Spirit of Embers, Spirit of Light, Spirit of Brilliance, Spirit of Wind and Fire, send forth the flame of your grace. 1 You want, kindle and set afire, you will raise hearts high: you will cast a torchlight into the darkness and dispel the darkness of sin. [...] 4. Your approach will blush us with the pulse of life, the growth of trembling. We will be born anew, darkness will become a ray" (Wanda Łakowicz – Polish text, Gabriela Rzechowska – music,

does not lose its nature. The image of the Spirit permeating the world of spirits created to resemble the radiance of the sun permeating and illuminating the air is similarly expressive. The indwelling of the Holy Spirit in man is the uncreated grace of God, but to speak of grace in separation from the Holy Spirit risks objectifying it, especially when we disconnect its effect from the personal action of the Spirit. The Spirit of Christ imprinted in the soul works synergistically with natural human faculties to transform human life. This new life is made visible in many ways, and we can develop it in the Holy Spirit. Through this, the fruit of the Spirit blossoms (Gal 5:22). Endowed with life in the Spirit and His gifts, people become persons that are subject to God and therefore free from the temptations of the flesh (2 Cor 3:17; cf. Gal 5:13,18; Rom 8:2,14). This freedom is neither mere assent nor mere conformity to an external law, but a complete convergence of desire and will with the love of God and is evident in the life of the Christian community. The Holy Spirit is the active presence of God in man, deepening the inner life and leading to communion with others. The natural desire to live in a relationship with others is raised to a superhuman level. This communion does not result in a confusion of beings, because the Spirit deepens the unique human being of a person, at the same time uniting people in love for one another. The communion in the Holy Spirit is evident in the communion of saints and in the performance of ordinary daily commitments. In the Spirit we can live together in love (cf. 1 Cor 13:4-5).[141]

The Holy Spirit supports the spiritual life of the Church and of all Christians. The New Testament speaks of the "divine life" imparted by Him in forms that are diverse and convergent at the same time. The first of these is adoption. St. Paul wrote: "you have received a spirit of adoption. When we cry, 'Abba! Father!' It is that very Spirit bearing witness with our spirit that we are children of God" (Rom 8:15-16). Then he reiterated: "And because you are children, God has sent the Spirit of his Son into our hearts, crying, 'Abba! Father!'" (Gal 4:6). This was also the experience of St. John: "See what love the Father has given us, that we should be called children of God; and that is what we are" (1 John 3:1). In this intimate experience, which makes us call God "our Father" according to the prayer Jesus taught us (Matt 6:9), the Holy Spirit does not appear, but He turns us towards the Father and gives us the awareness that we are His children.[142]

This adoption is not some external or juridical phenomenon, but is a presence, an indwelling. The Spirit of God dwells in you, writes the Apostle Paul (Rom 8:9,11; 1 Cor 3:16; 2 Tim 1:14), thus we are the temple of the Holy Spirit (1 Cor 6:19) and

---

"Duchu Ogniu, Duchu Żarze," in *Exsultate Deo. Śpiewnik mszalny. Wydanie siódme*, ed. Gisela Maria Skop (Carlsberg-Lublin, 1994), 193.

141 Cf. Guzowski, "Komunijna i dialogiczna struktura osoby. Perspektywa teologiczno-antropologiczna," in *Kościół i człowiek*, ed. Napiórkowski (Kraków: Salwator, 2021), 84–7.

142 Cf. Laurentin, *Nieznany Duch Święty*, 422–4.

more generally the temple of God (1 Cor 3:16-17; 2 Cor 6:16). The three Persons are inseparable, but the New Testament emphasises the special closeness of the Holy Spirit – spiritual indwelling – which does not mean it is unreal. St. Paul, similarly to St. John (3:3-7), does not speak of some sort of adoption of lesser value: "we should be called children of God; and that is what we are", he emphasises (1 John 3:1). This refers to the actual new birth (*palingenesia*) (Titus 3:5-7, Matt 19:28). "He saved us [...] according to his mercy, through the water of rebirth and renewal by the Holy Spirit. This Spirit he poured out on us richly through Jesus Christ our Savior, so that, having been justified by his grace, we might become heirs according to the hope of eternal life" (cf. Eph 5:26; 1 Pet 1:3 – "new birth" here has an eschatological meaning). God the Father saves us by being born in Jesus Christ (baptism), which is accomplished by the Holy Spirit identifying us with Jesus Christ. The progression of this adoption, together with the "inheritance", is expressed by Paul with the words: "justification", "sanctification", "revival" (2 Cor 3-6; cf. John 6:33; 1 Pet 3:18) and derived expressions. The apostle places particular emphasis on sanctification by the Holy Spirit. "But you were washed, you were sanctified, you were justified in the name of the Lord Jesus Christ and in the Spirit of our God" (1 Cor 6:11) – God (the Father) sanctifies us through the Spirit in the name of the Lord Jesus. This is a personal encounter, as in 1 Cor 12:4-6 and elsewhere.[143]

All these expressions testify to the deification,[144] as Christ Himself says (John 10:34-35) formally – albeit using an *ad hominem* argument: "Is it not written in your law, 'I said, you are gods'? If those to whom the word of God came were called 'gods'— and the scripture cannot be annulled [...]". Jesus juxtaposes the true sons of God with those who morally are sons of the devil. God's sonship is not only moral, it is also ontological – the disciples are one living being with Him: "I am the vine, you are the branches" (John 15:5). Paul defines deification in terms of knowing: "For now we see in a mirror, dimly, but then we will see face to face. Now I know only in part; then I will know fully, even as I have been fully known" (1 Cor 13:12). Paul speaks of knowledge in terms of identification and John states similarly: "What we will be has not yet been revealed. What we do know is this: when he is revealed, we will be like him, for we will see him as he is" (1 John 3:2). It is impossible to see God without one's nature fully being conformed to Him. Paul spoke on the same subject before the Areopagite, referring to the writings of Aratus. The unknown God, whom he proclaims in Jesus Christ, "does not live in shrines made by human hands [...] he himself gives to all mortals life and breath and all things. From one ancestor he made all nations to inhabit the whole earth [...] so

143 Cf. Laurentin, *Nieznany Duch Święty*, 424–5.

144 See Leon Siwecki, *Człowiek odczytany w Bogu Ojcu. Teologiczno-antropologiczne refleksje w nauczaniu Jana Pawła II* (Lublin: Wydawnictwo KUL, 2020), 40–6.

that they would search for God and perhaps grope for him and find him—though indeed he is not far from each one of us. For 'In him we live and move and have our being'; as even some of your own poets have said, 'For we too are his offspring'" (Acts 17:24-28).[145]

John Paul II wrote about this in his encyclical *Dominum et Vivificantem:*

> through the Holy Spirit God exists in the mode of gift. It is the Holy Spirit who is the personal expression of this self-giving, of this being-love. He is Person-Love. He is Person-Gift. Here we have an inexhaustible treasure […] At the same time, the Holy Spirit, being consubstantial with the Father and the Son in divinity, is love and uncreated gift from which derives as from its source (*fons vivus*) all giving of gifts vis-a-vis creatures (created gift): […] the gift of grace to human beings through the whole economy of salvation. As the Apostle Paul writes: 'God's love has been poured into our hearts through the Holy Spirit which has been given to us' (Rom 5:5).[146]

145 Cf. Laurentin, *Nieznany Duch Święty*, 426–31.

146 John Paul II, Encyclical *Dominum et Vivificantem*, 10. How God's involvement in our lives respects His transcendence. If the three Persons of the Trinity are one being and act identically to being Love, how can man come into personal contact with each of the Persons – here: with the Holy Spirit? R. Laurentin cites St. Thomas Aquinas, who explained that the identity of being does not prevent a differentiated relationship: "In God, each of the Persons enters indeed into a personal relationship with each of the Christians whom They indwell, just as They remains in a true personal relationship with the other two Persons. This multiplication of relations does not multiply a being but relates it. – In us, the peculiarity of the Spirit's action is not due to a difference in His action towards us, as if there were some division of work in the Trinity, but this communication bears the personal mark of each of the three Persons, according to their place in the Trinity; – The Father as Source has the initiative of mercy; – The Son as Word structures the creation; He came to save us from within, and we are identified with Him as children of the same Father; – The Holy Spirit, the Spirit of Love, gives us our own existence on the plane of nature and divine life on the plane of grace. It is through Him that we receive life from the Father and the Son" (Laurentin, *Nieznany Duch Święty*, 433). How does God deify us without losing anything of His divinity? The change takes place in an order of relationship "which does not change God's being, does not degenerate, does not transform our being, but completes it, according to the gratuitous and profound aspirations which God has placed in us and which we can measure only with difficulty, since the tremendous love of God, which lies at the source of this marvellous loving design, completely surpasses us. [...] Precisely because this fulfilment is internal and spiritual, and because it lies in the order of holiness, it depends on the Holy Spirit, according to His proper function in creation and in the order of grace. His role corresponds to His final position in the Trinity, which gives Him the most direct contact with the chosen ones, so that He causes the life of love of the Father and the Son to permeate them and be completed in Him. In this way, He stimulates everything from within the created being: this is what constitutes the difference between human production and divine creation" (Laurentin, *Nieznany Duch Święty*, 436).

Through the death of Jesus, the Holy Spirit "became" something that He had not been in this sense before. According to St. Paul, He became a "life-giving Spirit", just as the first Adam became a "living being" (cf. 1 Cor 15:45). Thus, with the historical event of the resurrection, the history of Jesus enters a new stage, and the history of the Holy Spirit also enters a new stage – played out externally as part of the expansion of Christ into the dimensions of the new people of God. From the incarnation until the death of Jesus, the Holy Spirit dwelt in Him as in a temple and accompanied His works; He had His history in the earthly Jesus. From the death of Jesus until the indefinite future, thanks to the fact that Jesus merited Him by shedding His blood and sent Him to earth, He has His earthly history in the history of the Church. As one and the same in the historical Jesus, in the glorified Lord and in the Church, his Body, He "expands" Christ by mediating the inclusion of Christians in Jesus' "fullness of the Spirit". This makes it possible to speak of the Church as "continuously living Christ", since the Holy Spirit present in the Church is not merely a substitute for Christ but is His presence, and by his unchanging continuance in time into the farthest future, He enables the work of salvation once accomplished by Christ to continue. In the Holy Spirit, the one-time person and work of Christ achieve universal efficacy and can be historically experienced by human beings. From His outpouring upon the disciples, the Spirit is always the Spirit of Christ, making His word and work present in history, friendship and communion with Christ. Through Him we can commune with Christ as Head of the Church.[147]

The Holy Spirit, as the Spirit of Christ (Rom 8:9; Gal 4:6; Phil 1:19), is the presence of the efficacious radiating power of the exalted Lord (cf. 2 Cor 3:17). He not only makes us realise who Jesus Christ is, but also represent His spiritual fullness. In Him we experience Christ as also present in the community today. He is the centre and the force providing access to Jesus Christ, allowing us to experience Him as the new Lord of the world, He is the personal environment of salvation.[148] What was accomplished once and for all in Jesus Christ is continued (cf. LG 48) by the Holy Spirit dwelling in the Church and in the hearts of believers (cf. AG 4) – it is realised from within and spread (cf. LG 4). His task is to integrate the reality of the world with the reality of Jesus Christ, or to universalise the reality of Jesus Christ. The Holy Spirit is the principle of the universalisation and assimilation of Christ's salvific mediation. Through "the Spirit of the Lord" (2 Cor 3:18) Christ can be and is the quintessence, culmination, reconciliation and mediation of all things. In love, the Father imparts Himself on the Son, and in the Spirit this love becomes Their inner freedom, which can impart itself externally. In the Spirit, however, the opposite

147 Cf. Czaja, *Credo in Spiritum Vivificantem*, 113–5.

148 Cf. Czaja, *Credo in Spiritum Vivificantem*, 116.

movement simultaneously takes place – the creation filled with the Spirit becomes in freedom the historical person through which the Son gives Himself to the Father. This devastating surrender of self "liberates" the Spirit from its particular historical form, so that Jesus' death and resurrection are at the same time a foreshadowing of the coming mediation of the Spirit (cf. John 16:7; 20:22). Thus Jesus Christ, who mediates between God and man in the Holy Spirit, through the Spirit becomes the universal mediator of salvation.[149]

From the words "Now the Lord is the Spirit, and where the Spirit of the Lord is, there is freedom" (2 Cor 3:17), it follows that Christ is present in the form of freedom – the Holy Spirit has a certain freedom and sovereignty.[150] LG 8 teaches that the work embodied by the Holy Spirit in close analogy resembles the mystery of the Incarnate Word. He is "another Paraclete", continuing the story of Jesus and His mission, but it is not an extension of the mystery of the Incarnation. "Another Paraclete" realises the historico-salvific anointing of Jesus as a mediator towards his "fullness". Furthermore, He is not only sent, but also gives Himself. He acts in His own proper way during the time of anticipation of Christ's second coming, arousing the faith that precedes baptism.[151] One cannot agree to completely identify the work of the Spirit with the work of Christ. According to the Scriptures, the Spirit expands the order of creation and salvation and thus opens the most universal perspective; He is the creative and continually re-creating power which, through Jesus Christ, progressively brings everything to eschatological fulfilment. He is not only the Spirit of Redemption, but also the Spirit of Creation. St. Irenaeus wrote that He makes Jesus constantly present in His newness.[152]

The whole essential content of what God has given to people in Jesus Christ is made present in our communication with Him, which takes place in the Holy Spirit

149 Cf. Czaja, *Credo in Spiritum Vivificantem*, 115–6.

150 Cf. Hryniewicz, *Nasza Pascha z Chrystusem*, 95–6. "The Holy Spirit is not the Spirit of the Church. He is and will remain forever the sovereign Spirit of God, the Spirit of Christ. The Son of God was sent into the world. God sends his Spirit continually into human hearts (Gal 4:4-6). The One who penetrates the depths of God (1 Cor 2:10) comes into direct contact with the human spirit and penetrates the intimate depths of humanity without violating them. The bodies of men become His tabernacle (1 Cor 6:19). Each human person is a unique reality, diverse, immeasurably rich, endowed with its own sensitivity and its own experience. No one else but the Spirit of God can unify from within so many separate consciousnesses. He does this not in spite of diversity, but precisely through and by means of it. This unifying action of the Holy Spirit brought the Church Fathers to a state of awe and thanksgiving. This work can only be accomplished by Him, the transcendent, omnipresent Spirit, permeating everything from within and filling everything; the One who respects human freedom and yet has the power to inspire and transform from within" (Hryniewicz, *Nasza Pascha z Chrystusem*, 96–7).

151 Cf. Czaja, *Credo in Spiritum Vivificantem*, 116–7.

152 Cf. Czaja, *Credo in Spiritum Vivificantem*, 118–9.

as the medium of this communication.[153] Prayer is a conscious effort to enter in a relationship with God. The Holy Spirit plays a central role in the relationship between man and God, since it is only in Him that a relationship with the Creator (God-Father) or Jesus Christ (God-Son) is possible. A direct relationship with God the Father or God the Son is unthinkable without the Holy Spirit. It is only in the Holy Spirit that God the Father is recognisable as Creator and Jesus the man as Christ. Just as the Holy Spirit is an intra-trinitarian relationship between the Father and the Son, so He represents the relational space between God and man. However, the Holy Spirit cannot be understood as an impersonal medium – He has a personal character and His own personal identity. Therefore, it is understandable to address the Holy Spirit as "Lord". Since the Holy Spirit is a personal relationship (intra-trinitarian), prayer is also not possible without Him and independently of Him. Therefore, Christian prayer must always be understood only in a trinitarian way. The Christian always prays to the Father with the Son in the Holy Spirit. Consequently, every prayer is a corresponding oscillation and imitation of an intrinsically trinitarian relational movement, and through it the Holy Spirit receives man into the relationship of the Father with the Son.[154]

The Holy Spirit constitutes a kind of mediating power in and through which Jesus most fully "enters" into man and becomes a universal reality. As part of the implementation of this process, the Church develops as the sacrament of salvation – which is thus also the sacrament of the Holy Spirit (M. Kehl). In men formed in the likeness of the incarnate Son, in the Holy Spirit, the Church achieves its basic shape of a historico-social space of love, a sacrament of divine communion.[155]

The Church derives from God's selection, from Christ's redemption and from sanctification by the Holy Spirit. The Church is not so much communal as communional in nature, and it is communion that is its fundamental dimension, which gives it its mystical character and makes it the Body of Christ. The Spirit of Christ animates and unites people in a community. He is the soul of the Church, constantly recalling the teachings of Christ and his salvific work, thus making it last in the history of the Church (cf. John 14:26). As the Spirit of Truth, he leads the faithful to the fullness of the truth and supports them in acting in accordance with the truth they have learned (cf. John 15:26; 16:13). "The Holy Spirit works extremely

153 Cf. Czaja, *Credo in Spiritum Vivificantem*, 119–20.

154 Cf. Keppler, "Der Heilige Geist – tatsächlich Gott, Person und Herr?," 187.

155 A related formulation can also be found by Gisbert Greshake. Realised in Christ, the perfect, indissoluble unity of man with God is brought into us by the Holy Spirit and made part of our life. As the Spirit of Christ, He realises in us such an inner likeness and giftedness ("new heart") which makes the "external" form of Christ and His "external" invitation to communion the inner form of the believer's life: "and it is no longer I who live, but it is Christ who lives in me" (Gal 2:20). Cf. Czaja, *Credo in Spiritum Vivificantem*, 120.

discreetly. He in no way restricts human freedom, on the contrary – He enlightens and strengthens it inconspicuously, He is invisible to the human eye as the growth and development of any plant which, thanks to the vital force develops to its fullness – its flower and fruit. The Holy Spirit initiates man's spiritual life and continues to sustain it, so that it may develop according to the will of the merciful Father and in the likeness of Christ. Therefore, without the Holy Spirit, neither the process of initiation of the individual man into the Christian life, nor the development of this life, nor the dynamism and self-sacrificing activity of the faithful in the community of the People of God can be understood".[156]

The Holy Spirit endows man with a new life – a life "in Christ" and a life "in the Spirit" – it is a life given by Christ as the exalted Lord in the Holy Spirit. The history of salvation cannot be understood without the participation of the Church in the Spirit of Jesus. Through the outpouring of the Spirit, Christ makes it possible for people to share in Him, in the fullness of grace embodied by the Spirit in Christ. From the moment of baptism, people share in the anointing of the Holy Spirit and through it they share Jesus' experience of the Spirit. He continually comes and gives people a share in the personal holiness of Jesus, in His divine sonship. He gives fulfilment to the deepest human longing, realises the new kind of being initiated by Christ. He leads people to resurrection by endowing them with the existence of a child of God. Through Him and in Him people are received into the communion of the Father and the Son, they are reborn and renewed in Christ.[157]

The Christians' existence is realised as "being in Christ" (2 Cor 5:21; Rom 14:12), i. e. in the sphere of influence of the Divine Kyrios. It shapes not only the ontic

---

156 Henryk Wejman, "Kościół wspólnotą zasłuchaną w słowo Boże," in *O Kościele Jezusa Chrystusa dzisiaj. Księga pamiątkowa dedykowana Księdzu Doktorowi Wojciechowi Wójtowiczowi*. ed. Sienkiewicz (Koszalin-Poznań: Pallottinum, 2020), 328.

157 Cf. Czaja, *Credo in Spiritum Vivificantem*, 121–2. Mühlen postulates a revision of the traditional theories of reception (assumption) or incorporation (inclusion), which assume that all human beings are "received" or "incorporated" into the one human nature of Jesus and they are united into one general person in the hypostatic union. The doctrine of inclusion was known to the Church Fathers but is not confirmed in the Scriptures. This does not mean that it is impossible to speak of the incorporation of all human beings into the humanity of Christ at all (cf. 1 Cor 15:45). The Incarnation is the real beginning of salvation, because at the moment of Jesus' anointing with the Holy Spirit, all were incorporated into the fullness of grace to which He is entitled. One can therefore speak not of direct but of pneumatological inclusion or assumption. Cf. ibid., 123–124; Czaja quotes H. Pottmeyer: "The pre-Paschal circle of disciples is not yet the Church, because Jesus is still singular. Having transcended historical existence through His death and resurrection, Jesus exists eschatologically. In this existence, from an individual Body he can become a spiritual Body. The Holy Spirit realises this eschatological existence; He makes Jesus present in the many and brings these many together in communion. In this way he is the co-constituting principle of the Church; together with Christ He co-creates the Church" (Czaja, *Credo in Spiritum Vivificantem*, 124).

condition of the Christians, but also their ethical orientation – in Christ can abide only those who allow themselves to be defined by the "Spirit" and not by the "flesh" (cf. Gal 5:13-26). Accordingly, the whole man touched by God abides "in Christ" (Rom 8:1), but also "in the Holy Spirit" (Rom 8:9), or more precisely "by the Holy Spirit in Christ", since from the moment of the resurrection man meets Christ in the Holy Spirit, and the Holy Spirit leads him to Christ.[158]

When the Scriptures speak of grace, the word primarily means God's benevolence, His love, which transforms and makes those whom He loves better.[159] Does God's created grace deify us? In a sense it does, for everything comes from God's supreme love, which creates in us a relationship that is real and alive. God loves us, comes inside us, unites us to Himself and identifies us with Himself. This love makes us participate in His life and He participates in ours. He therefore deifies us, but He lives less in us than we live in Him, as Paul says: "It is no longer I who live, but it is Christ who lives in me" (Gal 2:20). It is not we who bind God to us, but it is He who places us in the orbit of His Divinity, His perichoresis, as Paul and John express well when they speak of our life in God and God's life in us. And it is God's gift – the Holy Spirit, Love – that gives us the inspiration and makes us live and express this relationship that incorporates us into the Trinity itself.[160]

If man "allows" himself to be embraced by the Holy Spirit as a reciprocal reference of the Father and the Son, he is received "into" the Holy Spirit. This is why the Bible contains statements referring to the gift of the Holy Spirit as "receiving the Holy Spirit" and "being filled by the Holy Spirit". Since He is the "communion" mediating between the Father and the Son, the reception of man into it is also done on the basis of communion and itself generated communion. The Holy Spirit as Communion in God is the proper theological foundation of ecclesial communion, and it is precisely because of this that the community of the Church is fundamentally different from other communities. The prior gift of the common "life-space" of faith in the Church is thus not based on human striving for communion, but on the gift of the Holy Spirit, i. e. on the gift of participation in a pre-existing communion

---

158 Cf. Czaja, *Credo in Spiritum Vivificantem*, 124. The author cites, after B.J. Hilberath, an interesting metaphor of the Syriac Fathers concerning the birth of the Church from the pierced side of Christ, which does not interpret this fact from the Christologic-sacramental, but pneumatological perspective. The Church is not born directly from the side of the Crucified One, but is formed by the Holy Spirit, who was taken out of the side of the Logos as His rib. Just as Eve was created from Adam's rib and became the mother of life, so the Spirit as the 'rib of the Logos' is the Mother of new life who gathers all those born of her into the new community of life of the Church. Thus, it is neither the Church nor Mary, but the Holy Spirit who is analogous to Eve as mother of life. Cf. Czaja, *Credo in Spiritum Vivificantem*, 127–8.

159 See Siwecki, *Człowiek odczytany w Bogu Ojcu*, 32–9.

160 Cf. Laurentin, *Nieznany Duch Święty*, 436–7.

in God.[161] Therefore, the man of the Holy Spirit is the man of Communion, which is the Holy Spirit in God, and the man of the Church, which is a communion.[162]

> The personal uniqueness of man can only be guaranteed on the condition of being in relation to the eternally loving God. The personalisation of a human being through union with Christ in baptism can only take place in the Holy Spirit. Baptism marks the transition of existence from the 'truth' of being as an *individuum* towards the truth of personal being. The new birth is needed for existential truth to become personal and communal truth. The Holy Spirit as 'Power' and 'Giver of Life' opens the baptised one to relational existence. Christ comes to people as individuals and unites them to Himself so that they become persons open to relationships with other beings. Through baptism, a human being becomes a true person on the ecstatic and hypostatic level. The Church is not only the Body of Christ into which the faithful are implanted, but also the mother who gives birth to ecclesial persons. This birth takes place in the Spirit 'from the womb of the Church' and through community[163].

Life in communion would not be possible without the action of the Holy Spirit (cf. John 3:5; 14:16-18,26; 16:13-14; Rom 8:9; 1 Cor 12:3; 2 Cor 3:17; Gal 4:6). He anointed Jesus for messianic activity, and the glorified Christ sent Him to His disciples. In this light, man can perceive the specific dimensions of the work of the Holy Spirit (cf. Gal 4:4-6), while being created in Christ and the gift of being "incarnated" in Him through the Holy Spirit are distinct and interconnected dimensions of God's salvific plan. The Christian participates in the eternal sonship of the Incarnate Word, which is sustained and animated by the Holy Spirit who, as in the communication and communion between the Father and the Son, sustains and animates this sonship. Through baptism (cf. Rom 6:3-5; Gal 3:26-28) and the Eucharist (cf. 1 Col 10:16; 12:12), perceived as incarnation in the Church, a personal bond of living communion with the Son of God (cf. 1 Cor 1:9) and the Holy Spirit (cf. 2 Cor 13:13; Phil 2:3) is created; the reality of justification – as incarnation in Christ through the Holy Spirit – is expressed in the New Testament with the terms: "rebirth", "new birth" and "new creation".[164]

The idea of the new birth or birth in the Spirit was associated in the early Church with baptism. On the one hand, the deeper significance of baptism for the Christian life was associated with the death of "the old person", i. e. the way in which personal identity was acquired through biological birth. On the other hand, it was associated

161 Cf. Jagodziński, "Teologia komunijna. Człowiek Ducha Świętego," in *Kościół i człowiek*, 100–1.

162 Cf. Jagodziński, "Teologia komunijna. Człowiek Ducha Świętego," 102

163 Jagodziński, "Personalistyczno-komunijne wymiary kolegialności – synodalności w Kościele," *Studia Teologii Dogmatycznej* 5 (2019), 50–1.

164 Cf. Jagodziński, "Teologia komunijna. Człowiek Ducha Świętego," 102–3.

with birth, i. e. the emergence of identity through a new set of relationships provided by the Church as a communion of the Holy Spirit. While biological identity is always linked to necessity, spiritual birth involves freedom – a spiritual person acts differently from a physical person (1 Cor 2:14) – its personal identity is constituted in the freedom from the necessities of nature. The new identity conferred "in the Spirit" is constituted by incorporation into the Body of Christ, the Church, through a new set of relationships identical to Christ's relationship to the Father, and for this reason, baptism equates to obtaining the privilege of calling God "Father". "The new man" has no father on earth but "in heaven" (Matt 23:9) and his "brothers" are members of the Church; the new man has no citizenship on earth but in heaven (Phil 3:11), since his "city" will be the "future" (Heb 13:14) Kingdom. This was the existential meaning of baptism as the "death" of the "old" person and the birth of the "new" eschatological person. Against this background, we must also assess the significance of the Eucharist for Christian spirituality. The Eucharist gave positively what baptism meant negatively – the death of the old biological identity was replaced by the birth of a new identity given in the Eucharistic community. Because the old biological identity is based on natural necessity, it leads to death; the new identity given in the Eucharist gives eternal life. The Eucharist is eternal life primarily because it offers the very set of relationships that entail an eternal identity. Belonging to the Eucharistic community is therefore tantamount to obtaining eternal life. Christian spirituality is thus an ecclesial experience, not an individual one.[165] Therefore, without participation in Eucharistic communion there is no salvation. This is another way of expressing what the fourth Gospel emphasises – that unless we eat the flesh and drink the blood of the Son of Man, we cannot have life. But according to the same Gospel, it is the Holy Spirit who gives life, and thus it is the communion and fellowship of the Spirit – the Church that provides the proper context for spiritual life.[166]

Writing about the eschatological trinitarian perspective, J. Moltmann noted that God's historical presence among the people makes it possible to find the perichoresis of time that is in progress – His future in the present and the present in His future. If we understand Christ perichoretically as person and as space, we can discover in this formula both communion with Christ and His living space. If we "are in Christ", He is the space of the believers' life, the space of the new creation. Christians no longer live egocentrically, but eccentrically – in Christ. However, St. Paul states: "it is no longer I who live, but it is Christ who lives in me" (Gal 2:20), and this is already the other side of this relationship. Together with the experience of communion with Christ, and similarly in terms of structure, we also experience the presence of

165 Cf. Zizioulas, *The One and the Many*, 153–4.
166 Cf. Zizioulas, *The One and the Many*, 158.

the Holy Spirit – in the same perspective, He is person and space at the same time. If we are "in the Holy Spirit", we experience Him as an life-giving field of power, an illuminating light, a warming current of love, an embracing whirlwind. On the other hand, we discover God's Spirit "in us" – He is a person and we are His space in the world, the body and temple of the living Spirit who animates everything. In summary, it must be said that we are "in the Spirit" – here are our persons and the Spirit of our living space; God's Spirit is "in us" – here is the person of the Spirit, and we are His living space and His dwelling.[167]

2.5 The Pneumatological Dimension of Theology

Theology begins with reverence for God and the experience of communion with Him. The Church's task is to state how the teaching handed down in the Scriptures and the doctrine is to be understood and how to develop it in each situation.[168] Christian teaching must be in harmony with the historical revelation of Christ and His future coming in glory, and the preservation of this unity and the transformation of the past and the future is the special task of the Holy Spirit. The fulfilment of this task consists neither in mechanical or magical intervention nor in the perfecting of the human spirit, but in leading to a communion centred on the community that has horizontal and vertical dimensions. This is what the ecclesial work of the Holy Spirit consists in, the fruit of which is always the communion of Christ.[169]

We must decisively free ourselves from the widespread thinking that the Holy Spirit works in isolated individuals and then leaves them in the same state. It was in the Old Testament that the Spirit was given to individuals, prophets and kings, not to the whole people. In the New Testament, the Messiah gives the Holy Spirit to the whole people of God (St. Luke refers to the prophecy of Joel in his description of Pentecost, cf. Acts 2:17-18). The Holy Spirit with His charisms and gifts is therefore possessed by all the baptised, not just some. St. Paul rejected any elitism in his First Epistle to the Corinthians, claiming that even if someone had faith so great that

---

167 Cf. Moltmann, "Der dreieinige Gott," 193–4.

168 Cf. Zizioulas, *Lectures*, 7–8. See Jagodziński, "Pneumatologiczny wymiar Kościoła i teologii według Johna D. Zizioulasa," *Studia Teologii Dogmatycznej* 6 (2020), 11–21.

169 Cf. Zizioulas, *Lectures*, 10; Jagodziński, "Pneumatologiczny wymiar Kościoła i teologii według Johna D. Zizioulasa", 33–35; Małecki, "Kościół jako 'communio' w relacyjnej eklezjologii Johna D. Zizioulasa," *Studia Włocławskie* 1 (1998), 87: "The Church is the Body of Christ, but at the same time the space of the Holy Spirit. It is He, the Third Person of the Holy Trinity, who, by raising Christ from the dead, makes Him an eschatological person, already existing intrinsically with His Body, i. e. the Church. In this way, just as at the beginning of the mystery of the Incarnation, the Spirit brought Jesus into history, so now, through the Resurrection, He appears to free Him from its framework."

he could "move mountains" and had no love, he would be nothing.[170] The breath of the Holy Spirit always brings with it the end of individualism and elitism and creates communion. It is He who convenes the community and all His gifts serve the unity of the Church community. The revelation of truth always brings with it something of the communion of Christ. Christian teaching always points to this communion and teaches that communion means also to abide in the truth.[171]

The truth of God's revelation is an empirical reality in the body of the Church, which rejoices in the relationship of the Son to the Father. This relationship – constituting the community and forming the body of the Church – is actualised by the Spirit who reveals God in the world.[172] Truth is revealed and secured – and, in this sense, infallible – only when we submit to the communion of the Holy Spirit and are incorporated into the body of the Church,[173] for God does not exist outside the communion of the Holy Spirit and the love created by Him.[174]

The Holy Spirit acts within the framework of visibly graspable history and, remaining "hidden", never reveals His own face within the economy of salvation (He always remains, as it were, "in the shadows") while contributing to the fulfilment of God's plan of salvation. This is why Orthodox theologians speak of the "kenosis of the Holy Spirit"[175] or the "self-concealment" of His own face. According to B. Bobrinski, the Holy Spirit is the "Iconographer of the Church". Zizioulas even says that the Holy Spirit is the true "essence of the Church". It is for this reason that the Orthodox tradition links the creation of the Church with the event of Pentecost. The outpouring of the Holy Spirit is equivalent to the gathering back of the scattered people of God into the community of the Church.[176] For this reason, many Orthodox theologians have conceived of the Church as an "event of continual Pentecost".[177]

Christ revealed the truth about God and departed to the Father, but left the Church awaiting His second coming. He did not, however, leave the Church alone:

---

170 Cf. Zizioulas, *Lectures*, 11.

171 Cf. Zizioulas, *Lectures*, 12.

172 Cf. Zizioulas, *Lectures*, 13.

173 Cf. Jagodziński, "Komunijna mistyka eklezjalna według Johna D. Zizioulasa," *Roczniki Teologiczne* 67 (2020) 7, 13.

174 Cf. Zizioulas, *Lectures*, 16. "We have said that knowledge of God is offered to us within a loving relationship of the Father and die Son in which God is identified and known eternally, quite apart from us. We identify God in Christ as we become part of this existing relationship. This knowledge is the function of this relationship of love so God is known within the community constituted by these relationships. The Holy Spirit sustains the relationnships of love that make up the community of Christ" (Zizioulas, *Lectures*, 34).

175 See Evdokimov, *Duch Święty w tradycji prawosławnej*, 17–20.

176 Cf. Małecki, *Kościół jest wspólnotą*, 84–5.

177 Cf. Hryniewicz, "Duch Święty – Mistagog Bożego Królestwa," 12–4.

"And I will ask the Father, and he will give you another Advocate, to be with you forever. This is the Spirit of truth, whom the world cannot receive, because it neither sees him nor knows him. You know him, because he abides with you, and he will be in you. I will not leave you orphaned; I am coming to you" (John 14:16-18). When Christ sat down at the right hand of the Father, the Father sent another "Helper" – the Spirit of truth. The new experience of people's relationship with God began precisely with the arrival of the third Person – the Holy Spirit. The first disciples had to find a place for Him in their experience of God and thus a new community transcending all created limitations emerged, which the world had not known before His coming.[178]

For theology primarily concerned with the truth of God, the employment of the concept of person was of great significance.[179] Zizioulas continuously emphasises that it is not nature that is the origin of the Persons in God. It is the person of the Father who is the "cause" of God's existence as a Trinity – although 'Father' has no meaning outside the relationship with the Son and the Spirit, which in turn implies a Communion that does not allow for being in isolation. Personal Communion thus belongs to the very centre of being of God who is love,[180] and without this being Communion the incommunicable specificity of the individual Persons of the Holy Trinity could not exist.[181]

178 Cf. Zizioulas, *Lectures*, 44–5. "The Holy Spirit is not merely the life-giving and animating force of the Church. His salvific action stands at the very foundation of the Church's existence. He is, after all, the Spirit of communion, gathering the scattered children of God into one. In the present time, He reminds and represent in the Church the entire mystery of Our Lord. Being an eschatological gift, He simultaneously shows the Church its ultimate purpose and a kind of 'instrumentality' in relation to all created reality" (Małecki, *Kościół jest wspólnotą*, 77).

179 Cf. Zizioulas, *Lectures*, 50–1.

180 "Christianity did not invent the notion that God is love. [...] the phrase 'God is love' means that God is constituted by these personal relationships. God is communion; love is fundamental to his being, not an addition to it. [...] Love, or communion with other persons, is stronger than death and is the source of our existence. That 'God is love' means that God is the communion of this Holy Trinity. God the Father would lose his identity and being if he did not have the Son, and the same applies to the Son and to the Spirit. If we took away the communion of the Trinity to make God a unit, God would not be communion and therefore would not be love" (Zizioulas, *Lectures* , 53). "God is love in his very being. It is not however himself that he loves, so this is not self-love. The Father loves the Son and the Spirit, die Son loves the Father and the Spirit, the Spirit loves the Father and the Son: it is another person that each loves. It is the person, not the nature or essence, who loves, and the one he loves is also a person. Because divine love is a matter of personal communion this love is free: each person loved is free to respond to this love with love" (Zizioulas, *Lectures*, 53–4).

181 Cf. Zizioulas, *Lectures*, 58. "Thus each person of the Holy Trinity is unique and irreplaceable precisely because each is in an unbroken relationship with the other persons. If this communion is severed, that person is lost. Communion, therefore, is a condition for the person, indeed communion creates singularity" (Zizioulas, *Lectures*, 58).

The image of the Father in the Son is the ultimate content of being communicated in and through communion.[182] Zizioulas points to St. Augustine, who attributed to the Persons of the Trinity particular attributes of their action in the economy of salvation. According to Augustine, we can learn God through the Son, but the attribute of communion belongs to the Holy Spirit, who reveals that God is Communion.[183] However, as Zizioulas points out, the Greek Church Fathers avoided attributing personal attributes to the individual Persons of the Trinity.[184]

The incarnation of Christ can only be understood in relation to the Father and the Spirit. Zizioulas emphasises that the great error of earlier generations of dogmatists was to separate Christology from the doctrine of the Holy Spirit. In love, the Father decided on the Incarnation, the Son consented to the Father's will and descended upon men, and the Holy Spirit sustained this plan by supporting the Son in His suffering, abiding by Christ in all the moments affirming His freedom and constantly assisting Him.[185] For the presence of the Holy Spirit overcomes all constrictions of nature and liberates from all limitations. He was always with Christ during His entire existence in His most distinctive way, especially in the decisive moments for the realisation of God's plan concerning the salvation of the world.[186]

Salvation is accomplished through truth and depends ultimately on the identification of truth with communion.[187] It is realised in the Church, which is God's gath-

182 Cf. Zizioulas, *Being as Communion,* 101, 104; Jagodziński, "Communional Aspects of the Doctrine of the Holy Spirit according to John D. Zizioulas," *Teologia w Polsce* 14/1 (2020), 36–7.

183 Cf. Zizioulas, *Lectures*, 70; Jagodziński, "Communional Aspects of the Doctrine of the Holy Spirit according to John D. Zizioulas," 37–8.

184 Cf. Zizioulas, *Lectures*, 71.

185 Cf. Zizioulas, *Lectures*, 148. "A real 'de-individuation' of Christ takes place in the Resurrection [...]. [...] The Holy Spirit as 'power' and 'giver of life' makes Christ a relational being *par excellence*. Just as at the moment of the Incarnation the Holy Spirit 'brought' Christ into the framework of history, so now in the Resurrection, by the power of the same Spirit, He is freed from the framework of history to exist as a 'relational event', encompassing all humanity within Himself. All this is accomplished 'in the Spirit' since with the Spirit the 'last days' (cf. Acts 2:17) enter the confines of history. This new mode of Christ's existence opens the created reality united to Him to true life, which again regains its relational and communional character" (Małecki, *Kościół jest wspólnotą*, 67).

186 Cf. Zizioulas, *Lectures*, 106–8, 132–3. "The role of the Holy Spirit, though all-important, has been so underestimated that we could even say that it has been suppressed. The incarnation requires the whole doctrine of God. Trinity begins with the goodwill of the Father, continues with the Son taking on the fate of fallen creation and ends with Christ gathering us and all creation up by the Holy Spirit. The Holy Spirit always acts *through* Christ, because Christ is the point where all mankind and all creation are gathered up and brought into living communion with God on whom there are no confines. The incarnation is therefore not just about Christ's *receiving* the Holy Spirit, but also about Christ *giving* the Holy Spirit to all mankind..." (Zizioulas, *Lectures*, 108).

187 Cf. Zizioulas, *Being as Communion*, 101.

ered people representing the whole world united in Christ and the Holy Spirit.[188] Zizioulas writes that the incarnation of Christ would not be the ultimate realisation of the Church without the ensuing Pentecost and our personal incarnation in the Church. When St. Paul discusses the Body of Christ in 1 Cor 12, he writes that it is the people of God because the Holy Spirit calls its members to be together.[189] Therefore, ecclesiology cannot be practised in isolation from theology (the science of God).[190]

The Holy Spirit is the Spirit of communion, power and life; He demolishes the barriers separating all beings and makes communion possible.[191] Citing one of the hymns intended for the day of Pentecost, Zizioulas writes that the Holy Spirit keeps the whole institution of the Church united and it is no exaggeration to identify the Kingdom of God with the Holy Spirit.[192] When we pray for the coming of this Kingdom, we ask for the Holy Spirit. Connecting Him to the institution of the Church means that this "institution" itself and the framework within which it becomes a reality, i. e. the Eucharistic assembly, derive their meaning from the Kingdom of God. Zizioulas cites the teaching of Nicholas Kabazilas, who wrote that in the Eucharist the repetition of the Lord's words takes place "in the form of a narrative", but the transformation of the gifts into the Body and Blood of Christ belongs to the Holy Spirit. It is He who gathers "in one place" the eschatological community in which the Eucharistic transformation takes place.[193] The Eucharist is

188 "Zizioulas maintains that central to the Eucharist together with Christ, is the Person and work of the Holy Spirit, who comes to dwell in the Church (Eph. 2.22) through the Eucharistic *epiclesis* and, who brings the *eschaton* into her life and mission (Acts 2.17-21).42 This image of the Church as the *Temple of the Holy Spirit* (1 Cor. 6.19, 2 Cor. 6.16; Eph. 2.21-22) is founded upon the New Testament and according to Zizioulas, 'implies that the Church is not simply a unity, but a unity in diversity and personal freedom' In short, Zizioulas argues that the Holy Spirit *constitutes* the Church while Christ *institutes* her. The difference between these two prefixes: in- and con- 'can be enormous ecclesiologically', according to Zizioulas" (Wong Yee Kheong, *John Zizioulas' Ecclesiology of 'The One and the Many'*, VIII).

189 Cf. Zizioulas, *Lectures*, 126.

190 Cf. Zizioulas, *Lectures*, 132.

191 Cf. Zizioulas, *Lectures*, 136. "The Holy Spirit enables the communion of the created with the uncreated so this body can enable the communion of every being with every other. [...] the Holy Spirit enables us to exceed the limits of our creaturely being and enter that communion with God which is God's love. Beings must have boundaries so that they can be acknowledged as distinct, but they must surmount these boundaries in order to come into communion with one another and so live as a society. Creatures must be able to distinguish themselves from God who is the source of their communion. The Holy Spirit enables both this demarcation and its transcendence and so makes all community possible" (ibid., 139). Cf. Małecki, *Kościół jest wspólnotą*, 86.

192 Cf. Evdokimov, *Prawosławie* (Warszawa: PAX, 2003), 156.

193 Cf. Zizioulas, *The Eucharistic Communion and the World* (London-New York: T&T Clark, 2011), 73–4.

the Communion and participation in the Blood of Christ, which is "full of the Holy Spirit". Therefore, in it we share in Christ, but at the same time we also share "in the communion of the Holy Spirit" (the phrase comes from the Liturgy of St. Basil). The Holy Spirit descends not only upon the gifts presented, but also "upon us". In this way, Christ's "real presence" is extended to the Head and Body in the unity of the Holy Spirit, and the Eucharist as the communion of the Holy Spirit becomes "a communion of saints" – of holy things and holy people.[194]

Eastern theology strongly emphasises the eschatological dimension of the Church, which confesses that the Holy Spirit brings the future into history.[195] The worldly kingdoms are based on opposites and competition, but the Holy Spirit brings Christ's peace everywhere. Pentecost is the fulfilment of all times. And although many Christians believe that the sent Holy Spirit enlightens individuals, this is only a partial truth. For the Holy Spirit frees people from the various constraints of the history of individuals, nations or social groups. He brings them into much larger dimensions of the future, in which they are free to be for one another – without any limitations. The life given by the Holy Spirit is not fragmented, we receive it in its entirety, so that we also know that all Christians – past, present or future – are present to us in a communion unlimited by time or space.[196]

Zizioulas emphasises that when the Christian West somehow tried to develop pneumatology, it was not integrated into ecclesiology. Rather, the Church was treated as a primarily historical reality, to which the Holy Spirit brings a specific additional and almost cosmetic element. According to such a theology, the Church tended to be made of history, its community taking the form of the past, and the Holy Spirit only having the task of animating it. The truth, however, is that the Holy Spirit builds the Church together with the Son instead of only arriving in the Church when it is fully completed. If the Church is an indivisible work of the triune God in which all the persons of the Holy Trinity are involved, we must also not allow any trace of thinking about rivalry between the Divine Persons to be smuggled into theological thinking.[197]

The East, on the other hand, was arguing against the Christomonism of the West with its excessive emphasis on the Holy Spirit.[198] To demonstrate the difference in

---

194 Cf. Zizioulas, *The Eucharistic Communion and the World*, 75–6.

195 "Zizioulas emphasizes, 'The Holy Spirit is associated, among other things, with koinonia (2 Cor. 13.13) and the entrance of the last days into history (Acts 2.17-18), that is, eschatology.' There is a strong eschatological dimension to the presence and the activity of the Holy Spirit who is the spirit of liberty and who blows wherever He wills" (Wong Yee Kheong, *John Zizioulas' Ecclesiology of 'the one and the many'*, 106).

196 Cf. Zizioulas, *Lectures*, 154–5; Małecki, *Kościół jest wspólnotą*, 111.

197 Cf. Zizioulas, *Lectures*, 149.

198 Cf. Małecki, *Kościół jest wspólnotą*, 80–1.

relation to the West, Aleksey Khomyakov preached that the Church is a communion of the Holy Spirit, while completely ignoring its Christological basis. He taught that Orthodoxy must view the Church as a communion of the Holy Spirit and not as the Body of the historical Christ. This, of course, immediately introduced a contradiction between the Son and the Spirit and unacceptable divisions in God. It is sad to say that such a division has often sufficed as a basis for claiming that the Holy Spirit has nothing to do with the traditional institution of the Church and that the Gospel cannot be limited by an institutional framework. This is evident in the contrast occurring between the supposed freedom of charismatic ecclesial communities and churches with "institutional" apostolic and episcopal ministries, which is a disastrous result of the exaggerated emphasis on pneumatology at the expense of Christology.[199]

Zizioulas writes that every time a charismatic leader creates a new and more "spiritual" community, he divides the Body of Christ into spiritual and non-spiritual, or into charismatic and non-charismatic one – suggesting that he does not actually need half of that Body. Such a distinction between the "spiritual" and the "institutional" Church, however, is tantamount to forgetting "ordinary" Christians – if they can be called that. Are they not all members of the Body of Christ? Has the Holy Spirit deserted them? Charismatic leaders who place themselves outside the order and office in the Church[200] believe that the Holy Spirit is not given in baptism.[201]

---

199 Cf. Zizioulas, *Lectures*, 149, 151. As for the synthesis of Christology and pneumatology, Zizioulas refers to the work of N. Nissiotis and B. Bobrinskoy, who "unanimously emphasise that the salvific work of Christ and the Holy Spirit belong to each other. They are, as it were, two sides of one and the same mystery of salvation, which owes its origin to the initiative of the Father, realised by Christ in the Holy Spirit. It is not important that the mystery of Christ chronologically precedes the mystery of Pentecost. Indeed, the historical order of salvific events must not obscure the depth of the entire mystery of the Church. The doctrine of the Church should not therefore be guided by the mere logic of the succession of historical events. The mystery of the Church arises from a single, integrally understood, Christological-pneumatological event. The chronological priority of Christology over pneumatology is balanced by the fact that Christ Himself, from the beginning of His earthly activity, appears as a person "filled with the Holy Spirit" (cf. Luke 1:15; 4:1,18). In St. John's Gospel, the sending of the Holy Spirit is part of the Christological event (cf. John 7:39; 20:22). It is the Holy Spirit who reveals Christ, while Christ is the one who sends the Spirit from the Father. As Bobrinskoy notes, this law of reciprocity existing between the Spirit and the Son becomes the basic principle of the trinitarian economy of salvation" (Małecki, *Kościół jest wspólnotą*, 83).

200 On the Holy Spirit as the creator of order in the Church, see Małecki, *Kościół jest wspólnotą*, 136–139.

201 "The Greek theologian notes that all the baptismal connotations in the New Testament speak of baptism taking place 'in' (eis) Christ 'in' (en) the Holy Spirit. This grammatical distinction, which is difficult to render in other languages, points to the very essence of the sacrament of baptism. It is the incorporation 'into' Christ effected through (or 'by the power of') the Holy Spirit. From that moment, the Christian has the opportunity to realise his existence in a new, communional way in imitation of Christ. Through the sacrament of baptism, the newly baptised person himself also

But how can baptism not confer Him when it is the Holy Spirit who baptises and administers all the sacraments?[202] Protestants are not very interested in the institution of the Church and some even doubt whether Christ wanted it to exist. They regard the Holy Spirit as an inspirer who assists each person individually and the whole community in general, but virtually only so that they can receive the word of God.[203]

In the face of possible Christomonistic or charismatic narrowness, Zizioulas reminds us that Christ does not build the Church without the Holy Spirit, and that the Holy Spirit does not arrive in the Church until it already exists in full.[204] The institution of the Church came into being once and for all at a specific point in history, but it is also constantly constituted and renewed by the Holy Spirit.[205] It is He who gathers Christians around Christ, giving the Church its basic structures and offices through baptism, confirmation[206] and ordination. Episcopal ordina-

---

undergoes a process of 'de-individualisation'. He assimilates a new ecclesial hypostasis. Zizioulas states: it is only now that man has the chance to exist in a truly personal way, free of the necessity he carries with him through the fact of his biological birth since baptism, as a birth 'in' the Spirit, is different from biological birth" (Zizioulas, *Lectures*, 69).

202 Cf. Zizioulas, *Lectures*, 149–50. "Some generations later George Florovsky very justifiably corrected Khomiakov, but he did so equally without nuance, by insisting that ecclesiology should be understood merely as a sub-section of Christology. The emphasis returned to the history of Jesus Christ, again conceived as confined by history as much as any other individual. Others like Lossky, Nissiotis and Bobrinskoy responded to Florovsky by placing all the emphasis back *on* the Spirit again. However, ecclesiology is not a matter of either Christ or the Spirit, but of all the persons of the Trinity in indivisible unity. When we emphasise the Spirit we must be clear that we are speaking of the realisation of that recapitulation of all things *in The Son*. The choice is not between a christological ecclesiology on one hand and a pneumatological ecclesiology on the other, but between a christomonist *ecclesiology* and a fully *trinitarian ecclesiology* in which all the persons of God are at work. The proper basis of ecclesiology is the trinitarian doctrine of God. The role of the Holy Spirit should never lead this into an ecclesiology not founded in Christ; ecclesiology cannot be *Spirit-centred* because the Church *is* the recapitulation of everything *in Christ*" (Zizioulas, *Lectures*, 150). Cf. Zizioulas' reflections on the unity of baptism, confirmation and the Eucharist in: *The Eucharistic Communion and the World*, 114–6.

203 Cf. Zizioulas, *Lectures*, 156.

204 Cf. Zizioulas, *Being as Communion*, 111.

205 Cf. Zizioulas, *Lectures*, 157: "The Church is that congregation which is created by the Spirit as a portrayal of eschatological events, every time, in every place and whenever the divine Eucharist is performed. The Church is formed by the freely-willed gathering of Christians. [...] The structure, the institution of the Church is not something that is imposed by someone for we ourselves compose and constitute it. The Holy Spirit makes us all its founding members as he gathers us together as the Church, so the Church does not come into existence without us." Cf. Zizioulas, "The Pneumatological Dimension of the Church," *Communio. International Catholic Review* 2 (1972), 133–47.

206 The common tradition of the Church has always considered confirmation to be a sacrament of the Holy Spirit, with its rites visibly expressing and representing His action, although it was baptism that

tion is, after all, the manifestation of the foundation of the Church by the Holy Spirit and the renewal of Pentecost. The Holy Spirit, together with the Son, continually reconstitutes the Church, which thus also receives its continuity from the eschaton.[207]

In his reflections, Zizioulas presents a typically Eastern assessment of ecclesiastical teaching. He writes that when the bishops gather in synod, they are part of a greater whole constituted by the Holy Spirit, and that the authority of ecclesiastical teaching ultimately grows out of this Spirit who moves all the members of the Church. A particular decision or interpretation may turn out to be wrong, just as some historical opinion or interpretation by scholars may turn out to be wrong, thus only the Church as a whole has a sufficiently long existence which, through all the councils and through reverence to God, gives access to the full truth of God.[208]

The reception of the truth thus taught is of vital importance. The concept of theological reception is deeply rooted in the history and existence of the Church, which was born, grew and developed through it. The Church first receives everything from God – through Christ – in the Holy Spirit.[209] W. Hryniewicz wrote that whoever believes receives new life from Christ and allows himself to be penetrated by the Holy Spirit with His truth.

> In the Church there is a constant exchange of views, their critical reception or modification. Non-reception is also possible. This concerns various levels of ecclesiastical life. Most often, it concerned the reception of conciliar or synodal rulings by other ecclesial communities. Reception can furthermore be spoken of in relation to theological views received by theologians from one another. In addition to the reception of views, the reception of

---

from the beginning was understood as the new Pentecost. The power of the Holy Spirit conferred during confirmation becomes a personal power enabling the Christian to give testimony to the resurrection of Christ. Cf. Małecki, *Kościół jest wspólnotą*, 71–2.

207 Cf. Zizioulas, *Lectures*, 156. "The Church is always the creation by the Spirit in one place in time of the coming events of the eschaton. The Church is the summation and recapitulation of the world, so it is only through its continued incorporation in the Church that the world survives. The being of the Church is the outcome of the present work of the Holy Spirit, who enacts the labour of Christ, rendering the whole body of Christ alive and present for this specific time and place" (ibid.). The Eucharist has a special place there: "The Eucharist is the inaugural event of freedom and the moment in which eschatological reality becomes the actual presence of this assembly brought together by the Holy Spirit. This is the work of the Holy Spirit, which is why the invocation (*epiclesis*) of the Holy Spirit is fundamental. The gifts that bear the body and blood of Christ bring us into increasing participation in that body. This event of person-to-person relationship takes place in the Spirit, between each of us and Christ. These eschatological events are seen, felt and tasted in the gathering of the Church. This gathering is the event in which the Holy Spirit opens us to life together in freedom" (Zizioulas, *Lectures*, 161). Cf. Małecki, *Kościół jest wspólnotą*, 87.

208 Cf. Zizioulas, *Lectures*, 160.

209 Cf. Zizioulas, *Lectures*, 161.

> spiritual experiences also plays an important role. In some respects, it is even more important than the reception of theological formulations and statements. Until recently, all these facts of ecclesiastical life have not stimulated deeper reflection on their meaning and role in Christianity. The present ecumenical situation urges in a special way to undertake such a reflection and to draw from it all possible implications for the work of reconciliation and unification. Since reception – generally speaking – is an expression of spiritual exchange between individuals and whole communities, it cannot remain a matter of indifference for the future of ecumenism and the unity of the Church. It must be considered as an inherently ecclesial phenomenon – a vital process taking place in all Christian Churches.[210]

However, the question of the form of the reception of this teaching is one of the most difficult issues in the current ecumenical situation. God has given us the Son in the Holy Spirit and thus in the event of communion, but He does not force us to accept His gift. Truth is authoritative but not authoritarian – it comes to people in the event of communion, which is realised through the concrete community of the Church.[211] However, not every ecclesial community is the Church. No such community can isolate itself from the whole Church because the Church is structured in a particular way by the event of communion – and it is precisely in the Holy Spirit that everything happens as an event of communion.[212]

2.6 The Communional Aspects of Contemporary Pneumatological Thought

Pneumatology has experienced a renaissance in recent theology, which was made possible by the integration of theological reflection and spiritual experience, and above all by the new awakening of the ecclesiastical sense of union in the manner of "we", which has encouraged theologians to pneumatological reflections.[213] For

210 Hryniewicz, *Hermeneutyka w dialogu. Szkice teologiczno-ekumeniczne* (Opole: Wydawnictwo św. Krzyża, 1998), 2: 150.

211 Cf. Zizioulas, *Being as Communion*, 130–1: "Another important contribution of the Holy Spirit to the Christ event is that, because of the involvement of the Holy Spirit in the economy, Christ is not just an individual, not 'one' but 'many'. This 'corporate personality' of Christ is impossible to conceive without Pneumatology. It is not insignificant that the Spirit has always, since the time of Paul, been associated with the notion of *communion* (κοινωνια). Pneumatology contributes to Christology this dimension of communion. And it is because of this function of Pneumatology that it is possible to speak of Christ as having a 'body', i. e. to speak of ecclesiology; of the Church as the Body of Christ."

212 Cf. Zizioulas, *Lectures*, 162–3.

213 See Jagodziński, *Trynitologia komunijna*, 172–87.

H. Mühlen, a special role in this context played the experience of "We" in the Holy Spirit. He defined the Holy Spirit from the intra-trinitarian perspective as the divine „We", as the intimate union of the Father and the Son "in Person", as "We in Person". By analogy to this intra-trinitarian definition of the Holy Spirit he also explained His historico-salvific function: He appears to be the Divine "being-beyond-self", in a way God Himself, as if "coming out of Himself – the Holy Spirit understood as Divine self-giving".[214]

As the Gift, the Holy Spirit comes from the Father, while the Father gives to the Son all that He "possesses" – Himself in love. The riches of God are precisely the Holy Spirit. He flows from the perfect subjective-personal self-giving of the Father who keeps nothing for Himself, but as "Father" offers everything to the Son and remains "Father". This means that also the Son, to whom everything has been given from the Father, offers Himself completely to the Father. As subject, however, He remains offered to the Father as "Son". In this way, the mystery of the Holy Spirit is revealed: He is the Gift, not like the Father and the Son, who are both the Giver

---

214 Cf. Stubenrauch, *Pneumatologia*, 215–6; Laurentin, *Nieznany Duch Święty*, 360–2; Congar, *Wierzę w Ducha Świętego. Duch Święty w ekonomii Objawienia…*, 64–7; Czaja, *Credo in Spiritum Vivificantem*, 75–9; Guzowski, *Duch Dialogujący*, 389–92. K. Guzowski presents the theses of H. Mühlen as follows (pp. 390–1): "in the Trinity, the Holy Spirit is one person in two persons... [Mühlen] addresses the problem from the perspective of analysing the grammatical and anthropological functioning of personal pronouns in our verbal paradigms: I-you-he and We-you. The relationship between the Father and the Son is a I-you or me- you relationship; for example, this is the case in John 17:21-26. It is not possible to characterise the relationship of the Father and the Son with the Holy Spirit as a we-you relationship and, correspondingly: the relationship of the Spirit towards the Father and the Son as a I-you [plural] relationship. The Holy Spirit appears as the personal We between the I of the Father and the You of the Son, as the one who unites them in We. From the biblical analysis, Mühlen draws the conclusion: The Father and the Son appear as two I's who maintain an I-you relationship between them. Aware of the trinitarian context of his argument, Mühlen emphasises that the Father is the fundamental intra-trinitarian I, while the Son is the fundamental intra-trinitarian You. When Jesus utters We, it has a double dimension: it includes the Father, but never the people; it includes the Father and the Holy Spirit (cf. John 14:23). This linguistic analysis is of profound cognitive and theological value, since the We involving the Holy Spirit points to Him as a dialogical Person. In our speech, too, We is the most basic way of pointing to a person. In light of this, the Holy Spirit would be the intra-trinitarian We. This claim is based on the Western doctrine of the origin of the Holy Spirit, emphasising that in the Trinity we have '*duo spirantes sed unus spirator*'; this refers to active spiration. The action of the Father and the Son is in any case a subsistent act of We since it is performed by two persons. The expression of this act from the perspective of passive spiration is the Holy Spirit, who, as a personal Act-We subsists between the Father and the Son. The consequence of the Spirit's relation with the Father and the Son is the I-We relationship. The Holy Spirit is the *nexus* of the Father and the Son. This gives a picture of *two* forms of perichoresis within the Trinity: one occurring between the Father and the Son in the form of I-You, and the other occurring between the Father and the Son, and the Holy Spirit. Therefore, He is one Person in two Persons."

and the Gift to each other, but is the pure Gift. The Holy Spirit is the Gift dwelling wholly in the Father and wholly in the Son, making the relationship between Them possible and distinguishing Them from one another. He is also the Gift making God's being Divine in a unique and irreplaceable way, and thus making God's giving in Himself and externally possible. Since the Father offers Himself completely to the Son, and since the Son does the same in relation to the Father, and since in this relationship They do not lose each other, since as subjects they remain Givers to each other, the pure Gift cannot be Their mere reproduction, but rather constitutes "something" other, "Third" in relation to Them. He is God-Holy Spirit who, as a Person, unites in Himself the Father and the Son, but as a subject He is at the same time this Gift, but is also distinct from the Father and the Son.[215]

As has already been shown, according to H.U. von Balthasar, the mutual exchange of essence between the Father and the Son leads to Their dynamic union in the Holy Spirit. At the root of this union lies the kenotic, event-like process of self-giving. The essence of the love of the Father and the Son is their mutual "collision with each other" in the Holy Spirit, and it is in Him that the concretisation of God's essence is immortalised. It is He who causes the permanent "exchange" of the mutual being of the Father and the Son in each other. The dynamism of Divine love is expressed by the possession by the Divine essence of the property of "more and more" in relation to each Person. The Person of the Holy Spirit contributes to the unlimited interpenetration of the Persons of the Trinity, is the source of the energy of the mutual bestowal of the Father and the Son, the embodiment of mutual self-giving. Balthasar's specific conception of the drama of the distance between the Father and the Son finds its solution in the Holy Spirit, in whom the absolute distinction between the two becomes ever greater love. The breath of the Spirit is a fertile encounter of giving and receiving love, which, as if abandoning itself, in a common breath of love gives forth the very Spirit of love. Pardoxically, in the economy of salvation, the Spirit expresses the dynamically "growing" unity as pure distance.[216]

---

215 Cf. Stubenrauch, *Pneumatologia*, 227–8. Is the monarchy of the Father, and thus the biblical witness, preserved? The Father never becomes the Son and the Son never becomes the Father. Nor does the Holy Spirit enter, in the manner of the Son, into a Giver-Gift relationship with the Father. On this principle, the Father by giving Himself begets the Son and not another Father. Nor does the Son reflect Himself in the Father, but treats the Father as a constant dialogue partner. Finally, the Spirit does not "consist" of the Father and the Son – in which case He would not be a Spirit, but a kind of "Father-Son" – instead he is a Gift. This means that He realises God in the form of a pure gift. However, the Father remains *principium non de principio* – a beginning without a beginning. Otherwise, His subjectivity as Father would be reduced to an abstract principle, which could be juxtaposed at will with the names of the Son or the Holy Spirit or with some other metaphor, and consequently the essence of the dogma of the Holy Trinity would be violated. Cf. Stubenrauch, *Pneumatologia*, 228–9; Laurentin, *Nieznany Duch Święty*, 378–85.

216 Cf. Bokwa, *Trynitarno-chrystologiczna interpretacja eschatologii*, 105–6.

In the manifestation of the union of Father and Son's essence, they perceive Their unity "as the hypostatic essence of love". The Holy Spirit constitutes a concrete reality as "the subjective embodiment of the reciprocal love of the Father and the Son" – more than a "mutual inclination" of the Father and the Son or the fruit of Their love – He is the Gift. He enacts the love of the Father giving His whole essence to the Son, without being diminished in any way and remains the first, necessary act of the Divine going "outward". In the Person of the Holy Spirit, the love of the Father and the Son is enclosed in a whole that does not compromise Their personal properties, and this is all the more so since the Spirit does not wish to be "someone" for Himself, but only a pure declaration of the love of the Father and the Son.[217]

Balthasar conceives of the Holy Spirit as a trinitarian duality – as the supreme unity of the Father and the Son and as the separate, objective, personal "fruit" of Their love and eternal begetting, the "result" of that love and its witness. The Spirit exists eternally as the self-contained fecundity of divine love, as the unity of the ineffable love of the Father and the Son. The essence of God's love thus seems to "impose" a trinity in God – the breath of the Spirit constitutes a "process" that is "necessary", but at the same time absolutely free, and the Holy Spirit proceeds from it is an expression of God's unique freedom. The Spirit of God is identical with Himself and with the essence of God – He is God and, as Person, He is the "combined breath of the Father and the Son". The relationship between the Father and the Son is described as richness, gift, unity, communion of love. The Spirit of God contains the whole essence of God as love, He is "love as such and absolute", the poured out wholeness of being as love. The Spirit of love is the "essence of God", who is one precisely because of the unifying power of the Spirit of love, the "unity of imperishable love". The Spirit is the personification, the "prosopon" of the Divine, which is essentially the pure self-giving. The Spirit is the "culmination" of God's growing love – Balthasar writes of the "fecundity of love". It is in the power of the Spirit that God continually "attains" His eschatological fullness.[218]

Such a presentation of God as a unique and incomparable love giving itself unreservedly aims at an analogy between the structure of God's absolute love and the personal human encounter. The analogy is reciprocal. According to a "top-down" way of reasoning, it means to understand the trinitarian reality of God as the condition that makes interpersonal love possible, but this is only subsidiary, since Balthasar's main goal remains the conceptual-imaginative approximation of the trinitarian essence of God to people.[219] The Holy Spirit, as the love of the

217 Cf. Bokwa, *Trynitarno-chrystologiczna interpretacja eschatologii*, 106.
218 Cf. Bokwa, *Trynitarno-chrystologiczna interpretacja eschatologii*, 106–7.
219 Cf. Bokwa, *Trynitarno-chrystologiczna interpretacja eschatologii*, 107.

Father and the Son and the bond of Their unity, is Their eternal communication and communion.[220]

Analysing the contemporary pneumatological interpretation of the Church as communion, A. Czaja stated that it has experienced particular development under the influence of K. Rahner's thought.[221] Writing about the Holy Spirit as Co-Creator of ecclesial communion, Czaja presented a rich analysis of the communional development of contemporary pneumatology.[222]

Joseph Ratzinger wrote about the Holy Spirit as Communion, stating that He creates ecclesial communion by bestowing the Spirit and giving in the Spirit. Following St. Augustine, he emphasised that the Holy Spirit, being within the Trinity – by its

---

220 Cf. Laurentin, *Nieznany Duch Święty*, 319–20. In the conclusion to his work, K. Guzowski wrote that it collects "the best intuitions of the theological tradition and of personalist reflection, which allow us to see the person of the Holy Spirit in the entirety of personal and perichoretic dynamics, in communional unity and relation, and in relational and creative subjectivity" (Guzowski, *Duch Dialogujący*, 425).

221 M. de Salis draws attention to the pneumatological contribution of Y. Congar's thought in the post-conciliar period (cf. Salis, *Kościół wcielony w historii*, 187–94). He also shows the contribution of H.U. von Balthasar, the post-conciliar theology and the Magisterium of the Church – especially in the field of reflection on the relationship between the institution and the charism (cf. de Salis, *Kościół wcielony w historii*, 201–18).

222 This is especially true of the first chapter of his dissertation; Czaja, *Credo in Spiritum Vivificantem*, 35–129. In summarising part of this chapter on pp. 95–96, he wrote: "depending on one's understanding of the triune unity in God [...] some speak of participation in a different type of communion. [...] Out of the models [...] it is difficult to choose one and consider it as the only right one. However, the development of the understanding of trinitarian unity seems to be moving in the right direction: from speaking of intersubjective communion (Ratzinger), through intrapersonal inexistence (Mühlen), interpersonal communion (Kasper, Ganoczy, Müller), or inter-subjective communion (Stubenrauch), to teaching about a communion of inter-personal communication (Greshake, Kehl). It is linked to the conception of the person promoted by the respective authors, as well as to their concern for a more kerygmatic trinitological language. The search for a new language in trinitology, although it entails many ambiguities and even opposing opinions, essentially contributes to an increasingly dynamic understanding of unity in God ... [...] the understanding of the Spirit's mission for human participation in the Divine life is largely a product of the interpretation of His personality ('singularity') in the immanent Trinity. [...] the Spirit is presented as either the personal union of the Father and the Son or as one of the three mutually interpenetrating Persons. However, the one does not exclude the other. Rather, in my view, it represents the legacy of Augustinian thought, to which those discussed above clearly allude. Their slightly different approaches follow a greater emphasis on either understanding the Spirit as *communio* (bond of love) or understanding the Spirit as Gift (fruit of love) of the Father and the Son. Everyone is rather aware that Augustine has a certain dialectic in mind. However, it is difficult to enunciate it even when the dual character of the personhood of the Spirit is verbally emphasised. From this perspective, the account that best develops Augustine's intuition seems to be that of Kehl, who sees the specificity of the personhood of the Spirit in a kind of dialectic of His simultaneously being 'a previously given environment' and the 'social form' of the Divine *communio*."

very nature – always a Divine gift, comes and exists as the given one. Remaining within the Divine, He represents the opening of God to man and the history of salvation.[223] The Holy Spirit is the Gift whose reception makes all-embracing communion a reality; it is He who makes ecclesial communion possible, He co-creates it with Christ, mediating the participation of its members in God and His gifts by giving a share in Himself.[224]

Walter Kasper accused K. Rahner of extreme individualism which, within trinitological speculation, leads to granting the Persons of the Holy Trinity merely the status of "distinguished modes of subsistence", which cannot be invoked, worshipped or prayed to – in fact, one can only be silent towards them. In this view, they are merely moments of the economic self-giving of the Holy Trinity; there is no trace of subjectivity in them. However, something different follows from Christ's revelation of the Holy Trinity:[225] God is a communion of the Father, the Son and the Holy Spirit, and thus the starting point in the doctrine of the Holy Trinity should be the contemporary, relational understanding of person.[226] The Holy Spirit, according to the Augustinian trinitological tradition, is the eschatological gift to the world, but also "the personal Giver of that gift",[227] and His being gift and love is a reality in eternity.[228]

---

223 Czaja refers here (pp. 44–5) to Ratzinger, "Der Heilige Geist als Communio. Zum Verhältnis von Pneumatologie und Spiritualität bei Augustinus", in *Erfahrung und Theologie des Heiligen Geistes*, ed. Claus Heitmann and Mühlen (Hamburg-München: Kösel, 1974), 230–1.

224 Cf. Czaja, *Credo in Spiritum Vivificantem*, 44–6.

225 Cf. Czaja, *Credo in Spiritum Vivificantem*, 46–8.

226 Cf. Kasper, *Bóg Jezusa Chrystusa*, 353, 78.

227 Cf. Kasper, *Bóg Jezusa Chrystusa*, 277.

228 Cf. Czaja, *Credo in Spiritum Vivificantem*, 48–50. ibid. 50: "This view is shared completely by Bernd Jochen Hilberath. [...] God's self-giving as an offer to the rational creation reached its peak in the Incarnation, but it can only be accepted in the Holy Spirit. He cautions, however, that if one does not wish to fall into modalism in interpreting God's historico-salvific self-giving, it is necessary to speak explicitly of the personal self-giving of the Son and the Holy Spirit" (the author refers to Hilberath, *Der dreieinige Gott und die Gemeinschaft der Menschen. Orientierungen zur christlichen Rede von Gott* (Mainz: Grünewald, 1990), 33, 64). "The rightness and necessity of such a presentation of the historico-salvific activity of the Spirit derives, according to Christian Schütz, [...] from His status as a being in the immanent Trinity. [...] The Spirit, in His own personal way, not only makes something available from the Father and the Son, but He brings Them to Himself, confers Them, because He is the bond of Their love and knowledge. He is the love in which They love each other, the knowledge in which They recognise each other. He appears to represent the ecstasy of the Father and the Son. In Him the Father transcends Himself by going out towards the Son, and the Son transcends Himself by turning towards the Father. The Spirit is thus the original form and original content of their mutual self-giving" (the author cites Christian Schütz, *Einführung in die Pneumatologie* (Darmstadt: Wissenschaftliche Buchgesellschaft, 1985), 253).

Heribert Mühlen's pneumatological thought followed a similar direction. Just as there are two origins in God, there are also two missions – that of the Son and that of the Holy Spirit – in a well-defined order, revealed in *ad extra* action according to immanent trinitarian origins. The Holy Spirit performs the work of establishing personal communion with Christ as the One that has been sent and giving Himself. He is above all the Gift, but He disposes of Himself. He is the direct and ultimate Cause of every personal relationship between people and Christ. Mühlen described Him as the "self-giving Mediation", the "relational relation", the "immediacy of all immediacy", the "directness" with which Christians face Christ.[229] He Himself does not enter into personal relations but mediates according to His personal function of binding the Persons in the immanent Trinity.[230]

Alexandre Ganoczy defends the personal giving of the Holy Spirit within the doctrine of grace. He offers a trinitarian interpretation of the "fullness" from which all people received (cf. John 1:16) – it is the divine communion of love, which is "the eternal event of the interconnection and exchange of Three identical in essence but different, which opens itself to creation and constantly enriches it".[231] God seeks to give Himself in such a way that a man who accepts participation in His communional nature of love sees himself as a communal being, open to his co-recipients and accepting with gratitude the ministry of mediating grace. The Holy Spirit implants Divine love into the personal centre of man. Content-wise, His work is not different from Christ's – the Spirit fulfils it historically. Therefore, one can speak of Christological concentration and pneumatological expansion of God's giving. The Holy Spirit fulfils the eschatological function of actualisation, inspiration and strengthening.[232]

---

229 Here Czaja refers to Mühlen, *Una Mystica Persona. Die Kirche als das Mysterium der heilsgeschichtlichen Identität des Heiligen Geistes in Christus und den Christen: eine Person in vielen Personen* (München-Paderborn-Wien: Herder, 1968), 445, 451, 457.

230 Cf. Czaja, *Credo in Spiritum Vivificantem*, 50–6.

231 Alexandre Ganoczy, *Aus seiner Fülle haben wir alle empfangen. Grundriß der Gnadenlehre* (Düsseldorf: Patmos, 1989), 9. Cf. Czaja, *Credo in Spiritum Vivificantem*, 85.

232 Cf. Czaja, *Credo in Spiritum Vivificantem*, 56–8. "The difference in Ganoczy's position towards Mühlen's account is based on the trinitarian interpretation of 'fullness' and his preference for a different strand of biblical thought when it comes to the order of God's self-giving. However, the two positions are not at all mutually exclusive; they rather aspire to be complementary. The unifying element is the identification of the personal function of the Holy Spirit in the Divine self-giving. In both cases, it is grounded in a relational conception of person and grants the Holy Spirit the function of binding persons together. Both positions are also an interpretation of Paul's teaching, except that Ganoczy focuses his thought on the text of Rom 5:5: *God's love has been poured into our hearts through the Holy Spirit that has been given to us*, while Mühlen starts with Eph 2:18: *for through him [Christ] both of us have access in one Spirit to the Father*" (Czaja, *Credo in Spiritum Vivificantem*, 59).

According to Jürgen Werbick[233] the mission of the Son is to invite the mankind to communion with God, while God realises this communion in the Holy Spirit. The Holy Spirit opens the intra-trinitarian relationship of love and – in accordance with His intra-trinitarian function – unites in the economy of salvation. First, He hypostatically unites the Person of the Son to the human nature of Jesus and shapes the relationship between God and man in Christ, and after Easter – sent by the Father and the Son – He internally binds believers to the Exalted One and thus enables them to participate in His communion with the Father.[234]

Gerhard Ludwig Müller emphasises that the Holy Spirit, who within the Holy Trinity is the unity of the Father and the Son, mediates in the salvific economy the filial relationship of Jesus to the Father and gives men a share in it, introducing them to the divine-human communication of love realised in Christ. The triune God descends to men and bestows Himself directly on them through the Holy Spirit (cf. Rom 5:5). "He is communion and offers each person a share in the deepest communion with God and in the co-realisation of the Divine relationships of the Father, the Son and the Spirit".[235] As the One emerging from the innermost being of God, by giving Himself and entering the personal depths of man, the Holy Spirit mediates man's participation in the Divine life and thus makes the human co-realisation of the trinitarian communion of God possible.[236]

The most mature and comprehensive accounts of the role of the Holy Spirit in the communion of the Church can be found in Mederd Kehl's ecclesiology and Gisbert Greshake's trinitology; both very clearly link the occurrence of ecclesial communion to the personal action of the Holy Spirit.[237] For Greshake, God is a "relational structure" of three personally differentiated hypostases, "He is such a communion in which the three Divine Persons, in the trialogical dynamics of love, realise the one Divine life as mutual self-giving".[238] Through the Incarnation,

---

233 Cf. Werbick, "Trinitätslehre," 521, 562–4, 568.

234 Cf. Czaja, *Credo in Spiritum Vivificantem*, 60.

235 Müller, *Katholische Dogmatik. Für Studium und Praxis der Theologie* (Freiburg-Basel-Wien: Herder, 1995), 611.

236 Czaja refers to the above-cited work, pp. 49, 374, 410, 476; cf. Czaja, *Credo in Spiritum Vivificantem*, 61.

237 Cf. Czaja, *Credo in Spiritum Vivificantem*, 61.

238 Greshake, *Der dreieine Gott*, 179. Greshake speaks of "God as an 'interpersonal- communal unity', a 'mutually bestowing communion', 'being in a dialogue of love'. The divine being is a communion of love of the three Persons, i. e., 'it is such a communion in which the three divine Persons have, in the trialogical dynamics of love, one Divine life as mutual self-giving'. This reality neither derives from the substantial unity, nor is it rooted only in the Father. As a reciprocal mediation of unity and multiplicity, it constitutes 'the original [*ursprüngliche*] and indivisible reality of one Divine life'. In other words, what we have here is a relational unity of love 'in which three Persons mediate the Divine life to one another and in this exchange show both Their distinctiveness and Their supreme

the Son of God has incorporated the creation into the dynamics of the eternal life of God in mutual acceptance and devotion, gratitude and adoration, in the communion of the Holy Spirit, whose work consists in mediating the kenosis of the Son, binding Him to the Father and opening Him to all mankind.[239] Christ ties the knot of God's indissoluble unity with the mankind and implements the model of the mankind in communion with God, while the Holy Spirit realises the inner likeness and capacities that animate the figure of Christ and His invitation to communion.[240] In M. Kehl's ecclesiological reflection, the Holy Spirit is the mediating "Wherein" of the salvific work, the mediating power, by and through which Jesus Christ enters the personal centre of people and becomes a universal reality. The Holy Spirit is the space of personal communication from which the Church as communion grows. He does this as a personal "Environment" given previously by the resurrected Lord and given anew each time – a previously assumed, a priori space – a prior gift of common understanding and communication.[241] This gift in Person is precisely the Holy Spirit, and this constitutes the specificity of His personal mediation in salvation, which has its origin in the immanent life of God. For there He is the pre-given Environment of the mutual love of the Father and the Son and its "social form". In this way, the Father and the Son remain distinct, and the Holy Spirit is the principle of their unity and distinction. This is possible because – despite any dependence on the Father and the Son – the Holy Spirit is relatively independent. He is the embodied "unity" of Their love, and thus the intrinsic power and dynamism of the Father and the Son's transcending love.[242]

For J. Ratzinger, after the Resurrection, the Holy Spirit constitutes the mode of existence of the glorified Christ, He is the form of corporeality of the exalted Lord. When He implants people into Christ, He at the same time incorporates Them into Himself, into his own communional existence. By giving participation in Himself as love in person, He mediates our participation in the Divine Communion and its communication, and thus makes the communion of the Church real.

---

unity'. It is the kind of unity that *signifies* 'the communication of the many variously realised ones'" (Czaja, *Credo in Spiritum Vivificantem*, 90–1).

239 Cf. Czaja, *Credo in Spiritum Vivificantem*, 320, 322.

240 Cf. Czaja, *Credo in Spiritum Vivificantem*, 61–4. "The Holy Spirit realises this communion of God with the creation. from the very beginning, as God's immanent presence in the world, He opens the creation to intra-trinitarian life; He is the principle of its reception. As the Spirit of Christ, He brings into creation God's offer of perfect communion and makes it our life. The essence of His action in the mission *ad extra* can be expressed in the words: union [*Vereinigung*], being in [*In-Sein*], going beyond self [*Über-Hinaus*]. By constituting the dynamic of the Divine going beyond self, He actualises our union with God by giving us a share in the Divine being" (Czaja, *Credo in Spiritum Vivificantem*, 64).

241 Cf. Kehl, "Kirche – Sakrament des Geistes," 157.

242 Cf. Kehl, *Die Kirche*, 70–73; Czaja, *Credo in Spiritum Vivificantem*, 64–7, 94.

He builds the one Body of Christ by giving us a share in the trinitarian communion which He embodies. This body is the opposite of intra-historical corporeality, it is an open dynamic of communication, pure being for others, precisely because it is developed by the One who is the enabling and 'driving force' of personal dialogue. By analogy to the Trinity, He realises in us 'a love that unites until it lasts'; He makes it possible that 'the Church is love'".[243] A. Czaja notes critically that "unfortunately, with this kind of view of the triune unity of God as a communion of the Father and the Son in the Holy Spirit, Ratzinger – by the way, similarly to Augustine – adopts a purely relational conception of person. In the Trinity, he explains, the Father 'does not beget the Son, as if the act of begetting were added to the already full person'. The Father is Person not as the begetting one, but as an act of begetting. Similarly, 'the Son as Son and insofar as He is Son, He is nothing of Himself, has nothing of His own; He is an entity *from* and *towards*'. 'Father', 'Son" and 'Holy Spirit' are thus terms designating relations in the one and only substance of God. This *means* that the unity in God is not a differentiated unity of Persons standing in relation to each other – as the Cardinal claims in [...] the article *Der Heilige Geist als communio*. The conclusion is the opposite: 'Unity is in the plane of substance; trinity in the plane of relation, in the plane of what is relative'. If this is so, then the trinity of unity in God implies three relations in one subject. Thus, the Divine communion is reduced to the unity of one subject, an intra-subjective unity. Although the Cardinal recognises relations as being as primordial a form of being as substance, the simultaneity (*Gleichursprünglichkeit*) of the element of unity and trinity in God is clearly subjected to the domination of the all-embracing substance, since Persons as pure relations, having nothing of their own, cannot be conceived of outside of substance.[244]

W. Kasper writes of the Holy Spirit's participation in interpersonal communion (not intrapersonal communion – like Ratzinger, or intrapersonal inexistence – like Mühlen), which has no analogues in the human world, since being itself and co-existence are identical in God: "the three trinitarian persons are pure relationality;

---

243 Czaja, *Credo in Spiritum Vivificantem*, 72.

244 Czaja, *Credo in Spiritum Vivificantem*, 72–3. The author goes on to write: "The inconsistency of the Roman Prefect's thought, embedding the unity in God – once on the level of substance and, at other times, on the level of personal being, is not without resonance. A fundamental interpretative difficulty is related to what the Cardinal reproached Augustine for (which he himself, unfortunately, did not overcome): He enclosed the Divine Persons completely in the Divine interior and, consequently, conceded the action of God *ad extra* to the subjectivity of the Divine substance. When the persons are totally relational to one another, the whole activity of God can only be associated with the one subjective Self of the Divine nature. Thus, the very possibility of the historico-salvific self-giving of the Three Divine Persons revealed to us comes into question. If They do not have Their own personal being, how can we speak of Their historico-salvific activity?" (ibid., 73–4). Here Czaja recalls the objection of W. Kasper against Rahner's concept of distinguished modes of subsistence in God: Kasper, *Der Gott Jesu Christi* (Mainz: Grünewald, 1982), 353, 368.

they are relations in which the one essence of God subsists each time in an unchangeably different way. They are subsistent relations".[245] Czaja notes that in this statement Kasper reveals his helplessness, which is analogous to that found in the Eastern and Western Churches for centuries in all their attempts to reconcile unity and trinity in God. Aware of the difficulties of seeing the Divine Persons as pure relations, he accepts the Thomasian interpretation of relation as the only valid one and distinguishes between "being a relation" and "standing in relation". However, when he wants to express the essence of the Divine Persons, he describes them as "pure relationality" and this is not a one-time awkward formulation. He also describes the Father as pure self-expression, the Son as pure listening, and the Spirit as pure receiving. In doing so, he seems to accept Ratzinger's thesis that the Divine Persons are relations, while the human persons stand in relation. At the same time, Kasper speaks of the Divine Persons as modes of subsistence of the one Divine essence.[246]

In the Holy Spirit, God has "the possibility and reality of being outside of Himself" because in Him "what is most internal [in God] is simultaneously most external".[247] When the Spirit is sent and imparts Himself as God's eschatological gift to the world, we receive the gift of the Father through the Son to share in it. His "coming and staying is at the same time the second coming of Jesus and His indwelling in believers, by which the Father is in them as the Son is in the Father".[248] At the same time, the Holy Spirit, who penetrates the depths of divinity and knows it (cf. 1 Cor 2:11), opens up the triune essence of God, enabling us to know who God is. As the subjective possibility of Divine Revelation, the Spirit enables us to learn God ever more deeply, and helps us to accept and acknowledge in faith the revelation of the glory of the Father through the Son and of the Son through the Father. In this way, God is glorified in us and we are included in the eternal doxology of God.[249]

The trinitarian communion-unity itself is even "an excess of selfless giving, of bestowal, of loving self-effusion, a unity that does not exclude but implies an en-

---

245 Kasper, *Der Gott Jesu Christi*, 376. "He adopts the thought of modern personalism: 'a person exists only in relation, personality exists concretely only in interpersonality, subjectivity only in intersubjectivity'. Hence... [...] he favours a substantial-relational concept of person... [...] He speaks of the Father as the *speaking* one, presents the Son as the one *responding in obedience*, and the Holy Spirit is, according to him, the *purely receiving* one'" (Czaja, *Credo in Spiritum Vivificantem*, 82). Czaja supplements this opinion: "Miroslav Volf seems to rightly *point out* that Kasper does not explain how the self-speaking can be at the same time the speaking one and that, consequently, he does not overcome the difficulties arising from identifying the Divine Persons with relations; he seems to only verbally cover these difficulties" (Czaja, *Credo in Spiritum Vivificantem*, 82).

246 Cf. Czaja, *Credo in Spiritum Vivificantem*, 79–81.

247 Kasper, *Der Gott Jesu Christi*, 278.

248 Kasper, *Der Gott Jesu Christi*, 375.

249 Cf. Czaja, *Credo in Spiritum Vivificantem*, 83–4.

livening and loving being with and for one another".[250] Kasper speaks of the ecstasy of mutual love in God, of which the Spirit is the expression. In Him and through Him, God is eternally enthusiasm beyond Himself, self-giving love and kenotic existence of eternity, in which we can participate through Him. In the way that the Spirit is the God's way outward, He also makes all created reality return to God, and through Him soteriology ends again in the doxology.[251]

A peculiar and rather isolated interpretation of the Divine Communion is developed by Bertram Stubenrauch. On the one hand, the Father, the Son and the Holy Spirit, revealed in the history of salvation as bearers of concrete divine actions, are subjects, but on the other hand, as Persons, they are entirely relational, and are thus constituted not by what differentiates them, but by what unites them (the relational dimension). For this reason, God constitutes a unity as well as a *communio*, since the subjectivity of the Father, the Son and the Holy Spirit is not lost, since these Three, as Persons, are wholly directed towards one another, act together for Their own Divine being and receive this being from one another. Their personality is thus, in a way, owed to and constitutes a gifted form of being. It is a structure of being in which They are in relation to one another and are distinguished from one another in such a way that together They form the "Person" of the one God. The conclusion is surprising: instead of one God in three Persons, it would be more appropriate to speak of three subjective forms of realisation of being in one Person – the Divine reality. Such a conclusion, however, is not wrong if one takes into account the modern understanding of person as a self-conscious and free centre of acts. It corresponds to Bernard Lonergan's suggestion that in the Holy Trinity we deal with a single consciousness, which the three Divine entities "possess" each time in a different way.[252] Within such an understanding of unity in God as intersubjective

250 Kasper, *Der Gott Jesu Christi*, 380.

251 Cf. Czaja, *Credo in Spiritum Vivificantem*, 84. "Thus, in the current of the substantial-relational understanding of person (with a certain lack of its consistent application to the Divine Persons), Kasper perceives the Divine communion differently. He speaks of the mystery of trinitarian *communio*-unity. It denotes the communion of Persons interpenetrating one another within a single essence, and this understanding determines the account of the intra-trinitarian origin of the Spirit. The Father and the Son give origin to the Spirit in mutual love towards each other, and not, as Mühlen wants it, in a common act of Divine love, when the Father and the Son love the nature that is common to Them. However, despite this distinction, Kasper, similarly to Mühlen, speaks of the personal indwelling of the Spirit, which, through the mediation of Christ, gives us a share in the Father. He also speaks of that personal property of the Spirit which enables God to transcend Himself. In doing so, he distinguishes between the pneumatological mediation of the Divine opening to us and the pneumatological mediation of our opening to God. Moreover, a new element is the indication of the Spirit as the one who makes it possible for us to share in the eternal glory of the Triune One" (Czaja, *Credo in Spiritum Vivificantem*, 84–5).

252 Cf. Stubenrauch, *Pneumatologie*, 123–4.

communion, the intra-trinitarian status of the Spirit consists in being a pure gift. The Father and the Son subsist as subject-persons in a reciprocal relationship; in personal terms, They are completely devoted to each other, and in subjective terms, They give Themselves. The Holy Spirit is a pure Gift as subject and Person – His subjectivity and personality are realised in the eternal act of being given. He is a Gift dwelling wholly in the Father and wholly in the Son, and enabling Their union and differentiation, realising the Divine being and thus enabling God's self-giving internally and externally. In relation to the two Givers – the Father and the Son – He constitutes something "Third": He cannot be Their reproduction, because then the Father and the Son would lose their subjectivity. As subject, the Spirit is a Gift distinct from the Father and the Son, as such He is a specific way of realising the Divine being, and as Person He unites the Father and the Son in Himself.[253] "The Spirit realises God insofar as He goes out of Himself, insofar as He is outside of Himself [...] The Spirit is the intra-trinitarian being-beyond-self of the Father and the being-beyond-self of the Son, since He proceeds from both of Them and is thus a Person in two Persons"[254] and a Divine subject.[255]

Other theologians who further explore the communional unity in God speak of the communion-generating communication of the Persons. According to Jürgen Moltmann, unity is realised in a continuous process of mutual interpenetration of the Divine Persons, by the indwelling of one in the other two. They shape it by Themselves in the bloodstream of the Divine Life and therefore unity cannot be statically understood as an eternal circulation of the same.[256] Moltmann even speaks of a historical process of God's development.[257] For Wolfhart Pannenberg, the self-identity of the Divine Persons is realised through mutual interpersonal relations, while unity consists in that each of the Persons shares in one Divine essence through Their relation to the other two. The unity of God is therefore not something given in advance, it is realised in the communion of the Persons, in their mutual relation to each other.[258] Markus Knapp sees God as an "intersubjectively constituted reality of life". The triune God constitutes a kind of special existence realised in interpersonal communication – the mutual interpenetration of the Di-

253 Cf. Stubenrauch, *Pneumatologie*, 124–5.

254 Stubenrauch, *Pneumatologie*, 125.

255 Cf. Czaja, *Credo in Spiritum Vivificantem*, 86–8.

256 Cf. Moltmann, *Trinität und Reich Gottes*, 191.

257 Cf. Czaja, *Credo in Spiritum Vivificantem*, 88.

258 Cf. Wolfhart Pannenberg, "Die Subjektivität Gottes und die Trinitätslehre. Ein Beitrag zur Beziehung zwischen Karl Barth und der Philosophie Hegels," in *Grundfragen systematischer Theologie. Gesammelte Aufsätze*, ed. Pannenberg (Göttingen: Vandenhoeck & Ruprecht, 1980), 2: 111.

vine Persons, Their participation in one another, rooted in the simultaneity of Their being.[259]

For M. Kehl and G. Greshake, God is a communion of personal communication marked by the simultaneity of unity and multiplicity. According to Greshake, the Christ event reveals that God is life, relationship, communion.[260] In order to express the depth of communication in God, Greshake refers to the metaphor of a game-play to express the content of the concept of perichoresis. Divine communion can thus be understood as a "game-play" of Divine love that takes place between three Persons: the Lover, the Beloved and the Co-Beloved. These three Persons are apparently the "nodal points" among which the rhythm of love is realised: giving – receiving – giving back. In this rhythm of eternal love, the Father is the Original Gift, but He does not exist without the Son and the Spirit. Thus, He cannot be conceived of in isolation from the other Persons as Their – even if only logically prior – "Pre-Basis". His specificity is the "mystery of being the gift", He gives the whole Communion a "basis" in which the other Persons see their "centre", but not in the sense of a "genetic origin".[261]

With reference to the thought of Richard of Saint Victor, a phenomenology of perfect love emerges. The Father is bestowing love, the Son is receiving and bestowing love, the Holy Spirit is pure receiving love[262], but They are the same love in three rhythms.[263]

> In the rhythm of love, the Holy Spirit is, on the one hand, pure receiving, because He is the gift of the Father and the Son (in a different way) and a loving response in praise and adoration. On the other hand, He is the knot of love between the Father and the Son that constitutes their unity and oneness of being. He is the 'Third' (according to Richard of Saint Victor) who unites in the fire of selfless love the incomprehensible being of the other of the Father and the Son as Their 'unity in opposition', as the 'objectification of Their subjectivity', by which He acts against the possibility of Their blending or separation and directs Them towards each other. This is how the Holy Spirit, by being the gift of the Father to the Son and of the Son to the Father, confirms the identity of the givers – the identity in the difference between the Father and the Son, and thus identity in the difference of the Divine Communion of love. However, in the dual character of the knot of love between the Father and the Son and the fruit of that love as the Third guarantor of that love, the Holy Spirit is no duality. This dual character is two aspects of the same content in which

---

259 Cf. Knapp, "Die Theorie des kommunikativen Handelns als Denkmodell für den trinitarischen Gottesbegriff?," 335; Czaja, *Credo in Spiritum Vivificantem*, 88–9.

260 Cf. Greshake, *Der dreieine Gott. Eine trinitarische Theologie*, 192, 194–5, 204–5.

261 Cf. Czaja, *Credo in Spiritum Vivificantem*, 91.

262 Cf. Greshake, *Trójjedyny Bóg. Teologia trynitarna*, 184–5.

263 Cf. Laurentin, *Nieznany Duch Święty*, 377–8.

> the Spirit expresses the Divine 'We' of love. The Holy Spirit is the Person in whom the *Communio* of Divine love finds its full shape, and even more – in it, in going 'beyond oneself', the 'split' of the Father and the Son takes place. In the Spirit, the personal totality of the Divine life becomes comprehensible.[264]

M. Kehl has a different view on the "singularity" of the Holy Spirit in "the dynamism of God's threefold love".[265] He conceives of Him as the personal mediation (*communio*) of the giving (the Father) and receiving (the Son) love – also in intra-trinitarian communication he assigns to the Holy Spirit the function of uniting the "wherefrom" of love in God with its "whereto", as well as constitutes the "wherein" of divine love. The specificity of His personhood lies in the fact that He is not only the always pre-given and mediating "Environment" of mutual love between the Father and the Son, but at the same time also its "social form".[266] We could thus say that, on the one hand, the Holy Spirit constitutes the "womb" of divine love, the pre-given "space" in which the dynamic of mutual self-giving of the Father and the Son takes place and, on the other hand, that Their love takes in Him the shape of "We" which, despite all its dependence on the Father and the Son, has relative autonomy as simultaneously pre-given to Them and originating in Their mutual devotion. This love does not allow the two sides of the relationship between the Father and the Son to reduce one to the other – on the contrary, it reveals their immiscible personal difference. Therefore, the Holy Spirit is the principle of Their simultaneous unity and diversity, He constitutes the personal communion of love of the Father and the Son as well as Their inherent power and dynamic of transcending each other.[267]

264 Jagodziński, "Trialogiczno-komunijna koncepcja trynitologii," 70. Cf. Greshake, *Trójjedyny Bóg. Teologia trynitarna*, 185–6; Greshake, *Wierzę w Boga trójjedynego*, 35; Czaja, *Credo in Spiritum Vivificantem*, 92.

265 Cf. Kehl, *Die Kirche*, 72.

266 Cf. Czaja, *Credo in Spiritum Vivificantem*, 93.

267 Cf. Czaja, *Credo in Spiritum Vivificantem*, 94. "In the Spirit, the Father 'goes out' to the Son and the Son to the Father. Likewise, in this dynamic of self-transcendence that is proper to the Spirit, the Triune One gives Himself to the creation and realizes his salvific work. Therefore, the dialectic that constitutes the specificity of the personal being of the Spirit is also revealed in the economy of salvation. It is the dialectic of simultaneously being the 'space' and the 'effect' of divine love (the mutual self-giving of the Father and the Son). The Spirit is revealed as the personal 'environment' already given forever, in which the crucified and salvific love of the Father and the Son becomes the inner reality of man. Through Him, the universal history of humanity is received and incorporated into the history of the love of the Father and the Son, and becomes the historical figure of Divine love, the sacrament of Divine *communio*" (Czaja, *Credo in Spiritum Vivificantem*, 94).

3. The Pneumatological-Sacramental Structure of the Church's Communion

The Church's teaching about God does not bring any new concept of God, but rather continues the faith of Israel modified by Jesus Christ[1]. Christ is the Lord who sits at the right hand of God (cf. Ps 110:1), receiving all honour and glory, but upon departing to the Father He said: "I will not leave you orphaned; I am coming to you. [...] But the Advocate, the Holy Spirit, whom the Father will send in my name, will teach you everything, and remind you of all that I have said to you" (John 14:18,26). When Christ sits at the right hand of God, the Father sends another Advocate – the Spirit of Truth.[2]

The coming of the Third Person – the Holy Spirit – has initiated a new relationship of people to God. His Person verifies the presence of God Himself, gives gifts and demonstrates His power.[3] The first disciples were compelled to find a place in their understanding of God for the experience of the Holy Spirit, by whose power Christ breaks down the barriers of nature and forms the Church.[4] Thus we cannot continue to relate to God as Israel did without relating to the Son and the Spirit. We have the person of Christ who called Himself "the Son of God" and the person of the Holy Spirit who makes Christ present to us in the Church.[5] Through the experience of communion, the Church was led to profess faith in the Father, the Son and the Holy Spirit – this Trinitarian formula of faith became the proper name of the Christian God. Therefore, one must either reject it and remain with the form of faith found in Israel, or accentuate its Trinitarian character, which brings about a new communion of all creation through Christ.[6]

1 Cf. Zizioulas, *Lectures*, 40–4.

2 Cf. Zizioulas, *Lectures*, 44. In Chapter 15 of the Acts of the Apostles, the assembly of the Apostles addressed a message to the Christians containing very significant words: "For it has seemed good to the Holy Spirit and to us" (Acts 15:28). Zizioulas comments on the words "All scripture is inspired by God" (2 Tim 3:16) and writes that the teaching of the Church is equal to the Holy Spirit's work. One must not think that this is done in a mechanical or magical way, or as the work of the Holy Spirit leading to the development and improvement of the efforts of the human spirit over time. Rather, it must be seen as the work of the Holy Spirit that is an event of communion, which is centred in the community and has both horizontal and vertical dimensions (cf. Zizioulas, *Lectures*, 10).

3 Cf. Zizioulas, *Lectures*, 106–8.

4 Cf. Zizioulas, *Lectures*, 33, 45, 136; Zizioulas, *Being as Communion*, 110–3.

5 Cf. Zizioulas, *Lectures*, 148–53.

6 Cf. Zizioulas, *Lectures*, 45.

The work of the Holy Spirit is described by the Bible and tradition in various ways, mainly in terms of "power", "sanctification"; He is called "the Spirit of Truth", "the Spirit of Freedom" and, above all, "the Giver of Life" and "communion". Of these categories, "the Giver of Life" and "communion" seem to be the most significant ones for ecclesiology, especially since they actually include other categories as well. Besides, St. Paul and almost all the Church Fathers view the work of the Holy Spirit through the prism of these two terms. In fact, they have an identical meaning, because the Divine life which the Spirit gives is the life in the communion of persons. It is He who creates power and dynamic existence, as well as sanctification, miracles and prophecies, and leads to the truth – all this happens in Him.[7]

The significance and specificity of the pneumatological dimension of the Church lies precisely in the fact that it goes beyond linear historicism, making the eschaton part of the anamnesis (i. e. historical consciousness) of the Church. This happens "in the Spirit" and is so fundamental that it carries with it a warning to ecclesiology not to apply such unconditional linear historicism to the mystery of the Church. It is not caused by a pre-existing factor – whether Christological or pneumatological – but is constituted by both simultaneously. The chronological priority of Christological events over Pentecost is transcended in the Spirit – in the Gospel of John, the granting of the Holy Spirit is part of the Christological events. Going beyond linear history is precisely the Spirit's role, which does not make the Church any less Christological. The Church is the Body of Christ precisely because it is a "spiritual body". In this way, the Church becomes in the Spirit the image of the Trinity itself, in which the "essential" and the "existential", nature and person, are not causally related to each other, but are identical. This makes it impossible in ecclesiology to distinguish between "essence" and "event" and this is what the Holy Spirit does with the ontology of the Church.[8]

The Church is not simply inspired, animated or guided by the Holy Spirit – it is the Body of Christ established by Him. The Holy Spirit's proper and specific function – to create life during communion by implementing God's life here and now – means that, in constituting the Church as the Body of Christ, He makes the

---

7 Cf. Zizioulas, The *One and the Many,* 78. "The most important implication, therefore, of any synthesis between Christology and Pneumatology is one to which theology has not done full justice: in being conceivable only in the Spirit, Christ appears to be a relational being to an absolute degree; He cannot be conceived in terms of our empirical individualized existence. He is not an individual but a Person in the true sense of the word. His existence implies a body *by definition.* The Bible speaks of Him as the Messiah in terms of 'corporate personality' (Servant of God, Son of Man, etc.), and the Fathers, following Paul, describe Him as the recapitulation of all humanity, even of creation. But although this is a commonplace in theology readily admitted by all, it is hardly stressed that all this is inconceivable without Pneumatology. It is the Spirit that opens up reality to become relational, and this applies to Christ as well, if not par excellence" (Zizioulas, The *One and the Many*, 78).

8 Cf. Zizioulas, *The One and the Many*, 79–80.

totality of Christ a concrete existential reality in a particular environment, i. e. in the local community. In this way, this constitutive function of the Spirit fully transcends the dilemma of the relationship between locality and catholicity – both exist in each other at the very roots of the Church's existence. This is what allowed the early Church, from the time of St. Paul, to easily use the word *ecclesia* (ἐκκλησία) both to refer to the Church as a whole and to the local Church.[9] The first and, in a sense, ultimate form of this is the Eucharistic community. In no other form of its existence does the Church see from the beginning a complete synthesis of the Paschal (Christological) mystery with the Pentecostal (pneumatological) mystery. Although the Eucharist was instituted Christologically – at the Last Supper – it was not celebrated on the day of its institution, but on the day of the Resurrection – on the eschatological day of Sunday. Thus, in the Eucharist, the Body of Christ in its objective ontology becomes conditioned by the epiclesis – without Christ there is no community, but if there is no community to call upon the Holy Spirit, Calvary is no longer Calvary. The epiclesis (ἐπίκλησις) of the Spirit gives life the Body (John 6:63), and this removes any notion of causality from the sacramental reality of the Church; through the epiclesis, the Church embodies in itself the event of Christ without causing it or being caused by it. Thus, there is no question of priority between Christ and the Holy Spirit, which is also clearly shown by the epicleses of the early Church.[10]

Salvation is realised in communion.[11] However, entering Christ's pathway is accomplished not only through Him, but also – and in equal measure – through the gift of the Holy Spirit. There must be a certain interplay between Jesus Christ's "external" invitation and man's "internal" commitment to communion: eyes and ears must be opened, and man's heart must be touched to understand and respond in a personal and unique way to the sign that is Jesus.[12] And this is the work of the

---

9 "Thus, the Pneumatological dimension of the Church implies her local character in a constitutive sense. Yet, just as on the anthropological level the Spirit does not create individuals but persons in communion, in the same way ecclesiologically no individualistic isolation of the local community is conceivable in the Spirit. This is shown in the structure of the Church in two ways: (a) by a communion in time through apostolic succession, and (b) by a communion in space through conciliarity" (Zizioulas, *The One and the Many*, 81).

10 Cf. Zizioulas, *The One and the Many*, 80–1.

11 Zizioulas adds, however: "The basic view of the Fathers both in the West and in the East, that the operation of God *ad extra* should be regarded as one, leaves no room for a division of the Economy between Christology and Pneumatology. No matter how specific the role of the Spirit is – and we shall come to that in a moment – it is extremely dangerous for the unity of the Economy to speak of a special 'Economy of the Spirit.' With regard to the Church in particular, any such view would make it difficult to understand the biblical assertion that the Church is the Body of Christ and not of the Spirit" (Zizioulas, *The One and the Many*, 77).

12 Cf. Greshake, *Trójjedyny Bóg*, 324–5.

Holy Spirit.[13] In the confession of the Holy Spirit, the Church is conceived of as the place of the Spirit's action in the world.[14] The communication and communion that can be realised in the world has its ultimate justification in the trinitarian-Christological context,[15] and particularly in the pneumatological context.[16]

The Church has its source in the heart of God. Coming from such a source, "it is [...] a constant participation in the most intimate act of Jesus' being: in dialogue with the Father, in union with Him, in communion. And this communion of the Father and the Son is the Holy Spirit. And it is Him too, the Spirit of God, the One who is communion in God, who can make His Church a communion. And He does so. It is precisely from here – from His intrinsic communion with God and the capacity flowing from this to build interpersonal communion that the hope of the Church itself and all its hope-generating powers come from. J. Ratzinger/Benedict XVI emphasises that Church's salvation (today and always) does not come from tactics and strategies, compromise or adjustment, or from mere theories; 'salvation can only come from' an understanding of the truth about oneself and 'the depth of faith that opens the gate to the Holy Spirit and His unifying power'."[17]

The mystery of the Church's vitality is based on the constant presence in the Church of the resurrected Lord (cf. Matt 28:20), who lives and works through His Spirit. Christ established the Church while the Holy Spirit constituted the Church's being and nature.[18] The Second Vatican Council taught that the pilgrim Church "originates from the mission of the Son and the mission of the Holy Spirit".[19] J. Zizioulas emphasises that the salvific work of Christ and the Holy Spirit belong to each other, they are like two sides of the mystery of salvation, which owes its origin to the initiative of the Father carried out by Christ in the Holy Spirit. At the same time, it is not important that the mystery of Christ chronologically precedes

---

13 Cf. Greshake, *Trójjedyny Bóg*, 363–70.

14 Cf. Ratzinger, *Wprowadzenie w chrześcijaństwo*, 332.

15 Cf. Karl Grüner, "Überlegungen zu einer theologischen Kommunikationstheorie," *Communicatio Socialis. Zeitschrift für Publizistik in Kirche und Welt* 19 (1986), 211–2.

16 Cf. Jagodziński, *Communio dzięki komunikacji*, 340–342; Jagodziński, "Teologia a komunikacja," 73–4; Jagodziński, *Węzłowe zagadnienia chrystologii komunijnej*, 268–72.

17 Szymik, "Eklezjologia komunii. Kirche als koinonia, la Chiesa come communio, Kościół jako wspólnota w pismach J. Ratzingera/Benedykta XVI i W. Wójtowicza," in *O Kościele Jezusa Chrystusa dzisiaj*, 306. "'The Church cannot organise itself according to its own liking, but becomes itself only through the gift of the Holy Spirit, received through prayer in the name of Jesus Christ'. This is ultimately – in practice – decisive: The Church becomes itself through the liturgy, 'joining in the prayer of Jesus Christ, dwelling with him in the sphere of the Holy Spirit and speaking to the Father. It becomes the Church through adoration'" (Szymik, "Eklezjologia komunii," 316).

18 Cf. Congar, *Wierzę w Ducha Świętego. Duch Święty w "ekonomii" Objawienia*, 14–22; Jerzy Pałucki, *Trynitarny wymiar Kościoła. Studium patrystyczne* (Lublin: Wydawnictwo KUL, 2007), 91–9.

19 Cf. AG 2; Czaja, *Jedna Osoba w wielu osobach*, 371.

the mystery of Pentecost since the historical order of salvific events cannot obscure the depth of the whole mystery of the Church. The mystery of the Church arises from a single, integrally understood Christological-pneumatological event. The chronological priority of Christology over pneumatology is balanced by the fact that Christ Himself appears from the beginning of His earthly activity as a person "filled with the Holy Spirit" (cf. Luke 1:15; 4:1,18). According to the Gospel of John, the sending of the Holy Spirit is part of the Christological event (cf. John 7:39; 20:22). The Holy Spirit reveals Christ, while Christ sends the Spirit from the Father – this law of reciprocity has become a fundamental principle of the trinitarian economy of salvation.[20]

While discussing the presence of the Son and the Holy Spirit in the Church, H.U. von Balthasar also addressed the figurative designations of Christ as the "Head" and the Holy Spirit as the "Soul" of the Church. In the trinitologically important passage from Ephesians 3:16-19, St. Paul addressed a threefold request to the Father for the Christian community: "that [...] he may grant that you may be strengthened in your inner being with power through his Spirit, and that Christ may dwell in your hearts through faith, as you are being rooted and grounded in love [...] that you may have the power to comprehend, with all the saints, what is the breadth and length and height and depth, and to know the love of Christ that surpasses knowledge, so that you may be filled with all the fullness of God". Christ does not appear here as the "Head" of the Church, but as the innermost vital principle inseparable from the Holy Spirit. It is therefore necessary to go beyond the dualism of meaning and action in theological interpretation. The union of the glorified Christ with the Church ("Body" or "Bride") occurs certainly through imparting His Holy Spirit but also, in equal measure, through Christ's self-giving in the sacraments, above all in the Eucharist. It is thus necessary to look for the mutual interpenetration of the images of "Head" and "Soul", whereby it is not enough to consider the hypostatic union in Christ and the bestowal of the gifts of the Holy Spirit on the Church, and then leave it solely to the Holy Spirit to endow the Church with a living structure. It is only in the totality of what the pre-Paschal Jesus established and, as the resurrected Lord, bestowed on the Church that the structure of the Church wandering in the world can be fully grasped.[21]

---

20 Cf. Małecki, *Kościół jest wspólnotą*, 83. The content of this introduction is taken from Jagodziński, *Węzłowe zagadnienia chrystologii komunijnej*, 248–57.

21 Cf. Balthasar, *Teologika*, vol. III: *Duch Prawdy*, 269–72. Ibid., 272: "for us, dwelling in the flesh, everything spiritual-charismatic must be framed in visible structures, but these structures are internally filled with the goods of the resurrected, now spiritual Christ. To state this is more than to say merely that the Church is both visible and invisible at the same time; it must be said more specifically that, as long as it remains on earth, it is both pre- and post-Paschal. The point in which

The social form of the kingdom of God lives on in the post-Easter community of believers, gathered by the Resurrected One in the Holy Spirit because He did not descend only on the elect few, but on "the whole believing people". Believers are called "saints" and "the elect" because they have received a share in the common gift of the Spirit of God. Notably, the Church is not constituted by an assembly of pre-gifted people, but by the original (given to all) and joint participation in Spirit of the eschatological people of God.[22] This prior gift of community remains the basic structure of the Church[23] and of every intra-historical form of the Kingdom of God. Its relational, theological basis is the Holy Spirit Himself as the "formal principle" which is the unifying or communal form of the love of the Father and the Son. He unifies the Father and the Son (as the "wherefrom" and "whereto" of God's love) as well as the mediating, preceding and abiding "wherein" of that love. He "precedes" – because it is only in the "Environment" ("Medium") of common love (in the Holy Spirit) that the reference between the Father and the Son unfolds; He "abides" – because this "Environment" does not exist independently of the mutual reference between the Father and the Son (with all the relational independence of the Person of the Holy Spirit in God), but it continually flows from this reference.[24]

3.1 The Holy Spirit as the Co-Creator of the Church's Communion

J. Ratzinger writes that the Holy Spirit creates ecclesial communion[25] by bestowing Himself and giving in Himself ("in the Spirit"). Being always a Divine gift, He comes and exists as the Given One. Remaining within God, He represents at the

---

these two spheres meet is the death of Jesus, who concludes His earthly life with an act of supreme sacrifice, and thereby simultaneously gives the Holy Spirit from Himself to the Church."

22 "The term *kōinonia* in the Holy Spirit (2 Cor 13:13), which emphasises that the Church is a community of persons, united in the Holy Spirit, captures the truth of why this "external" or sociological community is at the same time an "'internal" community between the baptised. According to its original meaning, the term proposed by the Apostle signifies, firstly, the truth that it is the Holy Spirit who sanctifies the Church, making it a "communion of saints," and therefore it can be called the Temple of God, in which the Spirit dwells and works (cf. Eph 2:21; 2 Cor 6:16; 1 Cor 3:16-17). Secondly, it means that the Church is ontologically holy (sanctified in and by the Spirit) and existentially a pilgrim aiming at achieving the fullness of the gift of holiness deposited in it. Just as the Holy Spirit descended on the Incarnate Word, anointing Him, so He descends on each baptised person and on the Church, performing the holy anointing. Therefore, the Church can regard itself as the continuator of Christ's anointing by the Holy Spirit" (Guzowski, *Duch Dialogujący*, 207–8).

23 Cf. Kehl, *Und was kommt nach dem Ende? Von Weltuntergang und Vollendung, Wiedergeburt und Auferstehung* (Freiburg-Basel-Wien: Herder Verlag, 1999), 98–9.

24 Cf. Kehl, *Eschatologie* (Würzburg: Echter, 1986), 225–30; Jagodziński, *Węzłowe zagadnienia chrystologii komunijnej*, 335–6.

25 Pałucki, *Trynitarny wymiar Kościoła*, 172–87.

same time the opening of God to man and the history of salvation.[26] He is the Gift whose reception makes all-embracing communion real, makes ecclesial communion possible, co-creates with Christ and creates it,[27] mediating the participation of its members in God and His gifts by sharing Himself.[28]

J.D. Zizioulas emphasises that we must grant the Holy Spirit a co-constitutive role in the structure of the Church – He "acts as a force of communion (2 Cor 13:13)"[29]. It is necessary to stop treating the Church as an institution given by history, because such a view today can be perceived as a provocation to human freedom. The Church must be treated as something that is being continually constituted, i. e. emerging from the coincidence and convergence of relationships freely established by the Holy Spirit. There is nothing in the Church that is not given to it – offices, sacraments or other forms of structure – that do not have to be asked for, as if they were not given. This, too, is the epicletic nature of ecclesiology, clearly visible above all in the Eucharist, which, although based on the certainty flowing from the words of its institution, constantly needs the invocation of the Holy Spirit in order to be what it is. We are confronted at this point with a pneumatologically conditioned ontology, in which nothing exists of and in itself, except as a result of free communion, which is precisely the essence of the trinitarian doctrine in relation to God Himself. The

---

26 Czaja refers here (pp. 44–45) to Ratzinger, "Der Heilige Geist als Communio," 230–1. Cf. Guzowski, *Duch Dialogujący*, 209.

27 Cf. Napiórkowski, "Kościół i człowiek: tajemnica, wspólnota, misja," in Napiórkowski (ed.), *Kościół i człowiek* (Kraków: Salwator, 2021), 232–3: "Owing to centuries-long work by theologians, saints and mystics and the sense of faith of the People of God (*sensus fidei*), we can move away from a narrow view of the post-Paschal community as only the Church of Christ, called into existence by Jesus and equipped by the resurrected Lord. For the Church must be seen more as an event of the Holy Spirit than of Jesus of Nazareth. For Jesus unveiled and made present the mystery of the kingdom of God, but it was only after Pentecost that the apostles translated the teaching about it into that of the Church, making the latter the instrument and sign of the fulfilment of that kingdom in the temporal and earthly world. The Spirit, the main principle of unity with the Trinity and at the same time the source of the unity and reconciliation of creation, makes the Church the sacrament of intra-trinitarian relations."

28 Cf. Czaja, *Credo in Spiritum Vivificantem*, 44–6; Sienkiewicz, "Wierzę w święty Kościół powszechny," in *Wiara w świetle dokumentów II Soboru Watykańskiego*, ed. Jagodziński and Jerzy Karbownik (Radom: Wydawnictwo Diecezji Radomskiej AVE, 2013), 57: "the foundation of ecclesial communion, the emerging community in faith, is the Holy Spirit as Communion in God. Therefore, the community of the Church, which is the fruit of a relationship of love in the Holy Spirit and, at the same time, a space open to His action, is in a fundamental sense different from all other communities, constituting a historical form of communion with God and communion between people – built not separately; as it were, alongside this fundamental one, which is the source of communion and unity, but precisely in the Holy Spirit, in the relationship of the Father to the Son." Cf. Sienkiewicz, *Wspólnota Kościoła*, 300–6; Nastałek, "Słowo i Tchnienie. Konieczność duchowości inkarnacyjnej," 122–3.

29 Zizioulas, *The One and the Many*, 265.

Church must respect in everything, and above all in its being, in its ontology, that it is "the Church of God", i. e. the image or sign of the Holy Trinity.[30]

3.2 The Pneumatological-Communional Dimension of Faith

One of the constitutive elements of ecclesial communion is faith. Therefore, one can also speak of the Church's communion of faith.[31] It is quite rare in theology to point to faith as a work of the Holy Spirit, yet He is the animator of the universal faith of the Church and the personal faith of individuals. Ultimately, faith is brought to life by the Spirit's special work. He guarantees its permanence, identity and development. He reminds the disciples of all that Jesus told them (John 14:26) and leads them to the full truth (John 16:13; Luke 24:49), He is the principle for accepting revelation in faith and for confessing and witnessing.[32]

> In God's gift of faith, a supernatural infused virtue, we realize that a great love has been offered us, a good word has been spoken to us, and that when we welcome that word, Jesus Christ the Word made flesh, the Holy Spirit transforms us, lights up our way to the future and enables us joyfully to advance along that way on wings of hope. Thus wonderfully interwoven, faith, hope and charity are the driving force of the Christian life as it advances towards full communion with God.[33]

Faith is of communional nature and it is impossible to build a private communion with God. Nor can man believe of himself; by faith he joins the decision made in the community of believers. His participation in it is not a subsequent act – a corollary of faith, but it is part of faith as a personal act of man and a collective act of the Church. Zizioulas writes that the Church dogmas are not logical propositions to be tested and approved by the minds of individual believers, but doxological statements intended to glorify God and for the life of communities. Therefore, the

---

30 Cf. Zizioulas, *The One and the Many*, 15–6.

31 Cf. Czaja, *Credo in Spiritum Vivificantem*, 135–6.

32 Cf. Czaja, *Credo in Spiritum Vivificantem*, 140.

33 Francis, Encyclical *Lumen fidei*, 7. Thanks to the presence and action of the Holy Spirit, "the place where a living faith is present and can be experienced as 'the new light born of an encounter with the true God, a light which touches us at the core of our being and engages our minds, wills and emotions, opening us to relationships lived in communion' (No. 40). The unity of the faith is what creates and, at the same time, what expresses the unity of the Church as a community on pilgrimage in history and moving towards full communion with God. Therefore, 'to subtract something from the faith is to subtract something from the veracity of communion'" (No. 48) (Gardocki, "Encyklika 'Lumen fidei' Ojca Świętego Franciszka, Drukarnia Watykańska, Rzym 2013," *Studia Bobolanum* 3 (2013), 185–6).

Creed is not meant to be studied by theologians, but to be sung by communities.[34] The Holy Spirit guarantees, expands and deepens the memory of the Church, but He also animates the personal act of faith.[35] The profession of faith has its basis in the living relationship initiated by baptism and sustained by the Eucharist.[36] The faith professed by the candidate for baptism is not his own and individual action – it is a response to the Church's question. A person can only say "I believe" in response to the question of this community, faith is only possible within a community that asks about it.[37] It is a kind of giant "leap" towards Someone who, we believe, loves us, never leaves us, and we can only live based on this fact. For the first Christians who took this leap, faith meant participation in the community of the future, in the eschatological communion of God.[38]

Faith is realised in a personal encounter in which the presence of the Spirit embraces both parties and impels them to relate to each other. Therefore, reaching the faith in the Resurrected One, living in the fullness of the Spirit of God, is the fundamental experience of the Holy Spirit. He mediates the certainty of faith, hope and love to man. He makes it possible to enter into a relationship with Christ and wishes to order, ennoble and liberate it. The very readiness to receive Jesus flows "from the gift of grace, i. e. from the inspiration of the Holy Spirit" (Council of Orange – 529). This experience was clearly manifested at the beginning of the Church and involved the reception of the power of the Spirit (cf. Acts 1:5,8). People are filled with the Holy Spirit (Acts 2:4; 4:31; 9:17), they receive the Spirit (Acts 2:38; 8:15; 10:47; 17:19; 19:2), the Holy Spirit descends upon them (Acts 8:16; 10:44; 11:15). He describes this initial experience as the "baptism with the Holy Spirit" (Acts 1:5; cf. 11:16) by the exalted Lord. By imparting His Spirit, Jesus assures the disciples that He lives.[39]

A concrete example of anointing by faith is the outpouring of the Holy Spirit on the people of Caesarea (Acts 10:44-48). In the house of Cornelius, the Holy Spirit descended on those gathered and gave to all the same gift received earlier by the

---

34 Cf. Zizioulas, *The One and the Many*, 57.

35 Cf. Czaja, *Credo in Spiritum Vivificantem*, 141–2. "The self-awareness of the believer now expands because of the presence of another; it now lives in this other and thus, in love, life takes on a whole new breadth. Here we see the Holy Spirit at work. The Christian can see with the eyes of Jesus and share in his mind, his filial disposition, because he or she shares in his love, which is the Spirit. In the love of Jesus, we receive in a certain way his vision. Without being conformed to him in love, without the presence of the Spirit, it is impossible to confess him as Lord (cf. 1 Cor 12:3)" (Francis, Encyclical *Lumen fidei*, 21).

36 Cf. Zizioulas, *Lectures*, 33.

37 Cf. Zizioulas, *Lectures*, 34.

38 Cf. Zizioulas, *Lectures*, 37; Jagodziński, "Teologia jako komunijne nauczanie Kościoła według Johna D. Zizioulasa," in *O Kościele Jezusa Chrystusa dzisiaj*, 124.

39 Cf. Czaja, *Credo in Spiritum Vivificantem*, 143–5.

Apostles (cf. Acts 11:17). The people of Caesarea did not receive the Holy Spirit after having been baptised by laying hands on them (this was the case elsewhere – cf. Acts 8:12,14-17; 19:5-6), but when they had not yet heard the Good News. It then became clear to Peter that he could baptise them: "And as I began to speak, the Holy Spirit fell upon them just as it had upon us at the beginning. And I remembered the word of the Lord, how he had said, 'John baptized with water, but you will be baptized with the Holy Spirit'" (Acts 11:15-16). The coming of the Spirit before baptism leads people to faith, and His coming after baptism – later called confirmation – empowers believers to bear witness to faith. The activity of the Holy Spirit before baptism, which initiates faith in a person, is called "inner baptism", while sacramental baptism is regarded as the embodiment of this inner baptism. Karl Barth considered baptism with water to be the attestation of the prior "baptism with the Holy Spirit". The prior "illumination with the Holy Spirit" is also mentioned in the Tridentine "Decree on Justification". It describes an a priori event in the depths of the human heart that leads up to baptism and precedes the concrete preparation for receiving this sacrament. It signifies God's graciously granted inspiration for man to give an internal response to God's call. God addresses a person and the person becomes ready to receive baptism and to give a personal response to God's call in the act of confession of faith. It turns out that "inner baptism" – which is a priori, gifted and inner act of man's response to God – is not accomplished through the mediation of the word or the sacrament of baptism, but solely by the Holy Spirit. It signifies co-operation with the Holy Spirit and is actualised both by the Spirit's action and the will of the co-operating person.[40]

An interesting analysis of faith was made by M. Kehl,[41] according to whom the Holy Spirit transcendentally enables faith in Jesus. Through the Spirit's indwelling in us, we receive an enabling space for faith in God's revelation. Therefore, every encounter in faith always takes place "in the Holy Spirit". Without this prior space of encounter, there is no faith. If one allows oneself to be embraced by the Spirit, one can recognise in the historical Jesus the eternal Son of the Father. The Church, as a common reference to God in faith, can therefore exist and last if people allow themselves to be included in the "space" of the Holy Spirit. In Him the personal faith of the individual and the universal faith of the Church can develop. The Spirit of Christ includes the individual in the common space of faith, but this does not prevent the possibility of the personal realisation of faith. Wherever the Spirit makes communal and personal faith possible at the same time, the communion of the Church is realised as "the sacramental reflection of the prior gift of the Holy Spirit".

40 Cf. Czaja, *Credo in Spiritum Vivificantem*, 145–8.

41 See Jagodziński, *Komunijna "fenomenologia" Kościoła według Medarda Kehla SJ*, in *Communio w chrześcijańskiej refleksji o Kościele*, ed. Czaja and Marek Marczewski (Wydawnictwo KUL, Lublin 2004), 257–64; Jagodziński, *Komunijna wizja Kościoła według Medarda Kehla SJ*, 13–34.

Just as in the trinitarian communion the Holy Spirit is the pre-given "Environment" of mutual love between the Father and the Son, and at the same time constitutes its "social form", thus, by analogy, in the salvific economy the action of the Spirit is marked by the dialectic of prior giving and consequent commitment. In the intra-trinitarian context, the Holy Spirit acts as the "space" that enables love between the Father and the Son, and in history – as the prior endowment that makes faith possible; it is only in the Holy Spirit that the Father and the Son bind to each another in mutual loving surrender, and only in the Holy Spirit do people come to faith in God shared in Jesus Christ. The specificity of the Spirit's action is revealed in the Church as a sacrament of divine communion in that, in its social form, it is a pre-given "space" that enables the faith of individuals, while, on the other hand, the subjective being in faith is not prevented by common faith.[42]

As an existential "space" of faith, the Church is always given with each personal realisation of faith. The Church accommodates man and makes both his personal and communal faith possible. By itself, the Church cannot cut itself off from specific believers, for it materializes "out of believers" and in believers as a form of faith that is being constantly received and rooted anew. It thus constitutes a "communicative unity of believers". It is the Church for specific people when it leads them into communion in faith; it is also the Church out of specific people when it persists and develops in their subjective and personal forms of faith.[43] In this way, Kehl demonstrated the dialectical character of faith and thus also the dialectical (or dialogical) character of the Church as a community of faith. A consequence and significant achievement of such an approach is the enrichment of the pneumatological interpretation of the act of faith. It presents the Holy Spirit as Christ's prior gift which initiates the act of faith both by empowering man to respond to God and by including him in the space in which the response of faith can be realised. Kehl presents the Holy Spirit as the Live-Giver of personal and communal faith and shows how, through the mediation of this dialectic, the Spirit makes the Church real as a community of faith. On the one hand, the Spirit brings the space of communication; on the other hand, He simultaneously shapes communion out of the independent subjective being of believers.[44]

---

42 Cf. Czaja, *Credo in Spiritum Vivificantem,* 148–51; Jagodziński, "Kościół jako środowisko wiary," in *Wiara wobec współczesności,* ed. Bokwa and Jagodziński (Warszawa: Wydawnictwo UKSW, 2014), 162–8.

43 "In the communion of the one subject which is the Church, we receive a common gaze. By professing the same faith, we stand firm on the same rock, we are transformed by the same Spirit of love, we radiate one light and we have a single insight into reality" (Francis, Encyclical *Lumen fidei,* 47).

44 Cf. Czaja, *Credo in Spiritum Vivificantem,* 151.

3.3 The Pneumatological-Communional Dimension of the Word of God

The XXII Ordinary General Assembly of the Synod of Bishops in 2008 stated:

> The Word of God par excellence is Jesus Christ, God and Man. [...] The Word reveals the Mystery of the Triune God. Eternally spoken by God the Father through the love of the Holy Spirit, the Word carries on a dialogue which expresses communion and leads a person into the depths of the divine life of the Most Blessed Trinity. [...] The human person [...] is the masterpiece of creation, capable of entering into dialogue with the Creator, perceiving in creation the seal of its Author, the Creator-Word, and, through the Spirit, living in communion with the one who is [...] the Living and True God [...] every Christian is invited through the words of Sacred Scripture to discover the Word of God [...] Illuminated by the Holy Spirit [...] the faithful attentively read the Scriptures and draw out their full meaning in encountering the Word of God, the Person of the Lord Jesus Christ, who has the words of eternal life.[45]

The Word of God, therefore, is a means of interpersonal communication between God and men, carries the communicative dimensions of intra-trinitarian relations, serves to build a union of men with God, and generates faith, hope and love in the hearts of men, uniting men in the Church in truth and in life. The communicative function of the Word of God, having its deepest roots in the intra-trinitarian relations of the Divine Persons, serves to build a communion of God with men and a communion of the Church.[46]

In more recent theology, the source of the salvific and ecclesiogenic efficacy of the word of God is more and more clearly seen in the work of the Holy Spirit. When speaking of the event-like and salvific character of the proclaimed word, sometimes it is pointed to the Spirit as the One who makes the encounter of man with God possible through the word. The New Covenant is ultimately based not on the Scriptures but on the Holy Spirit. He makes Scriptures not only contain the words of Christ, but Christ-Word Himself – the Scriptures are virtually His incarnation, comparable to His incarnation in the Eucharist and in the Church, signifying the continued presence of Christ, who is now the Spirit (2 Cor 3:17).[47] For the Church's teaching to be a continuation of the word of God, it must be expressed and administered by the power of the Holy Spirit. "Reminding" it (cf. John 14:26) should be understood as making it present, revealing and explaining

---

45 XII Ordinary General Assembly of the Synod of Bishops, *The Word of God in the Life and Mission of the Church. Instrumentum laboris* (2008).

46 Cf. Jagodziński, "Komunijny wymiar słowa Bożego," in *Słowo Boże w Kościele*, ed. Roman Kuligowski and Jagodziński, and Daniel Swend (Warszawa: Wydawnictwo UKSW, 2009), 46.

47 Cf. Hryniewicz, *Nasza Pascha z Chrystusem*, 181–3.

it and making it available to experience. The anamnestic and salvific power of the proclaimed word has its source in the power of the Holy Spirit. Making Christ and His word present signifies the coming of the Kingdom of God, the personal encounter between God and man and the establishment of communion between Them in the power of the Holy Spirit. Thus, while interpreting the Church as the *creatura verbi*, the Spirit cannot be overlooked.[48]

> Evangelization will never be possible without the action of the Holy Spirit. [...] It is He who explains to the faithful the deep meaning of the teaching of Jesus and of His mystery. It is the Holy Spirit who, today just as at the beginning of the Church, acts in every evangelizer who allows himself to be possessed and led by Him. The Holy Spirit places on his lips the words which he could not find by himself, and at the same time the Holy Spirit predisposes the soul of the hearer to be open and receptive to the Good News and to the kingdom being proclaimed. [...] It must be said that the Holy Spirit is the principal agent of evangelization: it is He who impels each individual to proclaim the Gospel, and it is He who in the depths of consciences causes the word of salvation to be accepted and understood. But it can equally be said that He is the goal of evangelization.[49]

How is it possible that a "cold" mode of communication such as writing is the starting point and basis for personal communication in our encounter with Christ? The primary author of the Scriptures is the Holy Spirit – the Spirit of Jesus. It is He who speaks directly in the books and makes the direct presence of Jesus Christ in the text of the books,[50] He who is the great and present sender of the message contained in the books of the Bible, adapting the actions and words of Jesus to the current needs of each recipient, who is both the individual person and the ecclesial community. The Scriptures are therefore not a book or a collection of books about Christ, but an act, an action in the Holy Spirit. Thanks to the Holy Spirit, the Scriptures present a personal communication with Christ – the encounter with a human author or editor is more indirect and more concerned with the historical and cultural purposes of a particular text.[51]

---

48 Cf. Czaja, *Credo in Spiritum Vivificantem*, 158–62.

49 Paul VI, Exhortation *Evangelii nuntiandi* (1975), 75.

50 This "presence of Christ" refers to a supernatural relational reality, a relationship with Christ in faith, hope and love – through people and human texts – i. e. through direct and reciprocal communication with the resurrected and glorified Christ. It is direct communication because the presence of the glorified Christ surpasses the directness of communication with the people in whom He dwells, and besides, this presence takes away the character of indirect communication from the texts once written. Cf. Leszek Kuc, *Krótki traktat o teologii komunikacji* (Leszno k. Błonia: Lumen, 1997), 53; Jagodziński, "Komunijny wymiar słowa Bożego," 48–9.

51 Cf. Kuc, *A Krótki traktat o teologii komunikacji*, 50–2.

The Church, as a God-appointed community of believers, has a spiritual basis and a space for action[52] in a community of communication, which is realised in communicative action. The condition and consequence of communion is communication, and the Church is a communicative communion with a trinitarian basis.[53] Looking at the historical origins of the Church, one can see a link between its essence and verbal communication.[54] Since, from the beginning, salvation is realised in human forms of expression, the fulfilment of the essential ecclesial realities takes place among the systems of signs – these include linguistic signs (proclamation of the word of God) and written signs (the Scriptures), as well as non-verbal material signs (symbols and rituals). All these systems of signs (individually or in combination) convey information and make communion possible.[55]

The Divine authorship of the Scriptures means that God speaks using them through Christ in the Holy Spirit. This takes place not only during the creation of the books, but also in every instance of concretisation of the biblical literary text – when it is read and analysed in the Church.[56] The Church tradition allows us to hear the living Christ in the words of the Scriptures.[57] Thus, communication with Christ through the biblical books means true communion with Him.[58] Preaching

52 Cf. Jagodziński, *Communio dzięki komunikacji*, 335–43.

53 Cf. Jagodziński, "Trynitarne podstawy Kościoła jako komunii," 51–79; Jagodziński, "Komunijny wymiar słowa Bożego," 53–4.

54 Cf. Hans Otmar Meuffels, *Kommunikative Sakramententheologie* (Freiburg-Basel-Wien: Herder, 1995), 38. The testimonies of the women concerning the resurrection of Jesus (cf. Mark 16:6-11), the accounts of the disciples (cf. Luke 24:33-35) and the preaching of the Apostles (cf. Acts 2:14-16) – provided the basis for the kerygma and the Church.

55 Cf. Hans-Dieter Bastian, *Kommunikation. Wie christlicher Glaube funktioniert* (Stuttgart-Berlin: Kreuz, 1972), 120; Jagodziński, "Teologia a komunikacja," 80–5. Thanks to the very early process of objectification and formalisation taking place in the Church, the word of proclamation has been safeguarded from distortion, and the identity of the community gathering in common faith in this word crucially rests on the permanent identity of the word of God. Cf. Jagodziński, *Communio dzięki komunikacji*, 360–1.

56 Cf. Kuc, *Krótki traktat o teologii komunikacji*, 54–5, 207–8.

57 Cf. Second Vatican Council, *Constitution on Divine Revelation "Dei verbum,"* 8: "This tradition which comes from the Apostles develop in the Church with the help of the Holy Spirit. […] For as the centuries succeed one another, the Church constantly moves forward toward the fullness of divine truth until the words of God reach their complete fulfillment in her. […] Through the same tradition the Church's full canon of the sacred books is known, and the sacred writings themselves are more profoundly understood and unceasingly made active in her; and thus God, who spoke of old, uninterruptedly converses with the bride of His beloved Son; and the Holy Spirit, through whom the living voice of the Gospel resounds in the Church, and through her, in the world, leads unto all truth those who believe and makes the word of Christ dwell abundantly in them (see Col. 3:16)." Cf. ibid., 8–10.

58 Cf. Kuc, *Krótki traktat o teologii komunikacji*, 62; Jagodziński, "Komunijny wymiar słowa Bożego," 54.

has salvific power because Christ Himself speaks and acts by the power of the Holy Spirit. The word read in the Church is supported by the inner enlightenment and witness of the Holy Spirit.[59] Referring to the pneumatological sensibility of the Eastern tradition, we should say that Christianity is intrinsically a religion of the Spirit: "of a new covenant, not of letter but of spirit; for the letter kills, but the Spirit gives life" (2 Cor 3:6). This statement encapsulates the whole theology of the word written on the pages of the Scriptures and proclaimed in Church's living preaching. By the power of the Spirit, the living word of Christ, which is also the word of the Father Himself, can reach man. It has the power to resurrect from spiritual death and to bring a new life. However, it is not the letter alone that saves, but the word that has truly become the Holy Spirit' speech – the proclamation of the Gospels is not done by the word alone, "but also in power and in the Holy Spirit and with full conviction" (1 Thess 1:5). The Scriptures were written under the inspiration of the Holy Spirit (2 Peter l:21). Therefore, reading them in the community of the Church should follow a "spiritual" reading, in the same Spirit under whose influence it was edited. [60] There is no proper reading of the Scriptures without the inspiring role of the Holy Spirit. The Scriptures essentially speak of the all-embracing mystery of Christ (see John 5:39,46; 12:41; Luke 24:25-27; Acts 10:43). However, in order to perceive its deep meaning and call, the action of the Holy Spirit, the Spirit of Christ, is needed. The indissoluble bond between Christ and the Paraclete must also be seen in the mystery of the word of God read, preached and meditated upon in the Church. For the understanding of Scripture requires a "turn to the Lord", whose action is at the same time the action of the Spirit (see 2 Cor 3:16-17). Through Christ, God gives Himself, but always "in the Holy Spirit".[61]

J.D. Zizioulas points out that the West tends to treat Revelation as a rational or intellectual reality, with the Scriptures and the Church treated as repositories of accessible truths, as individual doses of information. For the Orthodox tradition, by contrast, the Scriptures and the Church are the testimonies of prophets and apostles who experienced Christ's truth. Truth, then, is not a matter of objective, logical propositions, but of personal relationships between God, the world and man. One does not arrive at it simply by assimilating it intellectually, but by the experience of being included in communion with God.[62] Therefore,

59 Cf. Hryniewicz, *Nasza Pascha z Chrystusem*, 185.

60 See KO 12.

61 Cf. Hryniewicz, *Nasza Pascha z Chrystusem*, 189–90.

62 Cf. Zizioulas, *Lectures*, 7. "Then we may realize that the Church's trinitarian doctrine of God faithfully articulates the truth of our experience in this communion that is the Church. Through such living experience, every member of the Church experiences the communion of God and is able to affirm that the doctrine of the Trinity is the truth of that reality. The revelation of God is an event in which man comes to experience, and share in, the life of God and of his fellow-man

> To practice theology means as much as to translate communion with God into the language of theology, to narrate its content. Of course, theology includes a doctrinal element, the *kerygma*, guidance and catechesis. But Church surrounds the vital juices of knowledge with greater reverence, listening to its saints and fathers, feeding on their experience of the Holy Spirit, their conversation with the word, and the Church offers these vital juices to all the faithful in the liturgy.[63]

The revelation of the true God is the person of Christ. Of course, it is always personal, however, it takes different shapes. In the New Testament, it has taken on a unique shape. In Jesus Christ, we can not only see and hear God, but also touch Him, feel Him and even relate to Him physically. It is not just a communion of mind or heart, but a communion of sight, hearing and touch: "[…] what we have heard, what we have seen with our eyes, what we have looked at and touched with our hands […]" (1 John 1:1). There is nothing higher than revelation in Christ according to His words: "Whoever has seen me has seen the Father" (John 14:9). The Church Fathers insisted that this communion is final and absolute.[64]

It is the Holy Spirit who leads the Church to the Truth (John 16:13), although Christ claims to be the Truth (John 14:6). To understand how the Church is "the pillar of the truth" (1 Tim 3:15), a proper synthesis of Christology and pneumatology is necessary. The claim that Christ is Truth, ceases in the Spirit to point to objectified

---

and the world, and this revelation brings new light and sense to all life" (ibid., 7–8). "The East has never cultivated the autonomy of natural reason – *lumen naturale rationis.* Addressing man in his revelation, God transformed the human spirit. God's knowledge, even 'natural', is always accompanied by love. According to Origen, '[the Scriptures], on the other hand, call the Wisdom of God that which raises the human soul from temporal affairs to the Divine happiness'. Slavophiles call the Divine knowledge 'the living knowledge', knowledge-life, knowledge-love and communion. They followed Eastern Patristics, which makes no distinction between "the way of love" and "the way of knowledge". According to the Tradition, thinking in truth is always accompanied by love (*caritas*), and in love – there is always wisdom. Both ways, in turn, reach their fullness in a single act of undivided love and wisdom. This is why the main principle of Hesychasm invites us to bring wisdom to the heart, so that the full powers of the human mind, elevated and enlightened by grace, come face to face with the mysteries of God, i. e. beyond any concept or mental image capable of standing between the heart-mind or the eye of the heart and the Creator. [...] faith in the East is never defined as an intellectual approach, but results from the transfiguration of the whole human being by the power of 'obviousness' or Pascalian 'certainty', lived in a particular 'experience of the Transcendent One'. Saint Maximus specified: 'I call experience true knowledge acquired beyond any concept [...], a participation in an object that is realised beyond all thought'. According to the Fathers, contemplative knowledge through participation is true theognosy" (Evdokimov, *Duch Święty w tradycji prawosławnej*, 40–2).

63 Evdokimov, *Duch Święty w tradycji prawosławnej*, 42. In other works, the author calls such an attitude "sapiential gnosis" (cf. Evdokimov, *Prawosławie*, 18–20).

64 Cf. Jagodziński, "Teologia jako komunijne nauczanie Kościoła według Johna D. Zizioulasa," 118–9.

and conceptualised truth and identifies Truth with life and communion, with the very life and communion of God. Given that "truth" never means anything less than true reality in the main tradition of the Greek Fathers, the application of "truth" to the eschaton simply points to the fact that if there is truth in history, it is only insofar as the eschaton enters history, and this can only happen in the Holy Spirit. In this way, Truth becomes a sacramental thing in history; it becomes sanctification (John 17:17-19) and life (John 3:21; 8:44), because the Spirit of Truth is also the Spirit of sanctification and communion. This is what makes truth an integral part of the Church's mystery.[65]

Therefore, the Word of God is not truth as a set of propositions or kerygmatic claims in themselves, but it is truth as life and community. The Church is not a place where truth is contained or "deposited", but is "of Truth", i. e. it is the real presence of Truth by virtue of being communion and community itself. Thus, truth is not imposed on us, but flows from our being – not as a product of social experience, but as a sacramental taste of the Divine life. Truth as word and Truth as sacrament are one and the same. Because Truth is not a conceptualised and comprehensible thing, Truth in the Spirit cannot be enslaved in some formulations. Dogmatic definitions are not systematic representations of Truth, which makes it difficult to speak of a "hierarchy of truths". In the Holy Spirit, dogmas are historical and cultural forms that are sanctified, being part of the event of communion, by means of which the original εἰκών of Christ – Truth, obscured by heretical distortions, is restored to be recognised and worshipped as the Truth in the community. This is what in all ancient council definitions required the exclusion from the community of heretics; this also shows that the councils did not aim at Truth as a propositional definition, but as communion in the community.[66]

Truth is epicletically conditioned and cannot be objectified or communicated in isolation from the community – whether by individuals or by systems of ideas. In order to become a pillar of the truth, the Church constantly needs the Pentecostal event and, in the context of this event the Church ordains bishops to an office endowed with *charisma veritatis*. This objective form of episcopacy in apostolic succession serves to embody this charisma, but it does not objectify the Truth – the infallibility that accompanies this is a charisma and as such is constantly subject to the epiclesis of the community. The bishop who exercises this "infallibility" is therefore not subject to the community as another objectified social structure (the Church is not a democracy), but to the community which is a charismatic event of communion. Infallibility thus appears in the Spirit as a dynamic circular movement. It does not rest statically on any structure or ministry, but is expressed through a

65 Cf. Zizioulas, *The One and the Many*, 85.

66 Cf. Zizioulas, *The One and the Many*, 85–6.

specific service, through a dynamic perichoresis in and through the whole Body. In this way, the faithful layman in his share in the Body, which by definition is charismatic, can point to the Truth, challenging any deviations from it by the bishops. However, if this is done in the Spirit, it can only be done by constantly strengthening the bonds of participation in the community. Thus, in the Holy Spirit, there is a paradoxical combination of witnessing to the Truth by each member of the Church with simultaneous devotion to the Body and its structure.[67]

Ultimately, Truth is transferred in the Holy Spirit from the mind to the heart, which is the centre of love. Since it is only in communion that the Spirit leads to Truth, the confession of Truth is a matter of the heart, which thus also acquires its own rationality. This does not mean that Truth becomes a matter of sentiment, but it is, in its entirety, concentrated in the place where love and communion take place. The current of spiritual tradition that makes the heart the centre of man has positively contributed in the East to the understanding of the Church as a pillar of Truth. In the teaching of the Desert Fathers, one can see how Truth manifested itself simultaneously as communion and sanctification. But this again can only happen in the Spirit, if only it is nourished by the bond of the Body – the Church, which is built in the Body of Christ, in the Eucharist.[68]

In Chapter 15 of the Acts of the Apostles, the assembly of the Apostles addressed a message to the Christians, containing very significant words: "For it has seemed good to the Holy Spirit and to us [...]" (Acts 15:28). Zizioulas emphasises that this reflects the Church's conviction that just as "all Scripture is inspired by God [...]" (2 Tim 3:16), so also the Church's teaching is equal to the work of the Holy Spirit. This, of course, cannot be understood in a mechanical or magical way, nor in the sense of the Holy Spirit's action leading to the development and improvement of the efforts of the human spirit over time. Rather, it must be seen as the work of the Holy Spirit – an event of communion, which is centred in the community and has both horizontal and vertical dimensions.[69] This can be called the ecclesial action of

---

67 Cf. Zizioulas, *The One and the Many*, 86.

68 Cf. Zizioulas, *The One and the Many*, 86–7. In another place, Zizioulas explains it as follows: "what is love? Here we must be very careful, for love is not a state of existence that can be created and sustained in the heart of the individual or of a group of individuals. It is neither a psychological nor an ethical-activistic phenomenon. It is an event that stems from the life of a community; in fact, it *is* a community. Here we arrive at the very fundamental equation: communion and community are identical. Communion is expressed only in terms of *historical* existence (this is the biblical mentality). The concrete structures of the community are not 'forms' of the expression of love – of a love or communion that is somehow conceivable in itself – but they *are* this love and this communion. You love only by being a member of a concrete structured community. This is ultimately the reason why theology as knowledge of the 'heart', identified with love and communion, is possible only as an expression of the Church – not of individuals" (Zizioulas, *The One and the Many*, 217–8).

69 Cf. Zizioulas, *Lectures*, 10.

the Holy Spirit, who brings the communion of Christ wherever He acts. Zizioulas insists that we must get rid of the conviction that the Holy Spirit acts in us as isolated individuals and then leaves us in the same state of isolation. Such an understanding of the Holy Spirit removes the person from the community and is so widespread that we must strongly oppose it. Those who think this way fail to notice the essential difference between His work in the Old Testament and in the New Testament. In the Old Testament, the Spirit of God was given to individuals, not to the whole people. In the New Testament, the Messiah gives the Holy Spirit to the whole people of God. That is why, in connection with Pentecost, St. Luke quoted the words of the prophet Joel: "'In the last days it will be', God declares, 'that I will pour out my Spirit upon all flesh, and your sons and your daughters shall prophesy, and your young men shall see visions, and your old men shall dream dreams. Even upon my slaves, both men and women, in those days I will pour out my Spirit; and they shall prophesy" (Acts 2:17-18).[70]

St. Paul rejects any elitism, writing that even if someone had such faith that they could "move mountains", without love they would be nothing. The First Epistle to the Corinthians in Chapters 11-14 shows that this love is a communion formed by the community of the Church. It does not refer to mere feelings or goodwill, but to the reciprocal relationship between the members of the Church, to that reciprocity which makes the communion one. Thus, no member of the Church can say to the others "I have no need of you" (1 Cor 12:21), because love means that all offices and ministries are exercised in mutual reference and in unity. Wherever the breath of the Holy Spirit reaches, it ends individualism and elitism and creates community.[71] He convenes community and all His gifts and actions serve the unity of the Church's community. Zizioulas concludes that the revelation of truth always brings communion – a special communion with Christ. Christian doctrine points to this communion and teaches that this communion is in itself the truth.[72] All members of the Church constitute this communion of the loving knowledge of

---

70 Cf. Zizioulas, *Lectures*, 11. "The New Testament teaches that all baptised Christians have the Holy Spirit, and with him, his charisms and gifts. The Apostle Paul explains in 1 Corinthians 12 that being a member of the Church means the possession of some particular gift and office of the Spirit for that Church. Paul clearly rejects the view of the Corinthians that some people may be more spiritual or more charismatic than others; he insists that everyone has some spiritual gift, even if it takes the form of an unostentatious service like administration" (ibid.). Cf. Jagodziński, "Teologia jako komunijne nauczanie Kościoła według Johna D. Zizioulasa," 120.

71 Cf. Zizioulas, *Lectures*, 11–2.

72 Cf. Zizioulas, *Lectures*, 12. "Knowledge of the revelation of God is an empirical reality within the body of the Church, which enjoys the relation of the Son to the Father, in which the entire world is embodied, making it the body of Christ. The relationships that constitute this community and make it this body are the actualisation by the Spirit of the revelation of God in the world" (Zizioulas, *Lectures*, 13).

God because only together do they form the Body of Christ which reveals Christ.[73] This knowledge in turn derives its authority from fidelity to the truth about the relationship between God and the world, revealed as the communion of God, the world and humanity in Christ – a communion that was experienced by the Apostles and their communities.[74] The synods of bishops, which formulate the Church's teaching that expresses the achieved reality of communion, play a special role in witnessing that truth.[75] Truth is revealed and secured – and thus it becomes infallible – only in submission to the Holy Spirit and in incorporation into the body of the Church. For God is not known outside of the Holy Spirit's communion and the love created by Him.[76]

Zizioulas states that in communion, the Holy Spirit brings the eschaton into history. If this is the meaning of Pentecost in the Acts of the Apostles, it means that the Church subsists in double existence. On the one hand, being an inherently eschatological reality, it is existentially opposed to this world at the profound level; the world hates it as it hated Christ (John 15:18; 17:14), but it must live; "the doors are locked" (John 20:19), and its "citizenship" is "in heaven" (Phil 3:20). On the other hand, by virtue of the same pneumatological dimension, the Church is intrinsically relational, its existence can only be ecstatic – it cannot reject anyone or anything, it can only receive – even that by which it is rejected. This dualism is perhaps the most acute problem arising from the pneumatological dimension of the Church. How to resolve it? Zizioulas writes that the Eastern Tradition tended to see the Church in terms of its eschatological nature as a triumphal theophany. The Western Tradition, on the other hand, tended to see the Church in terms of a relational reception of this world – it constantly emphasised the obligation to serve the needs of the world, creating an impression of activism and a utopian effort to build the Kingdom of God on earth. Of course, Zizioulas knows that these are generalisations, but they serve to illustrate the problem: Is it possible to combine these two mentalities? He notes first that, undoubtedly, both these tendencies belong to the same pneumatological dimension of the Church, and that the problem lies again in the synthesis of Christology and pneumatology. For if we allow the pneumatological aspect to determine the Christological-incarnate aspect in a fundamental way, the Church will acquire an eschatological mentality in its commitment to this world. Thus worship and social activity, sacred and secular, are no longer two different domains; the Church and the world are not ontologically divided; the problems of the world are at the

73 On the Church as communion, see e. g. Michelina Tenace, *Powiedzieć człowiek*, Part II: *Od obrazu Boga do podobieństwa. Zbawienie jako przebóstwienie* (Kraków: Salwator, 2015), 249–52.

74 Cf. Zizioulas, *Lectures*, 13.

75 Cf. Zizioulas, *Lectures*, 14.

76 Cf. Zizioulas, *Lectures*, 16; Jagodziński, "Teologia jako komunijne nauczanie Kościoła według Johna D. Zizioulasa," 120–1.

same time the problems of the Church; the Church's mission is not an attitude towards the world but a compassionate and sanctifying presence in it. All this will be part of the incarnational aspect of the Body of the Church and its relational nature in the Spirit. But in doing so, the Church must never equate the eschaton with history, trying to build the Kingdom as part of a historical process. At this point, the Church must be ready to confess its "tactical inferiority" compared to the Marxist view of history, precisely because of its pneumatological dimension. By bringing the eschaton into history, the Spirit makes the Church, through its sacramental structures, both the presence of the eschaton in history and the pointer directed beyond history, because pneumatology continually points to the non-objective, the uncontrollable, the extraordinary, the "beyond". This is another way in which the Spirit becomes the "spirit of prophecy" and remains "holy" or "separate" from this world – precisely in His communion. Likewise, the Church in the same Spirit becomes "holy" in its nature, being in this world, but not of this world.[77]

Through the word of God, the Christian participates in the mystery of Christ and in the mystery of the Holy Spirit's descent. The Spirit makes the word remain a living word, full of salvific power and strength. The Scriptures become a kind of "sacrament"[78] in the life of the Church, allowing "the voice of the Holy Spirit to resound" (DV 21) in it. Through Him "the living voice of the Gospel resounds in the Church, and through it, in the world" (DV 8). This conviction is increasingly becoming a common good for all Christians. The Holy Spirit protects the Scriptures from the danger of becoming a dead letter and ensures that they remain the living word of Christ Himself. In the light of Pascha and Pentecost, this word is alive and life-giving, full of the Paschal power of Christ and the Holy Spirit.[79]

The Holy Spirit is not only the guarantor of revelation and apparently the memory of the Church, He not only recalls but also actualises the events recalled. The concretisation of inspiration in the canon of the Scriptures has led over time to limit it only to the books of the Bible, whereas it is clear from the Gospel of St. John that the whole process of tradition is realised by the Holy Spirit and is associated with creative actualisation. The Scripture is made real in the Spirit, filled with the Spirit and effective in Him. His inspiration – i. e. the reality of the Holy Spirit – extends to the reading, hearing and heralding of its words: through them it develops its power of inspiration as it continues in the very same way as it was created – in the process of transmission and interpretation. The Holy Spirit not only preserves the transmission of the tradition, but also expands and deepens the memory of

77 Cf. Zizioulas, *The One and the Many*, 87–8.

78 See Michael Figura, "Sakramentalność słowa Bożego," *Communio. Międzynarodowy Przegląd Teologiczny* 21/5 (2001), 94–111.

79 Cf. Hryniewicz, *Nasza Pascha z Chrystusem*, 190.

the Church, taking care of its transmission and interpretation in the Church.[80] The proclamation of the Gospel is thus the work of the Holy Spirit through the medium of the proclaimed word. In order for it to fulfil its role, the epiclesis of the Spirit is needed, for only He can "open the heart" (Acts 16:14) of the listeners. The "anointing" of the Christian by faith (1 John 2:20,27; 2 Cor 1:21) comes from the Holy Spirit. It is He who makes the salvific mystery of Christ manifest in the words proclaimed to those who have experienced His mysterious closeness.[81]

The idea of the proclaimed word of God as the vehicle (Gift) of the Holy Spirit is very weakly presented in Catholic theology. Christ speaks in the proclaimed word, He awakens faith, calls for baptism and gives the Spirit. A. Czaja quotes an interesting passage from G. Sauter, who points out that the notions "word" and "spirit" are sometimes difficult to distinguish in biblical usage when they describe the coming of God to man.

> The word of God cannot be this kind of 'soulless' [*geistlos*] word, so that it will only be information and a pure statement of fact. It is much more an act of the word [Tat-Wort] and a word of action [Wort-Tat]: it materializes what it declares. God's Spirit, on the other hand, does not remain any impersonal, nameless and opinionless power, but penetrates human speech, makes Himself heard in everyday words, becomes a word that influences communication between people as He builds and develops the human way of speaking to and from God. Just as Jesus Christ, the Word of God, became flesh in order to dwell among men, so does the Spirit become the word in order to realise the communion between God and man, between people, and between people and the world, which also needs salvation in order to live.[82]

There are claims in Reformed theology that the Holy Spirit is not only the source of the salvific dimension of ecclesial prophesising, but also the first Gift of the word. The "miracle of the kenosis of the Spirit" takes place. The word proclaimed in the Church is the space of the Holy Spirit, who gives Himself in and through the proclaimed word, which is a kind of "kairos" – an event of the Spirit and a time of self-giving of the Holy Spirit.[83]

---

80 Cf. Czaja, *Credo in Spiritum Vivificantem*, 163–6.

81 Cf. Hryniewicz, *Nasza Pascha z Chrystusem*, 193.

82 Gerhard Sauter, "Die Kirche in der Krisis des Geistes," in *Kirche – Ort des Geistes*, ed. Kasper and Sauter (Freiburg – Basel – Wien: Herder, 1976), 59–106 (quoted in: Czaja, *Credo in Spiritum Vivificantem*, 168).

83 Cf. Czaja, *Credo in Spiritum Vivificantem*, 167–9.

3.4 The Church as the Sacrament of the Holy Spirit

In Catholic ecclesiology, the issues of treating the Church objectively and justifying the Church by referring only to the positive establishment of the Church by Christ have receded into the background. Today one sees the Church rather as the mystery[84] of the continuation of Jesus' work in the Holy Spirit.[85] In the newer vision of ecclesiology, the trinitarian dimensions assume great importance. In the space of creation, the Church is "the icon of the Holy Trinity", Their image, fruit, space of action and embodiment,[86] the people of the Father gathered by the Son and the Holy Spirit.[87] Through the Spirit the mission, the omnipotence received from the Father, the authority, the teaching and the action of the Son are internalised in people. Therefore, the Church is "the temple of the Holy Spirit" and "the Body of Christ" filled with the diversity of life in the Holy Spirit.[88] The "ontological" basis of its truth[89] is to abide in a living relationship with the self-giving of God in Jesus Christ and His presence in the Holy Spirit.[90]

The analogous concept of sacrament[91] was officially introduced into the Church's teaching via the words of the Dogmatic Constitution on the Church *Lumen Gentium* 1: "[...] the Church is in Christ like a sacrament or as a sign and instrument both of a very closely knit union with God and of the unity of the whole human race [...]". The concept of sacrament emphasises the inseparable unity and unconfused diversity of the Church against the self-giving of God in Jesus Christ and the Holy Spirit. As a "sacrament of salvation", it is a contingent and sinful sign, but since, after the exaltation of Jesus, God did not cease to give Himself to the world but remained present through the Holy Spirit, the entire content of salvation through Jesus Christ is made present – by the power of the Holy Spirit – in the

---

84 Pałucki, *Trynitarny wymiar Kościoła*, 199–204.

85 Cf. Jagodziński, *Communio dzięki komunikacji*, 223–6; Jagodziński, "Kościół – sakrament Ducha Świętego," in *Duch Kościoła. Kościół Ducha*, ed. Proniewski (Białystok: Wydawnictwo Uniwersytetu w Białymstoku, 2014), 136–55.

86 Cf. Moltmann, "Der dreieinige Gott," 188–90.

87 Cf. Nitsche, "Pneumatologie," 348–9.

88 Cf. Greshake, *Der dreieine Gott. Eine trinitarische Theologie*, 377–80; Guzowski, *Duch Dialogujący*, 213–5.

89 Cf. Kehl, "Kirche als Institution," 190.

90 Cf. Roman Słupek, *Jesteśmy Kościołem trójjedynego Boga. Kolegialność Kościoła według Yves'a Congara* (Lublin: Wydawnictwo KUL, 2004), 27–67; Guzowski, "Symbolika trynitarna Kościoła jako komunii i misji," in *Communio w chrześcijańskiej refleksji o Kościele*, ed. Czaja and Marczewski, 214; Jagodziński, "Trynitarno-pneumatologiczne pośrednictwo Kościoła," *Studia Diecezji Radomskiej* 10 (2010/2011), 73–4; Nitsche, "Pneumatologie," 349–50.

91 Cf. Antoni Nadbrzeżny, *Sakrament wyzwolenia. Zbawcze posłannictwo Kościoła w posoborowej teologii holenderskiej* (Lublin: Wydawnictwo KUL, 2013), 33.

essential acts of the Church's self-realisation. However, salvation itself cannot be unproblematically identified with these acts. By virtue of the incarnation, Jesus became the "Original Sacrament" of the triune God, and after the sending of the Holy Spirit, the Church became, in an analogous way, the "fundamental sacrament" of all sacramental acts of manifesting God's salvific work in the world.[92]

The Church represents the love of the Father and the Son communicated to people in the Holy Spirit.[93] As its structures express and realise this theological sense, it is thus the "universal sacrament of salvation" (LG 48).[94] The Holy Spirit chooses the human community as the instrument of His action,[95] hence the institutional dimension of the Church can also be justified pneumatologically, since the Holy Spirit is not only the "event of love" between the Father and the Son but also its lasting fruit operating in the institutional layer of the Church.[96]

Upon reflecting on the ecclesiological content of the concept of "communion", the trinitarian dimensions of this term for the Church have become more clearly realised.[97] The Christian experience of God has a trinitarian structure and leads to a trinitarian experience of communion.[98] Today, it has almost become obvious to speak of the triune communion of God as the prototype of the Church,[99] which is the "icon" of the Holy Trinity,[100] but it is not yet sufficient to base ecclesiology on trinitology from a methodological and content-related point of view, in order to demonstrate the analogy between the image of God and the image of the Church.[101]

92 Cf. Kehl, *Die Kirche*, 82–4; Jagodziński, *Komunijna wizja Kościoła według Medarda Kehla SJ*, 36–7.

93 Cf. Greshake, *Der dreieine Gott. Eine trinitarische Theologie*, 385–6; Jagodziński, "Komunijna 'fenomenologia' Kościoła według Medarda Kehla SJ," in *Communio w chrześcijańskiej refleksji o Kościele*, ed. Czaja and Marczewski, 257–64.

94 Cf. Kehl, "Kirche in der Kultur der Moderne," in *Christen an der Schwelle zum dritten Jahrtausend*, ed. Michael Sievernich and Johannes Beckermann (Frankfurt am Main: Knecht, 2000), 106–15.

95 Cf. Hilberath, "Vorgaben für die Ausarbeitung der Communio-Ekklesiologie," in *Communio – Ideal oder Zerrbild von Kommunikation?*, ed. Hilberath (Freiburg-Basel-Wien: Herder, 1999), 279; Ratzinger, *Wprowadzenie w chrześcijaństwo*, 332; Laurentin, *Nieznany Duch Święty*, 402–7.

96 Cf. Greshake, *Der dreieine Gott. Eine trinitarische Theologie*, 389–90, fn. 465; Anselmo Dalbesio, *Duch Święty w Nowym Testamencie, w Kościele, w życiu chrześcijańskim* (Kraków: WAM, 2001), 110–23.

97 Cf. Francis de Chaignon, "Kościół a Trójca Święta w doktrynie Soboru Watykańskiego II," in *Tajemnica Trójcy Świętej*, ed. Balter and Stefan Dusza, and Franciszek Mickiewicz et al. (Poznań: Pallottinum, 2000), 477–89; Volf, *Trinität und Gemeinschaft*, 182–247; Jagodziński, "Trynitarne podstawy Kościoła jako komunii," 51–79.

98 Cf. Moltmann, "Der dreieinige Gott," 186–92.

99 Cf. *Communio w chrześcijańskiej refleksji o Kościele*, 255–414.

100 Cf. Greshake, *Wierzę w Boga Trójjedynego*, 77–83; Lachner, "Communio – eine Grundidee des christlichen Glaubens," 243–5.

101 Cf. Nitsche, "Die Analogie zwischen dem trinitarischen Gottesbild und der communialen Struktur von Kirche. Desiderat eines Forschungsprogrammes zur Communio-Ekklesiologie," in *Commu-*

Indeed, in the light of the teaching of the last Council, the Church should be conceived of and implemented as "the sacrament of the community of the triune God", i. e. the strictly Christological context must be developed in the trinitarian and pneumatological perspective.[102]

The Christological interpretation of the sacramentality of the Church was post-conciliary complemented by a pneumatological interpretation, which showed that the Church is also the sacrament of the Holy Spirit[103]. This was pointed out above all by H. Mühlen, W. Kasper,[104] L. Boff, M. Kehl and Th. Schneider.[105] In his encyclical *Dominum et Vivificantem*, John Paul II calls the Church "the sign and instrument of the presence and action of the life-giving Spirit" (No. 64).

Pentecost, which is the "*Communio* in God"[106] is the foundation that makes the *communio* of the Church possible. Through the gift of the Holy Spirit, it is possible for the Church to participate in communion with God – in the love of the Father and the Son, in the unifying "We" of God. Owing to this, the Church as the communion of faith ("we") is – as the revealing and mediating sign of communion in God – "the sacrament of the Holy Spirit".[107]

The Church as the sacrament – the sign and instrument – is a social reality, and just as all theology is faced with the task of speaking responsibly about God, ecclesi-

---

nio – Ideal oder Zerrbild von Kommunikation?, ed. Hilberath (Freiburg-Basel-Wien: Herder, 1999), 81–3.

102 Cf. Czaja, *Credo in Spiritum Vivificantem*.

103 Cf. Gustave Martelet, *Zmartwychwstanie, Eucharystia, człowiek* (Warszawa: Pax, 1976), 226; Hryniewicz, *Nasza Pascha z Chrystusem*, 92; Guzowski, *Duch Dialogujący*, 220–2.

104 Walter Kasper's definition of the Church as a sacrament of the Holy Spirit is significant here: "Die Kirche ist also von ihrem Ursprung her beides: Stiftung Jesu Christi und deren Verwirklichung im Geist. Sie ist Institution und Ereignis. Sie besagt Bindung an den konkreten Ursprung und zugleich zu deren schöpferisch-geschichtlicher Vergegenwärtigung. Sie steht in der Spannung zwischen Buchstabe und Geist, sakramentaler amtlicher Struktur und lebendigem Charisma. Sie ist eine komplexe Wirklichkeit: Sie ist Kirche der Sünder und Gemeinschaft der Heiligen, d. h. Gemeinschaft durch Teilhabe am einen Heiligen Geist und seinen Gaben. Sie ist in einem sichtbaren menschlichen Gefüge die wirksame Gegenwart und geschichtliche Existenzform des Geistes Jesu Christi. Sie ist biblisch gesprochen 'Bau im Heiligen Geist' (1 Kor 3,16f.; Eph 2,22), dogmatisch formuliert 'Sacrament des Geistes'. Damit ist sie im Geist das unter den Völkern aufgerichtete Signal (Jes 11,12), die vorläufige Verwirklichung des Sinnziels der Geschichte: Einheit und Frieden (schalom) unter den Menschen und Völkern durch ihre Einheit mit Gott" (Kasper, "Die Kirche als Sakrament des Geistes," in Kasper, *Die Kirche Jesu Christi. Schriften zur Ekklesiologie I* (Freiburg-Basel-Wien: Herder, 2008), 296–7).

105 Cf. Czaja, "Traktat o Kościele," in *Dogmatyka*, ed. Adamiak and Czaja, and Majewski (Warszawa: Więź, 2006), 2: 395.

106 Cf. Mühlen, *Der Heilige Geist als Person*; Balthasar, *Pneuma und Institution*, 135–201; Ratzinger, "Der Heilige Geist als Communio," 223–38; Kehl, "Kirche – Sakrament des Geistes," 155–80.

107 Cf. Kehl, "Kirche als Institution," 191; Jagodziński, "Trynitarno-pneumatologiczne pośrednictwo Kościoła," 76–81.

ology is inevitably directed towards a dialogue with social philosophy.[108] However, it must preserve the trinitarian-pneumatological dimension of the Church, for without this, sociology will begin to play a desacralizing role in relation to the Church.[109] The essential concept and anthropological basis for such an ecclesiology of the sacrament is "communication"[110] – giving based on the human person's capacity to listen and open up to others, which leads to the formation of a community (*communio*[111]). However, the sociological and humanistic aspects of the Church receive their full depth of meaning only in the light of the Christological and trinitarian complement. Since Jesus Christ revealed Himself to the world as the Word who is the economico-salvific expression of the intra-trinitarian exchange-dialogue of love between the Father, the Son and the Holy Spirit – the concept of communication is something remarkably appropriate in theology,[112] and knowledge on communication provides a proper criterion for understanding communication as the realisation of love.[113] The essence of God is the personal communication of love – the self-giving and the exchange of love. The Father is the proper source of the communication of love, the Son is the Word of love, the Holy Spirit is the personified love of the Father and the Son and the personified communication of love – He is the intra-trinitarian node of love, which in economico-salvific inversion is turned towards people, the personal environment-medium of the communication of love between Christians and Christ. Since personal communication has a dialogical structure, it needs a "personal causality" presupposing the activity of an initiator and its recipient, who entrusts himself to the initiator. From this it follows that the communication of people with the Father is maintained through the personal relation of people to Christ and their formal filling with the Holy Spirit.[114]

---

108 Cf. Joachim von Soosten, "Zur theologischen Rezeption von Jürgen Habermas' 'Theorie des kommunikativen Handelns'," *Zeitschrift für Evangelische Ethik* 34 (1990), 139.

109 Cf. Jagodziński, *Communio dzięki komunikacji*, 296.

110 Cf. Emerich Coreth, "Lebensvollzug in Kommunikation und Interaktion," in *Theorie der Sprachhandlungen und heutige Ekklesiologie. Ein philosophisch-theologisches Gespräch*, ed. Hünermann and Richard Schaeffler (Freiburg-Basel-Wien: Herder, 1987), 16–22.

111 Cf. Greshake, *Der dreieine Gott. Eine trinitarische Theologie*, 176–7.

112 One can even speak of a trinitarian-Christological dimension to the ultimate justification of all communication. See Jagodziński, "Teologia a komunikacja," 73–102.

113 Cf. Meuffels, *Kommunikative Sakramententheologie*, 32–3; P. Hofmann speaks of the immanent Trinity as a model of an open community of communication, which is at the same time the prototype and goal of every human communication (Peter Hofmann, *Glaubensbegründung. Die Transzendentalphilosophie der Kommunikationsgemeinschaft in fundamentaltheologischer Sicht* (Frankfurt am Main: Aschendorff, 1988), 268).

114 Cf. Edward J. Kilmartin, *Christian Liturgy. Theology and Practice. I. Systematic Liturgy* (Kansas City: Sheed & Ward, 1988), 139–40; Jagodziński, *Communio dzięki komunikacji*, 299.

The Church has a dialectical character – it is the prior foundation of faith and is at the same time built on faith – and this corresponds exactly to its pneumatological dimension, i. e. the unity of communion given to it by the Holy Spirit.[115] In the intra-trinitarian context, the Holy Spirit is the "space" that makes the love between the Father and the Son possible, while on the historical plane, the Spirit is the prior gift to faith and the Church.[116] In the Holy Spirit, the Father and the Son relate to each other in mutual love, and it is only in the Holy Spirit that people accept faith in God revealed in Jesus Christ. This property of the Holy Spirit is visibly manifested in the Church, which is the sacrament of Divine Communion, since in the social reality of the Church, the Holy Spirit is always the pre-given space of life that makes faith possible.[117] On the intra-trinitarian level, the Holy Spirit can be understood as the "result", the "gift" of the love of the Father and the Son, a form of unity that "comes from the Father and the Son" and unites – while simultaneously personally differentiating – the Father and the Son.[118] This dimension of the Holy Spirit is expressed in the Church by the fact that unity arises from people as subjects in faith, while their personal being is not only undiminished by common faith but actually becomes itself in that faith.[119]

God's revelation transcends human communication to the historical community of people with God, the community of the Holy Spirit, the people of God.[120] The reception of the Gospel and entrusting oneself to God is tantamount to entering into a relationship with the triune God – it is a trustful "immersion" in and actual participation in the loving reference of the Son-Jesus to the Father. The Christian tradition called this reciprocal love-reference between the Father and the Son – the Holy Spirit. To explain the unity and differentiation of the trinitarian "structure of reference" in God, M. Kehl used a communicative scheme:

> 'The Father' is the beginningless direct Subject and Source [...] of infinitely self-giving love. 'The Son' is the Goal and Partner, originating in and mediated by the Father, [...] of infinitely receiving love. 'The Holy Spirit' is the unifying Environment, mediating between the Father and the Son and mediated by Them, [...] of this infinite love. Love itself, finally, is the Content [...] of that which exists between the Father, the Son and the Holy Spirit, and as such is identical with the divine 'Essence'"[121]. A consequence of this view of the

115 Cf. Guzowski, *Duch Dialogujący*, 223–6.

116 Cf. Hryniewicz, *Nasza Pascha z Chrystusem*, 92–4.

117 Cf. Jagodziński, *Komunijna wizja Kościoła według Medarda Kehla SJ*, 13–5.

118 Cf. M. Kehl, *Hinführung zum christlichen Glauben* (Mainz: Grünewald, 1987), 136–40.

119 Cf. Kehl, *Die Kirche*, 68–75, 158–9.

120 Cf. Kehl, *Die Kirche*, 328–31; Jagodziński, *Communio dzięki komunikacji*, 342.

121 Cf. Kehl, "Kirche als Institution – eine theologische Begründung," 121; Jagodziński, *Communio dzięki komunikacji*, 343.

> Holy Trinity is the view of the Church which "understands itself as 'the sacrament of Divine Communio'; as such, it forms a community of believers united by the Holy Spirit, modelled on the example of the Son, Jesus Christ, and called together with all creation into the kingdom of God the Father; a community of believers which is formed simultaneously 'hierarchically' and synodally.[122]

The Christian Tradition has called the Holy Spirit "Unity" (*unio*) or "Communion" (*communio*) in God.[123] Since the communion between the Father and the Son is a (relatively) self-contained (as person) existence of Divine Love, H. Mühlen writes that the Holy Spirit constitutes the "We" in God.[124] This communion between the Father and the Son – i. e. the Holy Spirit – possesses originally and exemplarily the property of a mediating agent, since God in Himself – in the Holy Spirit – is the all-creating and all-perfecting mediating event. On the one hand, the unity between the Father and the Son is always a pre-existing common "Space" (Spirit) of Their reference – since only in the Spirit of infinite love does the Father relate to the Son and the Son to the Father (God is always the Spirit of love, of mutual self-giving between the Father and the Son) – however, on the other hand, this common Spirit is "established" only through the mutual reference between the Father and the Son, He depends on this reference, and without it there would be no "We", no Community. If the believer allows himself to be embraced by this reciprocal reference of the Father and the Son – and thus also receives a share in this reference – he is received "into" the Holy Spirit as the Communion between the Father and the Son. Hence, the Bible refers to the gift of the Holy Spirit as "receiving the Holy Spirit" and "being filled with the Holy Spirit". This "filling with the Holy Spirit" takes place in communion. Since He Himself is the mediating "Communion" between the Father and the Son, reception into this Communion is community-based and, in turn, creates a community – the Holy Spirit as Communion in God is the proper theological foundation of the ecclesial communion in faith. The prior gift of the shared "life-space" of faith is thus not based on the human will to enter the community of faith, but on the gift of the Holy Spirit, the gift of participation in the Communion that exists in God. If the community of faith opens itself to the action of the Holy Spirit,

---

122 Kehl, *Die Kirche*, 51. Cf. Jagodziński, "Komunijna 'fenomenologia' Kościoła," 256.

123 Cf. Balthasar, *Pneuma und Institution*, 201–35; Ratzinger, "Der Heilige Geist als Communio," 223–38; Mühlen, "Soziale Geisterfahrung als Antwort auf eine einseitige Gotteslehre," in *Erfahrung und Theologie des Heiligen Geistes*, ed. Heitmann and Mühlen, 252–72; Mühlen, *Der Heilige Geist als Person*; Kehl, *Die Kirche*, 70–3.

124 Cf. Mühlen, "Der gegenwärtige Aufbruch der Geisterfahrung und die Unterscheidung der Geister," in *Gegenwart des Geistes. Aspekte der Pneumatologie*, ed. Kasper, 50; Kehl, "Kirche als Institution – eine theologische Begründung," 121; Kehl, *Hinführung*, 136; Jagodziński, *Komunijna wizja Kościoła według Medarda Kehla SJ*, 15–6.

it becomes the historical sign of intra-divine Communion – "the sacrament of the Holy Spirit". This is also the proper meaning of this communion – as a community of believers, it aims to represent, in a sign-sacramental way, the unity of the Father and the Son in the common Spirit and to mediate (as every sacrament does) – and it is for this reason that the Holy Spirit has been given to it.[125] The Church is thus "embraced" by the Holy Spirit as the mediating "Wherein" of salvation history, the mediating power in and through which Jesus Christ comes to man. The Holy Spirit mediates as the "Environment of Meaning" given before and permanently, yet given anew each time. He is the environment of meaning of the mutual love of the Father and the Son, as well as the "social form" revealed in Him and uniting Them. In the transcending power of this Spirit, the triune God gives Himself to the world as Mediator – as *Spiritus Creator*, He fills the world with the creative and life-giving power of God; as *Spiritus Redemptor*, He is the personal "environment of meaning" through which the salvific love of the Father and the Son is granted to man. Through him, the history of humanity is incorporated into the event of this love, so that it can become the perfect, historical form of communion that is identical with Him – the "social form" of the love of God Himself. This mediating power of the Holy Spirit finds its purpose in extending the love of the Father and the Son onto the universal communion of people with God and among people.[126]

The Church does not "possess" the Holy Spirit as an *a priori* incarnate or a "soul" belonging to it, He does not reside in the "material structure" of the Church either as its "inner form" (in the sense of an active super-quality) or as an anthropological principle of life or a sociological principle of the system. On the contrary, as the sacrament of the Holy Spirit, the Church points to and symbolises that which is beyond it, i. e. the infinitely transcending reality of that Spirit. He is present in the Church as the real "environment of meaning" of salvation, and by abiding in trust in Him, the Church actualises in itself the dynamics of the sacrament and sacramental self-growth, which awaits Him as a pure gift that is constantly being given and has to be constantly received anew. It is only in this attitude of waiting that the Holy Spirit can be present in the Church as the "environment of meaning" mediating in salvation, and that the Church can be His sacrament.[127]

How is it possible for the Church, as a large social system, to become – for the whole human community – an effective manifestation of the salvation-giving and unity-building power of the Holy Spirit? M. Kehl writes that the Church will be able

125 Cf. Kehl, "Kirche als Institution – eine theologische Begründung," 122–3, 139.

126 Cf. Kehl, "Kirche – Sakrament des Geistes," 155–61; Kehl, "Kirche als Institution," 190–1; Jagodziński, *Communio dzięki komunikacji*, 343–6; Jagodziński, *Komunijna wizja Kościoła według Medarda Kehla SJ*, 16–20.

127 Cf. Kehl, "Kirche – Sakrament des Geistes," 160–1; Jagodziński, *Communio dzięki komunikacji*, 347–8; Jagodziński, *Komunijna wizja Kościoła według Medarda Kehla SJ*, 17–20.

to fulfil this function if it actualises itself as the "concrete freedom of faith". Kehl drew the notion of "concrete freedom" from Hegel's philosophy of law, according to which the freedom of an individual becomes "concrete" when it is situated within a seemingly abstract social reality and animated and shaped with the spirit of freedom – when it is not "abstracted" from this social reality into privacy, but when it co-implements the tendency to formalise what is social in an interpersonal way. Of course, there is always a risk that the community of believers will close itself off from the Holy Spirit and cease to be a historical representation of the Communion of God Himself. Today this danger is particularly great because of the experience of the institutionalised and bureaucratic Church – "the institution" and "the Holy Spirit" even appear as almost insurmountable opposites. In such a situation, how can the Church defend its character as a sign of God's Spirit and of His communion-generating power? What is the specific service of the institutional dimension of the Church vis-à-vis its task of making the Holy Spirit present in the community of faith? To what extent is the Church "the sacrament of the Holy Spirit" as a mediating sign of the unity-building personal "environment" of salvation? Why is the social fabric of the Church a sacrament? M. Kehl believes that the service of the institution of the Church for the presence of the Holy Spirit in the communion of the Church is contained in the three specific functions of the institution: preserving the identity, integrating and liberating the Church.[128]

3.4.1 The Pneumatological-Communional Dimension of Institutionality at the Service of the Church's Identity

With the help of the institutional dimension, the Holy Spirit contributes to the preservation of the Church's identity[129] with the original events of the faith and its history,[130] and He introduces it ever more deeply into the truth of Christ (cf. John 14:17,26; 16:13-14). In this attachment, the faith finds its Christian basis, authenticity and identity in the Holy Spirit. This is done through the proclamation of the truth of the Gospel (cf. 1 Cor 1:23; 2:2), baptism (cf. Rom 6:3-4), participation in the "feast of the Lord" (cf. 1 Cor 11:26), the guidance of the Apostles (cf. Gal 6:2)

128 Cf. Kehl, "Kirche – Sakrament des Geistes," 167, 173; Kehl, "Kirche als Institution – eine theologische Begründung," 139; Kehl, *Die Kirche*, 394–402; Werbick, *Den Glauben verantworten*, 804–30; Jagodziński, *Communio dzięki komunikacji*, 352–4, 357–9; Jagodziński, *Komunijna wizja Kościoła według Medarda Kehla SJ*, 23–34; Jagodziński, "Trynitarno-pneumatologiczne pośrednictwo Kościoła," 81–2.

129 Cf. Sienkiewicz, *Wspólnota Kościoła*, 311–7.

130 Cf. Kehl, "Kirche in der Sorge um ihre Identität oder Kirche für die anderen," *Lebendige Seelsorge* 32 (1981), 60–2.

etc.[131] The basis for preserving the identity of faith is also the "sense of faith" of all believers, which is the Holy Spirit's work. It is the task of the Church's Magisterium to serve this "sense" – maintaining and sharpening it, protecting it from confusion and one-sidedness, setting it up as a signpost and a boundary.[132] The concern for the authenticity of prophesising (and thus of the community) is fulfilled by the episcopal office, the Church's *communio* and its leadership, as well as by the canon of the biblical books, the creed, the liturgical order, the law of the Church, the councils, the office of Peter and his authority etc. They all serve as identity marks of each new contemporaneity of faith. They do not have this power by themselves, but through the Holy Spirit, and they prove to be "instruments" of the identifying Spirit when they listen in faith to the Gospel and pay close attention to the "signs of the times".[133]

This also shows the criterion for distinguishing the true maintenance of the Church's identity from the danger of the Church's "preservation". The "identifying" power of the Holy Spirit demonstrates itself where the Church fearlessly enters with its message into a new historical situation and in it acquires a new – consistent with the original – identity in faith. The attitude of "preservation" only stiffens the Church, making it stagnant in the face of what has already been, and does not allow the Gospel to unfold its salvific and liberating action. The certainty that there will be no loss of identity in the new situation is based on hope owing to the presence of the Holy Spirit.[134] However, the formal criterion of the identity of faith is only legitimate if it serves the authenticity of its content; the common faith is authentic only if it is bound to formal criteria. However, this dialectic does not imply equivalence – the priority is given to the unambiguously content-oriented message of faith, and everything that is formal in the Church should serve it, whereby this service is all the better, the more inobtrusive it is; the essential message becomes evident in itself. Such subtle mediation can only be realised when both parties abide in an all-embracing communion – when the word of God is not deprived of the historical and contemporary context of faith, and when the formalised structures do not dominate over the community of faith. In this tension

131 Cf. Kehl, "Kirche – Sakrament des Geistes," 175; Kehl, "Kirche als Institution," 191–2.

132 Cf. Kehl, *Die Kirche*, 394–8.

133 Cf. Kehl, "Kirche als Institution – eine theologische Begründung," 89–112, 126–7, 319; Jagodziński, *Communio dzięki komunikacji*, 359–62.

134 Cf. Kehl, "Kirche in der Sorge," 57–65; Kehl, "Kirche als Institution – eine theologische Begründung," 128; Kehl, "Kirche als Institution," 192–3; Kehl, *Die Kirche*, 387–98; Guzowski, *Duch Dialogujący*, 222.

of the unity of the communion and its history, the "concretising" power of the Holy Spirit is revealed.[135]

3.4.2 The Pneumatological-Communional Dimension of Institutionality at the Service of Ecclesial Unity

Using the institutional forms of the Church, the Holy Spirit integrates the faithful into the original unity of the universal Church. He is the giver of diverse charisms and unites (cf. 1 Cor 12:1-31; Rom 12:4-8; 14; 15), while submission to His unifying power and inclusion in the unity of the Body of Christ is also a sign of the genuineness of the charism. Such unity is not something external or supplementary, but primary and given by the Holy Spirit; it does not destroy the diversity of charisms and the presence of the Holy Spirit in them, but it opposes sectarian obstinacy and complacency leading to alienation.[136] In the concern for the service of the charisms for the communal unity caused by the Holy Spirit's action, the particular responsibility of the institutional offices developed very early on. Following the apostolic office, the presbyters and bishops took over this service.[137] The celebration of the Eucharist was also linked to the office and took on an institutional form.[138] In its context the ministries of the episcopal office, the college of bishops, the councils and the office of Peter took shape over the course of history, and the local Churches were integrated into the all-embracing "Catholic" unity of the universal Church. The common confession of faith, dogma, law etc. also serve a similar purpose. The idea is that the faith of individual people, groups or local Churches can "expand" towards a larger, common faith of the whole Church. The four "marks" of the Church must always be linked – the "one" Church is at the same time "sanctified" by the Holy Spirit,[139] it mediates the "universal" (catholic) salvific will of God[140], and abides in the "apostolic" identity.[141] The Spirit of Christ bringing unity makes use of the institutional structures of the Church, which – by virtue of being objective and formalised (to a certain extent), relatively autonomous vis-à-vis the faith of an

---

135 Cf. Kehl, "Kirche – Sakrament des Geistes," 176–7; Jagodziński, *Communio dzięki komunikacji*, 362–4; Jagodziński, "Trynitarno-pneumatologiczne pośrednictwo Kościoła," 82–4.

136 Cf. Kehl. *Die Kirche*, 398–9; Sienkiewicz, *Wspólnota Kościoła*, 306–10, 317–21.

137 Cf. Kasper, "Die Funktion des Priesters in der Kirche," in *Die Kirche und ihre Ämter. Schriften zur Ekklesiologie II*, ed. Kasper (Freiburg-Basel-Wien: Herder, 2009), 163–71.

138 Cf. Kehl. *Die Kirche*, 288–90.

139 Cf. Guzowski, *Duch Dialogujący*, 226–9.

140 Cf. Guzowski, *Duch Dialogujący*, 229–30.

141 Cf. Guzowski, *Duch Dialogujący*, 231–2.

individual – become a weapon against the "charismatic" self-confidence, which is self-directed, closed and disregards greater unity.[142]

A typical danger of the "integrative" ministry of the Church institutions is that it is easily equated with "uniformity" or "harmonisation". Thus, in the process of integrating into the great unity of the Church, there must also be room for diversity (however, preserving the capacity to act). This implies a mutual openness – the Church must recognise legitimate differences, while individual believers and different lifestyles must recognise the greater unity. In this mutual orientation, the unifying power of the Holy Spirit is revealed, uniting all in intra-trinitarian and historical dimensions, making visible and guarding personal differences (between the Father and the Son, between Christ and Christians, between Christians themselves). Here, too, the capacity for mutual adjustment must be preserved. The diversity of charisms, communities and Churches serves the Holy Spirit to "uproot" the Church from the institutional pursuit of self-preservation and to open it to the "catholic" fullness of faith. In the willingness to do this, one can see the criterion for distinguishing proper integration from uniformity devoid of the Spirit. If the process of differentiation is balanced by the pursuit of integration, the Church will remain an "open system" for the Holy Spirit and will seek to secure unity not by means of perfect organisation, totalitarian "spiritual" integralism or purely formal understanding and obedience, but it will humbly and devotedly (while maintaining its "instrumental" interaction) allow itself to be offered this unity by the Holy Spirit. Since He acts both in the various forms of faith of concrete people (in charisms) and communities, and in the institutional ecclesial forms, it is necessary to maintain (despite all commonality) the inviolable and "open distinction" between individual faith and the common faith of the Church.[143]

However, internal differentiation has its limits – just as there is a danger of "uniformity", there is also a danger of "separation". For in the Church's life there are core values, in which its most intense realisation takes place. If one rejects them, one breaks the deepest link to the Church (whether in the form of a public abandonment of the Church or an act of excommunication). The same applies to the essential truths of faith – whoever does not accept them breaks the bond with the common faith of the Church, separates himself and his personal understanding of

142 Cf. Kehl, "Kirche als Institution – eine theologische Begründung," 128–31; Kehl, "Kirche als Institution," 193–4; Jagodziński, *Communio dzięki komunikacji*, 365–7; Guzowski, *Duch Dialogujący*, 215–20.

143 Cf. Karl Rahner, "Zur Struktur des Kirchenvolkes heute," in *Schriften zur Theologie*, ed. Rahner (Zürich-Einsiedeln-Köln: Benzinger, 1973), 11: 558–68; Rahner, "Der Glaube des Christen und die Lehre der Kirche," in *Schriften zur Theologie*, ed. Rahner (Zürich-Einsiedeln-Köln: Benzinger, 1972), 10: 262–85; Kehl, "Kirche als Institution – eine theologische Begründung," 131; Kehl, "Kirche als Institution," 194; Kehl, *Die Kirche*, 399; Jagodziński, *Communio dzięki komunikacji*, 367–8.

faith (no matter how original and creative it is) does not serve the common faith of the Church. In turn, it is up to the Church's Magisterium to declare the fact of deviation. It is this office that sets the "boundary posts" and determines how far an "open difference" between the common faith and one's individual understanding of it can go without shattering the unity of the Church. This does not mean there is a disbelief in the Holy Spirit and His action in the Church, on the contrary – it is to guard against replacing the Holy Spirit with one's own spirit. Through the competence of the Church's Office, the community of faith achieves its highest concreteness and objectivity – the Office gives the faith a clear shape to help believers to be Christians and to go beyond themselves in order to join the greater unity of the common faith.[144]

3.4.3 The Pneumatological-Communional Dimension of the Church's Liberating Institutionality

The institutionality of the Church is also a sign of the Holy Spirit liberating from the "necessity" of salvation by oneself. In Jesus Christ, human freedom has been fulfilled in the proper sense; He has "liberated" it from its entanglement in itself towards freedom proper. If one entrusts oneself to Jesus, God sends "the Spirit of his Son, crying Abba! Father!" (cf. Gal 4:6; Rom 8:15), the Spirit of free children of God who have freed themselves from the "Law" which imposes on everyone the obligation to secure salvation through their own abilities and "good deeds". The children of God are free because they receive salvation as a gift of God's and can pass it onto others without fear. This liberation takes place not only through the personal bestowal of the Holy Spirit, but also through the Church, above all through the word calling for freedom and through the sacraments of baptism and the Eucharist.[145] Although the history of the relation between the institutional Church and the freedom of the Spirit is not just glorious, it is the institutional form of the Church that bears the call to be an instrument of the liberating Spirit of Christ. However, it is not enough for the Church to be "concrete" only in its freedom. On the contrary, it rather fulfils its task as the sacrament of the Spirit when it takes the form of being there for others. The Church, of course, does not do this by itself – this is the work of Jesus Christ who is present and acting in the Holy Spirit. However, as a symbol of liberated freedom derived from Christ, the Church must at all times produce real signs announcing universal and ultimate liberation and reconciliation. The identity of faith with its origins and tradition liberates from the need to reproduce this

---

144 Cf. Kehl, "Kirche als Institution – eine theologische Begründung," 132–3; Jagodziński, *Communio dzięki komunikacji*, 368–9; Jagodziński, " Trynitarno-pneumatologiczne pośrednictwo Kościoła," 84–6.

145 Cf. Kehl, *Hinführung*, 122–4, 131–3.

identity in every moment of history and, in reference to the current "spirit of the times", it can liberate faith from a consciousness devoid of a historical dimension, susceptible to the vagaries of the moment. The "deep breath" of the tradition of faith relativises the present of faith, integrates it into the historical-social continuity and safeguards it from absolutizing the present. The same applies to the integrating role of institutionality. Being linked to the universal faith of the Church can liberate faith from subjective narrowness and amorphism to freedom, which allows one to be bestowed with faith and salvation "by grace" (cf. Rom 4:16).[146]

However, a distinction must be made between a liberating action and a "caring unburdening" from responsibility, decision and acceptance of faith. The Church should not liberate "from" but "to" responsibility in faith. It is not a question of emancipation from the Church, but of arranging the common space of faith so that man could be the subject and not merely the object of the salvific care. The criterion here is the possibility of co-responsible participation of the faithful in all the Church's achievements and decisions.[147] After all, the Holy Spirit is given in the reception of the word of God and the sacraments not by the grace of the Church, but by the grace of God who uses the Church. The greater the opportunity for this participation, the more the Church will experience itself as a community of liberated persons who owe their freedom to the freedom of Christ. The structures of the institution should take the diverse experiences of faith seriously and include "the people of God" as a responsible agent of the Christian service of salvation (cf. GS 10-12, 36). The more courageously the Church embarks on a path that allows for open discussion, the gradual separation of the various functions and responsibilities from their association with offices that accrued over the course of history (at the expense of other charisms), allowing for the co-determining function of charisms – the more it will be experienced as a real community of "owed and liberated freedom".[148] Such "concrete freedom of faith" in the Church also has its ambivalence. Institutional "concretisation" carries a certain risk, but the "charismatic" power of the Holy Spirit defends it against alienation, relativises it and opens it to the future offered by Him.[149]

---

146 Cf. Kehl, "Kirche als Institution – eine theologische Begründung," 134–7; Kehl, *Die Kirche*, 400–1; Kehl, "Kirche – Sakrament des Geistes," 173–9; Kehl, "Kirche als Institution," 195–6; Jagodziński, *Communio dzięki komunikacji*, 369–72; Sienkiewicz, *Wspólnota Kościoła*, 321–7.

147 Cf. Pottmeyer, "Theologie der Synodalen Strukturen," in *Fragen der Kirche heute*, ed. Adolf Exeler (Würzburg: Echter, 1971), 164–82; Kasper, " Kollegiale Strukturen in der Kirche," in *Glaube und Geschichte*, ed. Kasper (Mainz: Grünewald, 1970), 355–70.

148 Cf. Kasper, "Amt und Gemeinde," in *Glaube und Geschichte*, ed. Kasper (Mainz: Grünewald, 1970), 388–414; Kehl, "Kirche als Institution – eine theologische Begründung," 137–8; Kehl, "Kirche als Institution," 196–7; Kehl, *Die Kirche*, 401–2.

149 Cf. Kehl, "Kirche – Sakrament des Geistes," 179; Jagodziński, *Communio dzięki komunikacji*, 372–4; Jagodziński, "Trynitarno-pneumatologiczne pośrednictwo Kościoła," 86–8.

3.4.4 The Implications of the Pneumatological-Sacramental Vision of the Church

The identification of the Church as the sacrament of the Holy Spirit implies a decisive correction of its previous image. This gives rise to an important opening up of the Church and concrete aspects of its renewed form.[150]

Firstly, the Church is only a sacrament, a transitory reality until the coming of the eschatological kingdom of God, a sign of anticipation of its coming characterised by a dialogical missionary task. It must be attentive to the "signs of the times" created by the Holy Spirit in order to grasp His message more deeply and to create signs on its own, so that the world may read and realise them in the same Spirit of freedom and love. A well-thought-out pneumatological ecclesiology cannot lead to esotericism in the form of intra-ecclesial structural reform only or private mysticism, but amidst the confusion of the times it should be capable to filter out the universal dimensions of Christianity. The Church's task is to spiritually permeate the world, witnessing in love to the Spirit of freedom and inviting people to build, in solidarity in the world, the way to the coming kingdom. The responsibility for this must grow out of a life in the Spirit, and the spiritual saturation of the world is only possible by imitating Jesus who serves the Father and people in the evangelical attitude of "the poor in spirit".[151] Bearing credible witness to the kingdom of God is only possible through the renunciation of power and riches and in total trust in the Holy Spirit. Only a person filled with the Holy Spirit can be truly open to the world. W. Kasper suggests, following Roger Schutz, that the ancient rule "pray and work" (*ora et labora*) can be reinterpreted today as "fight and contemplate" and be presented as the shape of modern holiness.[152]

Secondly, the identification of the Church as the sacrament of the Holy Spirit has great ecumenical significance. The association of the Holy Spirit with a particular visible institution has always resulted in the resentment about its concreteness and visibility, and the effects of this must also be felt by the Church and its mission. Nonetheless, the Church must reckon with the fact that also outside its boundaries the Holy Spirit "blows wherever He pleases" and however He pleases. The Decree on Ecumenism *Unitatis redintegratio* proclaims that "the separated Churches and Communities [...] have been by no means deprived of significance and importance in the mystery of salvation. For the Spirit of Christ has not refrained from using them as means of salvation [...]" (No. 3). The conciliar teaching on ecclesial elements

150 Cf. Kasper, *Die Kirche als Sakrament des Geistes*, 298–9.

151 Cf. Gardocki, *Teologia wyzwolenia*, 135: "For the life of the Spirit of Jesus is nothing less than the imitation of Jesus and the attempt to recreate His way. Imitating Jesus is the paradigm of the Christian life and of life in the Spirit."

152 Cf. Kasper, *Die Kirche als Sakrament des Geistes*, 299–300.

outside the structure of the Roman Catholic Church is thus pneumatologically motivated, and the Church can only rejoice in the fruitfulness of the Holy Spirit's work there and acknowledge (often with shame) its existence. However, if one recognises not only the invisible but also the ecclesial action of the Holy Spirit, then, following *Unitatis redintegratio* and *Lumen gentium*, one must not only say that there is the Catholic Church in which the Church of Jesus Christ is concretely realised and, alongside it – the ecclesial elements mentioned, but also that the one Church of Jesus Christ is divided into Churches and ecclesial communities. This does not only mean that all these Churches and ecclesial communities are more or less equal branches of the one tree of the Church, and that their specificity (together with the Catholic Church, which claims to have retained the fullness of the salvific means) must simply be preserved. It also means that there is a true – albeit imperfect – unity in the Holy Spirit. A renewed pneumatology can become a source of stimuli that lead to the breaking of the contemporary ecumenical stagnation, without the blurring of differences or the preservation of existing Christian denominations, for this would only lead to new divisions. The right direction is the mutual recognition of all ecclesial realities as charisms of the Holy Spirit – including the visible, institutional form of the Catholic Church based on Peter, with its sacramental significance. The aim is thus to strengthen the unity in diversity that already exists in the Holy Spirit and, to be even more precise, to transform the divisive diversity into unity through mutual reception and acceptance.[153]

Thirdly, the Church is an improvisation of the Holy Spirit. The Christian allows himself to be guided by Him (cf. Rom 8:14) – he is a spiritual man – and there is no ready-made formula for this except faith, obedience and service. The conservatives believe the Holy Spirit only when He expresses Himself in forms they already know; the progressives are impatient and frustrated when history unfolds in ways they have not planned – and all lack courage and confidence. The dialectical middle stance too often only means mediocrity. Trusting the Holy Spirit requires the courage to endure adversity and uncertainty. This does not mean that everything is possible in the Church – but it is necessary to be open and to take advantage of real opportunities. Taking into account the unpredictability of the Holy Spirit's action does not mean, however, that the Church is to become entangled in protracted discussions that take away its concreteness. An important issue for the Church's future shape will always be the correct definition of the relationship between the communional-collegial and the jurisdictional-decisional elements. The last Council initiated this process, but these elements often exist side by side and cause much tension and controversy. Therefore, there is a need for greater openness and wise distribution of accents. This also requires a spirituality of "thinking with the Church", which can overcome

153 Cf. Kasper, *Die Kirche als Sakrament des Geistes*, 300–2.

conflicts and is open to change. Apart from the readiness to enter a dialogue and the ability to cooperate, what is needed is the openness to self-criticism and the acknowledgement of other experiences, realism of sensing a consensus and new possibilities, perseverance, patience and passion to stay on the right path. This has nothing to do with infantile devotion or pure fidelity to the adopted direction; instead, this spirituality grows out of love and suffering on the path to human and Christian maturity. Extreme ecclesial attitudes – individualism and centralism – are in fact egoistic. Individualism shatters and freezes everything, while centralism is cramped and breathless. Extreme attitudes must be hence avoided, so that not one or the other is all, but that all are whole in unity – this is the Catholic concept of the Church.[154]

3.5 The Pneumatological Dimensions of the Sacraments of Communion

Pneumatologically oriented sacramentology is a reflection rooted in the dynamics of the life of God that is pulsating in the communion of the loving Persons of the Holy Trinity. It leads to a dynamic, personal view of the sacramental mysteries as real symbols of Divine Love, as salvific events that open and introduce man and the liturgical assembly of the praying Church to the communion of life and love that is in God. Therefore, both the celebration of the sacraments and the participation in them initiate a dynamic process of participation in God's personal love, while the liturgical celebration can be interpreted as inclusion in the movement of the life and relationship of Jesus to the Father in the Holy Spirit.[155]

In the theological dialogue between the Catholic and Orthodox Churches, sacrament is seen as a sacramental mode of Christ's being enabled and sustained by the Holy Spirit, as a concretely realised form of the combined and mutual action of the Son and the Holy Spirit in the Church.[156] Is the Holy Spirit – as a gift – only the content of the sacraments or is He their proper and real dispenser? For a long time, Western theology did not develop a distinct economy of the Holy Spirit in the sacramental ministry of the Church since it focused exclusively on the mystery of Christ. Therefore, a pneumatologically oriented sacramentology asks about a distinct profile of the Holy Spirit's action in the sacraments – but it is neither completely independent from the economy of Christ, nor completely parallel with it. It is only a question of preserving the mission of the Holy Spirit and his action from

154 Cf. Kasper, *Die Kirche als Sakrament des Geistes*, 302–5.

155 Cf. Guzowski, *Duch Dialogujący*, 233–35; Krzysztof Gąsecki, *Jesteśmy napełnieni Duchem Chrystusa w sakramentach Kościoła. Pneumatologia a sakramentologia* (Pelplin: Bernardinum, 2018), 8, 19.

156 Cf. Pałucki, *Trynitarny wymiar Kościoła*, 102–5.

being functionalised and unreflectively subordinated to Christ's work. Sacramentology finds such a possibility in emphasising the personal character of the Holy Spirit's action.[157]

Contemporary personalist and communicative sacramentology shows that not only the sacraments of Holy Orders and marriage serve communion (as the current Catechism of the Catholic Church puts it), but that they all perform this service and are truly sacraments of communion. Following the Second Vatican Council, sacramentology strongly emphasises the relationship of the sacraments to faith, which is a subjective and personal factor. In recent sacramentology, a personalist understanding of the sacraments is increasingly prominent, which values the truth that they are always instances of real, current and historical communication between the Divine Persons and the human person. This approach reveals the truth about the bond between human persons with the Holy Trinity through the sacraments, about God's economy of salvation and incarnation, and at the same time seeks to recapitulate and synthesise the previous approaches, which sometimes tend to be contradictory. The personal dimensions give the dimensions of reality, meaning and sense to sacramental signs which are empirical, sacred liturgical signs binding man to Christ, actualising and realising salvation: "a sacrament constitutes the revealed trinitarian Economy of Salvation which is liturgically realized in seven evangelical signs that represent a living communion between God and man".[158]

The post-conciliar Catholic theology has recognised the salvific and ecclesiogenic work of the Holy Spirit in the administration and fruition of the sacraments. Particularly inspiring words for a pneumatological interpretation of the sacraments are contained in the encyclical *Dominum et Vivificantem*: "And yet it occurs by the power of the Holy Spirit, who makes it possible for Christ, who has gone away, to come now and for ever in a new way. This new coming of Christ by the power of the Holy Spirit, and his constant presence and action in the spiritual life are

---

157 "How can we explain this role of the Spirit in the sacramental mystery more clearly? What categories can express it? Let us start with the simple statement that the New Covenant is the Covenant of the Spirit (2 Cor 3:6) and the inner transformation of man into a new reality (2 Cor 5:17). God "anointed" with the Holy Spirit not only Christ (Acts 10:38), but also the Covenant community and each believer (2 Cor l:21-22; l John 2:20,27). One could speak also in this respect of a certain commonality of life and destiny between Christ, the Church and Christians. The Holy Spirit is not only a gift, but also the Giver. It is He who makes it possible for the Christian to participate in the new life, which is participation in the life of Christ and His salvific mysteries. Both cases involve the Spirit as a person (see l Cor 12:11). The action of the Spirit is by its nature transcendent, supra-historical. It becomes historical only in the history of Christ, the Church and individual persons. Without having its own personal incarnation similar to the incarnation of the Son of God, the Holy Spirit is nevertheless personally present through His action. This action is permanent and imperishable" (Hryniewicz, *Nasza Pascha z Chrystusem*, 276).

158 Cf. Bartnik, *Dogmatyka katolicka* (Lublin: Wydawnictwo KUL, 2003), 2: 593–5.

accomplished in the sacramental reality" (No.61). The encyclical goes on to explain that this

> sacramental ministry, every time it is accomplished, brings with it the mystery of the 'departure' of Christ through the Cross and the Resurrection, by virtue of which the Holy Spirit comes. He comes and works: 'He gives life'. For the sacraments signify grace and confer grace: they signify life and give life. The Church is the visible dispenser of the sacred signs, while the Holy Spirit acts in them as the invisible dispenser of the life which they signify (No. 63).

In other words, "the fullness of the salvific reality, which is Christ in history, extends in a sacramental way in the power of the Spirit Paraclete" (No. 64). Through Him and within His mission, the Church grows continually out of the Paschal mystery of Christ's "departure" and, at the same time, lives on through the continual new coming of Christ in the celebrated mysteries (cf. No. 63).[159]

The liturgical reform brings a clear increase in the awareness of the Holy Spirit in the dispensation of the sacraments. They are filled with the Holy Spirit and they participate in the mediation of the Holy Spirit. The Holy Spirit is the "Medium" of the liturgical presence of the Lord. The sacraments based on Christ's salvific work are structurally rooted in the action of the Spirit who initiates and supports the action of the Church. Since the Spirit raised Jesus from the dead, He has further realised His corporeality according to the given time and space. He presents Jesus to people and prepares them to receive His message, He initiates the encounter with Christ, sustains, supports and makes it real. He also uses human activity as a means and instrument.[160] It is the cause of Christ's communion with those receiving the sacraments.[161]

---

159 Cf. Czaja, *Credo in Spiritum Vivificantem*, 171–6.

160 On the *ars celebrandi* in the Holy Spirit, see Gąsecki, *Jesteśmy napełnieni Duchem Chrystusa w sakramentach Kościoła*, 117–9.

161 Cf. Czaja, *Credo in Spiritum Vivificantem*, 176–8. An additional issue is the relationship between word and sacrament. In a sacramental event, the word of preaching is necessary. The proclamation of the Good News is not only information about God's Revelation. Is the view of Protestant theology legitimate that the sacrament is accomplished by the living preaching of the word of God and the faith-filled reception of it? Why, then, does Eastern pneumatology maintain that salvation is made present through the action of the Holy Spirit and in so doing, it points to the epicletic-liturgical structure of God's economy? Is the sacrament realised more by the preaching word or more by the Holy Spirit acting in the liturgy? These questions seem not to have been precisely related to each other. After all, the sacrament is realised both by the word and by the Holy Spirit, because the word is proclaimed in the Spirit – the Holy Spirit Himself speaks through the word of God. This word is also present in experiencing the sacrament. For Protestants, it remains an open question whether the sacraments have the intrinsic efficacy to be mediated by the Spirit

of God. Catholic theology holds that the preached word is not just a homily – simple speaking based on the Scriptures read; preaching always has a broader sense, encompassing the whole ministry of salvation. Protestant theology simply states that the word and the sacrament cannot be interpreted against each other, for they are forms of the one word of God and differ not in kind but in modality – in the word and the sacrament, man experiences the manifested reality of God. It is the level of quality and intensity of the two means of salvation that remains an open question here. Is the pneumatological dimension really absent or only more strongly concealed in the tradition that emphasises the mediation of salvation through the Word? Perhaps the Eastern tradition should not accuse the West of "forgetting the Holy Spirit," since He is always implied there? In the word-centred liturgy, is the Holy Spirit merely the mediating power of Jesus' presence? Does He act as a Divine Person more independently in the trinitarian liturgy, which is based, inter alia, on the epicletic-liturgical dimension of prayer? The Western and Eastern traditions could come closer together if they attempted to interpret the essential categories – "Spirit," "word," "sacrament" – in a broader sense. If, for instance, the Reformed tradition speaks of the Word and of the mediation of salvation through the Word to emphasise that Christ is the one (and only) Sacrament, it could more clearly emphasise that He, as the Sacrament, is present in the Spirit through the sacraments given to us, in which His power is at work. However, also the East – while trying to emphasise the role of the Holy Spirit – should not forget the Christological centre of the economy of salvation. For the preaching of the word and supplication for the action of the Holy Spirit belong inseparably and constitutively to the sacramental rites. The sacraments flow directly from what has been revealed by the life-giving action of the Spirit of God and what has been said about the creative power of the word of God. The focus in sacramentological thinking on the word alone is often combined with an individualised path of self-knowledge and forgetting of the liturgy and the Church. The lack of clear distinctions between the preaching word and the sacramental word remains problematic in this conception; an explanation of the realisation of salvation through performative speech is favoured – the word makes itself present on the basis of its intrinsic power. Sacraments, however, cannot be confined to the realm of language or thought. Admittedly, they are linguistic events, but they must also involve putting oneself at the disposal of the Holy Spirit. Sacramentality requires theological justification – the action of the Divine Person of the Holy Spirit. Philosophical and anthropological underpinnings open analogous structures of thought that are conducive to theological reflection, but theological (pneumatological-trinitarian) explanation is ultimately indispensable. The power of the third Divine Person reveals the event of Christ – as a transcendental power and Divine act, not as a transcendental power of the temporal phenomenon of word, speech or utterance. The salvific work in Christ, with regard to the world, is conveyed in the Holy Spirit, who acts through word and sacrament, so that the Church is formed as a community of believers participating in the gifts of salvation. The manifestation of salvation through Christ in the Holy Spirit is carried by the initiative of the Spirit of God, who ignites faith in the participants of the liturgy. The Spirit – by uniting the exalted Lord with the believers during the liturgy – is a kind of medium of Christ's presence and His salvific acts. The Pneuma-Medium acts through the word of preaching in the symbolic actions of the Church and in the prayer of the gathered community. The word and the liturgical actions are indispensable elements. However, the action of the Spirit in the non-verbal sphere is not parallel to that which we experience in sacramental signs. A sacrament is not a mere confessional human act – it gives the space for the sanctifying action of the Spirit of God. Furthermore, the action of the Spirit should not be confined to the words of homiletic-catechetical preaching, it should not be understood only instrumentally as the power of Christ's action in man's journey of faith. The Holy Spirit is also at work in the

There are also attempts to look at the sacrament as an epicletic reality, that is, the fruit of the Church's call for the coming of the Holy Spirit.[162] The incoming Spirit makes the sacrament real, is the Giver of the sacrament and gives Himself – He is the Gift of the sacrament. Man's participation in "sacred things", in Christ and His offer of salvation, which is realized in the sacraments, is accomplished through mutual personal self-giving or even as a community of personal mutual self-giving. The principle of this mutual self-giving is the Holy Spirit. The One who shared in Jesus' sacrifice on the cross also shares in the sacramental realisation of this sacrifice. On the other hand, the Spirit liberates man to give himself to Christ, awakens the desire and enables him to become more and more like Christ.[163]

The sacramental mediation of God's self-giving to men takes place with the help of the Church, which, being the Church of Jesus Christ, communicates the incarnational presence of God's salvation in the power of his Spirit through signs. The incarnational structure of the salvific event is extended in the ecclesial interaction of word and symbol, and the Holy Spirit uses this as an instrument in making Christ present in his salvific action.[164] In such a perspective, the sacraments can be seen as visible and tangible signs of God's real closeness and presence, communication and communion, dialogue and fellowship with God, which also create communion and communication, dialogue and fellowship among people.[165]

All the essential elements of the Christian concept of communion can be seen in 1 John 1:3. The starting point is the encounter with the incarnate Son of God – Jesus Christ – who reaches people through the Church's preaching. This is how a human community based on the communion of the Triune God comes into being. The way to a communion with God leads through a communion of God with men, which is Christ in His Person. Jesus Christ – God-man – is also Himself a personal communion of deity and humanity. The encounter with Christ gives rise to a communion with Him and with the Father in the Holy Spirit, which then unites people to one another and leads to the perfect joy which is equivalent to the Holy Spirit. Thus, *communio* has a theological, Christological, pneumatological, historico-salvific and ecclesiological character, it also includes the sacramental dimension of God's closeness.[166] Everything that happens between God and people has a communional character; salvation is realised as salvation in communion. Entering

sacramental signs and in the symbolic actions of the community of believers who call upon Him to demonstrate and realise the redemptive work of Jesus Christ. Cf. Gąsecki, *Jesteśmy napełnieni Duchem Chrystusa w sakramentach Kościoła*, 108–14.

162 Cf. Gąsecki, *Jesteśmy napełnieni Duchem Chrystusa w sakramentach Kościoła*, 57–61, 99–108.

163 Cf. Hryniewicz, *Nasza Pascha z Chrystusem*, 275–7; Czaja, *Credo in Spiritum Vivificantem*, 178–80.

164 Cf. Herbert Vorgrimler, *Sakramententheologie* (Düsseldorf: Patmos, 1990), 88–9.

165 Cf. Lachner, "Communio – eine Grundidee des christlichen Glaubens," 230.

166 Cf. Lachner, "Communio – eine Grundidee des christlichen Glaubens," 247–8.

the way of Christ, however, is accomplished not only through Him, but also, and to an equal measure, through the gift of the Holy Spirit.[167]

The communion of the Church is substantially realised in the sacraments, with each of them developing a specific mode of communicative communion. Therefore, it is possible to speak of general communicative sacramentology as each of the sacraments is about communion-oriented communication.[168] Sacramental communication is thus as diverse as diverse are the different sacramental forms of communication taking place in different communicative situations.[169] Ecclesial acts of communication can be reproduced in new historical and personal conditions of the eternal event of the communion of the Father, the Son and the Holy Spirit. This event is realised in ecclesial communication, enlivening the dynamics of the currently lived communion (which in turn transitions again into communication), in which the Church, as sign and instrument of Divine communion, itself becomes "the sacrament of the universal communion of love".[170]

Since all sacraments, as communicative acts, serve to build communion – their communicative-communional character can be demonstrated in the groups pertaining to "initiation into communion", "healing of communion" and "service of communion". The following structure emerges: 1. Sacraments of initiation into communion: baptism – the sacrament of the beginning of communion; confirmation – the sacrament of the strengthening of communion; Eucharist – the sacrament of the building of communion. 2. Sacraments of healing of communion: penance – the sacrament of the restoration of communion; anointing of the sick – the sacrament of the maintenance of communion. 3. Sacraments at the service of communion: holy orders – the sacrament of the "official" service of communion; matrimony – the sacrament of the marital-familial service of communion.[171]

---

167 Cf. Greshake, *Der dreieine Gott*, 363–70.

168 Cf. Meuffels, *Kommunikative Sakramententheologie*, 309.

169 Cf. Lothar Lies, *Sakramententheologie. Eine personale Sicht* (Graz-Wien-Köln: Styria, 1990), 309.

170 Cf. Lies, *Sacramententheologie*, 350–1, 355–60. "A personal understanding of the role of the Holy Spirit revises not only the static image of God but also the role of the immanent Holy Trinity in the economy of salvation. The historico-salvific function of God in the Holy Spirit is to make the human experience of community a symbol of the Divine *Communio et Communicatio*. Then, the sacraments [...] owing to their pneumatological dynamics, can [...] be seen as dialogic-communicative actions of those who as subjects become participants in the communion of life and love with the Triune God. Therefore, sacramental worship – in such an explicitly personal-dialogical perspective – is not possible without communication" (Gąsecki, *Jesteśmy napełnieni Duchem Chrystusa w sakramentach Kościoła*, 132).

171 Cf. Jagodziński, *Sakramenty w służbie communio. Studium teologiczno-komunikacyjne* (Warszawa: Wydawnictwo UKSW, 2008), 319–408; Jagodziński, "Sakramenty komunii," *Ruch Biblijny i Liturgiczny* 4 (2009), 285–92; Jagodziński, "W komunii z Bogiem przez sakramenty," *Zeszyty Formacji Katechetów* 11/4 (2011), 36–8.

3.5.1 The Pneumatological Dimensions of the Sacraments of Initiation into Communion

St. Paul wrote that "in the one Spirit we were all baptized into one body" (cf. 1 Cor 12:13), forming one holy, universal and apostolic Church. The text of CCC 1212 is an introduction to the section on the sacraments of initiation[172] and quotes the words of Paul VI from the Apostolic Constitution *Divinae consortium naturae:*

> The sharing in the divine nature given to men through the grace of Christ bears a certain likeness to the origin, development, and nourishing of natural life. The faithful are born anew by baptism, strengthened by the sacrament of confirmation, and receive in the Eucharist the food of eternal life. By means of these sacraments of Christian initiation, they thus receive in increasing measure the treasures of the divine life and advance toward the perfection of charity.

These words can be perceived as a description of sacramental initiation into communion with God and people.[173]

If one tries to approach the sacraments of initiation as isolated acts, one can attribute some specific characteristics to them, but it is impossible to clarify many things about their origin and place in early Christianity. For example, it can be argued that confirmation is the rite of bestowing the Holy Spirit on the baptised. But then a question immediately arises: Does it bestow the Holy Spirit, while baptism and the Eucharist do not? In the account of Christ's baptism, the connection between the entrance into the water and the descent of the Holy Spirit is so considerable that it is difficult to separate one from the other. The same must be said of the descent of the Holy Spirit at Pentecost. Could we separate it from the baptism that follows St. Peter's sermon and the birth of the first Church in Jerusalem? In the New Testament times there was "baptism by water", but it was not Christian baptism.

---

172 Cf. Schneider, *Znaki bliskości Boga. Zarys sakramentologii* (Wrocław: Wrocławska Księgarnia Archidiecezjalna TUM, 1990), 69–83; Marino Qualizza, *Inicjacja chrześcijańska. Chrzest. Bierzmowanie. Eucharystia* (Kraków: WAM, 2002); Bartnik, *Dogmatyka katolicka*, 2: 670.

173 "The dispensation of the sacraments of initiation (baptism and the Eucharist) introduces into the very centre of the divine mysteries and, as Ambrose puts it, through them, man enters 'the sanctuary of rebirth.' For it is an introduction into the life of the Church and into the life of the Holy Trinity. The whole Trinity acts and is present in all sacraments and every action of sanctification is an action of the Trinity. Augustine concludes that the sacraments at the Church's disposal, though few in number, are nevertheless a sufficient instrument and give strength to guide the Church and to form one community – *communio* and *societas*" (Pałucki, *Trynitarny wymiar Kościoła*, 204–5).

The Church's baptism always involved the descent of the Holy Spirit (John 3:5). This was the belief that has lasted for centuries.[174]

The same problems arise when someone tries to isolate baptism from the Eucharist. It is no accident that Jesus used the term "baptism" in connection with His death (Matt 20:22; cf. Luke 12:50). The "cup" of His death and the "baptism" of His death can hardly be understood without the cup of the New Covenant from the Last Supper. In the story of the descent of the Holy Spirit, the baptism of thousands and the participation of them all in the "breaking of the bread" form one indivisible whole. The essential unified origin of all three sacraments of initiation is thus revealed and any attempt to look at them without this unity would cause serious theological and historical problems.[175]

What is the nature of this unity and what can be said about baptism, confirmation and Eucharist in its light? In a very general way, it can be said that Eucharist operated in the consciousness of the early Church in the context of Christology that encompassed the whole history of salvation realised eschatologically through the Pentecostal outpouring of the Holy Spirit.[176] It was only through the outpouring of the Holy Spirit "in these last days" (Acts 2:17) that Christian baptism could exist as a baptism of water and Spirit (John 3:5). When St. Paul spoke of baptism as participation in Christ's death and resurrection, he referred to the person of Christ both in the Fathers' Paschal crossing of the sea (1 Cor 10:1-2) and in baptism "in the one Spirit [...] into one body" (1 Cor 12:13). Baptism presupposes the Pentecostal community (Acts 2) in which it takes place. It should be remembered that, after all, "no one can say 'Jesus is Lord' except by the Holy Spirit" (1 Cor 12:3). It is impossible in the Church to worship God without the presence of the Spirit. Since both the historical and the eschatological aspects are united in Christ in the Holy Spirit, baptism seems ultimately to be an incorporation into that community which is the Body of Christ – the Church.[177] We can read in the baptismal liturgy of

174 Cf. Zizioulas, *The Eucharistic Communion and the World*, 114–5. "After discussing separately the three sacraments of Christian initiation: baptism, confirmation and the Eucharist, it is necessary to explain them together because, in accordance with New Testament theology, they are a single three-stage 'event' which one will not understand by separating one stage from the other. Hence, the emphatic saying that baptism is the most important sacrament should be replaced by the expression: 'these three are the most important for man'. Figuratively speaking: just as a mother who conceives a child should give birth to it and should provide for it, so the Church, receiving the new conception in God and helping it to be born in God, cannot fail to provide for its nourishment and upbringing. The same applies to Christian initiation, the author of which is the Holy Spirit, who gives man a new life that is completely and utterly immersed in Christ" (Guzowski, *Duch Dialogujący*, 246–7).

175 Cf. Zizioulas, *The Eucharistic Communion and the World*, 115.

176 Cf. Zizioulas, *The Eucharistic Communion and the World*, 115.

177 Cf. Zizioulas, *The One and the Many*, 94–5.

St. Hippolytus that it was after baptism and confirmation that the baptised could pray together with the faithful. This seems to minimise the specific nature of the Eucharist which authorises participation in common prayer. However, behind this there is the idea that the Eucharist, unlike baptism and confirmation, means essentially community, i. e. an ecclesial reality in which all that was individual in baptism and confirmation becomes communal by virtue of communion in the Body of Christ. It should thus be emphasised that the preservation of the unity of baptism, confirmation and the Eucharist was not intended to simply offer the Eucharist to the baptised immediately after confirmation, but primarily to bring the newly baptised person into the assembly of the faithful.[178]

The Eucharist, as the natural continuation of baptism and confirmation, appears as the sphere in which *the ordo* becomes a reality and ministry finds its basis of existence. It is no accident, then, that priestly orders appear in the early Church necessarily in the context of the Eucharist. The Eucharist in its communal and ecclesial character is a Pentecostal community, an eschatological community *par excellence*, which experiences and testifies to the entry of the eschaton into history and gives a foretaste of the future Kingdom. This communal character of the Eucharistic liturgy, which is "the common action of the whole Church" in a particular place, provides the proper context for priestly orders, since there is indeed no ministry or *ordo* that is outside or above the community of the Church. In the end, holy orders are an act of the whole Church, not just some part of it. The fact that all holy orders must take place in the Eucharistic context means that they cannot be seen as a self-explanatory sacramental whole, an objectified "sacrament" in itself, but as part of the one and indivisible mystery of Christ. The Eucharist guarantees this to an outstanding degree, since it is the only act of the Church which by its nature belongs to the whole community, it is a "Catholic" act of the universal Church. Entering holy orders is not just a matter of the bishop's laying on his hands, but it is a liturgical act of the whole community. Zizioulas notes that the Eucharist seems to be the only natural context for priestly orders, since the ordaining person is also the natural head of the Eucharistic assembly. It is no coincidence that from the beginning the bishop was the only person who could ordain – and this cannot be

178 Cf. Zizioulas, *The One and the Many*, 98–9. "This was the meaning given to the attachment of the Eucharist to Confirmation and Baptism by the early Church. The Eucharist was not simply the food and medicine of immortality to which every baptized and chrismated individual was immediately entitled, but at the same time – and this, I am afraid, we have lost sight of – it was the synaxis of the people of God, the ἐκκλησία τού Θεού, in the unity of which he was asked to enter and take his place. By virtue of his Chrismation, each baptised person becomes a member of the royal λαός of God, λαϊκόσ. It is only natural that he enters immediately the assembly of the Eucharist in order to occupy his proper τάζίς or τάγμα (=order) of the layman in this called and summoned people of God, the ἐκκλησία" (ibid.).

explained by a mere reference to "apostolic succession", because in such a case, the bishop in succession could ordain, for example, in his office. The fact that he can only do so in the Eucharistic context means that he does so primarily by virtue of being the head of the Eucharistic assembly. Therefore, the Eucharist is the proper context of the whole order in the Church.[179]

3.5.1.1 The Pneumatological-Communional Dimension of the Sacrament of Baptism

When we look at baptism in the light of the mystery of Christ, we see that baptism cannot be understood independently of the baptismal reality that pre-exists in the mystery of salvation. This is expressed in the New Testament idea of baptism of water. Added to this is the eschatological or pneumatological dimension – everything happens by virtue of the outpouring of the Holy Spirit "in the last days" (Acts 2:17) – Christian baptism can only exist as baptism of water and Spirit (John 3:5). The two dimensions were united in the person of Christ. When St. Paul speaks of baptism as participation in Christ's death and resurrection, he refers the person of Christ both to the Paschal crossing of the sea (1 Cor 10:1-2) and to the fact that "in the one Spirit we were all baptized into one body" (1 Cor 12:13). Two implications about baptism seem to follow from this basic observation. First, every baptism in the Church is linked to the participation in the history and vocation of the people of God. Secondly, baptism presupposes the existence of a community upon which the Holy Spirit has descended. Since the historical and eschatological dimensions are united in Christ in the Holy Spirit, it seems that baptism ultimately means an incorporation into the community that is the Body of Christ – the Church.[180]

The missionary imperative imposes the obligation to baptise all peoples and nations equally without any distinction or privilege: "Go therefore and make disciples of all nations, baptizing them in the name of the Father and of the Son and of the Holy Spirit" (Matt 28:19; cf. Mark 16:16). St. Peter's speech after Pentecost testifies to the same: "be baptized every one of you in the name of Jesus Christ" (Acts 2:38). The community of the baptised is a universal community of communication, with no division into Greek and Jew, slave and master, male and female. All "are one in Christ Jesus" (Gal 3:28), they are "one body": "For in the one Spirit we were all baptized into one body—Jews or Greeks, slaves or free—and we were all made to drink of one Spirit" (1 Cor 12:13; cf. Eph 4:4-5; Rom 12:5; Col 1:18-19; 2:19; 3:11). Baptism is administered so that all may, through "immersion into Christ Jesus",

179 Cf. Zizioulas, *The One and the Many*, 99–100.

180 Cf. Zizioulas, *The Eucharistic Communion and the World*, 116; Guzowski, *Duch Dialogujący*, 236–41; Pałucki, *Tryniatrny wymiar Kościoła*, 207–13.

"in the death of Jesus" (cf. Rom 6:3), constitute "one body" (1 Cor 12:13).[181] This involves a whole series of duties: "making every effort to maintain the unity of the Spirit in the bond of peace. There is one body and one Spirit, just as you were called to the one hope of your calling, one Lord, one faith, one baptism, one God and Father of all, who is above all and through all and in all" (Eph 4:3-6).[182]

Baptism anticipates the future, but it also takes account of and transforms the past – it is the gateway to salvation, which includes not only the past and the present, but also initiates the participation in the eschatological fullness of life: "he saved us […] according to his mercy, through the water of rebirth and renewal by the Holy Spirit. This Spirit he poured out on us richly through Jesus Christ our Savior, so that, having been justified by his grace, we might become heirs according to the hope of eternal life" (Titus 3:5-7). CCC 1215 teaches: "This sacrament is also called 'the washing of regeneration and renewal by the Holy Spirit' (Titus 3:5), for it signifies and actually brings about the birth of water and the Spirit without which no one 'can enter the kingdom of God' (John 3:5)" (cf. CCC 1216). Baptism is a bath of regeneration and cleansing in the Holy Spirit, and its supernatural effects are linked to the salvific passion of Christ: "Christ love and gave himself up for her, in order to make her holy by cleansing her with the washing of water by the word" (Eph 5:25-26). In a slightly different way, the thought is formulated in Titus 3:5-6: "he saved us […] according to his mercy, through the water of rebirth and renewal by the Holy Spirit. This Spirit he poured out on us richly through Jesus Christ our Saviour".[183] Baptism imprints the invisible seal of the Holy Spirit: "in him you also […] had believed […] and were marked with the seal of the promised Holy Spirit" (Eph 1:13; cf. 4:30; 2 Cor 1:22). Baptism is a new circumcision incorporating one into the new people of God (Col 2:11-12; cf. Eph 2:11-22). Finally, it means the reception of the pledge of the gifts of the Holy Spirit, the fullness of which has been promised to all believers in Christ (cf. 2 Cor 1:22; Eph 1:14).[184]

St. Paul writes in 1 Cor 12:13: "For in the one Spirit we were all baptized […] and we were all made to drink of one Spirit". We can see here the fulfilment of St. John the Baptist's prophesy: "One who is more powerful than I is coming after me […] He will baptize you with the Holy Spirit and fire" (Matt 3:11). Based on Romans 8:14, man is baptised "in the Holy Spirit" and receives the dignity of a child-son of God, with the Holy Spirit as an unfailing light and guide. Therefore, the baptised person does not only find himself in a new atmosphere and "breathes" or

181 Cf. Kazimierz Romaniuk, *Sakramentologia biblijna: zarys teologii sakramentów dla teologów, katechetów, duszpasterzy* (Warszawa: Wydawnictwo Salezjańskie, 1994), 20.

182 Cf. Kazimierz Romaniuk, *Sakramentologia biblijna*, 20–1; Jagodziński, "Das Sakrament der Taufe als Communio-Sakrament," *Roczniki Teologiczne* 63/7 (2016) 207.

183 Cf. Romaniuk, *Sakramentologia biblijna*, 20–1.

184 Cf. ibid., 22–3; Jagodziński, "Das Sakrament der Taufe als Communio-Sakrament," 208–11.

"lives" by the Holy Spirit. The fatherhood of God and the sonship of man, together with the aforementioned guidance, express something more, while the mention of "being infused with one Spirit" is not only an allusion to the Eucharist but, with reference to Joel 3:1, is regarded as a prophetic foreshadowing of the New Testament implications of baptism.[185] The immersion in the mystery of Christ's death and resurrection is also an immersion in the mystery of the Holy Spirit. The catechumen becomes a Christian through faith in Jesus and the gift of the Holy Spirit, who is the Spirit of Christ and works in people's lives.[186]

In St. John's Gospel there are allusions that interpret baptism. In His conversation with Nicodemus (John 3:1-21), Jesus said: "Very truly, I tell you, no one can enter the kingdom of God without being born of water and Spirit. What is born of the flesh is flesh, and what is born of the Spirit is spirit. Do not be astonished that I said to you, 'You must be born from above'" (J 3:5-7). In the conversation with the Samaritan woman (John 4:1-30), baptism is linked to the theme of "living water", usually signifying all grace, but primarily the grace of baptism. In the account of the healing of the man blind from birth, the allusion to baptism is made with the words "I went and washed and received my sight" (John 9:11). The metaphors of washing and enlightenment occur together here. The evangelist strongly emphasises the distinctiveness of John's baptism from the baptism commanded by Jesus, which he describes as being "born from above" (cf. John 3:3,7), "born of water and Spirit" (cf. John 3:5), "of God" (cf. John 1:13; 1 John 2:29; 3:9; 5:1,4,18), "of the Spirit" (cf. John 3:5,7-8). This baptism results in obtaining the dignity of a child of God (cf. John 11:52; 1 John 3:1-2).[187]

The implantation through baptism into Christ and immersion in His Paschal mystery means entering into communion with the entire Holy Trinity. The Paschal mystery of Christ is intimately linked to the Person and mission of the Holy Spirit. "The giving up of the Spirit" by Jesus at the moment of His death (John 19:30) is a foreshadowing of the "outpouring of the Spirit". The resurrected Jesus breathes the Holy Spirit upon His disciples (John 20:22) and grants them the authority to forgive sins, which in the Church is first realised through the sacrament of baptism. The necessary completion of the Paschal mystery was the sending of the Holy Spirit at Pentecost. One interpretation claims that the reception of the Holy Spirit on the day of Pentecost by the disciples meant for them the participation in the gifts that baptism provides in the sacramental life – thus it appears as the equivalent of the sacrament of baptism. The ritual sign expressing the reception of the Holy Spirit in baptism is the anointing with the consecrated Chrism oil. It is an

185 Cf. Romaniuk, *Sakramentologia biblijna*, 24.

186 Cf. Hryniewicz, *Nasza Pascha z Chrystusem*, 290.

187 Cf. Romaniuk, *Sakramentologia biblijna*, 24; Hryniewicz, *Nasza Pascha z Chrystusem*, 291–2; Jagodziński, "Das Sakrament der Taufe als Communio-Sakrament," 211–2.

expression of participation in the nature of Christ, who was anointed with the Holy Spirit. Baptismal anointing is at the same time a foreshadowing of the sacrament of confirmation, which actualises the Pentecostal grace. The participation in the Paschal mystery of Christ through baptism also establishes a relationship with the Father, since through Christ we gain access to the Father through boldness and confidence (Eph 3:12), and the Holy Spirit is the Spirit of adoption as sons of God, in whom it is possible to address God as "Abba! Father!" (Rom 8:15).[188]

The baptismal formula is an abbreviation for the communicative, relational structure of human existence and the trinitarian structure of being a Christian. For faith in Jesus Christ means recognising oneself as the addressee of a communicative offer on which one must rely completely. The measure of this offer are not human qualifications, qualities or capacities, but the reference of the Father to the Son. Man is incorporated into this reference, he is admitted to the Divine will of community, he is filled with the Holy Spirit, with the Divine references that create the community[189] and from that moment he begins his trinitarian existence in the name of the Father, the Son and the Holy Spirit.[190]

All sacraments celebrate ecclesial communion.[191] This applies in a special way to baptism, which is not only the gateway and foundation of this communion, but also of the other sacraments. God-given new life in baptism (cf. 2 Cor 5:17; Gal 6:15; John 4:14; Rom 8:11), realised as being born of the Holy Spirit (cf. Acts 2:38; John 32:5; 1 Cor 6:11; Titus 3:5; Rom 8:9.14), on the one hand signifies man's incorporation into the life of Jesus (in His death and resurrection[192]- cf. Rom 6; Col 2:11; Eph 5:25) and, on the other hand, incorporating him into the Body of Christ as a community of believers with Christ as its Head (cf. 1 Cor 12:13; Gal 3:26-29; Col 3:11; Eph 4:46; 2:13-16; Acts 2:41,47; 5:14; 11:24). Both of these fundamental dimensions of baptism are characterised by a prominently communicative structure – the Father makes Himself known to man through the Person

---

188 Cf. Maciej Zachara, "Sakrament chrztu," in *Znaki Tajemnicy. Sakramenty w teorii i praktyce Kościoła*, ed. Krzysztof Porosło and Woźniak (Kraków: WAM, 2018), 287.

189 Cf. Lies, *Sakramententheologie. Eine personale Sicht*, 296. "The true Mystagogue of baptismal initiation is the Holy Spirit Himself. Through Him the union of man with Jesus Christ and His fate is accomplished. Baptism becomes a 'personal Pentecost' of the baptised. In it, the resurrected Christ grants him His Spirit. Once baptised, He grants the Spirit continuously in the community of the Church, especially in the Eucharistic mystery. Thus, through baptism, the catechumen is introduced into the circle of the intimate life of the triune God. He may call Him Father. The sacrament of baptism thus becomes a sacrament of intimacy with God. The giver of this trinitarian intimacy is the Holy Spirit" (Hryniewicz, *Nasza Pascha z Chrystusem*, 296).

190 Cf. Hans-Joachim Höhn, *spüren. Die ästhetische Kraft der Sakramente* (Würzburg: Echter, 2002), 65; Jagodziński, *Sakramenty w służbie communio*, 44.

191 Cf. Meuffels, *Kommunikative Sakramententheologie*, 309.

192 Cf. Bartnik, *Dogmatyka katolicka*, 2: 613.

and achievements of Jesus Christ in the abiding action of the Holy Spirit (as Person and medium), so that the believer is called to respond to the offered message of salvation (salvific communication) and thus, through Christ acting in the Holy Spirit, to enter into communion with God (transcendental dimension). Man's response is a response of faith; this is why for St. Paul, faith and baptism are to some extent interchangeable (cf. Gal 3:26-27; Eph 3:17; Gal 3:2,14; Rom 6:4) – together and alternately they form a communicative structure of reference in which the communication of God's love calls man to the communication of faith (faith is a requisite for baptism (cf. Acts 8:12-13); baptism is a requisite for faith (cf. Rom 6:3-8; 1 Cor 10:1-13); the two realities interpenetrate each other (cf. Heb 6:4; 2 Cor 4:6; Eph 1:18; 3:9; 2 Tim 1:10). The life of God's love revealed and given in Christ has a communicative effect on human existence since the mystery of salvation unfolds in the concrete human existence.[193]

Similarly, the communicative structure of baptism can be demonstrated as inclusion in the Church. Initiation does not only mean the gradual integration of the individual into the Church but also the growth of the community towards the newly received individual[194]. Therefore, baptismal initiation is a communicative action of the community that brings the individual into the community of believers in Christ who recognise His lordship.[195] Included are both the biographical circumstances of the recipient of baptism and the whole social structure of the Church along with its words and symbols. The buckle that binds the spiritual and visible dimensions together is the Holy Spirit Himself.[196]

The Lima ecumenical document[197] states that

> The Holy Spirit is at work in the lives of people before, in and after their baptism. It is the same Spirit who revealed Jesus as the Son (Mark 1:10-11) and who empowered and united the disciples at Pentecost (Acts 2). God bestows upon all baptized persons the anointing and the promise of the Holy Spirit, marks them with a seal and implants in their hearts the first instalment of their inheritance as sons and daughters of God. The Holy Spirit nurtures the life of faith in their hearts until the final deliverance when they will enter into its full possession, to the praise of the glory of God (2 Cor 1:21-22; Eph 1:13-14)" (No. 5). "Baptism initiates the reality of the new life given in the midst of the present world. It gives

193 Cf. Jean-Marie R. Tillard, "Das sakramentale Handeln der Kirche," in *Neue Summe Theologie*, vol. III: *Der Dienst der Gemeinde*, ed. Eicher (Freiburg-Basel-Wien: Herder, 1989), 239–304.

194 Cf. Franz-Josef Nocke, *Sakramententheologie. Ein Handbuch* (Düsseldorf: Patmos, 1997), 119–20.

195 Cf. Ulrich Kühn, *Sakramente* (Gütersloh: Mohn 1990), 239.

196 Cf. Meuffels, *Kommunikative Sakramententheologie*, 310–1; Jagodziński, "Das Sakrament der Taufe als Communio-Sakrament", 214–6.

197 World Council of Churches, Faith and Order. Paper no. 111, the "Lima Text:" *Baptism, Eucharist and Ministry* (1982).

> participation in the community of the Holy Spirit" (No. 7). "Those baptized are called upon to reflect the glory of the Lord as they are transformed by the power of the Holy Spirit, into his likeness, with ever increasing splendour (2 Cor 3:18)" (No. 9). "In God's work of salvation, the paschal mystery of Christ's death and resurrection is inseparably linked with the Pentecostal gift of the Holy Spirit. Similarly, participation in Christ's death and resurrection is inseparably linked with the receiving of the Spirit. Baptism in its full meaning signifies and effects both. [...] All agree that Christian baptism is in water and the Holy Spirit (No. 14.).

Some theologians do not refer to baptism as the sacrament of the receiving of the Holy Spirit, but as the sacrament of the coming of that Spirit. Through His coming, God touches the heart of man and invites him into communion with Himself. Man can reject this offer or he can accept it in the power of the Spirit. God prepares man for the decisive event of sacramental baptism. In Him, man is transformed – from an enemy he becomes a friend of God; he receives from God the gift of communion; this begins a lifelong process of inner growth in the encounter with Christ. This also takes place through the Holy Spirit. It is more common to speak of a rebirth and renewal through the water in the Holy Spirit (cf. Titus 3:5). He is the Gift given in baptism and, at the same time, the space and dynamism of this event, His coming transforms man into the likeness of the dead and resurrected Christ and marks the beginning of his existence in the Spirit. By receiving the Holy Spirit in baptism, man receives the remission of sins and eternal life with the resurrected Christ, which shapes the community of the Church.[198]

3.5.1.2 The Pneumatological-Communional Dimension of the Sacrament of Confirmation

It is characteristic for biblical theology of the New Testament to combine baptism and confirmation. Hence, many authors do not even consider it necessary to distinguish between the two, and in many of St. Paul's statements about baptism they also see an allusion to confirmation.[199] Some even claim that the separation between confirmation and baptism in later theology was too sharp (the same accusation is levelled by Orthodox theology at Catholic theologians). All of this results in today's theology of confirmation being composed of more elements of later tradition than the actual biblical data.[200]

---

198 Cf. Czaja, *Credo in Spiritum Vivificantem*, 180–3.

199 Cf. Romaniuk, *Sakramentologia biblijna*, 27–31.

200 Cf. Romaniuk, *Sakramentologia biblijna*, 35; CCC 1290–92.

L. Bouyer noted that two stages of the Holy Spirit's action can be distinguished in the life of Jesus: at the very beginning at the Annunciation and then in the waters of the Jordan where He received His mission. F.-X. Durrwell, on the other hand, argues that the presence of the Holy Spirit in the life of Jesus consisted of "guidance by the Holy Spirit" towards fulfilment in death and resurrection. In the life of the Christian, the Holy Spirit also guides and supports spiritual growth so that communion with the Paschal Christ could become real.[201]

Confirmation by the laying on of hands or by the anointing with Chrism was understood from the beginning as the bestowing of the Holy Spirit on the baptised. This understanding was for a long time common to both East and West. But in the West, the emphasis was gradually directed at the idea of perfecting baptism by confirmation. The term *perfectio* (used in Pseudo-Ambrosian writings) was expressed by the adoption of the term *confirmatio*. The reason for the adoption of this term in the West was that confirmation was necessary because something was lacking in baptism itself – either in the rite itself or in the person receiving it (e. g. the appropriate age). This opened the way for an understanding of confirmation as an essential opportunity for an adult's response with faith, especially if they were baptised as a child. In the history of confirmation in the West, a separation between "baptism of water" and "baptism of the Spirit" developed. Confirmation, identified with the latter, became a self-contained whole and acquired a new meaning as a necessary complement to the former. At the same time, the reservation of the rite of the laying on of hands to the bishop linked confirmation (indirectly but fundamentally) to a penitential practice linked to the Western-specific understanding of secularity.[202]

Such a development was seen as strange in the East, where there is no conception of confirmation as a "completion" or "validation" of baptism in view of the liturgical and theological unity of baptismal administration. Confirmation has always been preserved there. The East understood and practised confirmation as the anointing with Chrism received by Christ (*Christos*) Himself. However, this can guide the understanding of confirmation also in another direction. The anointing of Christians was also associated with the anointing of priests and kings in the Old Testament. In the context of baptism, this anointing signified participation in the royal priesthood of Christ, by virtue of which the baptised person himself became a king and a member of the people of God as "the anointed one" (*Christos*) – a lay person in

---

201 Cf. Guzowski, *Duch Dialogujący*, 241. "In Confirmation, the Holy Spirit wants to guide everyone from the receptive stage, proper to the child, to a state of readiness to offer self-sacrifice; a state in which the believer shares with Christ in responsibility for the Church and for other people. Thus, in the sacrament of confirmation (the sacrament of maturity), the Holy Spirit seals the belonging to the Church initiated through baptism" (Guzowski, *Duch Dialogujący*, 242).

202 Cf. Zizioulas, *The Eucharistic Communion and the World*, 118–9.

the specific meaning of the word: not because he was ordained a priest, but as a "Christian" from "Christ". The implications of this understanding of confirmation in the East are significant, for it is at this point that the baptised person is introduced into participation in the Eucharist.[203]

The predestination of all people to confirmation is evidenced by a reference in Acts 10:44-45: "While Peter was still speaking, the Holy Spirit fell upon all who heard the word. The circumcised believers who had come with Peter were astounded that the gift of the Holy Spirit had been poured out even on the Gentiles". CCC 1306 states briefly: "Every baptized person [...] can and should receive the sacrament of confirmation".[204] The focus of confirmation on the universal community of communication is evidenced by St. Paul's significant statement in 1 Cor 12:13: "For in the one Spirit we were all baptized into one body – Jews or Greeks, slaves or free – and we were all made to drink of one Spirit" – although not all exegetes see the mention of "drinking of one Spirit" as a reference to the sacrament of confirmation.[205] Starting with the Jerusalem community, the word of God and the Church has expanded in all directions and transcended previously existing boundaries, and the apostles were at the source of this Spirit-filled community and the whole Church.[206]

The life of baptised and confirmed people (since it is difficult to distinguish the administration of the two sacraments in the early practice of the Church) is an early participation in the eschatological fullness of life. Therefore, the passage in Titus 3:5-7 can also be applied to confirmation: "he saved us [...] according to his mercy, through the water of rebirth and renewal by the Holy Spirit. This Spirit he poured out on us richly through Jesus Christ our Savior, so that, having been justified by his grace, we might become heirs according to the hope of eternal life". CCC 1296 speaks of a "mark" left by this sacrament:

> Christians are also marked with a seal: 'It is God who establishes us with you in Christ and has commissioned us; he has put his seal on us and given us his Spirit in our hearts as a guarantee' (2 Cor 1:21-22). This seal of the Holy Spirit marks our total belonging to Christ, our enrollment in his service for ever, as well as the promise of divine protection in the great eschatological trial.[207]

203 Cf. Zizioulas, *The Eucharistic Communion and the World*, 119.
204 Cf. Jagodziński, *Sakramenty w służbie communio*, 349.
205 Cf. Romaniuk, *Sakramentologia biblijna*, 31.
206 Cf. Nocke, *Sakramententheologie. Ein Handbuch*, 131.
207 Cf. Jagodziński, *Sakramenty w służbie communio*, 350.

All New Testament allusions to confirmation presuppose faith as a prerequisite for its reception (cf. Acts 8:12-13; 19:2-3; Heb 6:1), and true faith obviously requires deep repentance – a radical processing of the past.[208] And if St. Paul says that the full and true Christian life is firmly grounded and flows "in the Spirit" (*en pneumati*), he surely refers not only to the life of the baptised person, but also to the one endowed with the powers of the Holy Spirit through the sacrament of confirmation.[209] In turn, this life "in the Spirit" means – according to the unequivocal testimony of the whole New Testament – a critical attitude to the world and the emergence of a new configuration in the social space of life.[210]

The communicative nature of the sacrament of confirmation must be read in the context of its reciprocal relationship with the sacrament of baptism. Through the gift of the Holy Spirit, God perfects in it the work which He began with baptism,[211] while the nature of this completion, its effectiveness and depth depend on the situation of the person receiving this sacrament.[212] Just as Pentecost is the completion of the Paschal event of Christ, and both events have their deepest meaning in relation to the Church, in the sacraments of baptism and confirmation the goal of salvific action is the individual as a member of that Church. Completion through confirmation is aimed at the apostolic-missionary Church, living and growing in the world through the communicative witness of believers. It is, of course, a gift of God's grace, but the gift of God's personal love also demands readiness to receive and respond to it personally, as well as transforms people into witnesses and apostles.[213] A full-fledged conviction of faith, responsible, ready for action, bearing witness and making

208 Cf. Romaniuk, *Sakramentologia biblijna*, 32.

209 Cf. Romaniuk, *Sakramentologia biblijna*, 35.

210 Cf. Jagodziński, "Komunijna wizja sakramentu bierzmowania," in *Młodzież i doświadczenie wiary. Dialog w kontekście Światowych Dni Młodzieży w Krakowie*, ed. Marcin Składanowski, Tadeusz Syczewski and Jacek Połowianiuk, and Krzysztof Mielnicki (Lublin: Wydawnictwo KUL, 2017), 120–2.

211 Cf. Ganoczy, *Einführung in die katholische Sakramentenlehre* (Darmstadt: Wissenschaftliche Buchgesellschaft, 1979), 61. F. Courth writes of "extended initiation" which, in contrast to the writings of St. Paul, can be seen clearly in Acts (Courth, *Die Sakramente. Ein Lehrbuch für Studium und Praxis der Theologie* (Freiburg-Basel-Wien: Herder, 1995), 126–8).

212 Cf. Nocke, *Sakramententheologie. Ein Handbuch*, 136.

213 Cf. Mühlen, *Einübung in die christliche Grunderfahrung* (Mainz: Grünewald, 1978), 1: 63: Referring to confirmation as "the sacramental baptism of the Holy Spirit," he writes: " In der Geisttaufe werden wir eingetaucht in die göttliche Kraft zum Zeugnis, zum Selbstentäußerung und Selbstweggabe an andere. Wir könnten diesen Vorgang auch 'Zeugentaufe' nennen im Unterschied zur Sündertaufe mit Wasser." F. Courth believes that it is critical to contrast baptism by water, aimed at the remission of sins, with baptism of the Holy Spirit for Christian witness. At least Paul's account of baptism does not allow for this (cf. Courth, *Die Sakramente. Ein Lehrbuch für Studium und Praxis der Theologie*, 139).

sacrifice can only materialise in the Church by the power of the Holy Spirit.[214] The context of the community in which the effective – through confirmation – mission can fully develop communicatively is also relevant here,[215] since confirmation opens the active life of faith wide open. The Second Vatican Council further links baptism and confirmation with the Eucharist, which is "the sacrament of communion of the Church" developing the salvific reality within the world. By the power of the Eucharistic sacrifice, the priesthood of the baptised and the witness of the confirmed are developed and completed in it, and the Christian matures by the grace of the sacrament and constantly receives the gifts of the Holy Spirit.[216]

Confirmation is a sacrament grounded in the relationship to the historico-salvific Trinity, i. e. in the diakonia of the Holy Spirit in relation to the work of Jesus Christ. It has a unique genesis and structure, it can be viewed as an "incarnation" of the Holy Spirit consisting in the creation of a pneumatic environment which is aimed at demonstrating, continuing and disseminating Christ's salvific work. C.S. Bartnik called this "the sending of the Holy Spirit" upon a person (also an "ecclesiastical person"), "the small sending of the Holy Spirit" in a sacramental way, and he perceives the difference between confirmation and baptism in the ecclesiogenic nature of confirmation. For the confirmed man becomes a co-creator, co-constructor and co-author of the Church in all its dimensions. Confirmation gives him the grace of the fullness of the ecclesial Spirit and an official mission towards the Church and the world. It is a multiplication of the Spirit – above all the social Spirit – the spirit of service to people and the ecclesial community, of responsibility for the community of the Church and for the shape of people's lives on earth. Bartnik emphasises that this also results in the Catholic Church firmly tying the administration of this sacrament to the bishop, who is the head and foundation of the local Church.[217] He also gives an interesting account of the effects of confirmation – it confers a special and full ecclesiogenic personality at the particular and universal level; it is the source of a particular dynamism of the Christian life; it "personifies" Christians in the Holy Spirit who is the Personal Communion of the Father and the Son – it incorporates them into the sphere of

---

214 Cf. Lies, *Sakramententheologie. Eine personale Sicht*, 297. "Confirmation is the sacrament that highlights the relationship of believers to the Holy Spirit and reminds us of the truth of the Church as the Church of the Spirit, more precisely: that the Holy Spirit is the one who gives believers the power to continue Jesus' mission, by which He turns the Church into the missionary Church, i. e. one that is sent to the world" (Gardocki, *Teologia wyzwolenia*, 253).

215 Cf. Ganoczy, *Einführung in die katholische Sakramentenlehre*, 63.

216 Cf. Auer, *Die Sakramente der Kirche* (Regensburg: Pustet, 1972), 98–104; Lies, *Sakramententheologie. Eine personale Sicht*, 297–8; Jagodziński, *Sakramenty w służbie communio*, 350–1; Jagodziński, *Komunijna wizja sakramentu bierzmowania*, 124.

217 Cf. Bartnik, *Dogmatyka katolicka*, 2: 675–9.

the creative Love of the encounter between the Father and the Son. On the scale of the community of the Church, it elevates them to a messianic people, the people of the Spirit of God; it imprints the seal of the bearer of the Holy Spirit, which is a symbol of person; it perfects and "pleromizes" the common priesthood, strengthens it to profess and defend the faith; it makes it take up the task of a disciple and witness in the community of the Church and in the world, giving something from a higher view of temporal realities; it brings about ecclesial communion and unity, accomplishes the initiation of the particular Church into the universal Church, and makes it capable of social worship, active communal love and reform in accord with the Holy Spirit, and also empowers for Christian communal responsibility for the world.[218]

Among the many approaches to the specificity of confirmation, A. Skowronek opts for the biblical vision of "mission" that touches the very core of the Church's essence, structure and existence.[219] He notes that the main emphasis of Paul VI's Apostolic constitution *Divinae consortium naturae* rests on the claim that confirmation is precisely the sacrament of the special giving of the Holy Spirit by Christ together with the Father. A trinitarian-Christological account of the sending thus reveals its depth as a sacrament of sending – the sending of the Holy Spirit actualises the sending of Christians in the perspective of Jesus Christ, whose life was lived under the auspices of the same Spirit.[220]

Confirmation is a sacramental sign of the reception of Christians and their mutual reference to the divine reference of Jesus, a sign of the elevation and embracing of human being in the common being of the Father and the Son, which is the Holy Spirit. Confirmation, as the sacrament of the Holy Spirit, emphasises the communicative openness of man and the capacity for mutual references. God, who is "rich in references" and creates new references, in communion with people responds to them, as beings who live by references, with His reality of references. The purpose of confirmation is thus to fruitfully direct the practice of the Gospel to the tension-full relationship between man's individual dimension and his social dimension.[221] The laying on of hands, through which the Holy Spirit is given, clearly expresses belonging to the Church and the necessity of the ecclesial community's existence as a gift of this Spirit,[222] and this is sufficient for the Church to distinguish

218 Cf. Bartnik, *Dogmatyka katolicka*, 2: 680–2; Jagodziński, *Sakramenty w służbie communio*, 351–2, Jagodziński, *Komunijna wizja sakramentu bierzmowania*, 124–5.

219 Cf. Alfons Skowronek, *Sakramenty w ogólności. Chrzest. Bierzmowanie* (Włocławek: Włocławskie Wydawnictwo Diecezjalne, 1995), 216–22.

220 Cf. Skowronek, *Sakramenty w ogólności*, 222–7; Jagodziński, *Sakramenty w służbie communio*, 352–3.

221 Cf. Höhn, *spüren*, 66–7.

222 Cf. Schneider, *Znaki bliskości Boga*, 124.

two moments of Christian initiation: baptism and confirmation[223] as the sacrament of deepened incorporation into the Church.[224]

According to the basic principle of theology of confirmation, the Holy Spirit's role in confirmation for the individual person is the same as his original role for Christ and fundamental role for the Church. He thus offers the person the fullness of power to be a witness to Christ and a living inner formation and holiness. The fullness of initiation and the assumption of the mission of Christ and the Church are not mutually exclusive, since confirmation symbolically integrates the person into the Church filled with the Holy Spirit and makes him spiritually capable of taking up Christ's mission in the form of inner holiness and externally – in bearing the corresponding witness.[225]

Already during baptism, the anointing with oil signifies a call to responsibility, and this is even more true in the case of confirmation (cf. Acts 8:14-17; 10:44-48; 19:1-7). For confirmation is the second element of the same single initiation, in which the same Holy Spirit acts. The only difference may be the fact that the same reality of the Advocate can have different accents, so that the granting of the Holy Spirit in baptism (the salvific proclamation) invites the baptised person to live actively in the power of that Spirit (the salvific imperative), which is expressed in a separate sacrament. The gifts of the Holy Spirit, which are the fruit of the Father's communication with man, are supposed to result in the messianic attitude of Christians.[226] Baptismal communication and communion take on a new form again, in which the baptised persons – now ready for their own commitment – practice their own form of communicating faith (in relation to God and to their neighbours) and take an active part in building the kingdom of God and in ministerial tasks of the Church; in this way, communication becomes communion and communion becomes communication. The anointing in confirmation is thus focused on the communication of faith (its confession) and communicative action with faith in the Church and in the world (in connection with a specific apostolic succession).[227]

Confirmation is a sacrament of initiation, of communicative incorporation into the community of believers. The unifying power of the community makes it possible for references to be established and for communicative relationships to be

---

223 Cf. Qualizza, *Inicjacja chrześcijańska*, 102.

224 Cf. Skowronek, *Sakramenty w ogólności. Chrzest. Bierzmowanie*, 243; Jagodziński, *Sakramenty w służbie communio*, 353; Jagodziński, *Komunijna wizja sakramentu bierzmowania*, 126–7.

225 Cf. Courth, *Die Sakramente. Ein Lehrbuch für Studium und Praxis der Theologie*, 141; Hryniewicz, *Nasza Pascha z Chrystusem*, 315–6; Jagodziński, *Sakramenty w służbie communio*, 354.

226 Cf. Zdzisław Janiec, *Komunikacyjny wymiar liturgii* (Sandomierz: Wydawnictwo Diecezjalne w Sandomierzu, 2006), 316.

227 Cf. Meuffels, *Kommunikative Sakramententheologie*, 312; Jagodziński, *Sakramenty w służbie communio*, 354; Jagodziński, *Komunijna wizja sakramentu bierzmowania*, 128.

negotiated. Community enables the free co-existence of subjects when the unifying power is not theirs and does not belong to them alone. Moreover, such a community is only possible when the commonality and the diversity of the subjects find themselves in someone "third"; it is created when the different subjects have something in common and what is common is shared by the different subjects. The Holy Spirit guarantees both the commonality of the many and the diversity of what is common to the many; both the non-reducibility of the community to the subjects belonging to it and the openness of the community to other subjects; He defends the multiplicity in unity against the fatal lack of reference and He supports the unity in multiplicity against totalitarian equality. This is what the narrative of the event of Pentecost in Acts 2:1-13 conveys. The lack of reference and the social breakdown in the form of the confusion of languages at the Tower of Babel is here overcome in an assembly which, although it did not eliminate the plurality of languages, made it possible for everyone to communicate in many languages. Thus, a fact occurred in which community and individuality were not mutually exclusive, in which it was possible to remain oneself and be free while being with others, and furthermore, to perceive others in their own distinctiveness and understand them – something that had not been possible before. This is the "gift of the Holy Spirit" that makes the Church capable of plurality, and by enabling unity and plurality through the "social" experience of God, makes Christianity and the Church a multicultural reality.[228]

All the actions of the Holy Spirit – also in the sacrament of confirmation – in 1 Cor 12:7 boil down to one principle: "To each is given the manifestation of the Spirit for the common good". This primarily refers to the inner life of the community and its growth. Diversity is brought about by the Holy Spirit so that the life of the Church is not monotonous and flat, but rich and wonderful, full of action and imagination.[229] The experience of unity and plurality, similarly to the experience of self and the experience of community in their mutual orientation towards each other, has a "metaphorical" significance in itself – it "transfers" people into the realm of the Holy Spirit. People can then discover in each other that their likeness to God displays a social signature. The essence of God is openness, relationality, liberating community that is capable of plurality, and to be the image of God means for man to be adequate to His essence.[230] This communicative-communional character of the sacrament of confirmation corresponds precisely with the recommendations for its dispensation in the community of believers in the renewed rite.[231]

---

228 Cf. Höhn, *spüren*, 73–4; Jagodziński, *Sakramenty w służbie communio*, 354–5; Jagodziński, *Komunijna wizja sakramentu bierzmowania*, 128–9.

229 Cf. Qualizza, *Inicjacja chrześcijańska*, 100.

230 Cf. Höhn, *spüren*, 74–5.

231 Jagodziński, *Sakramenty w służbie communio*, 355; Jagodziński, *Komunijna wizja sakramentu bierzmowania*, 129–30.

According to contemporary theological interpretation, confirmation by the power of the Holy Spirit enables the Christian to announce a personal turn to God, the ecclesial community and service to others. It bestows the fullness of God's childhood, expressed in mutually contingent manifestations – as the power to bear witness to Christ outwardly and as an inwardly animating likeness to Christ. In this sacrament, the Spirit of Christ unites all the baptised to the past and future of the historical Jesus. It is a continuation of Jesus' anointing with the Spirit, which is the source of His messianic office, the inheritance of Christ's experience of the Spirit first imparted in the event of Pentecost. The confirmed receives a share in the elementary charismatic-missionary experience of the early Church. The Christian appears to be immersed in the Holy Spirit and, by the power of His gifts, he acquires the capacity to bear witness to Christ and fulfil His mission. By giving "more" of the Holy Spirit, God offers man a share in the service of the kingdom of God. This means a new call of God's grace. In Jesus Christ and in His Holy Spirit, God turns to man and gives him the chance to make a personal decision – if he does not respond with a full commitment in faith, God does not withdraw His call and permanently marks man with the "seal" of sacramental character.[232] Therefore, even if someone received confirmation without sincere intention – fruitlessly, he can always do so later. Then, through the Holy Spirit, he will be united more closely to Christ and his membership in the Church will be strengthened.[233]

232 "In the sacrament of confirmation, this internal marking is confirmed and, at the same time, is made evident to the world, because the Spirit grants the special grace to preach and live in the name of Christ. The principle behind interpreting the effects of confirmation is not only a reference to the outpouring of the Spirit on the apostles on the day of Pentecost, but also the messianic anointing unveiled in the Baptism of the Lord. The second outpouring of the Holy Spirit has the effect of conferring a sacramental character, since the Christian is no longer merely a child, which has primarily a personal significance, but also becomes a witness, i. e. a preacher of the Lord to the world. The same thing happens to him that took place in the lives of the disciples, who were first reconciled with the propitiated God and then, through Pentecost, became His apostles. Between the first and second stages, a radical, not merely formal, transformation took place in them. It is indeed a new state in which the Christian serves and which marks the relationship to the Master. Certainly, baptism unites one with God and thus gives access to all grace. Undoubtedly, however, confirmation 'creates' apostles" (Tomasz Grabowski, "Sakrament bierzmowania," in *Znaki Tajemnicy. Sakramenty w teorii i praktyce Kościoła*, 344–5).

233 Cf. Czaja, *Credo in Spiritum Vivificantem*, 194–6. The following statements are of communional significance: "The role of the parents is irreplaceable here, since the development of the grace of the Holy Spirit in the life of their child takes place through their witness of faith. The Holy Spirit shapes the child through the implanted grace of faith, causing integral personal development. The sacrament of confirmation – as one of the three sacraments of initiation – is meant to lead the child to the real discovery of the Holy Spirit, who unites us with Christ and gives us gifts and charisms. A one-sided emphasis on the gifts as graces for individuals, while forgetting the social dimension of our life in the Church and for the brothers, is reductive here. Those being prepared for confirmation are supposed to discover the Holy Spirit as a person and His guidance in individual and communal

3.5.1.3 The Pneumatological-Communional Dimension of the Sacrament of the Eucharist

What is striking about St. Hippolytus' baptismal liturgy is its insistence that it is exactly – and only – after baptism and confirmation have been received that the Christian prays with the other faithful. This seems to be a very reductive view, but it is supported by the truth that the Eucharist – distinguished from baptism and confirmation – is an ecclesial reality in which these individual acts become communal through the communion in the Body of Christ. The Holy Eucharist thus has a communal and ecclesial character as a "Pentecostal" community that experiences and witnesses the entry of history into the eschaton and offers a foretaste of the future Kingdom.[234] The Eucharist as a sacrament of communion thus also has a clear pneumatological dimension.[235]

In an article on the Eucharist, the *Catechism of the Catholic Church* mentions that, inter alia, through the celebration of the Eucharist

> we offer to the Father what he has himself given us: the gifts of his creation, bread and wine which, by the power of the Holy Spirit and by the words of Christ, have become the body and blood of Christ. Christ is thus really and mysteriously made present. We

life. For this reason, preparation for confirmation should be closely linked to the prayer of praise (the proclamation of the presence of the Holy Spirit in the life of the baptised) and to the living kerygma and witness of the action of the Holy Spirit in people's lives. Rational persuasion is not a sufficient prelude to the acceptance of the Spirit's inspirations and the observance the signs of His presence" (Guzowski, *Duch Dialogujący*, 243).

234 Cf. Zizioulas, *The Eucharistic Communion and the World*, 119–21. It was an unfortunate move in the East to offer the Holy Eucharist to newly baptised persons outside the Eucharistic assembly. Of course, this was the only possible solution when baptism and confirmation were separated from the Eucharistic liturgy, since an even worse alternative would have been to postpone the first Holy Communion until the first participation in the Eucharistic liturgy after baptism, which would have resulted in a separation of the unity of the sacraments of Christian initiation. The idea was mainly to introduce the newly baptised person into the community of the faithful. This was the meaning given by the early Church to the association of the Eucharist with confirmation and baptism. The Eucharist was not simply the food and medicine of immortality to which every baptised and confirmed person was immediately entitled. However, at the same time, this was related to the loss of awareness that it was the assembly of God's people, *ecclesia tou Theou*, the unity into which one was to enter and take one's place. By virtue of confirmation, every baptised person becomes a member of the royal family, God's *laos* – becomes the *laikos*. It is natural that the baptised person immediately enters the Eucharistic assembly in order to take the place of the laymen among the People of God (*ekklēsia*) thus called and summoned (cf. Zizioulas, *The Eucharistic Communion and the World*, 120).

235 Cf. Jagodziński, "Pneumatologiczny wymiar Eucharystii jako sakramentu komunii," in *Człowiek drogą Kościoła. Tradycja i współczesność*, ed. Piotr Turzyński and Wojciech Wojtyła (Radom: Łukasiewicz – Instytut Technologii Eksploatacji, 2020), 85–97.

must therefore consider the Eucharist as: – thanksgiving and praise to the *Father*; – the sacrificial memorial of *Christ* and his Body; – the presence of Christ by the power of his word and of his *Spirit* (CCC 1357-58).[236]

236 Cf. Figura, "Kościół i Eucharystia w świetle tajemnicy Trójjedynego Boga," *Communio. Międzynarodowy Przegląd Teologiczny* 20/2 (2000), 38–58. "It is clear from Jesus' speech that Jesus – as the glorified Son of Man – is the 'bread of life'. The question of how the Son of Man communicates life is fundamental here. He does so by means of the Spirit, which He, as the glorified one, possesses and bestows (7:39). 'The Son of Man, having ascended into heaven, will have the power to grant the life-giving Spirit (7:39; 17:2), the promised gift of life and the Eucharistic gifts'. [...] in the Eucharist the Spirit has a salvific effect in two ways: 1. The Eucharist involves not the flesh and blood of the earthly Jesus, but it involves the glorified Christ, filled with the Spirit. It is through the Holy Spirit that Christ enters the glory of the Father by rising from the dead (cf. Rom 8:11) and then, in this new state of life, He gives Himself to us in the Eucharist. 'In it we encounter Christ who is glorified by the Spirit, and thus we can say that in the Sacrament the Holy Spirit realises the real presence of the glorified Christ." It must be added at once, however, that the Eucharistic presence of Christ is a reflection and extension of the Incarnation, for the transubstantiation of the bread into the Body of Christ constitutes a renewal of that miraculous act by the Holy Spirit, by whose power He received a body in the womb of the Virgin Mary and made it a dwelling place for His person. Through this transubstantiation, Christ becomes present in time and space. 2. The condition for obtaining the gift of life is both eating the Body of Christ (John 6:53,54,57,58) and receiving the Spirit who 'gives life' (John 6:63). There exists a certain ambivalence here between the salvific function of Christ and that of the Spirit. It should be noted, however, which has already been stated above, that the glorified Christ whom we eat in the Eucharist is the 'Spirit-filled Christ' who gives life in his glorified humanity. This is why He unites us not only with His person, but also with the Spirit to whom we owe the gift of life. The tradition of the Syriac Church is clearly aware of the pneumatological dimension of this sacrament. St. Ephrem the Syrian wrote: 'Jesus took in His hands the bread, which at that moment was ordinary bread, blessed it, marked it and sanctified it in the name of the Father and the Holy Spirit, broke it and distributed it in pieces among His disciples in His unparalleled goodness; He called this bread His living body and filled it with Himself and the Spirit'. Elsewhere, Ephrem says that with the Eucharist we receive the Body of Christ and the Holy Spirit: 'Take, eat by faith without doubting, for this is my Body, and whoever eats it by faith, eats the fire and the Spirit in it ... Take and eat all of you, and consume the Holy Spirit in it; verily, this is my Body'. In general, it must be said that the Church is constantly in the state of epiclesis (invocation of the Holy Spirit), especially in the celebration of the sacraments, which 'are all the work of the Holy Spirit', most notably the Eucharist. The Eucharist and the Church are places where the energy of the Holy Spirit radiates. The Holy Spirit also brings into communion with the Body of Christ those who eat the same bread and drink from the same cup. Also, the words that Christ speaks come from the Spirit present in Him, and therefore, they by themselves, full of the Spirit, have the power to give life. Hence, the liturgy of the word at Mass is also the place of transformation. The Spirit works to make man accept Christ in faith, to live the life that is in Him, to live the love that is in Him. We believe what Christ said: 'The words that I have spoken to you are spirit and life' (John 6:63)" (Guzowski, *Duch Dialogujący*, 244–6).

The Eucharist is a specific communicative activity the aim of which is to enable communion to be achieved through the celebration of the "Lord's memorial".[237] The Eucharist is the culmination of human communication with God.[238] It is the effectively realised remembrance of Jesus' sacrifice for all people, which was intended to enable their communion with God.[239] The Eucharistic representation of Jesus' sacrifice enables and initiates this communion with God and among people,[240] has a dimension pointing to the present of communion with God, reaching into the past and towards the Lord's second coming. The Eucharist is the sacrament of the New Covenant as the communion of God with men, which has been uniquely and definitively realised in the person of Jesus Christ, who is its effectuating symbol.[241]

The "ideal" community of communication announced in the Old Covenant has found its counterpart in the "real" community of communication of the Father and the Son, who communicates it in the Holy Spirit to Christians.[242] The Church is the assembly of God, especially of Christ and the Holy Spirit. According to J. Ratzinger, the Church arose from its convocation by Church, i. e. it was formed from the sacrament and is thus itself the sacrament. The Eucharist, as the presence and sacrament of Christ, builds the Church. Consequently, the Church is present as a whole wherever the Eucharist is legitimately celebrated. Zizioulas maintains that the focal point of the Eucharist is – together with Christ – the Person and action of the Holy Spirit, who comes to dwell in the Church (Eph 2:22) through the Eucharistic epiclesis.[243] The image of the Church as a temple of the Holy Spirit (1 Cor 6:19; 2 Cor 6:16; Eph 2:21-22) is based on the New Testament and implies that the Church is not simply a unity, but a unity in diversity and personal freedom. In short, the Holy Spirit constitutes the Church, while Christ institutes it.[244]

---

237 Cf. Erhard Kunz, *Die Lehre von der Eucharistie. Skript zur Vorlesung im Sommersemester 1997* (Frankfurt am Main, 1997), 87–93; Jagodziński, "Teoria komunikatywnego działania a sakramenty," *Studia Diecezji Radomskiej* 6 (2004), 45–6; Jagodziński, *Sakramenty w służbie communio*, 356–60; Pałucki, *Tryniatrny wymiar Kościoła*, 214–19.

238 Cf. Janiec, *Komunikacyjny wymiar liturgii*, 316.

239 Cf. Courth, *Die Sakramente. Ein Lehrbuch für Studium und Praxis der Theologie*, 210–1.

240 Cf. John Paul II, *Ecclesia de Eucharistia*, 21: "The Apostles, accepting Jesus' invitation in the Upper Room: 'Take, eat [...] Drink from it, all of you [...]' (Matt 26:26-27), joined Him in sacramental Communion for the first time. From that moment until the end of time, the Church is built through this sacramental Communion with the Son of God, who gave Himself up for us."

241 Cf. Marc Quellet, "Trójca Święta a Eucharystia: tajemnica przymierza", *Communio. Międzynarodowy Przegląd Teologiczny* 20/2 (2000), 18–37; Jagodziński, *Sakramenty w służbie communio*, 360–3.

242 Cf. Kunz, *Die Lehre von der Eucharistie*, 232–3.

243 Cf. Hryniewicz, "Misterium Eucharystii w świetle teologii prawosławnej," *Ateneum Kapłańskie* 101/3 (1983), 375–7.

244 Cf. Wong Yee Kheong, *John Zizioulas' Ecclesiology of 'The One and the Many'*, VIII.

Zizioulas believes that Protestant Christianity should give the Eucharist a more central place in its life. Roman Catholic theology should liberate sacramental theology from the concepts of historical causality imposed by medieval scholastic theology in order to make the eschatological and pneumatological aspects of the Eucharist more visible. The Orthodox Church, on the other hand, should try to draw ethical implications from the Eucharist and perceive it as a source of life and not just as an experience of worship.[245]

Eating the Body and drinking the Blood of the Lord together results in personal communion with the Crucified and Exalted One.[246] The Eucharistic transubstantiation of bread and wine takes place to allow for the transfiguration of all those gathered.[247] Through eating and drinking as a sacramental action, the Eucharist is the most intense sign of mutual being in one another, the highest possible form of communication.[248] According to Zizioulas, the Church consists of concrete forms of ecclesial communion (baptism, Eucharist, holy orders) that reflect the relationship between communion and distinctiveness in the Holy Trinity, in Christ and in the Holy Spirit.[249]

In Orthodox theology, particular importance in the celebration of the Eucharist is given to the bishop, who in his person offers to God the world and all that is in it as the head of the Eucharistic assembly with which he celebrates the Eucharist and which constitutes the Body of Christ – the Church. Through the Holy Spirit, the bishop is not only a person who presides at the Eucharist, but an icon of Christ. Like Christ, he unites in himself everything and offers it to God in the Church by the power of the Holy Spirit who is present in him through the epiclesis. The bishop prays that the Holy Spirit may descend upon the assembly and sanctify all those present in the Body of the Son of God, so that the Church may truly have life and communion and be worthy of the name of the one, holy, universal and apostolic Church.[250]

The Catholic Church is the temple of the Holy Spirit and thus the place where the Holy Spirit descends through the epiclesis during each Eucharist.[251] When He descends in the Church during the Eucharist, each person receiving the Eucharist is transformed into the whole Body of Christ, and hence, in the same Spirit, the

245 Cf. Wong Yee Kheong, *John Zizioulas' Ecclesiology of 'The One and the Many'*, 127.

246 Cf. Courth, *Die Sakramente. Ein Lehrbuch für Studium und Praxis der Theologie*, 160–1.

247 Cf. Nocke, *Sakramententheologie. Ein Handbuch*, 176–7.

248 Cf. Gottfried Bachl, "Essen und Trinken als sakramentales Handeln," *Theologisch-praktische Quartalschrift* 1 (2007), 35–7; Skowronek, *Eucharystia sakrament wielkanocny* (Włocławek: Włocławskie Wydawnictwo Diecezjalne, 1998), 123; Jagodziński, *Sakramenty w służbie communio*, 363.

249 Cf. Wong Yee Kheong, *John Zizioulas' Ecclesiology of 'The One and the Many'*, 116.

250 Cf. Wong Yee Kheong, *John Zizioulas' Ecclesiology of 'The One and the Many'*, 124.

251 Cf. Hryniewicz, "Eucharystia – sakrament paschalny," *Ateneum Kapłańskie* 101/2 (1983), 243–8.

structure of the Church becomes the existential structure of each person.[252] "It must be remembered that the events which both commemorate the sacrament and make it present, are the work of the Holy Spirit."[253]

The celebration of the Eucharist takes place within the communicative-communional overlap in the structure of references.[254]

> [In the Eucharist] the *Deus Trinitas*, who is essentially love (cf. 1 John 4:7-8), becomes fully a part of our human condition. In the bread and wine under whose appearances Christ gives himself to us in the paschal meal (cf. Luke 22:14-20; 1 Cor 11:23-26), God's whole life encounters us and is sacramentally shared with us. God is a perfect communion of love between Father, Son and Holy Spirit. At creation itself, man was called to have some share in God's breath of life (cf. Gen 2:7). But it is in Christ, dead and risen, and in the outpouring of the Holy Spirit, given without measure (cf. Jn 3:34), that we have become sharers of God's inmost life. Jesus Christ, who 'through the eternal Spirit offered himself without blemish to God' (Heb 9:14), makes us, in the gift of the Eucharist, sharers in God's own life. This is an absolutely free gift, the superabundant fulfilment of God's promises. […] The 'mystery of faith' is thus a mystery of trinitarian love, a mystery in which we are called by grace to participate.[255]

Since in the Eucharist the surrender of Christ for men is made present, man not only gains access to this communion-building surrender for men but is also dialogically invited and drawn in to offer himself to God and men as a "spiritual sacrifice" (cf. Rom 1:11; 12:1; Phlm 2:17; 4:18; Heb 13:15-16).[256] The power of the Eucharist thus pulls people out of isolation and gathers them around the living centre of existence.[257] Since man personally encounters the real present Christ in the Eucharist, he is called to respond with thanksgiving to the communion given by God in Christ and to extend it to others.[258] The liturgical community, as a medium and subject of faith, is immersed in God's communication with people and thus becomes a communicative space for the communional exchange of love.[259] This gives rise to an ecclesiology that links the local Church to the mystery of the communion of the

---

252 Cf. Wong Yee Kheong, *John Zizioulas' Ecclesiology of 'The One and the Many'*, 125.

253 Guzowski, *Duch Dialogujący*, 243.

254 Cf. Meuffels, *Kommunikative Sakramententheologie*, 315–8.

255 Benedict XVI, *Sacramentum caritatis*, 8. Cf. Jagodziński, *akramenty w służbie communio*, 367–8.

256 Cf. Ganoczy, "Glaubwürdiges Feiern der Eucharistie," *Geist und Leben* 45 (1972), 106; Meuffels, *Kommunikative Sakramententheologie*, 318.

257 Cf. Ganoczy, *Einführung in die katholische Sakramentenlehre*, 77–9.

258 Cf. Ganoczy, *Glaubwürdiges Feiern der Eucharistie*, 107–8;

259 Cf. Franz Kohlschein, "Die liturgische Feier als Kommunikationsgeschehen," *Theologie der Gegenwart* 26 (1983), 5; Meuffels, *Kommunikative Sakramententheologie*, 319–20.

Holy Trinity. The Lord's feast thus appears as an ecclesial event of communion in and through Christ, who, as host, gives the guests the food that creates communion, a space of freedom to meet, exchange, bond and unite. This, of course, presupposes true interpersonal contact, reciprocity and willingness to communicate.[260]

Without the Holy Spirit, it is impossible to explain how the celebration of the Eucharist can realise the incarnation in the Body of the Lord and participation in the fullness of Divine life. It is the Eucharist of the glorified Lord, but it is celebrated in the Holy Spirit. It is the central ecclesiogenic event in which, through the Holy Spirit, the trinitarian form of existence is translated into ecclesial pre-existence. The degree of openness to the love of the Father and to people depends, to a large extent, on openness to the action of the Holy Spirit. The realisation of the catabatic and anabatic dimension of the Eucharist is made possible and effected precisely by the Holy Spirit. In the celebration of the Eucharist, He is the principle of effecting "God's blessing on men" and the principle of "blessing God by men" – of which St. Paul speaks when he writes of "the cup of blessing that we bless" (1 Cor 10:16). The purpose and effect of such an action of the Spirit is *koinonia* with and in Christ – in the sense of having a share in Christ and being internally united to Him, and ecclesially – as communion with others and in Christ (cf. CCC 1325). The question of God's self-giving in the Eucharist through the Holy Spirit is addressed in numerous ecclesial and ecumenical documents, emphasising the epiclesial understanding of the Eucharistic anamnesis and the presence of Christ in the Eucharist.[261]

The basis of the union asked for by the communional epiclesis is not simply the reception of the Holy Communion, but also the associated filling of the Holy Spirit. The body of Christ received in the Eucharist is, owing to the Resurrection, His body glorified by the Spirit. However, Christ's Body is now, through the Resurrection, His glorified body, for it is "the spirit that gives life; the flesh is useless" (John 6:63). Christ is "declared to be Son of God with power according to the spirit of holiness by

---

260 Cf. Ganoczy, *Einführung in die katholische Sakramentenlehre*, 79–84; Jagodziński, *Sakramenty w służbie communio*, 368–9.

261 Cf. Hryniewicz, "Eucharystia – sakrament paschalny," 237; Czaja, *Credo in Spiritum Vivificantem*, 184–90. "It is important not to separate the act of Christ, actualized by his priests, from the internal action of the Holy Spirit, who realises efficacy in the Host, the Body of Christ, and in the mystical body, i. e. in the Christians whom the Mass nourishes and identifies with Christ. These simple, obvious explanations should normally be enough to silence disputes: these illusory superstructures. Here, too, Christ and the Holy Spirit perform the same action, but imprint Their own mark in their creations. The words of institution: 'This is my Body', define the mark of Christ, who in substance takes the place of bread and wine without changing their form. The Holy Spirit performs the internal substantial sanctification (called transubstantiation) of the bread and wine and the sanctification of the souls fed by this sacrament. This is the hidden face of the Eucharist: its deep and transcendental dimension" (Laurentin, *Nieznany Duch Święty*, 412).

resurrection from the dead" (Rom 1:4), and therefore, He can give Himself to men as a gift in the Eucharist. In the Eucharist, the Body of Christ in its objective ontology becomes epicletically conditioned. Precisely because of this synthesis, the Eucharist reveals the "mastery" of the Church – without Christ there is no community, and if there is no community calling upon the Spirit, there is no Calvary. The epiclesis of the Spirit gives life to the Body (John 6:63), and this defends the sacramental reality of the Church against being associated with any other causality. Through the epiclesis, the Church realises the event of Christ within itself, whereby the epicleses of the early Church make no mention of any precedence between Christ and the Spirit.[262]

The epiclesis is also a request for the full fruit of believers' participation in Christ's mystery, their union with Him by the power of the Spirit. From this point of view, the theology of epiclesis is at the same time the theology of union and "communion" (*koinonia*). This makes it possible to discern the mysterious connection between the Holy Spirit and the participation in the Body and Blood of Christ. The mystery of Pascha and Pentecost is thus also reflected in the Eucharistic communion. It is not enough to perceive in the Eucharist only the Christocentric aspect of the real presence of the glorified Lord and the participation in His Body and Blood. It is also necessary to see their pneumatological, Pentecostal dimension – in receiving Holy Communion, believers also receive the Holy Spirit. Resorting to the language of images and symbols, the Syriac liturgical tradition often reiterated that in receiving the Body and Blood of Christ, believers also receive the Holy Spirit, His grace and the gift of immortality. Particularly eloquent and most frequently used was the image of fire, which is synonymous with the Holy Spirit. This was the origin of the expressions: "eating the Fire in the bread" and "drinking the Holy Spirit in the wine". Thanksgiving is also realised in the Eucharist by the Holy Spirit. This is why modern theology often speaks of the Eucharist as a gift of the Spirit – He is its possibility, the personal principle of its realisation.[263]

J.D. Zizioulas notes that it often escapes our attention that in the New Testament the Holy Spirit was sent to the Church after Christ's resurrection (John 7:39) – this is because the coming of the Spirit into the world signifies "the last days" (cf. Acts 2:17). He also stresses that it is no exaggeration to identify the kingdom of God with the Holy Spirit,[264] and that the Kingdom is linked to the whole structure of its realisation – together with the Eucharist. The liturgy of the Eucharist is usually approached from a Christological perspective, and in doing so the Holy Spirit is usually assigned only a subsidiary role (this is Western influence – this, of course,

262 Cf. Zizioulas, *The One and the Many*, 68.

263 Cf. Hryniewicz, *Nasza Pascha z Chrystusem*, 462–4; Czaja, *Credo in Spiritum Vivificantem*, 190–3.

264 He cites here the words of St. Maximus the Confessor in *Orationis dominicae brevis exposition*, PG 90, 885.

is related to the question of the epiclesis).[265] However, the Eucharist is not simply a repetition, a copy of a past event. While the repetition of Christ's words takes place in the form of a narrative, the work of transforming the gifts into the Body and Blood of Christ is the work of the Holy Spirit. The transformation, therefore, requires the descent of the Holy Spirit, and He comes – bringing the aforementioned "last days" into history. Christ's presence in the Eucharist is thus not realised without its pneumatological and eschatological structure – Christ's "real presence" presupposes and entails the gathering "in one place" of the eschatological community which the Holy Spirit holds together.[266] The Eucharistic community embodies the eschatological community. It has a definite shape and structure, which is revealed in the celebration of the Eucharist, where the eschatological community is made present by the Holy Spirit. The inseparability of the Eucharist and the Church is clearly manifested in an ecclesiology that is pneumatologically conditioned by the eschatology and ontology of communion.[267]

Zizioulas deplores that, throughout history, sacramental theology has somehow lost the memory that the Eucharist has the character of a vision, which has also resulted in a loss of expectation in it of a future event. The Eucharistic mystery has thus become incomplete. If we proclaim that Christ has died and stop there, the Eucharist becomes merely a psychological flashback involving a re-enactment of a past event. What about the present and future experience of the risen Christ and Christ as the One who will come again? The eschatological character of the Eucharist is lost here. Meanwhile, the Eucharist is a historical, eschatological event in which not only the past but also the memory of the future is present. This is made possible by the epiclesis, in which the Holy Spirit comes to the assembled Church to expand history and make it not only a linear course of time, but also to cause the eschaton to "intrude" into it.[268]

The Eucharist is a communion and participation in the Blood of Christ, which "is full of the Holy Spirit". We participate in Christ, but at the same time – according to St. Basil's anaphora – we participate in the communion of the Holy Spirit, and He descends not only on the gifts offered, but also on the whole liturgical assembly. In this way, Christ's "real presence" extends to the head and body in the unity of the Holy Spirit. The Eucharist as the communion of the Holy Spirit becomes the "communion of saints" in a double sense – the communion of holy things and the communion of holy people, realising itself as a mystery of love.[269]

---

265 See Evdokimov, *Duch Święty w tradycji prawosławnej*, 141–8.

266 Cf. Zizioulas, *The Eucharistic Communion and the World*, 74–5.

267 Cf. Wong Yee Kheong, *John Zizioulas' Ecclesiology of 'The One and the Many'*, 119.

268 Cf. Wong Yee Kheong, *John Zizioulas' Ecclesiology of 'The One and the Many'*, 121–2.

269 Cf. Zizioulas, *The Eucharistic Communion and the World*, 75–6.

The anamnesis of the Son and the epiclesis of the Holy Spirit are present inseparably in the Eucharistic sacrifice, although they have a separate place in leading to doxology – the giving of glory to the Father. The epicletic prayer asks the Holy Spirit to descend on the sacrificial gifts to transform them into the Body and Blood of Christ, and after the words of institution it asks for the transformation of those gathered. The Holy Spirit is thus invoked to effectuate the presence of Christ in the Eucharistic gifts and in the gathered faithful. The concluding Eucharistic doxology gives all "glory and honour" to the Father "through Christ, and with Christ and in Christ", "in the unity of the Holy Spirit". What is important here is the inseparable connection between the words of institution and the epiclesis (spoken over the Eucharistic gifts and over the assembled people). The second part of the epiclesis asks the Father to send the Holy Spirit upon the assembled community, so that its members may be transformed and incorporated as members of Christ's Body into his filial relationship to the Father. The Holy Spirit thus makes Christ present and brings the participants into an ever deeper communion with the Paschal mystery. The transforming power of the Holy Spirit brings people into a new "embodiment", into communion with the living body of the Son of God (first through baptism and then through the ever-deepening communion of the Eucharist).[270]

Thus understood Eucharist leads to the transformation of the world, but it directs us not only towards the past, but also into the future. Through the economy of the Holy Trinity, realised in the person and work of Jesus Christ with the participation of the Holy Spirit, space and time become transformable and become vehicles of life rather than death. Therefore, the Eucharist as the "communion of the end times" reveals that all creation is destined to be liberated from corruption and death, to live "for ever and ever" – to the communion of creation with God.[271]

3.5.2 The Pneumatological Dimensions of the Sacraments of Healing of Communion

The Catechism of the Catholic Church states that

> Through the sacraments of Christian initiation, man receives the new life of Christ. Now we carry this life 'in earthen vessels' (2 Cor 4:7), and it remains 'hidden with Christ in God'(Col 3:3). We are still in our 'earthly tent'(2 Cor 5:1), subject to suffering, illness, and death. This new life as a child of God can be weakened and even lost by sin (CCC 1420).

270 Cf. O'Collins, *Jezus nasz Odkupiciel*, 186–7.

271 Cf. Zizioulas, *The Eucharistic Communion and the World*, 80–1.

In the eternal plans of the Creator, there was the possibility of also bringing back and making in His likeness all those who were conceived and brought to the world in sin and then kept on falling. This possibility of returning to lost communion is called in the Bible the way of penance and repentance.[272]

The sacrament of penance and reconciliation is the remedy for the rupture and endangerment of the communion with God and people established after baptism. However, communion with God is sometimes threatened not only by the consequences of sin, but also in situations of illness and danger of death. "The Lord Jesus Christ, physician of our souls and bodies, who forgave the sins of the paralytic and restored him to bodily health, has willed that his Church continue, in the power of the Holy Spirit, his work of healing and salvation, even among her own members. This is the purpose of the two sacraments of healing: the sacrament of penance and the sacrament of anointing of the sick" (CCC 1421). Therefore, the sacrament of anointing of the sick can also be seen as a sacrament of healing of communion[273], especially since it was always mentioned alongside the sacrament of penance in the catalogues of the seven sacraments, and the Council of Trent discussed them together and called the anointing of the sick "the completion of penance".[274]

3.5.2.1 The Pneumatological-Communional Dimension of the Sacrament of Penance and Reconciliation

Discussing the "great Sacrament" of penance and reconciliation in the exhortation *Reconciliatio et paenitentia* (No. 29), John Paul II wrote:

> In the fullness of time the Son of God, coming as the lamb who takes away and bears upon himself the sin of the world appears as the one who has the power both to judge and to forgive sins, and who has come not to condemn but to forgive and save. Now this power to forgive sins Jesus confers through the Holy Spirit upon ordinary men, themselves subject to the snare of sin, namely his apostles: 'Receive the Holy Spirit. Whose sins you shall forgive, they are forgiven; whose sins you shall retain, they are retained' (John 20:22).

272 Cf. CCC 1426–1427; Romaniuk, *Sakramentologia biblijna*, 67–75.

273 Cf. Bartnik, *Dogmatyka katolicka*, 2: 613: "Penance allows us to deepen or regenerate our communion with God and the Church."

274 Cf. Sobór Trydencki, *Nauka o świętych sakramentach pokuty i ostatniego namaszczenia* (1551), in *Dokumenty Soborów Powszechnych. Tekst łaciński i polski*, vol. IV, ed. Baron and Pietras (Kraków: WAM, 2004), 501. Lies refers to these sacraments as the ones that "preserve the Church" (Lies, *Sakramententheologie. Eine personale Sicht*, 351). Cf. Jagodziński, *Sakramenty w służbie communio*, 369–70.

He added that each of the sacraments, in addition to its inherent grace, is also a sign of penance and reconciliation[275] – and therefore a "sacrament of mercy".[276]

The Catechism of the Catholic Church explains that

> The words *bind* and *loose* mean: whomever you exclude from your communion, will be excluded from communion with God; whomever you receive anew into your communion, God will welcome back into his. *Reconciliation with the Church is inseparable from reconciliation with God* (CCC 1445).

The sacrament of penance is intended for all sinners, but especially for those who, after baptism, have committed grave sin, thereby losing the grace of baptism and inflicting a wound on ecclesial communion. This sacrament offers a new opportunity to repent and regain the grace of mercy as a "second lifebuoy" after being shipwrecked (cf. CCC 1446).

In the Old and New Testaments, there was a conviction that sin was not something individual, but it affected the whole community. For Old Testament theology, it was clear that because God had made the covenant with the whole people and the whole community was sanctified, the individual could be sanctified on condition of belonging to God's holy community. The New Testament understands community on two levels – the individual attains communion with God by becoming a member of the Church, conceived of as the body of Christ. When a Christian commits a sin, he not only breaks the covenant with God, but also violates the holiness of the human community and excludes himself from it. This is why in the New Testament we can find traces of actions aimed at recovering a lost brother or sister and removing sin. The awareness that sin harms the community is also evidenced by the early practice of excommunication. An explanation of this attitude towards sin can be found in the theological vision of the Church as a "holy community".[277]

The New Testament statements on penance and reconciliation also contain pneumatological and communional themes. When specifying the anthropological aspects of reconciliation, St. Paul spoke not only of reconciling people with God, but also of removing all barriers between people: "For he is our peace; in his flesh he has made both groups into one and has broken down the dividing wall, that is, the hostility between us. […] So he came and proclaimed peace to you who were far off

275 John Paul II, Exhortation *Reconciliatio et paenitentia*, 27–8.

276 Cf. Jagodziński, "Sakramenty miłosierdzia," in *Oblicza miłosierdzia*, ed. Elżbieta Matulewicz (Warszawa: Wydawnictwo UKSW, 2010), 74–82; Jagodziński, "Komunijna wizja sakramentu pokuty i pojednania," in *Czy można dzisiaj wzywać do nawrócenia i pokuty? Chrześcijańska odpowiedź wiary*, ed. Składanowski and Syczewski, and Połowianiuk (Lublin: Wydawnictwo KUL, 2015), 74–5.

277 Cf. Guzowski, *Duch Dialogujący*, 248–9.

and peace to those who were near; for through him both of us have access in one Spirit to the Father" (Eph 2:14,17-18).[278] Repentance and penance include the idea of returning to God, but one must first turn away from evil: "Peter said to them, 'Repent, and be baptized every one of you in the name of Jesus Christ so that your sins may be forgiven; and you will receive the gift of the Holy Spirit'" (Acts 2:38). The salvation given to people already in the Old Testament had a social form, creating an inseparable unity of reference to God and people (cf. the law of the Decalogue, Deut 5-6), where sin signifies a disruption of Divine-human communal references (cf. Gen 20:6; 42:22; Judg 11:27; Ps 51:6), a fundamental defect in communication and communion (cf. Isa 59:2). Accordingly, penance and reconciliation are also a matter of the whole community (cf. Judg 20:26; 1 Sam 7:6; Jer 36:6-9; Joel 2:13-17; Hos 14:2-4). Penitential rituals, referring to sin and pleading for forgiveness, are deeply structured in terms of communication (verbal and non-verbal).

The Second Vatican Council restored the forgotten personal and ecclesial dimensions to the sacrament of penance and reconciliation. Guilt and sin are distortions of communication and wounds inflicted on communion in the totality of the relations between God, man and the world.[279] In the context of the demand for transformation and God's mercy, it is also necessary to systematically examine how human communication and the action of the Holy Spirit help people recognise the need for repentance. It is precisely here that the action of the Holy Spirit is needed, which, in the communication of love, places people in the presence of Christ and enables them to work out their partial faith, knowledge and cognition in the perspective of that truth which has been opened in Him for them to learn and to live in harmony with it. Both in finding the truth and in the symbolic communication of people lost in guilt and renewed in the truth, it concerns the accomplishments of the ecclesial community in which the individual subjects are involved, accomplished and sustained by the Holy Spirit.[280]

---

278 Cf. Romaniuk, *Sakramentologia biblijna*, 80.

279 Cf. Paweł Góralczyk, "Społeczny wymiar grzechu," *Communio. Międzynarodowy Przegląd Teologiczny* 4 (1984) 5, 35–47. "The theology of liberation fully shares the rediscovered ecclesial dimension of the sacrament of penance, while at the same time pointing out that both sin and reconciliation should not be seen as exclusively intra-ecclesial acts, because sin wounds not only the ecclesial body – it has a death dynamic that also wounds society and history. Therefore, sin destroys and kills both the life of personal and ecclesial grace and the life of the brother. It thus has not only an individual dimension, but also a social one. This is why repentance, to which the sacrament of penance obliges, should concern the repentance of both the heart and the social structures, insofar as these are marked by sin and their existence is its result" (Gardocki, *Teologia wyzwolenia*, 256).

280 Cf. Wolfgang Beinert, "Versöhnung als Lebensvollzug der Kirche," in *Theorie der Sprachhandlung und heutige Ekklesiologie. Ein philosophisch-theologisches Gespräch*, ed. Hühnermann and Schaeffler (Freiburg – Basel – Wien: Herder, 1980), 114–52; Meuffels, *Kommunikative Sakramententheologie*,

The liturgy of the sacrament of Penance shows the One God in the Holy Trinity acting in it, revealing His desire for reconciliation with the world and with man. The individual Persons of the Trinity are shown through Their action accomplished in the history of salvation. The Father is the source of mercy and forgiveness of sins. The Son of God, through the Paschal mystery of his passion, death and resurrection, sealed this desire of the Father and accomplished the restoration of unity with the Father, which was broken by sin. The Holy Spirit, on the other hand, becomes the guarantor that this reconciliation and forgiveness is being continually accomplished in the Church.[281]

In the sacramental act of penance, the Paschal dimension of baptism is apparently extended. The spiritually dead man is resurrected anew. The resurrected Christ calls for repentance and a change of mind, and the initiative to seek and to come forward also belongs to the Holy Spirit. The process of man's liberation from the bondage of sin and iniquity always takes place under the influence of the Holy Spirit – the purifying and transforming fire of His presence. Therefore, the sacrament of penance is realised under His creative breath. The renewed rite of penance introduced the formula of absolution, which is no longer purely declarative, but contains epicletic elements and also speaks of the sending of the Holy Spirit "for the remission of sins". Thus, at the very heart of sacramental penance, we find an important reference to the cleansing and sanctifying function of the Holy Spirit. Already St. Augustine attributed the remission of sins to the Holy Spirit and to the Church brought together by Him in unity, peace and love. The gift of the Holy Spirit – inherent in the sacrament of baptism – is also made present in the sacrament of penance.[282]

The forgiveness of sins is a unique work of the Holy Spirit. Christ gave the apostles a fourfold gift: peace, mission, the Holy Spirit and the power to forgive sins. The main purpose of Jesus' mission was "to take away the sin of the world" and to give the gift of salvation (cf. John 1:29; 3:16; 12:47; 10:10). In forgiving sins, the Holy Spirit does not magically or automatically make people a new creation, since sin is not a purely juridical fact, but a personal act resulting in a rejection of God's plan and closure to God. Therefore, the penitent needs repentance, i. e. a renewed openness to God's love and God's advocacy. The sacrament of reconciliation is

---

320–5; Jagodziński, *Sakramenty w służbie communio*, 378–9; Jagodziński, " Komunijna wizja sakramentu pokuty i pojednania," 76–88. Cf. CCC 1440.

281 Cf. Tomasz Bać, "Sakrament pokuty i pojednania," in *Znaki Tajemnicy. Sakramenty w teorii i praktyce Kościoła*, 412.

282 Cf. Hryniewicz, *Nasza Pascha z Chrystusem*, 341–3. A little-known formula for collective absolution contains an explicit exhortation to the Paraclete: "May the Spirit of the Comforter, given to us for the remission of sins, in whom we have access to the Father, purify your hearts and enlighten you with His radiance, so that you may proclaim the works of the power of Him who has called you out of darkness into His marvellous light" (Laurentin, *Nieznany Duch Święty*, 418).

therefore the fruit of the Holy Spirit, who grants the gift of repentance of heart and initiates a new existence. Jesus removes sin from the world because He is the most holy Lamb, filled with the Spirit and giving the Spirit. The gift of the Holy Spirit is a Paschal grace – it is through Him that we enter the mystery of the glorious death and resurrection through which Christ overcame sin and all guilt. In the sacrament of reconciliation, the Holy Spirit imparts the gift of unity in Christ and therefore the power to forgive sins becomes unfruitful without human repentance and love for God. Each sacrament must be understood personally as a process of developing friendship with Christ in the Holy Spirit. Any automatism or juridical treatment of the sacraments is the consequence of a lack of a living relationship with the Person of the Holy Spirit dwelling in those who were baptised.[283]

In the sacrament of Penance, the Holy Spirit continues to prove the world wrong about "sin and righteousness and judgment" (John 16:8). About sin – because of a lack of faith in Christ; about righteousness – because it has shone in His resurrection and exaltation; about judgement – because all hostility towards Christ has already been judged (cf. John 16:9-11). The sacrament of penance thus stands under the judging power of the Holy Spirit. The same Spirit, however, is also the Advocate, granting the human heart the grace of penance and repentance (CCC 1433). The transformation of the human heart is always the greatest and most difficult task and is thus the work of the One whom Christians profess as the "Lord and Life-Giver". Penance is a grace and a gift; the effort of purification leads to enlightenment, consolation and joy coming from the Paraclete (cf. Gal 5:22). He "helps us in our weakness; for we do not know how to pray as we ought, but that very Spirit intercedes with sighs too deep for words" (Rom 8:26). W. Hryniewicz comments on this in a beautiful statement: "The human epiclesis is matched by the epiclesis of the Spirit-Advocate Himself".[284]

The *Catechism of the Catholic Church* notes that

> Beneath the changes in discipline and celebration that this sacrament has undergone over the centuries, the same fundamental structure is to be discerned. It comprises two equally essential elements: on the one hand, the acts of the man who undergoes conversion through the action of the Holy Spirit [...] on the other, God's action through the intervention of the Church. The Church, who [...] forgives sins in the name of Jesus Christ and determines the manner of satisfaction, also prays for the sinner and does penance with him. Thus the sinner is healed and re-established in ecclesial communion (CCC 1448).

283 Cf. Guzowski, *Duch Dialogujący*, 250.

284 Cf. Hryniewicz, *Nasza Pascha z Chrystusem*, 343–4.

The sacrament of penance

> does not simply heal the one restored to ecclesial communion, but has also a revitalizing effect on the life of the Church which suffered from the sin of one of her members. Re-established or strengthened in the communion of saints, the sinner is made stronger by the exchange of spiritual goods among all the living members of the Body of Christ, whether still on pilgrimage or already in the heavenly homeland (CCC 1469).

3.5.2.2 The Pneumatological-Communional Dimension of the Sacrament of Anointing of the Sick

The richness of the metaphorical meaning of the anointing with oil stems from the widespread usefulness of olive oil in the lives of the people of the Middle East, where it was used to nourish, refresh and improve the body, it healed wounds, sustained the flame of the lamp, it was an expression of blessing, a symbol of joy, friendship and love. According to the Book of Enoch, oil will serve the saved to sustain their immortality.[285] The anointing with oil is a sign that the Holy Spirit wants to fill the sick person with new life and reunites him with the suffering and resurrected Christ and His Church.[286]

The sacrament of anointing of the sick has been treated very modestly by the New Testament authors, and the few statements that can be found there are quite ambiguous.[287] The biblical data need to be supplemented by the teaching of the Church, especially in this case. According to the Council of Trent, the anointing expressly represents the grace of the Holy Spirit, through whom the soul of man is invisibly anointed.[288]

Every human being without exception is exposed to illness and its consequences: "In illness, man experiences his powerlessness, his limitations, and his finitude. Every illness can make us glimpse death. Illness can lead to anguish, self-absorption, sometimes even despair and revolt against God" (CCC 1500-1). The Church in apostolic times knew of a special rite designed for the sick, and the Tradition has recognised it as one of the seven sacraments of the Church (cf. CCC 1510), in which "Christ continues to 'touch' us in order to heal us" (CCC 1504).[289]

The illness excludes man from the community – his activity decreases, he becomes dependent on others, he lacks self-disposition, autonomy, independence.

---

285 Cf. Romaniuk, *Sakramentologia biblijna*, 101–2.

286 Cf. Czaja, *Credo in Spiritum Vivificantem*, 196.

287 Cf. Romaniuk, *Sakramentologia biblijna*, 114.

288 Cf. Guzowski, *Duch Dialogujący*, 257.

289 Cf. Jagodziński, *Sakramenty w służbie communio*, 382.

The sick feels that he is a stranger, a hindrance and even a destructive element, he is a foreign body in his environment, he is aware of disintegration. His sense of inclusion in the social world is destroyed, he feels that he instils fear in the healthy.[290] People's reaction is often the simplest – to remove and isolate the sick person from society (the fear of contagion is often at the root of this phenomenon). This takes away the sick person's sense of belonging to the community, to life.[291] The Church's teaching on the connection of the sick with the whole community is very clear here: "By the sacred anointing of the sick and the prayer of the priests the whole Church commends those who are ill to the suffering and glorified Lord, that he may raise them up and save them (cf. Jas 5:14-16). And indeed she exhorts them to contribute to the good of the People of God by freely uniting themselves to the Passion and death of Christ (cf. Rom 8:17, Col 1:24, 2 Tim 2:11-12, 1 Pet 4:13)" (CCC 1499).[292]

> The Anointing of the Sick completes our conformity to the death and Resurrection of Christ, just as Baptism began it. It completes the holy anointings that mark the whole Christian life [...] This last anointing fortifies the end of our earthly life like a solid rampart for the final struggles before entering the Father's house (CCC 1523).

Early Christian prayers of consecration attribute the healing action in the bodily and spiritual spheres to the holy oil, which receives this power from the Holy Spirit invoked in the Church's epicletic prayer.[293]

In the new ritual of the sacrament of anointing, the Church has moved closer to an understanding of it that has long been accepted in the Orthodox Church. Of particular importance is the reference of the grace of anointing to the Holy Spirit: "Through this holy anointing and His most loving mercy, may the Lord assist you by the grace of the Holy Spirit, so that, freed from your sins, He may save you, and in His goodness raise you up". The Christological dimension is combined in this formula with the pneumatological and epicletic dimensions. In his entire life, the Christian relies on the resurrected Christ and the power of His Spirit; this also applies to the whole Church.[294] In the Orthodox Church, there is also the sacrament of the sick as a

---

290 Cf. Höhn, *spüren*, 94–5.

291 Cf. Höhn, *spüren*, 96.

292 Cf. Jagodziński, *Sakramenty w służbie communio*, 382–3.

293 Cf. Hryniewicz, *Nasza Pascha z Chrystusem*, 354. "Send down from the heavens your Holy Spirit, the Comforter, so that His power may penetrate this oil [...], so that this oil may become a protection for the soul and body of everyone who will be anointed with it" (Scheme 1). The laying on of hands is accompanied by the following words: "Grant that our brother, strengthened by the fullness of the Holy Spirit, may persist steadfastly in the faith [...] and testify to your love" (one of two formulas to choose from in Scheme 3) (Laurentin, *Nieznany Duch Święty*, 419).

294 Cf. Hryniewicz, *Nasza Pascha z Chrystusem*, 355–6.

salvific means of healing body and soul. The epiclesis of this sacrament occurs at the consecration of the oil, so that it acquires pneumatophoric properties – it becomes a vehicle for the Holy Spirit. Initially, the anointing of the sick was administered in the presence of the faithful – especially seven priests holding seven oil lamps symbolising the seven gifts of the Holy Spirit – and was the introduction to the celebration of the Eucharist.[295]

The effect of administering the sacrament of anointing of the sick is a special gift of the Holy Spirit –

> [the grace of] strengthening, peace and courage to overcome the difficulties that go with the condition of serious illness or the frailty of old age. This grace is a gift of the Holy Spirit, who renews trust and faith in God and strengthens against the temptations of the evil one, the temptation to discouragement and anguish in the face of death. This assistance from the Lord by the power of his Spirit is meant to lead the sick person to healing of the soul, but also of the body if such is God's will. Furthermore, 'if he has committed sins, he will be forgiven' (Jas 5:15) (CCC 1520).

and through the union with the passion of Christ

> the sick person receives the strength and the gift of uniting himself more closely to Christ's Passion: in a certain way he is consecrated to bear fruit by configuration to the Savior's redemptive Passion. Suffering, a consequence of original sin, acquires a new meaning; it becomes a participation in the saving work of Jesus (CCC 1521).

Ecclesial grace creates a new configuration in the social space of the Church: "the Church, in the communion of saints, intercedes for the benefit of the sick person, and he, for his part, through the grace of this sacrament, contributes to the sanctification of the Church and to the good of all men for whom the Church suffers and offers herself through Christ to God the Father" (CCC 1522).[296]

Human life is not limited only to the functioning of the organism, but it is above all a matter of communicative references – communion with God in the communion of people, being loved and being able to love, a creative exchange with the world.[297] The disintegration of vital relations in the sick person threatens to disintegrate the relationship with God, and yet the sick person as a Christian is hidden in God, nothing can threaten him, no powers of this world, neither illness nor death.[298]

---

295 Cf. Hryniewicz, *Nasza Pascha z Chrystusem*, 357.

296 Cf. Jagodziński, *Sakramenty w służbie communio*, 384.

297 Cf. Nocke, *Sakramententheologie. Ein Handbuch*, 232.

298 Cf. Höhn, *spüren*, 97–8.

The biblical basis for the sacrament of anointing of the Sick – James 5:14-15 – was originally an intercessory prayer by the presbyters of the community over the sick combined with a symbolic laying on of hands. It was thus a solidarity action of the faithful in a communicative word and a non-verbal communicative symbol. It was intended to intercede with God for the rescue of the seriously ill person from the sphere of death – as a breakdown of communication – and for the prolongation of life in communion with God and with people.[299] The sacrament is not about preventing the loss of health and beauty or the possibility of self-healing. It is involved in a process of communication that counteracts the physical, social and religious disintegration of the sick, demystifying the suspicion that God and people have abandoned them (cf. Jas 5:14). It does not underestimate pain and suffering, it calls by name that which brings misfortune, it does not raise rash hopes of healing, and it makes evil visible to all.[300]

The Second Vatican Council focused on ecclesial and Christological accents relating this sacrament:

> By the sacred anointing of the sick and the prayer of the priests the whole Church commends those who are ill to the suffering and glorified Lord, that he may raise them up and save them [...] and [...] exhorts them to contribute to the good of the People of God by freely uniting themselves to the Passion and death of Christ (CCC 1499).[301]

Anointing and prayer do not only create communication between two persons, but, through the ordained leaders of the community, they welcome the sick person into the community of prayer of the whole Church. It is precisely this all-embracing communication and communion in which the sick person is included that is also an argument for dispensing this sacrament even when the sick person is not conscious at the moment. The acute lack of communication that accompanies this situation is not an obstacle to making the communicative capacity of the community

299 Cf. Meuffels, *Kommunikative Sakramententheologie*, 327. The first sign of saving a life at risk and of communication is to be present with the sick person (cf. Nocke, *Sakramententheologie. Ein Handbuch*, 232). Instead of verbal consolation, the sacrament brings a gesture of tenderness – the anointing of the forehead and hands. In such a situation, words are hard to find, one has to be well guarded against any pushiness, great sensitivity is needed. It also requires overcoming the fear of suffering and touching the suffering. Touching has its origin in the pre-linguistic realisation of contact and communication – this "body language" is the earliest form of communication, it provides the basis for communication also in relation to "abstract" matters, it creates a bridge between feeling and thinking. Moreover, the intensity of the relationship is expressed in the intensity of tactile contact (cf. Höhn, *spüren*, 98).

300 Cf. Höhn, *spüren*, 99–100; Jagodziński, *Sakramenty w służbie communio*, 384–5.

301 Cf. Auer, *Die Sakramente der Kirche*, 206–7.

and of the whole Church fruitful.[302] Of course, the aforementioned community of communication does not grow out of itself, but is directed towards the Lord, who, as the one experienced in suffering and death – and yet the Victor – is the ideal dialogue partner able to offer consolation and hope. In the mystery of this communion with the (suffering) Lord, there lies the rescue of the sick person, and the fruitfulness of the suffering of the whole community of faith is foreshadowed.[303] Christ is thus the source of communication (the granting of salvation) through the sick person to the members of the community of the Church, and through the entrusting of the sick person to Christ, the eschatological-ministerial structure of the Church is manifested, which is also fruitful for the sick person.[304] It is thus a mutual, Christologically grounded communication between the individual and the community of believers, in which Christ is also always both the communicator and the communication partner.[305]

The Church retains the awareness that illness and death signify its own crisis – the physical death of its members would mean its own end. Hence, the prayer at the anointing also concerns the matter of the sick person's survival beyond illness and death in the life-giving Holy Spirit and in communion with the resurrected Christ. By this sacrament, the sick person is united to Christ, who, present in the members of his Body, builds his Church also in the sick. Sickness thus becomes a place of Christ's special presence in the Church. The great saints offered their sufferings for the Church. This means that sickness and death only outwardly signify a person's loneliness, but from the point of view of faith, they are a way of abiding in communion with Christ and with all those connected to Him, so that there is no individual, isolated or solipsistic dying among the baptised. The anointing of the sick therefore has a strictly ecclesiological reference, it is a celebration of the universal presence of the mission of the Son and the Holy Spirit in man and in the Church, beyond sickness and death; it is a celebration of the Church and a "preservation" of the Church.[306]

The sacramental work of the Holy Spirit is not "punctual", but involves the whole man. God never acts as a therapist or healer, but always as the saviour of man. This is why Christ, upon healing people of all weaknesses and diseases and casting out evil spirits, asked about the faith necessary for salvation. The Epistle of St. James also refers to the forgiveness of sins to the sick person. The healing and sanctifying

302 Cf. Meuffels, *Kommunikative Sakramententheologie*, 327.

303 Cf. Meuffels, *Kommunikative Sakramententheologie*, 327–8; Janiec, *Komunikacyjny wymiar liturgii*, 316.

304 Cf. Ganoczy, *Einführung in die katholische Sakramentenlehre*, 93.

305 Cf. Meuffels, *Kommunikative Sakramententheologie*, 328; Jagodziński, *Sakramenty w służbie communio*, 386.

306 Cf. Lies, *Sakramententheologie. Eine personale Sicht*, 362–4.

action of the Holy Spirit encompasses the whole person and penetrates down to the root of the illness, removing sin as well. The Jews believed that sins attract illnesses to people, whereby sin was understood as a transgression of God's Law. In particular, the enslavements due to addictions start with individual sins and then are the cause of illness. It is not God who punishes a person with illness for sins, but sin which separates the person from the influence of the Holy Spirit, who cleanses us and frees us from the evil effects of sin; sin can become the cause of demonic enslavement or illnesses of spirit and body. Therefore, through the prayer for healing, the whole history of the sick person is submitted to the influence of the Holy Spirit, who really knows what is inside a person.[307]

3.5.3 The Pneumatological Dimensions of the Sacraments at the Service of Communion

Man, as a religious being, feels the need to abide in a relation, a two-way relationship with God. From the human perspective there is thus a need for an intermediary to service this relationship. God revealed in Judaism and Christianity meets this need. The tasks of intermediaries included communicating God's will to people and offering sacrifices to God on behalf of people – "top-down" and "bottom-up" mediation.[308] The Christian notion of mediatorial ministry has many roots in the Old Testament priesthood[309], but is significantly based on the priesthood of Jesus Christ[310] – on whom the official mediatorial ministry of the sacrament of holy orders at the service of communion with God and people in the New Testament is also based.[311] Another type of service for communion that also has Divine-human dimensions is the sacrament of matrimony. The Catechism states briefly: "Two other sacraments, Holy Orders and Matrimony, are directed towards the salvation of others; if they contribute as well to personal salvation, it is through service to others that they do so. They confer a particular mission in the Church and serve to build up the People of God" (CCC 1534).[312]

307 Cf. Guzowski, *Duch Dialogujący*, 258–9.
308 Cf. Romaniuk, *Sakramentologia biblijna*, 116.
309 Cf. Romaniuk, *Sakramentologia biblijna*, 116–9.
310 Cf. Romaniuk, *Sakramentologia biblijna*, 119–25.
311 Cf. Romaniuk, *Sakramentologia biblijna*, 125–36.
312 Cf. CCC 11; Auer, *Die Sakramente der Kirche*, 288. L. Lies calls the sacraments of matrimony and holy orders the sacraments that sustain the Church (Lies, *Sakramententheologie. Eine personale Sicht*, 310).

3.5.3.1 The Pneumatological-Communional Dimension of the Sacrament of Holy Orders

The universal communion of the Church is situated in the context of the history of salvation, of God's constant striving for unity with people and unity among people. The specificity of the communication taking place in the sacrament of holy orders is the "official" ministry for this communion.[313] The Church is *communio* and the office within it is also *communio*.[314] This ecclesiastical office, like the sacrament of holy orders, is realised in three stages: bishop, presbyter and deacon.[315] The Second Vatican Council made it definitively clear that there is only one sacrament of holy orders and one sacramental-ecclesiastical office of ordination, which reaches its fullness in the episcopate.[316] The presbyterate and episcopate are priestly offices, while the diaconate is an office of ministry.[317] It is only in the pastoral ministry that the priesthood acquires its concrete shape, and it is necessary to distinguish between its biographical (personal) and socio-cultural contexts. The communional dimension pertains to the ministry of the preached word at all levels and the whole activity of the priest – with its culmination in the Eucharist – as well as to the office itself and the mission as a service to unity.[318] The priesthood is part of God's striving for universal communion and serves that communion, and because of that all its dimensions are inseparable, overlapping and illuminating one another, creating different dispositions and preferences in the exercise of pastoral ministry.[319]

In response to the question about the specificity of the priesthood, the priestly office is today pointed to as a charism of community leadership, with an ecclesial rather than a Christological basis. G. Greshake writes that "the priestly ministry has

313 Cf. Jagodziński, *Sakramenty w służbie communio*, 391–4.

314 Cf. Beinert, "Grundlagen des katholischen Amtsverständnisses," *Theologisch-praktische Quartalschrift* 4 (1973), 311, 316.

315 See Jacek Nowak, "Trójstopniowość sakramentu święceń," in *Kapłaństwo*, ed. Balter et al. (Poznań-Warszawa: Pallottinum, 1988), 94–112; Nitsche, "Pneumatologie," 350–3.

316 J.D. Zizioulas emphasises: "there is no *priesthood* as a *general and vague* term, as it was to become later on in theology under the name of *sacerdotium* – a term which acquired almost the meaning of a generic principle pre-existing and transmitted in ordination from the ordained to the ordained or from 'all believers' to a particular one. The true and historically original meaning of the term is this: as Christ (the only priest) becomes in the Holy Spirit a community (His body, the Church), His priesthood is realised and portrayed in historical existence here and now as a eucharistic community in which His 'image' is the head of this community offering *with and on behalf of* the community the eucharistic gifts" (Zizioulas, *Being* as *Communion*, 231).

317 Cf. Greshake, *Być kapłanem. Teologia i duchowość urzędu kapłańskiego* (Wrocław: Wydawnictwo *Wrocławskiej* Księgarni Archidiecezjalnej, 1983), 227–8.

318 Cf. Greshake, *Być kapłanem dzisiaj* (Poznań: "W drodze," 2010), 265–70.

319 Cf. Jagodziński, *Eklezjalne kształty komunii*, Wydawnictwo Diecezji Radomskiej AVE, Radom 2012, 108–15.

a sacramental character, because the Church is by nature a sacrament and makes its 'sacramentality' concrete and available through the sacraments – including ordination".[320] However, the functional justification of the sacrament of priesthood does not solve the problem. There needs to be an element of vocation and ordination for the priest to "represent" Christ.[321] The incarnational structure of all salvific mediation is revealed in the sacraments and does not need to originate in a pseudo-mystical identification of Christ with the ecclesiastical office. The office represents Christ by making Him present in sign, word and action, as a tangible and explicit symbol (sacrament) it lets His light shine through, in sacramental mediation people encounter God opening up towards the world. The Church and individual people experience in the office a sacramental-graphic "foretaste" of God's action and the authority of Jesus Christ. However, Christ is Priest[322] in such a different way that there can no longer be any other priesthood than the sacramental representation that enables the working of His priesthood. The interacting priest is the official sign of what the Lord does – the office in the Church is the "sacrament of Christ" – the priest is the effective sign that Christ lives in the Church and in His salvific gifts.[323] All these statements should be further expanded by an ecclesial-pneumatological dimension – the sacraments are not only sacraments of Christ but also of the Church, and since the salvific action has a Trinitarian dimension and the Church is drawn into this "great trinitarian movement" – the priestly office is situated at the intersection of Christ's authority and the Church community which is the work of the Holy Spirit.[324] Christ as Lord is present among us because the Incarnation was not His last word, it was completed in the cross and resurrection. This means that He was the first to enter the realm of the Holy Spirit and makes Himself known in and through Him. The new presence of Christ in the Holy Spirit is the condition for the existence of the sacrament and the sacramental presence of the Lord. The sacramental office never becomes the property of people, it is a sacrament of the

---

320 Greshake, *Być kapłanem*, 23.

321 Cf. Greshake, *Być kapłanem*, 25–9.

322 See Antonio Sicari, "Kapłaństwo Chrystusa," in *Kapłaństwo*, ed. Balter et al. (Poznań-Warszawa: Pallottinum, 1988), 15–22.

323 Cf. Greshake, *Być kapłanem*, 29–31, 39–41, 49, 74–6, 83–4.

324 Cf. Greshake, *Być kapłanem*, 91–2, 102–9; Greshake, *Der dreiene Gott. Eine trinitarische Theologie*, 411–9; Josef Hernoga, *Das Priestertum. Zur nachkonziliaren Amtstheologie im deutschen Sprachraum* (Frankfurt am Main-Berlin-Bern-New York-Paris-Wien: Peter Lang, 1997), 22–9, 124–6. Cf. Congregation for the Clergy, *Priest, Pastor and Leader of the Parish Community* (2002): "The identity of the priest must be pondered upon in the light of the salvific will of God. For this identity is the fruit of the sacramental action of the Holy Spirit and the participation in the salvific work of Christ, contributing to the extension of His work in the Church throughout its historical development. It is a three-dimensional identity: pneumatological, Christological and ecclesiological."

Holy Spirit.[325] John Paul II's exhortation *Pastores dabo vobis* therefore says that the identity of the presbyter is relational,[326] and the basic criterion for understanding it is ecclesiology of communion.[327]

As the Church proclaims the word of God, it needs preachers who act in the community as representatives of Christ. For the community to exist, there is a need for a ministry that gathers, inspires and awakens potential. The ordained priest stands "in front" of the community, but together with all its members he is subordinate to the word of God, which implies the essential equality of all the ordained.[328] Equality in the dignity of all the ordained, however, does not oppose the hierarchy of ministries which, according to the testimony of the Acts of the Apostles and the epistles of St. Paul, developed from the disciples and apostles instituted by Jesus Christ and the so-called apostles appointed by people, up to

325 Cf. Ratzinger, "Ruchy teologiczne i ich miejsce teologiczne," in Ratzinger, *Pielgrzymująca wspólnota wiary. Kościół jako komunia* (Kraków: Wydawnictwo M, 2003), 166. "The 'always' of the sacrament, the presence of the historical beginning in all times of the Church realised by the Spirit, presupposes a reference to [...] the one-time event of the beginning. [...] But, on the other hand, this one-time event reaches us in the gift of the Spirit, who is the Spirit of the resurrected Christ. It does not dissolve in what has happened, in the uniqueness of what is once and for all gone, but carries in itself the power of the present, because Christ has passed through 'the curtain of the flesh' (Heb 10:20) and thus in the one-time has given us the eternal" (Ratzinger, *Pielgrzymująca wspólnota wiary. Kościół jako komunia*, 166–7).

326 Zizioulas postulates a pneumatologically relevant understanding of ministry in the Church. Rather than first assuming the "Christ – ministry" schema and then trying to fill it with the action of the Holy Spirit, he wants to make it precisely the Spirit who is the foundation of this relationship. The general theological perspective shows that there is a fundamental interdependence between ministry and the concrete community of the Church, which is realised through the *koinonia* of the Holy Spirit. From a methodological point of view, this means that there is no way to understand the nature of ministry independently of the concrete community, and one cannot first assume the idea of a concrete community and only then look at ministry. Cf. Zizioulas, *Being as Communion*, 212. The same applies to the question of the validity of ordination. Cf. Zizioulas, *Being as Communion*, 243. If ordination is considered constitutive of community and if the community of *koinonia* of the Spirit is by its very nature a relational entity, ministry as a whole can be described as the complexity of the Church's relationship to the world. In fact, without the notion of "relation", ministry loses its character as a charism of the Holy Spirit, i. e. part of His *koinonia* and ministry (*diakonia*). Cf. Zizioulas, *Being as Communion*, 220.

327 Cf. John Paul II, Exhortation *Pastores dabo vobis* (1992), 12; Jagodziński, "Trwały skutek przyjęcia sakramentu święceń," *Collectanea Theologica. Kwartalnik Teologów Polskich* 74/3 (2004), 78–9. Zizioulas emphasises: "because of the relational nature of ordination, no ordained person realizes his *ordo* in himself but in the community. Thus if he is isolated from the community, he ceases to be an ordained person (no anathematized or excommunicated minister can be regarded as a minister)" (Zizioulas, *Being as Communion*, 233).

328 Cf. Höhn, *spüren*, 122–3.

deacons, presbyters and bishops.[329] The doctrine of the Church as Mystical Body and the conciliar category of "People of God" made it possible to go beyond the conception of the Church as a merely hierarchical institution governed by the clergy and to recognise the indispensable role of laymen and to dynamize their action in the whole space of ecclesial communion.[330] Here, the *Catechism* clearly distinguishes between two ways of participating in the priesthood of Christ:

> While the common priesthood of the faithful is exercised by the unfolding of baptismal grace – a life of faith, hope, and charity, a life according to the Spirit – the ministerial priesthood is at the service of the common priesthood. It is directed at the unfolding of the baptismal grace of all Christians. The ministerial priesthood is a means by which Christ unceasingly builds up and leads his Church. For this reason it is transmitted by its own sacrament, the sacrament of holy orders (CCC 1547).

St. John the Evangelist instituted as bishops those "whom the Holy Spirit pointed to" (St. Clement of Alexandria). The conferral of the three degrees of the sacrament of holy orders is accomplished by *epiclesis* and the laying on of hands. It is a consecration of the Christian – the immersion in the Paschal Christ and in the Holy Spirit, so that he belongs completely to the Father. The Holy Spirit consecrates the Christian in Christ's death and glory and makes him a sacrament of salvation,

---

329 Cf. Romaniuk, *Sakramentologia biblijna*, 171–6; Bernhard Mayer, "Die Kirche als Mysterium in ihren Ämtern und Diensten. Ansätze im Neuen Testament," in *Die Kirche als Mysterium in ihren Ämtern und Diensten*, ed. Mayer and Michael Seybold (Eichstätt-Wien: Sales, 1987), 9–42. "The Holy Spirit is the one who distributes the ministries, and without this sharing no charism is possible in the Church. But in this distribution, the Spirit takes everything from Christ (John 16:14) so that what seems to be a personal ministry in the Church is nothing other than a reflection of the ministry of Christ. It is striking to realise how many times the New Testament repeats that Christ is the 'minister' (Heb 8:2), the 'priest' (Heb 2:17; 5:6; 8:1; 10:21), the 'apostle' (Heb 3:1), the 'deacon' or 'servant' (Rom 15:8; Luke 22:77; cf. Phil 2:7; Matt 12:18; Acts 3:13; 4:27), the 'bishop' (1 Pet 2:25; 5:4; Heb 13:20), the 'teacher' (Matt 23:8; John 13:13), the one who has 'first place in everything' (Col 1:18). Christ remains the sole source of ministry because in the Eucharist he is the one who incorporates the many: every ministry and every order does not come from him simply to be then an individual possession, but to *reflect* him. And in order to reflect him, this ministry is diversified so that it is accommodated to the many. The work of the Holy Spirit, who is the bond of the body (Eph 4:3), assures the 'diversity of the ministries' (1 Cor 15:5, indeed, 'Are all apostles?' [1 Cor 12:29-31; cf. Jas 3:1; etc.]) so that no ministry can be considered objectively in and of itself or as an individual possession, but always must be understood *in relation to the others* that form the one body of Christ. This allows Paul to do what he forbade himself to do (cf. 1 Cor 12:22), that is, to speak of a hierarchy of worth in the gifts, by placing love over all others (1 Cor 12:12-31)" (Zizioulas, *The Eucharistic Communion and the World*, 23–4).

330 Cf. Napiórkowski, *Misterium communionis. Eklezjalny paradygmat dziejów zbawienia* (Kraków: WAM, 2006), 198–202.

transforms the presbyter into a sign of Christ to be a servant of all the faithful for their salvation, He sanctifies him in Christ, in His love and truth. Therefore, the priesthood is more than just an apostolic charism – the sacramental dimension speaks of sanctification in Christ by the power of the Spirit. The inseparability of personal sanctification and ministry results in the priest sanctifying himself by fulfilling the ministry of sanctification, he evangelises by evangelising himself, he consecrates himself by entrusting others to God as an "acceptable [offering], sanctified by the Holy Spirit" (Rom 15:16). It is worth noting the similarity between confirmation, the sacrament of maturity incorporating the Christian into the duties and mission of the Church, and the priesthood, which is bearing witness to the acceptance of responsibility for the further development of salvation through the ministry for people. The sacrament of holy orders makes the Christian an "elder" ("presbyter") as the Holy Spirit entrusts the Church of God to his care (Acts 20:28). The pneumatic dynamics of this sacrament can be better understood not so much starting with the notion of sacrament, but more with the gestures of Jesus and the act of handing over His own mission to the apostles: "Receive the Holy Spirit. If you forgive the sins of any, they are forgiven them; if you retain the sins of any, they are retained" (John 20:22-23). On the day of Pentecost, the apostles receive the fullness of the Holy Spirit not only for the remission of sins, but for the whole mission of Christ – from the proclamation of the Good News to the celebration of the Eucharist. Christ instituted the sacrament of holy orders to continue and accomplish His work in the power of the Spirit[331]. "The Holy Spirit, who infuses pastoral charity, introduces and accompanies the priest to an ever deeper knowledge of the mystery of Christ, which is unfathomable in its richness (cf. Eph 3:14-19) and, in turn, to a knowledge of the mystery of Christian priesthood".[332]

The pneumatic and charismatic character of the New Testament priesthood is not difficult to demonstrate since the chosen disciples are called "apostles" by Christ. This new name refers them to the prophets whom God chose, giving them His Spirit, transforming them into messengers of a new mission, so that they were even

331 Cf. Guzowski, *Duch Dialogujący*, 251–2. "By the power of the sacramental outpouring of the Holy Spirit, who sanctifies and sends, the priest is made in likeness of Jesus Christ, the Head and Shepherd of the Church, and sent to exercise the pastoral ministry. Marked in his very being with the perpetual and indelible mark of a servant of Jesus and of the Church, the priest is permanently and irreversibly incorporated into a particular state of life and charged with a pastoral ministry which, being rooted in his being and encompassing his whole existence, is also permanent. The sacrament of holy orders fills the priest with a sacramental grace which enables him to share not only in the salvific "power" and "ministry" of Jesus, but also in His pastoral "love; " at the same time, it serves for the priest as the guarantee of all those graces of God which will be granted to him whenever they are needed and useful for the worthy and perfect exercise of the ministry entrusted to him" (John Paul II, Exhortation *Pastores dabo vobis*, 70).

332 John Paul II, Exhortation *Pastores dabo vobis*, 70; cf. Guzowski, *Duch Dialogujący*, 252.

prepared to die for it. The ritual priesthood was abolished in Christ. Christ alone shed his blood in sacrifice and therefore became Prophet, Priest and Shepherd (cf. 1 Pet 3:18-25). The choice of the apostles was always the Holy Spirit's initiative (cf. Acts 1:2,21-26; 6:3-5; 16:6; John 15:16). In the case of the Twelve, Christ confirmed that selection by giving them the Spirit to mark the Paraclete's involvement in the continuation of His mission.[333]

For a long time, Western theology favoured the Christological key in interpreting the genesis and development of ecclesiastical ministries, while in the Eastern tradition more frequent reference was made to the Holy Spirit – today this is present in the West to a much greater extent.[334] If the Church is truly the sacrament of the Holy Spirit, the ecclesiastical office must be anchored in the Holy Spirit, must be the place of the Holy Spirit if it is to be the place of the Church.[335] The operation of the office "in persona Ecclesiae" is only the Spirit-illuminated historical concretisation of its Christological origins, its historically Christological continuity "in persona Christi".[336] According to Orthodoxy, the priesthood, the sacraments and all institutional forms are formed gradually and constitute a visible form of the Body in which everything is assured by the unchanging presence of the absolute Witness – the Holy Spirit revealing the absolute Lord – Christ.[337] During the ordination, the

333 Cf. Guzowski, *Duch Dialogujący*, 252–3.

334 Cf. Sienkiewicz, *Wspólnota Kościoła*, 414–8.

335 Cf. Seybold, "Die Kirche als Mysterium in ihren Ämtern und Diensten – Dogmatische Orientierung," in *Die Kirche als Mysterium in ihren Ämtern und Diensten*, 62. "Wenn der Heilige Geist die entscheidende Größe im ekklesialen Repräsentationsgeschehen des kirchlichen Amtes ist, dann ist dieses selbst nicht nur sakramental zu begreifen, sondern eben deswegen auch schon als christologische Repräsentanz. Das 'in persona Ecclesiae' ist gar nicht als solches möglich, wenn nicht zugleich als 'in persona Christi'. Denn: Zum ersten muß daran erinnert werden, daß der Geist wesentlich der Geist Christi ist und keine andere Organisationsfigur einbewohnt und heiligt als die von Christus gewollte. Nicht die Kirche schafft sich eigenmächtig ihr Amt, auch nicht einfach bloß mit Hilfe des sie belebenden Geistes, sondern der Geist sucht es sich als sein Organ, weil es der Kirche eingestiftet ist von Christus in den Aposteln und deren Nachfolgern. Zum anderen beinhaltet eine sakramental begriffene ekklesiale Repräsentationsfunktion des Amtes immer Universalität. Der Geist, der das 'in persona Ecclesiae' des kirchlichen Amtes fundiert, ist immer der Geist der ganzen Kirche, im Querschnitt wie im Längsschnitt" (Seybold, "Die Kirche als Mysterium in ihren Ämtern und Diensten – Dogmatische Orientierung," 62).

336 Cf. Seybold, "Die Kirche als Mysterium in ihren Ämtern und Diensten – Dogmatische Orientierung," 62–3.

337 Cf. Evdokimov, *Orthodoxy*, 175. The stability of the Church's being is based especially on the Eucharist: "In the Eucharist, therefore, the Body of Christ in its objective ontology becomes conditioned epicletically. The Eucharist portrays the mastery of the Church par excellence precisely because of this synthesis: without Christ there is no community, but unless there is a community to invoke the Spirit, Calvary is no longer Calvary. The *epiclesis* of the Spirit gives life to the Body (John 6:63), and this removes the sacramental reality of the Church from any notion of causality: thanks to the epiclesis, the Church realises in herself the Christ event without her causing it to

laying on of hands as a sign of the impartation of the Holy Spirit is done in silence, but while anointing of hands the following prayer is said: "The Father anointed our Lord Jesus Christ through the power of the Holy Spirit. May Jesus preserve you to sanctify the Christian people and to offer sacrifice to God" (*Roman Pontifical*).[338] The distinctly communal-communional dimension of the exercise of the ordained office also highlights the collegiality of ecclesiastical authority, which is linked to its apostolicity, it manifests itself in the relation of the episcopal ministry to the pope, in the unity of the bishop with the presbyters of the diocese and is ultimately an expression of the common concern for the community of the Church.[339]

Of particular significance to the disciples was the announced sending of the Holy Spirit: "It is not for you to know the times or periods that the Father has set by his own authority. But you will receive power when the Holy Spirit has come upon you; and you will be my witnesses in Jerusalem, in all Judea and Samaria, and to the ends of the earth" (Acts 1:7-8). Not surprisingly, many Eastern Church Fathers even regarded this descent as a kind of priestly ordination or episcopal consecration.[340] In the Epistle to the Ephesians, St. Paul presents a theology of the Church as the

---

happen and without her being caused by it. There is no issue of priority between Christ and the Spirit, and this is instructively shown by the epicleses of the early Church" (Zizioulas, *The One and the Many*, 81). This leads to the central role of the bishop in the Church, which cannot exist without a bishop. Everyone should participate in worship – laymen, deacons, presbyters – but the participation of the bishop is necessary for the Church to be fully catholic. A parish led by a presbyter is not in the full sense a local Church because it has, according to Zizioulas, an episcopocentric structure. At the centre of the Eucharistic assembly "on the throne of God" sits, as an icon of Christ, the bishop surrounded by presbyters. The Eucharist is not presbyterocentric but episcopocentric in its nature. The presbyters form a college surrounding the bishop, so that the whole Eucharistic assembly becomes an image of the worship of God in heaven described by the apostle John in the book of Revelation. Cf. Wong Yee Kheong, *John Zizioulas' Ecclesiology of 'The One and the Many'*, 112–3.

338 Laurentin, *Nieznany Duch Święty*, 419.

339 Cf. CCC 1559–60: "One is constituted a member of the episcopal body by virtue of the sacramental consecration and by the hierarchical communion with the head and members of the college. The character and collegial nature of the episcopal order are evidenced among other ways by the Church's ancient practice which calls for several bishops to participate in the consecration of a new bishop. In our day, the lawful ordination of a bishop requires a special intervention of the Bishop of Rome, because he is the supreme visible bond of the communion of the particular Churches in the one Church and the guarantor of their freedom. As Christ's vicar, each bishop has the pastoral care of the particular Church entrusted to him, but at the same time he bears collegially with all his brothers in the episcopacy the solicitude for all the Churches: 'Though each bishop is the lawful pastor only of the portion of the flock entrusted to his care, as a legitimate successor of the apostles he is, by divine institution and precept, responsible with the other bishops for the apostolic mission of the Church.'" Cf. Napiórkowski, *Misterium communionis*, 187–94; Jagodziński, *Sakramenty w służbie communio*, 388–9.

340 Cf. Romaniuk, *Sakramentologia biblijna*, 150.

Body of Christ, in which "The gifts he gave were that some would be apostles, some prophets, some evangelists, some pastors and teachers, to equip the saints for the work of ministry, for building up the body of Christ, until all of us come to the unity of the faith and of the knowledge of the Son of God, to maturity, to the measure of the full stature of Christ" (Eph 4:11-13).[341] The priestly ministry is concerned with the ministry of the word and the sacraments, which bring about the "realisation" of the word working through interpersonal communication (cf. 1 John 1:1).[342]

The priestly function is a ministry inextricably linked to the mystery of the resurrection and the descent of the Holy Spirit. It is not the property of the Church or an independent initiative of the Church, while the Holy Spirit ensures the permanence of this ministry in the Church. This ministry never manages to exhaust all the gifts of the Spirit and is a condition of the Church's fidelity to the Spirit of Christ. It serves to ensure that people are drawn by the power of the risen Christ and transformed by the action of His Spirit. Through the priesthood, the Paschal mystery is continually made sacramentally present in the community of the Church. Christ "through the eternal Spirit offered himself without blemish to God" (Heb 9:14) and, by the power of that Spirit, enables the members of His one priesthood to give themselves and their lives to apostolic service. Without the help of the Holy Spirit, man is unable to do this, and this is why the epicletic prayer for the filling with the Holy Spirit plays such a great role in the ordination rites: "The epiclesis of ordination directs towards the epiclesis of the whole life".[343] Sacramental ordination (diaconate, priesthood, episcopate) should not be understood as a point-like event. Each is a certain spiritual process, beginning with a choice and a call. This choice is the work of the Holy Spirit and therefore the Church prays and invokes the help of the Spirit so that the choice is the right one.[344]

Of vital importance in the rite of ordination is the gesture of laying on of hands as a sign of the impartation of the Holy Spirit. It was already used by the apostles and early disciples (Acts 6,6; 8:17; 13:3) with faith in the "charism of God" (1 Tim 4:14; 2 Tim 1:6). *The Apostolic Tradition* of St. Hippolytus of Rome reports that during the episcopal consecration, the assembled bishops laid hands on the chosen one,

---

341 Cf. Napiórkowski, *Misterium communionis*, 185–6.

342 Cf. Höhn, *spüren*, 129; Jagodziński, *Sakramenty w służbie communio*, 390–2.

343 Hryniewicz, *Nasza Pascha z Chrystusem*, 345.

344 Cf. Hryniewicz, *Nasza Pascha z Chrystusem*, 345. "It would undoubtedly be dangerous if the direct, pneumatological and thus sacramental character of concrete ordination were obscured by such a view, and if the mysticism of the community were thus overlooked. The community can do nothing of itself. It can only be pneumatological if every member is a pneumatic. However, the reverse is true when it comes to the individual: his communion with the whole Church, communion with the visible form of his primordial bond, is the place of the Spirit's presence and the guarantee of unity with the Holy Spirit" (Ratzinger, "Nauka Kościoła o 'sacramentum ordinis,'" in *Kapłaństwo*, ed. Balter et al. (Poznań-Warszawa: Pallottinum, 1988), 70–1.

while the priests and the people prayed silently for the descent of the Spirit. Then one of the bishops would lay his hand on the elect and pray for the outpouring of the power of the Holy Spirit, whom God once bestowed on Jesus Christ, and whom He in turn gave to His apostles. The text of this ancient prayer was restored by Paul VI's Apostolic constitution *Pontificalis romani* (1968), recognising it as a form of episcopal consecration. Many Church Fathers regarded Pentecost simply as the ordination of the apostles. The gesture of the laying on of hands and the request to grant the Holy Spirit also accompanied the ordination of priests and deacons. The liturgical reform in the Catholic Church restored to the gesture of the laying on of hands a profound pneumatological sense, expressed in the epicletic prayer for the descent of the Holy Spirit and the actualisation of the mystery of Pentecost.[345]

The Catholic teaching on the sacrament of holy orders refers to Jesus Christ, who was sent by the Father and passed on His mission to His disciples (cf. John 20:21; Matt 28:19-20). He thus laid the foundation for the new People of God.[346] St. Paul was also aware of this mission (cf. 2 Cor 5:20). The Apostles passed on the message they had received (cf. Acts 1:15-26), and the Pastoral Epistles reflect the already institutionally formed structure of the Church with bishops, presbyters and deacons (cf. 1 Tim 3:1-13; 5:17). *The Apostolic Tradition* of St. Hippolytus of Rome describes the extremely important – from the theological perspective – two-dimensionality of ordination: election is an ecclesial element, the laying on of hands and the prayer of epiclesis have a pneumatological dimension.[347] The sacramental mark, on the other hand, is not an ontological sign, but an ecclesiological distinction.[348]

---

345 Cf. Hryniewicz, *Nasza Pascha z Chrystusem*, 346. "The epicletic character of ordination is powerfully shown in the tradition of the Eastern Church. Here, the epiclesis is a request that 'the grace of the Holy Spirit' descend upon the ordained. The structure similar to sacramental ordination is also seen in the Orthodox Church in the rite of introduction to the position of hegumen (the head of a small monastery) and archimandrite (the abbot of a large monastery, now an honorary title). This rite has its epiclesis ('May the grace of the Holy Spirit elevate you to...') in contrast to the lower ordinations, which are devoid of it. Also the rite of monastic haircut (taking of vows, haircut, giving of a new name), which is similar to priestly ordination, has an epiclesis. The monastic state is a preparation for higher hierarchical degrees. It is regarded not only as a state of penance and asceticism, but also as an expression of a special union with Christ, which is granted a certain degree of sacramentality ('second baptism')" (Hryniewicz, *Nasza Pascha z Chrystusem*, 346).

346 Cf. Auer, *Die Sakramente der Kirche*, 349.

347 Cf. Meuffels, *Kommunikative Sakramententheologie*, 329.

348 Cf. Skowronek, *Małżeństwo i kapłaństwo jako spotęgowanie chrześcijańskiej egzystencji* (Włocławek: Włocławskie Wydawnictwo Diecezjalne, 1996), 206–7; Jagodziński, *Sakramenty w służbie communio*, 392. "A. Skowronek emphasises that the sacramental character of the priesthood was interpreted in a metaphysical sense and this ontological-static understanding of it causes a lot of difficulties in theology today. He believes that this sacramental mark is not an ontological mark but an 'ecclesiological distinction'. He adds, however, that functional statements must not be misunderstood – in a purely functionalist or actualist sense – and must not be won over against an

Zizioulas opts in this regard for a relational interpretation of the person of the bishop as *alter Christus*. He insists that he is not an image of Christ through the virtues and qualities contained in his own existence. According to the classical medieval conception, holy orders confer the grace possessed by the ordained; Zizioulas sees an extreme form of this concept in the theory that speaks of *chracter indelebilis*. He himself prefers the "iconological" approach to the matter. Ordination is first and foremost a relational reality – the ordained person is placed in the context of a particular set of relationships that are eschatologically transcended and exist in natural interdependence. In a typological or iconological approach, two conditions are necessary for a bishop to be an image of Christ. First, he acts *in persona Christi*, i. e. not based on *potestas* or qualities he possesses, but by virtue of the fact that through his actions he allows another person – Christ – to act. Secondly, he does not represent Christ as an individual, but as part of a community. Ordination does not give any person holding a ministry any rights that he might have individually, but gives him a special position in the community. The deeper justification for all this lies precisely in the vision of the Church as a sign of the eschatological community, which precedes the idea of *alter Christus*, for the eschatological Christ, of whom the bishop is the image, is not a mere individual but – and this is very important – part of the community. This essentially refers to the constitutive role played by the Holy Spirit in Christology, since the particular function of the Holy Spirit

---

ontological view of the sacrament of priesthood, with 'ontologicality' explained as 'first and foremost interpersonal relations', since these are the highest value of human reality" (Jagodziński, "Trwały skutek przyjęcia sakramentu święceń," 86). "More recent conceptions of the sacramental character attempt to situate it in ecclesiology, where it is treated as a visible continuation of the sacramental gesture, bringing people into a particular relationship with the Church, as a reality fundamental to its community of communication. [...] Communicative theology shows the effects of the reception of the sacrament of priesthood (character) as a reality that requires the development of the person towards being a medio-communicative sign of the grace offered by the Holy Spirit. This shows more clearly the relational (Christological and pneumatological) character of the sacrament of holy orders, emphasises the inseparable connection between sacramentology and ecclesiology, and makes it possible to apply reflection on the effects of receiving this sacrament to show the dimension of the life and action of priests [...] in the context of the theology of the Church as sacrament. The indicated theological foundations can have the effect of strengthening the sense of priestly identity in relation to Christ and the Holy Spirit, but also to the Church, and provide additional support for the corresponding priestly formation and spirituality. For they include the relationship between Christ – as the 'Original Sacrament' and the Church – as His 'fundamental sacrament', between Christ as creator and the sacrament in the proper sense – as His specific sign and instrument, and the relationship between the analogical-dynamic 'sacramentality' of the Church and the man who has received the sacrament. Integral to this is also the pneumatological dimension of all these relations, which more clearly reveals the fuller content of the dimension of ecclesial reality, pointing to the Church as the sacrament of the Holy Spirit" (Jagodziński, *Sakramenty w służbie communio*, 88–9).

is to be communion and to make Christ a collective person rather than a mere individual – Christ comes to His Kingdom as the first of many brothers, "many" as a community. The bishop as *alter Christus* is therefore unthinkable as a separate individual, i. e. without the community of which he is the head. The grace bestowed on him at ordination is not his individual property, but is a power given to him to bring about in history the presence of the eschatological Christ in the form which will be realised in the last days, i. e. as a community.[349]

Based on all primary data, it can be concluded that the whole office of ordination and its task stands under the sign of communicative giving and passing on in service of building the community.[350] The sacrament of holy orders expresses the hierarchical structure of the Church,which, starting with the episcopal office, communicates and must communicate all ordinations.[351] Its mission has a clear function in the communicative structure of references between God and people, and also within the community of believers. Consequently, the specific acts of the ordination office are the proclamation of Christ's message and guiding the community in the communication of faith and in building its communion. And since God and the Church meet here, the ordained person himself becomes the partner and medium of communication.[352]

The static-pyramidal understanding of the structure of the Church and of the priestly office, allowing only for vertical-universal communication and hierarchical-monarchical communion, was broken by the Second Vatican Council. As a result, a communicative-communional understanding of the Church and the sacrament of holy orders was made possible. First, instead of "priesthood", it generally speaks of "ministry"[353] at Christ's command (cf. PO 1-2, 12), or of "presbyter" in the context of the whole People of God (cf. LG 9). There is also the "common priesthood of the faithful", which is distinguished from the "ministerial priesthood" (cf. LG 10), the two being complementary to each other. This complementarity also includes the concept of three degrees of ordination and episcopal collegiality.[354] A. Skowronek stresses that the relationship between the degrees of ordination should be based on the principles of subsidiarity, solidarity and collegiality[355]. The constitution *Lumen gentium* and the decree *Presbyterorum ordinis* also value the function of preaching the word of God. The two-fold communicative function of this "ministry"

349 Cf. Zizioulas, *The One and the Many*, 243–4.

350 Cf. Auer, *Die Sakramente der Kirche*, 296; Bartnik, *Dogmatyka katolicka*, 2: 774.

351 Cf. Auer, *Die Sakramente der Kirche*, 357.

352 Cf. Meuffels, *Kommunikative Sakramententheologie*, 329; Hernoga, *Das Priestertum*, 175–9; Jagodziński, *Sakramenty w służbie communio*, 392–3.

353 Cf. e. g. LG 28–9.

354 Cf. LG 21–23; Ganoczy, *Einführung in die katholische Sakramentenlehre*, 97–100.

355 Cf. Skowronek, *Małżeństwo i kapłaństwo jako spotęgowanie chrześcijańskiej egzystencji*, 197–8.

thus manifests itself in the Christological point of intersection of the vertical and horizontal dimensions. Based on its Christological basis, the presbyter's position cannot be seen otherwise than in the communicative communion with all believers in Christ, and this also applies to the other two degrees of ordination. The ministry thus has a kind of catalytic function in creating interactive references in the area of the transmission and fulfilment of the Gospel and the making present of Christ's kingdom. Traditionally, these communicative interactions are said to be realised in *martyria*, *leiturgia* and *diakonia*.[356]

The reality of the duration of the sacrament can also be put in communicative-theological terms. The mediation of ordination is sacramentally perpetuated in the person who has received the charism of ordination (cf. 1 Tim 4:15), but it can only bear fruit through personal commitment. The life of the ordained person must become a sign of the grace offered to him by the Holy Spirit for the fulfilment of his ministry.[357] The mediating service for communication thus continues in the field of tension between Christology and ecclesiology.[358] The witness of the presbyter is realised in the sacramental, personal-communional celebration of the ministry for Christ with the aim to build a community.[359] W. Kasper sees the primary task of the sacrament of holy orders in the pastoral office, in guiding the community. The ordained priest is responsible for the unity of the community and

---

356 Cf. Meuffels, *Kommunikative Sakramententheologie*, 330.

357 Zizioulas writes: "it is important that the concept of 'order' and of ministry be freed from an objectifying sacramentalism that considers the gift of a charism or the ordination of a minister as 'sacraments' in themselves. If we consider the epicletic character of the sacrament – this is exactly what it means to relocate all ordination within the framework of the Eucharistic service – we are led to speak of the orders and ministers of the Church neither in ontological terms nor in functional terms (a dilemma in which many of the earlier controversies have been trapped), but in existential and personal terms, just as Paul speaks of the charisms in 1 Corinthians 12. By 'personal' and 'existential' (terms which, of course, are not ideal because they can have several meanings) I mean first, in a negative sense, no ministry is possible above or outside of the community as an individual and ontological possession and second, in a positive sense, that each ordination and each ministry is existentially linked to the Body of Christ. It is not defined by its 'utility' or by its 'horizontal social structure', but it is a reflection of the very ministry of Christ, the same energies of God the Father and the gifts of the Spirit (1 Cor 12:4-5) *in* and *for* the one body of Christ (1 Cor 12:12-30). This means that the concept of 'hierarchy' in the Church should not speak in terms of rank or merit (Paul firmly excludes this view of the charisms in 1 Cor 2:22-31), but in terms of personal charisms and of activities that put a person into profound existential relationships with others – something like the hierarchy existing in the Holy Trinity where obedience is not absent, but is based upon the activities of each person, themselves determined precisely by the relationships they have with one another and with the world they have created and love" (Zizioulas, *The Eucharistic Communion and* the *World*, 22–3).

358 Cf. Courth, *Die Sakramente. Ein Lehrbuch für Studium und Praxis der Theologie*, 294–9.

359 Cf. Meuffels, *Kommunikative Sakramententheologie*, 331.

this also defines his ministry in the Eucharist.[360] For K. Rahner, the teaching office is relevant here – the ministry of the word.[361] In this perspective, the priestly office is a condensed form of the preaching of the word.[362] Priestly ministry thus has significantly communicative dimensions – together with all the faithful, the priest is in need of the Lord's grace, he is directed towards them and bound to them by a deepened exchange of giving and taking, while his responsibility does not exclude that of the members of the community, but rather initiates and coordinates it.[363]

The deacon, bringing to the altar the worldly gifts offered by the congregation later distributes them as transformed, thus expressing the return to the world of that which comes from creation and returns as perfected, showing the way and nature of the transformation of the world. The symbolism of the breaking of bread in this perspective is not a sign constrained only to a momentary experience of communion. In the resurrected Jesus Christ, present in the breaking of bread, the Eucharistic assembly becomes the entrance of eschatology into the temporal dimension of the world, made possible by the space created by the Church acting in permanent relation to the Holy Trinity. Communion in this perspective is not an experience only of the ecclesial community or only of a particular Eucharistic assembly. It includes those coming from the world created by God and bringing with them symbolic elements derived from it in order to re-direct them to the world through the experience of communion with the Father in the Holy Spirit, proper to the Son, and to bring to it not only a message but a real unity based on the eschatological dimension, which infiltrates temporality through the Eucharist.[364]

The sacramental quality of the ecclesiastical office flows from the objective efficacy (owing to the indelible mark) embedded in the power of the Spirit of Christ Himself, but it also requires an existential adequacy in the personal holiness of the minister.[365] The same Holy Spirit who dwells in the office-bearer "according to power" also wants to dwell in him "according to holiness" and guide his whole life. The office's sacramental action "in persona Christi" and "in persona Ecclesiae", the double representation of Christ and the Church in which the minister is ordained by the Holy Spirit, is at the same time an existential appeal to him for an intense and comprehensive personal formation of Christ and His Church within himself. The office-bearer cannot seek personal salvation with the omission of his office – this

---

360 Cf. Kasper, *Glaube und Geschichte*, 364.

361 Cf. Rahner, "Der theologische Ansatzpunkt für die Bestimmung des Wesens des Amtspriestertums," in *Schriften zur Theologie*, ed. Rahner, (Einsiedeln: Benzinger, 1970), 9: 366–72.

362 Cf. Courth, *Die Sakramente. Ein Lehrbuch für Studium und Praxis der Theologie*, 298–9.

363 Cf. Nocke, *Sakramententheologie. Ein Handbuch*, 251; G. Greshake, *Priester sein* (Freiburg: Herder, 1991), 71; Jagodziński, *Sakramenty w służbie communio*, 393–4.

364 Cf. Sienkiewicz, *Wspólnota Kościoła*, 443.

365 See Jagodziński, *Eklezjalne kształty komunii*, 124–34.

would not only be a kind of personal schizophrenia, but also a pointless attempt to divide the Holy Spirit Himself. Thus the ordained person becomes the dwelling space of the Holy Spirit and the bridge between the Head and the Body, between Christ and His Church in the power of the Holy Spirit.[366]

The Congregation for the Clergy has included a passage in the *Directory on the Ministry and Life of Priests* specifically dedicated to the pneumatological dimension of priestly ordination:

> In priestly Ordination, the priest has received the seal of the Holy Spirit which has marked him by the sacramental character in order to always be the minister of Christ and the Church. Assured of the promise that the Consoler will abide 'with him forever' (John 14:16-17), the priest knows that he will never lose the presence and the effective power of the Holy Spirit in order to exercise his ministry and live with charity his pastoral office as a total gift of self for the salvation of his own brothers. It is also the Holy Spirit who by Ordination confers on the priest the prophetic task of announcing and explaining, with authority, the Word of God. Inserted in the communion of the Church with the entire priestly order, the priest will be guided by the Holy Spirit whom the Father has sent through Christ. The Holy Spirit teaches him everything and reminds him all Jesus has said to the Apostles. Therefore, the priest with the help of the Holy Spirit and the study of the Word of God in the Scriptures, with the light of Tradition and of the Magisterium, discovers the richness of the Word to be proclaimed to the ecclesial community entrusted to him. Through the sacramental character and the identification of his intention with that of the Church, the priest is always in communion with the Holy Spirit in the celebration of the liturgy, especially in the Holy Eucharist and the other sacraments. In fact, in each sacrament, Christ invoked by the priest who celebrates *in persona Christi* acts through the Holy Spirit with his efficacious power on behalf of the Church. Thus, the sacramental celebration finds its efficacy in the Word of Christ who has instituted it and in the power of the Holy Spirit which the Church invokes frequently in the epiclesis. This is particularly evident in the Eucharistic Prayer in which the priest, invoking the power of the Holy Spirit on the bread and on the wine, pronounces the words of Jesus and actualizes the mystery of the Body and of the Blood of Christ, really present through transubstantiation. It is thus in the communion with the Holy Spirit that the priest finds the strength to guide the community entrusted to him and to maintain it in the unity wanted by the Lord. The prayer of the priest in the Holy Spirit can be patterned on the priestly prayer of Jesus Christ (cf. John 17). Therefore, he must pray for the unity of the faithful so that they

366 Cf. Seybold, "Die Kirche als Mysterium in ihren Ämtern und Diensten – Dogmatische Orientierung," 76–7.

may be one in order that the world may believe that the Father has sent the Son for the salvation of all.[367]

St. Paul emphasises that no one is commissioned without being gifted to do so. Such an action is attributed to the Holy Spirit. The life of Jesus, anointed and sent to carry out the mission of salvation in the power of God's Spirit (Luke 4:18-19; Isa 61:1-2), and the apostles chosen to continue Christ's mission (John 17:17) with St. Paul (Rom 1:1-5), Peter (1 Pet 1:1), Timothy (1 Tim 4:1), Titus (Tit 1:5) and Jude (Jude 1:1), are placed on this line of effective transformation. In the Church, those in priestly ministry receive the permanent anointing of the Spirit so that Christ is constantly present through them. Sacrificing oneself to Christ and sanctification by the Spirit go hand in hand, and for this reason the Church demands of those called a personal consecration, so that their priestly ministry is not merely exercised outwardly, but encompasses their whole life (cf. Heb 8). Christ's action in the person of the priest is always carried out in the power of the Holy Spirit. And since sanctifying grace is a work of the Spirit, the sacramental priesthood (the sacramental manifestation of Christ in the ordained priest) is clearly a work of the Holy Spirit. "The priesthood [...] is conferred by that special sacrament; through it priests, by the anointing of the Holy Spirit, are signed with a special character and are conformed to Christ the Priest in such a way that they can act in the person of Christ the Head" (PO 2).[368]

3.5.3.2 The Pneumatological-Communional Dimension of the Sacrament of Matrimony

The Catholic Church counts marriage among the sacraments mainly because redemption (also referred to as "new covenant" or "new creation") profoundly renews man himself and his relationships to God, to other people, to himself and to creation, and is the building block of a sacramental life based on divine love, not merely on human effort. We can only experience this newness in the power of the Holy Spirit, who pours true love into our hearts. Redemption is the grace of "adoption", i. e. love permeating the whole of human nature. This can only be experienced in the presence of the Holy Spirit. Sacramental marriage is grounded in this love of the Holy Spirit and is therefore the source of His gifts and charisms. The author of this sacrament is the Holy Spirit, because the resulting communion is the beginning of a new life which we do not possess on our own but receive from Him. Love and life

367 Congregation for the Clergy, *Directory on the Ministry and Life of Priests* (1994), 8–11. cf. Hernoga, *Das Priestertum*, 173–5.

368 Cf. Guzowski, *Duch Dialogujący*, 253.

divinised and sanctified by the Holy Spirit become a sign of God's presence if the spouses allow Him to guide them.[369]

The sacrament of matrimony is the work of the Holy Spirit because through him God created man and woman. He is the love and communion of God, he arouses love and unity in people, He seeks to personalise everything and the relationship of sexes becomes a covenant between persons.[370] He has created a world of symbols, among which the most sublime is marriage, the "great mystery" that expresses Christ's reference to the Church (Eph 5:32). Therefore, Christian spouses will be all the closer to each other the more they love Christ and the Church, and this common "passion" will unite their bond of love.[371]

Modern anthropology takes into account the personal and interpersonal reality of man[372] and even makes a new interpretation of the human person. According to it, man becomes himself in communication with another person and through this, the community necessary for being oneself is created.[373] Theology emphasises that the communicative and communal essence of God is reflected in man,[374] and the result is the communicative[375] and communional dimension of being human.[376]

---

369 Cf. Guzowski, *Duch Dialogujący*, 254–5.

370 "Every sacrament should be understood dynamically as a constant interaction with the Holy Spirit, for every action of His in our world involves 'personalisation' and not objectification. Where the Holy Spirit descends, the object reality is transformed into a personal reality. However, this process of personalisation is to continue unceasingly, and therefore a necessary condition for the development of the sacramental bond of marriage is the common daily prayer of the spouses, who thus constantly invoke the help of the Holy Spirit, professing faith in His sanctifying and healing power" (Guzowski, *Duch Dialogujący*, 255–6).

371 Cf. Guzowski, *Duch Dialogujący*, 255.

372 Cf. Andrzej Perzyński, *Włoska anthropologia teologiczna. Studium historyczno-dogmatyczne* (Łódź: Archidiecezjalne Wydawnictwo Łódzkie, 2012), 12–3.

373 Cf. Eicher, *Die anthropologische Wende. Karl Rahners philosophischer Weg vom Wesen des Menschen zur personalen Existenz* (Freiburg (Schweiz): Universitätsverlag, 1970), 98–110; Schneider, *Znaki bliskości Boga*, 1112; Jagodziński, *Sakramenty w służbie communio*, 171–2.

374 Cf. Lachner, "Communio – eine Grundidee des christlichen Glaubens," 239.

375 Cf. Hryniewicz, *Pascha Chrystusa w dziejach człowieka i Wszechświata*, 241.

376 Cf. Carlos Valverde, *Antropologia filozoficzna* (Poznań: Pallottinum, 1998), 349: "Man is attributed to man and only in the other man does he find himself. Only by transcending himself in the search for 'you' does man realise his own being. [...] The 'I-you' relationship is a relationship in the full sense of the word. It is an encounter between persons; it does not mean making the other person into an object to be owned or manipulated. It means contemplation and respectful acceptance, an enlightening presence, a direct relationship without intermediaries (economic, political, erotic etc.) that would interfere with a true encounter with 'you'. It is a relationship in which everyone retains freedom but involves the whole person. When I say 'you', I also say 'I'. 'You' makes 'I'. In a reciprocal relationship we both gain an awareness of our own existence as persons. In it we feel ourselves to be learning and being learnt, loving and being loved, in it we choose and are chosen, we exercise our freedom towards the other person and they recognise us as free. In this

The creation of man had already a communional dimension.[377] There is also a communional dimension to the human person. It has a relational and ecstatic character, which is confirmed even by the linguistic analysis itself – the Greek *prósopon* meant a direct relation to someone or something. The original content of the word precludes an understanding of the person as an individual without any reference to another reality. What is meant here is the relation of generic difference in the sense of an event that puts a person into a state of reference. The concept of person is thus a relational ontological concept and presupposes a relation of the person to another subject or object. Therefore, it is necessary to conceive of the person as an existential relation, a specific mode of existence of nature manifested in relation and in the capacity to enter into contact and into communion.[378] The person involves not only being and abiding, but also being directed towards communion with others, and human nature is the condition and basis for mutual solidarity, empathy, shared experience, complementarity and building communion.[379] The Christian, in particular, is an ecstatic human being that has unmistakably communional features.[380]

This is of great importance for marriage since the human person is characterised by sexuality.[381] According to John Paul II's letter *Mulieris dignitatem*, man and woman are the image of God also as a union of two. The Pope extended the classical

relationship, I want you to be you, that is, someone other than me, and you want me to be me, someone other than you. In this way, we both form 'we', a communion of persons, based on an identity of co-responsibility. The ontological category that provides the rationale for the sufficiency of 'we' is the in-between – the true fundamental aspect of human existence in the Heideggerian sense. But the deepest reality of the 'in-between' is love, understood not only as affection but also as communion." Cf. Jagodziński, "Komunijny wymiar osoby ludzkiej," *Roczniki Teologiczne* 61/2 (2014), 51–63; Jagodziński, *Antropologia komunijna* (Lublin: Wydawnictwo KUL, 2015), 5–7.

377 Cf. Jagodziński, *Antropologia komunijna*, 15–20.

378 Cf. Hryniewicz, *Pascha Chrystusa w dziejach człowieka i Wszechświata*, 67.

379 Jagodziński, *Antropologia komunijna*, 47.

380 Cf. Szymik, "Religio vera. Rzeczywistość chrześcijaństwa – chrześcijański wymiar rzeczywistości według Josepha Ratzingera/Benedykta XVI," *Teologia w Polsce* 7/2 (2013), 8–10; Jagodziński, *Antropologia komunijna*, 21–8; Jagodziński, "Komunijna wizja sakramentu małżeństwa," *Studia Teologii Dogmatycznej* 2 (2016), 50–1; Królikowski, "Trynitarno-chrystologiczne perspektywy teologii małżeństwa," *Studia Teologii Dogmatycznej* 2 (2016), 18–20.

381 Jagodziński, *Antropologia komunijna*, 59–60: "man is not a monad, but rather is constituted as a relational being, based on communication, transmission, communion, mutual participation, community. Already in the fact of the existence of two genders his relational and communal dimension is revealed. Being human is realised in being male and female in mutual correlation. The difference between the sexes is not only related to the mutual discovery of each other's identity, but also allows the realisation of the essential characteristic of the human person, which is the ability to give oneself and to build a communion of persons. 'The reality of God's image is not exhausted in the structure of man's being, but demands the adoption of a dynamic, dialogical, communal perspective'. Man is the image and likeness of God not only through his humanity, but

vision of man as a personal subject by treating primary sexual differentiation as a constitutive part of God-likeness: "man was made in the image and likeness of God not only through its humanity, but also through the communion of persons constituted from the beginning by man and woman".[382] In this way also human procreation is different from animal procreation, for the fruit of the conjugal communion of love is not an individual but a human being who is the image of God. Every human being is a communal person, ontologically open to communion with others since they are ontologically dependent on communion with the Creator. The communion between man and woman, which is the primordial expression of all possible communion between human beings, realises the image of the Holy Trinity when it is based on the love of God. Adopted sons and daughters of God who live in communion actualise this dimension of the image of God, which is fulfilled in an outstanding way in marital communion.[383] Gender difference thus makes the *communio personarum* possible. Through the creation of the communion of persons of the first parents, the work of creation was apparently brought to completion[384]. The loneliness of man in the Yahwistic description of man points not only the first discovery of the transcendence proper to the person, but also to the discovery of the relationship to the person as an opening and expectation of the communion of persons. Unity through the body also points to the embodied communion of persons and postulates this communion.[385] In his letter to families *Gratissimam sane* (no. 8), John Paul II wrote that, according to Genesis 2:24, two somatically different subjects become "one flesh", participate in the capacity to live in truth and love. This capacity reflects the personal constitution of man and predisposes him to form a communion of persons. The man's exclamation at the sight of the woman

---

also through the communion of persons; he reflects God not in the act of solitude, but in the act of this communion."

382 John Paul II, *Mężczyzną i niewiastą stworzył ich. Odkupienie ciała a sakramentalność małżeństwa*, ed. T. Styczeń (Lublin: Wydawnictwo KUL, 2008), 33.

383 Cf. Angelo Scola, *Osoba ludzka. Antropologia teologiczna* (Poznań: Pallottinum, 2005), 188–90; S. Kunka, *Teologiczna wizja cielesności człowieka w nauczaniu Karola Wojtyły – Jana Pawła II* (Lublin: Wydawnictwo KUL, 2012), 36–65; Królikowski, "Trynitarno-chrystologiczne perspektywy teologii małżeństwa," 20–2.

384 Cf. Sławomir Kunka, *Teologiczna wizja cielesności człowieka*, 39.

385 Cf. Kunka, *Teologiczna wizja cielesności człowieka*, 41–2; Jagodziński, *Antropologia komunijna*, 51: "The body expresses femininity for masculinity and masculinity for femininity and facilitates the reciprocity and communion of persons. Marital communion is rooted in the natural bonds of flesh and blood. The body in itself is not an expression of God's likeness and image – God does not have a body. However, since the body belongs to the nature of the human person and participates in the realisation of the human person through communion with other persons, it participates in that image and likeness. The trinitarian perspective, which presupposes the objective ('structural') status of God's image in man, implies its communional ('relational') status."

"This at last is bone of my bones and flesh of my flesh" (Gen 2:23) means that the flesh expresses femininity for masculinity and masculinity for femininity, and thus it facilitates reciprocity and communion of persons.[386]

Indissolubility is not so much a normative expectation, but rather a demand placed on each other by spouses trusting in their love. Such a life decision presupposes a free and definite determination of the will to place no limits on the growth of their love. The proper basis for an indissoluble and irrevocable lifelong union is that it is an expression of the personal truth of two people who wish to respect and recognise each other as persons. The indissolubility of marriage and its unity are based on the partners' unconditional acceptance and confirmation.[387] "The grace of the sacrament transforms human love into divine love. Only the Holy Spirit, as St. Paul writes, is able to transform human hearts to such an extent that the law of commandments will be replaced by a new law, the law of the Spirit, which is the law of freedom".[388] The essential features of marriage – its exclusivity (monogamy), the absence of any reservations and the readiness for a future together – stem from what in the language of the social sciences is called "the inclusion of the whole person" (Niklas Luhmann). Thus, it is not a question, as in other forms of human socialisation, of a temporary interaction in some segment of life, but of the unconditional acceptance of man and woman with all aspects of their being persons. This implies a demand for total belonging and the utmost transparency of one's

386 Cf. John Paul II, *Mężczyzną i niewiastą stworzył ich*, 48; Jagodziński, *Antropologia komunijna*, 28–9; Jagodziński, "Komunijna wizja sakramentu małżeństwa," 52–3; Skrzypczak, "Sakrament małżeństwa," in *Znaki Tajemnicy. Sakramenty w teorii i praktyce Kościoła*, 528–31.

387 "St. Paul shows that both the permanence of human bonds and the power of love have their source in God, the Apostle addresses Christian believers (faith is a condition of the marital covenant) to 'put on' Christ (Rom 13:14), and those who have already put Him on (Gal 3:27) with the encouragement that men should love their wives as their own flesh, and that the union of the two should be so close that they constitute one flesh (Eph 5:28,31). To use contemporary terms: that they become one spiritual person, with moral, spiritual and physical unity. This is also how Jesus understood marriage in the light of the will of the Creator – a unity so close that nothing can separate it. However, this unity, possible at the level of nature, has been weakened by sinfulness and is too fragile to be maintained without the help of the Holy Spirit. For this reason, Christian spouses must show sufficient faith to constantly receive this Gift, which is the Spirit of holiness and unity. This sacrament is actualised by *praying together* (not so much individually), which is an image of a living faith, which makes God their 'everyday life'. Therefore, receiving the sacrament means both a gift and a task. The spouses should really show their love for the Church and their desire to save people (at least themselves and their children), following the example of Christ, so that this sacrament will reveal its power and fruitfulness in their lives. The love of the Holy Spirit is salvific, which is why theology interprets conjugal love not so much as a natural one, leading to physical birth and caring for temporal well-being, but as a reality rooted in and having its source in the love of the Trinity" (Guzowski, *Duch Dialogujący*, 256).

388 Guzowski, *Duch Dialogujący*, 257.

own being as a self, which seeks its fulfilment in love, and whose "machinery" is sexuality.[389]

The significant basis for the necessity of including sexual experiences in the space of a partnership characterised by lasting fidelity is the fact that we are dealing with another person and not an object to be "used". It is thus also necessary, in sexual intercourse characterised by pleasure, to "enjoy" the presence of the other, which corresponds to the dignity of that person. The existential significance of sexual desire lies in the fact that it is directed towards a person of the opposite sex and can become the basis for a lasting reference. Therefore, sexuality cannot be conceived analogously to hunger and thirst, but rather in terms of language and communication. As the most intense form of human communication, it is subject to the basic requirement of truthfulness, in which man and woman express their mutual inclination. Sexuality is thus always, also as lustful love in sexual form, a relationship between persons in their fullness of being. It serves the fulfilment of the basic human need to build a protective space for intimacy and entrusting oneself and additionally provides the basic sense of shelter, security, as well as responsibility and devotion to the other. It helps people discover, as men and women, a specific place where they find their life task and connect being themselves with being in the world. On the other hand, the mere fact that a man or woman then also becomes an object of desire does not yet destroy their personal dignity. For the loving partner also wants to be mutually desired, he or she does not want to meet with indifference or respect only. Rather, the experience of one's attraction to one's partner contributes to the experience of self-worth, is expected and in the language of sexual desire means: "I want you because it is good for me that you are here". Mutual desire presupposes that partners are useful to each other, however, not in the sense of using an object. If desire is rooted in a personal, enduring and faithful reference, it implies a mutual affirmation of the partners in love. It does not equate having a partner for oneself but desiring someone to whom one has given oneself and expects their mutual devotion. "In love there is no possession that does not grow out of devotion".[390] If the sexual desire of another person is combined with love, it goes beyond the self, which corresponds to the ecstatic structure of desire combined with being with the other person, which characterises the desire for love.[391]

The fundamental truth about the person is revealed by an analysis of the interpersonal encounter. The human person seeks a personal "you" through which one becomes aware of one's otherness and separateness. By transcending oneself and

389 Cf. Eberhard Schockenhoff, "Liebe auf Abwegen? Zum Verhältnis von Sexualität und Liebe in intimen Beziehungen," *Theologisch-praktische Quartalschrift* 4 (2015), 339–43.

390 Eberhard Jüngel, *Gott als Geheimnis der Welt* (Tübingen: Mohr, 1977), 437.

391 Cf. Schockenhoff, "Liebe auf Abwegen?", 343–5; Benedict XVI, Encyclical Letter *Deus caritas est* (2005), 11; Jagodziński, "Komunijna wizja sakramentu małżeństwa," 53–4.

entering into dialogue with another person – in ultimate relation to God as the "eternal You" – the human person actualises and constitutes oneself. This means revalorising the category of relationship, introducing love into the definition of person and pointing to the dependence of the human self on the encounter with "you" and "we". When God created man, He entered into dialogue with him. He opened Himself to man and saw in him a conversation partner. Man must therefore seek the measure of himself in God. In this way, the image of God in man contains a relationship, a partnership, a communion of persons.[392] Relationality is a constitutive feature of personal being, for which it is essential to be open to other persons, to be closely connected and deeply united (*communio personarum*). The divine persons share their personal being with human beings, are a model of full personal perfection for them and include them in their communion.[393] The original category of the reality of person is thus not the ancient substance or the modern subject, but relation.[394]

An in-depth analysis of inter-personal communion shows that between "I" and "you" there is always an "in-between", which is different from and at the same time indicative of the two essential members of the relationship, without which (as the "third" in which they both merge into "we") they cannot exist – persons even become themselves in something "third" that unites them. This "third element" always has something deeper at its core – a new personal bond. In love, for example, one does not love only the other (and oneself), but also the mutual commonality. This bond reaches its peak when it becomes a person,[395] which "represents" the personally shared world of the relationship partners and their supra-personal connection.[396] Thus, it turns out that every interpersonal event is not only bipolar

392 Cf. Grzegorz Barth, *Hermeneutyka osoby* (Lublin: Wydawnictwo KUL, 2013), 137–9.

393 Cf. Marian Rusecki, "Personalizm. II. W teologii," in *Encyklopedia katolicka*, ed. Edward Gigilewicz et al. (Lublin: TN KUL, 2011), 15: 333–5; Jagodziński, *Antropologia komunijna*, 34–5.

394 Cf. Gacka, *Znaczenie osoby w teologii Josepha Ratzingera – Benedykta XVI*, 25–30, 124–5; Jagodziński, "Komunijna wizja sakramentu małżeństwa," 54–5.

395 Cyprian Kamil Norwid, *Człowiek*: "- Rodziców miłość, jak trzecia istota, Z dwóch serc ku niebu powstająca kwiatem…" (http://www.poezja.org/utwor-4661.html).

396 Cf. Greshake, *Trójjedyny Bóg*, 134–44; Jagodziński, "Trialogiczno-komunijna koncepcja trynitologii," 60–1. Barth, *Hermeneutyka osoby*, 174: "The significance of the *third factor* constituting the relation to the world becomes clearer when it moves towards and into the personal bond. It arises […] 'between' 'I' and 'you' as a kind of 'result' of the relation and the encounter. Of course, it acquires its external expression both in the form of a new experience and the shaping of the world, and in language, but its basis and simultaneously content is love. As a matter of fact, 'I' and 'you' not only love each other, but also love that which is 'between' them, i. e. the *personal commonality* of 'I' and 'you'. This *third* is crystallised as a bond that represents the (personal!) shared world of 'I' and 'you', which can take the form of a concrete person (God as an instance of the two spouses, or a child vis-à-vis the parents) or some particular value that unites the world of persons. Being two not only does not exclude *the third/the third person*, but welcomes and includes it so that it can

in a significant way, but actually tripolar. This is also the essence of interpersonal communion – all constitutive elements individualise each other and at the same time achieve the unity of the whole; in fact, the individual elements and the whole can only be grasped trialectically.[397]

However, there is also a deeper dimension to the aforementioned "third-in-between", which is also of great significance for sacramental marriage. It refers to the triune God, without whose "trialogical life" and its reflection in the human world of the person the trialogical structure of personal being and the realisation of the trialogical-"trinitarian" communion would not be possible.[398] J. D. Zizioulas argues that a person achieves full humanity by being able to participate in the trinitarian life of God.[399] Since the essence of God is communion, the essence of the human person is also communion, which also makes it necessary to deepen the theology of person and marriage by placing it within the trinitarian hermeneutic of the concepts of "relation" and "community".[400] Of course, the turning point in the discovery of this personal structure was the Christian revelation. In this way, something was brought out to the surface of consciousness that neither modern philosophy nor even Christian philosophy itself had managed to capture in a sufficient manner.[401]

---

develop. The two even experience the joy of giving it space in this development. *The third*, on the other hand, rejoices in its being gifted as a shared being of two."

397 Cf. Greshake, *Trójjedyny Bóg*, 139–40; Jagodziński, *Antropologia komunijna*, 39–41; Jagodziński, "Komunijna wizja sakramentu małżeństwa," 55–6.

398 Cf. Greshake, *Trójjedyny Bóg*, 141–2.

399 Cf. Zizioulas, "Human Capacity and Human Incapacity: A Theological Exploration of Personhood," *Scottish Journal of Theology* 28 (1975) 407–8. The person cannot exist without *communio*, "is stuck not in an individual existence but in an interaction to God and creation: man is not a living *entity* without a connection to other persons. Man becomes a relational creature and realises his being as a creature in communion. Only then does he acquire a truly ontological existence..." (Barth, *Hermeneutyka osoby*, 164–5).

400 Cf. Barth, *Hermeneutyka osoby*, 162–3. These concepts "are based on an ontological foundation found in the trinitarian being of God, which ultimately signifies perichoretic communion. We have historical access to this ontological image of communion [...] primarily in the incarnate Son and the Church. The top-down path [from Divine to human communion] is the basis for understanding human personhood – each member of the Church, and then the personhood of all people in the world. [...] if the Church contains the image of the divine community and if human beings are persons made in the image of God and ultimately – in the image of God who is communion, then man is theologically a *person* only if his personhood reflects the personhood of God as community" (Barth, *Hermeneutyka osoby*, 163).

401 Barth, *Hermeneutyka osoby*, 168–9: "J. Ratzinger claims that in Christianity there is no simple dialogical principle in the modern sense of 'I'-'you', nor is there such a principle in the case of man put into the context of history, in the broad 'we', nor in the case of God, who [...] is not a mere 'You', but the proper 'We' of the Father, the Son and the Holy Spirit. The human 'I' and even our human 'I'-'you' as a dialogical relationship are implicit in the divine 'We'. [...] with the trinitarian 'We', a place has been prepared for every human 'we' [...] It pulls the person from the still (!) individualistic

The communional-anthropological dimension of marriage has received much attention in the reflection on its reality, but little thought has been given to the pneumatological dimension of sacramental marriage. W. Hryniewicz was absolutely right when he wrote that

> without deep pneumatological awareness, theology is produced as if there were only one Divine mission (*missio divina*) in the history of salvation, namely the mission of the Incarnate Word. Meanwhile, the only economy of salvation is *de facto* the economy of the Son and the Spirit in a total reciprocity of action and interpenetration. The participation of believers in the Paschal mystery is always accomplished by the power of the Holy Spirit. *En Christo* and *syn Christo* are inseparable from *en Pneumati* just as much as death and resurrection are inseparable from the sending of the Spirit, which completed the salvific work of Christ.[402]

Therefore, pneumatology is indispensable to properly illuminate the problem of representing the salvific mysteries.

The a priori sense of true communication is mutual recognition of each other. If two people promise something to each other, they recognise this assumption and put it into practice in their lives. Therefore, a marriage vow cannot be made unilaterally and cannot even be revoked bilaterally.[403] The monogamous equality of the spouses is most clearly emphasised in St. Paul's teaching, according to which a woman and a man are allowed to bind themselves in marriage to only one person, and the spouses have the same mutual rights to their spouse's body (cf. 1 Cor 7:3-4). A possible decision for temporary abstinence in cohabitation must therefore also be agreed bilaterally (cf. 1 Cor 7:5).[404] The same rights apply to widowers and widows who are allowed to remarry (cf. 1 Cor 7:8-9). The woman is not allowed to leave the man and the man is not allowed to leave the woman (cf. 1 Cor 7:10-11). The same rules apply to the consent to cohabitation or departure of the non-believing party (the so-called Pauline privilege[405]) (cf. 1 Cor 7:12-13,15). The celibate state of

---

'I'-'you' relationship, in which the 'you' can even be lost. [...] it is a matter of capturing an essential moment which, from the point of view of the Divine-human relationship, sheds essential light to the understanding of the personal relation, where 'I' and 'you', the common being with each other, the true *communio* will be the most primordial mode of all personal being. The triadic structure and dynamics (*triadicity*) of the person is then revealed. Between 'I' and 'you' there enters a *third element* through which and only in which 'I' and 'you' can relate to each other and to themselves in full freedom and with recognition." Cf. Jagodziński, *Antropologia komunijna*, 41–3; Jagodziński, "Komunijna wizja sakramentu małżeństwa," 56.

402 Hryniewicz, *Nasza Pascha z Chrystusem*, 274.

403 Cf. Höhn, *spüren*, 119–21.

404 Cf. Romaniuk, *Sakramentologia biblijna*, 226.

405 Cf. Romaniuk, *Sakramentologia biblijna*, 217–20.

a man and a woman is assessed in the same way: (cf. 1 Cor 7:27.33-34).[406] Although St. Paul writes that "the husband is the head of his wife" (1 Cor 11:3) and that "Indeed, man was not made from woman, but woman from man. Neither was man created for the sake of woman, but woman for the sake of man" (1 Cor 11:8-9), a few verses further he adds: "Nevertheless, in the Lord woman is not independent of man or man independent of woman. For just as woman came from man, so man comes through woman" (1 Cor 11:11-12). The same thought is expressed in a different context in Galatians 3:28: "There is no longer Jew or Greek, there is no longer slave or free, there is no longer male and female; for all of you are one in Christ Jesus". The equality of spouses is also evidenced by the command" "Be subject to one another out of reverence for Christ" (Eph 5:21).[407]

By the will of God, a man and a woman are united for life, forming an indissoluble community of marriage and family (cf. Mk 10:6-9). The *Catechism* comments on the resulting task of fidelity:

> It can seem difficult, even impossible, to bind oneself for life to another human being. This makes it all the more important to proclaim the Good News that God loves us with a definitive and irrevocable love, that married couples share in this love, that it supports and sustains them, and that by their own faithfulness they can be witnesses to God's faithful love. Spouses who with God's grace give this witness, often in very difficult conditions, deserve the gratitude and support of the ecclesial community (CCC 1648).[408]

The spouses are thus not alone since through the sacrament they have the support of God, while their community of marital communication is incorporated into the communicative community of the whole Church.[409]

The marriage vow establishes a relationship and a social meaning that encompasses the present and the future and needs time to be realised.[410] The passage from Ephesians 5:25-32 is very rich in content. Through the "great mystery" of the union of two people, compared to the union of Christ with the Church, the spouses cease

406 Cf. Romaniuk, *Sakramentologia biblijna*, 212–3.

407 Cf. Romaniuk, *Sakramentologia biblijna*, 226–7; CCC 1645: "The unity of marriage, distinctly recognized by our Lord, is made clear in the equal personal dignity which must be accorded to man and wife in mutual and unreserved affection" (Catechism cites GS 49). Cf. Jagodziński, *Sakramenty w służbie communio*, 395–396; Jagodziński, "Komunijna wizja sakramentu małżeństwa," 57–8.

408 Cf. Carlo Caffarra, "Sakramentalna ontologia a nierozerwalność małżeństwa", in *Pozostać w prawdzie Chrystusa. Małżeństwo i Komunia w Kościele katolickim*, ed. Roberto Dodaro (Poznań: Księgarnia Św. Wojciecha, 2015), 166–7.

409 Cf. Jagodziński, *Sakramenty w służbie communio*, 396; Jagodziński, "Komunijna wizja sakramentu małżeństwa," 58.

410 Cf. Höhn, *spüren*, 118–9.

to be mere human beings, and all their actions and the essence of marriage are elevated to the realm of quite different values, to the supernatural world.[411] The spouses also have their own gift in the life of the Church:

> This grace proper to the sacrament of Matrimony is intended to perfect the couple's love and to strengthen their indissoluble unity. By this grace they 'help one another to attain holiness in their married life and in welcoming and educating their children' (CCC 1641).[412]

The most revolutionary moment in Jesus' teaching on marriage was the requirement of indissolubility (cf. Mark 10:2-9).[413] This is confirmed by the statements of St. Paul (cf. 1 Cor 7:10-11). This teaching of Jesus was (in relation to the Old Testament) not so much a novelty, it merely restored to marriage its original perfection relegated to the background because of the hardness of hearts. The restoration of this original perfection of marriage also implies a transformation of the defective communicative relations that occurred after the fall of people in the social space. The decidedly religious dimension of sacramental marriage is also evidenced by its New Testament mystique, based essentially on Old Testament symbolism, especially the metaphor of God's marriage with Israel.[414]

According to the Old Testament laws, only the man could in principle be the subject in a divorce procedure and only he could take another wife, whereas according to Jesus' teaching, each party commits the sin of adultery if they leave their spouse (Mark 10:11-12; cf. Luke 16:18). This principle creates a new reality in the social space of marriage. The New Testament marriage law presents itself modestly compared to the detailed rules of the Old Testament law, but it brings a great deal of bright light to the joint life of spouses, guarantees the equality of their rights and duties and respects the dignity of each person.[415] Jesus' teaching particularly emphasised the idea of the unity of both spouses (cf. Matt 10:7-8). In accordance with the Semitic mentality, "one flesh" means simply man, and the communion of flesh also implies a communion of thoughts and desires. It is also

---

411 Cf. CCC 1639; Romaniuk, *Sakramentologia biblijna*, 230–1, 233.

412 Cf. CCC 1653: "The fruitfulness of conjugal love extends to the fruits of the moral, spiritual, and supernatural life that parents hand on to their children by education. Parents are the principal and first educators of their children. Cf. Second Vatican Council, decl. Gravissimum educationis, 3. In this sense, the fundamental task of marriage and family is to be at the service of life." Cf. Jagodziński, *Sakramenty w służbie communio*, 396–7; Królikowski, "Trynitarno-chrystologiczne perspektywy teologii małżeństwa," 23–6.

413 Cf. Romaniuk, *Sakramentologia biblijna*, 200.

414 Cf. Romaniuk, *Sakramentologia biblijna*, 229–30.

415 Cf. Romaniuk, *Sakramentologia biblijna*, 201–6.

worth emphasising Jesus' words referring to the beginnings of humanity: "Therefore what God has joined together, let no one separate" (Matt 19:6). He was not just referring to the creation and union of the first two people. Every marriage is a work of God. He accompanies the act of its creation and establishes (creates) the institution of marriage.[416] The sacrament of marriage works throughout the lives of the spouses, transforming the familial community into a communion of life and love.[417] CCC 1643 quotes Tertullian's words:

> Conjugal love involves a totality, in which all the elements of the person enter – appeal of the body and instinct, power of feeling and affectivity, aspiration of the spirit and of will. It aims at a deeply personal unity, a unity that, beyond union in one flesh, leads to forming one heart and soul; it demands indissolubility and faithfulness in definitive mutual giving; and it is open to fertility. In a word it is a question of the normal characteristics of all natural conjugal love, but with a new significance which not only purifies and strengthens them, but raises them to the extent of making them the expression of specifically Christian values.[418]

The *Catechism* goes on to say that through all its members, the family home becomes

> the first school of Christian life and 'a school for human enrichment'. Here one learns endurance and the joy of work, fraternal love, generous – even repeated – forgiveness, and above all divine worship in prayer and the offering of one's life (CCC 1657).[419]

The communicative-theological dimensions of the sacrament of marriage should be shown on the basis of the biblical rationale.[420] The creation of woman (cf. Gen 2:18,21-25) gave man a personal partner. The later account of creation (cf. Gen 1:27) shows both human sexes as the image of God. For the prophets, conjugal union was a sign of the covenant with God and His faithfulness, but at the same time the unfaithfulness of the Chosen People (cf. e.g. Hos 1; 3; Jer 2; 3; Ezek 16; Isa 54; 62). In the theology of creation and covenant, the communion of man and woman (cf. Gen 2:12) has a special theological value.[421] Love needs a promise that

---

416 Cf. Romaniuk, *Sakramentologia biblijna*, 201.

417 Cf. Napiórkowski, *Misterium communionis*, 251–7.

418 Cf. FC 13.

419 Cf. Jagodziński, *Sakramenty w służbie communio*, 397–9; Jagodziński, *Antropologia komunijna*, 136–7.

420 Cf. Sienkiewicz, "Małżeńskie communio w sakramentalnym urzeczywistnieniu," *Studia Teologii Dogmatycznej* 2 (2016) 30–45.

421 Cf. Meuffels, *Kommunikative Sakramententheologie*, 331–2; Jagodziński, *Sakramenty w służbie communio*, 399.

saves individuals from the destructive effects of individualism. It is about love, fidelity and justice.[422] According to Catholic theology, the sacrament is dispensed by the spouses themselves through a mutual "consensus". The solemnity of love[423] demands unconditional recognition of the dignity of the other person, which is expressed precisely in the mutually pronounced marriage vow,[424] and since it cannot be withdrawn,[425] the sacrament of matrimony becomes the basis of the family as a communion of life and love.[426]

The proper sacramentality of marriage is based on Christ (cf. Mark 10:2-9; Eph 5:21-33). Man is assigned to the Lord in imitation of His relationship to people, and the basis of this bilateral communional relationship (including the conjugal relationship) is the mystery of salvation.[427] 1 Cor 7:3-5 describes a close communion of the sexes based on constant communication. On the other hand, Eph 5:21-33 must be interpreted in the light of Eph 4:5, which shows baptism as the foundation of faith and marriage. The description of marriage became a bridge to introduce the Christ-Church analogy. The mention of the "great mystery" (Eph 5:32), which refers to the Christ-Church relationship, makes it possible to understand the sacramentality of marriage in relation to baptism and the Eucharist as a kind of condensation of the mystery of salvation.[428] This interactive event of communication is incorporated into the encompassing relationship between God and people and thus receives its proper character.[429] The triune God is the source and model of all authentic communion between people.[430]

The theology of marriage is characterised by considerable diversity in the Christian Churches. In the Catholic Church, mutual consent and marriage vows are of decisive importance. In the Eastern Churches, however, the most important moment is placing of crowns on the spouses' heads. It has an epicletic character, it is a supplication for the coming of the Holy Spirit and a sign of His coming and of the

---

422 Cf. Höhn, *spüren*, 118.

423 It refers to "love" in combination with the freedom of mutual gift and acceptance, the realisation of self-determination to the highest degree, the proper place of eroticism in relation to *agape*, and the strength to endure adversity (cf. Nocke, *Sakramententheologie. Ein Handbuch*, 270).

424 Cf. Höhn, *spüren*, 119–20.

425 Cf. Höhn, *spüren*, 121.

426 Cf. Napiórkowski, *Misterium communionis*, 251–7; Jagodziński, *Sakramenty w służbie communio*, 399–400; Jagodziński, "Komunijna wizja sakramentu małżeństwa," 60–1.

427 Cf. Skowronek, *Małżeństwo i kapłaństwo jako spotęgowanie chrześcijańskiej egzystencji*, 55–9.

428 Cf. Nocke, *Sakramententheologie. Ein Handbuch*, 272–3.

429 Cf. Meuffels, *Kommunikative Sakramententheologie*, 332–3; Skowronek, *Małżeństwo i kapłaństwo jako spotęgowanie chrześcijańskiej egzystencji*, 63.

430 Cf. Jacek Salij, "Sakrament małżeństwa a sakrament Eucharystii," http://www.kongres-eucharystyczny.mkw.pl/salij.pdf; Jagodziński, *Sakramenty w służbie communio*, 400; Jagodziński, "Komunijna wizja sakramentu małżeństwa," 61.

spouses' participation in the fertility of the Father.[431] The Eastern tradition teaches that this sacrament is administered by a priest. His role is similar to that fulfilled in the celebration of the Eucharist. The crowns are a symbol of the sacramental Pentecost – the descent of the Holy Spirit upon the spouses, the priest's posture and the prayer he utters are epicletic in character.[432]

The following words apply to the conjugal bond between man and woman: "This is a great mystery [*to mysterion*], and I am applying it to Christ and the church" (Eph 5:32). The *mysterion* is the salvific plan of God realised in the person and work of Christ, the salvific reality made present in the Church by the power of the Holy Spirit, the permanent union of Christ with the Church. Marriage shows in all its clarity the interpenetration of the mystery of creation and redemption. Conjugal love is the eschatological sign of God's own love and fidelity, shown once and for all in the mystery of Christ permanently present in the Church. Two people have already been embraced by the Holy Spirit in the sacrament of baptism and incorporated into the salvific reality of the risen Lord, and through marriage their mutual union is also incorporated into this reality, becoming a sign of a new life permeated by the Paschal mystery of Christ and the Holy Spirit.[433]

In the mystery of true love, the mystery of man himself is revealed. Going beyond the sensual sphere, love gives extraordinary depth to the human body, overcoming distance, alienation and loneliness. True human love has its ultimate source in God: "its flashes are flashes of fire, a raging flame" (Song 8:6) – fire is a symbol of the Spirit and His gifts. Marriage is a sacrament of love transformed by the power of the Holy Spirit, giving love new dimensions in the mystery of Christ and the Church. The rite of sacramental marriage is a request for the transformation of human eros into pure conjugal love, bearing the mark of charisma and the grace of the Holy Spirit required to overcome the egocentric state of isolation.[434]

---

431 Cf. Laurentin, *Nieznany Duch Święty*, 420.

432 Cf. Hryniewicz, *Nasza Pascha z Chrystusem*, 347.

433 Cf. Hryniewicz, *Nasza Pascha z Chrystusem*, 347–8.

434 Cf. Hryniewicz, *Nasza Pascha z Chrystusem*, 348–9. "Marriage is thus a mystery, a mystery of love between two people and of Christ's love for His Church. This is why 'love never ends' (1 Cor 13:8). Since marriage reflects God's love for creation, monogamy is its prerequisite. Union in God leads to immortality, and immortality demands love. Love responds to love and I am only because I love. People enter the world with a loving sense of their body, of their masculinity and femininity. Man and woman were given to each other in order to achieve a *koinonia* of persons: 'It is not good that the man should be alone' (Gen 2:18). They also develop each other through their bodies, which bear the dignity flowing not only from the fact of creation, but also from the fact of Christ's Incarnation. Love not only signifies the mutual communion of persons, but is also immortality, since it is the negation of death: 'Set me as a seal upon your heart, as a seal upon your arm; for love is strong as death, passion fierce as the grave" (Song 8:6). Without love one cannot realise one's humanity, and this

Marriage is also a charismatic participation in the salvific mission of the Holy Spirit in the Church. The liturgy of this sacrament according to the Polish rite emphasises the Spirit's role by singing the hymn *Veni Creator* just before the very act of marriage (the original rite lacks this element). The Holy Spirit sanctifies the union, strengthens love, makes it a sign of the love of Christ and the Church, and gives the grace to persevere. The participation of the spouses in the mystery of the Holy Spirit ultimately consists in their charismatic service in the Church through faith, communion of love and mutual sanctification. Sacramental marriage symbolises, represents and reveals the truth of the Incarnation and the sending of the Holy Spirit.[435]

By giving rise to the domestic Church, the sacrament of matrimony appears to demand its own Pentecost (the rite of the placing of the crowns refers to this). In the Orthodox Church, the priest asks for the sending of the Holy Spirit: "Lord, our God, crown them (the spouses) with glory and honour". These words, taken from the Bible (Ps 8:6; Heb 2:7), constitute a proper epiclesis of the sacrament of marriage. It is easy to find in them an allusion to Jesus' prayer: "The glory that you have given me I have given them, so that they may be one, as we are one" (John 17:22). The glory of the resurrection is the culmination of Christ's salvific work completed in the mystery of the descent of the Holy Spirit, a sign of the manifestation of the Spirit and a manifestation of the "Pentecostal charism of unity". Praise and worship are the Spirit's gifts. The newlyweds experience the time of their "conjugal Pentecost", which unites them into a new reality of the "domestic Church" (see Rom 16:5). The sacramental descent of the Holy Spirit makes them witnesses to this new reality. In the Coptic Church, this sense is validated by the anointing of the newlyweds, which resembles the anointing at confirmation and is a sign of the gifts of Pentecost and the priesthood of all believers.[436]

In the early Church, there was no special rite of matrimony – this role was fulfilled by both spouses-to-be participating in the Eucharist. The Eucharist is the nuptial celebration of the Church, the celebration of the union of people with God. Communion therefore completes and seals the sacrament of marriage.[437]

Living in the world, Christian spouses also have a special mission to descend with Christ into the hell of human fall in order to bear witness to the unlimited salvific presence of the resurrected Christ. "The sin of the world" is, after all, born of insensitivity to what has been accomplished in the mystery of His death and resurrection, and in the descent of the Holy Spirit. Christian marriage is prophetic

---

requires full acceptance of the other person" (Henryk Paprocki, "Sakramentologia prawosławna," in *Znaki Tajemnicy. Sakramenty w teorii i praktyce Kościoła*, 552).

435 Cf. Hryniewicz, *Nasza Pascha z Chrystusem*, 350.

436 Cf. Hryniewicz, *Nasza Pascha z Chrystusem*, 350–1.

437 Cf. Hryniewicz, *Nasza Pascha z Chrystusem*, 352.

and eschatological, a sign of hope pointing to the ultimate fulfilment of the Divine plan. It belongs to the reality of the pilgrim Church and endures the hardships of daily life, pointing constantly to eschatological joy, realising the tension between the "already" and the "not yet" that characterises the whole sacramental life of the Church.[438]

The first and immediate effect of sacramental marriage is the bond of a typically Christian communion of persons, with love as the principle and power of family communion.

> Its first task is to live with fidelity the reality of communion in a constant effort to develop an authentic community of persons. [...] The love between husband and wife and, in a derivatory and broader way, the love between members of the same family – between parents and children, brothers and sisters and relatives and members of the household – is given life and sustenance by an unceasing inner dynamism leading the family to ever deeper and more intense communion, which is the foundation and soul of the community of marriage and the family (FC 18).

Marital communion has its roots in the natural complementarity of man and woman, it is the fruit and sign of a deeply human need.

> But in the Lord Christ God takes up this human need, confirms it, purifies it and elevates it, leading it to perfection through the sacrament of matrimony: the Holy Spirit [...] offers Christian couples the gift of a new communion of love that is the living and real image of that unique unity which makes of the Church the indivisible Mystical Body of the Lord Jesus. The gift of the Spirit is a commandment of life for Christian spouses and at the same time a stimulating impulse so that every day they may progress towards an ever richer union with each other on all levels-of the body, of the character, of the heart, of the intelligence and will, of the soul – revealing in this way to the Church and to the world the new communion of love, given by the grace of Christ (FC 19).
>
> In that it is, and ought always to become, a communion and community of persons, the family finds in love the source and the constant impetus for welcoming, respecting and promoting each one of its members in his or her lofty dignity as a person, that is, as a living image of God. [...] the moral criterion for the authenticity of conjugal and family relationships consists in fostering the dignity and vocation of the individual persons, who achieve their fullness by sincere self-giving (FC 22).

Life in a family should become an experience of communion: "the spiritual communion between Christian families, rooted in a common faith and hope and given

438 Cf. Hryniewicz, *Nasza Pascha z Chrystusem*, 352.

life by love, constitutes an inner energy that generates, spreads and develops justice, reconciliation, fraternity and peace among human beings" (FC 48).[439]

Late medieval and scholastic theology reduced the personal communion of life, based on diverse communication, to the so-called purposes of marriage. The new view of the Second Vatican Council[440]presents marriage as a covenant of personal communion of life and love in mutual self-giving, correlation and exchange and, on this basis, develops the sacramental dimensions of marriage as an encounter between the spouses and Christ.[441] This refers not only to the act of concluding a marriage, but to the whole marital existence.[442] The marital community is a perichoretic sign and reflection of the intra-trinitarian perichoresis.[443] Therefore, not a single trace of the patriarchal mentality remains, while the incorporation of the achievements of modern personalism has resulted in the centrality of the reciprocal exchange among all the existential correlates of conjugal love.[444] On the other hand, the expression "domestic Church" (LG 11) extends the Christological-ecclesial understanding of the sacramentality of marriage to the ministry of faith of the entire family community.[445]

A new view of the sacrament of matrimony, emphasising its unity and love and its purpose,[446] is developed in two aspects – communication of faith and communication of life. Marriage is a faith-fulfilled communicative action between a man and a woman taking place in an ecclesial celebration in which Christ is also involved. In this context, the spoken consent is the medium in which the encounter between the man and the woman (at the initiative of God) becomes the space for the encounter between God and people. The sacrament, in this sense, signifies the established and unending dynamic of life, which enables communication with Christ in faith and makes interpersonal and intergender communication a symbol

439 Cf. Jagodziński, *Antropologia komunijna*, 69–73; Jagodziński, "Komunijna wizja sakramentu małżeństwa," 61–2.

440 Cf. LG 11; GS 47–52.

441 Cf. GS 48; *Obrzędy sakramentu małżeństwa dopasowane do zwyczajów diecezji polskich* (Katowice: Księgarnia św. Jacka, 1974), 1–4.

442 Cf. GS 49. Commenting on this passage, A. Skowronek (*Małżeństwo i kapłaństwo jako spotęgowanie chrześcijańskiej egzystencji*, 19) notices the communicative dimension of the carnality of the conjugal acts: "The purpose of pleasure combined with bliss is thus to bring man beyond himself, so that he opens himself to the other and communicates to him; pleasure and delight are nothing else than a call to establish a communal bond."

443 Cf. Lies, *Sakramententheologie. Eine personale Sicht*, 148–50.

444 Cf. Ganoczy, *Einführung in die katholische Sakramentenlehre*, 103–4; Skowronek, *Małżeństwo i kapłaństwo jako spotęgowanie chrześcijańskiej egzystencji*, 45–9.

445 Cf. Schneider, *Znaki bliskości Boga*, 321–2; Meuffels, *Kommunikative Sakramententheologie*, 333; Bartnik, *Dogmatyka katolicka*, 2: 788; Jagodziński, *Sakramenty w służbie communio*, 400–1.

446 Cf. LG 11; GS 48.

of God's faithfulness. By contrast, disrupted communication in marriage becomes a symbol of disrupted reference to God (which, however, points to the possibility of penance and renewed communion with Christ). Implied in marital consent, the potential planes of communication signify, on the one hand, the elevation and transformation of the socio-biological dimensions of the partnership in reference to God, and on the other hand, the self-realisation in mutual co-existence. Unity and love, however, are not easy to realise due to risks, tensions, challenges and changes. Faced with the demands of faith and in the presence of God (the transcendental dimension), the spouses must constantly define their references in a communicative discourse (action dimension) so that their relations could be an expression (aesthetic dimension) of human and divine love and correspond to their life situation (historical dimension).[447]

The Church is the space in which the life of the triune God is realised in the human world in the mystery of conception and love, creation, salvation and sanctification executed on the foundation of the sacrament of matrimony. Consequently, marriage is in a sense the communional foundation of the Church. Spouses-to-be confer it on each other on the basis of the common priesthood flowing from baptism, but in the presence of an ordained representative of the Church. This shows the deep and communal connection between the horizontal order of the People of God and the vertical order of the hierarchical structure of the Church.[448] With reference to Pius XI's encyclical *Casti conubii*, one can also see the communional analogies between the sacraments of matrimony and the Eucharist in terms of permanence, development and being a sign of Christ's inseparable union with the Church. In these sacraments, holistic union, love and happiness are realised, as well as readiness for mutual self-giving and the replication of God's love. Marriage is a sacrament of mutual human sanctification and an act of worship, hence John Paul II pointed out its connection with the Eucharist, the sacrament of penance and reconciliation, and family prayer.[449] Through the sacrament, the family becomes a small Church

---

447 Cf. Meuffels, *Kommunikative Sakramententheologie*, 333–5; Jagodziński, *Sakramenty w służbie communio*, 401–2; Jagodziński, "Komunijna wizja sakramentu małżeństwa," 63–4.

448 Cf. Auer, *Die Sakramente der Kirche*, 287–9.

449 "In the Eucharistic gift of love, the Christian family finds the basis and the spirit that animates its 'communion' and its 'mission'; the Eucharistic bread makes the various members of the family one body, a revelation of and participation in the wider unity of the Church; participation in the Body 'given' and Blood 'shed' by Christ becomes the inexhaustible source of the missionary and apostolic dynamism of the Christian family" (FC 57). The celebration of the sacrament of penance brings about "the discovery, in a spirit of faith, of how sin opposes not only the covenant with God, but also the marital covenant and family communion, leading the spouses and all the members of the family to encounter God, 'rich in mercy', who, extending his love that is more powerful than sin, restores and perfects the marital covenant and family communion" (FC 58). Family prayer "is the communal prayer of husband and wife, parents and children. Communion in prayer is at the

(*ecclesiola*), "a living edition of the whole Church": "The conjugal love [...] is one of the realisations of the unifying love of the Church; it is equally ecclesiogenic and conveyed by the Church" (K. Rahner).[450]

---

same time the fruit and requirement of that communion received in the sacraments of baptism and matrimony" (FC 59).

450 Cf. Skowronek, *Eucharystia sakrament wielkanocny*, 185–9; Jagodziński, *Sakramenty w służbie communio*, 402; Jagodziński, *Antropologia komunijna*, 137–9; Jagodziński, "Komunijna wizja sakramentu małżeństwa," 64–5.

4. The Pneumatological-Communional Dimensions of the Church's Unity

According to *Lumen Gentium*

> Christ, the one Mediator, established and continually sustains here on earth His holy Church, the community of faith, hope and charity, as an entity with visible delineation through which He communicated truth and grace to all. But the society structured with hierarchical organs and the Mystical Body of Christ, are not to be considered as two realities, nor are the visible assembly and the spiritual community, nor the earthly Church and the Church enriched with heavenly things; rather they form one complex reality which coalesces from a divine and a human element (LG 8).

This text has become the basis for interpreting the Church as a communion encompassing the reality of God and people (as the sacrament and communion of saints) and communion in the dimensions of the internal structure of the basic forms of realisation in earthly society – the communion of believers, the communion of Churches and the hierarchical communion. According to the ecclesiology of communion, the Church is a gathering of believers in Christ who receive the share in the goods of salvation offered to them in the Holy Spirit (especially baptism and the Eucharist) and form a unity in the diversity of believers and Churches (*communio fidelium*) and are gathered around Christ represented in the power of the Holy Spirit by the community of ministers (*communio hierarchica*). This ecclesial unity is dynamic, it is a continuous process of communion building by the Holy Spirit, and His role is to invigorate the visible structures founded by Christ[1].

---

1 Cf. Czaja, *Credo in Spiritum Vivificantem*, 199–206. In order for people to measure up to this task, "Jesus gives them the Holy Spirit, who represents in history the saving fruits of His life, passion, death and resurrection, and makes disciples into apostles and proclaimers of the great works of God. [...] This Spirit is also present and active in the Church today. He forms in it determined and courageous missionaries and 'indicates the places that should be evangelised and chooses those who should do it'. He is 'the soul of the evangelising Church' and 'the inner Master who leads to the knowledge of all truth' and the One who gives light and life through the sacraments. He is the gift given to us by the Father that identifies believers with Jesus as the Way, the Truth and the Life. It animates and sustains missionary zeal, 'helps us in our weakness' (Rom 8:26) and heals all that weakens us in the fulfilment of the missionary task. He enriches the whole Church which evangelises by giving it various charisms and gifts which are incorporated into the body of the Church and provide the impetus for evangelisation. All this shows that evangelisation, which is the main task of the Church and thus of the disciples of Jesus, must be done with the spirit. It is an evangelisation led by the Holy Spirit, animated by Him and open to Him. It is conducted by evangelisers who pray and work, which makes them true

The communion in the Holy Spirit does not unify the Church, but it personalises and pluralises it in unity. The Church-communion should reflect the richness of the forms of God's grace (cf. 1 Pet 4:10) – only then will the Church be truly catholic.[2]

The unity of the Church must be interpreted in the context of the trinitarian faith and the pneumatological context of the third article of the Creed. It is an attribute of the Church through faith in the presence of the resurrected Christ and in the work of the Holy Spirit. Through His work, He unites, sanctifies, permeates all things and involves people in the salvific mission. The unity of the Church is the result of His work in all members, in every place and at every time, it results from the unifying action of Christ (Gal 3:28) and is at the same time "the unity of the Spirit" (Eph 4:3).[3]

The cultic formula of the nascent Church – "The grace of the Lord Jesus Christ, the love of God, and the communion of the Holy Spirit be with all of you" (2 Cor 13:13) – links the confession of the free gift of the Father's love in Jesus Christ with the confession of the communion effected by the Holy Spirit.[4] This communion presupposes both participation in the life of the Spirit and the brotherhood that results from it – a fraternal communion aroused, nourished and animated by the gift of the Spirit. Grace, love and communion are here different aspects of participation in the trinitarian life from which the Church of love was born – willed by the Father, gathered by the grace of the Son, and expressed in history in the form of communion in the Spirit. In particular, the Gospel of St. John conceives of Christian brotherhood as the direct fruit of communion with Divine life, realised through the encounter with Jesus in the Spirit. The communion of love, binding the Son to the Father and to people, is the model and source of

---

evangelisers with the Spirit. Living in the Spirit opens the disciples of Jesus to other people and to the mission and makes them 'generous and creative persons, happy in their evangelising and missionary service'" (Gardocki, "Misyjność Kościoła w świetle Adhortacji apostolskiej Evangelii Gaudium i Dokumentu z Aparecidy 'Jesteśmy uczniami i misjonarzami Jezusa Chrystusa, aby nasze narody miały w Nim życie'," *Studia Bobolanum* 2 (2017), 93). Cf. Laurentin, *Nieznany Duch Święty*, 407. On the pneumatological and communal dimensions of the institution of the Church according to Orthodoxy, J.D. Zizioulas wrote: "Authority in the Church was always placed in the context of worship, particularly the Eucharist, and was thus conditioned by the eschatological outlook in two main respects: through Pneumatology, which makes of the institution an event, and through communion, which makes the authority of the institution constantly dependent on the community to which it belongs" (Zizioulas, *The One and the Many*, 366–7).

2 Cf. Joaquín Losada, "Wspólnota w Kościele-komunii," *Communio. Międzynarodowy Przegląd Teologiczny* 9/3 (1989), 64.

3 Cf. Hryniewicz, *Nasza Pascha z Chrystusem*, 85–91; International Theological Commission, *Synodality in Life and Mission of the Church* (2018), 46.

4 Zizioulas points out very emphatically: "The love of God the Father and the grace of our Lord Jesus Christ cannot be separated from the *koinonia* of the Holy Spirit: they form one reality" (Zizioulas, *The One and the Many*, 60).

fraternal communion between the disciples (John 15.12; cf. 13:34), "that they may be one, as we are one" (John 17:22) – Communion as the fruit of the Son's grace and the Father's love, made visible in mutual love, is "the communion in the Holy Spirit" (2 Cor 13:13). Thanks to the Holy Spirit, the disciples will be witnesses to the Teacher (John 15:26-27) if they maintain a fraternal communion: "By this everyone will know that you are my disciples, if you have love for one another" (John 13:35). The Church of love – the icon of the Holy Trinity – is thus the Church of the Holy Spirit, who brings about the communion among the disciples and the disciples' communion with God by giving Himself through the word of life, the sacraments of faith and the ministry of priests. However, the communion of the Holy Spirit has not only a synchronic dimension, but it spans all times and enables the unity of faith and communion between generations in the one Lord.[5]

4.1 The Pneumatological Dimensions of the Communion of the Faithful

With reference to the documents of the last Council, the communion of the people of God is presented as a solidary communion of saints (the sanctified), a universal brotherhood of believers, a communicative unity of people committed to the cause of Jesus Christ, sharing in the active and subjective being of the Church. Active participation in the building of the Church is an obligation derived from the reception of the sacrament of confirmation, while the ultimate source of the dignity and subjective being of the faithful is the anointing:

> The Lord Jesus, 'whom the Father has sent into the world' (John 10:36) has made his whole Mystical Body a sharer in the anointing of the Spirit with which he himself is anointed (cf. Matt 3:16; Luke 4:18; Acts 4:27;10:38). In him all the faithful are made a holy and royal priesthood; they offer spiritual sacrifices to God through Jesus Christ, and they proclaim the perfections of him who has called them out of darkness into his marvelous light (PO 2).

"The baptized, by regeneration and the anointing of the Holy Spirit, are consecrated as a spiritual house and a holy priesthood [...]" (LG 10). This reveals the basis and need for a pneumatological interpretation of the *communio fidelium* – the community of people anointed with the Holy Spirit, Christians (*communioi christianorum* – the communion of the anointed).[6] It is a messianic people, a people

5 Cf. Forte, *Istota chrześcijaństwa*, 130–3.

6 J. D. Zizioulas emphasises: "it must be stated emphatically that there is no such a thing as 'non-ordained' person in the Church. Baptism and especially confirmation (or chrismation) as an inseparable aspect

anointed with the Holy Spirit in the sacrament of baptism (cf. LG 10). He causes the people to come together (cf. LG 9) and unites the faithful scattered throughout the world (cf. LG 13). He does this through mediation leading to the participation of all in the priesthood of Christ (cf. PO 2), guarding them from error (cf. LG 12) and empowering them "to undertake a variety of works and functions aimed at the renewal and further useful expansion of the Church" (LG 12).[7]

The love that comes from the Holy Spirit is the guarantee of unity while preserving diversity. Neither uniformism, nor the massification of the ecclesial community, nor individualism as a "sublimated form of egoistic culture" come from Him. It is necessary to be reasonable and theologically precise so that the Church's charism of love does not nullify the structures that sustain the Church's unity.

> There is no measure that can be used to examine to what extent unity in the Church is due to unitary structures and the centralisation of authority, and to what extent the Holy Spirit also uses these structures which, as we know from history, have been forged by holy and enlightened men endowed with charisms of governance and leadership. It would be wrong to unilaterally assess the existing structures as devoid of the motif of love, or to pay homage to subjectivism, which leads to decoupling. The so-called 'enthusiasts', who did not recognise the mediation of the Church, tended to become a source of division and the absolutisation of their beliefs as inspired.[8]

The past teaches that unity based solely on legal compulsion produces negative effects in the Church, and the lack of appreciation for charisms and talents is due to a lack of love for the Holy Spirit – the generous giver of gifts. On the other hand,

---

of the mystery of Christian initiation involves a 'laying on of hands' ('chrismation' in this respect is another form of the same thing). The East has kept these two aspects (baptism – confirmation) not only inseparably linked with one another but also with what follows, namely *the eucharist.* The theological significance of this lies in the fact that *it reveals the nature of baptism and confirmation as being essentially an ordination*, while it helps us understand better what *ordination itself* means. As we can see already in Hippolytus' *Apostolic Tradition*, the immediate and inevitable result of baptism and confirmation was that the newly baptised would *take his particular 'place' in the eucharistic assembly*, i. e. *that he would become a layman.* That this implies ordination is clear from the fact that the baptised person does not simply become a 'Christian', as we tend to think, but he becomes a *member of a particular 'ordo'* in the eucharistic community. Once this is forgotten, it is easy to speak of the laity as 'non-ordained' and thus arrive at the possibility – witnessed to by the history of the Church in a dramatic way – of either making the layman an unnecessary element in the eucharistic community (hence the 'private mass' and the entire issue of clericalism) or of making him the basis of all 'orders', as if he were not himself a specifically defined order but a generic source or principle (hence the prevailing view of 'the priesthood of all believers' in all its variations)" (Zizioulas, *Being as Communion*, 217–8).

7 Cf. Czaja, *Credo in Spiritum Vivificantem*, 206–9.

8 Guzowski, *Duch Dialogujący*, 225.

attention to the purity of doctrine, uniformity of teaching and encouragement of obedience for the advancement of the kingdom of God have always borne fruit in the form of spiritual revival. Love for God, the Church and people always enables the Holy Spirit to work effectively in people and to invigorate ecclesial structures.[9]

The Church is a living organism made up of living persons united in love with their Head. Love for the Holy Spirit should precede love for people so that the Holy Spirit can shape it. When love is lacking, charisms are wasted, and a person endowed with charisms but acting to the detriment of unity misappropriates the will of the Giver Himself, who gives the gifts for the building of the Church.

The source and basis of the unity of the faithful is the same Spirit residing in Christ and Christians. *Lumen gentium* speaks of the Spirit given by Christ, one and the same in the Head and members, who animates, unites and moves the whole Body. In connection with his pneumatological-ecclesiological formula of the one Person in many persons (the Holy Spirit in Christ and Christians), H. Mühlen cites the biblical statement: "All these are activated by one and the same Spirit, who allots to each one individually just as the Spirit chooses" (1 Cor 12:11).[10] In interpreting his thesis, he refers to the biblical-patristic idea of anointing: Jesus, anointed with the Holy Spirit at the moment of the Incarnation, in the Easter events imparts His Spirit, who in turn imparts Himself. This anointing took place on the day of Pentecost and continues to be realised in history until the second coming of Christ. We can therefore speak of the Church as a continuation of the anointing and an extension of Pentecost. In baptism, people receive a share in the anointing and form a community of the anointed with the Holy Spirit – sharing in Christ's fullness of the Spirit or Christ's experience of the Spirit. This participation signifies a community of people who are adopted in Christ, endowed with Christ's grace and predisposed to carry out His mission through the presence of the Holy Spirit in them. The identity of the Holy Spirit in all of them (in the historical Jesus, in the glorified Lord and in the members of His Body) – despite their diversity and various endowments – "extends" Christ to the "great self" of the Church and constitutes the basis of unity (including the unity of charisms) as well as universal equality and fraternity.[11]

Mühlen notes that the Spirit of Christ binds us to Christ in a different way than Christ to us. Christ, as the Head of the ecclesial community, "extending" into His Body, relates to us personally through the sending of His Spirit. The hypostatic function of the Spirit in this case reveals its "proceeding" character since He, who is present a priori as the Fullness present in Christ, "proceeds" from the Head and is

9 Guzowski, *Duch Dialogujący*, 224–6.

10 Cf. Mühlen, *Una Mystica Persona*, 433. Czaja points out that the conciliar document does not cite this text.

11 Cf. Czaja, *Credo in Spiritum Vivificantem*, 209–11.

shared by all the members of the Body. On the other hand, in the realisation of the Church as the Bride of Christ, the same Spirit puts us vis-à-vis Christ in a bridal relationship – His salvific mediation this time shows a contradictory feature since, by uniting many persons into a community of "We", He puts it vis-à-vis Christ the Bridegroom. The Spirit unites Christians to Christ and to one another because He is the "treasury of all grace" that cannot be received apart from Him. In this way, the Holy Spirit realises the communion of the faithful as the same One in all of them, but also as One and the same Giver of their endowment.[12]

The pneumatological element belongs to the institutional structure of the Church since through baptism all its members are especially endowed with the Holy Spirit – they receive His anointing (cf. 1 John 2:20,27), which realises the fundamental and indestructible equality of all members of the Church.[13] This refers not only to the identity of the Spirit, but also to the specificity of His personal being as the personification of Divine communion and love. The Church constitutes the fraternal community of the new people of God, which is realised in the Eucharistic union of love, i. e. in the eating of the Body of the Lord, and is closely connected with the power of the Holy Spirit's action. It brings together those who share in the Spirit. This community is the place of a shared experience of the Spirit's working in the world and is the necessary condition for the existence of this community. It involves His paradoxical personhood, His being communion and love itself. By the power of the inner dynamism of His being in the manner of communion, the Holy Spirit enables and mediates communication and communion between believers. In Him it is impossible to live apart from dialogue and communion, and furthermore, abiding in Him excludes being solely for oneself. Since the Holy Spirit is present and acts in the manner of unifying love, the community of believers realises in Him its being "for" – abiding in pro-existence and unity for the world.[14] Precisely because the Holy Spirit is given to the Church, the fraternity of believers in Christ constitutes the basic structure of the Church. Jesus Christ is the principle and foundation of this fraternity, while it is realised in the Spirit. W. Kasper emphasises the communional character of the personhood of the Spirit, "which is the love of God in Person and

12 Cf. Czaja, *Credo in Spiritum Vivificantem*, 211.

13 LG 32; CCL 208. Cf. Beinert, "Der Heilige Geist und die Strukturen. Die Spannung von Amt und Charisma in der Kirche," in *Wo der Geist des Herrn wirkt, da ist Freiheit*, ed. Günter Koch and Josef Pretscher (Würzburg: Echter, 1997), 115. Cf. also Kehl, *Die Kirche*, 106–7; Schneider, "Die dogmatische Begründung der Ekklesiologie nach dem Zweiten Vatikanischen Konzil," in *Kirche. Ursprung und Gegenwart*, ed. Heinz Althaus (Freiburg im Breisgau: Herder, 1984), 90.

14 Cf. Ratzinger, "Der Heilige Geist als Communio," 225–6, 232–3.

the eternal communion of the Father and the Son, it is also the principle and source of the unity of the Church in faith and love".[15]

According to LG 12, the filling of the whole Church and of each believer with the Holy Spirit is concretised in two ways – the Holy Spirit brings the "sense of faith" (*sensus fidelium*) and grants charisms. He is the principle of the unity of the *communio fidelium* on both the diachronic (the development of the tradition and safeguarding the truthfulness of the faith) and the synchronic plane (the distribution of gifts and cohesiveness of the faith). According to LG 25, "on account of the activity of that same Holy Spirit […] the whole flock of Christ is preserved and progresses in unity of faith". This text stems from the doctrine of the anointing of the faithful with the fullness of the Spirit and sees in His indwelling in them all the ultimate source of their conformity in faith.[16] According to the vision of the Church as a communicative unity of believers, consent in faith can be realised in the dialectic of the previously given and constantly developing social space of faith, guaranteed by the Holy Spirit. This consent must grow out of a free agreement of all, matured in dialogue, which makes it possible to refer unambiguously to the truth of God revealed in Jesus Christ. This consent is not the fruit of our will to reach a communicative consensus but stems from a readiness to open up to the God-given capacity to communicate, it stems from the acceptance of God's liberating gift for communication. In this, the unifying power of the Holy Spirit is revealed, who enables the whole people of God to share in the prophetic office of Jesus Christ and guards its fundamental identity of faith.[17]

The Holy Spirit helps the Church to continually identify with the original message of the Gospel and the specificity of the community of Jesus Christ, and in doing so He uses the institutionalised structures of the Church. This has been the case

15 Kasper, *"Der Geist macht lebendig." Theologische Meditationen über den Heiligen Geist*, (Freiburg: Informationszentrum Berufe der Kirche, 1982), 15. Cf. Czaja, *Credo in Spiritum Vivificantem*, 212–3.

16 Cf. Czaja, *Credo in Spiritum Vivificantem*, 213. "The anointing with the Holy Spirit is manifested in the *sensus fidei* of the faithful. 'In all the baptised, from the first to the last, the sanctifying power of the Spirit is at work, impelling them to evangelise. God's people are made holy by this anointing which makes them *infallible 'in credendo'*. This means that when they believe, they do not err, even if they do not find the words to express their faith. The Spirit leads them in the truth and draws them to salvation'. Part of the mystery of His love for people is that God endows *the faithful with a sense of faith – sensus fidei* – which helps them to discern what truly comes from God. The presence of the Spirit provides Christians with a kind of union with the reality of God and wisdom that enables them to grasp this reality intuitively, even if they do not have the tools to express it precisely. This characteristic of the faithful is expressed in *sentire cum Ecclesia*: to feel and perceive in harmony with the Church. This is required not only of theologians but of all the faithful; it unites all members of the People of God in their pilgrimage" (Międzynarodowa Komisja Teologiczna, *Synodalność w życiu i misji Kościoła*, 56).

17 Cf. Kehl, *Die Kirche*, 148–59.

from the very beginning of the Church. Despite the emergence of enthusiastic and gnostic tendencies, the original Christian community maintained that the Holy Spirit was the Spirit of the historical and crucified Jesus of Nazareth. Therefore, the Spirit does not liberate believers from history, but liberates by guiding people on the path of the crucified love of Jesus. From the very beginning, the rediscovery of Christian identity is accomplished through the institutional structures of the Church in the ever-changing circumstances of human history. The identifying power of the Holy Spirit is revealed precisely in the fact that the Church fearlessly faces constantly new historical situations with the message of salvation and, in the process, finds each time the identity of its common faith.[18]

Without the Holy Spirit, we would be in constant danger of moulding the image of God in our own likeness. Contrary to this, the Spirit realizes the *communio fidelium* as the principle of the common faith – He initiates our response to God's call, allows us to experience His love and rejoice in it, and at the same time makes present and communicates the essence of the faith.[19] The Church's identity of faith is dynamic, and the Holy Spirit has a critical function in the process of its realisation through the signs of the times and their correct interpretation[20]. He is the subject of ecclesial renewal and, by the power of the Gospel, keeps the Church constantly young and allows its members to live and act.[21]

The Holy Spirit also unites the communion of the faithful by realising the plurality and complementarity, endowing the faithful with the riches of His gifts, "allotting to each one individually just as the Spirit chooses" (1 Cor 12:11) – especially the charisms making people "fit and ready to undertake the various tasks and offices which contribute toward the renewal and building up of the Church" (LG 12). Charisms, together with the Word of God, the sacraments and the ecclesiastical office, form an indissoluble whole. Charisms are special gifts of the Holy Spirit, which He gives to specific persons for the benefit of all, while at the same time He manifests Himself through them. Their multiplicity does not threaten the unity of the *communio fidelium* – and not just because they come from a single source. Their purpose is to build a communion, and their diversity, which expresses the richness of the Spirit, also signifies for the community a complementarity of gifts

---

18 Cf. Kehl, "Kirche als Institution," 191–2.

19 Cf. Kasper, *"Der Geist macht lebendig,"* 11–2, 42.

20 Cf. Figura, "Duch Święty a Kościół," *Communio. Międzynarodowy Przegląd Teologiczny* 18/2 (1998), 94.

21 Cf. Ganoczy, "Kirche im Prozeß der pneumatischen Erneuerung," in *Glaube im Prozeß. Christsein nach dem II Vaticanum*, ed. Elmar Klinger and Wittstadt (Freiburg im Breisgau: Herder, 1984), 198–9.

that develops and enriches the unity of the faithful. They serve the good of the community and are given in such a way that all may benefit from them.[22]

The immediacy of the experience of the Holy Spirit and His gifts, however, does not give believers a basis for forming a separate Church or even considering themselves as distinct from those already in existence. This statement also applies to the Charismatic Renewal movement. Those belonging to this movement often simply believe that the Church is where the experience of the presence of the Holy Spirit is, that the unity of Christians can be realised without the unity of Churches – as if on a different plane. Spiritual unity is thus separated from visible unity, and consequently, the pneumatological dimension gains a certain autonomy at the expense of the Christological dimension. The Church becomes rather a fact of spiritual internalisation and a direct experience of the Spirit. This, however, runs the risk of being reduced to the individual experience of even a larger number of persons, but without considering the requirements of the theology of the people of God as a whole. There is something of real unity in this, achieved independently of or rather across confessional divisions, which can be of great importance for the Christian reunion.[23] Internalisation and the direct experience of spiritual reality should not

---

22 Cf. Czaja, *Credo in Spiritum Vivificantem*, 216–7.

23 Zizioulas emphasises how crucial the proper synthesis between the Christological and pneumatological dimensions of the Church is here. Perhaps one can say that the institutional elements of the Church (e. g. sacraments and ministry) are closely related to Christology, but if one does not make pneumatology an integral part of Christology, this inevitably leads to a distinction between "institution" and "charismaticism". This has in fact been the case, especially in the West, where even in our time the dimensions of "ordination" or "institutionality" are contrasted with the "charismatic" dimension, and Pentecostalism seems to flourish precisely by exploiting this opposition. Cf. Zizioulas, *The One and the Many*, 82. Zizioulas adds: "The institutional becomes, in the Spirit, charismatic and the charismatic institutional: *'Ubi Ecclesia ibi et Spiritus Dei, et ubi Spiritus Dei, illie Ecclesia'*. The Spirit blows where He wills (John 3:8), but we know that He wills to blow in the direction of Christ (John 16:14). At the same time, He is the Spirit of communion, and wherever He blows, He does not create good individual Christians but a community (cf. Acts 2). All this suggests that the movements of the Spirit cannot be predicted, but their ultimate direction can. Extraordinary ministries are not only possible but necessary, yet as Paul says (1 Cor 14:3-26) they should be part of the body. This means that all such extraordinary ministries (wrongly called 'charismatic' as if the ordinary ones were not) should not be discouraged by the Church. Nevertheless, they must all be integral parts of the body, and it is significant that in the apostolic communities all these gifts, like prophesy, glossolalia, etc., were expressed during the eucharistic gatherings (1 Cor 10-14). But the Spirit conditions the ordinary ministries, too, in exactly the same way. The mystery of the Spirit is one of personalization and this means that in dividing the Church into 'orders', He renders a relational entity in which every member is charismatic precisely because he is a member, i. e., related to the others (in 1 Cor 12, Church membership equals charisma), and this without confusion of ministries (1 Cor 12:29). This is a paradox, and the only way we can express it is, it seems to us, by calling the ministry a *specificity* of *relationship* within the body" (Zizioulas, *The One and the Many*, 82–3).

be underestimated; hence, the charismatic movement has the opportunity to contribute to finding such a balance, should become a source of revival and lead to reunion and reconciliation. The charismatic awareness of the manifold gifts of the Holy Spirit (see Rom 12:6; 1 Cor 12:4-11,28-31) should foster mutual enrichment through a lively exchange of spiritual values. This will often require a clarification of one's own way of understanding and living the charisms, while awareness of the presence of the Holy Spirit is one of the factors that can transform the face of the whole Church.[24]

However, the institution is inescapable not only because it represents an ordinance from Christ, but because it is at the same time a charismatic requirement of the communion created by the Spirit. Because it is charismatic, the institution (ministry, sacrament, Scriptures etc.) is not intended to create objectified security – it constantly depends on the Holy Spirit and exists only epicletically. Thus, although it is based on a particular form, it is never that form itself and cannot be separated from the charismatic event of communion. The institution cannot exist apart from the community; it is clothed with prayer, that is, with the request that what is given in it be given as if it did not exist at all – this is what a proper Christological-pneumatological synthesis requires. The purpose of institutions is not to create objective authorities for security and obedience, but to provide the means for personal and free life in communion. One must free oneself from the idea of freedom as a choice and understand it as a movement towards communion. The Spirit gives freedom – but the freedom of God Himself, which does not consist in choosing between different possibilities, and certainly not between good and evil, as the freedom of the fallen existence does. It involves the liberation from personhood and individualism that the Spirit grants in the Church, and this makes Him once again the Spirit of freedom and the Creator of communion. The freedom of the Spirit means that the structure of the Church is not an objectified, imposed thing, but the fulfilment of the personality of each believer. As in baptism or confirmation, each person becomes the whole Christ, and in the Eucharist each person receiving it is transformed into the whole Body of Christ; in the same Spirit, the very structure of the Church becomes the existential structure of each person.[25]

The divine Spirit wants to give Himself and, through His gifts, unites all into the "Body of Christ", a communion in which individual endowment serves the benefit of all. The Spirit, which is the source of diversity and plurality in the Church, is revealed in the variety of charisms, in which the fullness of being given by the Spirit for the building of the community can be experienced in different ways. The integrating power of the Holy Spirit is revealed in the mutual openness of

---

24 Cf. Hryniewicz, *Nasza Pascha z Chrystusem*, 98–9.

25 Cf. Zizioulas, *The One and the Many*, 84–5.

the members of the Mystical Body to one another, when He guards the personal differentiation between Christ and Christians and between individual Christians and gives it an appropriate profile. Through such integration, the Church maintains its specific character as an open system – it achieves its unity not through perfect organisation or integralism, but because, as a gift of the Holy Spirit, it allows itself to be continually endowed.[26]

Through the distribution of charisms, the Holy Spirit realises the communion of the mutual complementarity of the faithful – being at the same time the principle of plurality and unity. He is not the principle of anarchic formlessness, but of the creative power of God. His work is unity, which is realised not by abolishing plurality but by assembling plurality into an all-embracing communion. The union of peoples in a universal faith, in a Church speaking all languages, understanding and embracing in love all languages and overcoming the dispersion of the Tower of Babel, has been revealed at Pentecost (AG 4). The Holy Spirit is the principle of synchronic and diachronic plurality, the principle of continuous renewal stimulating the Church to find new forms and to walk new paths. Through Him "the living voice of the Gospel resounds in the Church and through the Church in the world" (DV 8).

For centuries the community of the faithful abides securely in Christ's truth thanks to the hermeneutical function of the Holy Spirit and His special freedom – He "blows where He wills". He is the principle of the ecclesial unity of communion, plurality, diversity and newness, and the catholic principle of the Church. The unity realised by the Holy Spirit does not remove the intrinsic value of individuals, for it is not a unity devoid of all differences, but a voluntary human response to the work of Jesus Christ. Such a unifying action also protects the Church from historical or institutional ossification. Through the dissemination of the event of Christ, the Holy Spirit makes and preserves the Church as catholic, and this catholicity also serves Him in revealing the fullness of Christ's grace, riches and gifts. This kind of the Spirit's action is essential to the existence of Christians and of the whole Church: He is the principle of the union – and at the same time He gives birth to plurality, He is the principle of diverse abilities and vocations for all – and at the same time He is the source of direct relations to God. The perfect Christian, however, is not a cloned Christ – the Holy Spirit prevents such "cloning" and creates unity in the plurality of forms and abilities.[27]

The plurality brought about by the Spirit of Christ does not lead to divisions or splits, but forms one living organism of the Body of Christ. The division of the Church into denominations is a consequence of sin. But the Holy Spirit can

---

26 Cf. Kehl, "Kirche als Institution," 194.

27 Cf. Greshake, *Wierzę w Boga Trójjedynego*, 80–81; Czaja, *Credo in Spiritum Vivificantem*, 219–20.

cause salvific realities to appear everywhere; in Him the supra-denominational unity of all the faithful is realised. Being a community of those who "have the Spirit of Christ" (LG 14), the Church appears as an institution, a sacrament and a place of special action of that Spirit who desires and causes (sustains) unity even in externally divided Churches. His action is the source of the dynamic that directs Christians towards visible unity.[28] In *Ut unum sint*, John Paul II pointed out that the Spirit realises the fraternity and communion of the faithful – including the faithful of Churches and Communities that are not in full communion with the Catholic Church.[29] One can thus speak of the universal presence and unity of the saints across denominational boundaries as a consequence of the transcendent action of the sanctifying power of the Holy Spirit: "Where there is a sincere desire to follow Christ, the Spirit is often able to pour out his grace in extraordinary ways" (UUS 84). He creates an inner, spiritual space for the realisation of holiness above any divisions; as the "conscience of unity" of the Church, He makes Christians into a community of faith and life – a fraternal communion.[30]

The Holy Spirit dwells in the faithful and perfects their personality – He grants all the same dignity and commits all to a common mission. This is why all Christians – endowed with the same Spirit – are "clergy". He forms a communion of freedom, equality and fraternity in faith through anointing by Him (the specificity of the ecclesial office lies only in the uniqueness of the pastoral ministry). All are called to participate in the life, liturgy and mission of this communion animated by the Holy Spirit – He is the source of the unity realised in the communicative process of reception and transmission.[31] In his pneumatological interpretation of the subjectivity of the Church and of all the faithful, M. Kehl believes that the post-Easter genesis of the Church's institutionalisation shows that the gathering of the "true" Israel is linked to the Pentecostal experience of the disciples – God pours out the Spirit of Christ upon them and through Him the Church is constituted as a community in faith. The Holy Spirit, as a prior Gift, is the enabling principle of this ecclesial communion – its source are not socially objectified signs of faith.

28 Cf. Ulrich Willers, "Kościół jako instytucja Ducha Świętego. Tajemnica, którą żyjemy," *Communio. Międzynarodowy Przegląd Teologiczny* 9/2 (1989), 27–43. "Of course, it is not difficult to see that Willers' opinion reflects the conciliar interpretation of the grounds or reasons for the universal union of all Christians (cf. LG 15). Pottmeyer refers to the conciliar texts directly and in his commentary explains: 'The Spirit is the principle that binds the plurality of divided Christians. There even arises among them 'a true bond in the Holy Spirit, for he by his graces and gifts among them also works by his sanctifying power' (LG15)'. Those who 'possess' Him realise a communion that anticipates the institutional union of the Churches, as is revealed in certain charismatic groups, religious communities or in Taizé" (Czaja, *Credo in Spiritum Vivificantem*, 221).

29 Cf. UUS 42.

30 Cf. Czaja, *Credo in Spiritum Vivificantem*, 221–2.

31 Cf. Czaja, *Credo in Spiritum Vivificantem*, 222–4.

The participation in the love of the Father and the Son imparted by the Holy Spirit unites the gifted from the outset and thus the Church can come into being in its relative autonomy from the individual. However, the Holy Spirit does not destroy the individual's subjectivity, but guards and guarantees it. His "liberating" power frees one from coercion and empowers one to be responsible – not only to be the object of pastoral care, but also to actively participate in all forms of Church life.[32]

More recent accounts of the pneumatological interpretation of the subjectivity of the Church and in the Church point to the Holy Spirit as the Life-Giver of the *communio fidelium* in the sense of the principle of the subjective unity of the "whole Christ" and in the sense of the principle of the unity, diversity and freedom of the community of subjects.[33] According to Miroslav Volf, the social dimension of salvation can only be explained pneumatologically. The resurrected Christ lives in Christians through the Holy Spirit (cf. Rom 8:10-11) and Christians live through Him in Christ (cf. 1 Cor 12:12-14). Upon raising objections to the thesis of the collective personality of the Church, Volf suggests looking at the Church as a community of interpenetrating subjects, of which the trinitarian communion is the prototype. The Holy Spirit realises in the Church the phenomenon of mutual personal being in Him – being present in Christians, He opens them to Himself.[34] Therefore, it is necessary to see in the Church a polycentric community and a polycentric participation of all the faithful in its life, rooted in Christian vocation and charisms. Christians receive from the Holy Spirit the disposition and abilities for their mission. Only the forms of its realisation change, just as the people called to it and the situations in which they live change. The single task in the Church and in the world has its origin in the Christian vocation, and the type of ministry depends on the Spirit's gift received at a particular time.[35] The need for the salvific commitment of all the faithful arises from the fact that although all possess some charisms, no one possesses them all. Therefore, the Christian life should be characterised by reciprocity, which should also apply to official charisms. For the faithful endowed

32 Cf. Kehl, "Kirche als Institution," 167–8, 190–1, 195–6; Kehl, *Die Kirche*, 400–2. A different conception of the subjectivity of the Church and in a different context was presented by H. Mühlen. Cf. Czaja, *Credo in Spiritum Vivificantem*, 225–7: "both the subjectivity of the Church as a whole (the personal unity of *Totus Christus*) and the subjectivity within the Church involving all the faithful have their origin in the Holy Spirit. On the one hand, the Spirit of Christ does not destroy the personalities of the individual faithful, but develops them, is the life-giving source of the realisation of Christ's threefold mission to the extent of the bestowal of charismatic grace, and at the same time brings each of them into such a close personal relationship with Christ that it signifies living the life of Christ, the unique mutual abiding of Christ and Christians in each other precisely in the Spirit, i. e. the pneumatological inclusion in Christ" (Czaja, *Credo in Spiritum Vivificantem*, 227).

33 Cf. Czaja, *Credo in Spiritum Vivificantem*, 229–30.

34 Cf. Volf, *Trinität und Gemeinschaft*, 179–80.

35 Cf. Volf, *Trinität und Gemeinschaft*, 215–7.

with an office do not act by virtue of that office, but in the act of exercising their ministry, and therefore their action is not fundamentally different from that of any other member of the Church. However, this does not mean that the polarity between the ministry *in persona Christi* and the community is eliminated, though it is decentralised.[36]

One cannot completely agree with all of Volf's theses, especially with his undermining of the sense of speaking of a single subjective being of the Church. It is perhaps more difficult to see this subjective being within the framework of interpreting the Church as communion, but the conciliar principle of using multiple images and metaphors applies here, which only together can express the truth about the Church.[37]

> The Church, considered from the perspective of Christ, is *Christological* because it is, in the biblical sense of the word, the Bride of Christ, His beloved *vis-à-vis* reflecting His reality in itself; on the other hand, because of the Spirit's unifying work, it is *pneumatological* and is hence the Body of Christ.[38]

All in this Body "are bound together as closely as the members of one body are bound together by their vital functions, and thus – together with Christ as the Head and the Holy Spirit as the Soul – they form one Body to the glory of God the Father".[39] Failure to respect this truth causes the communion of its members to disintegrate into individuals, each of whom invokes the Spirit they have received. Volf's proposal, therefore, must be viewed in the light of the question of the possibility of drawing conclusions by analogy from the perichoretic model of the unity of the Divine Persons. Undoubtedly, the Holy Trinity is the source and prototype of the Church, which is supposed to be the reflection of the trinitarian communion, but it must be remembered that the shape and structure of the Church cannot be presented as a simple schematic representation of the Divine communion. It must be stressed, however, that certain elements of Volf's concept are compatible with the attempts at a pneumatological interpretation of the subjectivity of the faithful and clearly demonstrate that the Church lives by the dynamic of the Holy Spirit, who distributes the gifts to each one as He chooses (1 Cor 12:11) and determines the role and place of each believer. It is He who animates and shapes ecclesial structures, which in turn reveal their pneumatological character.[40]

---

36 Cf. Volf, *Trinität und Gemeinschaft*, 221–2.

37 This is also the central thesis of de Salis' work: *Kościół wcielony w historii*.

38 Greshake, *Wierzę w Boga Trójjedynego*, 80.

39 Greshake, *Wierzę w Boga Trójjedynego*, 57.

40 Cf. Czaja, *Credo in Spiritum Vivificantem*, 232–5.

4.2 The Pneumatological Dimensions of the Communion of Particular Churches

Among the many forms of the Church's presence, there are particular Churches. The Church is not only the Body made up of the Head and many members, but also the "Body of the Churches" (LG 23) and thus – by analogy – it is possible to apply the concept of communion to the unity existing between the particular Churches and to conceive of the Church as *communio ecclesiarum*, a union of a mysterious nature incomparable to other unions in human society. Zizioulas writes that the Holy Spirit particularises the one Body of Christ, making each of the local Churches the full and "catholic" Church.[41] John Paul II spoke of the relationship of interpenetration between the universal Church and the particular Churches – and it is not difficult to see in this a reference to the concept of perichoresis. It recognises the link between the structure of ecclesial communion and the specificity of the trinitarian communion, characteristic of the ecclesiology of communion, which also has a great ecumenical significance.[42] In the interpretation of the "perichoresis" of the universal Church and the particular Churches, German theology rather excludes the possibility of some kind of pre-eminence of the universal Church in relation to the local Churches. At the same time, the communion of the Churches is pneumatologically grounded.[43]

The exception here is J. Ratzinger, who is recognised as the author and promoter of the thought on the ontic and temporal pre-eminence of the universal Church in relation to the particular Churches, although he does not question the interdependence of these Churches. A. Czaja notes that Ratzinger's thesis is primarily concerned with the genesis rather than the working of the communion of Churches. Ratzinger links the internal temporal origin of the Church to the power and action of the Holy Spirit. The community gathered at Pentecost was not the local Church of Jerusalem, but the universal Church. From the totality of his interpretation of *communio ecclesiarum*, it is quite clear that the Holy Spirit is the principle of the catholicity of the Church, which as one is realised in the many diverse local

41 "Whenever Pneumatology is weak or dependent in relation to Christology (a sort of 'Filioquism' in ecclesiology), there is bound to be a submission of the local Church to a universal Church structure. The '*koinonia* of the Holy Spirit' suffers in this case. Equally, if the local Church is not related to the one Church of God in the world, this is a sign of submission of Christology to Pneumatology (a sort of 'Spirituquism' in Triadology as well as in ecclesiology). If we attach to Christology and Pneumatology an equal importance, we are bound to attribute full catholicity to each local Church (the *totus Christus*) and, at the same time, seek ways of safeguarding the oneness of the Church on the universal level" (Zizioulas, *The One and the Many*, 55).

42 Cf. Czaja, *Credo in Spiritum Vivificantem*, 235–8.

43 Cf. Czaja, *Credo in Spiritum Vivificantem*, 238–42.

Churches, which in turn derive their ecclesiality from the Church permeating the whole of history.[44]

H. Mühlen, in line with *Lumen gentium*, argues that the Church of Christ "subsists in the Catholic Church", but that its elements can also materialise outside its boundaries. Although only the Catholic Church constitutes the most concrete form of the existence of the one Church of Christ, it cannot be ruled out that the separated Churches are also forms of its existence, which involves the action of the Holy Spirit in them, however, the efficacy of the Eucharist on which the communion of the Churches depends, relies upon Him. Mühlen clearly gives a pneumatological orientation to Eucharistic ecclesiology and develops the idea of the a priori unity of the one Church in reference to Paul's idea of the Church as the "Fullness" of Christ – the Church is such "Fullness" manifesting the "fullness of Christ" through the Spirit, who is the power that "expands" Christ's "Original Self" into the "Great Self" of the Church.[45] The condition for the development of the a priori unity of the Church in history is the entrance of the supra-historical Spirit, which is linked to the sending of Him into human hearts. This exhibits a structure similar to that of the Incarnation of the Son (the Son exists in two natures – the Spirit in many persons or in particular Churches) and reflects the divine "order" of diversified unity in the created world. At the same time – by analogy to its mediating function in unifying the differing modes of existence of the one Divine nature – through its manifold gifts and functions it differentiates the particular Churches within the universal Church, animating and shaping its structure. The Spirit is the principle of the distinctiveness of the particular Churches, of their relative autonomy; His action does not destroy unity and, in the endowed Churches, is the source and basis of catholicity. The Holy Spirit Himself realises the differentiation of ecclesial wholeness in them – this wholeness is present in them (the whole Spirit of Christ), although they do not represent it completely, but only in the multiplicity of the various elements.[46] In this way, Mühlen offers a qualitative understanding of catholicity and points to the dynamic character of the catholic unity of the Church. The pursuit of it can be accomplished in openness to the Holy Spirit, in embracing that a priori unity of the one Church of Christ, which is precisely what the Spirit realises by giving Himself in the word, the sacraments and the apostolic office. In this way, he provides access to the "Fullness" of Christ personified in Himself and communicates the historical heritage of the Church, which is Jesus Himself. In doing so, the Spirit is not only the power by which Jesus performs His salvific work, but as Person He is also the inseparable fullness of all that is unfolding in the

44 Cf. Czaja, *Credo in Spiritum Vivificantem*, 242–7.

45 Cf. Mühlen, *Una Mystica Persona*, 156–69.

46 Cf. Mühlen, "Der eine Geist und die vielen Kirchen nach den Aussagen des Vaticanum II," *Theologie und Glaube* 55 (1965) 354–5.

various traditions.[47] There can thus be the history of word, office and sacrament in the Church because the Spirit of Christ has its own history in the ecclesial-human tradition and makes it possible. And because He does not merge with this history and, at the same time, is not separated from it, He enters truly into human freedom and places Himself in human hands. This is why human freedom is a constitutive and intrinsic moment in the history of the Holy Spirit, and this forms the basis of the incomprehensible mystery that the one and whole Spirit can be present in separate Churches and ecclesial communities. With the entirety of His self, He realises the *communio ecclesiarum* and is, as it were, torn apart by human sin causing schism.

> And seeking in this perspective an understanding of the identity of the one Spirit of Christ in the many Churches, in the twofold sense of an incomprehensible mystery: as the revealed mystery of faith and, at the same time, as the mystery of human guilt recognised in the light of this revelation, the reference to the 'fullness' entrusted only to the Roman Church will be very cautious, and then this Church will openly acknowledge the 'wholeness' of the separated Churches realised by the Spirit. And if the wholeness of the one Church of Christ is realised in them and revealed in a 'broken' way, then the Roman Church will also confess the same about itself. [...] the difference between the separated Churches will not be determined first by the question of how many elements (*vestigia Ecclesiae*) have been preserved, but by the question of how far the one and whole Spirit of Christ is actually historically manifested in them.[48]

In this way, within the horizon of understanding the trinitarian communion as an intrapersonal internal existence in the Spirit, Mühlen offers a distinctly pneumatological interpretation of the catholic unity of the *communio ecclesiarum*. He bases this on the intra-trinitarian functions of the Holy Spirit – these of binding and differentiating – who, as the embodiment of the "fullness" of Christ, realises the a priori unity of the Church and, by providing a share in it through the giving of Himself, makes it possible to draw on the ecclesiality of the Church which permeates history and, through His entry into time, shapes the unity and catholicity of the individual particular Churches.[49]

According to W. Kasper, the Church exists in and is built on many local Churches. There is thus mutual conditionality without any prior form. The "ecclesial elements" scattered in the Churches are gifts or fruits of the Holy Spirit in whom the real (albeit incomplete) communion of the Christian Churches continues. The Church and its

---

47 Cf. Mühlen, *Una Mystica Persona*, 533.

48 Mühlen, "Der eine Geist und die vielen Kirchen nach der Aussagen des Vaticanum II," 359 (quoted by Czaja, *Credo in Spiritum Vivificantem*, 250).

49 Cf. Czaja, *Credo in Spiritum Vivificantem*, 247–51.

offices must first be understood pneumatologically as realities that are historically formed in this Spirit and realised anew in charismatic ways.[50] The Spirit is the principle of diversity, distinctiveness and richness in the Church as the dispenser of charisms, offices and ministries.[51]

The role of the Holy Spirit as the Life-Giver of the communion of the particular Churches can be demonstrated in accordance with the approach of G. Greshake and M. Kehl, who analyse the communion of the Churches from the perspective of the trinitarian communion. The Church, as the image of the Holy Trinity, is supposed to realise the communion of mutual communication and embody it in its structure, so that its unity must be in harmony with the plurality and the Christological dimension with the pneumatological dimension. For both, the pneumatological dimension is a necessary condition for a balanced interpretation of the communion of the Churches, in which there is room for the universal Church and the plurality, diversity and distinctiveness of the particular Churches, without the need for mutual subordination.[52] Greshake recognises that the fundamental cause of the centralist and pyramidal concept of the Church and the post-conciliar subordination of the particular Churches to the universal Church was the deficit of the pneumatological dimension. It is therefore necessary, without forgetting the Christological perspective, to discover the role and specific activity of the Holy Spirit in the life of the Church and to give Him a greater place in it. He is creatively active in the faithful and in local communities and is the guarantee that unity is realised in the plurality of the most diverse forms and that diversity creates unity in mutual exchanges.[53] Kehl emphasises the unifying and differentiating activity of the Holy Spirit, through which the Church is a community of Churches ensuring the fullness of unity in diverse plurality.[54]

Another way to capture the interpenetration of the universal Church and the particular Churches can be seen in B. Stubenrauch's proposed reinterpretation of the trinitarian communion on the basis of the simultaneity of subjectivity and relationality of human being, which must never be separated because they cannot be reduced to one another – subjectivity expresses itself in a relation which does

---

50 Cf. Kasper, "Dienst an der Einheit und Freiheit der Kirche," in *Wozu noch einen Papst? Vier Plödoyers für das Petrusamt*, ed. Heinz-Joachim Fischer (Köln: Communio, 1993), 53.

51 Cf. Czaja, *Credo in Spiritum Vivificantem*, 251–4. Czaja notes that Kasper sees the Holy Spirit as the Life-Giver of the Catholic communion of Churches, but his insights are rather general. Instead, he points to a greater development of the pneumatological dimension of the Church by Zizioulas, "Die pneumatologische Dimension der Kirche," *Internationale katholische Zeitschrift Communio* 2 (1973), 138–42.

52 Cf. Czaja, *Credo in Spiritum Vivificantem*, 254–8.

53 Cf. Greshake, *Wierzę w Boga Trójjedynego*, 88.

54 Cf. Kehl, *Die Kirche*, 75–6; Czaja, *Credo in Spiritum Vivificantem*, 258–9.

not diminish the fullness of being of the subject.[55] By analogy, one would have to assume that the communion of Churches neither develops in such a way that first there are local Churches, nor in such a way that the one universal Church is realised first. An interpretation that does not allow for any precedence in ecclesial perichoresis would have to be considered as the only correct one. However, such an interpretative possibility was not adopted by Stubenrauch with regard to the communion of the Churches, and thus it can only be regarded as a probable one, deductively derived from his trinitology, based on the assumption that there exist an analogy between the structure of the trinitarian Communion and the ecclesial communion. Czaja believes that Stubenrauch would have probably approved of the pneumatological threads in the interpretation of the *communio ecclesiarum* developed by H. Mühlen.[56]

In the conclusion of his analysis of approaches to the work of the Holy Spirit in the communion of the Churches based on the achievements of German theologians, A. Czaja writes: "The Spirit of Christ undoubtedly deserves to be called the Life-Giver of the catholic unity of the communion of Churches. They [theologians] see in Him the principle of the simultaneous differentiation and unity of the Churches, the source of their identity with the apostolic origin; they see the One who enables them to draw on the ecclesiality of the Church permeating history. He is the source of the mutual interpenetration of unity and plurality, and as such shapes the vitality and dialectic of the ecclesial perichoresis; He constantly animates the dynamism and tension of the mutual interpenetration of the universal Church and the particular Churches. His activity also involves creative action, not only at the birth of the *communio ecclesiarum*; He has constant influence on the shape and structure of the communion of the Churches [...]"[57]. And regarding the ecumenical dimensions of the problem discussed here, he quotes the well-known words of archbishop Alfons Nossol that we all need "Catholic breadth, Evangelical depth and Orthodox dynamism in the sense of the pneumatological dimension".[58]

4.3 The Pneumatological Dimensions of the Hierarchical Communion

The universal community of believers realised as a communion of Churches can only be led by Christ and gathered around Him as its Head. This implies a specific need for the ongoing representation of Christ in the Holy Spirit. This is why Christ

55 Cf. Stubenrauch, *Pneumatologia*, 266.

56 Cf. Czaja, *Credo in Spiritum Vivificantem*, 259–60.

57 Czaja, *Credo in Spiritum Vivificantem*, 261–2.

58 Alfons Nossol, *Ekumenizm jako imperatyw chrześcijańskiego sumienia. Przez dialog i pojednanie ku ekumenicznej jedności* (Opole: Wydział Teologiczny UO, 2001), 158–9.

sent us this Spirit, He lives in Him, works in and among us, He is the perfect Representative of Christ, Christ comes and is constantly present in Him.[59] To the same end, Christ instituted the Twelve as the visible representation of the Apostles capable of acting in His name, endowed them with the special gift of the Holy Spirit and equipped them with the sacred pastoral authority in relation to the people of God (cf. LG 18). In turn, through the Apostles "themselves, [He] made their successors, the bishops, sharers in his consecration and mission. The office of their ministry has been handed down, in a lesser degree indeed, to the priests. Established in the order of the priesthood they can be co-workers of the episcopal order for the proper fulfillment of the apostolic mission entrusted to priests by Christ" (PO 2).[60] In the complementarity of the office and the community of the faithful, a kind of perichoresis of these two realities is realised and the mutual attribution of the common priesthood of the faithful and the hierarchical priesthood, as well as the relational and servile character of the collegially exercised office are outlined[61] (Zizioulas writes of the "perichoresis of ministries"[62]).

The term "hierarchical communion" refers to the community of those exercising the office of priest in the Church, i. e. those who, through ordination, receive from Christ the special gift of the Holy Spirit and the power to act in relation to the Church *in persona Christi*. The identity of the office in the Church can only be described within the framework of a pneumatologically conditioned Christology – it is the Holy Spirit who constitutes the Body of Christ by realising the ministry of Christ as the ministry of the Church. This means, writes Zuzioulas, that

---

59 This is particularly true of the whole tradition and structure of the Church – cf. Zizioulas, *Being as Communion*, 207: "Tradition is not just passed on from one generation to another; it is constantly reenacted and re-received in the Spirit. This will bring out the importance of the Church as a *community* – the community which results from the communion of the Spirit – and of the basic *structure* of this community – the structure which emerges from the vision of the eschatological community as the complex of the specific relations (ministries) in and through which the Spirit constitutes this community." Cf. Zizioulas, *Being as Communion*, 216–7.

60 "If all ministry in the Church is nothing but the ministry of the One 'sent from God', Christ, and is realized here and now by the movement of the Spirit in this communion, this ministry is not to be seen as of human origin but as a gift of the Spirit coming *from God*" (Zizioulas, *The One and the Many*, 182).

61 Zizioulas emphasises that just as Christ (the only Priest) becomes a communion (the Body, the Church) in the Holy Spirit, so is His priesthood realised and shown concretely in the historical existence of the Eucharistic community, in which its head, with it and on its behalf, offers the sacrificial gifts. Cf. Zizioulas, *Being as Communion*, 231.

62 Zizioulas, *The One and the Many*, 54.

> instead of *first* establishing [...] a 'Christ – ministry' scheme and *then* trying to fill it with the action of the Holy Spirit, we have made the Spirit a *constitutive element of the very relationship between Christ and ministry.* [...] This means that there is a fundamental *interdependence between ministry and the concrete community of the Church*, which is realised through the *koinonia* of the Spirit.[63]

Hierarchical communion is realised collegially on two levels – in the universal Church as the hierarchical communion of bishops with the pope[64] and in the local Church as the hierarchical communion of presbyters with the bishop.[65]

63 Zizioulas, *Being as Communion*, 211. Cf. ibid., 211–4. "By being the sole ordainer to the ministry, the bishop becomes *alter Christus* in the double Christological function: he unites the Church in one body, and at the same time he diversifies this unity by distributing the ministries and orders in the Church. Ecclesiologically speaking, it is due to the ministry of the bishop that the local Church acquires its catholicity and fullness as the 'Church of God' in one place. For since he is the εἰκών of the eschatological Christ in his Church, the bishop makes his Church a full image or εἰκών of the eschatological community. Nothing is lacking in this image for man to experience and 'taste' the eternal life that is the Kingdom of God" (Zizioulas, *The One and the Many*, 246).

64 Analysing the question of primacy in the Church from an Orthodox point of view, Zizioulas emphasises that the Church must be simultaneously a unity of one and many Churches: "This principle stems from Trinitarian theology as well as from Christology in its relation to Pneumatology. It is also supported by the eucharistic nature of ecclesiology. In the triune God there is unity, but this unity does not precede multiplicity (the three Persons). The priority of the 'One God' over against the 'triune God', which we encounter in traditional dogmatic manuals in the West – and, also, in the academic dogmatic theology of the East – was rightly shown by theologians such as Karl Rahner to be wrong. We do not first speak of the One God (as divine substance) and *then* of the three Persons as relations *within* the one substance – a favorite approach of medieval theology. The Trinity is just as primary as the one substance in the doctrine of God: the 'many' are constitutive of the one, just as the one is constitutive of the 'many'" (Zizioulas, *The One and the Many*, 265).

65 Cf. Czaja, *Credo in Spiritum Vivificantem*, 264–70.

The existence of hierarchical communion[66] is based on three factors – apostolic succession,[67] unity among the bishops[68] or presbyters[69] and unity with the pope or one's own bishop. The essence of the structure of the Church office thus includes community, communication, common good and common action, and the prototype of this specific perichoresis is the trinitarian perichoresis. Analogously, the unity of the Church consists in the perichoresis of the local Churches and the perichoresis of the spiritual office, while the hierarchical communion is the spokesperson of the Catholic unity of the Church, the richness of its life and the reflection of Christian brotherhood. It is a grace for the whole Church, a necessary condition of the *communio sanctorum* and a sacrament of its Catholic unity. It must not be forgotten, though, that the invisible principle and node of hierarchical communion is the Holy Spirit. It is He who guides the chosen people that undertake the apostolic ministry.[70]

---

66 "It is precisely the uniqueness and specificity of the person that makes the ministry *hierarchical.* The notion of hierarchy is usually connected with a classification established with the help of objective criteria of value, etc. But if we get our notion of hierarchy from, for example, Trinitarian theology, we see that this notion is determined not by such criteria but by the specificity of each divine person. In this sense, hierarchy is an essential result of ordination, and it is in this light that the distinction between clergy and laity or the development and existence of the threefold ministry, etc., should be placed. The distinctions inherent in the multiplicity of ministries bear no value judgment. Those ministries that for historical reasons do not fall under the established categories of ministry are not inferior in any way. The role of the bishop in this action of hierarchy is precisely to transcend in the communion of his community any division that may occur because of the multiplicity of ministries. Those of us who attach great importance to the bishop should do so precisely in the sense that, in his being the head of the concrete community – especially as this community manifests its character of communion in the eucharistic assembly over which he presides – he is the one who safeguards the unity of the body through the multiplicity of the ministries and the charismata. His exclusive right to ordain, notably conditioned by the fact that he does so only in the context of the community, can only be justified by this role if ordination is viewed in the light of communion" (Zizioulas, *The One and the Many*, 188–9).

67 Cf. Guzowski, *Duch Dialogujący*, 231–2.

68 "The bishop is a minister whose responsibility transcends the local Church. He is the instrument of the catholicity of the Church, not only in terms of eschatology *(alter Christus)* and of history *(alter apostolus),* but also in terms of catholicity. In order for each local Church to be catholic, it must be in communion with all the other local Churches in the world. This, too, is entrusted to the bishop: he brings his Church into communion with the other local Churches in the whole '*oikoumene*'" (Zizioulas, *The One and the Many*, 249).

69 Zizioulas emphasises the Orthodox view of the presbyter and his relation to the bishop: "The presbyters never cease to be a college, even if they perform the Eucharist separately. The crucial difference between them and the bishop is that they are many, whereas he is one in his Church. They cannot, therefore, assume the *alter Christus* function, for this function is one of unity and requires singularity. Just as there is one God and one Christ, there can be only one bishop in the typology suggested by the Eucharist" (Zizioulas, *The One and the Many*, 251).

70 Cf. PDV 15; Czaja, *Credo in Spiritum Vivificantem*, 270–3.

One of the institutional manifestations of the realisation of the hierarchical communion are episcopal conferences placed at the level between the diocesan Church and the universal Church. These have been introduced by the Catholic Church but are also of interest in the Orthodox Church. Zizioulas stresses that, according to the Orthodox view, they must be meetings not of bishops but of the Churches they represent. He believes that they would be extremely helpful in restoring full communion between the two Churches if they were put in the context of the ecclesiology of the local Church.[71] The pneumatological dimension of ecclesiology requires a Church structure that combines unity and diversity. A universalist or pyramidal ecclesiology risks sacrificing diversity for the sake of unity. In a pneumatic ecclesiology, "the one and the many" exist independently, and this is not possible outside of the canonical system in which synods at all levels complement and correct each other.[72]

The gesture of laying on of hands and the words accompanying the ordination have a pneumatological meaning – the laying on of hands is a gesture of petition for the Holy Spirit, the words of the preface bear traces of epiclesis. The true Giver of the power of ordination is hence the Holy Spirit invoked in the sacramental prayer of the Church. The Christian laying on of hands signifies a union with Jesus Christ and the apostolic beginning of the Church. The Spirit given through the mediation of the Church fills the ordained person and receives that person for service in the Church. He empowers the person to master and hand himself over to God for His ownership and service towards a special mission, whereas the propagated alternative "office or charism" is totally unjustified. Moreover, the laying on of hands introduces one into the college that is a formal and material successor to the apostolic office, and succession is not only a mechanical chain of laying on of hands, but also a continual invocation of the Holy Spirit.[73]

---

71 Cf. Zizioulas, *The One and the Many*, 254–5.

72 Cf. Zizioulas, *The One and the Many*, 260.

73 Cf. Czaja, *Credo in Spiritum Vivificantem*, 274–7. "This permanent presence of Christ in His people, which is the work of the Holy Spirit through the ministerial structures, the Word and the sacraments of the Church, is referred to in theological terms as 'apostolic tradition'. It is not merely a material transmission of what was given at the beginning to the Apostles, but an active presence of the Lord, crucified and risen, throughout the history of the community gathered by Him. *Tradition*, rightly distinguished from particular and secondary traditions, is the communion of the Holy Spirit in its temporal dimension; it is the unity established by Him between the experience of apostolic faith shared in the first community of disciples and the present experience of Christ in His Church. Tradition is the living Gospel proclaimed by the Apostles in its purity, coming from the fullness of their unique and unrepeatable experience, and finding expression among Christians – in time and in space – under the influence of the Holy Spirit who animates them. Tradition is the history of the Spirit acting in the history of His Church..." (Forte, *Istota chrześcijaństwa*, 133).

Zizioulas notices that speaking of apostolic succession as a chain of episcopal ordinations without indispensably linking these ordinations to the community in which the Eucharistic assemblies take place would imply an absolute conception of ministry. However, it is no coincidence that the early Church did not know episcopal ordination outside the Eucharistic context or without explicit mention of the place to which the bishop would be assigned. Therefore, we must conclude that there is no apostolic succession that is separated from a particular community.[74] Zizioulas believes that the so-called episcopal letters of successors did not merely serve to promote the orthodox faith (the teachers were primarily presbyters), but they showed that the concern for the survival of orthodoxy was not isolated from the life of the Church as a community led by bishops. As successors of the apostles, they were not the promoters of ideas (similarly to the heads of philosophical schools or teachers) like the presbyters, but the superiors of communities whose whole life was – by design – to express their office.[75]

---

74 Cf. Zizioulas, *Being as Communion*, 166. According to the Orthodox view, due to the relational nature of ordination, an ordained person cannot realise his *ordo* except in community – when isolated from the community, he ceases to be an ecclesiastical minister. Cf. Zizioulas, *Being as Communion*, 233. Zizioulas cites historical circumstances to confirm the necessity of the relationality of the ecclesiastical office: "authority in the Church resides not in any office per se, but in the event of communion created by the Spirit as the Spirit forms the believers into the Body of Christ, both locally and universally. It is traditionally admitted, at least by Roman Catholics and Orthodox, that the highest authority in the Church lies in the Ecumenical Council. But no Ecumenical Council is authoritative simply as an institution. Reception of its decisions by the local Churches is required for it to be authoritative. The examples of Ephesus 449 and Ferrara-Florence, which possessed all the institutional requirements of an Ecumenical Council (universal representation, etc.) and yet were not received by the Church as a whole, are well known. It is true that without some kind of institution, which would teach and decide authoritatively, there could be no unity in the Church. But the final decisions of such an institution must be tested through their reception by the communities before they can claim frill and true authority. Like everything else in an ecclesiology of communion, *authority must be relational*" (Zizioulas, *The One and the Many*, 58).

75 Cf. Zizioulas, *Being as Communion*, 166–7. Zizioulas believes that originally it was spoken not of "apostolic succession" but of "apostolic successions," just as in the language of that time the catholicity of the Church was understood in the plural as "catholic Churches," and the corollary of this was that each episcopal community was considered to reflect not only the "whole Church" but also the entire succession of apostles. And indeed, Zizioulas emphasises that it is very significant that each bishop was recognised not as the successor of a particular apostle, but of all the apostles (cf. ibid. 168). "This means that apostolic succession can never be a result of *adding up* die various episcopal successions. The apostolic college in its succession was not divided into parts so that each bishop would be ascribed to one part and all bishops together to the whole of this college. Episcopal collegiality, therefore, does not represent a *collective* unity, but a *unity in identity*, an organic unity. It is the identity of each community with the Body of Christ expressed in historical terms through the continuity of the apostolic presence in the *locus apostolicus* of each episcopal community" (Zizioulas, *Being as Communion*, 168–9).

H. Mühlen believes that it is the Holy Spirit who is the ultimate guarantor of apostolic succession and not the historical chain of its transmission. Each recipient of the charismatic grace of ordination enters into a direct personal relationship with Christ, which is brought about by the Holy Spirit, whose identity in Christ and Christians constitutes the uninterrupted transmission of word, sacrament and office. Through his presence in the entire history of the Church, the Holy Spirit ensures that Christians share in Jesus' consecrating anointing. It can be concluded from this that there is some form of apostolic succession in all the divided Churches. Since it is the Holy Spirit who is the ultimate guarantor of it, it is possible by His power even where there is no historical continuity, and an extraordinary way of its development cannot be excluded.[76]

The post-conciliar ecclesiology recognises that the Holy Spirit is the power that enables the members of the hierarchical communion to fulfil the mission entrusted to them. Significant contributions to the pneumatological interpretation of the service-like nature of the office as a constitutive element of the hierarchical communion were made by W. Kasper, H. Mühlen and G. Greshake. Kasper initially did not expose the pneumatological dimension of the office, but later he saw that the representation of Christ can only be understood pneumatologically. The Spirit given to the Church is the Spirit of the Church or the Spirit in the Church. The Spirit was given to the Church by Christ once and for all and, since it is bound to Christ's model, the Spirit can actualise Christ's authoritative "towards" or "vis-à-vis" the Church precisely through the ecclesiastical office, enabling and realising, introducing apostolic ministry by including the Christian in the office-making relation of Christ's "vis-à-vis" the Church. In this way, the office-bearer is a member of the Church and at the same time stands "in relation to" the Church as a representative of Christ in hierarchical communion.[77]

The moment of pro-existence of ecclesiastical office holders in the context of the universal bestowal of the Holy Spirit on all the faithful was also discussed by H. Mühlen. He emphasised that no human being is capable of representing the fullness of the Spirit and he also referred this to the ecclesial community and even postulated desacralization of the word, sacrament and office in order to reach in them the experience of that Spirit in whose service they mediate.[78] He argued that in the so-called Constantinian era of the Church, the search for the theocratic image of God (the so-called pre-trinitarian monotheism) led to the monarchical understanding and absolutisation of the office in the Church. Meanwhile – since

---

76 Cf. Mühlen, *Una Mystica Persona*, 564; Czaja, *Credo in Spiritum Vivificantem*, 274–80.

77 Cf. Kasper, "Sein und Sendung des Priesters," *Geist und Leben* 51 (1978) 197–202; Czaja, *Credo in Spiritum Vivificantem*, 281–2.

78 See Mühlen, *Entsakralisierung: Ein epochales Schlagwort in seiner Bedeutung für die Zukunft der christlichen Kirchen* (Paderborn: Schöningh, 1970).

Christ pointed to Himself as the place of God's presence and the proper temple of the Father – the proper place of worship and experience of transcendence is no longer the Jerusalem temple, but the Christian community and each of its members as the concretisation of the sacred experience, i. e. the union with the Father through the Son in the Holy Spirit. It is the Holy Spirit who, without being incarnate, makes the actual experience of God possible; He constitutes the gracious and enlivening fascination by which Christians face one another; in Him everyone is a temple shining with God's glory. Therefore, the desacralisation and re-sacralisation of the office advocated by Mühlen, should lead to the rediscovery of its pneumatological dimension. "It is necessary [...] to undertake personalisation (a total de-divinisation of the office to turn towards Christ) and so-called pneumatisation [...], that is, to get fascinated anew by the Spirit of Christ".[79]

G. Greshake points out that the ecclesiastical office-bearer exercises his *ecclesial* pro-existence not only in the name of and as a substitute for Christ, since he also does so within the structure of the Church, and thus acts not only in *persona Christi* but also *in persona Ecclesiae*.[80] Greshake submits this to a trinitarian interpretation and claims that a purely Christological view of the office under the *auctoritas et potestas Christi* would be alienating. If, on the other hand, we perceive it purely pneumatologically, we view it as one of many spiritual ministries in the Church. Through the sacrament of holy orders, a person enters into a double relationship – with Christ and the Church: as a representative of Christ, he stands before the faithful, but at the same time he is carried by the communion of the Church as its member. He then testifies to the faith of the Church, demonstrates the priestly character of the entire Christian people, presides over the liturgical celebration and represents the unity created by the Holy Spirit. The Church's approval is not secondary to the office itself but is an expression of the Church's internal trinitarian structure, in which the Christological and pneumatological dimensions overlap – the people of God approve and present for ordination persons in whom they are convinced to have recognised, through the power of the Holy Spirit, the qualities that predestine them to fulfil the functions related to the office.[81]

J.D. Zizioulas emphasises that ministry in the Church cannot be interpreted in isolation from the context of communion.[82] Affirming the belonging of the ministry

---

79 Czaja, *Credo in Spiritum Vivificantem*, 285. Cf. ibid, 282–4; Mühlen, *Entsakralisierung*, 95–105.

80 Cf. Greshake, *Być kapłanem*, 92–102.

81 Cf. Czaja, *Credo in Spiritum Vivificantem*, 284–6.

82 Cf. Zizioulas, *Being as Communion*, 163–4: "It is not an accident that the early Church applied to Christ all forms of ministries that existed. He was the apostle, the prophet, the priest, the bishop, the deacon, etc. A Christologically understood ministry transcends all categories of priority and separation that may be created by the act of ordination and 'setting apart.' Another fundamental implication is that no ministry in the Church can be understood outside the context of the community.

to the community means placing the question of ordination outside the dilemma of choosing between an ontological or functional understanding of the priesthood. It has long been debated whether ordination endows a person with something indelible that is one's personal property (permanent or temporary), or whether it simply empowers one to act for a certain purpose. Zizioulas believes that, in the context of the Eucharistic community, such a dilemma makes no sense or leads in the wrong direction, since there is no charism that can be individually owned, and yet there is no charism that can be conceived or acted upon other than individually. He explains that the paradox of the incarnation of the "many" into the "one", on which the Eucharistic community and perhaps even the whole mystery of Christ is based, can only be understood and explained in terms of "personal existence". Individuality is a category presupposing separation and separateness – individuality is revealed in distinction from other individualities (M. Buber), while person is a category presupposing unity with other persons. The Holy Spirit makes ministry a personal reality.[83] The Eucharistic community and the Church as communion in general can only be understood in terms of personal existence.[84]

This should not be explained in terms of representativeness and delegation of authority, for these terms being basically juridical finally lead to a separation of the ordained person from the community: to act *on behalf of* the community means to stand *outside* it because it means to act *in its place*. But what is precisely denied by this communal dimension we want to point out here, is that there is no ministry that can stand *outside* or *above* the community."

83 Cf. Zizioulas, *The One and the Many*, 188. "But when we say that the ministry becomes personal and that this is the only way through which Christ's ministry expresses itself in the Church, we must distinguish very sharply between the 'personal' and the 'individual'. The latter is defined by its being separated from all the other individuals, whereas the former is characterised by the fact that it exists only in communion with other persons. Ordination, therefore, while – or because of – making the ministry personal, existentially relates the ordained person to a community" (Zizioulas, *The One and the Many*, 188).

84 Cf. Zizioulas, *Being as Communion*, 164–5. "It is impossible to say whether ordination bestows an objective grace ontologically possessed by an individual or simply delegates authority to function and minister in a certain way in the Church. Both these options presuppose an objectification of the charisma and make of the ordained person an *individual* who stands outside or above the community, as if he could be understood in himself. In the light of love and in the context of the notion of communion, ordination *binds* the ordained person so *deeply* and *existentially* with the community that in his new state after ordination he cannot be conceived in himself at all – he has become a *relational entity*. In this state, existence is determined by communion, not by ontology or function. In the state of love and the bond created by it, can we ever say one simply 'functions' in a certain way or 'represents' someone without his very being having been affected deeply and decisively by this bond? Or can we in such a state speak of something ontologically possessed by an *individual*? Can we ever isolate and objectify this state created by love and speak of some *thing* given through it? Ordination is like marriage, and the historical development [...] and preservation in the Eastern Orthodox liturgy of an ordination service basically similar to that of matrimony seems to be a strikingly profound and revealing thing" (Zizioulas, *The One and the Many*, 185).

Ordination to ecclesiastical ministry in the context of the Eucharistic communion means that the received "seal of the Holy Spirit" cannot exist outside of the existential relationship of the ordained person with the community. It is not a mere function performed outside of a deep bond with the community. It is a bond of love, like any gift of the Holy Spirit, and its indelible character can only be compared to that which is possessed or given through love. Apart from this existential bond with the community, this bond is doomed to die, just as the Holy Spirit, who gives this charism and constantly sustains it, does not live apart from the community because it is a bond of love. In this sense, the Holy Spirit "owns" the Church exclusively, and all ministry is His gift. All this means going beyond the divisions caused by the diversity of ministries and the distinctiveness of ordained ministry in the Church. The bishop's exclusive right to ordain priests must also be considered in this context. It derives from the fact that he is the head of the Eucharistic community – hence he cannot ordain outside that community – as the one who offers the whole community to God in the Eucharist. His exclusive right to ordain, indeed his whole life as bishop, makes no sense apart from this role as the one through whom all divisions, including those arising from ordination, are overcome. His task is always to bring about the universality of the Church that is realised in a particular place, thus he must be existentially bound to the community. Therefore, there is no ordained ministry in the universal Church that can exist *in abstracto* – in separation from the community.[85]

There can be no absolute ordination. Ordination in the context of communion implies a commitment to the community. A communion that does not express itself in the form of community is not existential, because it is the concrete local situation, with all the details of historical existence, which is expressed in the here and now, that makes up the existential context of our life. It is because of this existential understanding of the Church that "catholicity" was unthinkable outside the local Church in the early centuries, and ordination was reserved for the Eucharistic assembly, in which communion is realised to the highest degree along with all its divine and human dimensions. In the light of communion, ordination is a commitment – it is not a commitment to ideas, ideals or a vague "humanity", but to concrete human beings, towards whom, in particular circumstances, the ordained person is to be committed in an absolute and unconditional way, as love in its existential character demands.[86]

A. Czaja emphasises that the interpretations of Kasper, Mühlen and Greshake point to the Holy Spirit as the power that enables the members of the hierarchical communion to be permanently open to the universal community of the Church,

85 Cf. Zizioulas, *Being as Communion*, 165–8.

86 Cf. Zizioulas, *The One and the Many*, 186–7.

the source of their inclusion and continuance in relation to the Church as the Bride and to act on behalf of the Church as the Body.[87] However, the pro-existence of bishops and presbyters as members of the hierarchical communion does not end with the fulfilment of their mission – it still requires collaboration and collegiality. For the Church is not about uniformity, but about the communion of the Spirit bringing about unity in the synchronic and diachronic order. The grace of the Holy Spirit unites the bishop with the presbyters, He is the basis of the unity of the college, and the diversity within the college has its source in His manifold gifts. In the hierarchical communion, there are natural tensions between the person and the demands of the office, and between primacy and synodality. Through the Holy Spirit, these can develop dynamically and creatively for the good of the hierarchical communion itself and the community of the Church. Only in the power of the Holy Spirit can the office exercise its ministry of unity in the space of freedom of faith. Its power unifies and differentiates, binds and liberates, and is the condition for the effectiveness of the official ministry of unity. The realisation of hierarchical communion therefore requires constant openness of all its members to the Holy Spirit and a permanent fascination with Him.[88]

Interesting aspects concerning the pneumatological dimension of the place of the hierarchy in the Church appear in Orthodox theology. J. Zizioulas emphasises that it is an assembly created by the Holy Spirit[89] and its structure – the institution

87 Cf. Czaja, *Credo in Spiritum Vivificantem*, 286–7.

88 Cf. Czaja, *Credo in Spiritum Vivificantem*, 287–90. Zizioulas emphasises the communal significance of the office of bishop: "If we arrive at the importance of the episcopal succession via the idea of continuity of *structure*, we can appreciate the traditional assignment to the bishop of the role of the sole ordainer. Because of his place in the structure of the community, especially in its eucharistic form, the bishop is the one through whom all charismatic manifestations of the Church must pass, so that they may be manifestations not of individualism but of the *koinonia* of the Spirit and of the community created by it. Extraordinary or (as they are called today) "charismatic" ministries have their place in the Church and must be encouraged. But it is only if they are parts of the structure of the community that they are not in danger of becoming the kind of individualistic manifestations which St. Paul fought so vigorously in Corinth. All these extraordinary ministries, therefore, become integral parts of the apostolic continuity in the synthesis I am expounding here, if they go through the bishop, in whom the entire structure converges and the 'many' become 'one' in a particular existential milieu" (Zizioulas, *Being as Communion*, 199).

89 Cf. Zizioulas, *Lectures*, 160–1: "The Church is the gathering of God's people in a specific place and time, which portrays the complete assembly of all created things. It is summoned by the Holy Spirit who makes the Church new every time it gathers, and so sustains the constantly life-renewing body of Christ on earth. In this way, we are neither defined by history nor in denial about it. The Eucharist is the inaugural event of freedom and the moment in which eschatological reality becomes the actual presence of this assembly brought together by the Holy Spirit. This is the work of the Holy Spirit, which is why the invocation (*epiclesis*) of the Holy Spirit is fundamental. The gifts that bear the body and blood of Christ bring us into increasing participation in that body. This event of person-to-person relationship takes place in the Spirit, between each of us and Christ. These

of the Church – is not imposed or composed and constituted by someone of the people. The Holy Spirit makes people its fundamental members when He gathers them as the Church and therefore the Church cannot exist without them. For this reason, Zizioulas emphasises that Orthodoxy has no problem with clericalism or secularism (which is in fact a reaction directed against clericalism). The people must be present in order for priests to celebrate the Eucharist or even exist as such. It is the gathered people who enable the priests not only to perform the ritual but also to act effectively with authority. The charismatic action and authority of the clergy thus depends on the presence of the whole people, who lend authority to the priests and accept and recognise their action. Ordination is not a separate rite, but takes place during the celebration of the Eucharist, and so it is the action of the whole Christian people participating in the action of the Holy Spirit, through which He makes the representatives of the office the servants of the people. For this reason, there are no "private" or "clerical" liturgies in which the laypersons are absent. The Church is constituted by the people and therefore its existence presupposes the necessity of people's presence and involvement. Their "Amen" is necessary to give validity to the actions and words of the clergy and makes them the actions and words of the people of God. Thus, when the priest says "Peace be with you", the response "And also with your spirit" must come from someone who is not the priest – the people and the priest are in dialogue. The assembled people must – with their "Amen" – actively affirm that the prayers being offered are their prayers.[90]

> If ordination is approached in this way, ministry ceases to be understood in terms of what it *gives* to the ordained and becomes describable only in terms of the particular relationship in which it places the ordained. If ordination is understood as constitutive of community, and if the community being a *koinonia* of the Spirit is by its nature *a relational whole*, then *all* ministry can be described as a complexity of relationships within the Church and in relation to the world. In fact, without the notion of 'relation', ministry

---

eschatological events are seen, felt and tasted in the gathering of the Church. This gathering is the event in which the Holy Spirit opens us to life together in freedom."

90 Cf. Zizioulas, *Lectures*, 157. "The Eucharist realizes and reveals the Church as a *community*. If the Christian people do not gather, or do not participate in the worship or do not affirm the decisions and teaching with their 'Amen' the identity of the Church is lost. Then we do indeed start to refer to the clergy as though they were the Church, as the media do every time they say that 'the Church has announced', with all the resulting division and confusion that we see around us. Without a theology of Christ and Spirit, and head and body, we are of course only able to pit clergy and people against one another, so every news story about the Church is about the individual opposing the hierarchy. But it is by their being gathered together into one that the people of God are brought into being" (Zizioulas, *Lectures*, 160).

loses its character – both as a charism of the Spirit, i. e. part of His *koinonia*, and as a service (*diakonia*).[91]

As far as the authority deriving from ministry is concerned, by recovering its relational character in the light of the Eucharistic community, the struggle against the "institution" (which is very topical today) becomes pointless, since the institution will then not only be valid but also relational. The authority associated with ministry understood as an objectified office and as *potestas* is naturally associated with oppression and provokes resistance. On a relational view of ecclesiastical ministry, authority arises directly from relations – the Church is hierarchical in the sense that the Holy Trinity itself is hierarchical because of the specificity of the trinitarian relations. As a reflection of God's love in the world, the Church reflects precisely this kind of authority through its ministry. Hierarchy and authority thus derive from communional relations, not from "ontological" or "moral" authority (*auctoritas* or *potestas*).[92]

God's existential involvement in human history has shifted the question of His authority from the objective ontological level to the existential level – instead of being an objective authority who speaks, acts and governs "authoritatively" from within His own self-defined being – He has become a participant in human destiny until death.[93] Only in Christ does God become authoritative, but Christ can only be an existential authority for man through the Holy Spirit: "no one can say 'Jesus is Lord' except by the Holy Spirit" (i. e. no one can recognise His authority; 1 Cor 12:3). This means much more than just the help given to people by the Holy Spirit to recognise the lordship of Christ in their life. The Holy Spirit is connected to the very roots of the reality of Christ as God's personal involvement in our lives,

---

91 Zizioulas, *Being as Communion*, 219–20.

92 Cf. Zizioulas, *Being as Communion*, 223–4.

93 Cf. Zizioulas, *The One and the Many*, 172. "This existential involvement implies an 'authority' that is no longer *auctoritas*. This authority does not stem from a being or a principle objectively conceived, but from a *relationship* in the deepest and existential sense of the word. It may be called the authority of love, if by love we do not imply a moral or sentimental category, but an ἔκστασις (cf. Heidegger's *ek-sistieren*), i. e., a going out of one's self in order to come to personal *communion*. The authoritative element in this situation lies in the fact that this communion affirms the order's presence as an existential necessity – the 'I' can exist personally only because there is a 'Thou'. This authority that is defined by the power of mere existential presence 'imposes' itself *from within* as an affirmation of authentic existence; it is *authority as authenticity. [...]* God Himself, by sharing our existence in Christ, has made it impossible for us to conceive of Him as an *auctoritas*, i. e., as a claim to submission coming from without our existence. He is an authority only in the sense that by participating in our *existence personally*, i. e., as the *Logos* and not as God (the latter would suggest an objective ontological reality on the level of 'nature'), He allows us to be in communion with Him and thus *authenticates our personal existence*" (Zizioulas, *The One and the Many*, 172).

because He worked in the very fact of Christ's incarnation, baptism and His entire ministry (Matt 1:18-20; Mark 1:10; Luke 1:35; 4:18 etc.). Our communion with God in Christ is therefore a communion also in the Holy Spirit, whereas Christ's existential authority over us, i. e. the authentic affirmation of our personal existence as children of God, is ultimately the authority of the Father, the Son and the Holy Spirit at the same time.[94]

That the Holy Spirit makes the lordship or authority of Christ existential for us has important implications for our understanding of "authority". Zizioulas points out that the fundamental error committed by theology – which has influenced its entire development – has been to forget that the Holy Spirit is a bond of love and wherever He "blows", He does not create good individual Christians but persons abiding in communion with God and with people, i. e. He creates a community. In this sense, it remains a fundamental and indisputable truth that the Spirit exists only in the Church, in community, in the Body of Christ, and that all spiritual gifts, such as inspiration, charism, ministry etc., cannot be seen as the property of individuals since they can only exist in persons abiding in communion, i. e. in the context of the ecclesial community. Therefore, St. Paul's claim that the lordship of Christ, i. e. His authority, is recognised only in the Spirit, is another way of expressing the fact that the authority of God in Christ is an authority only in a relative sense – the Church as the community of the baptised does not consist of many individuals professing the objective authority of God but is a community that actually makes this authority a reality. By giving birth to this community, the Holy Spirit creates this personal communion with God's personal existence, which realises God's authority and dominion in our lives.[95]

In this understanding, all "authorities" in the Church who claim to represent the authority of God cease to be objective, authoritative subjects in themselves and become authoritative only in the context of the community. According to Zizioulas, the structure of the Church cannot allow for the possibility of authority outside or above the community. The Church cannot be structured along the lines of secular organisations in the name of "efficiency" by introducing objective authority, which will sooner or later be felt as a yoke and therefore be rejected by people. Its structure must be a reflection of the communion of God with man in Christ, and all ministries can only be authoritative in the sense that they realise the authority that flows from the communion itself.[96]

94 Cf. Zizioulas, *The One and the Many*, 172–3.

95 Cf. Zizioulas, *The One and the Many*, 173.

96 Cf. Zizioulas, *The One and the Many*, 173–4. "In the same manner, truth and doctrine cannot be an authority in themselves. For the Christian, truth bears no authority whatsoever; in fact it only exists – significantly enough – as a Person ('I am the truth', John 14:16). This means that truth exists only in so far as it shares personal existence, i. e., only in the context of community based

The sin of individualism engulfing the Church, which is the communion of the Holy Spirit, is no lesser with regard to the community than with regard to the individual. According to this principle, a Eucharistic community that separates itself from the rest of the communities is not an ecclesial community – according to the old Latin maxim *unus christianus nullus christianus*. Orthodox theology stresses that unity in time and space cannot destroy the unity of local communities.[97] Only the diocesan bishop can vote at the synod because he participates in the synod as the head of his community, with none of the synodal decisions being authoritative until accepted by the communities.[98] On the other hand, reception – organically linked to conciliarism – is inevitable when we view conciliarism as the identity of the communities expressed in charismatic terms. It is hence not a question of legal but of charismatic recognition. For this reason, a true council is realised only *a posteriori* – it is not an institution but an event in which the whole community participates and which shows whether its bishop has acted in accordance with his *charisma veritatis*.[99] From the point of view of episcopal ministry, this demonstrates again how relational is that which is given or realised in ordination.[100]

God has given us his Son in the Holy Spirit. From an ecclesiological point of view, the most important thing is that the Spirit is *koinonia*. Therefore, if the reception of the gift of God takes place in the Spirit, it must always take place in and

---

on communion, since it is the Spirit again that leads us 'to all truth' – or rather to the 'whole, integral truth' (*εἰς πᾶσαν τὴν ἀλήθειαν* – John 16:13). Doctrines appear only within the context of communion ('it seemed good to the Holy Spirit and to us' – Acts 15:28); they have no authority in themselves but only in relation to the community. [...] This leads us to a specific consideration of the authority of the Bible. Should the Bible have any authority for a non-Christian? And what does it mean that it has 'authority' for a member of the Church? The authority of the Bible can be conceived only 'in the Spirit,' i. e., in the context of the communion existing in the community. Without the descent of the Holy Spirit at Pentecost and the community that was created, any record of the words and acts of God would be objectively possible but not existentially authoritative. Like divine authority in general, biblical authority is only relevant for the Church. In its original appearance and composition, the Bible was essentially a witness recorded by persons who were themselves witnesses not in an individualistic sense but 'in the Spirit,' i. e., in their personal, existential relationship to the community created by the Spirit. Their authority, therefore, was not an individual possession, objectively imposed upon the community, but it was an authority that emerged from the reality of Christ's presence and communion in this community" (Zizioulas, *The One and the Many*, 174).

97 Cf. Zizioulas, *Being as Communion*, 236–7.

98 Cf. Zizioulas, *Being as Communion*, 241.

99 Zizioulas emphasises that the task of conciliarity in the Church was not so much to throw anathemas, but rather to constantly strive to maintain communion: "I have stressed this aspect of conciliarity not only because we often tend to overlook it under the impression of the 'anathemas' pronounced by the councils, but because it fits into the picture of primitive conciliarity that always involved a persistent effort at communion and not simply an action of exclusion from communion" (Zizioulas, *The One and the Many*, 210).

100 Cf. Zizioulas, *Being as Communion*, 245.

through communion. In giving His Son to humanity as His own love, God does not impose the reception of this gift on us. The Holy Spirit is freedom. Truth is not authoritarian – it is authoritative as flowing from the event of communion. Communion is concretely a community, thus the reception of truth must pass through the particular community or communities of the Church. No matter how universally something is received in the Church, if it is not received in the context of the Eucharist, it has not yet been received. Hence, all creedal and conciliar formulas only reach their ultimate goal when they become an integral part of the Eucharistic community. The reception of truth does not take place at the level of individuals, but at the level of communities, and therefore, a certain ministry expressing the unity of the community is needed. In the classical model of reception, such a function is performed by the bishop. Each local Church has received the Gospel as one body through one bishop, who ensures that reception has been consistent with earlier communities dating back to the first apostolic communities and shared with other ecclesial communities around the world. In this way, the episcopal office became essential to the mode of reception. Since in the Holy Spirit everything takes place as an event of communion, the classical model of reception stipulated that every decision of the bishop or bishops at the council should be received by the community. This created a form of vicious circle – the community could do nothing without the bishop, and the bishop had to accept the "Amen" of the community in everything he did. In doing so, reception must not be limited to the local level, but must be universal. A ministry of universal reception is therefore also needed, which should meet the requirements of communion.[101]

Ordination is necessarily linked to the mission of the Church. Zizioulas notes that throughout history both the concepts of mission and ordination have adopted meanings that separated them. Ordination came to be associated more with a static view of the life of the Church, while mission was identified more with the idea of sending out, of the Church going out into the world to evangelise and convert people. But in the light of communion, ordination signifies an act leading to an existential engagement with the world and brings the Church into a deep relationship with the world, its needs, anxieties and possibilities. Through ordination, the Church becomes a community that connects the world to God – and this is essentially what mission should mean. Mission, then, is not a method, but an attribute related to the nature of the Church. It can thus be practised though a variety of methods, insofar as it presupposes and realises that communion which God willed the world to have with Him in Christ, and to which ordination commits the ordained and, through

101 Cf. Zizioulas, *The One and the Many*, 122–3. In this context, Zizioulas did not hesitate to add: "In these circumstances, one should not hesitate to seek such a ministry in the Bishop of Rome" (ibid, 123).

them, the Church. Through ordination, the Church goes beyond itself. This is the ecstasy of communion, which should also be "going beyond" with a mission. The ecstasy that would leave itself behind, any spatial "sending out" that would not also be a "presence", would not be the ecstasy of communion. Ordination in the light of communion makes the Church missionary precisely in the sense of its existential engagement in the world and its deep connection with the world.[102] This attitude is very strongly expressed in the teaching of Pope Francis in his exhortation *Evangelii gaudium.*[103]

4.4 The Pneumatological Dimensions of the Shared Ecumenical Vision of the Church as Communion

The Council's *Decree on Ecumenism* states that "It is the Holy Spirit, dwelling in those who believe and pervading and ruling over the Church as a whole, who brings about that wonderful communion of the faithful. He brings them into intimate union with Christ, so that He is the principle of the Church's unity" (No. 2). Connected with the quest to recover the visible unity of the Church is the necessity of converting the hearts of believers, which can only be achieved by the Holy Spirit, who will only then bring people into communion with their brothers and sisters from other Christian confessions: "Repent, […] and you will receive the gift of the Holy Spirit" (Acts 2:38). The Holy Spirit provides the mankind with access to the resources of salvation in Christ and watches over its realisation and the sanctification of people.

> The Church, which the Spirit guides in way of all truth (cf. John 16:13) and which He unified in communion and in works of ministry, He both equips and directs with hi-

---

102 Cf. Zizioulas, *The One and the Many*, 187. "From the moment God Himself chose the way of communion in order to transform the world by being personally and existentially involved in the world, the Church had no other choice in her way of mission but to do the same. This 'incarnational' or, one might call it, 'eucharistic' understanding of the ministry is what ordination leads to, if placed in the light of communion" (Zizioulas, *The One and the Many*, 189).

103 Cf. e. g. Francis, Exhortation *Evangelii gaudium*, 31: "The bishop must always foster this missionary communion in his diocesan Church, following the ideal of the first Christian communities, in which the believers were of one heart and one soul (cf. Acts 4:32). To do so, he will sometimes go before his people, pointing the way and keeping their hope vibrant. At other times, he will simply be in their midst with his unassuming and merciful presence. At yet other times, he will have to walk after them, helping those who lag behind and – above all – allowing the flock to strike out on new paths. In his mission of fostering a dynamic, open and missionary communion, he will have to encourage and develop the means of participation proposed in the Code of Canon Law, […] the principal aim of these participatory processes should not be ecclesiastical organization but rather the missionary aspiration of reaching everyone."

> erarchical and charismatic gifts and adorns with His fruits (cf. Eph 4:11-12; 1 Cor 12:4; Gal 5:22). By the power of the Gospel He makes the Church keep the freshness of youth. Uninterruptedly He renews it and leads it to perfect union with its Spouse (LG 4).

The Holy Spirit's role in building the unity of the Church must be placed in the context of His close association with the Church. He does this in the process of sanctifying people not in a uniform manner but in accordance with the richness of individual human persons of infinite variety. The Holy Spirit watches over the distribution of grace in the Church through the hierarchical priesthood and the special charismatic gifts as well as guarantees full unity and harmony (cf. 1 Cor 12:11).[104]

Developed through strenuous effort and an extraordinary ecumenical achievement, the document of the World Council of Churches entitled *The Church. Towards a Common Vision*[105] recalls at the outset the words of St. Paul: "For just as the body is one and has many members, and all the members of the body, though many, are one body, so it is with Christ. For in the one Spirit we were all baptized into one body – Jews or Greeks, slaves or free – and we were all made to drink of one Spirit" (1 Cor 12:13). It emphasises that, according to the Bible, man and woman were created in the image of God (cf. Gen 1:26-27), bearing the inherent element of the capacity for communion (*koinonia* in Greek) with God and with each other. The dynamic history of the rebirth of communion found an irreversible achievement in the incarnation and Paschal mystery of Jesus Christ. The Church, as the body of Christ, acts by the power of the Holy Spirit to continue its life-giving mission of participating in God's work of healing the broken world. Communion, whose source is the very life of the Holy Trinity, is the gift by which the Church lives and to which it is called.[106] The Acts of the Apostles cite the words of Jesus spoken to the

---

104 Cf. Napiórkowski, *Teologia jedności chrześcijan*, 133.

105 World Council of Churches, Faith and Order: Paper No. 214, *The Church. Towards a Common Vision* (2013). "For twenty years, the delegated representatives of the Orthodox, Protestant, Anglican, Evangelical, Pentecostal and Roman Catholic churches in a World Conference on Faith and Order (1993), three Plenary Commissions on Faith and Order (1996, 2004, 2009), eighteen meetings of the Standing Commission, and countless drafting meetings have sought to uncover a global, multilateral and ecumenical vision of the nature, purpose, and mission of the Church. The churches have responded critically and constructively to two earlier stages on the way to a common statement. The Commission on Faith and Order responds to the churches with *The Church. Towards a Common Vision*, its common – or convergence – statement on ecclesiology. The convergence reached in *The Church* represents an extraordinary ecumenical achievement" (ibid., VIII).

106 Cf. *Towards a Common Vision*, 1, 23–4: "The Church is fundamentally a communion in the Triune God and, at the same time, a communion whose members partake together in the life and mission of God (cf. 2 Pet 1:4), who, as Trinity, is the source and focus of all communion. Thus the Church is both a divine and a human reality. While it is a common affirmation that the Church is a meeting place between the divine and the human, churches nonetheless have different sensitivities or even

Apostles before His departure to the Father: "But you will receive power when the Holy Spirit has come upon you; and you will be my witnesses" (Acts 1:8) (cf. No. 2). The Spirit descended upon the disciples on the morning of Pentecost and equipped them with the power to begin the mission entrusted to them (Acts 2:1-41),[107] and they went throughout the world and fulfilled it, incorporating into the Church and transforming – as necessary under the guidance of the Holy Spirit – the cultural heritage of their listeners.[108]

The second chapter of this document, entitled "The Church of the Triune God", states that all Christians share the conviction of the normativity of the Scriptures, and that the same Holy Spirit who guided the earliest communities in producing inspired biblical texts is the guide of the later followers of Jesus as they seek to be faithful to the Gospel. This is what the "living Tradition" of the Church is all about.[109]

The Church is the Church of the triune God as *koinonia.*[110] It is called into existence by God, who sent the Holy Spirit to guide believers into all truth, reminding them of all that Jesus taught (cf. John 14:26). In the Church of the Holy Spirit, believers are united to Jesus Christ and thus share a living relationship with the Father, who speaks to them and calls them to a trusting response. The biblical concept of *koinonia* has become central in the ecumenical search for a common understanding. Communion refers not simply to the unification of the existing Churches in their present form. The noun *koinonia* (communion, participation, fellowship, sharing), from which the verb meaning "to have something in common", "to share", "to take part in" or "to act together" is derived, appears in passages describing mutual sharing (cf. 1 Cor 10:16-17; Gal 2:7-10; Rom 15:26; 2 Cor 8:3-4; Acts 2:42-45). As a community established by God, the Church belongs to God and does not exist for itself. It is called and sent to bear witness with its own life to that communion which God has intended for all people and all creation in His kingdom.[111] Through the preaching of the Gospel (cf. Rom 10:14-18) by the power of

---

contrasting convictions concerning the way in which the Holy Spirit's activity in the Church is related to institutional structures or ministerial order."

107 Cf. *Towards a Common Vision*, 3.

108 Cf. *Towards a Common Vision*, 6.

109 Cf. *Towards a Common Vision*, 11.

110 "If we are to seek unity on a stable and healthy basis, we need a sound doctrine of God as Trinity and of the divine Economy in Christ in relation to the work of the Holy Spirit. These doctrines are not simply dogmatic formulations for theologians, but indispensable presuppositions for an ecclesiology of communion – as well as for all efforts to overcome division with the help of such an ecclesiology" (Zizioulas, *The One and the Many*, 59).

111 Cf. *Towards a Common Vision*, 13.

the Holy Spirit (cf. 1 Cor 12:3) people come to the salvific faith and the sacraments, i. e. they are incorporated into the Body of Christ (cf. Eph 1:23).[112]

Christ prayed to the Father to send the Holy Spirit upon the disciples to guide them into all truth (John 15:26; 16:13). The Spirit not only bestows faith and other charisms on individual believers, but also equips the Church with its essential gifts, qualities and order. The Holy Spirit nourishes and animates the Body of Christ with the living voice of the proclaimed Gospel and through sacramental communion, especially in the Eucharist, and through the official ministry.[113] The Church is "a chosen race, a royal priesthood, a holy nation, God's own people" (1 Pet 2:9-10). Recognising the unique priesthood of Jesus Christ, whose single sacrifice established the new Covenant (cf. Heb 9:15), believers are called to express with their lives what has been called the "royal priesthood", offering themselves as "a living sacrifice, holy and acceptable to God" (Rom 12:1). Every Christian receives the gifts of the Holy Spirit for the building of the Church and participation in Christ's mission. These gifts are given for the common good (cf. 1 Cor 12:7; Eph 4:11-13) and oblige one to be responsible for each individual and local community, and for the Church as a whole. Empowered by the Holy Spirit, Christians are called to live as disciples in various forms of service.[114] From the earliest times, certain believers have been chosen under the guidance of the Holy Spirit and given special authority and responsibility. Ordained ministers build the Body of Christ by preaching the Word of God, celebrating the sacraments and guiding the community's liturgical life, worship, mission and caring ministry. All members of the Body, ordained and lay, are members of the priestly people. Ordained ministers remind communities of their dependence on Jesus Christ, the source of unity and mission, and understand their ministry as dependent on Him. They can only fulfil their vocation in and for the Church and need the Church's recognition, support and encouragement.[115]

---

112 Cf. *Towards a Common Vision,* 14. "While there is wide agreement that God established the Church as the privileged means for bringing about his universal design of salvation, some communities believe that this can be suitably expressed by speaking of the 'Church as sacrament', while others do not normally use such language or reject it outright. Those who use the expression 'Church as sacrament' do so because they understand the Church as an effective sign and means (sometimes described by the word *instrument)* of the communion of human beings with one another through their communion in the Triune God" (*Towards a Common Vision,* 27).

113 Cf. *Towards a Common Vision,* 16.

114 Cf. *Towards a Common Vision,* 18.

115 Cf. *Towards a Common Vision,* 19. "There is widespread agreement among churches of different traditions about the vital place of ministry. This was succinctly expressed in the Faith and Order 5 *Baptism, Eucharist and Ministry,* Geneva, WCC, 1982, section on Ministry, §13. document, *Baptism, Eucharist and Ministry* (1982), which stated that 'the Church has never been without persons holding specific authority and responsibility', noting that, 'Jesus chose and sent the disciples to be witnesses of the kingdom. The mission which Jesus entrusted to the eleven in Matthew 28

Christ is the Head of his Body, the Church (cf. Eph 5:26). He is intimately united to it, animating all believers in the Holy Spirit (Rom 12:5; cf. 1 Cor 12:12). The Holy Spirit gives the members of the Church a variety of gifts and ensures unity in the process of building the Body (cf. Rom 12:4-8; 1 Cor 12:4-30). He renews their hearts, equipping them with strength and calling them to good works, thus enabling them to serve the Lord in spreading the kingdom of God in the world. Thus, the image of the "body of Christ" implies a deep connection with the Holy Spirit, as evidenced in the whole New Testament. A vivid example of this is the description of the descent of tongues of fire upon the disciples gathered in the Cenacle on the morning of Pentecost (cf. Acts 2:1-4). Through the power of the Holy Spirit, believers grow as a "holy temple in the Lord" (Eph 2:21-22), "a spiritual house" (1 Pet 2:5). Filled with the Holy Spirit, they are called to live a life worthy of their vocation in worship, witness and service, desiring to preserve the unity of the Spirit through the bond of peace (cf. Eph 4:1-3). The Holy Spirit animates and equips the Church with power to preach and bring about the holistic transformation awaited by the whole creation (cf. Rom 8:22-23).[116]

The Church is one because God is one (cf. John 17:11; 1 Tim 2:5). Jesus prayed that all His disciples would be one so that the world would believe (cf. John 17:20-21) and He sent the Holy Spirit to form them into one body (cf. 1 Cor 12:2-13). The current divisions within and between the Churches contradict this unity and must therefore be overcome with the gifts of faith, hope and love from the same Spirit.[117]

---

entails 'a ministry of word, sacrament and oversight given by Christ to the Church to be carried out by some of its members for the good of all. This triple function of the ministry equips the Church for its mission in the world'. Agreed statements are making it clear that the royal priesthood of the whole people of God (cf. 1 Pet 2:9) and a special ordained ministry are both important aspects of the church, and not to be seen as mutually exclusive alternatives. At the same time, churches differ about who is competent to make final decisions for the community; for some that task is restricted to the ordained, while others see the laity as having a role in such decisions" (*Towards a Common Vision*, 20).

116 Cf. *Towards a Common Vision*, 21. "It is God's design to gather humanity and all of creation into communion under the Lordship of Christ (cf. Eph 1:10). The Church, as a reflection of the communion of the Triune God, is meant to serve this goal and is called to manifest God's mercy to human beings, helping them to achieve the purpose for which they were created and in which their joy ultimately is found: to praise and glorify God together with all the heavenly hosts. This mission of the Church is fulfilled by its members through the witness of their lives and, when possible, through the open proclamation of the good news of Jesus Christ. The mission of the Church is to serve this purpose" (*Towards a Common Vision*, 25).

117 Zizioulas writes that the Church is not a reality that lives outside of time, while communion is not just a matter of mutual references between local Churches in the space of a given time but *a koinonia* with communities of both the past and the future. Therefore, this concerns a communion in time. Without this, there would be no true communion. Cf. Zizioulas, *The One and the many*, 57–8.

The Church is holy because God is holy (cf. Isa 6:3; Lev 11:44-45) and Jesus "loved the church and gave himself up for her, in order to make her holy by cleansing her with the washing of water by the word, so as to present the church to himself in splendor, without a spot or wrinkle or anything of the kind—yes, so that she may be holy and without blemish" (Eph 5:25-27). The essential catholicity of the Church is undermined by the divisions, thus Christians are called to remove all obstacles that stand in the way of realising the fullness of truth and life that the Church has received by the power of the Holy Spirit. The Church is apostolic because the Father sent the Son to establish it, and the Son in turn chose and sent the apostles and prophets endowed with the gifts of the Holy Spirit at Pentecost to serve as its foundation and oversee its mission (cf. Eph 2:20; Rev 21:14). The apostolic succession under the guidance of the Holy Spirit is intended to serve this apostolicity of the Church.[118]

Communion is realised in unity and diversity. The legitimate diversity in the life of communion is a gift from the Lord. The Holy Spirit endows the faithful with diverse, complementary gifts for the common good (cf. 1 Cor 12:4-7). Disciples are called to full unity (cf. Acts 2:44-47; 4:32-37) respecting the diversity and richness of the gifts (1 Cor 12:14-26).[119] Therefore, each local Church remains in communion with the local Churches of all places and times. The issues of unity and diversity have been a major concern ever since the Church, with the help of the Holy Spirit, saw that pagans should be accepted into communion (cf. Acts 15,1-29; 10,1-11,18).[120] The ecclesiology of communion provides a helpful framework for considering the relationship between the local Church and the universal Church. Christian community is essential to living in communion. From the very beginning, communion between the local Churches has been maintained and nurtured. Thus, such communion of the local Churches is not an additional element. The universal Church is the communion of all local Churches united in faith and worship throughout the world. It is not merely a sum, federation or collection of local Churches, but all of them together constitute the same Church that is present and active in this world. Catholicity refers not only to the geographical scope, but also to the manifold diversity of local Churches united in *koinonia*.[121]

The Church is an eschatological reality which already anticipates the kingdom of God but does not yet fully realise it. It is only when we look at the present in the

118 Cf. *Towards a Common Vision*, 22.

119 Cf. *Towards a Common Vision*, 28.

120 Cf. *Towards a Common Vision*, 28–30.

121 Cf. *Towards a Common Vision*, 31. "Within this shared understanding of the communion of the local churches in the universal Church, differences arise, not only about the geographical extent of the community intended by the expression 'local church' but also in relation to the role of bishops" (ibid, 32).

light of the action of the Holy Spirit, guiding the whole historico-salvific process to the final union in Christ to the glory of the Father, that we begin to grasp the mystery of the Church.[122] The path to the full realisation of God's gift of communion requires Christian communities to agree on fundamental aspects of the life of the Church – the aim of the ecumenical movement is communion in the fullness of apostolic faith in sacramental life, in one and mutually recognised ministry, in conciliar structures, in decision-making structures and in common witness and service in the world.[123] Faith is awakened by the word of God, inspired by the grace of the Holy Spirit, attested in the Scriptures and handed down through the living tradition of the Church. The Holy Spirit inspires and guides all Churches to rethink and reinterpret their traditions in dialogue, seeking to embody one Tradition in the unity of the Church of God.[124]

As far as the sacraments are concerned, through baptism of water in the name of the triune God – the Father, the Son and the Holy Spirit – Christians are united to Christ and to each other in the Church of every time and place. Baptism is the introduction and celebration of new life in Christ and participation in His baptism, life, death and resurrection (cf. Matt 3:13-17; Rom 6:3-5). "The water of rebirth and renewal by the Holy Spirit" (Titus 3:5) incorporates believers into the body of Christ and enables them to participate in the kingdom of God and the life of the world to come (cf. Eph 2:6). Baptism involves confession of sins, conversion of heart, forgiveness, cleansing and sanctification; it consecrates the believer as a member of "a chosen race, a royal priesthood, a holy nation" (cf. 1 Pet 2:9). Baptism is thus the fundamental bond of unity. The document adds that some Churches see the gift of the Holy Spirit as given in a special way through chrismation or confirmation, which they regard as one of the sacraments of initiation. General agreement on baptism has led some involved in the ecumenical movement to call for mutual recognition of the validity of this sacrament.[125]

There is a dynamic and profound relationship between baptism and the Eucharist. The communion into which the newly initiated Christian enters is more fully expressed and nourished by the Eucharist, which confirms baptismal faith and gives grace.[126] In ecumenical dialogue, it is accepted that the Lord's Supper is the

---

122 Cf. *Towards a Common Vision*, 33.

123 Cf. *Towards a Common Vision*, 37.

124 Cf. *Towards a Common Vision*, 38.

125 Cf. *Towards a Common Vision*, 41.

126 Zizioulas emphasises that there can be no full communion without communion in the sacramental life of the Church, above all in the Eucharist. In ecclesiology of communion, the word "intercommunion" should be replaced by the word "communion". "Full communion means, in the first place, eucharistic communion, since the Eucharist is the recapitulation of the entire economy of salvation, in which past, present, and future are united and in which communion with the Holy Trinity and

celebration during which Christians receive the Body and Blood of Christ. It is the proclamation of the Gospel, the glorification of the Father (doxology), the commemoration of the death and resurrection of Jesus Christ and of what was accomplished once and for all on the cross (anamnesis) and the invocation of the Holy Spirit to transform both bread and wine and the participants themselves (epiclesis).[127]

Some Churches maintain that the ministry of holy orders stands in a special relationship with Christ's unique priesthood, which is distinct from the royal priesthood described in 1 Peter 2:9, even if it is related to it, and that some persons are ordained to a specific priestly function through the sacrament of holy orders. Others do not regard ordained ministers as "priests" and some do not understand ordination in a sacramental way. However, there was a time when the Holy Spirit guided the Church to tailor its ministry to particular needs (cf. Acts 6:1-6) and various forms of ministry were blessed with His gifts.[128] The authority that Jesus Christ shares with those in leadership roles is a gift of the Spirit intended for the ministry (diakonia) of the Church in love. Decision-making in the Church seeks and elicits the consensus of all and depends on the guidance of the Holy Spirit, who resolves possible ambiguities in the process of active reception over time. The close relationship between the ordained ministry and the community should find its expression in the communal dimension and requires the effective participation of the community in discovering the will of God and the guidance of the Holy Spirit. Under the guidance of the Holy Spirit, the whole Church is synodal and conciliar at all levels of ecclesiastical life, and the structures of the Church should realise the life of the community as communion.[129]

The source of passion for the transformation of the world is the communion of the faithful with God, who is absolute love, mercy and justice, and can work through them by the power of the Holy Spirit.[130] The unity of the Church lies in the gift of communion and there is a growing consensus that *koinonia* as communion with the Holy Trinity manifests itself as unity in faith, sacramental life and service. The celebration of the Eucharist serves as a dynamic paradigm of what such *koinonia* looks like in the present day. In it, the people of God experience communion

with the rest of the Churches, as well as with creation, takes place. Baptism, Chrismation or Confirmation, and the rest of the sacramental life, are all given *in view of* the Eucharist. Communion in these sacraments may be described as 'partial' or *anticipatory* communion, calling for its fulfilment in the Eucharist" (Zizioulas, *The One and Many*, 59).

127 Cf. *Towards a Common Vision*, 42.

128 Cf. *Towards a Common Vision*, 26–49.

129 Cf. *Towards a Common Vision*, 51–3; Andrzej Dobrzyński, "Synodalność w nauczaniu i pontyfikacie Jana Pawła II," *Teologia w Polsce* 15/2 (2021), 127–8.

130 Cf. *Towards a Common Vision*, 64.

with God and fellowship with Christians of all times and places.[131] One of the blessings of the ecumenical movement has been the discovery of the many aspects of being a disciple of Jesus in different Churches that have not yet been living in full communion. Schisms and divisions are contrary to Christ's will and hinder the Church's mission. This is why the restoration of unity among Christians under the guidance of the Holy Spirit is such an urgent task. The development of communion unfolds within this wider community of believers, which extends into the past and into the future, embracing the whole communion of saints. The Church's ultimate destiny is to be included in the communion of the Father, the Son and the Holy Spirit, to be part of the new creation glorifying and rejoicing forever in God (cf. Rev 21:1-4; 22:1-5).[132]

131 Cf. *Towards a Common Vision*, 67.

132 Cf. *Towards a Common Vision*, 68.

Summary

The concept of pneumatology presented in this monograph first discussed the place of the Holy Spirit in the Communion of the Holy Trinity. The analysis of the biblical data made it possible to show the communal pneumatological potential contained therein, which forms the basis for distinguishing the communional aspects of the historical development of pneumatology. This in turn made it possible to show first the communional position of the Holy Spirit in the light of the first trinitological concepts, and further the communional-pneumatological aspects in the further development of trinitology – from medieval pneumatology to Vatican II pneumatology and contemporary theology. This led first to the description of the Holy Spirit as a Person in the Communion of the Holy Trinity and presenting Him in the context of the other Persons of that Communion, the communional trinitarian perichoresis and the interplay of communional unity and trinitarian plurality. This was followed by a discussion of the origin of the Holy Spirit in the context of the trinitarian Communion and problems with the traditional view of the Persons of the Holy Trinity, as well as the specificity of the Holy Spirit within the trinitarian Communion and the communional view of the properties of the Holy Spirit. The new trinitarian thinking starts with the inter-personal and communicative action of the Divine Persons. Since God is perfect love, the Holy Spirit is the personal environment (medium) of the love of the Father and the Son, connecting them by a knot, a "Communion in God" that mediates the communicative unity and diversity of the Persons. According to the scheme drawn from the model of communicative action, "the Father" is the subject and source ("Wherefrom") of infinitely sacrificial love, "the Son" is the goal and partner ("Whereto") of infinitely received love proceeding form the Father. "The Holy Spirit" is the unifying and mediating environment ("Wherein") of this infinite love. And finally, love itself is the content ("What") of that which exists between the Father, the Son and the Holy Spirit and is identical with the Divine "essence". The Holy Spirit as Communion in God is the proper theological foundation of ecclesial communion, and the Church becomes the historical sign of intra-Divine Communion – the "sacrament of the Holy Spirit". The Holy Spirit is the mediating "Wherein" in the history of salvation, the communicative "environment of meaning" of the mutual love of the Father and the Son. Through the Holy Spirit, human history is incorporated into the event of this love in order for it to become the perfect form of the Communion that is identical with Him – the "social form" of God's love. This mediating power of the Holy Spirit finds its purpose in extending the love of the Father and the Son onto the universal communion of people with God and among people.

Important for pneumatology of communion is the issue of the communional-trinitarian aspects of the Holy Spirit's action in the history of salvation. Above all, it is the question of so-called Christological pneumatology or, put differently, pneumatological Christology. The proper synthesis achieved in theology shows that Christology and pneumatology must exist simultaneously. This has been pointed out by the great theologians of more recent times. In addition, the exegetical discoveries have shown conclusively that a significant place in the New Testament Christologies is given to the question of presenting Christ in relation to the Holy Spirit. Contemporary personalist Christology links Jesus' historicity and uniqueness with His intra-trinitarian identity. The Holy Spirit, who mediates between God's inner life and His work in the world, prepares creation for the Incarnation, guides Jesus through earthly life to glory and enables all human beings to participate in the life of the triune God. Pneumatological Christology reveals the universal and timeless meanings of Jesus for all people. His mission involves the mission of the Holy Spirit and the Kingdom of love, justice and peace arising in His power. Also the fruits of redemption are born in the lives of people of every era through the Holy Spirit continuing the work of salvation today. There is no Christ without the Holy Spirit and no Holy Spirit without Christ – He is "the pneumatic Christ". Even the Body of Christ in a Christological (incarnational) and ecclesiological sense is a historical reality "only in the Holy Spirit". Any division between Christology and pneumatology thus disappears in the Holy Spirit. This was clearly confirmed by an analysis of the Holy Spirit's role in revelation and His joint action with the Son, and the work of the Holy Spirit in the mysteries of Christ. Jesus' death was the glory and exaltation of God and the cross of Christ is called a kind of liturgy of obedience, in which the unity between the Father and the Son in the eternal Holy Spirit is shown.

Another issue was the reflection on the pneumatological dimension of human life in the communion with Christ and theology – with particular emphasis on the communional aspects of contemporary pneumatological thought, such as deification, sanctification, grace, filiation, new life, subsisting in Christ and in the Holy Spirit. The whole essential content of what God has given to human beings in Jesus Christ is made present in our communication with Him, which takes place in the Holy Spirit as the medium of this communication. Pneumatology has experienced a renaissance, mainly due to the integration of theological reflection and spiritual experience, and a new awakening of the ecclesial sense of union as communion. The study briefly outlined the main communional impulses present above all in the works of H. Mühlen, H.U. von Balthasar, K. Rahner, J. Ratzinger, A. Ganoczy, J. Werbick, G.L. Müller, M. Kehl, G. Greshake, W. Kasper, B. Stubenrauch, B. Lonergan, J. Moltmann, W. Pannenberg and M. Knapp.

The words spoken in 1968 at the General Assembly of the Ecumenical Council of Churches in Uppsala by Metropolitan Ignatius of Laodicea are widely known: "Without the Holy Spirit, God is distant, Christ is merely a historical figure, the

Gospel is a dead letter, the Church is just an organisation, authority is domination, mission is propaganda, liturgy is only nostalgia, and the work of Christians is slave labour. But with the Holy Spirit, Christ is risen and present, the Gospel is a living force, the Church is a communion in the life of the Trinity, authority is a service that sets people free, mission is Pentecost, the liturgy is memory and anticipation, and the labour of Christians is divinised". Modern theology can fully subscribe to these words. If this is the case, the Holy Spirit can be sought in the pneumatological-sacramental structure of the Church's communion.

The Holy Spirit is the co-creator of the communion of the Church and thus faith and the word of God, which are fundamental to this communion, have pneumatological dimensions. The Holy Spirit guarantees, expands and deepens the memory of the Church, but He also animates the personal act of faith. The Church as a common reference to God in faith can come into being and persist where people join in the communional "space" of the Holy Spirit. According to more recent theology, the salvific and ecclesiogenic efficacy of the word of God also rests on the Holy Spirit's work. Communication with Christ through books is true communion with Him, because Christ speaks and acts by the power of the Holy Spirit. Truth is not arrived at by merely acquiring it intellectually, but through the experience of being included in communion with God. Truth subsists only in submission to the Holy Spirit and in communion with the body of the Church. For God is not known apart from the communion of the Holy Spirit and the love created by Him. The Church, as the sacrament of the Holy Spirit, is also characterised by the pneumatological-communional dimensions of its institutionality which serve its identity, unity and freedom, while its sacraments – which are the sacraments of communion – have important pneumatological dimensions.

According to the ecclesiology of communion, the Church is an assembly of believers in Christ who accept the share in the goods of salvation offered to them in the Holy Spirit and form a unity in the diversity of believers and Churches. This unity is a continuous process of building communion through the Holy Spirit who animates the visible structures. Communion in the Holy Spirit does not unify the Church, but rather personalises and pluralises it in unity. It is for this reason that the final chapter is devoted to the pneumatological-communional dimensions of the Church's unity realised as the communion of the faithful, the communion of particular Churches and the hierarchical communion. This communion presupposes participation in the life of the Holy Spirit and the resulting fraternal communion. It is owing to the Holy Spirit that there is a sense of faith and charisms; in Him it is impossible to live apart from dialogue and communion, only for oneself.

The monograph concludes with the presentation of the pneumatological dimensions of the common ecumenical vision of the Church as communion based on the World Council of Churches document, entitled *The Church. Towards a Common Vision*. The Church works by the power of the Holy Spirit to heal the broken world and bring it into communion. Divisions must be overcome with gifts from this Spirit. One of the blessings of the ecumenical movement is the emergence of a desire to restore unity among Christians under the guidance of the Holy Spirit, who guides them to join in the communion of the Father, the Son and the Holy Spirit. In this great work we can clearly see the incomprehensible power of His action and the accompanying hope.

List of abbreviations

AG — Second Vatican Council, Decree on the Missionary Activity of the Church *Ad gentes divinitus* (1965).

CCC — *Catechism of the Catholic Church* (1993).

CCL — *Code of Canon Law* (1983).

DV — Second Vatican Council, Dogmatic Constitution on Divine Revelation *Dei Verbum* (1965).

FC — John Paul II, Exhortation *Familiaris consortio* (1981).

GS — Second Vatican Council, Pastoral Constitution on the Church in the Modern World *Gaudium et Spes* (1965).

LG — Second Vatican Council, Dogmatic Constitution on the Church *Lumen Gentium* (1964).

PDV — John Paul II, Exhortation *Pastores dabo vobis* (1992).

PG — *Patrologiae Cursus Completus. Series Graecae*, ed. P. Migne, Vols. 1–167, Paris 1857–1866.

PL — *Patrologiae Cursus Completus. Series Latina*, ed. P. Migne, Vols. 1–217, Paris 1878–1890.

PO — Second Vatican Council, Decree on the Ministry and Life of Priests *Presbyterorum ordinis* (1965).

STh — S. Thomae Aquinatis, *Summa theologica*, I–III (Taurini 1939).

UUS — John Paul II, Encyclical *Ut unum sint* (1995).

List of Abbreviations

Bibliography

1. Bible

Holy Bible. The New Revised Standard Version. Catholic Edition (2007).

2. Church Documents

Sobór w Bazylei – Ferrarze – Florencji – Rzymie. *Bulla unii z Koptami* ("*Cantate Domino*," *Decretum pro Jacobitis*) (1442). In *Dokumenty Soborów Powszechnych. Tekst łaciński, grecki, arabski, ormiański, polski*, vol. III (1414–1445), edited by Arkadiusz Baron and Henryk Pietras (Kraków: WAM, 2003), 570–619.

Sobór Trydencki. *Nauka o świętych sakramentach pokuty i ostatniego namaszczenia* (1551). In *Dokumenty Soborów Powszechnych. Tekst łaciński i polski*, vol. IV, edited by Arkadiusz Baron and Henryk Pietras (Kraków: WAM, 2004), 483–513.

Leo XIII. Encyclical Letter *Divinum illud munus* (1897).

Pius XI. Encyclical Letter *Casti conubii* (1930).

Pius XII. Encyclical Letter *Mystici Corporis Christi* (1943).

Second Vatican Council. Decree on Ecumenism *Unitatis redintegratio* (1964).

Second Vatican Council, Dogmatic Constitution on the Church *Lumen gentium* (1964).

Second Vatican Council. Pastoral Constitution on the Church in the Modern World *Gaudium et spes* (1965).

Second Vatican Council. Decree on the Ministry and Life of Priests *Presbyterorum ordinis* (1965).

Second Vatican Council. Decree on the Missionary Activity of the Church *Ad gentes divinitus* (1965).

Second Vatican Council. Constitution on Divine Revelation *Dei verbum* (1965).

Paul VI. Constitution *Pontificalis romani* (1968).

Paul VI. Constitution *Divinae consortium naturae* (1971).

Obrzędy sakramentu małżeństwa dopasowane do zwyczajów diecezji polskich. Katowice: Księgarnia św. Jacka, 1974.

Paul VI. Exhortation *Evangelii nuntiandi* (1975).

John Paul II. Exhortation *Familiaris consortio* (1981).

John Paul II. Exhortation *Reconciliatio et paenitentia* (1984).

John Paul II. Encyclical Letter *Dominum et Vivificantem* (1986).

John Paul II. Apostolic Letter *Mulieris dignitatem* (1988).

John Paul II. Exhortation *Pastores dabo vobis* (1992).

John Paul II. Letter to Families *Gratissimam sane* (1994).
Congregation for the Clergy. *Directory on the Ministry and Life of Priests* (1994).
Catechism of the Catholic Church (1994).
John Paul II. Encyclical Letter *Ut unum sint* (1995).
Pontificial Council for Promoting Christian Unity. *Greek and Latin Traditions Regarding the Procession of the Holy Spirit* (1995).
Congregation for the Clergy. *Priest, Pastor and Leader of the Parish Community* (2002).
John Paul II. Encyclical Letter *Ecclesia de Eucharistia* (2003).
Benedict XVI. Encyclical Letter *Deus caritas est* (2005).
Benedict XVI. Exhortation *Sacramentum caritatis* (2007).
Jan Paweł II. *Mężczyzną i niewiastą stworzył ich. Odkupienie ciała a sakramentalność małżeństwa*, Tadeusz Styczeń (ed.), Lublin: Wydawnictwo KUL, 2008.
Synod of Bishops. XII Ordinary General Assembly. The Word of *God in the Life and the Mission of the Church* (2008).
Francis. Encyclical Letter *Lumen fidei* (2013).
Francis. Exhortation *Evangelii gaudium* (2013).
International Theological Commission. *Synodality in Life and Mission of the Church* (2018).

3. Literature

Alves, Manuel Isidro. "Dam wam Ducha nowego." *Communio. Międzynarodowy Przegląd Teologiczny* 8/1 (1988): 14–31.
Andia, Ysabel de. "Święty, Pan i Dawca życia." *Communio. Międzynarodowy Przegląd Teologiczny* 8/1 (1988): 32–48.
Arens, Edmund. "Was kann Kommunikation?" *Stimmen der Zeit* 6 (2002): 414–17.
Auer, Johann. *Die Sakramente der Kirche.* Regensburg: Pustet, 1972.
Auer, Johann. *Gott - Der Eine und Dreieine.* Regensburg: Pustet, 1978.
Auer, Johann. *Jesus Christus - Gottes und Mariä "Sohn"*." Regensburg: Pustet, 1986.
Bachl, Gottfried. "Essen und Trinken als sakramentales Handeln." *Theologisch-praktische Quartalschrift* 1 (2007): 30–8.
Bać, Tomasz. "Sakrament pokuty i pojednania." In *Znaki Tajemnicy. Sakramenty w teorii i praktyce Kościoła*, edited by Krzysztof Porosło and Robert J. Woźniak (Kraków: WAM, 2018), 389–418.
Balthasar, Hans Urs von. *Pneuma und Institution. Theologische Skizzen IV.* Einsiedeln: Johannes Verlag, 1974.
Balthasar, Hans Urs von. *Teologika*, vol. II: *Prawda Boga.* Kraków: WAM, 2004.
Balthasar, Hans Urs von. *Teologika*, vol. III: *Duch Prawdy.* Kraków: WAM, 2005.
Barth, Grzegorz. *Hermeneutyka osoby.* Lublin: Wydawnictwo KUL, 2013.
Bartnik, Czesław Stanisław. *Dogmatyka katolicka*, vol. I. Lublin: Wydawnictwo KUL, 2000.
Bartnik, Czesław Stanisław. *Dogmatyka katolicka*, vol. II. Lublin: Wydawnictwo KUL, 2003.

Bartnik, Czesław Stanisław. "Osoba a dusza." *Personalizm* 12 (2007): 21–6.
Bartnik, Czesław Stanisław. *Personalizm*. Lublin: Wydawnictwo KUL, 2008.
Bastian, Hans-Dieter. *Kommunikation. Wie christlicher Glaube funktioniert.* Stuttgart-Berlin: Kreuz, 1972.
Beinert, Wolfgang. "Der Heilige Geist und die Strukturen. Die Spannung von Amt und Charisma in der Kirche." In *Wo der Geist des Herrn wirkt, da ist Freiheit*, edited by Günter Koch and Josef Pretscher (Würzburg: Echter, 1997), 83–120.
Beinert, Wolfgang. "Grundlagen des katholischen Amtsverständnisses." *Theologisch-praktische Quartalschrift* 4 (1973): 305–17.
Beinert, Wolfgang. "Versöhnung als Lebensvollzug der Kirche." In *Theorie der Sprachhandlung und heutige Ekklesiologie. Ein philosophisch-theologisches Gespräch*, edited by Peter Hühnermann and Richard Schaeffler (Freiburg-Basel-Wien: Herder, 1980), 130–49.
Bokwa, Ignacy. *Trynitarno-chrystologiczna interpretacja eschatologii w ujęciu Hansa Ursa von Balthasara*. Radom: Radomskie Wydawnictwo Diecezjalne AVE, 1998.
Bouyer, Louis. *Duch Święty Pocieszyciel. Duch Święty i życie w łasce*. Kraków: Wydawnictwo M, 2000 [French original: *Le Consolateur. Esprit Saint et Vie de grace*. Paris: *Cerf*, 1980].
Bouyer, Louis. *Ojciec niewidzialny. Drogi do tajemnicy Boga*. Kraków: Wydawnictwo M, 1998.
Bouyer, Louis. *Syn Przedwieczny*. Kraków: Wydawnictwo M, 2000.
Breuning, Wilhelm. *Nauka o Bogu*. Kraków: Wydawnictwo M, 1999.
Caffarra, Carlo. "Sakramentalna ontologia a nierozerwalność małżeństwa." In *Pozostać w prawdzie Chrystusa. Małżeństwo i Komunia w Kościele katolickim*, edited by Roberto Dodaro (Poznań: Księgarnia Św. Wojciecha, 2015), 161–73.
Chaignon, Francis de. "Kościół a Trójca Święta w doktrynie Soboru Watykańskiego II." In *Tajemnica Trójcy Świętej*, edited by Lucjan Balter, Stefan Dusza, and Franciszek Mickiewicz et al. (Poznań: Pallottinum, 2000), 477–89.
Chevalier, Max-Alain. "Biblische Pneumatologie." In *Neue Summe Theologie*, vol. 1: *Der lebendige Gott*, edited by Peter Eicher (Freiburg-Basel-Wien: Herder, 1988), 341–78.
Congar, Yves. *Słowo i Tchnienie*. Kraków: WAM, 2018.
Congar, Yves. "Systematische Pneumatologie." In *Neue Summe Theologie*, vol. 1: *Der lebendige Gott*, edited by Peter Eicher (Freiburg-Basel-Wien: Herder, 1988), 379–406.
Congar, Yves. *Wierzę w Ducha Świętego. Duch Święty w "ekonomii" Objawienia i doświadczenie Ducha*, vol. I. Warszawa: Wydawnictwo Księży Marianów, 1995.
Congar, Yves. *Wierzę w Ducha Świętego. "Panem jest Duch i daje życie" (2 Kor 3,17)*, vol. II. Warszawa: Wydawnictwo Księży Marianów, 1995.
Congar, Yves. *Wierzę w Ducha Świętego. Rzeka życia płynie na Wschodzie i na Zachodzie płynie na Wschodzie i na Zachodzie (Ap 22,1)*, vol. III. Warszawa: Wydawnictwo Księży Marianów, 1996.
Cordes, Paul Josef. *Communio – Utopie oder Programm?* Freiburg-Basel-Wien: Herder, 1993.

Coreth, Emerich. "Lebensvollzug in Kommunikation und Interaktion." In *Theorie der Sprachhandlungen und heutige Ekklesiologie. Ein philosophisch-theologisches Gespräch*, edited by Peter Hünermann and Richard Schaeffler (Freiburg-Basel-Wien: Herder, 1987), 11–26.

Courth, Franz. *Bóg trójjedynej miłości*. Poznań: Pallottinum 1997.

Courth, Franz. *Die Sakramente. Ein Lehrbuch für Studium und Praxis der Theologie*. Freiburg-Basel-Wien: Herder, 1995.

Czaja, Andrzej. *Credo in Spiritum Vivificantem. Pneumatologiczna interpretacja Kościoła jako komunii w posoborowej teologii niemieckiej*. Lublin: Wydawnictwo KUL, 2003.

Czaja, Andrzej. *Jedna Osoba w wielu osobach. Pneumatologiczna eklezjologia Heriberta Mühlena*. Opole: Wydawnictwo Świętego Krzyża, 1997.

Czaja, Andrzej. "Traktat o Kościele." In *Dogmatyka*, edited by Elżbietata Adamiak, Andrzej Czaja and Józef Majewski (Warszawa: Więź, 2006), 2: 289–569.

Dalbesio, Anselmo. *Duch Święty w Nowym Testamencie, w Kościele, w życiu chrześcijańskim*. Kraków: WAM, 2001.

Daniélou, Jean. *Teologia judeochrześcijańska. Historia doktryn chrześcijańskich przed Soborem Nicejskim*. Kraków: WAM, 2002.

Dobrzyński, Andrzej. "Synodalność w nauczaniu i pontyfikacie Jana Pawła II." *Teologia w Polsce* 15/2 (2021): 109–30.

Durwell, François-Xavier. *L'Esprit Saint de Dieu*. Paris: Cerf, 1983.

Eicher, Peter. *Die anthropologische Wende. Karl Rahners philosophischer Weg vom Wesen des Menschen zur personaler Existenz*. Freiburg (Schweiz): Schweiz Universitätsverlag, 1970.

Evdokimov, Paul. *Duch Święty w koncepcji prawosławnej*. Poznań: "W drodze," 2012.

Evdokimov, Paul. *Prawosławie*. Warszawa: PAX, 2003.

Fiedorowicz, Michael. *Teologia ojców Kościoła. Podstawy wczesnochrześcijańskiej refleksji nad wiarą*. Kraków: Wydawnictwo UJ, 2009.

Figura, Michael. "Duch Święty a Kościół." *Communio. Międzynarodowy Przegląd Teologiczny* 18/2 (1998): 79–95.

Figura, Michael. "Kościół i Eucharystia w świetle tajemnicy Trójjedynego Boga." *Communio. Międzynarodowy Przegląd Teologiczny* 20/2 (2000): 38–58.

Figura, M., "Sakramentalność słowa Bożego." *Communio. Międzynarodowy Przegląd Teologiczny* 21/5 (2001): 94–111.

Forte, Bruno. *Istota chrześcijaństwa*. Lublin: Wydawnictwo KUL, 2007.

Freitag, Josef. *Geist-Vergessen – Geist-Erinnern. Vladimir Losskys Pneumatologie als Herausforderung westlicher Theologie*. Würzburg: Echter, 1995.

Gacka, Bogumił. *Znaczenie osoby w teologii Josepha Ratzingera – Benedykta XVI*. Warszawa: Wydawnictwo UKSW, 2010.

Ganoczy, Alexandre. *Aus seiner Fülle haben wir alle empfangen. Grundriß der Gnadenlehre*. Düsseldorf: Patmos, 1989.

Ganoczy, Alexandre. *Einführung in die katholische Sakramentenlehre*. Darmstadt: Wissenschaftliche Buchgesellschaft, 1979.

Ganoczy, Alexandre. "Glaubwürdiges Feiern der Eucharistie." *Geist und Leben* 45 (1972): 98–110.

Ganoczy, Alexandre. "Kirche im Prozeß der pneumatischen Erneuerung." In *Glaube im Prozeß. Christsein nach dem II Vaticanum*, edited by Elmar Klinger and Klaus Wittstadt (Freiburg im Breisgau: Herder, 1984), 196–206.

Gardocki, Dariusz. "Boska świadomość Jezusa w ujęciu współczesnej chrystologii." In *Sens ludzkiej przygody*, edited by Zbigniew Kubacki and Waldemar Cisło (Warszawa: Rhetos, 2008), 161–81.

Gardocki, Dariusz. "Cierpienie Boga w ujęciu Jürgena Moltmanna," *Studia Bobolanum* 1 (2010): 49–65.

Gardocki, Dariusz. "Misyjność Kościoła w świetle Adhortacji apostolskiej Evangelii Gaudium i Dokumentu z Aparecidy "Jesteśmy uczniami i misjonarzami Jezusa Chrystusa, aby nasze narody miały w Nim życie." *Studia Bobolanum* 2 (2017): 79–100.

Gardocki, Dariusz. "Oblicze współcierpiącego Ojca w ujęciu Jeana Galota." *Studia Bobolanum* 2 (2010): 21–31.

Gardocki, Dariusz. *Teologia wyzwolenia jako odpowiedź na epokowe wyzwania czasu.* Kraków: WAM, 2020.

Gardocki, Dariusz. „Encyklika "Lumen fidei" Ojca Świętego Franciszka." Drukarnia Watykańska, Rzym 2013. *Studia Bobolanum* 3 (2013): 181–8.

Gąsecki, Krzysztof. *Jesteśmy napełnieni Duchem Chrystusa w sakramentach Kościoła. Pneumatologia a sakramentologia.* Pelplin: Bernardinum, 2018.

Gomes, Cirilo Folch. "Jezus a dar Ducha Świętego." *Communio. Międzynarodowy Przegląd Teologiczny* 7/1 (1988): 3–13.

Góralczyk, Paweł. "Społeczny wymiar grzechu." *Communio. Międzynarodowy Przegląd Teologiczny* 4/5 (1984): 35–47.

Grabowski, Tomasz. "Sakrament bierzmowania." In *Znaki Tajemnicy. Sakramenty w teorii i praktyce Kościoła*, edited by Krzysztof Porosło and Robert J. Woźniak (Kraków: WAM, 2018), 303–46.

Gregory of Nazianzus, St., *Carmina dogmatica*, PG 37, 397–522.

Gregory of Nyssa, St., *Ad Ablabium*, PG 45, vol. II, 115–36.

Greshake, Gisbert. "Communio – Schlüsselbegriff der Dogmatik." In *Gemeinsam Kirche sein. Theorie und Praxis der Communio. Festschrift der Theologischen Fakultät der Universität Freiburg i. Br. für Erzbischof Dr. Oskar Saieri*, edited by Günteher Biemer, Bernhard Casper and Josef Müller (Freiburg-Basel-Wien: Herder, 1992), 90–121.

Greshake, Gisbert. *Priester sein.* Freiburg: Herder, 1991 [Poznań: "W drodze," 2010)].

Greshake, Gisbert. *Być kapłanem. Teologia i duchowość urzędu kapłańskiego.* Wrocław: Wydawnictwo Wrocławskiej Księgarni Archidiecezjalnej, 1983.

Greshake, Gisbert. *Der dreieine Gott. Eine trinitarische Theologie.* Freiburg-Basel-Wien: Herder, 1997 [*Trójjedyny Bóg. Teologia trynitarna.* Wrocław: Wydawnictwo Wrocławskiej Księgarni Archidiecezjalnej, 2009].

Greshake, Gisbert. *Wierzę w Boga trójjedynego. Klucz do zrozumienia Trójcy Świętej.* Kraków: Znak, 2001.

Grüner, Karl. "Überlegungen zu einer theologischen Kommunikationstheorie." *Communicatio Socialis. Zeitschrift für Publizistik in Kirche und Welt* 19 (1986): 206–19.

Guzowski, Krzysztof. *Duch Dialogujący. To dialegomenon Pneuma. Zarys pneumatologii dialogalnej.* Lublin: Wydawnictwo KUL, 2016.

Guzowski, Krzysztof. "Komunijna i dialogiczna struktura osoby. Perspektywa teologiczno-antropologiczna." In *Kościół i człowiek*, edited by Andrzej A. Napiórkowski (Kraków: Salvator, 2021), 73–89.

Guzowski, Krzysztof. *Symbolika trynitarna Brunona Fortego.* Lublin: Wydawnictwo KUL, 2004.

Guzowski, Krzysztof. "Symbolika trynitarna Kościoła jako komunii i misji." In *Communio w chrześcijańskiej refleksji o Kościele*, edited by Andrzej Czaja and Marek Marczewski (Lublin: Wydawnictwo KUL, 2004), 213–33.

Hemmerle, Klaus. *Thesen zu einer trinitarischen Ontologie.* Einsiedeln: Johannes Verlag, 1976.

Hernoga, Josef. *Das Priestertum. Zur nachkonziliaren Amtstheologie im deutschen Sprachraum.* Frankfurt am Main-Berlin-Bern-New York-Paris-Wien: Peter Lang, 1997.

Hilberath, Bernd Jochen. *Der dreieinige Gott und die Gemeinschaft der Menschen. Orientierungen zur christlichen Rede von Gott.* Mainz: Grünewald, 1990.

Hilberath, Bernd Jochen. *Der Personbegriff der Trinitätstheologie in Rückfrage von Karl Rahner zu Tertullians "Adversus Praxean."* Innsbruck-Wien: Tyrolia, 1986.

Hilberath, Bernd Jochen. "Pneumatologie." In *Handbuch der Dogmatik*, edited by Thomas Schneider (Düsseldorf: Patmos, 1992), 1: 445–551.

Hilberath, Bernd Jochen. "Vorgaben für die Ausarbeitung der Communio-Ekklesiologie." In *Communio – Ideal oder Zerrbild von Kommunikation?*, edited by Bernd Jochen Hilberath (Freiburg-Basel-Wien: Herder, 1999), 277–97.

Hofmann, Peter. *Glaubensbegründung. Die Transzendentalphilosophie der Kommunikationsgemeinschaft in fundamentaltheologischer Sicht.* Frankfurt am Main: Aschendorff, 1988.

Höhn, Hans-Joachim. *spüren. Die ästhetische Kraft der Sakramente.* Würzburg: Echter, 2002.

Hryniewicz, Wacław. *Chrystus nasza Pascha. Zarys chrześcijańskiej teologii paschalnej – tom 1.* Lublin: TN KUL, 1981.

Hryniewicz, Wacław. "Duch Święty – Mistagog Bożego Królestwa." In *Duch Święty w tradycji prawosławnej*, edited by Paul Evdokimov, 7–25. Poznań: "W drodze," 2012.

Hryniewicz, Wacław. "Eucharystia – sakrament paschalny." *Ateneum Kapłańskie* 101/2 (1983): 231–48.

Hryniewicz, Wacław. *Hermeneutyka w dialogu. Szkice teologiczno-ekumeniczne*, vol. 2. Opole: Wydawnictwo św. Krzyża, 1998.

Hryniewicz, Wacław. "Misterium Eucharystii w świetle teologii prawosławnej." *Ateneum Kapłańskie* 101/3 (1983): 366–80.

Hryniewicz, Wacław. *Nasza Pascha z Chrystusem. Zarys chrześcijańskiej teologii paschalnej - tom 2*. Lublin: TN KUL, 1987.

Hryniewicz, Wacław. *Pascha Chrystusa w dziejach człowieka i wszechświata. Zarys chrześcijańskiej teologii paschalnej - tom 3*. Lublin: TN KUL, 1991.

Hünermann, Peter. *Jesus Christus. Gottes Wort in der Zeit*. Münster: Aschendorff, 1994.

Jagiełło, Jarosław. "Metodologiczna odnowa dogmatyki: egzystencjalno-antropologiczny punkt widzenia." In *Dogmat i metoda. Wprowadzenie do badań interdyscyplinarnych w teologii dogmatycznej*, edited by Robert J. Woźniak (Kraków: WAM, 2020), 207–36.

Jagodziński, Marek. *Antropologia komunijna*. Lublin: Wydawnictwo KUL, 2015.

Jagodziński, Marek. *Communio dzięki komunikacji. Teologiczny wymiar teorii komunikatywnego działania w eklezjologii Medarda Kehla SJ*. Radom: Wydawnictwo Diecezjalne w Sandomierzu, 2002.

Jagodziński, Marek. "Communional Aspects of the Doctrine of the Holy Spirit according to John D. Zizioulas." *Teologia w Polsce* 14/1 (2020): 31–45.

Jagodziński, Marek. "Komunijna "fenomenologia" Kościoła według Medarda Kehla SJ." In *Communio w chrześcijańskiej refleksji o Kościele*, edited by Andrzej Czaja and Marek Marczewski (Lublin: Wydawnictwo KUL, 2004), 255–77.

Jagodziński, Marek. "Teologia komunijna. Człowiek Ducha Świętego." In *Kościół i człowiek*, edited by Andrzej A. Napiórkowski (Kraków: Salvator, 2021), 90–105.

Jagodziński, Marek. "Das Sakrament der Taufe als Communio-Sakrament." *Roczniki Teologiczne* 63/7 (2016): 201–19.

Jagodziński, Marek. *Eklezjalne kształty komunii*. Radom: Wydawnictwo Diecezji Radomskiej AVE, 2012.

Jagodziński, Marek. "Komunijna mistyka eklezjalna według Johna D. Zizioulasa." *Roczniki Teologiczne* 67/7 (2020): 5–18.

Jagodziński, Marek. *Komunijna wizja Kościoła według Medarda Kehla SJ*. Kraków: Unum, 2009.

Jagodziński, Marek. "Komunijna wizja sakramentu bierzmowania." In *Młodzież i doświadczenie wiary. Dialog w kontekście Światowych Dni Młodzieży w Krakowie*, edited by Marcin Składanowski, Tadeusz Syczewski, Jacek Połowianiuk and Krzysztof Mielnicki (Lublin: Wydawnictwo KUL, 2017), 115–32.

Jagodziński, Marek. "Komunijna wizja sakramentu małżeństwa." *Studia Teologii Dogmatycznej* 2 (2016): 48–67.

Jagodziński, Marek. "Komunijna wizja sakramentu pokuty i pojednania." In *Czy można dzisiaj wzywać do nawrócenia i pokuty? Chrześcijańska odpowiedź wiary*, edited by Marcin Składanowski, Tadeusz Syczewski and Jacek Połowianiuk (Lublin: Wydawnictwo KUL, 2015), 73–93.

Jagodziński, Marek. "Komunijny wymiar osoby ludzkiej." *Roczniki Teologiczne* 61/2 (2014): 51–63.

Jagodziński, Marek. "Komunijny wymiar słowa Bożego." In *Słowo Boże w Kościele*, edited by Roman Kuligowski, Marek Jagodziński and Daniel Swend (Warszawa: Wydawnictwo UKSW, 2009), 45–57.

Jagodziński, Marek. "Kościół jako środowisko wiary." In *Wiara wobec współczesności*, edited by Ignacy Bokwa and Marek Jagodziński (Warszawa: Wydawnictwo UKSW, 2014), 149–68.

Jagodziński, Marek. "Kościół – sakrament Ducha Świętego." In *Duch Kościoła. Kościół Ducha*, edited by Andrzej Proniewski (Białystok: Wydawnictwo Uniwersytetu w Białymstoku, 2014), 136–55.

Jagodziński, Marek. "Personalistyczno-komunijne wymiary kolegialności – synodalności w Kościele." *Studia Teologii Dogmatycznej* 5 (2019): 41–54.

Jagodziński, Marek. "Pneumatologiczny wymiar Eucharystii jako sakramentu komunii." In *Człowiek drogą Kościoła. Tradycja i współczesność*, edited by Piotr Turzyński and Wojciech Wojtyła (Radom: Łukasiewicz – Instytut Technologii Eksploatacji, 2020), 85–97.

Jagodziński, Marek. "Pneumatologiczny wymiar Kościoła i teologii według Johna D. Zizioulasa." *Studia Teologii Dogmatycznej* 6 (2020): 9–23.

Jagodziński, Marek. "Sakramenty komunii." *Ruch Biblijny i Liturgiczny* 4 (2009): 285–92.

Jagodziński, Marek. "Sakramenty miłosierdzia." In *Oblicza miłosierdzia*, edited by Elżbieta Matulewicz (Warszawa: Wydawnictwo UKSW, 2010), 73–82.

Jagodziński, Marek. *Sakramenty w służbie communio. Studium teologiczno-komunikacyjne*. Warszawa: Wydawnictwo UKSW, 2008.

Jagodziński, Marek. "Teologia a komunikacja." *Studia Theologica Varsaviensia* 41/2 (2003): 73–102.

Jagodziński, Marek. "Teologia jako komunijne nauczanie Kościoła według Johna D. Zizioulasa." In *O Kościele Jezusa Chrystusa dzisiaj. Księga pamiątkowa dedykowana Księdzu Doktorowi Wojciechowi Wójtowiczowi*, edited by Edward Sienkiewicz (Koszalin-Poznań: Pallottinum, 2020), 117–26.

Jagodziński, Marek. "Teoria komunikacyjnego działania w nauce o Trójcy Świętej." *Studia Koszalińsko-Kołobrzeskie* 15 (2010): 47–69.

Jagodziński, Marek. "Teoria komunikatywnego działania a sakramenty." *Studia Diecezji Radomskiej* 6 (2004): 33–50.

Jagodziński, Marek. "Trialogiczno-komunijna koncepcja trynitologii." *Studia Diecezji Radomskiej* 10 (2010/2011): 59–72.

Jagodziński, Marek. "Trwały skutek przyjęcia sakramentu święceń." *Collectanea Theologica. Kwartalnik Teologów Polskich* 74/3 (2004): 77–89.

Jagodziński, Marek. "Trynitarne podstawy Kościoła jako komunii." *Studia Theologica Varsaviensia* 42/1 (2004): 51–79.

Jagodziński, Marek. "Trynitarno-pneumatologiczne pośrednictwo Kościoła." *Studia Diecezji Radomskiej*, 10 (2010/2011): 73–88.

Jagodziński, Marek. *Trynitologia komunijna*. Lublin: Wydawnictwo KUL, 2021.

Jagodziński, Marek. *Węzłowe zagadnienia chrystologii komunijnej*. Radom: Wydawnictwo Diecezji Radomskiej AVE, 2013.

Jagodziński, Marek. "W komunii z Bogiem przez sakramenty." *Zeszyty Formacji Katechetów* 11/4 (2011): 36–42.

Janiec, Zdzisław. *Komunikacyjny wymiar liturgii*. Sandomierz: Wydawnictwo Diecezjalne w Sandomierzu, 2006.

Jüngel, Eberhard. *Gott als Geheimnis der Welt*. Tübingen: Mohr, 1977.

Kasper, Walter. "Amt und Gemeinde." In *Glaube und Geschichte*, edited by Walter Kasper (Mainz: Grünewald, 1970), 388–414.

Kasper, Walter. *Bóg Jezusa Chrystusa*. Wrocław: TUM Wydawnictwo Wrocławskiej Księgarni Archidiecezjalnej, 1996) [*Der Gott Jesu Christi*. Mainz: Grünewald, 1982].

Kasper, Walter. "Die Funktion des Priesters in der Kirche." In *Die Kirche und ihre Ämter. Schriften zur Ekklesiologie II*, edited by Walter Kasper (Freiburg-Basel-Wien: Herder, 2009), 153–72.

Kasper, Walter. "Dienst an der Einheit und Freiheit der Kirche." In *Wozu noch einen Papst? Vier Plödoyers für das Petrusamt*, edited by Heinz-Joachim Fischer (Köln: Communio, 1993), 21–56.

Kasper, Walter. *"Der Geist macht lebendig." Theologische Meditationen über den Heiligen Geist*. Freiburg: Informationszentrum Berufe der Kirche, 1982.

Kasper, Walter. "Die Kirche als Sakrament des Geistes." In *Die Kirche Jesu Christi. Schriften zur Ekklesiologie I*, edited by Walter Kasper (Freiburg-Basel-Wien: Herder, 2008), 281–305.

Kasper, Walter. *Glaube und Geschichte*. Mainz: Grünewald, 1970.

Kasper, Walter. *Jezus Chrystus*. Warszawa: Pax, 1983.

Kasper, Walter. "Kollegiale Strukturen in der Kirche." In *Glaube und Geschichte*, edited by Walter Kasper (Mainz: Grünewald, 1970), 355–70.

Kasper, Walter. "Sein und Sendung des Priesters." *Geist und Leben* 51 (1978): 162–222.

Kehl, Medard. *Die Kirche. Eine katholische Ekklesiologie*. Würzburg: Echter, 1994.

Kehl, Medard. *Eschatologie*. Würzburg: Echter, ^{3}1986.

Kehl, Medard. *Hinführung zum christlichen Glauben*. Mainz: Grünewald, ^{2}1987.

Kehl, Medard. "Kirche als Institution." In *Handbuch der Fundamentaltheologie*, vol. III: *Traktat Kirche*, edited by Walter Kern, Hermann Josef Pottmeyer and Max Seckler (Freiburg-Basel-Wien: Herder, 1986), 176–97.

Kehl, Medard. "Kirche als Institution – eine theologische Begründung." In *Kirche als Institution, Studienbrief* II/1, edited by Medard Medard Kehl, Norbert Glatzel and Norbert Mette (Tübingen: "Deutsches Institut für Fernstudien an der Universität Tübingen. Fernstudium Katholische Religionspädagogik," 1984), 48–150.

Kehl, Medard. "Kirche in der Kultur der Moderne." In *Christen an der Schwelle zum dritten Jahrtausend*, edited by Michael Sievernich and Johannes Beckermann (Frankfurt am Main: Knecht, 2000), 99–115.

Kehl, Medard. "Kirche in der Sorge um ihre Identität oder Kirche für die anderen." *Lebendige Seelsorge* 32 (1981): 57–65.

Kehl, Medard. "Kirche – Sakrament des Geistes." In *Gegenwart des Geistes. Aspekte der Pneumatologie*, edited by Walter Kasper (Freiburg: Herder, 1979), 155–80.

Kehl, Medard. *Und was kommt nach dem Ende? Von Weltuntergang und Vollendung, Wiedergeburt und Auferstehung.* Freiburg-Basel-Wien: Herder, 1999.

Keppler, Cornelius. "Der Heilige Geist – tatsächlich Gott, Person und Herr? Eine Spurensuche." *Stimmen der Zeit* 3 (2016): 181–90.

Kijas, Zdzisław Józef. *Traktat o Duchu Świętym i łasce.* Warszawa: Więź, 2007.

Kilmartin, Edward J., *Christian Liturgy. Theology and Practice. I. Systematic Liturgy.* Kansas City: Sheed & Ward, 1988.

Knapp, Markus. "Die Theorie des kommunikativen Handelns als Denkmodell für den trinitarischen Gottesbegriff?" In *Communio Sanctorum. Einheit der Christen – Einheit der Kirche,* edited by Josef Schreiner and Klaus Wittstadt (Würzburg: Echter, 1988), 323–37.

Knapp, Markus. "Trinitätslehre und Handlungstheorie." In *Gottesrede – Glaubenspraxis. Perspektiven theologischer Handlungstheorie,* edited by Edmund Arens (Darmstadt: Wissenschaftliche Buchgesellschaft, 1994), 49–68.

Kohlschein, Franz. "Die liturgische Feier als Kommunikationsgeschehen." *Theologie der Gegenwart* 26 (1983): 1–13.

Królikowski, Janusz. *Tajemnica Trójjedynego. Studia z teologii trynitarnej.* Kraków: Wydawnictwo Naukowe UPJP II, 2015.

Królikowski, Janusz. "Trynitarno-chrystologiczne perspektywy teologii małżeństwa." *Studia Teologii Dogmatycznej* 2 (2016): 15–27.

Kuc, Leszek. *Krótki traktat o teologii komunikacji.* Leszno k. Błonia: Lumen, 1997.

Kunka, Sławomir. *Teologiczna wizja cielesności człowieka w nauczaniu Karola Wojtyły – Jana Pawła II.* Lublin: Wydawnictwo KUL, 2012.

Kunz, Erhard. *Die Lehre von der Eucharistie. Skript zur Vorlesung im Sommersemester 1997.* Frankfurt am Main, 1997.

Kühn, Ulrich. *Sakramente.* Gütersloh: Mohn 1990.

Lachner, Raimund. "Communio – eine Grundidee des christlichen Glaubens. Ein Beitrag zur Elementarisierung im Fach Dogmatik." In *Qualitätsmanagement in der Theologie. Chancen und Grenzen einer Elementarisierung im Lehramtsstudium,* edited by Raimund Lachner and Egon Spiegel (Kevelaer: Butzon & Bercker, 2003), 231–51.

Laurentin, René *Nieznany Duch Święty. Odkrywanie Jego doświadczenia i Jego Osoby.* Kraków: Znak, 1998.

Leśniewski Krzysztof. "Przebóstwienie człowieka w teologii prawosławnej." In *Kościół i człowiek,* edited by Andrzej A. Napiórkowski (Kraków: Salwator, 2021), 191–208.

Link-Wieczorek, Ulrike. "Warum trinitarisch von Gott reden? Zur Neuentdeckung der Trinitätslehre in den heutigen Theologie." In *Der lebendige Gott. Auf den Spuren neueren trinitarischen Denkens,* edited by Rudolf Weth (Neukirchen-Vluyn: Neukirchener Verlag, 2005), 11–30.

Lies, Lothar. *Sakramententheologie. Eine personale Sicht.* Graz-Wien-Köln: Styria, 1990.

Liszka, Piotr. *Duch Święty, który od Ojca (i Syna) pochodzi.* Wrocław: Papieski Wydział Teologiczny, 2000.

Losada, Joaquín. "Wspólnota w Kościele-komunii." *Communio. Międzynarodowy Przegląd Teologiczny* 9/3 (1989): 58–68.

Łakowicz, Wanda (text) and Gabriela Rzechowska (music). "Duchu Ogniu, Duchu Żarze." In *Exsultate Deo. Śpiewnik mszalny. Wydanie siódme*, edited by Gizela Maria Skop (Carlsberg-Lublin, 1994), 193.

Łukaszuk, Tadeusz Dionizy. *Ty jesteś Chrystus, Syn Boga żywego. Dogmat chrystologiczny w ujęciu integralnym.* Kraków: Papieska Akademia Teologiczna, 2000.

Małecki, Roman. "Kościół jako "communio" w relacyjnej eklezjologii Johna D. Zizioulasa." *Studia Włocławskie* 1 (1998): 84–93.

Małecki, Roman. *Kościół jest wspólnotą. Dogmatyczno-ekumeniczne studium eklezjologii Johna Zizioulasa.* Lublin: Wydawnictwo KUL, 2000.

Matwiejuk, Kazimierz. *Liturgiczna celebracja zbawczych ingerencji Boga.* Ząbki: Apostolicum, 2014.

Martelet, Gustave. *Zmartwychwstanie, Eucharystia, człowiek.* Warszawa: Pax, 1976.

Maximus the Confessor, St, *Orationis dominicae brevis exposition*, PG 90, 871–910.

Mayer, Bernhard. "Die Kirche als Mysterium in ihren Ämtern und Diensten. Ansätze im Neuen Testament." In *Die Kirche als Mysterium in ihren Ämtern und Diensten*, edited by Bernhard Mayer and Michael Seybold (Eichstätt-Wien: Sales, 1987), 9–42.

Meuffels, Hans Otmar. *Kommunikative Sakramententheologie.* Freiburg-Basel-Wien: Herder, 1995.

Moltmann, Jürgen. *Bóg nadziei.* Lublin: Wydawnictwo KUL, 2006.

Moltmann, Jürgen. "Der dreieinige Gott." In *Der lebendige Gott. Auf den Spuren neueren trinitarischen Denkens*, edited by Rudolf Weth (Neukirchen-Vluyn: Neukirchener Verlag, 2005), 178–96.

Moltmann, Jürgen. *Trinität und Reich Gottes.* München: Kaiser, 1980 [*Trinity and the Kingdom of God: The Doctrine of God*, London 1981].

Munteanu, Daniel. "Das Filioque – ewige Streifrage oder Herausforderung der ökumenischen Trinitätslehre?." In *Der lebendige Gott. Auf den Spuren neueren trinitarischen Denkens*, edited by Rudolf Weth (Neukirchen-Vluyn: Neukirchener Verlag, 2005), 233–49.

Mühlen, Heribert. "Der gegenwärtige Aufbruch der Geisterfahrung und die Unterscheidung der Geister." In *Gegenwart des Geistes. Aspekte der Pneumatologie*, edited by Walter Kasper (Freiburg-Basel-Wien: Herder, 1979), 24–53.

Mühlen, Heribert. *Einübung in die christliche Grunderfahrung*, vol. I. Mainz: Grünewald, ^{4}1978.

Mühlen, Heribert. *Entsakralisierung: Ein epochales Schlagwort in seiner Bedeutung für die Zukunft der christlichen Kirchen.* Paderborn: Schöningh, 1970.

Mühlen, Heribert. "Der eine Geist und die vielen Kirchen nach der Aussagen des Vaticanum II." *Theologie und Glaube* 55 (1965): 329–66.

Mühlen, Heribert. *Der Heilige Geist als Person. Beitrag zur Frage nach der dem Heiligen Geiste eigentümlichen Funktion in der Trinität, bei der Inkarnation und im Gnadenbund.* Münster: Aschendorff, 1989.

Mühlen, Heribert. "Soziale Geisterfahrung als Antwort auf eine einseitige Gotteslehre." In *Erfahrung und Theologie des Heiligen Geistes*, edited by Claus Heitmann and H. Mühlen (Hamburg-München: Kösel, 1974), 252–72.

Mühlen, Heribert. *Una Mystica Persona. Die Kirche als das Mysterium der heilsgeschichtlichen Identität des Heiligen Geistes in Christus und den Christen: eine Person in vielen Personen.* München-Paderborn-Wien: Herder, 1968.

Müller, Gerhard Ludwig. *Chrystologia – nauka o Jezusie Chrystusie.* Kraków: Wydawnictwo M, 1995.

Müller, Gerhard Ludwig. *Katholische Dogmatik. Für Studium und Praxis der Theologie.* Freiburg-Basel-Wien: Herder, 1995 [*Dogmatyka katolicka*, Kraków: Wydawnictwo WAM, 2015].

Nadbrzeżny, Antoni. *Sakrament wyzwolenia. Zbawcze posłannictwo Kościoła w posoborowej teologii holenderskiej.* Lublin: Wydawnictwo KUL, 2013.

Napiórkowski, Andrzej A. "Kościół i człowiek: tajemnica, wspólnota, misja." In *Kościół i człowiek*, edited by Andrzej A. Napiórkowski (Kraków: Salwator, 2021), 227–51.

Napiórkowski, Andrzej A. *Misterium communionis. Eklezjalny paradygmat dziejów zbawienia.* Kraków: WAM, 2006.

Napiórkowski, Andrzej A. *Teologia jedności chrześcijan. Podręcznik ekumenizmu.* Kraków: Salwator, 2011.

Nastałek, Julian. "Słowo i Tchnienie. Konieczność duchowości inkarnacyjnej." In *Współczesne oblicza duchowości. Nova et vetera*, edited by Bogdan Ferdek and Paweł Beyga (Wrocław: Papieski Wydział Teologiczny, 2020), 115–28.

Nitsche, Bernhard. "Pneumatologie." In *Dogmatik heute. Bestandsaufnahme und Perspektiven*, edited by Thomas Marschler and Thomas Schärtl (Regensburg: Pustet, 2014), 321–60.

Nitsche, Bernhard. "Die Analogie zwischen dem trinitarischen Gottesbild und der communialen Struktur von Kirche. Desiderat eines Forschungsprogrammes zur Communio-Ekklesiologie." In *Communio – Ideal oder Zerrbild von Kommunikation?*, edited by Bernd Jochen Hilberath (Freiburg-Basel-Wien: Herder, 1999), 81–114.

Nocke, Franz-Josef. *Sakramententheologie. Ein Handbuch.* Düsseldorf: Patmos, 1997.

Norwid, Cyprian Kamil. *Człowiek*, http://www.poezja.org/utwor-4661.html.

Nossol, Alfons. *Ekumenizm jako imperatyw chrześcijańskiego sumienia. Przez dialog i pojednanie ku ekumenicznej jedności.* Opole: Wydział Teologiczny UO, 2001.

Nowak, Jacek. "Trójstopniowość sakramentu święceń." In *Kapłaństwo*, edited by Lucjan Balter et al. (Poznań-Warszawa: Pallottinum, 1988), 94–112.

O'Collins, Gerald. *Chrystologia. Jezus Chrystus w ujęciu biblijnym, historycznym i systematycznym.* Kraków: Wydawnictwo Uniwersytetu Jagiellońskiego, 2008.

O'Collins, Gerald. *Jezus nasz Odkupiciel. Chrześcijańskie ujęcie zbawienia.* Kraków: Wydawnictwo Uniwersytetu Jagiellońskiego, 2009.

Oeing-Hanhoff, Ludger. "Hegels Trinitätslehre. Zur Aufgabe ihrer Kritik und Rezeption." *Theologie und Philosophie* 52 (1977): 378–407.

Pałucki, Jerzy. *Trynitarny wymiar Kościoła. Studium patrystyczne.* Lublin: Wydawnictwo KUL, 2007.

Pannenberg, Wolfhart. "Die Subjektivität Gottes und die Trinitätslehre. Ein Beitrag zur Beziehung zwischen Karl Barth und der Philosophie Hegels." In *Grundfragen systematischer Theologie. Gesammelte Aufsätze*, edited by Wolfhart Pannenberg (Göttingen: Vandenhoeck & Ruprecht, 1980), 2: 96–111.

Pannenberg, Wolfhart. *Systematische Theologie*, vol. III. Göttingen: Vandenhoeck & Ruprecht, 1993.

Paprocki, Henryk. "Sakramentologia prawosławna." In *Znaki Tajemnicy. Sakramenty w teorii i praktyce Kościoła*, edited by Krzysztof Porosło and Robert J. Woźniak (Kraków: WAM, 2018), 537–56.

Perzyński, Andrzej. *Włoska antropologia teologiczna. Studium historyczno-dogmatyczne.* Łódź: Archidiecezjalne Wydawnictwo Łódzkie, 2012.

Piotrowski, Eligiusz. "Traktat o Trójcy Świętej." In *Dogmatyka*, vol. IV, edited by Elżbieta Adamiak, Andrzej Czaja and Józef Majewski. Warszawa: Więź, 2007.

Pottmeyer, Hermann Josef. "Der eine Geist als Prinzip der Einheit der Kirche in Vielfalt. Auswege aus einer christomonischen Ekklesiologie." *Pastoral-theologische Informationen* 5 (1985): 253–84.

Pottmeyer, Hermann Josef. "Theologie der Synodalen Strukturen." In *Fragen der Kirche heute*, edited by Adolf Exeler (Würzburg: Echter, 1971), 164–82.

Quellet, Marc. "Trójca Święta a Eucharystia: tajemnica przymierza." *Communio. Międzynarodowy Przegląd Teologiczny* 20/2 (2000): 18–37.

Qualizza, Marino. *Inicjacja chrześcijańska. Chrzest. Bierzmowanie. Eucharystia.* Kraków: WAM, 2002.

Rahner, Karl. "Der Glaube des Christen und die Lehre der Kirche." In *Schriften zur Theologie*, edited by Karl Rahner (Zürich-Einsiedeln-Köln: Benzinger, 1972), 10: 262–85.

Rahner, Karl. "Der theologische Ansatzpunkt für die Bestimmung des Wesens des Amtspriestertums." In *Schriften zur Theologie*, edited by Karl Rahner (Einsiedeln: Benzinger, 1970), 9: 366–72.

Rahner, Karl. "Zur Struktur des Kirchenvolkes heute." In *Schriften zur Theologie*,edited by Karl Rahner (Zürich-Einsiedeln-Köln: Benzinger, ^{2}1973), 11: 558–68.

Ratzinger, Josef. *Bóg Jezusa Chrystusa. Medytacje o Bogu Trójjedynym.* Kraków: Znak, 2006.

Ratzinger, Josef. "Der Heilige Geist als Communio. Zum Verhältnis von Pneumatologie und Spiritualität bei Augustinus." In *Erfahrung und Theologie des Heiligen Geistes*, edited by Claus Heitmann and Heribert Mühlen (Hamburg -München: Kösel, 1974), 223–38.

Ratzinger, Josef. *Dogma und Verkündigung.* München-Freiburg: Wewel, 1973.

Ratzinger, Josef. "Nauka Kościoła o 'sacramentum ordinis.'" In *Kapłaństwo*, edited by Lucjan Balter et al. (Poznań-Warszawa: Pallottinum, 1988), 65–76.

Ratzinger, Josef. *Nowe porywy Ducha. Ruchy odnowy w Kościele.* Kielce: Jedność, 2006.

Ratzinger, Josef. "O kwestii historyczności dogmatów." In Josef Ratzinger, *Opera omnia*, edited by Krzysztof Góźdź and Marzena Górecka (Lublin: Wydawnictwo KUL, 2018), IX/1: 527–38.

Ratzinger, Josef. "Ruchy teologiczne i ich miejsce teologiczne." In *Pielgrzymująca wspólnota wiary. Kościół jako komunia*, edited by Josef Ratzinger (Kraków: Wydawnictwo M, 2003), 159–88.

Ratzinger, Josef. *Wprowadzenie w chrześcijaństwo*. Kraków: Znak, 1994.

Ratzinger, Josef/Benedykt XVI. *Kościół. Pielgrzymująca wspólnota wiary*. Kraków: Wydawnictwo M, 2005.

Richard de Saint-Victor, *De Trinitate. Texte critique avec introduction, notes et tables*. Paris: Librairie Philosophique *J. Vrin*,1958.

Rojek, Paweł. "Dogmatyka a metafizyka. Założenia i implikacje teologii trynitarnej." In *Dogmat i metoda. Wprowadzenie do badań interdyscyplinarnych w teologii dogmatycznej*, edited by Robert J. Woźniak (Kraków: WAM, 2021), 237–75.

Romaniuk, Kazimierz. *Sakramentologia biblijna: zarys teologii sakramentów dla teologów, katechetów, duszpasterzy*. Warszawa: Wydawnictwo Salezjańskie, 1994.

Rusecki, Marian. "Personalizm. II. W teologii." In *Encyklopedia katolicka*, edited by Edward Gigilewicz et al. (Lublin: TN KUL, 2011), 15: 338–41.

Salis, Miguel de. *Kościół wcielony w historii. Elementy do ponownego odczytania Konstytucji dogmatycznej o Kościele Lumen gentium*. Kraków: WAM, 2021.

Salij, Jacek. "Sakrament małżeństwa a sakrament Eucharystii." http://www.kongres-eucharystyczny.mkw.pl/salij.pdf.

Sauter, Gerhard. "Die Kirche in der Krisis des Geistes." In *Kirche - Ort des Geistes*, edited by Walter Kasper and Gerhard Sauter (Freiburg-Basel-Wien: Herder, 1976), 59–106.

Scharer, Matthias. and Bernd Jochen Hilberath. *Kommunikative Theologie. Eine Grundlegung*. Mainz: Grünewald, 2002.

Scheffczyk, Leo. *Der Gott der Offenbarung. Gotteslehre*. Aachen: MM Verlag, 1996.

Scheffczyk, Leo. "Sens Filioque." *Communio. Międzynarodowy Przegląd Teologiczny* 8/1 (1988): 49–60.

Schneider, Theodor. "Die dogmatische Begründung der Ekklesiologie nach dem Zweiten Vatikanischen Konzil." In *Kirche. Ursprung und Gegenwart*, edited by Heinz Althaus (Freiburg im Breisgau: Herder, 1984), 79–118.

Schneider, Theodor. *Znaki bliskości Boga. Zarys sakramentologii*. Wrocław: Wrocławska Księgarnia Archidiecezjalna TUM, 1990.

Schockenhoff, Eberhard. "Liebe auf Abwegen? Zum Verhältnis von Sexualität und Liebe in intimen Beziehungen." *Theologisch-praktische Quartalschrift* 4 (2015): 339–46.

Schoonenberg, Piet. "Duch Boży w historii zbawienia." *Communio. Międzynarodowy Przegląd Teologiczny* 8/1 (1988): 76–88.

Schulz, Michael. *Sein und Trinität: Systematische Erörterungen zur Religionsphilosophie G.W.F. Hegels im ontologiegeschichtlichen Rückblick auf J. Duns Scotus und I. Kant und die Hegel-*

Rezeption in der Seinsauslegung und Trinitätstheologie bei W. Pannenberg, E. Jüngel, K. Rahner und H.U. v. Balthasar. St. Ottilien: EOS Verlag, 1997.

Schütz, Christian. *Einführung in die Pneumatologie.* Darmstadt: Wissenschaftliche Buchgesellschaft, 1985.

Scola, Angelo. *Osoba ludzka. Antropologia teologiczna.* Poznań: Pallottinum, 2005.

Sicari, Antonio. "Kapłaństwo Chrystusa." In *Kapłaństwo*, edited by Lucjan Balter et al. (Poznań-Warszawa: Pallottinum, 1988), 15–22.

Siwecki, Leon. *Człowiek odczytany w Bogu Ojcu. Teologiczno-antropologiczne refleksje w nauczaniu Jana Pawła II.* Lublin: Wydawnictwo KUL, 2020.

Skowronek, Alfons. *Małżeństwo i kapłaństwo jako spotęgowanie chrześcijańskiej egzystencji.* Włocławek: Włocławskie Wydawnictwo Diecezjalne, 1996.

Skowronek, Alfons. *Sakramenty w ogólności. Chrzest. Bierzmowanie.* Włocławek: Włocławskie Wydawnictwo Diecezjalne, 1995.

Skowronek, Alfons. *Eucharystia sakrament wielkanocny.* Włocławek: Włocławskie Wydawnictwo Diecezjalne, 1998.

Skrzypczak, Robert. *Osoba i misja. Podstawy eklezjologii misyjnej w świetle personalizmu papieża Jana Pawła II.* Warszawa: Wydawnictwo Sióstr Loretanek, 2005.

Słupek, Roman. *Jesteśmy Kościołem trójjedynego Boga. Kolegialność Kościoła według Yves'a Congara.* Lublin: Wydawnictwo KUL, 2004.

Soosten, Joachim von. "Zur theologischen Rezeption von Jürgen Habermas' "Theorie des kommunikativen Handelns""." *Zeitschrift für Evangelische Ethik* 34 (1990): 129–43.

Strumiłowski, Jan. *Między Bogiem a człowiekiem. Teologia relacji w kontekście późnej nowoczesności.* Kraków: WAM, 2018.

Szczurek, Jan Daniel. *Trójjedyny. Traktat o Bogu w Trójcy Świętej jedynym.* Kraków: Wydawnictwo Naukowe PAT, 2003.

Szymik, Jerzy. "Eklezjologia komunii. Kirche als koinonia, la Chiesa come communio, Kościół jako wspólnota – w pismach J. Ratzingera/Benedykta XVI i W. Wójtowicza." In *O Kościele Jezusa Chrystusa dzisiaj. Księga pamiątkowa dedykowana Księdzu Doktorowi Wojciechowi Wójtowiczowi*, edited by Edward Sienkiewicz (Koszalin-Poznań: Pallottinum, 2020), 303–26.

Szymik, Jerzy. "Filioque i dia tou Hyiou u progu trzeciego tysiąclecia". In *Duch Odnowiciel*, edited by Lucjan Balter et al. (Poznań: Pallottinum, 1998), 83–100.

Szymik, Jerzy. ""Na bliskość tchnienia": kluczowe tezy pneumatologii Josepha Ratzingera." *Śląskie Studia Historyczno-Teologiczne* 44/2 (2013): 337–51.

Szymik, Jerzy. "Pneumatologiczna communio. Po stronie Logosu (pistis), przeciwko anarchii (gnosis)." In *Duch Kościoła. Kościół Ducha*, edited by Andrzej Proniewski (Białystok: Wydawnictwo Uniwersytetu w Białymstoku, 2014), 19–34.

Szymik, Jerzy. "Religio vera. Rzeczywistość chrześcijaństwa – chrześcijański wymiar rzeczywistości według Josepha Ratzingera/Benedykta XVI." *Teologia w Polsce* 7/2 (2013): 3–22.

Seybold, Michael. "Die Kirche als Mysterium in ihren Ämtern und Diensten - Dogmatische Orientierung." In *Die Kirche als Mysterium in ihren Ämtern und Diensten*, edited by Bernhard Mayer and Michael Seybold (Eichstätt-Wien: Sales, 1987), 43–88.

Sienkiewicz, E. "Małżeńskie communio w sakramentalnym urzeczywistnieniu". *Studia Teologii Dogmatycznej* 2 (2016): 28–47.

Sienkiewicz, Edward. "Wierzę w święty Kościół powszechny." In *Wiara w świetle dokumentów II Soboru Watykańskiego*, edited by Marek Jagodziński and Jerzy Karbownik (Radom: Wydawnictwo Diecezji Radomskiej AVE, 2013), 37–58.

Sienkiewicz, Edward. *Wspólnota Kościoła*. Szczecin: Feniks, 2013.

Skrzypczak, Robert. "Sakrament małżeństwa." In *Znaki Tajemnicy. Sakramenty w teorii i praktyce Kościoła*, edited by Krzysztof Porosło and Robert J. Woźniak (Kraków: WAM, 2018), 501–35.

Splett, Jörg. "Dialektik des Tuns - Dialog - Person-Sein in trinitarischer Analogie: L'Action (Blondel) als con-dilectio (Richard v. St. Victor)?," *Theologie und Philosophie* 61 (1986): 161–75.

Stubenrauch, Bertram. *Pneumatologia - traktat o Duchu Świętym*. Kraków: Wydawnictwo M, 1999.

Szczurek, Jan Daniel. *Bóg Ojciec w tajemnicy Trójcy Świętej. Elementy patrylogii*. Kraków: Wydawnictwo M, 2003.

Tenace, Michelina. *Powiedzieć człowiek*, part II: *Od obrazu Boga do podobieństwa. Zbawienie jako przebóstwienie*. Kraków: Salwator, 2015.

Tertulian, *Adversum Praxean*, PL 2, 153–96 C.

Thomae Aquinatis S., *Summa theologica*, I-III. Taurini, 1939.

Tillard, Jean-Marie R. "Das sakramentale Handeln der Kirche." In *Neue Summe Theologie*, vol. III: *Der Dienst der Gemeinde*, edited by Peter Eicher (Freiburg-Basel-Wien: Herder, 1989), 239–304.

Valverde, Carlos. *Antropologia filozoficzna*. Poznań: Pallottinum, 1998.

Volf, Miroslav. *Trinität und Gemeinschaft. Eine ökumenische Ekklesiologie*. Mainz - Neukirchen-Vluyn: Neukirchener Verlag, 1996.

Vorgrimler, Herbert. *Sakramententheologie*. Düsseldorf: Patmos, 1990.

Wagner, Harald. *Dogmatyka*. Kraków: WAM, 2007.

Warzeszak, Józef. *Bóg Jedyny w Trójcy Osób*. Warszawa: Wydawnictwo Archidiecezji Warszawskiej, 2006.

Wejman, Henryk. "Kościół wspólnotą zasłuchaną w słowo Boże." In *O Kościele Jezusa Chrystusa dzisiaj. Księga pamiątkowa dedykowana Księdzu Doktorowi Wojciechowi Wójtowiczowi*, edited by Edward Sienkiewicz (Koszalin-Poznań: Pallottinum, 2020), 327–40.

Werbick, Jürgen. *Den Glauben verantworten. Eine Fundamentaltheologie*. Freiburg-Basel-Wien: Herder, 2000.

Werbick, Jürgen. "Trinitätslehre." In *Handbuch der Dogmatik*, edited by Theodor Schneider (Düsseldorf: Patmos, 2000), 2: 481–576.

Willers, Ulrich. "Kościół jako instytucja Ducha Świętego. Tajemnica, którą żyjemy." *Communio. Międzynarodowy Przegląd Teologiczny* 9/2 (1989): 27–43.

Wilski, Teofil. ""Tajemnica osoby" – klucz do rozumienia siebie i Boga." *Communio. Międzynarodowy Przegląd Teologiczny* 2/2 (1982): 24–44.

Wong Yee Kheong, Jeffrey. *John Zizioulas' Ecclesiology of 'The One and the Many'*, Otago (Ph.D. Diss., 2019).

World Council of Churches. Faith and Order. Paper No. 111, the "Lima Text:" *Baptism, Eucharist and Ministry* (1982).

World Council of Churches. "Faith and Order" Paper No. 214, *The Church. Towards a Common Vision* (2013).

Woźniak, Robert J. *Praca nad dogmatem. Wybrane aspekty odnowy teologii dogmatycznej.* Kraków: WAM, 2022.

Zachara, Maciej. "Sakrament chrztu." In *Znaki Tajemnicy. Sakramenty w teorii i praktyce Kościoła*, edited by Krzysztof Porosło and Robert J. Woźniak (Kraków: WAM, 2018), 245–304.

Zizioulas, John D. *Being as Communion. Studies in Personhood and the Church.* Crestwood-New York: St. Vladimir's Seminary Press, 1985.

Zizioulas, John D. *Communion and Otherness. Further Studies in Personhood and the Church.* London-New York: T&T Clark, 2006.

Zizioulas, John D. "Die pneumatologische Dimension der Kirche." *Internationale katholische Zeitschrift Communio* 2 (1973): 133–47.

Zizioulas, John D. "Human Capacity and Human Incapacity: A Theological Exploration of Personhood." *Scottish Journal of Theology* 28 (1975): 401–48.

Zizioulas, John D. *Lectures in Christian Dogmatics.* London-New York: T&T Clark, 2009.

Zizioulas, John D. "Preface." In *Lectures in Christian Dogmatics*, edited by John D. Zizioulas, IX-X. London-New York: T&T Clark, 2009.

Zizioulas, John D. *The Eucharistic Communion and the World.* London-New York: T&T Clark, 2011.

Zizioulas John D. *The One and the Many: Studies on God, Man, the Church, and the World Today.* Los Angeles: Sebastian Press, 2010.

Author Index

Subject Index

D

E

R

S

T